THE NEW MARITIME HISTORY OF DEVON

Volume I

Grant of Arms to Sir Francis Drake, 1581. (Private collection)

THE NEW

MARITIME HISTORY

of

DEVON

Volume I: From Early Times to the Late Eighteenth Century

Edited by

MICHAEL DUFFY
STEPHEN FISHER
BASIL GREENHILL
DAVID J STARKEY
JOYCE YOUINGS

CONWAY MARITIME PRESS
in association with
THE UNIVERSITY OF EXETER

Frontispiece: Grant of Arms to Sir Francis Drake, 1581. (Private collection)
Note the sea battle depicted in the lower border.

Transcript of the text with abbreviations extended:

Wheras it hath pleased the Queenes most excellent majestie graciouslie to regarde the praisworthie desertes of Sir Francis Drake knight & to remunerate the same in him not onely with the honorable order of knighthoode and by sundrie other demonstrations of her highnes especiall favor, but allso further desirous that the impressions of her princely affection towardes him might be as it were immortallie derived and conveighed to his offspringe and posteritie for ever, Hath assigned and geven unto him armes and tokens of vertue and honor answerable to the greatnes of his desertes & meet for his place and callinge. That is to say, Of Sable and fece wavy betwene two starres argent, The helme adorned with a Globe terrestriall Upon the height whereof is a Shipp under saile trained aboute the same with goulden haulsers by the direction of a hande appearinge out of the Cloudes all in proper colour with theis woordes *Auxilio Divino*. The said armes with all other the partes and ornamentes thereof in maner heere above depicted, with theise wordes *sic parvis Magna*, I Robert Cooke, alias Clarencieulx king of Armes of the Este, West and South partes of this realme of England, accordinge as the duties of myne office bynde mee, have caused to be registred entred and recorded for perpetuall memorie [with] the armes and other honorable and heroicall monuments of the nobilitie and gentrie within my said province and marches. In witnesse whereof I have heereunto subscribed my name the xxi[th] daye of June in the year of our Lord God Mccccclxxxi and in the xxiii[th] yere of the prosperous reigne of our most gracious Sovereigne lady Queene Elizabeth etc.

ROBERT COOKE ALIAS CLARENCIEULX ROY DARMES

Title page: Seal of the Vice-Admiralty of Devon, *c*1600 (PRO, HCA1,101/39).

First published in Great Britain 1992 by
Conway Maritime Press Ltd,
101 Fleet Street, London, EC4Y 1DE
in association with the University of Exeter

British Library Cataloguing in Publication Data
The New Maritime History of Devon – Vol. 1:
From Early Times to the Late Eighteenth Century
I. Duffy, Michael *et al.*
387.509423

ISBN 0 85177 611 6

Maps drawn by Rodney Fry, Department of Geography, University of Exeter
Designed and typeset by The Word Shop, Bury, Lancashire
Printed and bound in Great Britain by The Bath Press

Contents

List of Contributors

PETER ALLINGTON, Master (HT), Shipkeeper and Skipper of the Tamar sailing barge *Shamrock*, National Maritime Museum, Cotehele Quay.

J L ANDERSON, BA, Senior Lecturer in Economic History, La Trobe University, Australia.

JOHN C APPLEBY, BA, PhD, Lecturer in History, Liverpool Institute of Higher Education, co-Editor of *The Irish Sea* (1989).

G T BOALCH, BSc, PhD, Phycologist, Plymouth Marine Laboratories, Visiting Professor, Austral University, Chile, and Editor of *Botanica Marina*.

ALAN P CARR, BSc, PhD, formerly of the Institute of Oceanographic Sciences, Taunton.

WENDY R CHILDS, BA, PhD, FRHistS, Senior Lecturer in History, University of Leeds, author of *Anglo-Castilian Trade in the Later Middle Ages* (1978).

the late E A G CLARK, BA, PhD, lately Professor of Education, Rhodes University, South Africa, author of *Ports of the Exe Estuary* (1960).

JONATHAN COAD, MA, FSA, Inspector of Ancient Monuments, English Heritage, author of *The Royal Dockyards, 1690–1850* (1989).

PETER CORNFORD, BA.

J D DAVIES, MA, DPhil, Bedford Modern School, author of *Gentlemen and Tarpaulins: the Officers and Men of the Restoration Navy* (1991).

MICHAEL DUFFY, MA, DPhil, Senior Lecturer in History and co-Director of the Centre for Maritime Historical Studies, University of Exeter, Editor of the *Mariner's Mirror* and author of *Soldiers, Sugar and Seapower: the British Expedition to the West Indies and the war against Revolutionary France* (1987).

R A ERSKINE, BA, formerly University of Exeter, Hon. Treasurer, Fortress Study Group.

STEPHEN FISHER, BSc (Econ), PhD, FRHistS, Senior Lecturer in Economic History and co-Director of the Centre for Maritime Historical Studies, University of Exeter and author of *The Portugal Trade: a study of Anglo-Portuguese Commerce, 1700–1770* (1971 and Portuguese edn 1984).

IAN FRIEL, MA, PhD, Museum Services Officer, Arun District Council and co-Editor of the *Armada* Exhibition Catalogue (1988).

ALISON GRANT, BA, PhD, FSA, Chairman, North Devon Maritime Museum, author of *North Devon Pottery: the Seventeenth Century* (1983).

TODD GRAY, BA, PhD, Research Fellow, Department of History, University of Exeter, editor of *Early Stuart Mariners and Shipping: The Maritime Surveys of Devon and Cornwall, 1619–35* (1990).

ALAN G JAMIESON, MA, DPhil, Editor and principal author of *A People of the Sea: the Maritime History of the Channel Islands* (1986).

MARYANNE KOWALESKI, MA, PhD, Associate Professor of History, Fordham University, New York, author of *Local Markets and Regional Trade in Medieval Exeter* (forthcoming).

the late A J MARSH, MA, author of 'The Navy and Portsmouth under the Commonwealth', *Hampshire Studies* (1981).

SEÁN MCGRAIL, MA, PhD, DSc, FSA, Professor of Maritime Archaeology, University of Oxford, author of *Ancient Boats in North-West Europe* (1987).

KENNETH MORGAN, BA, DPhil, Lecturer at the West London Institute of Higher Education, editor of *An American Quaker in the British Isles* (1991).

ROGER MORRISS, BA, PhD, Curator, Naval and Mercantile History, National Maritime Museum, author of *The Royal Dockyards during the Revolutionary and Napoleonic Wars* (1983).

RONALD POLLITT, PhD, Professor of History, University of Cincinnati, Ohio, author of 'The Mobilization of English Resources, 1570–85', in W Cogar ed., *New Interpretations in Naval History* (1989).

PETER POPE, BA, MLitt, PhD, Assistant Professor of History, Memorial University of Newfoundland.

WILLIAM RAVENHILL, MA, PhD, FSA, FRGS, Emeritus Reardon Smith Professor, University of Exeter, author of many papers on the cartography of the South West of England.

N A M RODGER, MA, DPhil, Anderson Fellow, National Maritime Museum.

A J SOUTHWARD, BSc, PhD, DSc, FIBiol, Marine Biological Association, Plymouth, Visiting Professor, University of Liverpool and Adjunct Professor, University of Victoria, British Columbia.

DAVID J STARKEY, MA, PhD, Leverhulme Research Fellow in Maritime History, University of Exeter, author of *British Privateering Enterprise in the Eighteenth Century* (1990).

ALAN STIMSON, National Maritime Museum, Greenwich, author of *The Mariner's Astrolabe* (1988).

ANDREW THRUSH, BA, PhD, History of Parliament Trust.

HELEN WALLIS, OBE, MA, DPhil, FRHistS, FSA, formerly Map Librarian, British Library, author of *Maps and Text of the Boke of Idrography presented by Jean Rotz to Henry VIII* (1989).

JOYCE YOUINGS, BA, PhD, FRHistS, Emeritus Professor, Exeter University, author of *Sixteenth-Century England* (1984).

Lists of Figures and Maps

List of Figures

Permission to use copyright material has been granted by the Trustees of the National Maritime Museum; the British Library; the Controller of Her Majesty's Stationery Office; the National Portrait Gallery and English Heritage. These and all other sources of illustrations are acknowledged in the captions.

List of Maps

List of Tables and Abbreviations

List of Tables

Abbreviations

BL	British Library
CPR	*Calendar of Patent Rolls*
CSP	*Calendar of State Papers*
DAT	*Devonshire Association Transactions*
DCNQ	*Devon and Cornwall Notes and Queries*
DCRS	Devon and Cornwall Record Society
DRO	Devon Record Office, Exeter
EHR	*English History Review*
EcHR	*Economic History Review*
HCA	High Court of Admiralty
MM	*Mariner's Mirror*
NDRO	North Devon Record Office, Barnstaple
NMM	National Maritime Museum
NRS	Navy Records Society
Oppenheim	M Oppenheim, *Maritime History of Devon* (1968)
PRO	Public Record Office
WDRO	West Devon Record Office, Plymouth
WCSL	Westcountry Studies Library, Exeter

Editors' Foreword

Early in this century Michael Oppenheim, having already published his *History of the Administration of the Royal Navy* (1896), prepared a substantial chapter on maritime history for the projected second Devon volume of the *Victoria History of the Counties of England*. One of the best of his many county studies, unlike the others it never appeared as intended and it was not to be published until 1968, by the University of Exeter.[1] A new maritime history of Devon is long overdue, one that is more detailed, more comprehensive in its coverage of topics, and, most important, in line with late-twentieth-century scholarship. Devon can now claim to be the first English county to produce a modern study of the relations of its land and people with the sea.[2]

For Basil Greenhill it was a study undertaken in the 1960s, of the interaction between the developing shipbuilding industry of the Canadian province of Prince Edward Island in the early nineteenth century and the activities of some merchant families of north Devon,[3] which led him to the conviction that a thorough investigation of all aspects of Devon's maritime history would lead to a radical revision of many entrenched beliefs. Contact was established with Stephen Fisher of the Department of Economic History in the University of Exeter, a specialist in the history of overseas trade, but at that time the idea of launching a major project was premature. During the following years the Dartington maritime history conferences organised by the department became well established, and a number of collections of research papers, on West Country as well as on wider themes, were published by the University.[4] In 1984 the need for a modern reassessment of Devon's maritime history was again put forward by Basil Greenhill in his Presidential Address to the Devonshire Association.[5] This was taken up in the University with enthusiasm, among others by Joyce Youings of the Department of History and Archaeology, whose own work as a social historian had made her aware of the potentialities of research on the nature of the maritime community, especially in a manageable local context. These three original directors of the project were later joined by Michael Duffy, also of the Department of History and Archaeology, whose special interest is naval warfare.

A Steering Committee (whose names are listed below) was formed, representative of a wide range of interests and expertise both within and outside the county and the University, to whose continuing support and encouragement the project owes a great deal. With a substantial grant from the Leverhulme Trust, indicative of its confidence in the importance of the proposal, and without whose help an investigation of this magnitude could not have been attempted, the keel of 'The New Maritime History of Devon', from antiquity to the present day, was laid down. Necessary additional funding was provided by the University, the British Academy, Devon County Council, the Devonshire Association, Bideford Town Council and Devonport Management Ltd, and contributions towards printing costs were received from Lord Courtenay, Claude Pike esq., John Holman and Sons, Watts Blake Bearne & Co plc and The Twenty-Seven Foundation, to each of whom we are most grateful. In 1985 David Starkey, an economic historian, was appointed for four years to the post of Research Fellow, and from 1989 his appointment was extended through the generous support of Television South West to enable him to conduct further research into the later-modern maritime history of the South West. Besides making his own substantial contribution to the writing and editing of the History, he has acted as Secretary to the Steering Committee and as the day-to-day administrator of the project. A second Research Fellow, Peter Hilditch, was appointed for two years to examine Devon and the Navy in the nineteenth and early-twentieth centuries. The two departments of history at Exeter have co-operated to the full, each devoting postgraduate research funding to Devon's maritime history, and the contributions of these young scholars has added greatly to the enterprise. Conway Maritime Press, whose managing director, Ray Blackmore, became an enthusiastic supporter, exchanged a contract with the University for the publication of a two-volume work, and this was not only an enormous encouragement but also provided deadlines for completion.

At an early stage it became clear that many more hands would be needed, and the directors found little difficulty in obtaining the services of a wide range of expert and willing contributors, many of them already known to them through the Dartington conferences, not only in Devon and the West Country but all over Britain and also in America and other parts of the world. In all, some sixty contributors have completed chapters of varying lengths, and many of them have attended and read papers at one or more of the three weekend symposia which have been held at the University and which have resulted in some valuable preliminary publications.[6] Contributors have received only minimal expenses, and all royalties received will be placed by the University in a trust fund to further the study of maritime history through the recently-established Centre for Maritime Historical Studies.

Certain principles were laid down at an early stage: the History was to be authoritative and provided with a scholarly apparatus of references, tables and maps, but it was also to be written so as to be readable by non-specialists. Contributors were urged to set their subjects in as wide a regional, national and indeed international context as possible, and by agreement with the publishers the two volumes were to be extensively illustrated. For the most part quotations from original sources, both manuscript and printed, were to be in modern spelling. All contributors have risen admirably to these requirements so that, in general, only the minimum of editing has been necessary. As almost every chapter touches on themes elaborated elsewhere, the Editors have introduced cross-references where these seemed likely to be helpful to readers. They are not, of course, responsible for the opinions expressed.

The extent to which the contributors to this History are indebted to generations of modern scholars, and to some of an earlier vintage, will be evident from the references. The worldwide transformation in the study of maritime history in the late-twentieth century has been made possible very largely by the availability of a far greater range of documentary sources than were known to Oppenheim and his contemporaries. To the official custodians of these records, to the archivists in both local and national repositories, to all those who have provided the invaluable finding aids, and to the editors of texts, all the contributors are greatly indebted. Their work would not have been possible without the services of countless librarians, nor in most cases would it have reached the printer without the many secretaries who typed and word-processed their scripts. The wide range of sources of photographic illustrations is acknowledged in the captions, particular thanks being due to the National Maritime Museum at Greenwich; the Imperial War Museum; HM Naval Base Museum, Devonport;

RMCTC Lympstone; RNEC Manadon; RNC Dartmouth; Devonport Management Ltd; the Devon Record Office; Devon Library Services; Devon Property Department; the City of Plymouth Museums and Art Gallery; the Devon and Exeter Institution; the *Western Morning News*, the *Express and Echo* (Exeter) and the *Herald Express* (Torquay); the owner of the Grant of Arms to Sir Francis Drake used as the Frontispiece in volume 1 and to John Saunders and Tony Fisher of the Photographic Department in the University Library. All maps have been drawn by Rodney Fry of the University's Department of Geography, for whose ready help and professional expertise we are most grateful.

There has been something of a tacit agreement among contributors that the well-known maritime heroes of Devon should steal less of the limelight than has been their wont in much popular historical writing and that, as far as the sources permit, more attention should be devoted to the rank and file of the county's seafarers, thus making *The New Maritime History of Devon* truly popular in its content as well as in its appeal. If it be argued that this detracts from the romance of the subject, let it be remembered that until very nearly our own time it was by sea that the riches of the world came to Great Britain and that every putting out to sea, especially from the hazardous estuaries and coasts of Devon, and indeed every return to the county's waters, was and still is an adventure, incurring risks to all involved, to the owners of the ships and their cargoes, to the passengers and, of course, to the officers and crew. What can be more exciting than the history of the gradual widening of the maritime horizons of all those who through the centuries have set out from Devon by sea: to fish, to trade, to travel, to explore, to found colonies, to prey on other seafarers and to defend the realm?

Inevitably there are gaps in the coverage of so vast and varied a subject. By and large the two volumes have emerged from what was forthcoming: there are themes for which no author could be found, and others which could not be satisfactorily covered for lack of source material. This latter limitation is particularly true of the early centuries, and indeed much more space has been devoted to relatively modern times, although it has also emerged that the twentieth century has as yet attracted little attention from maritime historians and hence all findings for this period are pioneering and must be regarded as provisional. An obvious gap midstream is the lack of a chapter on seventeenth- and eighteenth-century merchant shipbuilding, and readers will no doubt identify other lacunae. We have done our best to fulfil the task upon which we embarked such a short time ago, and we shall feel happy if, as a result, there is aroused in the minds of mainstream historians a greater awareness of the maritime preoccupations of an island race. We have no doubt that all Devonians, at home and abroad, will discover in these two volumes a great deal they did not know about the maritime involvement of their ancestors.

Exeter
July 1992

Michael Duffy
Stephen Fisher
Basil Greenhill
David J Starkey
Joyce Youings

Editors' Foreword References

1 M Oppenheim, *The Maritime History of Devon*, with an Introduction by WE Minchinton (Exeter, 1968). The unpublished text was drawn upon very extensively by WG Hoskins for his *Devon* (1954), chapter XI.

2 Some precedence must be allowed to AG Jamieson, ed., *A People of the Sea: The Maritime History of the Channel Islands* (1986).

3 Basil Greenhill and Ann Giffard, *Westcountrymen in Prince Edward's Isle* (Toronto and Newton Abbot, 1967).

4 HES Fisher, ed., *The South West and the Sea* (Exeter, 1968); *Ports and Shipping in the South West* (Exeter 1971); with WE Minchinton, *Transport and Shipowning in the West Country* (Exeter 1973); *West Country Maritime and Social History: Some Essays* (Exeter 1980) and *British Shipping and Seamen, 1630–1960: Some Studies* (Exeter 1984).

5 Basil Greenhill, 'Towards a New Maritime History of Devon', *DAT*, 116 (1984).

6 David J Starkey, ed., *Sources for a New Maritime History of Devon* (Exeter, 1986) and *Devon's Coastline and Coastal Waters: Aspects of Man's Relationship with the Sea* (Exeter, 1988).

Members of the Steering Committee

Benefactors

The following made grants towards the cost of research:
Bideford Town Council
The British Academy
Devon County Council
Devonport Management Ltd
The Devonshire Association
The Leverhulme Trust
University of Exeter

and towards the cost of printing:
Lord Courtenay
Claude Pike esq.
John Holman & Sons
Watts Blake Bearne & Co., plc
The Twenty-Seven Foundation

Introduction

The frontiers between land and sea in Britain are everywhere long and varied, but the section of the south-west peninsula known for a thousand years as the county of Devon has always had the distinction of having two quite separate coasts. That in the north faces across the Bristol Channel (the old 'Severn Sea') towards Wales and beyond to Ireland, while the other, much longer, on the south, borders the English Channel (the one-time 'Sleeve'), western Europe's busiest seaway, looking towards western France and beyond to the Iberian peninsula. Further west of both lie the Atlantic and access to the ocean highways of the world. In the first chapter in this volume Alan Carr goes back far beyond the relatively short period of Devon's human habitation and pursues the laying down of the extraordinarily diverse geological structure of the county, explaining thereby the very varied appearance of its coasts and the hazards they have offered to seafarers down the ages.

Like its most famous seaman, Sir Francis Drake, the historic county of Devon is 'broad-breasted', in nautical terms 'broad in the beam', her 12,600 square miles occupying by far the widest part of the south-west peninsula, measuring 70 miles from Foreland Point in the north to the southernmost tip at Prawle Head, and almost as far from east to west. Even allowing for the great moorland waste of Dartmoor and the foothills of Exmoor, which extend well into north Devon and enclose the upper reaches of the river Exe, much of the county lies many miles from the sea. In fact only 65 of Devon's 430 or so parishes are bounded by the coast or by the tidal reaches of her many rivers. It is the coastal parishes, most of them stretching far inland, and their immediate neighbours, which have always been the most densely populated and indeed among the first to be settled. Domesday Book and later taxation records show a high concentration of population and wealth in the valleys of the river Exe and its tributaries, with an extension westwards as far as the river Dart. By the early sixteenth century this relative density had spread across the South Hams and as far as the Cornish boundary along the river Tamar. North Devon, by comparison, has always been sparsely populated. The extension of so many coastal parishes inland has been explained by the need for early settlers, most of them arriving by sea, to keep out of sight of later comers or passing marauders. Hence few of the county's oldest parish churches are to be found at the water's edge to serve as landmarks for seafarers. The village of Tormohun, a good mile and a steep climb inland, existed as the centre of a thriving community nearly a thousand years before its little seaside causeway for fishing boats gave way to the Victorian resort of Torquay, and even Dartmouth had its beginnings sometime in the twelfth century at Townstall, half a mile uphill from the riverside. The early seamen of Devon really did 'go down to the sea'.

In north Devon the port of Barnstaple, itself situated some way up the Taw estuary, must give precedence as a settlement to its present inland suburb of Pilton, whose ancient 'Causeway' still carries traffic into the town. In more settled times people moved nearer to the water and ships and their moorings became very much part of many Devon townscapes, although at Exeter, the county's capital and largest centre of population, and at other places on river estuaries, silting and other natural coastal changes would leave former ports beyond the reach of seagoing vessels. Sea views and the supposed benefits of sea air are relatively modern attractions, and only in the second half of the twentieth century has the rapid growth of residential development on the coast made it necessary for the National Trust, through its Operation Neptune, to step in to halt the seaward migration. Long stretches of Devon's coast are now safe from predatory landsmen, so that today, just as their forbears did in 1588, the people of Devon have access to cliffs and beaches from which to watch the world's flotillas pass by.

How odd it would have seemed to the Elizabethans that in less anxious times their descendants would look to the beaches and to the sea for their recreation. Until the advent of the seaside holiday and the appearance of the amateur sailor the sea, off Devon as elsewhere, was important primarily as a means of livelihood and of communication. Inshore fishing by hook and line was no doubt always a relatively leisurely and at times even an enjoyable activity for many, as well as providing additions to the household diet, but trawling the deeper waters was essential if the poor were to subsist and the godly to observe the Lenten and other fasts. Ferries, about whose early history little is known, must in the early middle ages have been more numerous than bridges, and barges and rowing boats more convenient for local traffic than unmade tracks and green lanes, the terrible state of Devon's early roads being notorious. Until the age of railways and trunk roads water was the main commercial highway and the sailing ship the fastest, cheapest and most efficient transporter of both men and goods. Until very recently the sea remained the only means of international communication for the British, and indeed holiday traffic is still considerable between Devon's south coast ports and the continent, though modern container transport of goods has largely passed her by. The sea once supplied Devon's farmers with their main artificial fertiliser in the form of seaweed and sea-sand, and Domesday Book records saltpans at 22 places in Devon, with saltworkers being mentioned in six others. Not until the county was able to offer its own marketable commodity, woollen cloth, could it afford to import this essential food preservative from abroad.

The sea provided, but it also demanded. One of the continuous themes in *The New Maritime History of Devon* is the relationship between the sea and the county's economy, the latter being an amalgam of its natural and human resources, its scale of production of raw materials and manufactured goods, and the viability of its markets both at home and abroad. This involved not only the coastal population, but also those far inland who worked the tin on Dartmoor, tended sheep on the hillfarms of mid-Devon, spun and wove their wool and yarn and trudged weekly to market, and indeed the whole network of dealers and merchants on whom the port towns depended. For travel and transport to and from foreign countries and other parts of England there had to be available ships and all the facilities they needed by way of havens, deep-water harbours and wharves, and, by no means the least essential, men possessed of sufficient skill and muscle to sail the ships and to load and unload their cargoes. It is in the rank and file of usually anonymous seafarers and those landsmen upon whom they relied that the strength of Devon's maritime tradition rests.

Exactly when, in the mists of antiquity, people first lived in what we know as Devon, let alone built seaworthy craft, cannot be ascertained with any precision. Seán McGrail, in the first of the more wide-ranging chapters in this volume, tells us that it was about 7 millenia BC that Britain became separated from the rest of what can for convenience be called the mainland of Europe, making it necessary for future inhabitants of south-west England to communicate with the continent by sea. The coast as we see it today is probably about five thousand years old, one of the near-certainties being that men of the Bronze Age lived on land at the mouth of the river Plym which two millenia later was to be named, after a Civil War admiral, Mount Batten. The first men who sailed to south-west England probably came in search of tin, but of early vessels it can only be assumed that they were akin to those few which have survived in other parts of England and of the continent. Of Devon's own involvement with the sea before the Norman Conquest and for at least a century thereafter little is known at present, save that in the event of the mounting of a royal expedition by sea or land the three Domesday boroughs of Totnes, Barnstaple and Lydford were required to perform the same service as Exeter, but this was probably in cash terms. Much of Devon's early maritime history may yet be uncovered through archaeological fieldwork on or immediately above the shoreline, especially in the former estuaries. Some of their loss of water perhaps had a long history, but when the farmers of the Axe valley reported to Queen Elizabeth the finding of ships' anchors when they ploughed their fields, they spoke as though the silt had arrived only in the time of their grandfathers. There is clearly scope here for an interdisciplinary approach, including ecology.

At this point readers will find themselves brought back to reality with a short but immensely vivid account, written by an experienced sailor, Peter Allington, especially for the landsman, of what is involved in the safe conduct of sailing ships, even those equipped with modern aids, no amount of which can give total protection against the hazards of the sea. As an additional help to the landsman's understanding, Alan Stimson traces the technology available to seafarers over the centuries. Although it is not peculiar to Devon, what he has to say explains the limitations under which her seamen operated until the invention of the modern electronic techniques to be described in volume 2. Early navigational progress in the northern hemisphere owed a very great deal to three Elizabethan Devonians whose careers are briefly sketched by Joyce Youings. Details of the construction of the Devon ships, even those of the later-medieval period, are scarce, but Ian Friel concludes that they were mostly small by the standards of the day and of no recognisably local design. Indeed, he thinks that all vessels of any size were built elsewhere, being either purchased or captured as prizes. He finds Dartmouth and Plymouth as home ports equal to, if not actually in advance of the Exe estuary, especially in their contributions to royal fleets, which largely comprised converted merchantmen. This comparative standing of the three main ports is borne out again and again in other chapters.

There is no doubt (and in this she does not stand alone among the maritime counties of England) that in actual numbers Devon's medieval and early-modern shipping consisted very largely of small boats of ten tons or less, used occasionally for cross-Channel and coastal trips, but largely for fishing. They do not figure in the few early shipping lists, being of no interest to the Crown as naval auxiliaries. The early placing in this volume of the chapter by Alan Southward and Gerald Boalch on marine resources, largely fish, though it is based mostly on modern data, is intended to underline the importance of fishing in the process whereby Devonians overcame their natural fear of the sea. Not only have the two coasts always provided their own distinct range of marine fauna and flora, but in terms of water temperature, and hence of ecology, the south coast of Devon marks the meeting point of southern and northern marine habitats. As fish have never been a prime target for royal taxation, it will probably never be known just how much was brought ashore until comparatively modern times, but the *Valor Ecclesiasticus* of 1535 has many references to the payment of tithes on fish landings, and certainly does not tell the complete story. Todd Gray puts his finger firmly on the county's maritime pulse by tracing her fisheries from the mid-sixteenth century, underlining not only their dual importance in home and foreign markets, but the growing need by 1600 for new sources of supply. Devon fishermen had long been sailing as far afield as the North Sea, and probably even longer to the coast of Ireland. By the third quarter of the sixteenth century the trickle of ships going annually to Newfoundland was beginning to look like a fleet, especially those from Dartmouth. By the end of the century – a probable starting date of 1597 has come to light – Devon ships were diverting southwards to the shores of New England, and within a few decades the annual migration was turning into emigration, that is settlement, albeit on a limited scale. Here, as elsewhere, firm evidence is emerging that Devon seamen not only moved easily between fishing and other maritime pursuits but also, largely but not always seasonally, to and from employment on the land, both at home and overseas, Devonians being traditionally multi-skilled. On Richmond Island in the Gulf of Maine, of which Todd Gray provides a short account, the fisheries were for a while big business, with Plymouth providing both the entrepreneurs and the workforce.

Devonian success in New England, though shortlived, was in stark contrast to the far more risky and very much less successful colonial ventures of Sir Walter Raleigh and his contemporaries elsewhere on the eastern seaboard of North America. Although nothing had been achieved by 1600, some useful soundings had been taken and courses charted which, under better management and carrying Devonians as well as the Londoners upon whom Raleigh largely relied, provided the basis for a fresh start under the new dynasty. This is a story taken up by Alison Grant, who describes the more highly-organised conveyance of emigrant settlers, first to Ireland, where Raleigh had had some success with his fellow-Devonians, and then to Virginia, Bermuda and the West Indies. Certain seaports specialised in the traffic, as they had done two centuries earlier in the carriage of pilgrims. Actual numbers fell somewhat after the interval of the Civil War, and by the end of the seventeenth century the traffic had almost dried up altogether, except for the transportation of convicts described by Kenneth Morgan, a 'trade' much resorted to by eighteenth-century Devon magistrates, using in particular the ports of north Devon and complementing its trade in tobacco.

The one part of North America where Devonians maintained a continuous sea-link from the mid-sixteenth to the end of the eighteenth century and beyond was Newfoundland. The attraction here, as in New England, was fish, almost entirely cod, but ships did not sail out with empty holds. David Starkey describes how the catching, drying and the shipping of the catch to Europe was complemented by the transportation of supplies for an increasingly resident population. Though not without its hazards and fluctuations, the Newfoundland trade, very largely monopolised by Devonians, employed many thousands of seamen, paid good dividends to shipowners, and was much favoured in government circles as one of the great nurseries of naval manpower. Dartmouth men led the way, and it is therefore no surprise to learn from Peter Pope's account of archaeological excavations at Ferryland in Newfoundland that Totnes pottery figured among the finds. Here, surely, is a most promising way forward in the study of early colonial history along the whole length of the eastern seaboard of North America. Indeed, glazed pottery and clay pipes from north Devon are already on display in American museums.

These, then, are some of the more enterprising aspects of Devon's early maritime history. Also featuring prominently in this volume is the continuous story of Devon's overseas trade, a story of steady achievement starting, where the records permit, in the early middle ages and reaching its modern heyday in the early eighteenth century. It will no doubt surprise some readers to learn how much can be recovered, largely from royal and town customs records, about the activities of the merchants who handled Devon's medieval seaborne trade, and about the ships which plied her commercial seaways. Maryanne Kowaleski concentrates on the fourteenth century and identifies not only the merchandise which passed into and out of the port towns but also their respective industrial and commerical hinterlands, establishing the comparative economic importance of the leading port towns of Devon which, with only slight variations, is reflected in all the general chapters which follow. Exeter, with its considerable markets, seems to have held its own only by dint of its extensive coastal trade and faced stiff competition from Dartmouth, already in use as an assembly point for royal fleets. Plymouth, too, grew phenomenally as a seaport during the early stages of the Hundred Years War, and in the 1390s there was even a challenge from the north Devon region centred on Barnstaple, already a hub of coastal trade up and down the Bristol Channel. Then, as always, physical factors were paramount, especially immediate access from deepwater harbours to markets. In writing of Devon's maritime trade in the fifteenth century, a period long regarded as one of nationwide economic recession caused partly by internal and external conflict, Wendy Childs describes and quantifies not only considerable local buoyancy but, in the closing decades, as already noted by E M Carus-Wilson for Exeter, quite unprecedented expansion, especially in the export of woollen cloth, now establishing itself as Devon's major marketable product. Neither in the middle ages nor later did any Devon port depend upon the resort of alien ships and merchants: both make their occasional appearance in the records, but never as prominently as in London and other ports further east. Least of all did the Devon cloth industry owe anything to alien expertise or investment, especially the latter, for this was an industry of small master craftsmen, many of them also primarily engaged in farming.

In a chapter covering the sixteenth century Joyce Youings shows that the high level of conventional overseas trade achieved around 1500 was maintained, though with a slower growth rate, until well into the mid-century, and that by continuing to concentrate on the established cross-Channel links with France and Spain the merchants of Devon were able to weather the depression which, around 1550, dealt such heavy blows to London and the South East with their dependence on the Low Countries. The 1560s even saw one of those very occasional leaps forward in north Devon, but even there the Spanish War beginning in 1585 brought setbacks not entirely compensated for by the profits from privateering, substantial as these occasionally were. The limited commercial expansion which had characterised the sixteenth century was a foretaste of even more solid achievement in Devon from 1600 to 1689. Alison Grant shows how the county's leading merchants, notably Richard Delbridge of Barnstaple, took the lead in England's outports in challenging the longstanding overseas predominance of London. Real success, especially for Exeter, came only after the Restoration, but even before the Civil War the city's cloth exporters were exploring the Netherlands markets, still officially closed to them. By the time Dutch William passed through their city in 1688 they were poised to enter that heyday of their trade in serges which so impressed Daniel Defoe. There is still much to be seen in the buildings, not only of Exeter and its outport, Topsham, to remind us of the county's prodigious commercial wealth around 1700, but it must always be remembered that, without the traditional skills of the people of the Devon countryside in the making of woollen cloth of a quality to satisfy discriminating foreign purchasers, the merchant ships and their crews would have found it hard to make a living.

It was a success story which, even by 1800, had not entirely faded. Stephen Fisher describes a commercial scene in the eighteenth century which would not have been unrecognisable even in the medieval period, though it was now more far-flung, reaching out not only to the Low Countries, but to the Baltic, to southern Europe and, of course, to North America. The old concentration on the cross-Channel trade was now past history. But from the 1730s Devon was losing ground, despite some further growth in the 1770s, notably and rather curiously at Plymouth. Possibly developments in the naval dockyard there were acting as a temporary spur to local merchants. Strangely, little or no attempt was made to breach the Londoners' monopoly of the East India trade, nor was there much continuing interest in the West Indies, perhaps because Devonians preferred to leave the slave trade to their less-sensitive neighbours at Bristol. The effects of the French wars at the turn of the century have still to be worked out in detail, but certainly by 1815 Devon was no longer a major overseas trading county. The causes will probably be found partly in her now comparatively scanty population, but principally in the stagnation of her woollen cloth industry. This had social and economic causes deep in the countryside, there now being more money to be made in farming. Other provincial ports, notably Bristol, Liverpool, Glasgow and Hull, with more populous and vigorously-developing hinterlands, were leaving the Devon ports irrevocably behind in both the Atlantic and European trades. That there was, however, still some sign of life is shown by Arthur Clark's short contribution on the activities of three Exeter pioneers in the Italian trade in the 1770s.

With the patterns of Devon's overseas trade from 1300 to 1800 now fairly clearly established, there still remains a great deal of scope for the investigation of the handling of shipments, their profitability, and so on. Sources will probably be largely legal, but it is already clear from the port customs particulars that the medieval and early modern Devon merchants not only shared the ownership of shipping but consistently spread their cargoes between ships, and even between ports. Such was their bread-and-butter livelihood, and Exeter men in particular eschewed the taking of unnecessary risks. Only men of the self-confidence of the Hawkinses of early Tudor Plymouth would send their own ships, carrying largely their own goods, to the shores of South America.

Of course the development of transatlantic links, whoever was responsible, did have consequences for Devon, if only in the increase in shipping of all nationalities passing close to her shores. Shipping preferred to travel along the north side of the English Channel partly because the coasts of Britanny were even more dangerous than those of Devon and Cornwall, but largely because sailing ships were driven by the prevailing southwesterly winds and the coastline from the Lizard to Start Point was a vital landfall on the seaway between northwest Europe and the rest of the world. Torbay was one of the safest refuges against westerly storms, probably the best between Lands End and the Isle of Wight. This resulted in a good deal of casual trade: it is clear from the small size of many of the cargoes entered in the Devon port books that ships' masters frequently engaged in a little business when calling in for water and other necessities. Such considerations no doubt engendered in the minds of strangers, especially the Dutch, the need for accurate charting of the Devon waters. In a study of the county's maritime cartography from Tudor times William Ravenhill, together with Helen Wallis, who has selected and described some of the best of contemporary maps and charts, shows that in this respect the South West as a whole was rather better served than others among the maritime counties of England, and that as time went on there was local talent equal to that of most foreign makers of charts. Along with developments in ship design and rigging, and also in navigation, marine cartography was part of the new technology which long before the Industrial Revolution on land was slowly but surely revolutionising the English seaman's art.

However, strangers entered Devon's ports or sailed her coasts with some trepidation on other counts, for they were always, of course, regarded as fair game by local residents. As John Appleby shows, it was not a far cry from occupying one's ship in legitimate merchandising to engaging in wartime privateering and also in peacetime piracy. Gentlemen and other adventurers indulged in what they called 'the keeping of the seas', ostensibly in the service of the Crown, but it was usually unpaid service, and what they captured they reckoned to be their own. After reaching a peak during the Spanish wars of Elizabeth's reign, privateering declined somewhat in the seventeenth century, when naval service offered an alternative employment. But in the eighteenth century Devonians again invested in private warships for profit. The size of this business emerges in David Starkey's second chapter. A veritable fleet of privateers operated from Devon's ports, in particular from Dartmouth and Plymouth, harvesting the seas for prizes and through their captures actually adding goods to the trading stock acquired by more peaceable enterprise. The powers-that-be encouraged this activity, directing it against specific targets as an instrument of public policy. Queen Elizabeth and her medieval predecessors had done likewise, but now more than ever Devon's privateering venturers were well placed to profit at the expense of French, Spanish and, on occasion, Dutch vessels sailing through the county's waters.

One must not forget, too, the not-inconsiderable volume of contraband goods which, again following long-established tradition, were entering Devon in the eighteenth century, either through the larger ports under the very eyes of customs officers (if not with their positive connivance) or run ashore on the two coasts with their multiplicity of small bays and coves. This highly-organised trade was largely in goods of high value and in great demand, principally brandy, tobacco, silks and tea, all of them now subject to high and rising excise duties such as would have amazed medieval and sixteenth-century smugglers, who had to make do largely with the less-profitable illegal export of grain in times of high prices. On occasion, however, in the eighteenth century, even salt, also dutiable, was smuggled ashore. Alan Jamieson's chapter on this very popular but often over-romanticized subject is particularly revealing about the career of Jack Rattenbury of Beer in east Devon. Throughout the centuries such marginal trades were always combined, as occasion offered, with more legitimate occupations on sea and land.

With Devon's undoubted maritime wealth, to which must be added her extremely important strategic position commanding the western end of the English Channel, it was inevitable that throughout the period covered by this volume, and indeed beyond, she would be a regular target for seaborne attacks, either hit-and-run or with the objective of landing an invasion force. The story of Devon's coastal defences down the ages is closely linked with that of governmental administration, but Devon was a long way from Westminster and her vulnerability as a 'place of descent' by an enemy was rarely properly appreciated, at any rate by those who might have provided most of the funding. Except during the Civil War there was little co-operation between those responsible for land defences and such naval forces as were anywhere in the vicinity. Nor is there a single example of shore defences actually preventing an invasion. Reginald Erskine's chapter pursues a tale of local apathy and central brinkmanship from the end of the medieval period right up to the twentieth century. However, as he makes clear, much of what was built, usually by occasional feats of central and local collaboration, was of magnificent proportions. Much of the work remains, especially the great Citadel overlooking Plymouth Sound, the availability of good local building stone being in this as in other respects an important ingredient of Plymouth's visual image through the centuries. Indeed, the very grandeur of Plymouth Hoe and the Sound, together with the surrounding 'heights' with their scope for artillery defences, was enough to deter an enemy and to protect Plymouth from the fate of many of her less-well-favoured Devon neighbours.

The use of warships to defend the realm against enemy attack was only very rarely practicable. It was rather the ships which needed support from the shore. Medieval royal navies were in fact ephemeral phenomena, largely composed of converted merchant vessels hastily commandeered in a national emergency, the Crown relying for its sea-keeping on the occasional services of such men as the extraordinarily versatile Hawleys of Dartmouth. But long before 1500 the south Devon ports, in particular Dartmouth and Plymouth, were regularly used as points of assembly for royal fleets, especially those bound for western France and the Iberian peninsula. This was still the county's primary naval role in the early wars against France of Henry VIII. Ronald Pollitt describes the process whereby, in the later sixteenth century, the county came to play a more active naval role, Devon's leading maritime entrepreneurs, notably Sir John Hawkins and Sir Francis Drake, inviting Spanish hostility by their efforts to carve a place for their fellow countrymen in the New World. Although held in check by a tight royal rein, the seamen of Devon, he argues, were instrumental in persuading the nation as a whole of its aggressive maritime capabilities. By 1630 such local leadership was again lacking and Plymouth was no longer in the front line, except once again as a reception area. The county's maritime resources, however, were an ongoing and, indeed, an appreciating asset. Although there had been a limit to the degree of reliance placed by Drake and his fellow admirals on Devon ships and Devon crews, there is no doubt that at Westminster the county was now more than ever regarded as a recruitment area for able seamen. Devon's actual potential as a source both of mariners and of shipping is revealed by a newly-discovered survey of the county's southern parishes made in 1619 for the Duke of Buckingham and here briefly analysed by Todd Gray. Although, as expected, the county's maritime resources were concentrated at Plymouth and Dartmouth, there were mariners resident quite long distances inland and shipwrights at Otterton in east Devon, a port no longer accessible by seagoing vessels. Presumably they were either engaged in building small boats or worked in the ports of the Exe estuary.

It is easy to assume that the occasional presence of a naval squadron put money into the pockets of local dealers and suppliers of victuals, to say nothing of owners of timber, shipwrights and the labour force generally. But Drake in his day had been hard put to obtain supplies locally and in 1588 in particular most victuals had had to be sent from London, whence also came the greater part of his fleet. Beer of a kind was available in Plymouth, but was not to the seamen's taste. Part of the trouble was that the Crown expected to buy at its own price. Half a century later, as Andrew Thrush shows in a short contribution on 'Bottomless' Sir James Bagg, the naval agent at Plymouth and a local man, problems stemmed also from the Treasury's slowness in providing cash for what could be obtained. The Dutch wars of the 1650s further delayed Plymouth's rise as a naval base by taking some of the strategic pressure off the whole southwestern region. However, David Davies, in a chapter devoted to the years from 1642 to 1688, suggests that the establishment by Parliament in the 1640s of a new western squadron to guard the western approaches to the Channel pointed the way towards a more permanent westcountry naval commitment by the restored Stuart monarchy, especially for the defence of trade. In 1678 Devon headed the list of quotas fixed for the recruitment of naval seamen, and for the first time there are recorded in the country's Quarter Sessions records the suffering of some of those Devonians who served on the lower deck. Towards the end of the seventeenth century there was a growing interest in the county in full-time professional service in the Navy, although most recruitment was still via the merchant service. The same author's short study of the naval agents who succeeded Bagg shows that little had changed except that the larger scale of naval supply and impressment now offered even more handsome pickings for royal officials.

John Anderson's short note on Prince William of Orange's landing at Brixham in 1688 focusses attention on an event which in many respects was to prove a landmark in Devon's maritime history – literally so in the establishment of a naval dockyard immediately to the west of Plymouth. It was, of course, the re-emergence of France as England's major enemy, both on sea and land, as in the later middle ages, that dramatically changed the whole strategic position of the South West. Every part of southern England was exposed to the threat of attack, but that by sea, if it came, would be based on France's great naval arsenals in the Bay of Biscay, waters long familiar to Devon seamen. The example of the King's own success was not lost on his enemies; large and powerful French fleets, not just small raiding parties as had appeared three hundred years earlier, actually attacked the south Devon coast in 1690 and again in 1779. These details of naval strategy and their very important implications for Devon are brought out in Michael Duffy's pivotal chapter covering the period from 1689 to the final defeat of Napoleon in 1815. The Emperor himself made only a brief appearance off the Devon coast, as a captive, but a century and a half before this the steadily-increasing size, armament and sophisticated equipment of purpose-built English warships had shown up the limitations of the existing naval bases of Devon for operational purposes, the new ships of the line requiring extensive and expensive servicing facilities for repair and supply to keep them seaworthy. Such facilities could be provided only by purpose-built dockyards, and, of paramount importance, with the very considerable capital investment in them which only the state could provide. So far these were to be found only in the Thames, the Medway and the Solent: for Devon it now had to be everything or nothing vis-a-vis the Navy. Various considerations led to the rejection of all other competitors and to the selection in 1689 of Plymouth as the site of William and Mary's new dockyard. Here their ships could not only anchor but also be efficiently repaired, rebuilt, and even newly created. Most importantly, from Plymouth close blockade of the cross-Channel naval bases became practicable, and with hazards equal to those faced by Drake a century and more earlier. Nor did Plymouth steal the whole show, Torbay proving a useful and popular naval resort and refuge, as Sir John Gilbert had suggested to Queen Elizabeth it would be for the Spanish Armada. However, many towns way inland found the obligation to receive French prisoners something of a mixed blessing.

All in all the century up to 1815 had seen changes in Devon's maritime commitment more revolutionary than those in the whole of the previous five hundred years. The permanent naval presence was even reflected in her employment pattern. Nicholas Rodger, in a chapter neatly complementing that of Michael Duffy, shows that in 1795, although Devon was only fifth-largest in the county quotas for the provision of seamen, she was consistently in the top two or three counties supplying recruits for the naval officer corps, thus continuing an earlier trend. And although Georgian Devon failed to produce a naval commander of national renown to set beside General George Monck, the second tier was not lacking naval officers of Devon birth nor newcomers with the means to retire to Devon in the comfort made possible by the capture of enemy vessels.

With no fewer than three substantial chapters devoted to its development in the eighteenth and early-nineteenth century, Plymouth Dockyard is given a prominence in local history which it has hitherto lacked. Jonathan Coad traces the stages by which state investment was built up in the various units which made up the whole repairing enterprise, including the naval hospital built at Stonehouse in 1758–62. The late John Marsh describes the uses to which these facilities were put, with particular emphasis on the local supply of timber and other materials and the assembling of a skilled labour force. Both placed considerable demands on the local economy and presented opportunities not quickly perceived locally. Finally, Roger Morriss examines the problem of Dockyard labour relations, concluding that, although there were moments of considerable tension, in true eighteenth-century fashion the situation never reached crisis point. By 1815 Plymouth Dockyard was rivalling Portsmouth as the largest naval base in Europe, and as the British government's most substantial capital investment and employer of labour. Devonport, the town which by then had grown up outside the dockyard, was the largest urban community in Devon, and the new permanent naval presence was now beginning to transform the economic and social life of its hinterland and beyond. That the county's rise to naval prominence took place at almost the same time as it was declining industrially and commercially points the difference between state-generated and locally-generated economic activity. That there was apparently so little evidence of local enterprise to meet the new challenge was due in large part, no doubt, to the fact that, in the crucial 1690s, the county's overseas trade in woollens was extremely buoyant, and indeed was still expanding, and that even thereafter it was a long time dying. During the latter part of this long decline a great deal of the capital accumulated from the manufacture and sale of woollen cloth, especially in Exeter, found its way into areas of the economy which were anticipating the Victorian age, banking and the import of luxury goods such as wine. Queen Elizabeth would have expected, though only grudgingly rewarded, more local initiative in serving her Navy, especially in the provision of ships, but the revolution in warship construction meant that the eighteenth-century armed merchantman had no place in the line of battle, and Devon ship owners and masters could only contribute in a lesser privateering role. Moreover, while ordinary seamen were easily transferable, naval officers were now required to be professional sailors as well as fighting men. Devonian versatility was wearing a little thin.

Much had indeed changed since Devon's connections with the sea had first been revealed in any detail in the records five hundred years earlier, but an epilogue to this volume by Arthur Clark leaves the reader very conscious of how much had remained the same. Tides still ebbed and flowed with predictable regularity and the very appearance of the sea's surface, even more than that of the land, still reflected the alternating of the seasons. Navigational aids had improved almost out of all recognition but pilotage, especially in home waters, still depended on local knowledge. In 1800 revolutionary technological changes in the propulsion and handling of ships were only just around the corner, but it would always be necessary for the seafarer, professional or amateur, whether conducting a large or a small vessel, to respect the Rhythms of the Sea.

Michael Duffy
Joyce Youings

1 *The Environmental Background*

ALAN P CARR

THE PHYSICAL FACTORS, BOTH TERRESTRIAL and marine, which have helped to influence the maritime history of Devon are spatial; geological and sedimentological; geomorphological; and oceanographical. The structure of the land means that ease of access varies from one place to another (and has varied substantially more in the past) so that the effects of distance *per se* are distorted. If this is true of the terrestrial environment, then the maritime one compounds the situation still more, especially in the case of a county which 'faces both ways'. The precise effect of each physical component has also varied over time as technology has developed and human response has altered. For example, the existence of or potential for really deep-water channels and harbours became important when large, steam-powered, iron vessels plying deep-sea routes supplanted the earlier small, wooden-hulled, sailing craft.

The Land

Geology

'Whosoever drew the county boundaries of Devon . . . had little regard for topography and even less for geology.'[1] Similar difficulties apply to the South West as a whole. Although the administrative boundaries are clear, the definition of the southwest peninsula is not, and is dependent upon the context in which the term is used. Primarily on altitudinal grounds, Steers drew his eastern boundary for the province as a line running from approximately west of the river Parrett in the north to Budleigh Salterton in the south[2] (Map 1.1). While this has some validity with respect to the Bristol Channel coast, it is less tenable elsewhere because it omits the area of southeast Devon which must, perforce, be included in the present context.

The solid rocks of the southwest peninsula date from the Pre-Cambrian to the Cretaceous (Map 1.2), together with a limited number of later deposits, notably the Tertiary granite of Lundy and other, local, sedimentary outliers extending to the Lizard area. As far as Devon itself is concerned, the vast bulk of the rocks were laid down between two and four hundred million years ago, although they were often substantially modified thereafter. The Start Bay schists may be older, but Selwood and Durrance suggest a Lower Devonian age and Mottershead a Carboniferous one.[3] All periods from the Lower Devonian to the end of the Cretaceous are represented in the county or adjacent to it but, from the Permian onwards, presence on the coast is limited to the southeast. The Cretaceous oversteps the Jurassic deposits to rest directly on the Triassic and the Permian. This helps to explain the distribution of rock types east of the river Exe.

Devonian rocks make up much of the north and south coastlines. Indeed, with the possible exception of the Start Point area, all of the coast west of Tor Bay is of Devonian age. Similarly, the north coast from near Croyde eastwards as far as Minehead, Somerset, is of comparable age, the down-faulted Triassic deposits around Porlock excepted. The Lower Devonian is composed predominantly of sandstones and slates, but volcanics become a significant element within the Middle and Upper Devonian, while limestones occur in and around Tor Bay. Similar materials were deposited during the succeeding early Carboniferous (Dinantian) Period. This was followed in turn by the laying down of turbidite sandstones and shales in deep-sea conditions, approximately corresponding to the Millstone Grit of the Pennines. Thereafter, the granite of Dartmoor was intruded, while the Variscan orogeny had the effect of deforming the Carboniferous basin into a synclinorium (a long trough) trending east-west.

Map 1.1 Relief Map of the South West

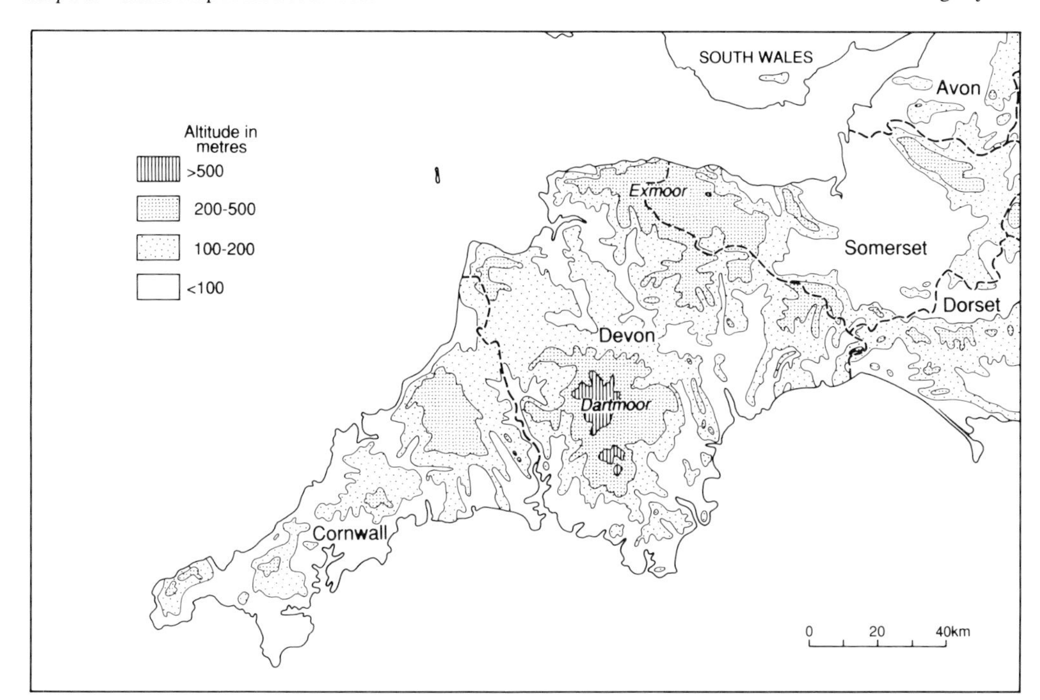

The end of the Carboniferous period saw various forms of igneous activity and some further orogenic movement. It also marked the beginning of desert conditions which continued through the Permian to the Triassic. Both the latter two periods were marked by torrential deposits (breccias and conglomerates), together with sandstones and mudstones. Between the deposition of clays and limestones of the following period, the Jurassic, and that of the glauconitic sand (Upper Greensand), Gault clay, and chalk during the Cretaceous, some folding, faulting, and erosion occurred. The Cretaceous was, in turn, succeeded by minor folding and faulting in the early Tertiary. Later in the Tertiary period, the Eocene was marked by erosion, gravel formation, and the intrusion of the Lundy granite. Thereafter, in the Oligocene, freshwater clays, sand, and lignite were laid down locally in basins. Faulting took place during this period, and thereafter.

The last 1.5 million years or so, which mark the Quaternary, represent a mixture of phases of erosion and localised deposition (eg of boulder

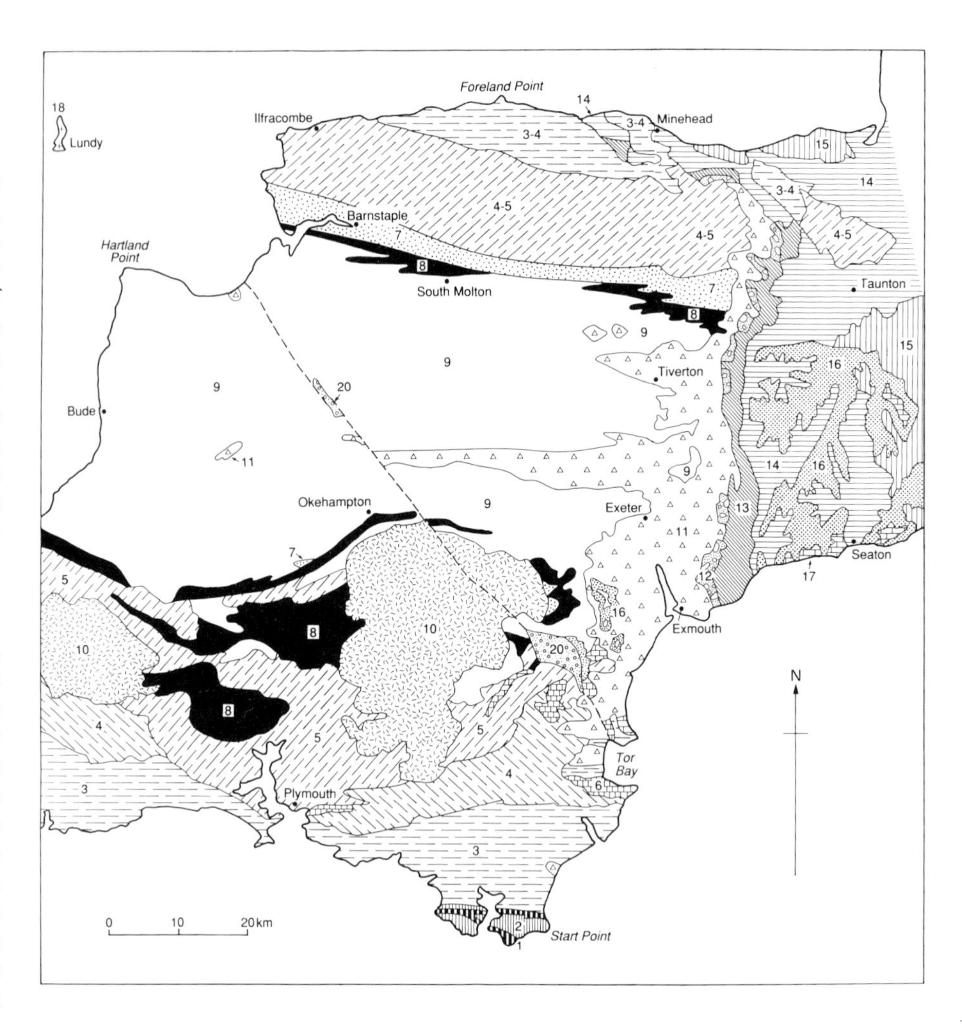

Map 1.2 The Geology of Devon. Based, with permission, on E M Durrance and D J C Laming (eds), *The Geology of Devon (Exeter 1982)*.

clay, head, peat, silt, clays and gravel), largely reflecting the presence or absence of glacial stages and the inter-related, oscillating, sea levels.[4] The net result of this long succession of events is that the northern rock coastline, approximately south and west of Croyde, is made up almost exclusively of Upper Carboniferous sandstones and slates. (This is the unproductive counterpart of the Coal Measures in South Wales). The southern coast, east of Tor Bay, is of systematically younger age towards the east, progressing from the Permian, through the Triassic, to the Cretaceous. It is upon this framework, and that for the county as a whole, that the detailed form: scalloped headlands and bays, raised beaches (stranded shorelines) and rock platforms; sand dunes, barriers, and bars; and so on, has developed.

Geomorphology

With the notable exception of the Taw-Torridge river system, virtually all of the rivers in the county drain towards the south coast (Map 1.3). Even in the case of the Torridge, the tributary river Waldon and the upper Torridge itself flow southeast and east from just landward of Hartland Quay to near Hatherleigh, where they join the river Okement. The whole is then redirected to the north coast at Bideford. Both the Tamar and the Exe rise within 5 or 6 kilometres of the north coast between Hartland Quay and Bude, and between Lynton and Porlock on Exmoor, respectively. Thus there are two main elements in the fluvial drainage of Devon and the neighbouring area: this pronounced tendency for the streams and rivers to flow to the south, and the radial drainage pattern of streams off Dartmoor. In large measure these two tendencies are complementary, and reflect the superimposition of the drainage regime from an earlier geological cover and topography. The net effect is that those drainage channels that do reach the north coast are small, short, and steeply graded, often culminating in small waterfalls wherever the coastline is cliffed. They contrast markedly with the far more substantial, gentle river networks which flow southwards.

Particularly in an agricultural context, these south-directed valleys have provided far greater economic potential while they, and the rivers as such, ensured a more viable means of communication than that feasible within the less hospitable environment of the land areas adjacent to the greater part of the northern coast.

It has already been observed that the coastline of both north and south Devon is closely related to the geology of which it is composed: for example, the variability in hardness of the sedimentary rocks, especially that of the grits and sandstones of the Lower Devonian and the Culm. But it also reflects the area's complex physical evolution. Steers wrote: 'Although there is a close relation between geological structure and coastal scenery, it is usually not so evident as in South Wales'.[5] Nor, indeed, as in the neighbouring county of Cornwall, where headlands often reflect the existence of igneous dykes, sills, and bosses. Yet it is still clear.

In general there is the contrast of the high, inhospitable, northern coast with the softer, more mellow, southern one. Again, this is a gross simplification of the picture, and most elements and coastal features can be found at certain locations on each coast. Steers and Kidson have each described the coastal milieu[6] as a whole, while other authors have examined certain areas (EAN Arber for north Devon)[7] or specific features (MA Arber; Durrance regarding cliffs and cliff profiles, and buried channels of the Exe and the Taw-Torridge,[8] respectively). While it is important to look at each coastline as an entity, it is also necessary to examine the diversity contained within each one since both aspects help to account for the constraints in, and the potential for, development in Devon's maritime history, insofar as that may relate to the physical environment. Steers commented that the 'coast of the Southwest peninsula . . . differs from (most of) that of the rest of the country in that it is far more crenulate and indented' reflecting old rocks, young form, and a drowned shoreline. He wrote that '. . . lines of cliffs in Somerset, Devon and Cornwall are very diverse in form'.[9] While in Cornwall this diversity is, in large measure, a reflection of the geological constituents, this is less obviously true of Devon, where structural elements are probably as important.

North Devon

Kidson regarded the cliffs of the Hartland area of north Devon as 'some of the finest sea cliffs in England', while Steers described those of north Devon as a whole as 'perhaps the most imposing in England and Wales'.[10] The centre of the elongated trough referred to above runs in a line very approximately from Tiverton to Bude, so that the age of the rocks becomes systematically older to the north (and to the south) and the folds become progressively more inclined.[11] The major folds have a wavelength of 2 to 10 kilometres, but minor folds vary depending upon their relative position and the coherence of the rock material, with wavelengths of a few metres for shales and a few hundred metres for sandstones. The folded cliffs are cut by faults, those running in a northwest-southeast direction being particularly prominent. The throw of the faults is highly variable, ranging from several metres to several kilometres in the case of those at Sticklepath and Lustleigh.

The gentle land surface of the Hartland peninsula truncates the geological structure. Keene regarded the surface as marine and Pleistocene in age, unlike the older, probably sub-aerial higher surfaces of the South West, and with a maximum elevation of some 200 metres.[12] The severe wave attack from the Atlantic ensures that the west-facing cliffs of the Hartland coast form an abrupt boundary to the terrestrial landscape, although the detail is determined by differential erosion of the particular rock, and the structural form. The coastline, like that of Lundy Island, has been the scene of many shipwrecks in the past. Coastal waterfalls and hanging valleys occur intermittently all the way from Boscastle, Cornwall, to Lynton, Devon, and

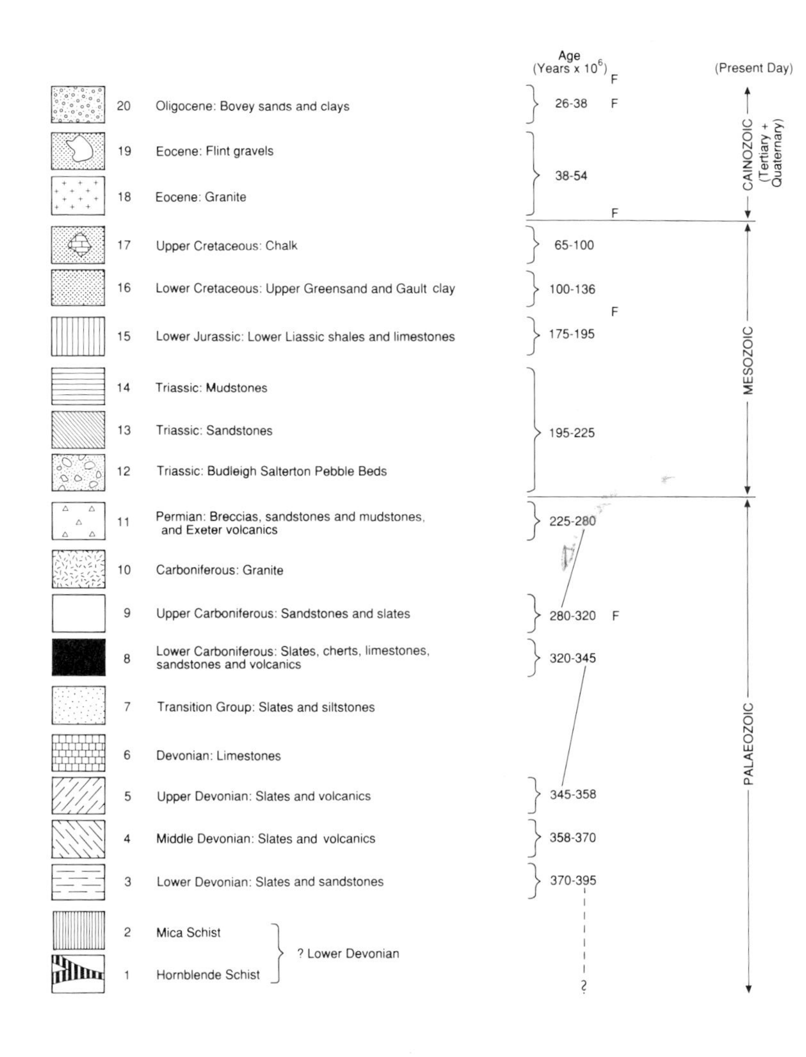

are a response to the inter-relation of coastal erosion rates, rock resistance, and the capacity of streams, with only the larger valleys at base level. There is a marked contrast between the exposed west-facing Hartland coast and the north-facing one, as at Clovelly. This reflects the short northeast fetch and the highly refracted waves of the latter (see below). Keene believed that sub-aerial erosion predominates and that landslips are more prevalent in the relatively protected, Clovelly, area.[13] Wooded, incised, combes are typical.

The other major area of cliffs extends continuously from just north of the Taw-Torridge estuary into the neighbouring county of Somerset. In places this area rises to over 300 metres close to the coast and thereafter more gently to exceed 500 metres in the highest parts of Exmoor. In general, the cliffs tend to be of hog's back form representing the scarp edge of inland-dipping rocks. Only the base of these cliffs relates to modern coastal processes. That above reflects structural and sub-aerial processes. Even along the stretch of Middle and Lower Devonian cliffs which run from roughly east of Combe Martin to near Porlock, and again beyond, there is some diversity (eg the Valley of Rocks, near Lynton), and this is enhanced from Combe Martin westwards as geology becomes more varied and sandstones and shales/slates each dominate alternating stretches of coast. Thus there are the complex coastline of Ilfracombe, the slate reefs of Morte Point, the resistant headlands of Baggy Point and Down End, and the embayments of Woolacombe and Croyde. Nevertheless, Keene thought that although there was a relationship between coastal configuration and geology it was not necessarily the one that might logically have been anticipated.[14] Both Woolacombe and Croyde are fronted by sand dunes, but the best dunes in the whole South West are found at Braunton Burrows, where the 30 metre-plus high, 5 by 2 kilometres in area, system forms the northern flank of the Taw-Torridge estuary.

On the other side of the estuary are the less-imposing Northam Burrows and the well-known Westward Ho! pebble ridge with its history of erosion and retreat over the past 150 years. Evidence for environmental change is provided by the raised beaches and 'head' deposits flanking the cliffs immediately north of Braunton Burrows and west of Westward Ho! as well as in the till and clay up-estuary at Fremington. The inter- and pre-glacial rock channel of the Taw-Torridge is buried to a depth of −24 metres at Appledore Pool, while the channel can be traced some 12 kilometres offshore,[15] where it terminates in a buried cliffline.[16]

Parts of the Taw-Torridge estuary are subject to marked change at the present day, for example the erosion of the southwest and south flanks of the Braunton Burrows dune system. This retreat can be traced for over a century or so at varying rates, and may be linked directly to sand and gravel extraction in the neighbourhood, principally at Crow Point. Tracer experiments showed that sand, transported by waves, renourished Crow from the north, and that there was some sediment exchange from the shoreline at the Burrows to Bideford Bar.[17] Other sand was detected having travelled upstream towards Bideford from Instow, opposite the port of Appledore.

South Devon

Although there are drowned valleys on the north coast, it is on the southern one that they are both more numerous and best developed. Here there is a full spectrum, ranging from the almost totally infilled feature (such as that underlying Slapton Ley and the 8-kilometre-long adjacent coastal barrier), through partially infilled valleys and channels (the Tamar, Kingsbridge, and Teign estuaries are examples and are, in some respects, analogous to that of the Taw-Torridge in the north), to relatively sediment-free systems such as that of the lower Dart with its deepwater anchorage. Such drowned valleys, or rias, form a major element in the coastal landscape – only the scale varies – and reflect the complex geological history. The valleys were carved out at a time, or times, of lower relative sea level than that prevalent today, while the infilling (which may include tin deposits) has been related to various periods in geological notably Quaternary, history.[18] Again, as on the north coast, the changing sea levels of the Quaternary Period are also reflected in raised

Map 1.3 The Drainage Pattern of Devon

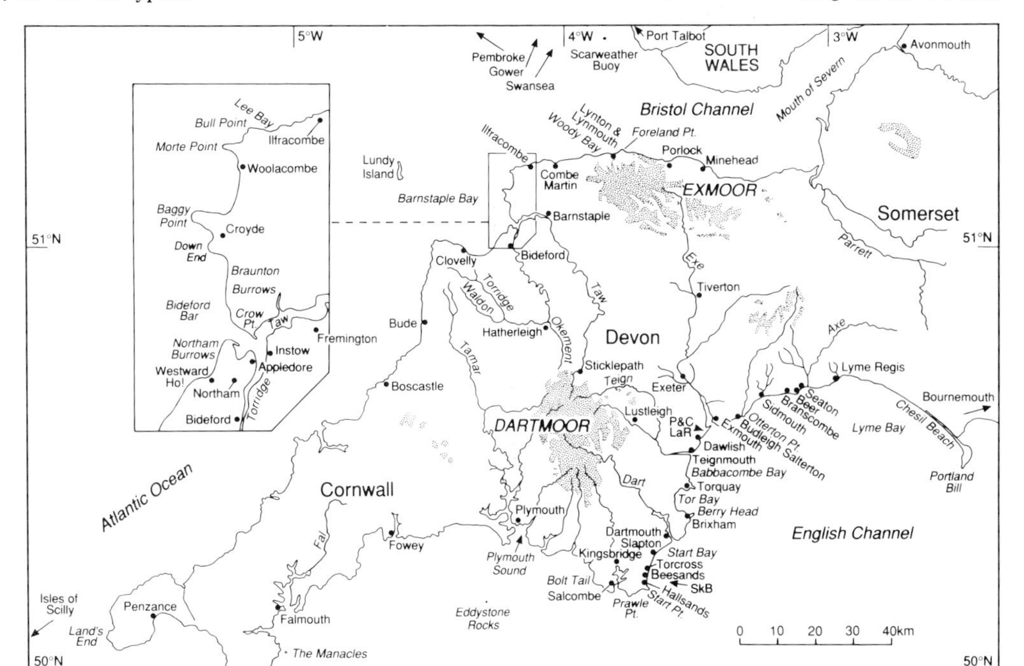

beaches and inter-tidal platforms. Good examples are found at various locations in the Start Bay area (eg near Prawle Point, at Lannacombe, and at Hallsands), and elsewhere (eg Hope's Nose, near Torquay). Mottershead thought that there was evidence of coastal platforms at three levels in the Start district.[19] If his suggestion that the 500-metre, the widest of these discontinuous platforms, took some one million years to develop is accurate, then at least part of the sequence almost certainly has to be pre-Quaternary or composite in origin. The last phase, which began about ten thousand years ago, was one of relatively rising sea level, and is demonstrated by areas of submerged forest, the upper parts of which can still be seen under favourable conditions at extreme low tides (eg at Blackpool Sands and in part of Tor Bay). Once again there are counterparts of these features along the Bristol Channel, as at Bridgwater Bay, Somerset.

However, there are two major differences between the north and south coasts of Devon. These are relative height and degree of diversity. Thus the north coast is generally of substantially greater elevation and displays more continuity of form than that of the south. While there are contrasts, as between the Atlantic and Barnstaple Bay facing western flank of the county, or between the unconsolidated sediments infilling the valley system of the Taw-Torridge and the solid geological framework, such contrasts are on a coarser scale than those along the south coast. This is especially true of the latter west of the river Exe as far as, and beyond, the county boundary. The Kingsbridge estuary provides a case in point. Even within a single estuary the width, slope, and height closely relate to the underlying geological structures, with the narrow entrance to Salcombe harbour cut through the relatively resistant, vertically-bedded, schists. The copious sediment deposited within the valley system is, according to Mottershead, the result of the yield attributable to the high relief further upstream towards Dartmoor.[20] In the west the coastal cliffs are up to 150 metres high; towards the eastern county boundary this figure may be slightly exceeded.

In traversing the southern coast from west to east one passes from the mainly sedimentary Devonian rocks of the Plymouth Sound area, through the highly metamorphosed schists of Bolt Tail and Start Point, via faulted slates in part of Start Bay, to the diverse Lower and Middle Devonian geology of the area around, and east of, the entrance to the river Dart. The shales and igneous rocks of the latter have been subject to markedly different rates of erosion so that stacks and resistant headlands are characteristic features. The Devonian limestones of Berry Head are succeeded by the softer Secondary Permian and Triassic deposits of Tor Bay, but Devonian rocks again form the headland at the north of the bay. In the Tor Bay district structural factors (particularly the complex faulting) and the presence of igneous and metamorphic rocks (dolerite at Black Head; igneous sills; slates) all contribute to the detailed variety of the geomorphology.

From Babbacombe to the county boundary in the east the solid geology is all of Secondary age; Permian, Triassic, and Cretaceous. While the geological units are somewhat larger, diversity still persists within them, and is augmented by unconsolidated deposits such as the soft, mainly muddy sediments infilling the Teign and Exe estuaries. The red coloured Permian clays, marls, breccias, and conglomerates which extend as far east as the Exe estuary provide a sequence of features, such as the Parson and Clerk stacks, and Langstone Rock, which alternate with the softer, seawall-clad, coastal stretches.

The bar at the mouth of the Teign has been widely considered as 'cyclical' in nature,[21] while the Dawlish Warren sandspit, which flanks the west side of the entrance to the Exe estuary, has had a long history of depletion and only survives in its present form as a result of extensive coast protection works in the late 1960s and 1970s.[22] The precise inter-relationship between the embankment on which the main railway line from Exeter to the South West runs, and Dawlish Warren, has been a subject of controversy because the spit is really only one, albeit prominent, component of the estuarial system, and no direct link can be readily drawn between railway and sandspit.

Exmouth, and its compact docks, lie opposite to Dawlish Warren, with a deep channel between. There are some minor dunes to the east before solid geology is once more exposed at the surface. Notable here are the Budleigh Salterton Pebble Beds, which are thought to be a minor constituent of Chesil Beach, Dorset, although Carr and Blackley have cast some doubt about this.[23] From Otterton Point, through Sidmouth and Branscombe to Beer Head, there is a succession of changes in the detailed geology and in the form of the coastline with small pebbly bays, stacks and arches, and reefs offshore being typical. Steers noted that erosion of the coastline here is of the order of 8 feet per century.[24]

The most westerly extension of the classic landslip area of Devon and Dorset is represented in the short stretch between Branscombe and Beer Head, where sandy Cretaceous deposits overlie Triassic clays. Nearby, faulting results in the juxtaposition of Red Marls and Greensand, and the consequent erosion of Seaton Bay. At the east side of the bay is the deflected exit of the river Axe. Landslip areas reoccur, and extend beyond the county boundary near Lyme Regis, into Dorset. The slips there are complex in form, with both slumping and rotational shear being important processes in their development. In common with coastal landslips elsewhere they reflect the inter-relation of porous sands and limestones, and impermeable clays; geological structure; rainfall; and sea level, notably through the erosion of the toe by marine processes. In the coastal stretch east of Seaton the Lias clay (of early Jurassic age) tends to play the same role as the Triassic clays to the west of the town. In both areas substantial slips have occurred. Steers relates the loss of 7 to 10 acres in 1790 at South Down common near Beer Head, while other, even larger, slips took place in the nineteenth century at Bindon and Dowlands, east of Seaton.[25]

A wide range of geological types; a diversity of processes which have varied through time in relative importance, one to another: these have combined to give the Devon landscape, especially the coastline, its almost unique kaleidoscopic character.

The Sea Floor – Form and Composition

Bathymetry

Once away from the immediate coastline, the slopes on the seabed (Map 1.4) are rarely as severe as those on land. The bathymetry directly adjacent to Devon's coast represents a hesitant progression from the ruggedness of Cornwall in the west to the mainly gentler contours off Somerset and Dorset to the east. Yet within this 'hesitant progression' much diversity occurs. Further offshore the picture is somewhat similar, with the rock-strewn Isles of Scilly giving way to only the occasional irregularity that manifests itself above the sea surface in features such as the Eddystone Rocks or the island of Lundy. Seawards of the coast of southeast Devon and west Dorest the seabed is smoother again and, where rock outcrops occur, they provide little obvious topographic response. On the north coast, as Devon merges into Somerset, the bathymetry begins to reflect the dynamic sediment regime of the Bristol Channel. The nature of the sediments comprising the seabed is

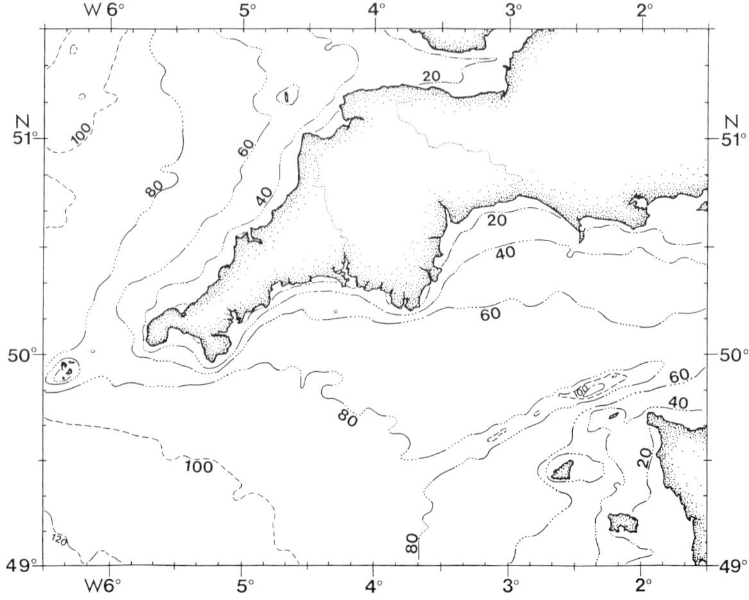

Map 1.4 Generalised Bathymetry of the Southwestern Approaches (in metres).

discussed below. It is sufficient to point out here that the rocky intricacies of the Cornish coast produce near-permanent, known hazards, whereas soft shorelines (e.g. the Skerries Bank, Start Bay, or Bideford Bar, at the mouth of the Taw-Torridge estuary) result in changing, less predictable ones.

North coast

Three Admiralty Charts cover the broad outline of the north coast of Devon,[26] although more detailed surveys are available for local areas. In the west the form of the offshore seabed is fairly straightforward, but the prevalence of wrecks, and names such as Tense Rocks, testify to the inhospitable nature of the immediate coastline. The 20-metre isobath is generally a little more than 2 kilometres offshore. Thereafter slopes are rather irregular but, with the exception of the area north of Hartland, depths eventually reach approximately 50 metres at 15 to 20 kilometres offshore.

Further to the east there is the juxtaposition of the best haven, that of the Taw-Torridge estuary, and the most complex bathymetry both near and offshore. Much of this offshore irregularity is not critical, because of depths greater than 25 metres, but this is not universally true. The most conspicuous exception is the 5-kilometre-long, north-south trending island of Lundy. It is not merely the island itself which presents a hazard to shipping, but also the banks related to it. Although Stanley Bank is covered by over 8 metres of water, and the North West Bank by still more, both generate tide rips which are a navigational hazard.

All of Barnstaple Bay is less than 30 metres deep at low water, and most of it less than 20 metres. Between Clovelly in the south and Down End in the north the ten-metre contour is of the order of 1.5 kilometres offshore, and occasionally slightly more. This distance reflects the gently shelving coast, but the southern boundary of the bay from Clovelly to Westward Ho! is all rocky cliffs. Elsewhere the coast is composed of pebbles and sand, and liable to shift. The relevant chart notes 'changing depths' on Bideford Bar.

From Down End northwards the bathymetry becomes more complex; for example, Asp Rock is covered by only 4 metres of water at low tide but is 1.5 kilometres off the Down End coastline. Similarly, Baggy Rock is about 1 kilometre off Baggy Point. There are reefs off Morte Point. But, as in the case of Lundy, it is not merely the absolute depths that are important; again it is the tide rips and overfalls that result from the form of the seabed, and the navigational hazards related thereto. From Bull Point eastwards the coast takes on essentially east-west orientation. There are small, relatively sheltered, bays, as at Lee and Combe Martin, and a fairly substantial harbour at Ilfracombe. Nevertheless, there are problems both as to the size of vessels and drying out. West of Foreland Point the 20-metre contour is mostly 1.5 to 2.5 kilometres offshore; east of Foreland, as far as Minehead, Somerset, it is 6 to 7 kilometres offshore, and the seabed becomes even shallower further to the east. There are complications inshore of the 20-metre isobath. For example, Copperas Rock, which has only 2.4 metres clearance, is located approximately 1 kilometre offshore, east of Combe Martin; there are shallows with some 4 metres depth off Woody Bay; and there is a drying sand ridge which runs west from Foreland Point, while Foreland Ledge extends off the Point itself for about 2 kilometres. Yet again, tide rips and overfalls are associated with much of this coastline.

South coast

Three other Admiralty Charts cover the general outline of the south coast from Falmouth to the Bill of Portland[27] although, once again, more detailed bathymetry is available for coastal areas such as Plymouth Sound. There are notable areas of wrecks off the Manacles, near Falmouth harbour, and also south of Plymouth Sound, ie southeast of Eddystone Rocks. In general the offshore seabed topography there is fairly straightforward and slopes progressively downwards to about 40 to 70 metres away from the coast. The principal exceptions are the Eddystone Rocks themselves, which dry out, and Hands Deep to the northwest. The coastline west of Plymouth Sound is mainly indented and rocky. East of the Sound the coastal and nearshore bathymetry is again complicated, as at Renney Rocks and Great Mewstone island. There, the 20-metre isobath varies in its distance offshore, but is typically of the order of 2 kilometres or so as far east as Start Point. Seawards of 20 metres, depths tend to increase progressively once more, but there are exceptions, with East Rutts being covered by less than 9 metres, yet located some 9 kilometres off the coast.

The Skerries Bank trails northeast from Start Point. This 7 kilometre-long structure is typically covered by some 5 metres of water, but with a minimum of barely 2 metres. From Start Bay to Tor Bay the distance offshore of the 20-metre contour is highly variable, ranging from 1 to nearly 6 kilometres. East of Dartmouth as far as, and including, Tor Bay, the offshore seabed is some 25 to 45 metres deep. While this is rather shallower than further west, it nevertheless retains a similar simple topographic expression. Between the Dart estuary and Berry Head there are a number of rocks and ledges, some of which dry out or are permanently exposed. However, all of these features are close inshore. Although there are rocky elements along the coast between Teignmouth and Dawlish, the shoreline in general is less accidented north of Hope's Nose, Torquay. Difficulties of port access to the Teign and the Exe are due to shifting channels rather than solid geometry. The bathymetry away from the coast continues, in the main, to shelve yet more gently with the 10-metre contour up to 1.5 kilometres offshore, and the 20-metre one up to 10 kilometres, but typically in the range of 5 to 6 kilometres. Because the tidal range is smaller along the south coast, tide rips and overfalls are less well developed, but they may be present as in the neighbourhood of Start Point and the Skerries Bank, where they contribute to the navigational problems.

Offshore of both the north and south Devon coasts there are comparatively few bathymetric hazards but, where they do occur, they tend to be dramatic in scale. Nearer the shore the risks are greater and more varied. But it is the degree of exposure of the south west peninsula as a whole which magnifies the potential difficulties to seafarers.

Geology of the Seabed

The constituents of the sea floor are important for such diverse industries as fishing and aggregate extraction. Although, in recent years, the seabed geology has become much better known, it remains far less well-defined than that of the land,[28] partly from the relative paucity of boreholes and the uneven coverage of geophysical surveys. The description that follows is based largely on the British Geological Survey 1:250,000 solid and seabed sediment map series.[29]

The north coast

The solid rock version of the Lundy sheet is a good example of the problems of generalization, in that the detailed zonation of the Devonian and Carboniferous rocks on land (eg in the case of the Devonian, the Morte Slates; Ilfracombe Slates; and Hangman Grits) become less elaborately classified offshore as part of the Pilton Beds. The sheet shows severe faulting in the Jurassic deposits immediately north of the Cainozoic (Tertiary) granite of Lundy island. An extensive basin stretches to the west where younger Cretaceous rocks are prominent.[30]

Various sources indicate a relatively complicated picture of sediment distribution with an irregular 'rough rock floor' exposed on the seabed off most of the northeast coast of Cornwall and almost the whole of north Devon apart from Barnstaple Bay.[31] This complex sediment pattern extends towards the Bristol Channel although, in general, gravels there skirt the remaining north Devon, and west Somerset, coast.[32] These areas of coarse aggregate extend as far west as Lundy island. The Lundy surface geology sheet shows sediment varying from a few centimetres to more than 20 metres deep, with the thickest area in a line drawn from Pembroke to Bideford.[33] Sandwaves and sandbanks shown on this sheet are mostly confined to due west of the Gower peninsula although, in fact, they are also known from Barnstaple Bay.

The south coast

The solid geology of the south coast (Portland sheet[34]) continues logically outwards along the whole coast from the so-called Isle of Portland in the east, through Sidmouth, to Tor Bay, where the offshore geology is once more shown in simplified form. The schists of the Start complex are labelled offshore as 'basement undivided'. In the case of the Start area *sensu stricto* this group extends about 12 kilometres south of the coastline. With the exception of bedrock outcrops west of Start Point a virtually continuous sand cover is indicated along almost the whole coast. Areas of sandwaves, furrows, and ridges mostly occur further offshore, with a maximum sediment thickness of up to 5 metres, corresponding to the sandwaves. However, sandwaves are also prominent immediately seawards of the Tor Bay–Exmouth coastline, where they reach, and occasionally exceed, 10 metres in thickness.

Superimposed upon the broad brush outlines, as shown on the 1:250,000 scale geology maps, detailed sediment distribution patterns occur in localised areas such as the Taw-Torridge estuary or the tidal current-moulded sand and shell bank of the Skerries spawning ground in Start Bay. While most of these detailed features are naturally generated, this is not always the case. Human modifications of existing sediment circulations, resulting from habitations, port and harbour construction, fishing facilities and the like are of importance, at least on a local scale.

On resistant, hard rock, coasts erosion is not an important source of sediments. The beach deposits are more likely to have been derived from offshore as sea level rose relative to the land during post-glacial times, but inland sources brought down by river can also be of significance. Estuarine mud and silt are probably often from this source. In the case of Dawlish Warren, Kidson believed that the sand source was from along and offshore; Mottershead thought it came from inland via the river Exe.[35] Paramount, however, is the likelihood of simple redistribution of what is already there.

Sea Level, Tides and Waves

Sea level

On the open coast, such as that of north and south Devon, high and low tides occur twice each day (diurnally). They are amplified every two weeks at Springs and reduced on the alternate weeks between (Neaps), dependent upon the phases of the moon. Extreme ranges occur at, or about, the equinoxes, while secular variations, in the form of both positive and negative surges; seiches within harbours; and time delays, are a response to atypical meteorological conditions. Positive surges (ie sea level above prediction) occur with severe winds and low barometric pressure, and produce flooding. Negative surges may result in the grounding of vessels because the ships' draught exceeds actual, as distinct from predicted, seabed depth. But much greater fluctuations of sea level have occurred over geological time with the resulting coastline far offshore of the present coast during low stands corresponding to the maximum volume of water being locked up in icesheets and glaciers during glacial phases. Similarly, there is evidence of at least slightly higher sea levels during earlier inter-Glacial stages of the 1.5 million-year Quaternary Period. Whatever the timespan involved, the effect of varying sea level and tidal height is to shift the relative level at which coastal and offshore processes took, and continue to take, place. Both the short-term, diurnal, variations and the longer-term changes have had, and continue to have, their effects on Devon's maritime history.

Tidal range

Although in the open ocean the range between high and low water is as little as 30 centimetres, substantial increases may occur as a response to tidal phase and coastal configuration. The author has recently reviewed the implications in the context of the Devon coastline, and it is the intention here merely to summarize that work.[36]

The tidal range of the north and south coasts of Devon reflects, in the former case the amplifying effects of the funnel-shaped Bristol Channel/Severn estuary, and in the latter the more open southern coastline between Fowey and Portland. Thus, in the Bristol Channel, tidal range increases fairly progressively eastwards so that, at Avonmouth near Bristol, the mean spring tidal range is 12.3 metres.[37] However, on the southern coast, where overall range is less, such changes as take place result in a relatively systematic diminution in the same eastwards direction culminating in a range of only some 2.0 metres at the amphidromic point near Bournemouth. Tidal ranges are correspondingly less on Neaps. For example, at Plymouth (Devonport) the mean spring range is 4.7 metres, but that at Neaps is only 2.2 metres. Similarly, along the Bristol Channel coast, the mean spring ranges at Ilfracombe and Avonmouth are reduced from 8.5 to 3.9 metres, and from 12.3 to 6.5 metres, respectively.

Where a river estuary occurs there are two conflicting tendencies: an increase owing to convergence and a decrease attributable to frictional losses of energy. The topographic and bathymetric form of the estuary is relevant in this context. In the case of the Taw-Torridge estuary in north Devon the mean Spring tidal range falls from 7.3 metres at Appledore to 5.9 and 3.8 metres at Bideford and Barnstaple, respectively. This reduction in tidal range is also attributable, in some measure, to both the freshwater flow from the upper reaches and the increasing elevation of the river bed upstream. While, in theory, the diminution in tidal range up-estuary provides certain logistic advantages, in practice these are outweighed by the short period at the top of the tide during which navigation is possible and the erratic nature of the freshwater input subsequent to precipitation events in the respective river catchment. In the open ocean the tidal curve is sinusoidal in form, and in the case of both the north and south Devon coasts is only slightly modified from this ideal pattern. As a result, while the tidal ranges may vary, the duration during which a given percentage of the maximum tidal level is reached remains much the same throughout, estuaries excepted. However, variations in tidal velocities are more significant. The implications of tidal range are in harbour engineering, cargo handling, and ship design and handling, but the response is not necessarily the same under different levels of technology and different economic circumstances.

Tidal currents

The tides are primarily the sum of the gravitational attraction of the moon and the sun, and the gravitational attraction and centrifugal force of the earth. However, a whole series of harmonics are generated. In addition, the geoidal form of the Earth, and the Earth's plasticity play a small role.[38]

In the open North Atlantic the current is especially susceptible to wind. Wind-generated currents are approximately one-thirtieth of the speed of the wind which produces them and, because of the Earth's rotation, at 30 degrees to the right in the Northern Hemisphere. Thus the *West Coasts . . . Pilot* states that winds would have to blow at Force 6 for 12 hours to give a wind-drift current of about 0.5 knots and at Force 9 for 48 hours to give one of some 1.25 knots.[39] Lag effects continue once the generating wind has ceased to blow. The *Channel Pilot* notes that once the tidal currents are removed from the computations there remains a weak up-channel set.[40] In the Western Approaches to the English Channel tidal streams are more or less rotatory clockwise with little variation in direction and rate at different locations. However, further up-channel tides become progressively more rectilinear. The rates correspond with width, so that at the narrowest parts of the English Channel the maximum velocity at springs is approximately 3.5 knots, whereas in wider areas it is limited to 2.0–2.5 knots.[41]

Maximum tidal velocities along the open coast are approxmately twice as great on spring tides as on neaps (eg Ilfracombe: Flood 3.1; 1.7 knots; ebb 2.9; 1.6 knots: Start Point: Flood 1.9; 1.1 knots; ebb 2.1; 1.2 knots: Tor Bay/Exmouth: Flood 0.8; 0.4 knots; ebb 0.9; 0.5 knots[42]). The high velocities and coastal bathymetry are such as to produce tidal races and overfalls at various locations such as Hartland Point, Lundy, Morte Point, Bull Point and Foreland Point along the north coast, especially in bad weather. Complex local eddies and circulation may occur over parts of the tidal cycle, as in the Dartmouth area, and in the approaches to Teignmouth. In the latter case the channels make it impossible for ships to enter the estuary in bad weather and indeed, with southerly or southeasterly gales, there is no shelter between Start Point and Portland Bill except in Dartmouth, Brixham, and Torquay harbours.[43]

The tidal current regime within estuaries may be more complex, reflecting such factors as the degree of tidal mixing of fresh and salt water; the horizontal juxtaposition of ebb and flood channels; and the effect of varying cross-channel width at different water levels. Tidal mixing, in particular, is a three-dimensional effect with denser, saline, water often underlying fresher, surface water, so that tidal currents at the surface and near the seabed may be partially out of phase. This phenomenon is not restricted to river estuaries, while in both estuaries and the open sea tidal current velocities are normally substantially reduced near the seabed.

Sea waves

Sea waves are caused by the wind blowing over the water surface. Their height is proportional to the strength of the wind and the length of the water surface (fetch) across which it blows without obstruction. This simple statement has to be qualified in four respects: geographical and physical limits, the presence of swell, friction, and refraction. The last two are closely related.

Draper has noted that the British Isles are situated 'at the downwind end of one of the windier sea areas of the world, with the result that wave conditions can be severe and the average values of wave energy are high'.[44] On the exposed areas of the Continental Shelf wave motion can reach the seabed. In the UK the quietest open water areas are in the southeast of the British Isles. While windspeeds are not appreciably lower there, fetches are more limited and the shallower water depths mean that friction reduces the wave energy. Characteristic short-period steep waves give rise to choppy seas. This contrasts with the relatively deep waters exposed to the Atlantic Ocean, where swell is a frequent constituent. Swell, unlike locally generated windwaves, is the legacy of wave-forming processes outside the immediate area. It is typically of long period and length, but often of relatively low amplitude. As Draper observes, there is very little difference between the wave climate of the deep ocean off the Hebrides or southern Ireland.[45] However, once the Continental Shelf is encountered, deformation becomes a possibility. Where direct measurement is not feasible, eg by pressure transducers on the seabed or by surface-following buoys, or where a specific storm event is to be examined, wave characteristics are hindcast from the windfields prevailing at the time of interest. Statistical procedures enable the probabilities of extreme wave heights to be calculated, and these are employed for determining the design heights of structures such as sea defence works and oil production platforms. However, there is evidence that wave heights are non-stationary.[46] That is, over a period of years there is a tendency for the average and/or extreme wave heights to increase (or decrease). Such a trend appears to be evident from the Atlantic since the 1960s. It seems likely that such non-stationarity will have occurred in times past, so that during earlier centuries Devon's shipping may have been systematically more prone to environmental hazards at certain times than at others.

The longest UK data set for sea waves is also that from the most exposed light vessel station, 'Sevenstones' off Land's End. Even so, whereas significant wave height (the average height of the highest one-third of the waves, [H_s]) reaches 4.0 metres in winter at the Ocean Weather Stations, it is already reduced to 2.4 metres at 'Sevenstones' and falls still further, to 0.9 metres, in the eastern English Channel. In summer (July–September) wave heights are approximately half those of winter (January–March), but this relationship does not necessarily apply elsewhere. Mean wave period in the open Atlantic in winter is of the order of ten seconds falling to eight seconds in summer but, because of the selective attenuation of long-period waves, there is less seasonal variation at the coast.[47]

Relatively long-term (ie a year or more) wave records are available for coastal sites in Devon, such as Slapton Sands, Start Bay, and Budleigh Salterton, Lyme Bay. Other peripheral locations such as Swansea Bay, South Wales, and Wyke Regis and West Bexington, both along Chesil Beach, Dorset, give an indication of the values to be expected at more exposed locations including those for the Devon coast. Data for Start Bay show that, for wave period [T_s], the largest class falls between 6.0 and 6.5 seconds, but that the distribution is highly skewed towards long-period waves.[48] At Slapton 50 per cent exceeded 0.16 metres in height, with approximately 5 per cent exceeding 1 metre, but virtually none 2 metres.[49] The offshore Skerries Bank has the effect of causing marked variation in the height, period, and direction of waves at the coast as between high and low water. At Wyke Regis, Chesil Beach the peak T_z falls between 10.0 and 10.5 seconds, with 50 per cent of the waves (as H_s) exceeding 0.26 metres and 2.7 per cent exceeding 2.0 metres. The maximum wave height during the observation period was calculated as about 8.0 metres.[50]

Thus, while median wave heights are not unduly large, maximum storm wave heights can be substantial and, coupled with relatively long wave periods, are capable of providing considerable energy at times.[51]

Budleigh has a 'wave regime somewhat intermediate between that of Chesil and Start Bay'.[52] Scarweather Sands, some 13 kilometres off the coast of Swansea Bay, South Wales, experiences a winter monthly mean wave height (as H_s) of between 1.8 and 2.2 metres, yet virtually no waves exceeding 3.5 metres.[53] The closely related, nearshore, wave recorder site at Port Talbot has a winter monthly mean of 1.4 metres, thus giving a tangible measure of frictional energy losses between the two sites.[54] The comparable summer figures for Scarweather and Port Talbot are 0.5 and 0.4 metres, respectively.[55]

Along the north Devon coast it is only the stretch that faces southwest, west, or northwest that is subject to the maximum effective fetch of some 3,800 kilometres from the Atlantic. Elsewhere there are only narrow windows where such conditions can prevail and, particularly on the coastline facing due north, most waves are relatively small and short-period in character, having been generated largely over the short fetch of the Bristol Channel and adjacent areas. Any long-period windwaves and swell there are heavily refracted and, as a consequence, have lost much of their energy. In the case of the south Devon coast analogous conditions apply. The most exposed area is between the Tamar estuary and Salcombe, where the coastline is once more subject to maximum fetch from the Atlantic. In contrast, the whole shoreline from Start Bay eastwards is affected almost exclusively by the choppy wave regime generated by winds from the south and southeast. It is only east of the county border that the coastline is again subject to maximum fetch from the Atlantic, as at Chesil Beach and the Isle of Portland. The fact that the southeast-facing coast of Devon is, under most circumstances, relatively well sheltered, only throws into relief the atypical event. For example, the storms affecting Torcross and its coastal defences in 1979, when easterly gales are alleged to have generated waves up to 5.5 metres high,[56] or the arrival at the coast of severely refracted, long-period swell from the northeast. Such swell would focus on Hallsands and Beesands and is likely to have been part of the cause of the final demise of Hallsands following the ill-advised extraction of the foreshore for the construction of Devonport docks at the turn of the century.[57]

Because of the greater tidal range of the north coast, relative to the south, the response to waves of a given height and period to an identical coastal feature will not be the same. The effects of waves will be spread over a greater altitudinal (and therefore spatial) range during the tidal cycle. As a consequence, at high water wave forces will be more, and at low water less effective because of the relative degree of attenuation through friction compared with the case where the tidal range is smaller. Under relatively severe conditions sea water may be trapped inshore between headlands, so warping the mean sea level of the sea surface. This phenomenon, known as wave 'set-up', allows wave crests to operate from an abnormally high level before breaking. The process can have economic consequences such as the over-topping of sea defences. Trapped water flows seaward at systematically distributed points alongshore in the form of 'rip currents'. These are often a hazard to bathers. Another type of hazard is the abnormally high breaker which occurs from time to time within a given wave regime. These are attributable to the interaction of two wave trains, or of waves and swell, having different periods and directions of approach. Because of the differing frequencies the two trains come into and out of phase one with another, initially complementing and thereafter decrementing each other.

The Environment and Man

The environment has provided both opportunities and constraints. For example, rocky coastlines have presented hazards of shipwreck but also the possibility of sheltered havens. Similarly, shifting sand and gravel banks have acted as both navigational dangers and economic stimuli, whether as a source of aggregate or fish spawning grounds. The scope and limitations have varied over time as technology has developed. But it is not just the immediate coastline that is relevant. Nor can one consider Devon as an entity. Thus there is the contrast between the relatively inhospitable north coast – the Taw-Torridge estuary almost alone excepted – and the gentler southern one. And even within the limits of the latter there is much diversity and differing potential reflecting the respective hinterlands. Where broader, gentler, rivers debauched on the coast they could provide marketing scope for agriculture and the woollen industries, as well as enabling easier communications generally. Here was no maritime cul-de-sac, as the Bristol Channel tended to be, but an opportunity to develop and capitalize upon the sea routes extending westwards across the Atlantic, and eastwards to southeast and eastern England and the mainland of Europe. The ways in which the physical endowments as a whole were utilised is the subject of much of the rest of this volume.

1: The Environmental Background

1 EM Durrance and DJC Laming, eds, *The Geology of Devon* (Exeter, 1982), 3.
2 JA Steers, *The Coastline of England and Wales* (Cambridge, 1946), 205.
3 EB Selwood and EM Durrance, 'The Devonian Rocks', in Durrance and Laming, eds, *Geology of Devon*, 20–2; D Mottershead, *Classic Landforms of the South Devon Coast* (Sheffield, 1986), 15.
4 While the series of glaciations of the Quaternary is not representative of the longer-term geological picture, the complications which it reflects may be more typical than the apparent simplicity of earlier times. It could be that these events are simply closer to the geological present and therefore more readily discernible.
5 Steers, *Coastline*, 205.
6 Steers, *Coastline*, 205–68; C Kidson, 'The Coasts of South and Southwest England', in JA Steers, ed. *Field Studies in the British Isles* (1964), 26–42.
7 EAN Arber, *The Coast Scenery of North Devon* (1911).
8 MA Arber, 'Cliff Profiles of Devon and Cornwall', *Geographical Journal*, 114 (1949), 191–7; MA Arber, 'The Cliffs of North Devon', *Proceedings of the Geological Association*, 85 (1974), 147–57; EM Durrance, 'The Buried Channels of the Exe', *Geological Magazine*, 106 (1969), 174–89; EM Durrance, 'Gradients of Buried Channels in Devon', *Proceedings of the Ussher Society* 3 (1974), 113–119.
9 Steers, *Coastline*, 210.
10 Kidson, 'Coasts of Southwest England', 26; Steers, *Coastline*, 205.
11 P Keene, *Classic Landforms of the North Devon Coast* (Sheffield, 1986), 6.
12 Keene, *North Devon Landforms*, 7.
13 Keene, *North Devon Landforms*, 10.
14 Keene, *North Devon Landforms*, 31.
15 Durrance, 'Gradients', 117; PB MacFarlane, 'Survey of Two Drowned River Valleys in Devon', *Geological Magazine*, 92 (1955), 419–29.
16 The subject of the Quaternary history of the county of Devon is discussed by RA Cullingford, 'The Quaternary', in Durrance and Laming, eds. *Geology of Devon*, 249–90; that of the South West as a whole is dealt with by C Kidson, 'The Coast of South West England', in C Kidson and MJ Tooley, eds, *The Quaternary History of the Irish Sea* (Liverpool, 1977), 257–98.
17 MWL Blackley, AP Carr, and R Gleason, *Tracer Experiments in the Taw-Torridge Estuary with Particular Reference to Braunton Burrows NNR* (Unit of Coastal Sedimentation Report 1972/22, Taunton).
18 EML Hendriks, 'The Physiography of South-West Cornwall', *Geological Magazine*, 60 (1923), 21–3; Steers, *Coastline*, 259; Cullingford, 'The Quaternary', 287.
19 Mottershead, *South Devon Landforms*, 22.
20 Mottershead, *South Devon Landforms*, 10.
21 Steers, *Coastline*, 251; AHW Robinson, 'Cyclical Changes in Shoreline Development at the Entrance to Teignmouth Harbour, Devon, England', in J Hails and A Carr, eds, *Nearshore Sediment Dynamics and Sedimentation* (Chichester, 1975), 181–200.
22 C Kidson, 'Dawlish Warren: A Study of the Evolution of Sand Spits Across the Mouth of the River Exe in Devon', *Transactions of the Institute of British Geographers*, 16 (1952), 69–80.
23 AP Carr and MWL Blackley, 'A Statistical Analysis of the Beach Metaquartzite Cherts from Budleigh Salterton, Devon', *Proceedings of the Ussher Society*, 3 (1975), 311.
24 Steers, *Coastline*, 264.
25 Steers, *Coastline*, 264.
26 Hydrographic Department, Taunton (hereafter HD), Admiralty Charts: 'Trevose Head to Hartland Point', 1156 (1973); 'Hartland Point to Ilfracombe', 1164 (1974); 'Worm's Head to Watchet', 1165, (1976). All on Scale 1:75,000.
27 HD, Admiralty Charts: 'Falmouth to Plymouth', 1267 (1972); 'Eddystone Rocks to Berry Head', 1613 (1972); 'Berry Head to Bill of Portland', 3315 (1973). All on Scale 1:75,000.
28 G Warrington and B Owens, *Micropalaeontological Biostratigraphy of Off-shore Samples from South West Britain*, Institute of Geological Sciences Report 77/7 (1977). Cited in Durrance and Laming, eds, *Geology of Devon*, 6, where an outline bedrock geology map of the south-west peninsula and surrounding area is reproduced.
29 British Geological Survey, Offshore Geological Map Series (hereafter BGS). Scale 1:250,000. Solid: Guernsey (1980); Lands End (1985); Lundy (1983); Portland (1983). Seabed Sediments: Bristol Channel (includes Quaternary Geology) (1986); Lizard (1983); Lundy (1983); Portland (1983).
30 BGS, 1:250,000 (1983).
31 DN Langhorne and NH Kenyon, *Collation of Data on the Form and Composition of the Sea Bed in the South-Western Approaches to the British Isles and the Celtic Sea*, Institute of Oceanographic Sciences (hereafter IOS), Internal Document 45, (Taunton, 1979). Note particularly Diagrams 2 and 4. MA Johnson, NH Kenyon, RH Belderson and AH Stride, 'Sand Transport', in AH Stride, ed. *Offshore Tidal Sands* (1982), 58–94.
32 BGS, 1:250,000 (1986).
33 BGS, 1:250,000 (1983).
34 BGS, 1:250,000 (1983).
35 C Kidson, 'Dawlish Warren, Devon: Late Stages in Sand Spit Evolution', *Proceedings of the Geological Association*, 75 (1964), 167–84; Mottershead, *South Devon Landforms*, 43–4.
36 AP Carr, 'The Implications of Tidal Range', in DJ Starkey, ed., *Devon's Coastline and Coastal Waters: Aspects of Man's Relationship with the Sea* (Exeter, 1988), 25–32.
37 HD, *Admiralty Tide Tables, Volume 1: European Waters* (1985).
38 For a detailed treatment of the subject see DT Pugh, *Tides, Surges, and Mean Sea Level* (Chichester, 1987).
39 HD, *West Coasts of England and Wales Pilot* (11th edn. 1974), Section 1.57.
40 HD, *Channel Pilot* (2nd edn. 1977), Section 1.82.
41 HD, *Channel Pilot*, Section 1.84.
42 HD, *Admiralty Tidal Stream Atlas: The English and Bristol Channels* (3rd edn, 1973), Figures 19 and 34.
43 HD, *Channel Pilot*, Section 4.1.
44 L Draper, 'Wave Climatology of the UK Continental Shelf', in FT Banner, MB Collins, and KS Massie, eds, *The North-West European Shelf Seas: The Sea Bed and the Sea in Motion, II, Physical and Chemical Oceanography, and Physical Resources* (Amsterdam, 1980), 354.
45 Draper, 'Wave Climatology', 354.
46 DJT Carter and L Draper, 'Has the North-east Atlantic Become Rougher?', *Nature*, 332 (1988), 494.
47 Draper, Wave Climatology', 354.
48 R Gleason, MWL Blackley, and AP Carr, 'Beach Stability and Particle Size Distribution, Start Bay', *Journal of the Geological Society of London*, 131 (1975), 86.
49 AP Carr, 'Differential Movement of Coarse Sediment Particles', *14th Conference on Coastal Engineering* (American Society of Civil Engineering, New York), 2 (1975), 859; Gleason, 'Beach Stability', 86.
50 PJ Hardcastle and AC King, 'Chesil Beach Sea Wave Records', *Civil Engineering*, 67 (1972), 299–300; AP Carr and MWL Blackley, 'Ideas on the Origin and Development of Chesil Beach', *Proceedings of the Dorset Natural History and Archaeological Society*, 95 (1974), 9.
51 AP Carr, 'Chesil Beach: Environmental, Economic and Sociological Pressures', *Geographical Journal*, 149 (1983), 54.
52 Carr, 'Differential Movement', 863.
53 BCH Fortnum and PJ Hardcastle, *Waves Recorded at Scarweather Bank in the Bristol Channel* (IOS Report 79, Taunton, 1979).
54 BCH Fortnum and PJ Hardcastle, *Waves Recorded at Port Talbot on the South Wales Coast* (IOS Report 78, Taunton, 1979).
55 AD Heathershaw, AP Carr, and HL King, *Swansea Bay (Sker) Project Topic Report 5: Wave Data: Observed and Computed Wave Climates* (IOS Report 99, Taunton, 1980); with the exception of the records from the offshore buoy at Scarweather Sands, Swansea Bay, all the figures quoted are strictly comparable, having been obtained by seabed pressure recorders. Surface buoys are able to detect very short-period waves, with the result that mean wave periods for recorders at such sites are apparently shorter than elsewhere.
56 Mottershead, *South Devon Landforms*, 31. These values may, in any event, be deformed breaker heights, and as such would not be strictly comparable with 'offshore' wave heights.
57 JR Hails, 'Sediment Distribution and Quaternary History', *Journal of the Geological Society of London*, 131 (1975), 31; AHW Robinson, 'The Hydrography of Start Bay and its Relationship to Beach Changes at Hallsands', *Geographical Journal*, 127 (1961), 63–77.

2 History of Navigation

ALAN STIMSON

> The art of navigation demonstrateth how by the shortest good way, by the aptest direction and by the shortest time a sufficient ship . . . [may] . . . be conducted.

THIS DEFINITION OF NAVIGATION WAS WRITTEN in 1570 by the great Elizabethan scholar Dr John Dee, at a time when the application of astronomical and mathematical principles and the skills of the instrument maker had made it possible for seamen to find their way to all corners of the known world and return safely. Admittedly seamen could not yet calculate their longitude at sea and would not be able to do so for a further two centuries, but regular trading voyages, such as those to the East Indies via the southern tip of Africa and to the riches of the South American continent across the wide Atlantic, were commonplace.

Progress towards accurate navigation by the sun and stars had been slow and halting, and very little evidence of early methods has survived, chiefly because seamen were often illiterate and rarely set down the secrets of their trade. What written clues there are tend to be found in the works of poets and clerics who did not fully understand the scenes they were recording.

The invention of the magnetic compass is probably the single most important improvement in navigation technique, and yet there is still considerable argument as to its origin. A strong tradition links its invention with Amalfi in northern Italy, sometime in the twelfth century, but the earliest written reference is made by an English monk, Alexander Neckham, in 1187. At this time the magnetised iron needle was used only in overcast conditions, when it was impossible to see the sun or stars. At first the secret of the lodestone, a naturally occurring magnetic ore, was treated as a form of magician's trick. Vincent of Beauvais in about 1240 wrote:

> when clouds prevented sailors from seeing the Sun they take a needle and rub its point on the magnet stone. They then thrust it through a straw and place it in a bowl of water. The stone is then moved round and round the bowl faster and faster until the needle which follows it is whirling swiftly. At this point the stone is suddenly snatched away, and the needle turns its point towards the Stella Maris. From that position it does not move.[1]

The Age of Discovery

The Portuguese, inspired by Prince Henry the Navigator (1394–1460), became the originators of the next phase of navigational improvements when they undertook extensive voyages of exploration down the West African coast and out into the Atlantic. The Canary Islands were colonised by 1402, and by 1433 the Azores, too, were visited and colonised. During this early period the wind systems in the North Atlantic were thoroughly investigated, and as soon as the mariner was confident of being able to return to Portugal safely a determined attempt was made to round Cape Bogador and push down the African coast.[2]

The new techniques meant that the 'dead reckoning', a progressively less accurate estimation of the ship's position, could be checked by observation of the height of the Pole star above the horizon with a simplified version of the astronomical quadrant. This was a wooden quarter circle with two sights fixed on one straight edge and a plumb-line suspended from its apex so as to read over a scale of 90 degrees marked upon its limb. With this instrument seamen were at first taught to observe the Pole star at their port of departure and mark on the limb the place where the plumb-line cut the scale. During the course of the voyage they marked the height of the star at successive headlands, river estuaries, and islands so that on their return the astronomers gradually built up a table of coastal latitudes expressed as 'altura' or height of the Pole. Because of its circumpolar motion the navigator was warned to observe the Pole star only when the 'Guards' (pointing stars in the constellation of the Little Bear) were in a certain position. When he wished to visit a port or place of known 'altura' all he had to do was look for its name on the scale of his quadrant, and when the height of the Pole agreed with the mark he was east or west of his destination. Later he was taught to convert the number of degrees of 'altura' into distance by multiplying each degree by $16\frac{2}{3}$ leagues, a league being reckoned as three miles, in order to find the distance sailed south (or north) and eventually, as his understanding increased, to think in terms of degrees of latitude.

By 1471 the equator, from where the Pole star was no longer visible, had been reached by Europeans. What was the navigator to do? The problem of how to navigate in the southern hemisphere was resolved by the Commission

2.1 Shooting the Pole Star with a Cross Staff. From Pedro Medina's *Regimento de Navegacion*, 1552. *(National Maritime Museum)*

set up by King John II of Portugal in 1485. A *Regiment of the Sun* was drawn up which enabled the navigator to use the sun as a means of latitude determination. The *Regiment* gave the sun's declination (its seasonal distance north or south of the equator) for each day of the year so that, by measuring the altitude of the sun at noon and correctly applying its declination for that day, a navigator could find his latitude everywhere on the Earth's surface. Additional rules were necessary to explain how to work the calculation for the various cases of the observer being to the north or south of the sun when it lay in either the northern or southern hemispheres, and when the observer and the sun were in differing hemispheres. Mercifully, this was often expressed as a diagram which most practical seamen found much easier to understand than the written word.[3]

Its plumb-bob made the quadrant a difficult instrument to use at sea, and an unwanted visit ashore was often necessary to get a satisfactory result. The astronomer's astrolabe was eventually simplified for use at sea and soon proved itself to be a superior instrument. First recorded in 1481, the mariner's astrolabe was initially made of wood, but was eventually cast in bronze or brass.[4] It was a heavy circular instrument, from six to eight inches in diameter, suspended by a hinged suspension ring which allowed it to hang vertically. A sighting alidade was pivotted at its centre in such a way that pointers at each end could in turn read from a scale of degrees marked on the upper limb.

A further altitude instrument, the cross-staff, was introduced into Portugal early in the sixteenth century, possibly based on the Arab *kamal* which Vasco de Gama had encountered in the Indian Ocean after he had rounded the Cape of Good Hope in 1498. The cross-staff consisted of a square-sectioned staff approximately 30 inches long, on which three transversals or crosses could be mounted, each appropriate to an altitude scale in degrees and minutes engraved upon the staff. In using it the observer selected the cross appropriate to the altitude and placed one end of the staff to his eye. He then slid the cross in, or out, until the top end of the cross just covered the sun or star while at the same moment the lower end rested in line with the horizon. The altitude was read from where the cross cut the scale. Although much more accurate than the astrolabe, its one major defect was ably expressed by William Bourne in his *A Regiment for the Sea* (1574):

> . . . but if it [the altitude] doe exceed 50 degrees then by the means of casting your eye upwardes and downwardes so muche, you may soone commit error and then in like manner the degrees be so small marked, that if the Sunne doth pass 50 or 60 degrees in height, you must leave the cross staffe and use the Mariner's ring, called by them the Astrolaby which they ought to call the Astrolabe.[5]

The new Portuguese methods quickly spread to Spain, which, after Columbus' epic voyage of 1492, rapidly built up an empire in the New World across the Atlantic. The Portulan chart of the Mediterranean was expanded to accommodate the new discoveries and progressed from being based on direction and estimated distance only to incorporating the latitude of places and a latitude scale. Some charts also carried longitude scales, but these were almost always in error because it was not yet possible to find longitude at sea.

By the middle of the sixteenth century altitude observations and charts were beginning to be used by north European seamen, although not without a certain amount of resistance by the more conservative elements. This resistant attitude is succinctly described by William Bourne in the preface to his *Regiment* (1574):

> I have known within this twenty years that them that were ancient masters of ships hath derided and mocked them that have been busy with their cards and plats [charts] and also the observation of the altitude of the Pole, saying that they care not for their parchments for they could keep a better account upon a board. And when that they did take the latitude they would call them star-shooters and sun-shooters, and would ask if they had hit it.[6]

Fortunately this resistance to new methods does not seem to have pervaded all English seamen, for by the 1540s ships owned by William Hawkins of Plymouth had made 'three long and famous voyages unto the coast of Brazil, a thing in those days very rare, especially for our nation'[7] and not many years later Francis Drake, by common consent the greatest of Devon seamen, became the first Englishman to circumnavigate the globe.

For the next two centuries very little progress in method or technique was made. Seamen could generally find their latitude to within about 15 miles and found their destination by practising the art of 'running down the latitude', that is sailing well to seaward of a desired landfall of known latitude, observing the sun or Pole star until that latitude was reached and then sailing east or west, until land was sighted ahead. The English contribution to such improvements as there were consisted of a development of the cross-staff by the Devonian, Captain John Davis, in the 1590s into a more versatile altitude instrument known as the backstaff.[8] It was also in the second half of the sixteenth century that the 'English log' for estimating a ship's speed through the water was invented (see below, p. 34). This consisted of a triangular piece of wood which was streamed over the stern of the ship attached to a length of light line. The line was marked at intervals by knots which were timed over the stern by a sandglass originally running for 30 seconds. The length of line run out in half a minute was proportioned to the distance the ship had sailed in an hour. A ship's speed is today still expressed in 'knots'.

2.2 The Mariner's Astrolabe. This instrument was found under a rock on the island of Valencia off the west coast of Ireland in 1845. It is thought to be Spanish and may have come from an Armada wreck. *(National Maritime Museum)*

The Finding of Longitude

> They have one great imperfection yet in their arts, and hitherto by no man supplyed, and that is the wante of exact rules to knowe the Longitude . . . without the which they can not truely geeve the place or situation of any Coaste, Harberough or Towne, ne yet in saylinge discerne how the place they sail unto beareth . . . .[9]

Thomas Digges, writing in 1576 in his *Errors in the Arte of Navigation*, clearly defined the last major navigational problem to be conquered, little knowing that the solution still lay some two hundred years in the future. Longitude is basically distance east or west on the Earth's surface, and can be expressed as the difference in time between two places. In order to find

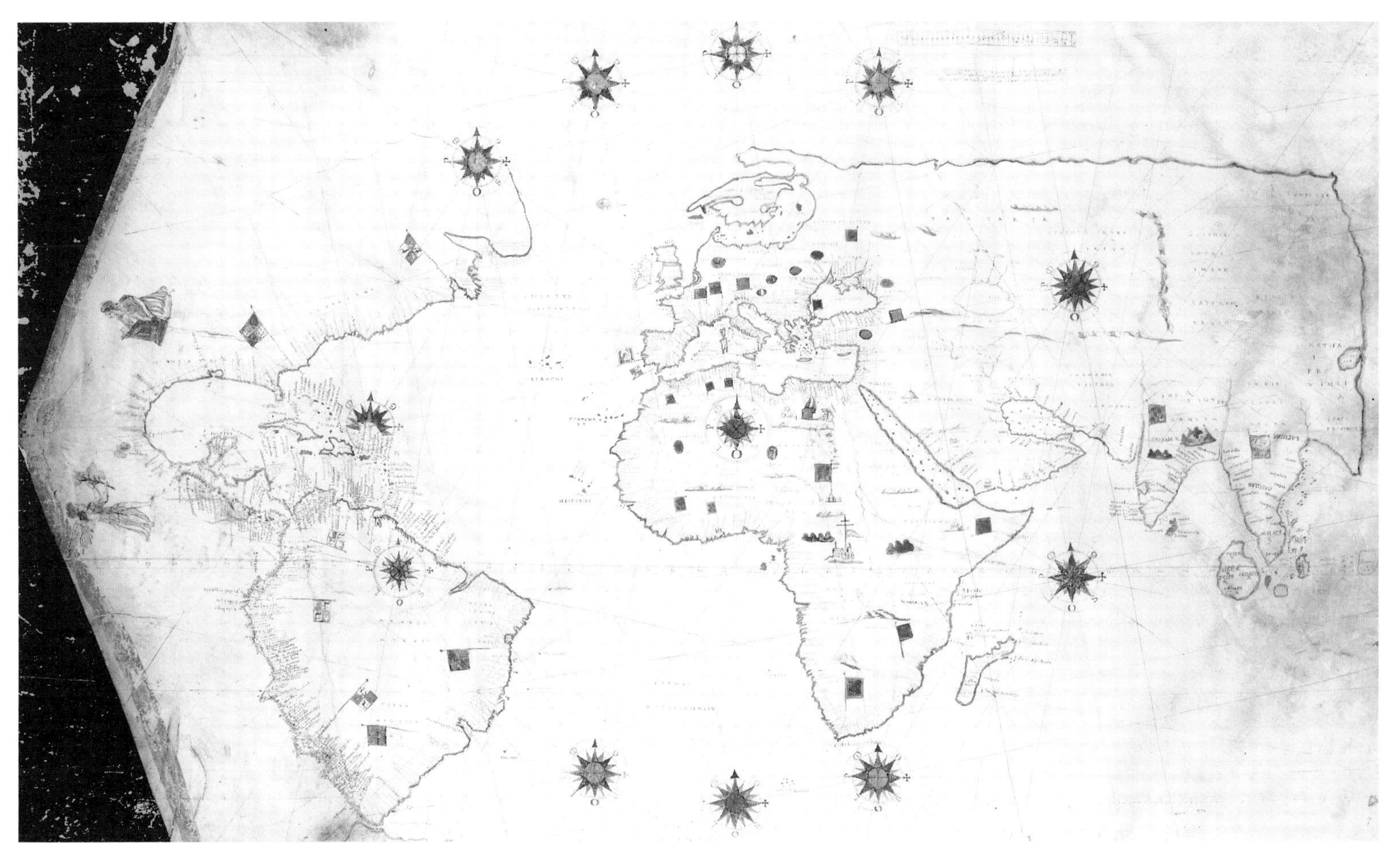

2.3 Portulan Chart of the world by Girolamo Verrazzano, 1529, corrected to 1540. *(National Maritime Museum)*

how far east or west his ship has sailed a navigator must be able to find the time at his ship and at the same instant be able to calculate the time at his place of departure or the time at a standard meridian.

In 1675 Charles II made the first official step in England towards a solution of the longitude problem by establishing a Royal Observatory at Greenwich. The first Astronomer Royal, John Flamsteed, was directed to:

> . . . apply himself with the utmost care and diligence to the rectifying the tables of the motions of the heavens and the places of the fixed stars so as to find out the so much to be desired longitude of places for the perfecting the art of navigation.[10]

Flamsteed was paid a salary of £100 each year, out of which he had to purchase his own astronomical instruments and pay his assistants. Progress was slow, and it was to be another forty years before his star catalogue was published.

A series of maritime disasters culminating in the wrecking of part of a returning squadron of Naval ships under the command of Sir Cloudesly Shovell on the Scilly Islands in 1707 eventually led to the British Parliament setting up a committee to examine the problem. This, in turn, resulted in the Act of 1714, which offered a prize of £20,000, a fortune in the eighteenth century, for any method of determining a ship's longitude to within half a degree. A panel of commissioners, known as the Board of Longitude, was constituted at the same time to examine and adjudicate on proposed solutions.[11] The offer of this great sum of money concentrated the minds of scientists and instrument makers throughout Europe, although the Board of Longitude had to contend with a succession of ludicrous proposals. The first useful consequence of the prize was the invention in 1731 of the reflecting quadrant by John Hadley (1682–1744), a country gentleman of a scientific turn of mind and a fellow of the Royal Society.

Hadley's quadrant, as it was generally called by seamen, measured up to one quarter of a circle, 90 degrees, on the principle of double reflection. The actual arc of the instrument therefore was only one eighth of a circle, so that it is sometimes called an octant. It made use of two mirrors so that the sun (or star) and the sea horizon could both be seen at the same instant. This allowed accurate measurements to be taken at sea for the first time, whatever the movement of the vessel, and Hadley was confident that when the theory of lunar prediction was perfected his octant could be used to measure the necessary 'lunar distances'.[12]

At much the same time that Hadley was working on his reflecting octant, a Yorkshire carpenter and self-taught clockmaker named John Harrison (1693–1776) began work on a series of sea clocks, and later watches, which were eventually to win him the longitude prize. John Harrison completed his first sea clock, known as H1 today, in 1735, incorporating into it many original ideas. It was temperature-compensated by a gridiron compensator, it was fitted with interconnected balances to nullify the motion of the ship, and it had a new frictionless escapement, as well as many other devices to reduce friction. Reducing friction lessened the need for lubricating oil, which had the tendency to clog and slow a clock.

Harrison was encouraged by the Board of Longitude, who paid him to continue developing his ideas. Two other clocks followed, the last (H3) being completed in 1757. However, while working on this last clock Harrison had at the same time made some watches which incorporated some of his inventions. These performed so well at sea that he was persuaded to produce a large silver watch and submit this for the prize. The watch (H4) was completed in 1759 and was tested by the Board of Longitude on voyages to Jamaica in 1762 and Barbados in 1764, on both occasions surpassing the conditions of the competition. Indeed, on its arrival in Jamaica in 1762 it was found to have lost only five seconds after allowing for its rate of going, an error of 1¼ minutes of longitude or less than one nautical mile in the latitude of Jamaica. Although Harrison had fulfilled the requirements of the Act, the

Board of Longitude refused to award him the prize, maintaining that the performance of his watch was something of a fluke and it was not therefore of general use. The Board demanded that Harrison explain the principles of his watch to a committee of clockmakers, so that further examples could be made and tested. After much heated argument Harrison complied in August 1765, after which the Board paid him half the prize money. In 1767 Larcum Kendall was commissioned to make a copy of H4, a task he completed by 1769. The watch was tried at the Royal Observatory and then sent to sea with Captain Cook on his second voyage to the Pacific in 1772. Meanwhile, Harrison continued to demand that the Board of Longitude pay him the balance of the £20,000, but they were adamant that he must make two more watches for testing before this could happen.

By 1772 Harrison had made another watch (H5), but at 79 he was a very old and tired man. It was obvious he would not be able to complete another, but his fight with the Board of Longitude had captured the interest of George III, who took up his case and tested H5 at his own observatory at Kew. The following year, 1773, Harrison petitioned Parliament, which, while not disputing the Board's decision, felt that the old man had done enough and granted him a further £8,750. This sum, together with earlier payments, meant that Harrison at the age of 80 eventually received the full amount of the prize. He died three years later.[13] Throughout his heated exchanges with the Board of Longitude Harrison felt that he and his method were being discriminated against because the Board favoured the 'lunar distance' approach to the longitude problem. This was understandable, because one of the Board members was Nevil Maskelyne, Astronomer Royal from 1765 and an advocate of the rival method.

The second half of the eighteenth century was a period of intense geographical exploration, with France and Great Britain equipping and sending out expeditions to many parts of the world. In 1768 the *Endeavour* was sent to the Pacific with Lieutenant James Cook in command and a party of scientists led by Joseph Banks, ostensibly to observe the transit of the planet Venus across the sun's disc at Tahiti, but also to search for a supposed southern continent in the South Seas. The expedition was equipped partly by the Royal Society and partly by the Board of Longitude to carry out a number of scientific experiments to try new equipment and instruments, but also to test the new lunar distance method of finding longitude at sea. Cook was equipped with the *Nautical Almanac* and the requisite sextants for the observations.[14]

2.5 Harrison's first timekeeper, H1, with the prize-winning watch H4 (centre) flanked by Larcum Kendall's copy, K1, and his simplified watch, K2. *(National Maritime Museum)*

2.4 John Harrison, 1693–1776. Mezzotint by Tassaert after a painting by King. Harrison is seated with H4 on the table and the clock H3 in the background. *(National Maritime Museum)*

The results of the first Pacific voyage were far reaching. Not only did Cook achieve his objectives at Tahiti, but he also discovered the east coasts of New Zealand and Australia and partially dispelled any ideas of a great southern continent. Most important of all, though, was that here for the first time was a man able to fix his position at sea and also fix the position of newly discovered land so that it was possible to lay it down accurately on a chart for future reference. On his second voyage (1772–75) Cook was equipped with the recently finished copy of Harrison's watch by Larcum Kendall and with three other longitude watches or chronometers by John Arnold. As considerable sums of money were at stake, elaborate precautions were taken to ensure they were not tampered with or damaged at sea. Special boxes were made, and at the daily winding the Captain, Lieutenant and the Astronomer had all to be present.[15] The Kendall watch performed magnificently, and when the voyage was nearly over Cook wrote enthusiastically to the Secretary of the Admiralty:

> Mr Kendall's watch has exceeded the expectations of its most zealous advocate and by being now and then corrected by lunar observations has been our faithful guide through all the vicissitudes of climates.[16]

Perhaps the most significant navigational action of the whole voyage was on the passage from the Cape of Good Hope to St Helena. The eighteenth-century practice to find a small island in a large ocean was to sail to the correct latitude, which was easily found, but well to the westward or eastward of it, and then sail east or west until land was sighted ahead. This was known as 'running down the latitude'. Cook now had the means to sail directly for the island, and thus save much valuable time. His journal records:

> Depending on the goodness of Mr Kendall's Watch, I resolved to try to make the island by a direct course, it did not deceive us and we made it accordingly on the 15th May at Day-break.[17]

For his third voyage (1776–80) Cook was equipped with two longitudinal watches by Lacum Kendall, the proven K2 and a less expensive, simplified watch known today as K3. The third voyage confirmed the practicality of the methods tried on the two earlier voyages and William Wales, the astronomer on Cook's second voyage, was able to write in 1788:

> there were few, even of the 'Petty' Officers, who could not observe the distance of the moon from the Sun, or a star, the most delicate of all the observations, with sufficient accuracy . . . who would not, whatever his real skill may be, feel ashamed to have it thought that he did not know how to observe for, and compute the time at sea, though but a short time before these voyages were set on foot such a thing was scarcely ever heard of among seamen and even first rate astronomers doubted the probability of doing it with sufficient exactness.[18]

The 'new' navigation had certainly arrived, although it was to be some years before most navigators had the education or the ability to equip themselves with the necessary instruments and tables to put it into effect.

The Lightning Age

> The days of navigating by a carpenter's two foot rule had gone by, and accurate time-keeping chronometers are a necessity of the 'lightning age' in which we live.

This definitive statement was made by S T S Lecky, master mariner, in his famous *Wrinkles* of 1881. He went on to say:

> not only has the chronometer been perfected in a high degree, as a reliable timekeeper, but its price has been reduced so low by excessive and unhealthy competition that to be without one, on any over-sea voyage would be considered almost criminal negligence.[19]

John Harrison's and Larcum Kendall's expensive timekeepers had been quickly followed by other makers' products. The initial high cost was soon reduced by simplification of the mechanism and by the commercial production introduced by such makers as John Arnold and Thomas Earnshaw in England and by Berthoud, Breguet, and Motel in France. By 1800 many merchant captains in the East India trade had purchased them and, by combining them with the 'lunar distance' method of finding longitude, made their voyages to India and the Far East in much greater safety.[20] However, it was not until 1818 that chronometers were issued to all ships of the Royal Navy, their Lordships, no doubt, being reluctant to expend the considerable sums of money required to equip their ships with the new devices.[21]

With the increasing use of chronometers it became necessary to devise some methods of checking their rate of gaining or losing. Astronomical observatories displaying daily time signals were set up around the world at most major ports, the time ball at Greenwich being the first, in 1833.

As well as improvements to astronomical navigation, the nineteenth century produced better ways of calculating the dead reckoning position of a ship. Various types of mechanical log for estimating a ship's speed through the water had been tried in the second half of the eighteenth century, the most promising being that of William Foxon in 1772.[22] None was completely satisfactory until, in 1802, Edward Massey patented the first commercially-successful mechanism. It consisted of a towed rotator which was connected to a box containing the registering wheelwork. The whole mechanism was towed astern of the ship and had to be hauled in to be read and reset at each alteration of course or change of watch. Minor alterations were effected over

2.6 Edward Massey's Mechanical Log for recording distance sailed, first patented in 1802. *(National Maritime Museum)*

the years until, in 1878, T F Walker patented a taffrail log which could be read from a dial mounted at the stern of the ship and, by 1890, from the bridge.[23]

It is strange that the most important instrument in a ship, its magnetic compass, was for centuries the least improved and perhaps the least understood. In the 1750s Dr Gowin Knight developed a method of permanently magnetising steel needles and designed an improved compass which was tried by Captain James Cook on his voyages of discovery between 1768 and 1780.[24] Ralph Walker's improved compass was introduced into the Royal Navy in 1793, and that of Captain Phillips in 1825, but as the nineteenth century proceeded and an increasing amount of iron was used in the construction of ships its effect on the compass became a real hazard.[25]

Despite the work of Matthew Flinders between 1801 and 1814,[26] little was done until 1836, when the Admiralty conducted a series of experiments in iron ships, at first under Commander Edward Johnson and later under the Astronomer Royal, George Biddell Airy. A committee was set up in 1837 to investigate the whole matter of magnetic compasses and their errors.[27] The debate on whether a compass should be corrected for errors induced by the ship or whether a standard compass of known errors on different headings should be used continued throughout the middle years of the nineteenth century. In 1855 the Liverpool Compass Committee was set up by the local ship owners to investigate the problems, and its report in 1861 disclosed some alarming facts. It reported that most merchant ship officers rarely used an azimuth compass to discover the compass error, but instead used the magnetic variation printed on the chart. Even worse, some ship's masters estimated compass error by comparing their dead reckoning position with that obtained by sights. The publication of the Liverpool Compass Committee's report resulted in a more scientific approach to compass construction and magnetic theory.[28] By 1876 Sir William Thomson, later Lord Kelvin, had patented his famous dry card compass and binnacle which

2.7 A Thomson 8in Compass and Binnacle designed for small vessels, made by H White, Glasgow, in 1882. *(National Maritime Museum)*

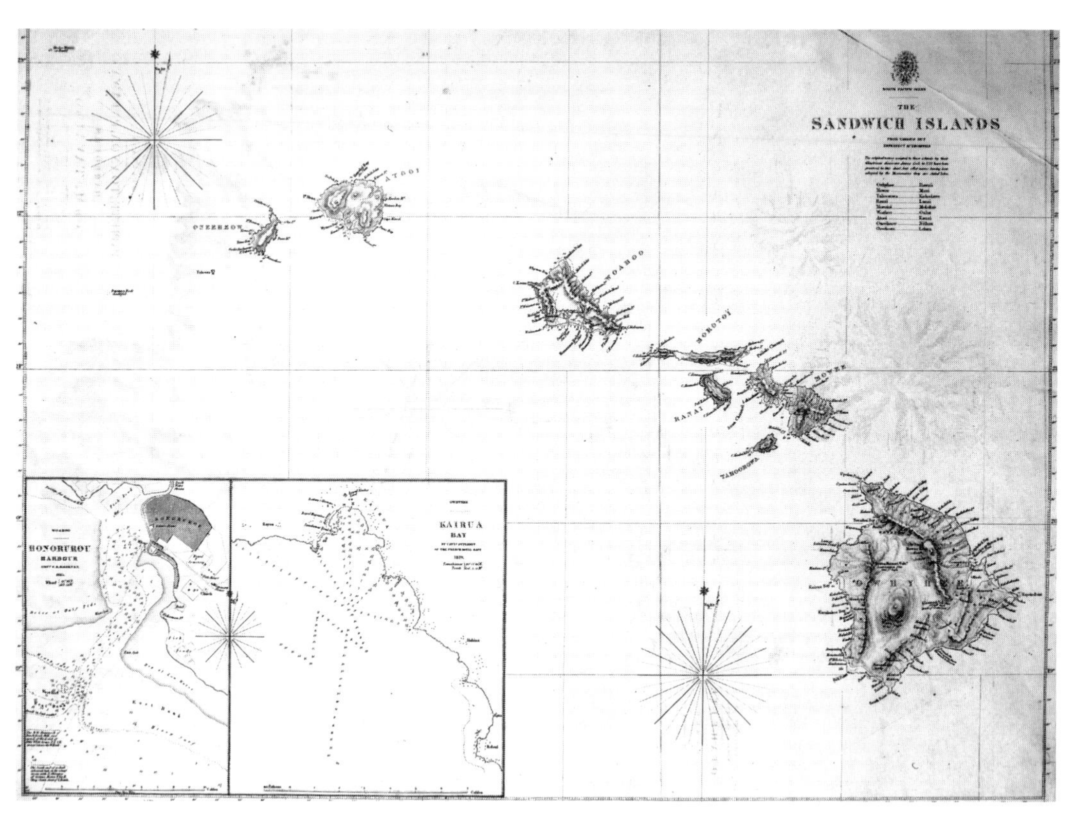

2.8 British Admiralty Chart of the Sandwich (Hawaiian) Islands, 1843. *(National Maritime Museum)*

was much used in the Merchant Service, although many sailing ships still mounted the standard compass high on a wooden pole above the upper deck in an attempt to escape the magnetic effect of the ship.

The nineteenth century saw the rapid growth of the British Admiralty Hydrographic Department, established in 1795, whose survey vessels worked in practically every part of the world. The zeal and dedication of such hydrographers as Fitzroy, Ross and Lort Stokes, using the new navigational methods, produced charts of undreamed-of excellence, which from 1823 were also available to the merchant service. It is from this time that the demise of the private chart seller can be traced. The last representative is the firm of Imray, Laurie, Norie and Wilson Ltd, whose famous blue-back charts are still produced, though now only for yachtsmen and fishermen. Admiralty surveying and charting probably reached its peak under Admiral Beaufort in the 1850s. By the 1880s over 70 per cent of the world's shipping was using their charts.[29]

The growing number of steam powered ships of iron construction in the latter part of the nineteenth century with, for the navigator, the dual properties of magnetic interference and vibration, accelerated the use of the liquid-damped compass first suggested by the German Ingen Housz in 1779. Indeed, it became virtually impossible to fit a magnetic compass of adequate performance in the 'iron clad' warships constructed at that time, and experiments with gyroscopic compasses were begun. Work by Anschutz Kaemf in Germany between 1904 and 1912, and later Sperry in the USA and Brown in the UK led to the gyroscopic compass being adopted by the navies of their respective countries during the First World War, but they were not fitted in many merchant vessels until after the Second World War.[30]

During the nineteenth century, with the development of the powered iron ship and steam tugs to assist sailing ships to berth at the conclusion of their voyages, seafaring gradually became a safer occupation. The adoption of the new navigational techniques and improved charts, the setting up of lighthouses and the mooring of light vessels and the laying of many more buoys (lighted from 1880) all helped to improve the safety record.[31] In addition, in the 1840s, it was recognised that merchant seamen required properly organised training in the new skills, and a system of examinations for Masters and Mates was introduced by the British Government under the supervision of the Board of Trade. These examinations were made compulsory in 1854.[32]

The twentieth century has seen even greater changes in the way that ships are navigated. Radio navigation at sea was pioneered by Guglielmo Marconi, who succeeded in sending a signal across the English Channel in 1899.[33] This quickly led to the broadcasting of radio time signals, the earliest on a regular basis being from Washington DC in January 1905. Chronometers could now be checked frequently at sea, and this development sounded the death knell of the by now little used lunar distance longitude method, whose tabulations disappeared from the *Nautical Almanac* in 1906. The first serious rival to astronomical navigation, radio direction finding, was developed during the First World War, but it was the Second World War which accelerated the development of many electronic aids to navigation. The long-range hyperbolic radio position fixing system, Loran, and the German long-range rotating radio beacon, Sonne, later to be called Consol, were developed, together with perhaps the most important of shipborne aids, radar. Radar was first fitted only to warships, but became available commercially in 1949.[34]

The first artificial satellite navigation system, Transit, became operational in 1964 with five satellites in polar orbit. These allow a navigator to fix his ship's position in any weather with an accuracy of about one quarter of a mile merely by the touch of a button. The successor to Transit, the Navstar Global Positioning system, which requires 24 satellites, when it becomes fully operational, will fix a ship's position to within a few metres. Lecky's 'lightning age' has certainly arrived for the navigator, with satellite navigation systems, even for the yachtsman, offered at less than £1,000. The old astronomical position fixing systems are still taught and used, but for how much longer it is difficult to predict.

2: *History of Navigation*

1 WE May and HL Hitchens, *From Lodestone to Gyro-Compass* (1955), 94; EGR Taylor, *The Haven Finding Art* (1971), 94.
2 DW Waters, *The Art of Navigation* (New Haven, 1958), 39, 40.
3 DW Waters, *Science and Techniques of Navigation in the Renaissance* (1976).
4 DW Waters, 'The Sea or Mariner's Astrolabe', *Agrupamento de Estidos de Cartigrafia Antiga*, XV (Coimbra, 1966).
5 William Bourne, *A Regiment for the Sea* (1574).
6 Bourne, *Regiment*, preface.
7 Richard Hakluyt, *Principal Navigations* (1599).
8 See also below, p. 34.
9 T Digges, 'Errors in the Arte of Navigation commonly practiced', in *A Proganostication Everlasting* . . . (1576); Waters, *Art of Navigation*, 533.
10 EG Forbes, *Greenwich Observatory: Origins and Early History* (1, 1975).
11 *Act for providing a Public Reward for such Person or Persons as shall Discover the Longitude at Sea*, 13 Anne, cap. 15 (1714).
12 J Hadley, 'The Description of a New Instrument for Taking Angles', *Phil. Trans.* 420 (1731).
13 H Quill, *John Harrison, the Man who Found Longitude* (1966).
14 JC Beaglehole, *The Journals of Captain James Cook on his Voyages of Discovery*, (Cambridge, 1959) I.
15 Beaglehole, *Journals of Captain Cook*, 11.
16 Beaglehole, *Journals of Captain Cook*, 22.
17 HD Howse, 'Captain Cook's Marine Timekeepers: The Clocks and Watches of Captain James Cook, 1769–1969, *Antiquarian Horology* (1969).
18 W Wales, *Astronomical Observations made in the Voyages . . . for making Discoveries in the Southern Hemisphere* (1788).
19 STS Lecky, *Wrinkles in Practical Navigation* (1881), 25.
20 WE May, *A History of Marine Navigation* (Henley-on-Thames, 1973), 33.
21 May, *History*.
22 May, *History*, 114, 115.
23 JE Willmott, *Thomas Walker & Sons Ltd: A Short History* (Birmingham, 1951).
24 G Knight, 'A Description of a Mariner's Compass contrived by Gowin Knight, MB, FRS', *Phil. Trans.* 46 (1750).
25 AN Stimson, 'The Development of the British Admiralty Standard Compass, 1740–1840', *Anais Hulroyraficos*, Tomo xli (Suplemento), (Rio de Janeiro, 1984).
26 M Flinders, 'An account of some experiments to ascertain the effects produced on the compass . . . by Matthew Flinders, Captain in the Royal Navy, 1812', PRO, ADM 1/1809, X/1 9318.
27 *Report of the Admiralty Compass Committee, 1840*, Appendix AP9. (NMM, ACO 9/24).
28 *First and Second Reports of the Liverpool Compass Committee to the Board of Trade, 1855 and 1856* (1857).
29 HD Howse and M Sanderson, *The Sea Chart* (Newton Abbot, 1973), 12.
30 AE Fanning, *Steady As She Goes* (1986), 175–180.
31 HP Mead, *Trinity House* (1947).
32 PG Parkhurst, *Ships of Peace: A record of some problems which came before the Board of Trade . . . from early days to 1888* (New Malden, 1962); S Foreman, *Shoes and Ships and Sealing Wax: An Illustrated History of the Board of Trade, 1786–1986* (1986).
33 HE Hancock, *Wireless at Sea* (Chelmsford, 1950).
34 L Holder, 'Modern Developments', in May, *History of Marine Navigation*, 222–66.

3 *Three Devon-born Tudor Navigators*

JOYCE YOUINGS

UNTIL THE MIDDLE OF THE sixteenth century the few English ships which ventured beyond the traditional western European seaways depended on the engagement, if not the capture, of foreign pilots, especially Portuguese. Indeed, as late as 1577 Francis Drake relied upon one Nuna da Silva of Lisbon to get him to the Pacific, and on Spanish charts for the crossing thereof.[1] By the later 1570s, however, London was becoming a centre for the academic study of oceanic navigation, although few Englishmen could speak with practical experience. Among those who could were three Devonians, Stephen and William Borough, and John Davis.

The Borough brothers came of a minor landed family long settled in the parish of Northam in north Devon. An earlier generation had produced John Aborough (the surname used on occasion by Stephen and William), a master mariner employed by Viscount Lisle, Lord Deputy of Calais, who had connections with north Devon through his wife, the former Honor Grenville. John was one of two experienced seamen employed by Henry VIII in 1539, in preparation for the coming to England of Ann of Cleves, to compile in great secrecy sailing directions for, and a sketch of, a part of the Zeider Zee.[2] This resulted in the construction of the first sea chart known to have been by an Englishman.[3] Both Stephen (1525–84) and William 1536–99), whose exact relationship with John has not been established, moved to London and entered the service of the Company of Merchants trading to Russia, whose Governor was no less a navigator than Sebastian Cabot. In 1553 Stephen Borough sailed as master of the *Edward Bonaventure* in a fleet commanded by Richard Chancellor and Hugh Willoughby to search for a North East Passage to China.[4] The voyage became transformed by circumstances into one establishing important diplomatic and commercial contacts with Russia. Borough came to be regarded as the real discoverer of the sea route to Muscovy, no doubt finding in the shallow waters and sandbanks of the White Sea conditions similar to those he had known as a boy at the confluence of the rivers Taw and Torridge (Fig. 3.1). It was he who named the North Cape, and his later discovery, the Kara Gate, was originally known as Borough Strait.[5]

Such was Stephen's reputation that in 1558 he was received with great courtesy at the School of Navigation in Seville, where he observed instruction in oceanic navigation of a kind unknown in England. He was also able to study the school's collection of the latest in navigational instruments.

3.1 An aerial view of the mouth of the rivers Taw and Torridge looking seaward towards the Bristol Channel, with Appledore, historically in the parish of Northam, in the left foreground. *(RV Tait)*

He returned to England with a copy of Martin Cortes's manual, published in 1551, which he persuaded the Muscovy Company to have translated by another of its employees, Richard Eden, and to publish in a cheap and handy edition in 1561 as *The Arte of Navigation*. In a preface Eden drew attention to Borough's insistence, unusual at this time, that all available navigational science should be made generally available.[6] In pleading for the practical examination of mariners, Borough deplored the fact that in England anyone:

> . . . when he can apparel himself like a mariner, to have a whistle and chain of silver about his neck, and . . . can something talk of the art, . . . thinketh then to be a good mariner, whereas indeed he is far from good and necessary in the same.

With a view to obtaining an appointment as the Queen's Pilot-Major, with the sole right of examining and licensing mariners, Borough declared his belief both in the 'subtlety', that is the skill, and the 'certainty', that is the exactitude, of the navigator's art, describing how a ship, caught in a storm 300 leagues from land:

> . . . the day being very much overshot with clouds and mists, and also the night so extremely dark that a man standing in the poop of the ship shall not see the foreships and scantly the masts, giving many *bueltas* [reverses], turns in the sea, running from one part to the other, heaving and setting with the vehemence of the winds and force of the seas, notwithstanding these, by the certainty of the art, the expert pilot shall know the way that the ship hath gone and the place where he is and also truly how to direct his course.

The Seamans Secrets.

A Table shewing the Order how the Seamen may keep his Accompts, whereby he may at all times distinctly examine his former practises, for in every 24 hours, which is from noon to noon, he doth not only lay down his Latitude, with the Corse and Leagues, but also how the Wind hath blown in the same time.

The first Column is the months and dayes of the time; the second is the observed Altitude, the third is the Horizontal Corse or motion of the Ship, the fourth the number of Leagues that the Ship hath sayled, the fifth is a space wherein must be noted, by what Wind those things have been performed; and the next great space is to lay down any brief Discourse for your memory.

Moneths and dayes of the Moneth	Anno. 1593. Latitude. G.	M.	Corse.	Leagus	Wind	The 13 of March cape S Augustin in Brasil, being 16 leagues East from me, I began this accompt.
March. 24	7	30	N.N.E.	25	East.	
25	5	44	N.b.E.nor	36	E b.N.	Compasse varied 9 degrees the South point westward.
26	4	1	N. b. N.	35	E.b N.	
27	2	49	N.	24	E.b.N.	Compasse varied 8 degrees, the South point westward.
28	1	31	N.easterly.	26	E.b.N.	
29	1	4	N.N.W.	9	N.E.	
Aprill. 31	0	0	N. b. W.	21	E N.E.	Compasse varied 6. deg. 40. min. the South point westward.
4	0	39	N.W.b.N.	15	N. E.	
7	1	53	N.N.W.	28	N. E.	Observation, the Pole Artick above the Horizon.
9	3	5	N.W.b.N	30	N.e.b.E	
10	4	5	N.W.b.N.	22	N.e.	
11	4	45	N. W.	18	N.e.b.N	
12	5	16	N.W.	14	N.e.b.N	Compasse varied 7. degrees, the North point Eastward.
13	6	11	N.W.b.N.	23	N. e.	
14	7	16	N.W.b.N.	34	N.e.	

3.2 John Davis's Model Log, printed in his *Seamen's Secrets* (1595). Note that longitude is not logged and that there are two methods of recording variation. *(National Maritime Museum)*

A little optimistic perhaps, but this was no armchair navigator. Himself a maker of sea charts, he could marvel at the way great expanses of the oceans could be depicted on paper no greater in size than the palm of a man's hand. Truly, declared this pious son of Devon, the office of pilot is like that of a Bishop: 'the one travailleth to the port of Heaven, the other to a port on Earth'.[7] Borough is thought to have played some part in the drafting of the parliamentary statute of 1562 which began to establish the professional status of mariners. In 1563 he became Chief Pilot of the Queen's ships in the Medway, and both he and his brother William were to be Master of the

118 The English Voyages, Nauigations, *M. John Dauis.* 3.

Moneth	Dayes.	Houres.	Course.	Leagues.	Elevation of the pole. Deg.	Min.	The winde.	THE DISCOVRSE.
Iuly.	31	24	S. by W	27	62		N.W.	This 31 at noone, comming close by a terriando or great cape, we fell into a mightie rase, where an iland of ice was carried by the force of the current as fast as our barke could saile with lum wind, all sailes bearing. This cape as it was the most Southerly limit of the gulfe which we passed over the 30 day of this moneth, so was it the North promontory or first beginning of another very great inlet, whose South limit at this present wee saw not. Which inlet or gulfe this afternoone, and in the night, we passed over: where to our great admiration we saw the sea falling downe into the gulfe with a mightie overfal, and roring, and with divers circular motions like whirlepooles, in such sort as forcible streames passe thorow the arches of bridges.
August								
Noone the	1	24	S.E. by S.	16	61	10	W.S.W.	The true course, &c. This first of August we fell with the promontory of the sayd gulfe or second passage, having coasted by divers courses for our safegard, a great banke of the ice driven out of that gulfe.
Noone the	2	48	S.S.E.	16	60	26	Variable.	
Noone the	6	72	S.E. Southerly.	22	59	35	Variable with calme.	The true course, &c.
	7	24	S.S.E.	22	58	40	W.S.W.	The true course, &c.
	8	24	S.E.	13	58	12	W. fog.	The true course, &c.
	9	24	S. by W.	13	57	20	Variable & calme.	The true course &c.
	10	24	S.S.E.	17	56	40	S.W. by W.	The true course, &c.
	11	24	S.E. easterly.	40	55	13	W.N.W.	The true course, &c.
	12	24	S.E. easterly.	20	54	32	W.S.W.	The true course &c.
	13	24	S.S.E.	4	54		N.W.	This day seeking for our ships that went to fish, we strooke on a rocke, being among many iles, and had a great leake.
Noone the	14	24	S.S.E.	28	52	40	N.W.	This day we stopped our leake in a storme. The 15 of August at noon, being in the latitude of 52 degrees 12 min. and 16 leagues from the shore, we shaped our course for England, in Gods name, as followeth. *
*Noone ye	15				52	12	S.S.W.	The true latitude.
	16	20	E.s.e. halfe point s.	50	51		S.W.	The true course, &c.
	17	24	E. by S.	30	50	40	S.	The true course, &c. This day upon the Banke we met a Biscaine bound either for the Grand bay or for the passage. He chased us.
	18	24	E by N northerly	40	51	18	W.	The true course, &c.
	19	24	E halfe point northerly	51	51	35	Variable W. & S.	The true course, &c.
	20	24	E.S.E.	31	50	50	S.W.	The true course, &c.
Noone the	22	48	E. by N.	68	51	30	S.S.W.	The true course, &c.
	23	24	E by N. Northerly	33	51	52	S.	The true course, &c.
	24	24	E. by N.	31	52	10	Variable.	The true course, &c. This 24 of August observing the variation, I found the compasse to vary towards the East, from the true Meridian, one degree.
Noone the	27	72	E. Northerly.	40	52	22	Variable & calme.	The true course, &c. for 72 houres.
Noone the	29	48	E.S.E.	47	51	28	Variable W. & N.	The true course, &c.
Noone the	31	48	S.E. by E. Easterly	14	51	0	Variable.	The true course, &c.
September	2	48	E. Southerly	05	51		N.W.	The true course, &c.
	3	24	E. by S. Easterly.	24	50	50	W.N.W.	The true course, &c.
	4	24	S.E. by E.	20	50	21	N.N.E.	The true course, &c.
	5	24	S.E. by E.	18	40	48	N.N.E.	The true course, &c. Now we supposed our selves to be 66 leagues fro Sillie.
	6	24	E. by S.	15	49	40	N.	The true course, &c.
	7	24	E.S.E.	20	49	15	N.N.W.	The true course, &c.
	8	24	N.E.	18	49	40		
	9	24	W.S.W.	7	49	42		
	10	24	S.E. by E.	8	40	28	Variable.	
	11	24	N.E. by E.	10	40	45	Variable.	
	12	24	N.W. by W.	6	50		N.E.	
	13	24	E. by S. Southerly	15	40	47	N.E.	
	15							This 15 of September 1587 we arrived at Dartmouth.

Under the title of the houres, where any number exceedeth 24, it is the summe or casting up of so many other dayes and parts of dayes going next before, as conteine the foresayd summe.

A repor

3.3 John Davis's Tabular Log Book printed in Richard Hakluyt's *Principal Navigations* (1599–1600). This is the earliest example of a tabular log book, and the devising and first use of this essential record of a ship's course and distance sailed each watch can be attributed to Davis. Earlier surviving log books are essentially narrative. It is a practical reflexion of his mathematical ability: by systematising the numerical entries of courses and distances sailed, etc, it simplified and facilitated the calculation and plotting of the ship's course and position at noon daily (DW Waters, 6 March 1990). *(National Maritime Museum)*

Corporation of Trinity House at Deptford.[8] He died and was buried at Chatham.

As a boy of 16 William Borough served under his brother on the Muscovy run, and he was ultimately to surpass Stephen in combining practical experience with scholarship, studying in particular the problem of compass variation. His *Discourse of the Variation of the Compass or Magnetical Needle* (1581) set out in language comprehensible to the ordinary mariner how to calculate with the use of the astrolabe and cross staff the sun's true bearing. He also did much to encourage the making of England's own charts to replace faulty foreign imports.[9] It is significant that both brothers appear among a list of ships' masters on the Thames in 1582, but William was to go on to command the *Lion* in Drake's attack on Cadiz in 1587 – and to presume to argue with his chief – and perhaps for this reason he commanded only the much smaller *Bonovalia* against the Spanish Armada.[10] Stephen's son, Christopher, was employed by the Muscovy Company as an interpreter, and in 1579–81 he chronicled an expedition from the White Sea to Persia, accompanying his text with celestial calculations which showed that he, too, had received a thorough technical training.[11] They were a truly remarkable family.

At about the same time that the Boroughs were exploring the North East there was born at Sandridge in the parish of Stoke Gabriel, on the river Dart in south Devon, one whose maritime exploits were to be largely to westwards. John Davis's family was also modest but well-established, near neighbours of the Gilberts at Greenway. John was almost certainly taken to London as a boy by Humphrey Gilbert: certainly by 1579 he was acquainted with the learned Dr John Dee. Where, if indeed at all, he obtained his practical experience as a mariner is not known, but it is difficult to believe that mere booklearning could have prepared him to lead three expeditions between 1585 and 1587 in search of a North West Passage to the Orient.[12] He and his principal patron, Adrian Gilbert, did in fact return to Devon from time to time and were more successful than the Gilberts' halfbrother, Walter Raleigh, in tapping the financial resources of the merchants of Exeter and other westcountry towns for their project.[13] With great persistence Davis reached Baffin Bay and sighted the Hudson Strait, thereby preparing the way for others to follow in his wake. He excelled in making friends with the Inuit of Greenland, and, true to his Devon origins, showed considerable interest in the region's whaling and fishery potential.

Following royal service in 1588–9 Davis became involved with Thomas Cavendish in Pacific ventures, reputedly, on his way home, discovering the Falkland Islands. He subsequently sailed to the Far East, and it was off Sumatra in 1605 that he was murdered by Japanese pirates. Meanwhile, he had found time to commit his nautical experience to print, publishing two important manuals, *The Seaman's Secrets* (Fig. 3.2) in 1594 and *The World's Hydrographical Description* the following year. A tabular log book kept by him in 1587 was printed by Hakluyt (Fig. 3.3) as a model for others to follow. Finally, not the least important of John Davis's achievements was the invention of a navigational instrument, the back staff or Davis quadrant (Fig 3.4), which replaced the sea astrolabe and was to be in use by seamen for over two centuries.[14]

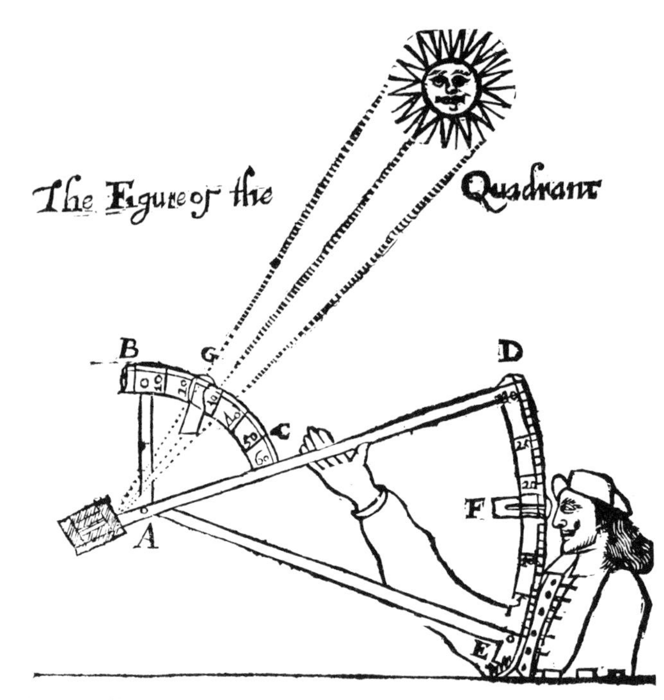

3.4 A Backstaff, an instrument for finding the sun's altitude by using its shadow. It was invented by John Davis about 1590 and was much used by English seamen. From *The Mariner's Magazine*, by Samuel Sturmy, 1669. *(National Maritime Museum)*

It was no coincidence that three of Devon's most distinguished navigators made their mark largely in Arctic waters. Had they been successful, either way, in reaching 'Cathay' they would have opened up not only by far the shortest, but politically the least hazardous route to rich markets for Devonshire kersies. What they also undoubtedly shared was an ability to combine practical experience with 'mathematical' science, and this should ensure them an honoured place in Devon's, and indeed England's, maritime history.

3: Three Devon-born Tudor Navigators

1 DW Waters, *The Art of Navigation in England in Elizabethan and Early Stuart Times* (1958), 120–1. See also the same author's 'Elizabethan Navigation', in Norman J Thrower, ed., *Sir Francis Drake and the Famous Voyage, 1577–80* (California 1984), 12–32. I am most grateful for David Waters's helpful comments on a draft of this chapter, and for additional and hitherto unpublished material on John Davis appended to Fig. 3.3. See also below, chapter 21.

2 R Dymond, 'Stephen Borough the Navigator', *DAT* XII (1881), 332–60; M St Clare Byrne (ed.), *The Lisle Letters*, 6 vols (Chicago 1981), v, 74–6; Alwyn Ruddock, 'The Earliest Original Seaman's Rutter and Pilot's Chart', *J(ournal of the) I(nstitute of) N(avigation)* XIV (1961), 409–31.

3 DW Waters, 'The English Pilot: English Sailing Directions and Charts and the Rise of English Shipping, 16th to 18th Centuries', *JIN* 42 (1989), 319.

4 KR Andrews, *Trade, Plunder, and Settlement, 1480–1630* (Cambridge 1984), 64–75.

5 Borough kept a journal in which he noted both sea and land marks, and one of his charts was printed by Hakluyt as a model for others to follow: Andrews, *Trade, Plunder and Settlement*, 70. For a recent appreciation of Borough's talents as a mapmaker see Samuel H Baron, 'William Borough and the Jenkinson Map of Russia', *Cartographica*, 26, ii (1989), 72–85.

6 Waters, *Art of Navigation*, 103–4, 100.

7 Dymond, 'Stephen Borough', 349 (also in part in Waters, *Art of Navigation*, 513), 351, 352, 354.

8 Waters, *Art of Navigation*, 102–3 and GG Harris, *The Trinity House of Deptford Strand* (1969), 273.

9 Waters, *Art of Navigation*, 341, 154–8, 97–8.

10 PRO, State Papers Domestic, Elizabeth, SP12/156/45/fo.105; *Dictionary of National Biography*, sub William Borough.

11 *DNB*, sub Christopher Borough.

12 AH Markham (ed.), *Voyages and Works of John Davis the Navigator*, Hakluyt Society, LIX (1878) contains most of what is known of Davis's early career. I am indebted to Professor David Quinn for further details of his connections with the Gilberts.

13 Markham, *Voyages*, xx.

14 Waters, *Art of Navigation*, 205–6. The chart he constructed of the Isles of Scilly and to which he drew attention in *The Seamen's Secrets* is no longer extant. It points to another of his competences, that of hydrography: ex inf. DW Waters.

4 *From the Ice Age to Early Medieval Times*

SEÁN McGRAIL

IN HIS *Maritime History of Devon* Oppenheim gave scant treatment to the period before the Normans, saying little about Roman times and nothing at all about the prehistoric period. Today it is known that Man has been in south-western Britain for some 50,000 years, intermittently at first but continuously since *c*8000 BC. During the cold periods which constituted the greater part of the Palaeolithic period (ie up to the end of the last Ice Age) Britain was a westward extension of continental Europe. During the 17th millennium BC the land connection with Ireland was broken, and in the 8th/7th millennium BC Britain became separated from the Continent by rising sea levels.[1] Thus early travel to Britain during the inter-glacial periods from the south and east could have been by land, but after *c*7000 BC any such movements would have had to be by water transport.

The evidence for early man in Devon is limited and patchy, much of it being based on material recovered before scientific methods of excavation and recording had been introduced.[2] For land-based activities a much wider area (Map 4.2) than that defined by the present-day county boundaries must be used to present anything like a coherent picture. For maritime affairs it is equally necessary to use evidence from elsewhere to supplement the meagre Devon materials: for example, no boat has survived in Devon that can be unambiguously dated to the period under review. In addition, in this early period, it is impossible to differentiate clearly between Cornwall and Devon. In the late–1st millennium BC the *Dumnonii* people occupied the southwest peninsula from *Belerion* (Lands End) to the Parrett-Axe line,[3] and it seems likely that this reflects the situation in much earlier times. Geomorphologically, economically, and culturally, the southwest peninsula appears as relatively homogenous until almost the end of the period, when sub-Roman *Dumnonia* became increasingly dominated by English culture from the east, and Devon, east of the river Tamar, became recognizably different from Cornwall. Furthermore, it is impracticable when dealing with these early times to make a distinction between seafaring and the use of inland waters: thus, this chapter deals with lakes and rivers as well as the sea.

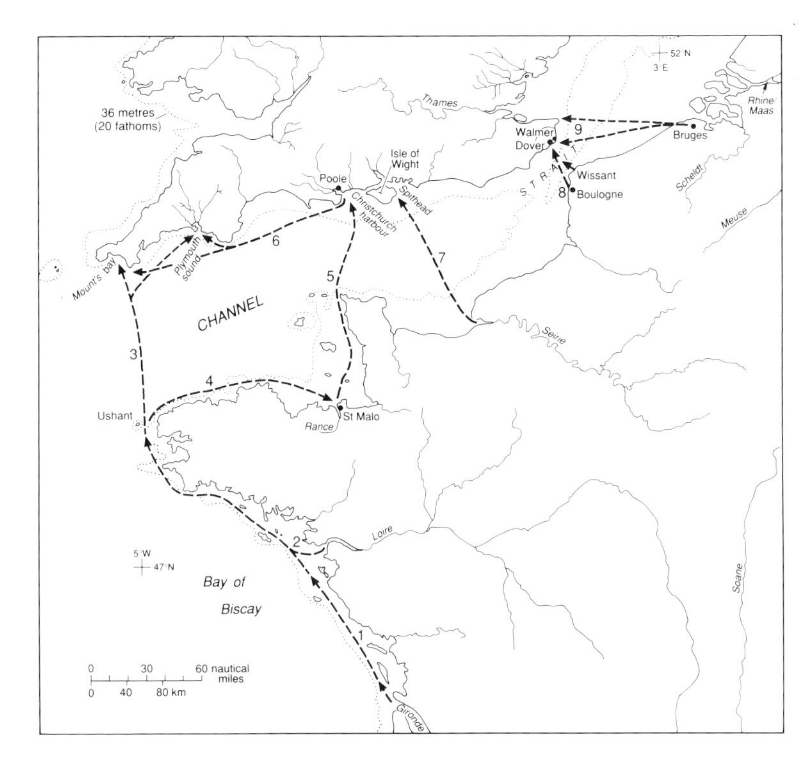

Map 4.1 Trade Routes between Northwest France and Southwest Britain in the 1st century BC

Environmental Changes

In the other historical chapters in this book the geomorphological features of land and sea and the climate of the Devon region may be taken as a relatively unchanging background against which to discuss events. This is not so in this chapter: there have been marked changes to the environment in the period under discussion, so that the coastline and the coastal waters of Devon as known today differ considerably from those in early prehistoric times, owing to variations in sea level and to erosion and deposition.

In southern Britain there has been a general rise – though with significant oscillations – in sea level in post-glacial times (ie from *c*8000 BC), due mainly to the melting of the ice sheets and glaciers (eustatic rise), modified by local (isostatic) changes in the relative height of the land, which rose when released from the weight of ice (a factor of more significance in northern Britain), but fell where inundated with water. The combined effect of these factors varies at different times and places, but a general picture for southwest Britain may be obtained from data published by Heyworth and Kidson.[4] This shows that there has been a general rise in sea-level, but at a diminishing rate, from the 8th millenium BC to the present date, totalling about 31 metres. Before *c*3000 BC mean high water spring tides (MHWST) were appreciably below today's lowest of spring tides – for example, in *c*7000BC MHWST was probably somewhere in the region of the present day 10 to 15 fathoms line. Early landsmen thus knew a different Devon from the Devon we know today. And early seamen had a different seascape to face: the coastal topography and depths of water would have been different and these factors, together with the distance of open water to windward of a place (fetch), would have resulted in different tidal patterns from today's.

Another significant difference from today is that, in early times, lakes and rivers had imprecise boundaries, and in wet seasons considerably extended their basins and channels. Rivers were faster flowing and there was less silting. Subsequently, rising sea-levels drowned lower river valleys which were then re-shaped by tidal flows, and, as river gradients and velocities decreased, silting increased which, when combined with longshore drift of foreshore material, formed spits and bars partly blocking estuaries, such as at Dawlish Warren on the river Exe (see below, chap. 11). Mining activities and deforesting increased the rate of inland erosion and intensified this siltation. A further effect of rising sea levels is that much of the evidence for man's activities on the coastal plains in early times is now under water. Occasionally, at times of unusually low water, such sites and the remains of coastal woodlands are exposed, as at Westward Ho! in north Devon.[5]

The climate has also changed appreciably during the past, and a summary of the variations experienced in post-glacial times may be quoted from Lamb:[6]

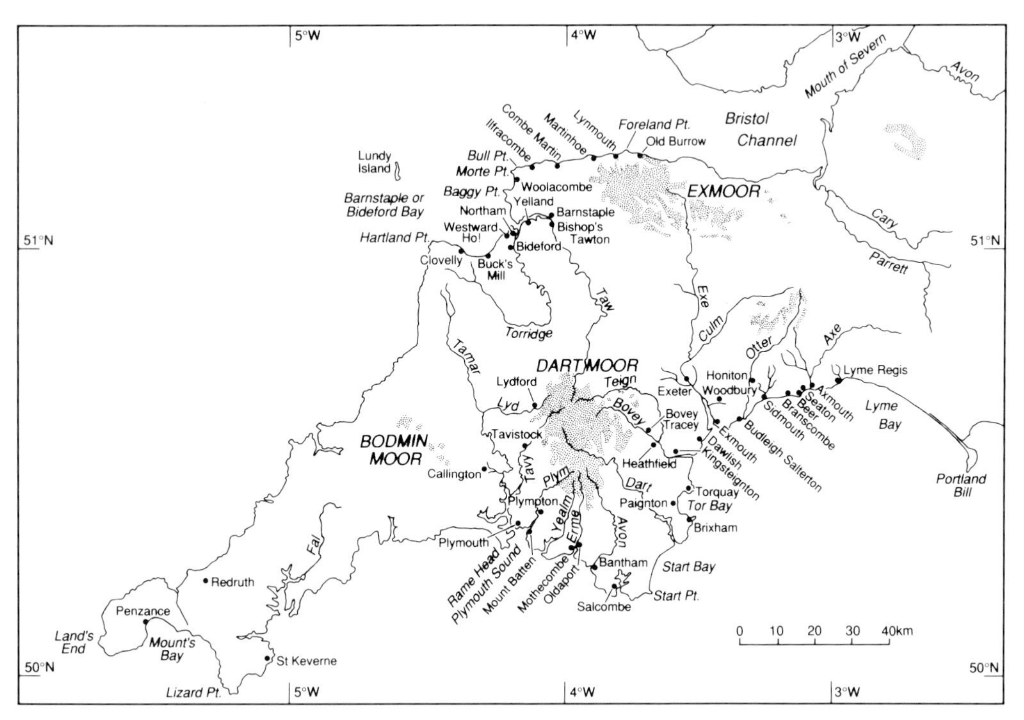

Map 4.2 The Natural Features of Devon, showing location of early archaeological sites

7th millennium BC	Temperature rise with winters generally milder and summers warmer than today.
6th to mid-4th millennium BC	Climatic optimum with mild winters. The wind was generally westerly.
mid-4th to 1st millennium BC	Generally warm and settled but with significant fluctuations at *c*200-year intervals.
1st millennium BC to AD 100	Decisive shift to colder, wetter climate so that weather became comparable with today's. Winds in the westerly and NW sector.
AD 100 to 400	Some increase in temperature and a tendency to be drier.
AD 400 to 800	Reversion to colder, wetter weather.
from AD 800	Improvements culminating in a warmer 12th/13th century. Then, apart from some exceptional periods, climate became much as it is today.

Today the predominant winds and the resultant swell off south west Britain are from between southwest and northwest throughout the year, although travelling depressions generally moving northeastwards can result in a wind from the south through west to north, or even east. We may assume, on the evidence now available, that similar conditions generally prevailed in Devon waters back to *c*1000 BC. In that same period, and even as far back as *c*3000 BC, it also seems likely that tides and tidal streams in the English and Bristol channels were much as they are today.

Havens and Landing Places

By *c*3000 BC, when more than 80 per cent of the total post-glacial rise in sea level had been achieved, the Devon coastline would have been generally similar to today's. From the maritime viewpoint the north and south coasts differ. The south coast is generally open to the southwest with a long fetch of open water across which winds blow and waves travel and consequently build up energy. The Bristol channel part of the north coast is generally exposed to short fetches only, but the coast to the west is more exposed. The generally-converging nature of the Bristol channel can make for some vicious seas. In the Severn estuary, east of Devon, are some of the greatest tidal ranges in Britain, up to 14 metres at springs, 6 metres at neaps. However, these ranges are less on the north Devon coast, being generally 10 to 7 metres at springs, with 6 to 4 metres in Barnstaple Bay. On the south coast spring ranges are *c*5 metres in the west, decreasing to *c*3 metres in the east.

McKee has classified the British coastline according to its relative suitability for operating sailing boats from natural harbours and unimproved beaches. His analysis for Devon is that there are exposed sections from Lyme Regis to Sidmouth, and from Start Point to Rame Head on the south coast, and Westward Ho! to Morte Point on the north; with sheltered sections from Sidmouth to Start Point in the south, and Hartland Point to Westward Ho!, and Morte Point to Foreland Point in the north.[7] There are fewer problems in operating a boat under oars or sail from a sheltered beach or natural harbour than from an exposed one, and thus it may be argued that sheltered stretches of coast would be preferred. This may be true in general, but this analysis miscasts such places as Seaton and Beer, which are in a generally exposed sector but gain some protection from a locally different coastal alignment. Additionally, some rivers on sheltered coasts have relatively limited hinterlands, whilst others in exposed stretches, such as the Tamar, have a large and economically important catchment area and thus attract sea traffic.

Sites which would evidently have made good landing places for boats in early times from, say, 3000 BC, include:

South coast: Axe estuary, Beer, Seaton, Branscombe, Sidmouth, Budleigh Salterton, Exe estuary, Tor Bay, Start Bay, Dart estuary, Salcombe harbour, and the Avon, Erme, Yealm, and Tamar estuaries.

North coast: Clovelly, Bucks Mills, Taw/Torridge estuaries, Ilfracombe, Combe Martin, and Lynmouth.

Except for the Roman period, boats and ships in prehistoric and early medieval northwest Europe generally used informal landing places, beaching, anchoring off, or mooring to a pole or stone. Formal harbours with waterfront structures began to be built, for the first time since the Romans, in the 9th century AD, and most economic regions seem to have had at least one such place by the 12th century.[8] There is every reason to believe that Devon conformed to this general pattern, but evidence has not so far been uncovered.

The Palaeolithic Period

During the colder parts of this period, which extended down to the end of the last Ice Age, *c*8000 BC, Britain was a peripheral peninsula of continental Europe. There is evidence that man visited Devon intermittently and sporadically when fluctuations in the position of the ice sheet permitted. These Palaeolithic people came to Devon seasonally, following animal herds northwards and westwards in the warm season and returning with them in the winter. Sites used in the Lower and Middle Palaeolithic (before 40,000 BC), such as Kent's Cavern, Torquay and Windmill Hill cave, Brixham, have been recognised by the types of stone tools found, although precise dating is not possible. Finds elsewhere suggest that Lower Palaeolithic man moved along the valleys of such rivers as the Axe (where Greensand chert was readily available for tools), the Exe, Otter, Culm, and Tavy.

During the Upper Palaeolithic (*c*40,000 BC to *c*8000 BC) movement appears to have been along the valleys of the Teign, Dart, and possibly the Plym. Antler harpoon blades are known from this period, including two from Kent's Cavern dated to *c*12,000 BC and 10,000 BC: these suggest the hunting of fish and sea mammals.[9] Fish bones are, however, very sparsely represented in reports of bone finds from the Palaeolithic, but it may be that nineteenth and early-twentieth century excavators were unable to recognise them.

Palaeolithic water transport

A theoretical analysis of the tools and techniques needed to make the various types of water transport – floats, rafts, and boats – suggests that late Palaeolithic man would generally have been capable of making floats of logs, bundles of reeds or hides; simple log rafts; and simple, frameless, hide boats. The raw materials for such craft were available to Palaeolithic man, but no direct evidence for the use of water transport has survived anywhere. Whether these float rafts or boats were indeed used depends upon whether the idea had arisen of using available tools and techniques to make water transport; whether the idea had been conceived of forming multiple units by fastening together individual units of buoyant material, or of using the buoyancy properties of a 'leather bag'; and whether purposeful methods of steering and propulsion had been evolved.[10]

There seems little likelihood that Palaeolithic man used water transport extensively in British coastal waters. Rafts and floats of even the most advanced design are nowadays seldom, if ever, used at sea outside the zone enclosed by latitudes 40°N and 40°S, as low air and sea temperatures combined with wind and wetness soon make a man numb.[11] In addition, the simple frameless hide boat is insufficiently sturdy to be used in anything but the calmest of seas. Thus Palaeolithic man in Devon would have used any water transport he had evolved on lakes, rivers, and estuaries, and possibly in the shallows on favoured coasts. This putative ability would have given him access to a wide variety of food sources and could have been of great use in his exploration of coastal and inland environments for raw materials.

The Mesolithic Period

This technological stage lasted in Devon from the late-9th millennium to the late-5th, that is the early post-glacial period, when the retreat of the Ice Sheet caused beneficial changes in the climate leading to an increased range of available raw materials and a wide range of food sources obtainable by hunting, fishing, and gathering. As the climate improved, people whose ancestors had visited Britain seasonally could now remain there the year round. Todd estimates that the southwest peninsula could have supported up to 100 people at any one time during the earlier Mesolithic, with some increase in the later period.[12]

Faunal remains from a number of sites in northwest Europe show that, *inter alia*, sea mammals, birds, and fish were eaten in the Mesolithic period. For example, at a coastal site at Morton, Fife, remains of cod, haddock, turbot, sturgeon, and salmon were found. Many of the cod bones were from fish longer than 1 metre, which were probably caught in relatively deep water away from the coast. The excavator John Coles has suggested that birds such as the guillemot may also have been taken at sea. From this and from other sites in Britain and elsewhere it seems clear that Mesolithic man was nomadic or at best semi-sedentary, exploiting a range of seasonal food sources.[13] We may visualize people in Devon exploiting estuaries in late spring and early summer for shellfish, sea fish, salmon, and sea birds. In later summer they followed the deer to upland pastures, returning in autumn to the coast for sea birds and shellfish. In winter and early spring they alternated between taking sea fish and seals on the rocky coast, and hunting hoofed mammals in inland wooded areas. Thus it can be seen that estuaries could be a source of food almost throughout the year, being the meeting point of several ecological zones: marine, coastal, riverine, and terrestrial.

The earliest known Mesolithic site in Devon is at Woodbury Common, overlooking the Exe estuary. There are also sites at Northam, north of Bideford, Woolacombe Sands in Morte Bay, Yelland in the Taw estuary, and Westward Ho!, north-west of Bideford (exposed at low water); other sites are known near some of the south coast rivers. At the Westward Ho! site a midden of shells and animal bones has been dated to the mid-5th millennium bc.[14] Other Mesolithic sites undoubtedly remain to be found underwater, near the mouths of now-inundated estuaries. Flint and stone microliths are found in abundance on Mesolithic sites, and the principal hunting weapons of this period seem to have been arrows, throwing spears and fish spears, tipped and barbed with microliths.

Mesolithic rafts and boats

During the Mesolithic stage of technology it was theoretically possible to build bundle rafts and log rafts of substantial timbers, as well as simple log boats and framed hide boats made from several skins.[15] As the Mesolithic progressed substantial trees became available, but the simple forms of logboats that it was technically possible to build would probably not have been seaworthy. A narrow, hollowed pine log from Pesse, in the Netherlands, which could well be a logboat has survived from this period and has been dated to *c*6315 bc.[16] Thus it would theoretically have been possible to use hide boats in the seas off Devon; and rafts of logs or reed bundles and simple logboats as well as hide boats could have been used on inland waters. In the early stages of the Mesolithic, until the final land bridge across the channel was breached in the 8th/7th millennium, people could have made their way from and to continental Europe on foot. After this time, travel would have had to be by hide boat. Seafaring was indeed practised off northwest Europe during this period, as we know indirectly from the settlement of such islands as the Hebrides, and from the evidence for deep-sea fishing.

The Neolithic Period

In Devon the Neolithic lasted from *c*4000 to *c*2000 BC, its characteristic features being ground and polished stone tools and weapons, the production of pottery, and crop and animal husbandry which led to a relatively settled way of life. A question posed in recent years is whether migrants from the Continent brought these innovatory ideas and sheep and corn to Britain, or whether the indigenous Mesolithic Britons absorbed ideas prevalent on the Continent and adapted them to suit local conditions.[17]

Whether it was only ideas that crossed the Channel or whether it was migrants, some form of water transport had to be used. The question then must be asked, where did such voyages take place? Clark pointed out the possibility of the transfer of ideas by contacts between fishermen following migrating fish in mid-channel.[18] Such contacts would theoretically be possible anywhere in the Channel, from the Strait of Dover (18 to 29 nautical miles wide) to the crossings from Normandy/Brittany to Devon/Cornwall, where the distance nowadays is not less than 70 nautical miles. As the sail appears not to have been known in northwest European waters at this time, and as pilotage is less demanding than navigation out of sight of land,[19] contacts in the eastern Channel seem more likely than in the Devon region. For similar reasons any migrants are likely to have crossed near the Strait, where both sides can generally be seen from a position in mid-Channel. Channel fishing was undoubtedly undertaken off the south Devon coast in the Neolithic period, but probably only in those waters from which the Devon coast, or coastal indications such as orographic cloud, could be seen.

That voyages were also undertaken along the Devon coast may be deduced from the evidence for the dispersal of stone from sources now underwater in the Penzance/Mounts Bay region of Cornwall in the 3rd millenium BC.[20] Although several tools of this type of stone have been found in Cornwall and Devon, the great majority are found further east, in Wessex and eastern England. As Mercer has pointed out, the surviving sample of *c*200 may be a minute proportion of the output, and thus the plotted distribution may be unrepresentative.[21] Nevertheless, on present evidence the distribution does suggest that there were coastal entrepôts or centres of distribution in or near Poole Harbour, Dorset, and in the Thames and possibly Humber estuaries. The implication is that these tools were moved by sea, rather than overland, with the possibility of a return cargo of Beer flint from east Devon and Portland chert from Dorset.[22] Furthermore, Peacock has shown that pottery found at Hembury near Honiton, at Maiden Castle and Hambledon Hill in Dorset, and at Windmill Hill and Robin Hood's Ball in Wiltshire, in contexts of *c*3000 BC, was made near St Kevern on the Lizard peninsula. Mercer considers that such delicate pottery must have been moved by water transport.[23] An alternative hypothesis is that clay from Cornwall was distributed to Devon, Wiltshire, and Dorset, where it was made into pots.

This south coast traffic between Cornwall and Wessex in stone tools and pots (or possibly clay) could well have involved the use of landing places on the south coast of Devon, either as planned breaks in a voyage or for safety when bad weather seemed likely. The landing place for the embarkation of flint for the westward journey could have been within the Axe estuary or near Beer or Seaton; Budleigh Haven near the mouth of the River Otter may have been a staging post for Hembury; shelter and watering places *en route* could have been found in the estuaries of the Exe, Teign, and Dart, in Start Bay, Tor Bay, or at Salcombe, or in the Avon, Erme, Yealm, and in Plymouth Sound. The remains of what was probably a fish weir discovered off Westward Ho! and recently dated to *c*2800 BC,[24] are a sign of the continued use of coastal waters and rivers by Neolithic man.

Neolithic rafts and boats

During this Neolithic period *all* known forms of water transport became technologically possible. Thus, in addition to those postulated for earlier times, pots used as floats, complex logboats, and plank-built boats[25] could theoretically have been built. The earliest known plank-built boats from Britain are dated to the Bronze Age (see below) but the skills to build them and the raw materials were evidently there in Neolithic Britain and thus it is possible that they, and complex logboats, were built and used. If this were so, it seems probable that such craft were suitable for inland waters and estuaries rather than for seafaring, which probably continued as in earlier times to be undertaken in hide boats. Propulsion, as in the Mesolithic and Palaeolithic, would have been by paddle and, in shallow water, by pole.

*The Bronze and Iron Ages: c*2000 BC to the 1st century AD

The introduction of copper, and more especially the copper/tin alloy known as bronze, for tools and weapons, stimulated international trade both in raw materials and in finished products. Finds from Britain's southwest peninsula of imported artifacts indicate relations not only with Wales and Ireland, but also with the Continent, including Mycenean Greece, Cyprus, and the east Mediterranean, probably indirectly via northwest France.[26] The concentration of finds at Mount Batten, a peninsula site on the eastern side of Plymouth Sound, suggests that this was a major landing place and entrepôt from the Late Bronze Age[27] (see below).

During 1978–81 a group of seven bronzes was found underwater off Moor Sands, to the southeast of the entrance to Salcombe Harbour. These included a bronze sword blade, common in central Europe in *c*1000 BC, and bronze tools probably from Brittany. In 1982 a sword handle was recovered.[28] These finds not only demonstrate cross-Channel trade, in either bronze artifacts or scrap, but also suggest that this was a wreck site, although no trace of a boat has yet been found.

Copper has relatively wide distribution in Europe, but tin is known from few sources, notably northwest Spain, Brittany, and southwest Britain on the Atlantic seaboard.[29] When demand for tin by the Mediterranean civilisations exceeded supplies available from sources such as northern Italy, north Greece, central Germany, and possibly the Middle East, these Atlantic seaboard sources came to be exploited. There are readily available tin and copper (and also lead) deposits in the southwest peninsula; tin in west Cornwall, Bodmin Moor, and Dartmoor, while there is copper on Exmoor and Dartmoor.[30]

During the 1st millennium, from about 700 BC onwards, there was a gradual change from bronze to iron, but bronze long continued to be in demand, right into the Roman period. The 4th century AD Latin poem *Ora Maritima* contains extracts from a 6th century BC 'pilotage handbook' known to us as the *Massaliote Periplus*, which describes coastal features on the sea route between the west European seaboard and *Massalia* (Marseilles), at a time when there was increasing commercial competition between Phoenicians from Carthage and Greeks from *Massalia*.[31] From this *periplus* we learn of islands adjacent to Cape *Oestrymnis* (possibly Ushant) where Greek traders from *Tartessus* (near Huelva in southwest Spain) obtained tin and lead brought there by northern seamen in hide boats from Brittany, Britain, and Ireland. There are problems in precisely identifying the places named and routes given in this account; nevertheless it seems clear that in the first half of the 1st millennium metal was exported by sea from southwest Britain. Finished artifacts and fine pottery were probably imported in exchange. If the route taken was direct to Ushant, as seems likely, rather than via staging posts further up channel, then the problem of open-sea navigation must have been solved by this time.

In the later fourth century BC Pytheas sailed from *Massalia* to explore the northern seas and to bring back commercial and navigational information.[32] Pytheas's subsequent book is now lost, but Latin authors such as Diodorus Siculus and Strabo of the first century BC, and Pliny of the first century AD, quote from him and from Timaeus of the fourth century BC. From these accounts it is deduced that, after leaving the continent, probably in the vicinity of Ushant, Pytheas made a landfall at *Belerion* (Lands End in Cornwall), followed by a landing somewhere else in the southwest peninsula. Here he learned that tin mined in the South West was taken by hide boat to *Mictis*, an island some six days' sail up channel, ie to the east, where it was made available to foreign merchants. It is generally thought that this entrepôt and landing place must have been on or near the Isle of Wight (*Vectis* in later times). The practice of using an island or a promontory as a mart or entrepôt for foreign trade is widespread:[33] on such isolated and readily defended sites traders can be segregated, protected, and supervised, justice dispensed, and tolls imposed.

Diodorus also mentions an island called *Ictis* connected at low water to the mainland of Britain by a causeway, where tin was brought in wagons for foreign merchants to buy and transport to the Mediterranean via Gaul. This practice may well refer to the 1st century BC rather than earlier. Sixteen and more places have been suggested for the location of *Ictis*,[34] the two considered most likely being St Michael's Mount in Mounts Bay, Cornwall, and the peninsula of Mount Batten on the eastern side of Plymouth Sound. The difficulty is to establish whether, in the 1st millennium BC, either of these sites would have been an island which dried at low water, leaving a natural causeway to the mainland. Although neither site has been extensively excavated in recent times, there are a number of finds from Mount Batten which provide some support for its identification as *Ictis*.[35] These show links with southwest France or northwest Spain in the fourth or third century BC, and later contacts with northwest France, as well as suggesting a coastal trade with the Poole/Hengistbury Head region of Dorset. Mount Batten seems to have been prominent in the seaborne trade from the fourth century BC until just before the Roman Conquest. The rivers Tavy and Tamar gave access to the tin and copper deposits on Dartmoor and around Callington, and it thus seems likely that the preferred method of transporting metal to Mount Batten would have been by boat. The overland approach to Mount Batten from the north is more circuitous, as, amongst other problems, a way has to be found across the river Plym to the northeast, and it is difficult to visualise circumstances when wagons would be used. On the other hand, they could well have been used to load ships anchored or moored in the shallows off both Mount Batten and St Michael's Mount.[36] Future excavations at these two sites may throw more light on the location of 1st century BC *Ictis*.

Christie, discussing the early 1st millenium BC, and Cunliffe describing the end, both see southern Britain in general, and the southwest peninsula in particular, as more closely integrated culturally, politically, and economically with Armorica than with neighbouring parts of Britain.[37] Mutual exploitation of Channel fishing grounds and the overseas trade contacts described above would have made a significant contribution to this. Diodorus (v.22, 1–4), writing in the 1st century, BC noted:

> The inhabitants of Britain who dwell throughout the promontory called *Belerion* are more than usually friendly to strangers . . . and through their intercourse with foreign traders they have been made peaceable in their ways. (Translated by C Hawkes.)

Bronze Age boats

The Classical sources quoted above seem to suggest that hide boats were the principal seagoing craft of Britain in the 1st millennium BC and possibly earlier, but the archaeological evidence for this is thin, even when we consider the whole of northwest Europe: some rock carvings in Scandinavia, a small shale bowl from Caergwrle, Wales, and the minute gold models from Nors, Denmark, may represent hide boats.[38]

Theoretical analysis suggests that sea-going plank boats could also have been built in Bronze Age Britain, but the four boats that survive from this period are river and estuary craft. Remains of three sewn plank boats were found at North Ferriby, North Humberside (Fig. 4.1) and excavated by EV and CW Wright between 1937 and 1946, and in 1963,[39] and samples from them have been dated by radiocarbon assay to the mid-second millennium BC: they are thus the oldest known planked boats in northwest Europe. A related boat, the so-called 'raft' from Brigg, South Humberside, was found in 1888. The remains, excavated in 1974, proved to be the bottom of a flat-bottomed boat (Fig. 4.2), dated *c*800 BC.[40] These four boats were built of flush-laid oak planking, sewn with withies (yew at Ferriby, hazel at Brigg), with moss caulking and longitudinal laths at the plank seams, and transverse timbers through cleats left proud of the planking. They were flat-bottomed boats, without keel or stems, probably used as ferries for men, animals and cargo within the Humber estuary and its tributaries. It is theoretically possible that similar boats could have been used in the estuaries and rivers of southwest Britain.

There is some slight evidence for another Bronze Age plank boat tradition in Britain: one of the boat-shaped, log coffins from the Early Bronze Age site at Loose Howe, northeast Yorkshire, has the shape of 'stem' and 'keel' worked in the solid log. This pseudo-stem is similar to the one worked at the forward end of the Iron Age logboat from Poole, Dorset.[41] Such features are non-functional in logboats and therefore must be skeuomorphs: their occurrence suggests that plank boats (or possibly hide boats) with keels and stems were known in Bronze Age Britain. Such boats seem more likely to have had sea-going potential than the stemless tradition of the Humber estuary, and may have been used off the coasts of the southwest peninsula. On the other hand, it may be that these Bronze Age British coffin makers were acquainted with *foreign* boats with keel and stems, and that such craft were not yet built in Britain.

Logboats, for inland waters rather than sea-going, have survived from the Bronze Age in parts of Europe: for example, Denmark in the late fourth millennium BC and France in the early third millennium.[42] The earliest dated British logboat, from Locharbriggs, Scotland, is from the early second millennium BC.[43] Only four logboats have been recorded from the southwest peninsula: two from Cornwall, at Tolcarne near Penzance and Tuckingmill near Redruth; and two from Devon, at Bovey Heathfield and Plympton.[44] None of them has survived, scanty details were recorded, and none is dated. It may be that these boats were prehistoric, but it must be borne in mind that of the logboats dated so far in northwest Europe approximately three-fifths have proved to be Roman Age or later.

Iron Age boats

There is documentary and iconographic evidence for the types of boat used in British waters in the late Iron Age. In *Bello Civile* (1.54) Caesar records how he built hide boats similar to those he had seen in Britain; and both Caesar (*BG* III 13) and Strabo (4.4.1) have left descriptions of the sea-going boats of the Veneti, a Celtic people of northwest France who regularly sailed in the Channel. These broad and flat-bottomed boats with rising ends were propelled by sails of hide. Their oak planking was caulked with seaweed (possibly moss), and heavy frames were fastened to the planking by stout iron nails. There are representations of boats on two pre-Roman coins of Cunobelin of the Catuvellauni (Fig. 4.3) dated early first century AD, from Canterbury[45] and Sheepen near Colchester. These British craft have mast, yard, and rigging, and a horizontal projection from the bottom of the bow which may represent a protruding forefoot to facilitate beaching or to increase speed potential or improve weatherly performance. Boats resembling these Latin descriptions and Celtic depictions may well have been used in Devon waters in the late–1st millennium BC.

Propulsion

Models and other representations of ships show that sail was used in Bronze Age Egypt and Mesopotamia (before 3000 BC) and in the Mediterranean (before 2000 BC); but in northwest Europe the earliest evidence for sail is not until the Iron Age, in the first century BC, when Caesar and Strabo described the leather sails of the Venetic ships. The small model boat (Fig. 4.4) from Broighter, Co Derry, of that same century, which may represent a hide boat, is further evidence for mast and yard.[46] However, it seems likely that the hide boats that took tin and lead from southwest Britain across the Channel (possibly to Ushant – see above, p. 38) in the sixth century BC, had sails. The first evidence of the oar in northwest Europe is from the fifth century BC, on a model boat from Dürrnberg, near Hallein.[47] It thus seems likely that both oar and sail were known in northern waters by the mid–1st millenium BC, and used on sea-going and inland craft.

4.1 Ferriby (North Humberside) boat 1 during excavation from the river Humber foreshore in 1946. *(National Maritime Museum)*

Trade routes

Descriptions by late-Roman authors, and excavations on key sites, suggest the sea routes by which the trade between the classical world and Britain was carried out in the second half of the 1st millennium BC.[48] Those involving southwest Britain (Map 4.1, above p. 35) include the river Loire or river Gironde via Ushant to Mounts Bay or Plymouth Sound; Alet (St Malo) to Poole or Christchurch Harbours; Christchurch Harbour to Plymouth Sound and Mounts Bay.

As in earlier times, pilotage methods were used when in sight of land on

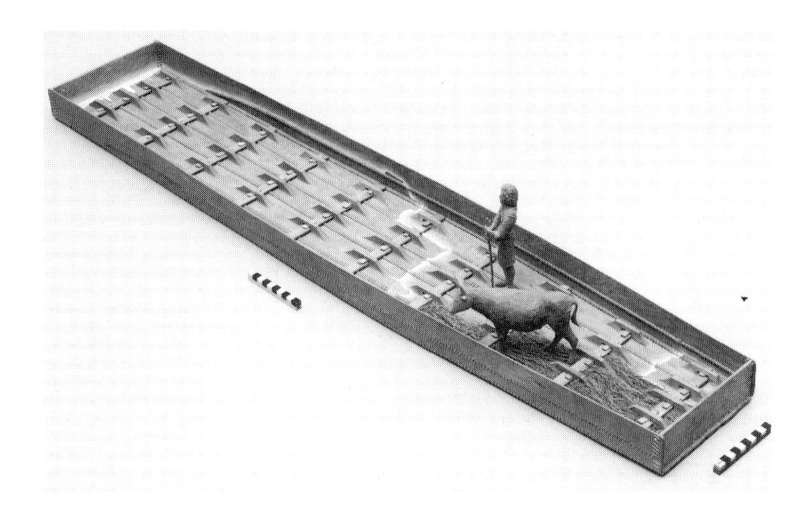

4.2 1:10 scale model of the flat-bottomed boat from Brigg (South Humberside). The parts outlined in white represent what was excavated. *(National Maritime Museum)*

4.3 Pre-Roman coin of Cunobelin. *(Colchester, Essex, Museum)*

the coastal routes, but navigational techniques were needed on the open-sea sections of cross-Channel routes. A boat on the Ushant to southwest Britain route would be out of sight of land for about 52 nautical miles out of a total of 95 to 120 nautical miles, even in the best of weather, whereas on the Alet to Dorset route this would be only 10 nautical miles out of 130. Crossings at the western end of the Channel thus not only called for good seamanship but also for high standards of navigation using a form of dead reckoning and every conceivable environmental clue. This would include using the zenith sun, and the position of sunrise and sunset to give directions in daylight; and the swell, wind, and stars, especially *Polaris*, at night. Estimates of distance gone and speed made good were probably expressed as faster or slower than usual.[49]

These traditional cross-Channel routes appear to have been disrupted by the Roman advance into France and especially by Caesar's defeat and dispersal of the Veneti at Quiberon Bay in 56 BC (men from southwest Britain fought with the Veneti (Caesar *BG* 3.9). The subsequent Roman invasions of southeast Britain in 55 and 54 BC and 43 AD diverted the main trade routes to the eastern Channel, to the river Rhine and Belgic Gaul on the Continent, and the rivers Thames, Stour, Blackwater, and Colne in southeast Britain.

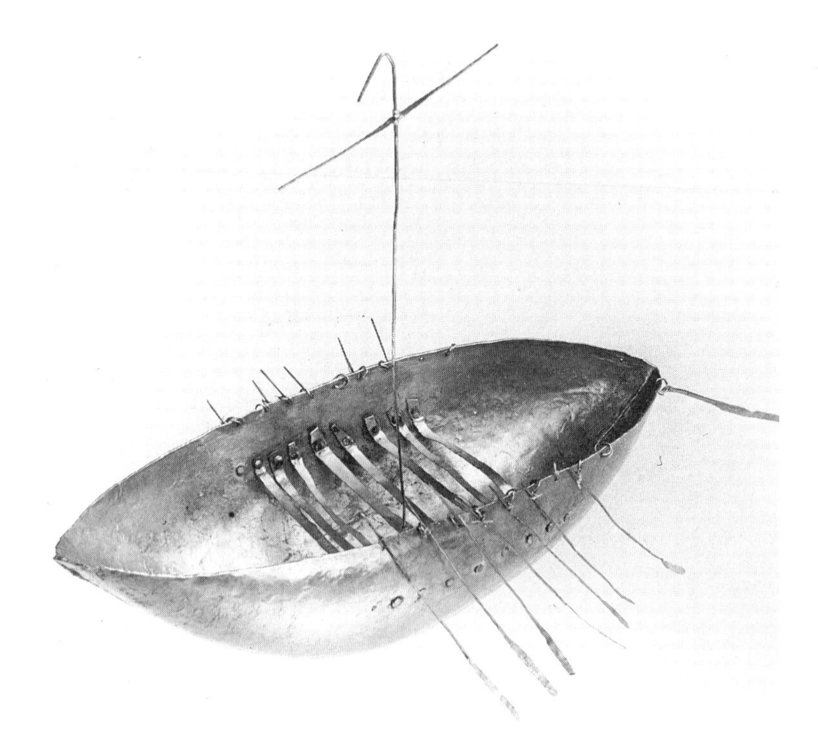

4.4 Small gold model boat from Broighter, Co Derry, with oars, mast and yard, and steering oar. *(National Museum of Ireland)*

The Roman Period: 1st to 4th centuries AD

The Roman occupation of Devon appears to have taken place within a decade of Claudius' invasion.[50] This was primarily a land campaign, but subsequently the Roman army was at least partly supplied by sea, for example at Exeter (*Isca Dumnoniorum*), at the head of the Exe estuary, the river probably being tidal that far in those days.[51] Fortresses, possibly with waterfront facilities, may also have been established at the head of the Taw estuary, possibly at Barnstaple or Bishop's Tawton, and at the head of the Tamar estuary, but neither has yet been located. Aerial reconnaissance has recently revealed other possible forts.[52] Roman signal stations, or fortlets, of the 1st century AD have been recognised on the north coast of Devon at Martinhoe and Old Burrow, west and east of Foreland Point.[53] These stations command a view across the British Channel to South Wales, and there are possibly beach landing places nearby where they could have been supplied. Similar stations may remain to be found near headlands further west, such as Bull, Morte, Baggy, and Hartland Points – the last is probably the *Herculis Promontorium* of Ptolemy.[54]

The first Devon seaman, in fact the first Devon person, whose name is known to us lived during the Roman occupation. Aemilius, a citizen of Dumnonia and son of Saenus, was a sailor in the Roman fleet of the Lower Rhine. He was buried near Cologne in the early second century AD.[55]

Although the principal axis of continental trade may have moved eastward (see above) during the 1st century AD, imports continued to reach Mount Batten and a site on the western side of Plymouth Sound. There may have been another trading place at Sutton Pool, across the Cattewater from Mount Batten.[56] It is also possible that Axmouth and Sidmouth were used in this period.

Roman Age boats

A group of a dozen or so boats, excavated principally from the Rhine region and the lower Thames, are dated to the first to third centuries AD.[57] These Romano–Celtic boats are not all well-documented but, in general, they were flat-bottomed, keel-less boats, with flush-laid planking fastened to the floor timbers by iron nails which were clenched in a distinctive way by turning the point through 180 degrees back into the timber (Fig. 4.5). We should learn more, especially about sea-going variants of this tradition, when details of the Roman Age wreck from St Peter Port Harbour, Guernsey, are published. Boats such as these may have been used on the Devon rivers and estuaries, whilst other sea-going craft may have been similar to the ship from the County Hall site by the Thames in London, which was built in the classical Mediterranean tradition with flush-laid planking fastened by wooden draw-tongue joints (a form of mortice and tenon).[58]

The sub-Roman Period: 4th to 7th centuries AD

From the late third century AD North Sea pirates raided coastal sites and harassed the eastern cross-Channel trade routes, and it may be that, as a result, sea routes across the western Channel became more attractive to traders.[59] However, by the end of the fourth century all Channel routes became disrupted as raiders spread into the western seas from the Continent and from Ireland. Nevertheless, and despite the collapse of the western Roman Empire in the 5th century AD, the western cross-Channel routes continued to be used, at least intermittently. Amphorae containing wine or oil, and a distinctive style of red pottery, were shipped, probably indirectly, from west Turkey and North Africa to the southwest peninsula in the late-fifth and sixth centuries AD,[60] and Byzantine coins dating from the end of the fifth to the beginning of the seventh century have been found in Exeter, Exmouth, and Plymouth.

Trade contacts with northwest France also continued during the sixth century and up to *c*AD 700. For example, French pottery has been found at the clifftop site of High Peak, three miles west of Sidmouth. Imported pottery and other objects have also been found at Mothecombe at the mouth of the river Erme, and Bantham Ham in the Avon estuary.[61] Mothecombe may be related in some way to Oldaport (*Yoldeport* in the fourtheenth century) near Modbury. This possibly pre-medieval fortified site overlooks a silted-up harbour at the confluence of two streams with the river Erme.[62]

Further evidence for sea travel in this period is contained in the writings of Gildas (*De Excidio*) and Procopius (VIII.20.8). Taken together, these sources describe a migration of Celtic people from southwest Britain to northwest Gaul and to Galacia in northwest Spain. The settlement in northwest Gaul was so significant that *Armorica*, its name in Roman times, became *Britannia*, and the northwest part of this Brittany/Bretagne subsequently became known as *Dumnonia*. The Breton language developed from the Celtic language of southwest Britain, and is clearly related to Welsh and to the old Cornish language. These late-fifth and early-sixth century migrations may have been caused by the general disturbance of those times, or more specifically by the threat of the Saxons advancing inexorably from the east.[63]

Ogham inscriptions and memorial stones recording Irish names indicate cross-channel relations between Devon and Ireland, either direct or via South Wales.[64] Although there is some evidence from Exeter of Christianity in Roman times, it does not seem to have become general until after 500 AD. Possibly the impetus came from Ireland via Wales, or from western Gaul.[65] In subsequent centuries missionaries appear to have travelled extensively between Ireland, Wales, southwest Britain and northwest Gaul.

Clearly, in this period, the seamen of the north and south coast of Devon retained, and indeed extended, their knowledge of coastal and cross-channel passages. What boats they used must remain conjectural, but it seems likely that they included both hide and plank-built versions, using as analogous evidence the sixth-century boats used by St Columba and St Brendan in the seas around Ireland and Scotland.[66]

The Early Medieval Period

The Anglo-Saxon settlement of England began in the South East in the mid-fifth century, and by the mid-seventh century had progressed as far west as Wiltshire and Dorset. Although there were undoubtedly strong English influences in east Devon by the end of the seventh century – St Boniface, born *c*675, was educated at an English monastery in Exeter, for example – the documentary, place name, and excavated evidence suggests that there was no swift conquest but a gradual colonisation of Devon from the east. A more formal absorption of Devon into England probably occurred in the early ninth century, when Ecgbert of Wessex attacked *Dumnonia*, and this was reinforced in 936 when Athelstan expelled the remaining Britons from Exeter and re-asserted English overlordship over lands west of the Tamar, which ever since has effectively remained the border between Devon and Cornwall.[67]

Early Viking raids

The Vikings first raided England in 789, landing somewhere on the south coast, probably east of Devon. The Scandinavian fleet first appeared in southwest waters in 838, when an army allied itself with some Britons against the Wessex forces of Ecgbert. The site of the ensuing battle, which was won by the English, appears to have been at Hingston Down near Callington, which may mean that the Viking ships used the river Tamar. In 851 another Danish army was defeated by Ealdorman Ceorel and the men of Devon at *Wicgeanbeorg*, possibly Wickaborough, some five miles inland from Tor Bay, where the Viking fleet could have been beached. In 876 Exeter was taken by a Danish army which had ridden from Wareham, south west of Poole, Dorset. Its fleet sailed from Poole Harbour with the intention of making Exeter, but 120 ships were lost at sea in a storm off Swanage. It does not appear that any ships that survived this storm went on to Exeter as, after the Vikings in Exeter had agreed a truce with Alfred, they moved overland into Mercia.

In 878 the brother of Ivor and Halfdan (possibly the Ubba of north Devon folklore) sailed with 23 ships across the Bristol Channel from south Wales to north Devon, where he was defeated by Odda, Ealderman of Devon, at a place called *Arx Cynuit*, which may have been Kenwith near Bideford or Countisbury Hill, south of Foreland Point and east of Lynmouth Bay. Foreland Point is 'bold off the outer point' and would have made a good landfall.[68] The fact that Odda was able to meet the Vikings soon after they had landed may mean that, as in Roman times, lookouts had been stationed along the north Devon coast.

In 893 the Vikings who had settled the Danelaw in Northumbria and East Anglia effected near-synchronised attacks on the north and south coasts of Devon. One hundred ships sailed from the east coast south-about to Exeter, and 40 north-about to a fort which may have been Pilton, near Barnstaple.[69] Alfred marched his army to Exeter and the Vikings withdrew by ship. As Binns has pointed out, these attacks on Devon may have been a diversionary tactic to draw Alfred away from two Viking armies which had landed the previous year in Kent from Boulogne.[70]

In 897 Alfred changed his tactics from pursuit on horse and on foot to interception by ship. He ordered warships to be built, bigger, swifter, and steadier than the Viking ships. The chroniclers state that these ships were of Alfred's own design, different from the Viking ships and from those of the Frisians. Frisian seamen, however, were masters of at least three of the nine King's ships which, later that year, blockaded six Viking ships beached within an estuary somewhere on the coast of Dorset or south Devon. As a result of the ensuing land battle, two Viking ships were seized in the harbour; two others were subsequently lost at sea off the Sussex coast.

Later Viking attacks

No further Viking raids on England were recorded until the late tenth century. In 981 there were raids at several places on the north Devon coast, and in the following year Aethelred decided to use ships, as Alfred had aimed to do, to intercept the Viking ships at sea: he did not have the same success. In 997 the Vikings sailed westwards along the English Channel and

4.5 Romano-Celtic boat from Druten, the Netherlands, during excavation in 1973. *(L Th Lehman)*

around into the Bristol Channel, where they raided Wales as well as Devon and Cornwall. Subsequently they returned to the English Channel and entered the river Tamar, evidently taking their ships 25 miles or so up that river to its confluence with the river Lyd, and possibly a further five miles up that tributary to Lydford. After burning Lydford and the abbey at Tavistock they returned to the sea with their plunder. In 1001 a Viking fleet, together with some ships which had deserted from the English, entered the river Teign and destroyed *Teignton*, probably modern Kingsteignton. They then entered the Exe where, if they had intended to take or raid Exeter, they were thwarted and instead raided and burnt Pinhoe and Broad Clyst to the north west of Exeter.

Swein of Denmark invaded England in 1003 and later that year his army took Exeter, but it seems unlikely that this was a seaborne assault. More raids followed in many parts of England during the next decade, and Aethelred's response was to alternate between paying 'danegeld' to the Vikings and attempting to fight them. In 1008 he followed Alfred's example and ordered ships to be built throughout England, one warship (*scegd*) having to be provided from every 310 hides.[71] That large ships were owned, and possibly built, in Devon in this period may be seen in the will of Aelfwold, bishop of Crediton, who died in 1012 and bequeathed to the king, *inter alia*, a 64-oared ship.[72] By 1016 the Danish armies and fleets had triumphed, and Cnut son of Swein was chosen as king of the English.

Viking ships

The general characteristics of the ships used by the Scandinavians for raiding and for trading in early medieval times are reasonably well-known. A series of Danish and Norwegian finds, from bogs, underwater sites, and grave mounds, extending from the pre-Viking Nydam boat of *c*AD 400 to the Skuldelev wrecks of the tenth/eleventh century, differ in detail but have sufficient in common to define a Scandinavian or Norse tradition of boat and ship building.[73] These craft were double-ended, with the keel blending into curved stems; the distinctive curve of the top edge of the sides gave the hull a pronounced sheer towards the ends; in cross-section these craft had a generally rounded bottom and flared sides. The hull was built in the shell sequence with overlapping (clinker) planking fastened to a 'backbone' of keel and stems, and supported by an internal structure of symetrically-placed floor timbers, slender cross-beams and knees. The keel protruded well below the planking, even on oared vessels, and was fastened, from at least the eighth century, by vertical scarfs to the stems. Propulsion was by oars pivoted about tholes on the sheerline of the smaller boats, or through oar ports in an upper strake of the larger vessels. Sailing craft had a mast stepped near amidships and a single square sail. Steering was by a side rudder, usually over the starboard quarter. Although the larger of the craft in this tradition were capable of North Sea crossings, and indeed Atlantic voyages, they remained until the end of the Viking period 'open boats'. Those built as cargo vessels, with greater beam and depth measurements than warships, had a hold amidship and half-decks under which stores could be carried, but there was no shelter for the crew other than possibly a covering of hides.

Three ships from the burial mounds near Oslo, Oseberg, Gokstad, and Tune have survived from the ninth century, a period of intensive Viking activity in the British Isles.[74] Those ships, powered by oar and sail, give a *general* impression of the sort of vessel used by Viking raiders. However, it seems probable that the tenth/eleventh-century Ladby boat (Fig. 4.6) and Skuldelev wrecks 2 and 5 with a length/breadth ratio of *c*6.5 rather than the *c*4.5 of Gokstad and Oseberg, are more representative of the warships used in the ninth, tenth and eleventh-century Viking raids.[75]

The Viking boatbuilder selected his timber carefully so that the grain ran the length of each member, no matter whether it was straight or curved. Such timbers were strong and therefore could be slender: thus weight was saved. With such light scantlings (dimensions of individual timbers) and a buoyant hull form, the Viking warship had relatively slight displacement – thus even when a full crew was on board she drew little water and could venture into the upper reaches of rivers, as we see frequently mentioned in the Anglo-Saxon and Irish chronicles.

English ships

There are only two boat finds of any consequence from early medieval England: the *c*600 AD impression of a buried boat (Fig. 4.7) excavated from a royal grave mound at Sutton Hoo, Suffolk; and the *c*900 AD cargo boat (Fig. 4.8) excavated from a tributary of the river Thames at Graveney, Kent.[76] It has been argued on the basis of these two finds, statements in the Anglo-Saxon Chronicles, and some later material, that there is an Anglo-Saxon tradition of boat-building which can readily be distinguished from the contemporary Scandinavian or Norse tradition.[77] However, in the present stage of knowledge it seems wiser to regard any Anglo-Saxon 'tradition' as a regional variant within a broad northwest European tradition which embraced the Baltic as well as the North Sea countries. Indeed the variations found in some of the boat finds from the eastern Baltic – treenails as plank fastenings, moss as caulking, and the mast stepped in a transverse timber – demonstrate that such sub-groups existed.[78] The persistent features of the mainstream northwest European tradition may be seen on the eleventh-century Bayeux Tapestry, twelfth to fourteenth-century town seals (see below, p. 65, Figs 7.4a, b, c), and the boat remains from twelfth/thirteenth-century Wood Quay, Dublin, and twelfth/fifteenth-century Bergen.[79]

4.6 *Imme Gram*, a twentieth-century replica of the Ladby boat, after unloading horses on the Danish coast.
(Viking Ship Museum, Roskilde)

4.7 Excavation of the boat burial at Sutton Hoo, Suffolk, 1939. *(British Museum)*

4.8 The Graveney (Kent) boat during excavation from a former tributary of the river Thames in 1970. *(National Maritime Museum)*

The ships which Alfred had built in 897 may have been longer than contemporary Viking ships – 60 oars suggests an overall length of over 100 feet (30 metres), and the Gokstad ship with 32 oars was about 23 metres – and possibly broader, but structurally they could well have been in the same technological tradition. Fragments of clinker planking now in Torquay Natural History Museum, which are all that remains of a boat uncovered near Kingsteignton in 1898, may be from this early medieval period: the results of radiocarbon dating are awaited.

Trade routes

During the Anglo-Saxon settlement phase, and even during the periods of Viking raids, trade still continued across the English and Bristol Channels. However, trade in the eastern English Channel and the North Sea from the seventh century until the late-ninth century came to be dominated by the Frisians with their principal port at Duurstede (Dorestad) at the junction of the river Lek with the Rhine. The Frankish port of Quentovic on the river Canche upstream of Etaples in northern France also had a strong influence on trade patterns from the seventh century until it became silted in the tenth century, when it was replaced by Wissant.[80] Thus English ports such as Ipswich, London, and Southampton flourished, and it may be that in this period goods traded to and from Devon were carried by coastal shipping via these ports rather than on direct cross-Channel routes.

4: From the Ice Age to Early Medieval Times

1 RJ Devoy, 'Analysis of the Geological Evidence for Holocene Sea-Level Movements in SE England', *Proc. Geologists' Association*, 93 (1982), 65–90; RM Jacobi, 'Britain Inside and Outside Mesolithic Europe', *Proc. Prehistoric Society* 42 (1976), 72–3. In this present paper calendar years are given as BC and AD, and radiocarbon years as bc and ad. I am grateful to Professor Barry Cunliffe, Dr Andrew Sherratt, and Professor Malcolm Todd for their criticism of an earlier draft.

2 M Todd, *South West to AD 1000* (1987), and *Cornish Archaeology* 25, (1986) are useful sources for the southwest peninsula generally.

3 B Cunliffe, *Iron Age Communities in Britain* (2nd edition 1978), 111–4, 3rd ed. 1991.

4 IG Simmons and MJ Tooley, eds, *Environment in British Prehistory* (1981), 83–9; A Heyworth and C Kidson, 'Sea-Level Changes in SW England and in Wales', *Proc. Geol. Assoc.*, 93 (1982), 91–111.

5 Todd, *South West*, 63.

6 HH Lamb, *Climate* Vol. 2 (1977), 372–4, 384–5.

7 E McKee, *Working Boats of Britain* (1983).

8 S McGrail, 'Early Landing Places', in AE Herteig, ed., *Conference on Waterfront Archaeology* (Bergen, 1985), 12–18; S McGrail, 'Medieval Boats, Ships and Landing Places' in G Milne and B Hobley, eds, *Waterfront Archaeology in Britain and N Europe* (1981) 17–23; and R Hodges, *Dark Age Economics* (1982).

9 Todd, *South West*, 41–4, 53.

10 S McGrail, *Rafts, Boats, and Ships* (1981), Table 1; S McGrail, *Ancient Boats in NW Europe* (1987), Tables 5.1, 9.3, 10.6, 10.10, p. 53.

11 S McGrail, *Ancient Boats*, 5.

12 Todd, *South West*, 65–66.

13 JM Coles, 'Early Settlement of Scotland', *Proc. Prehistoric Society*, 37 (1971), 284–366; P Mellars, *Excavations on Oronsay* (Edinburgh, 1987); RM Jacobi,

'Early Flandrian Hunters in the South West', *P[roc]. D[evon] A[rchaeological] S[ociety]*, 37 (1979), 48–93; P Mercer, 'Neolithic in Cornwall', *Cornish Archaeology*, 25 (1986), 35–80; N Johnson and A David, 'A Mesolithic Site on Trevose Head and Contemporary Geography', *Cornish Archaeology*, 21 (1982), 67–103; SH Andersen, 'En stenalderbäd fra Tybrind vig', *Antikvariske Studies*, 6 (1983), 162–172.

14 Todd, *South West*, 63, Fig. 3.1; PJ Berridge, 'Mesolithic Sites in the Yarty Valley', *PDAS* 43 (1985), 1–21; P Berridge and A Roberts, 'Mesolithic Period in Cornwall', *Cornish Archaeology*, 25 (1986), 12.

15 S McGrail, *Ancient Boats*, Tables 5.1, 6.4, 7.5, 9.3, 10.8.

16 M van Zeist, 'De Mesolithische boot van Pesse, *Nieuwe Drentse Volksalmanak* (1957), 4–11; Ref Gro-486. See also F Reick and O Crumlin-Pedersen, *Bade fra Danmarks oldtid* (Roskilde, 1988), 28.

17 R Bradley, *Prehistoric Settlement of Britain* (1978), 89; R Dennell, *European Economic Prehistory* (1983), 186.

18 JGD Clark, 'Economic Context of Dolmens and Passage Graves in Sweden', in V Marcotic, ed., *Ancient Europe and the Mediterranean* (1977).

19 S McGrail, 'Cross-Channel Seamanship and Navigation in the Late–1st Millennium BC', *Oxford Journal of Archaeology*, 2 (1983), 299–337.

20 WA Cummins, 'Neolithic Stone Axe Trade in Britain', *Antiquity*, 48 (1974), 201–5; WA Cummins, 'Neolithic Stone Axes' in THMcK Clough and WA Cummins, eds, *Stone Axe Studies* (1979), 5–12.

21 Mercer, 'Neolithic in Cornwall', 44.

22 Todd, *South West*, 82; Mercer, 'Neolithic in Cornwall', 44.

23 DPS Peacock, 'Neolithic Pottery Production in Cornwall', *Antiquity*, 43 (1969), 145–9; Mercer, 'Neolithic in Cornwall', 49.

24 Todd, *South West*, 63.

25 S McGrail, *Rafts, Boats, and Ships*, Table 1; S McGrail, *Ancient Boats*, Tables 6.5, 6.6, 7.6, 7.7, 9.4, 10.10, 10.11.

26 Todd, *South West*, 110, 134, 146, 153, 219; PJ Clark, 'Neolithic, Bronze, Iron Age and Romano-British Finds from Mount Batten', *PDAS*, 29 (1971), 137–62.

27 Todd, *South West*, 153–4; B Cunliffe, 'Ictis', *Oxford Journal of Archaeology*, 2 (1983), 123–6.

28 K Muckelroy and P Baker, 'Bronze Age Site off Moor Sand, near Salcombe, Devon', *International Journal Nautical Archaeology*, 8 (1979), 189–210; K Muckelroy, 'Two Bronze Age Cargoes in British Waters', *Antiquity*, 54 (1980), 100–9; K Muckelroy, 'Middle Bronze Age Trade Between Britain and Europe', *Proc. Prehistoric Society*, 47 (1981), 275–97; Martin Dean, personal communication.

29 T Champion *et al*, *Prehistoric Europe* (1984), Fig. 6.11.

30 Todd, *South West*, 4, 5, 109, Fig. 1.1.

31 CFC Hawkes, *Pytheas* (Oxford, 1977).

32 Hawkes, *Pytheas*; CFC Hawkes, 'Ictis Disentangled, and the British Tin Trade', *Oxford Journal of Archaeology*, 3 (1984), 211–33.

33 S McGrail, 'Cross-Channel Seamanship', 311–3.

34 IS Maxwell, 'Location of Ictis', *Journal Royal Institute of Cornwall*, 6 (1972), 293–319; B Cunliffe, 'Ictis'; CFC Hawkes, *Pytheas*.

35 Clarke, 'Neolithic Bronze'; Cunliffe, 'Ictis'; C Gaskell-Brown and T Hugo, 'Prehistoric and Romano-British Finds from Mount Batten, Devon', *PDAS*, 41 (1983), 69–74; B Cunliffe, *Mount Batten, Plymouth* (Oxford 1988), 26.

36 D Ellmers, 'Loading and Unloading Ships using a Horse and Cart Standing in the Water', in Herteig, *Waterfront Archaeology*, 25–30.

37 PM Christie, 'Cornwall in the Bronze Age', *Cornish Archaeology*, 25 (1986), 105; B Cunliffe, *Iron Age Communities*, 111–4.

38 S Marstrander, *Østfolds Jordbruksristninger* 2 vols. (Oslo, 1963); JM Coles and AF Harding, *Bronze Age in Europe* 1979, 317; GT Denford and AW Farrell, 'Caergwrle bowl', *International Journal of Nautical Archaeology*, 9 (1980), 183–92; P Johnstone, *Seacraft of Prehistory* (1980), 126.

39 EV Wright, *North Ferriby Boats*, 1976; EV Wright, 'North Ferriby Boats – a revised basis for reconstruction', in S McGrail and E Kentley, eds, *Sewn Plank Boats* (Oxford, 1985), 105–144; EV Wright, *North Ferriby boats: seacraft of prehistory* (1990); S Parry and S McGrail, 'Prehistoric plank boat fragment and a hoard from Caldicot Castle Lake, Gwent, Wales', *Internat. Journal of Nautical Archaeology* 20 (1991), 32–4. This find is somewhat older than the Ferriby boats.

40 S McGrail, ed., *Brigg 'raft' and her prehistoric environment* (Oxford, 1981); S McGrail, 'Brigg 'raft' – problems in reconstruction and the assessment of performance', in McGrail and Kentley, *Sewn Plank Boats*, 165–194.

41 HW and F Elgee, 'EBA burial in a boat-shaped wooden coffin from NE Yorkshire', *Proc. Prehistoric Soc.* 15 (1949), 87–106; S McGrail, *Logboats of England and Wales* (Oxford, 1978).

42 SH Andersen, 'En Stenalderbad'; J Gomez, 'Une pirogue momoxyle néolithique dans le lit de la Charente', *Bull. Soc. Préhistorique Francaise*', 79 (1982), 61–3.

43 WG Jardine and LJ Masters, 'Dugout canoe from Catherinefield Farm, Locharbriggs, Dumfries', *Trans. Dumfries and Galloway Nat. Hist. and Antiquarian Soc.*, 52 (1976–7), 56–65.

44 McGrail, *Logboats of England and Wales*; RN Worth, 'Presidential Address', *DAT*, 23 (1891), 25–101.

45 K Muckelroy, *et al*, 'Pre-Roman coin from Canterbury and the ship represented on it', *Proc. Prehistoric Soc.*, 44 (1978), 439–444.

46 AW Farrell and S Penny, 'Broighter Boat', *Irish Archaeological Research Forum* 1975, 2.2, 15–26.

47 D Ellmers, 'Shipping on the Rhine during the Roman Period' in J du P Taylor and H Cleere, eds, *Roman Shipping and Trade*, (1978), 1–14.

48 McGrail, 'Cross-Channel Seamanship'; Hawkes, 'Ictis Disentangled'.

49 McGrail, 'Cross-Channel Seamanship'.

50 Todd, *South West*, 189–200.

51 CG Henderson, *Archaeology in Exeter* (Exeter 1983/4).

52 Todd, *South West*, 199; FM Griffith, 'Aerial Reconnaissance in Devon', *PDAS*, 42 (1984), 7–32.

53 A Fox and WD Ravenhill, 'Early Roman Outposts on the North Devon Coast', *PDAS*, 24 (1966), 3–39.

54 ALF Rivet and C Smith, *Place-Names of Roman Britain* (1979), 118, 135, 372.

55 VA Maxfield, 'Early Devonians?', *DAT*, 116 (1984), 127–33.

56 J Barber and C Gaskell-Brown, 'Plymouth', in Milne and Hobley, *Waterfront Archaeology*, 144; Todd, *South West*, 202, 219; OAW Dilke, *Greek and Roman Maps* (1985), 118.

57 McGrail, *Rafts, Boats, and Ships*, 23–4; S McGrail (ed.), *Maritime Celts, Frisians and Saxons*, CBA Research Report 71 (1990), papers by M Rule (49–56) and P Marsden (66–74).

58 PRV Marsden, 'County Hall Ship', *Trans. London and Middlesex Archaeology Society*, 21 (1965), 109–17.

59 B Cunliffe, 'First Eight Thousand Years', in AG Jamieson, ed., *People of the Sea* (1986), 15–16.

60 C Thomas, *Provisional List of Imported Pottery in Post-Roman Western Britain and Ireland* (Redruth, 1981); Todd, *South West*, 255; C Thomas, 'Gallici Nautae de Galliarum Provinciis: A 6th/7th century trade with Gaul reconsidered', *Medieval Archaeology* 34 (1990), 1–26.

61 Todd, *South West* 253, 266; A Fox, 'Some Evidence for a Dark Age Trading Site at Bantham, near Thurleston, S. Devon', *Antiquaries Journal*, 35 (1955), 55–67 and '25th Report on the Archaeology and Early History of Devon', *DAT*, 93 (1961), 79; FM Griffith, 'Salvage Observations at the Dark Age Site at Bantham Ham, Thurlestone in 1982', *PDAS*, 44 (1986), 39–57.

62 ME Farley and RI Little, 'Oldaport, Modbury', *PDAS*, 26 (1968), 31–6.

63 Todd, *South West*, 238–9.

64 Todd, *South West*, 250–2.

65 C Thomas, *Christianity in Roman Britain* (1981), 89, 108, 168; Todd *South West*, 240, 249–50.

66 AO and MO Anderson, eds, *Adoman's Life of St. Columba* (1961); JJ O'Meara, *Voyage of St. Brendan* (Dublin, 1978); G Ashe, *Land to the West* (1962), 64.

67 Todd, *South West*, 273–4.

68 A Grant and P Christie, *Book of Bideford* (Buckingham, 1987), 12; Todd, *South West*, 276; JS Hobbs, *British Channel Pilot* (1859).

69 Todd, *South West*, 276.

70 A Binns, 'Towards a North Sea Kingdom' in A Bang-Anderson *et al.* eds, *North Sea* (Oslo, 1985), 53–4.

71 Translations of the *Anglo-Saxon Chronicle* by GN Garmonsway (1954) and D Whitelock (1961) differ, the latter (p. 88) being followed here.

72 D Whitelock, ed., *English Historical Documents*, 1 (1955), 536.

73 McGrail, *Rafts, Boats and Ships*, 31–3; McGrail, *Ancient Boats*, Chap. 8.

74 AW Brogger and H Shetelig, *Viking Ships* (Oslo, 1953).

75 O Olsen and O Crumlin-Pedersen, Skuldelev Ships II, *Acta Archaeologica*, 38 (1967), 73–174.

76 R Bruce-Mitford, *Sutton Hoo Ship Burial*, I (1975); V Fenwick, *Graveney Boat* (Oxford, 1978).

77 PN Cameron, 'Saxons, Sail and Sea', *International Journal Nautical Archaeology*, 11 (1982), 319–332; DM Goodburn, 'Do we have Evidence of a Continuing Saxon Boat-Building Tradition?', *International Journal Nautical Archaeology*, 15 (1986), 39–47.

78 O Crumlin-Pedersen, *Das Haithabuschiff*, Ausgrabungen in Haithabu, Bericht 3 (Neumunster 1969).

79 DM Wilson, *Bayeux Tapestry* (1985); H Ewe, *Schiffe Aug Siegeln* (Rostock, 1972); S McGrail, *Medieval boat and ship timbers from Dublin*, Royal Irish Academy (Dublin, 1992); AE Christensen, 'Boat Finds from Bryggen', (Bergen, 1985), 47–280.

80 Hodges, *Dark Age Economics*; S McGrail (ed.), *Maritime Celts, Frisians and Saxons*, papers by Lebecq (85–90) and Elmers (91–2).

5 *The Principles of Shiphandling*

Peter Allington

This chapter employs many technical terms and as far as reasonably possible they are explained in context, but some readers coming to the subject for the first time may find them difficult. These words and expressions are the classic terminology of the sailing ship seaman, and there is no other language in which the technology can be explained, except at interminable length. The difficulties some readers may experience underlines a point made in the preface to the second volume of this history – that the seaman was isolated from the land community not only by the nature of his occupation, which took him away from normal human society ashore for long periods of time, but also by his very manner of speech, in which he used many of his sea terms to describe situations and events ashore. The chapter also underlines another aspect of seafaring for a living under sail in past ages – that the technology was immensely complicated and could be mastered only by immersion in it from a very early age.

The achievements of mariners were circumscribed throughout history by the limitations of the performances of the vessels in which they sailed. From the beginning of water transport until the development of powered ships in the nineteenth century the mariner was forced to use a fickle and ever changing source of energy, the wind, or his own muscle power, to supply the motive force. In areas of higher latitude this wind is mostly unpredictable. In other parts of the world, depending on the season, the trade winds or monsoons blow with some regularity. Certain parts of the oceans are subjected to calms and light variable breezes, making it difficult to predict the length of a passage. Furthermore, there could be a delay of days or even weeks at the outset of a passage, waiting for the wind to change to a favourable direction. All these delays were often prolonged by the poor sailing performance of many ships.

Sailing ships depended primarily on the wind for their motive power, but when engaged on deepwater voyages advantage could be taken of the ocean currents. In a similar way the tidal ebb and flow around our shores was of great assistance, especially to those with local knowledge. Although the direction changes approximately every six hours, the adverse set can often be 'cheated' while full use is made of the fair trade. Compared with the wind, the tides have an important advantage; they are at least predictable. The twice-daily rise and fall which governed the depth of water had to be considered and related to the vessel's draught, and both the strength and direction of the stream and wind remain to this day of vital importance when manoeuvring in a close quarters situation.

Sometimes, the only option for larger vessels which had to be moved in the confines of a small harbour was kedging or warping. Kedging involved running out a light anchor to the desired spot and heaving on a line attached to it. Instead of an anchor, moorings marked by buoys were often laid in strategic positions for the sole purpose of shifting vessels. Warping involved taking a long rope to the buoy or ashore to move the vessel. In calm conditions and slack water it was possible to tow a vessel using one or two large open boats with up to a dozen or so men in each pulling away at the oars.

In this chapter I shall concentrate on 'shiphandling' as it effects the pure sailing ship, which, until the 1870s, comprised the majority of merchant tonnage. I therefore define shiphandling as: the art of manoeuvring a vessel by control of her sails and rudder using wind and tide, the working of anchors, both for maintaining position and regulating her movement, and the getting on and off a buoy or berth by warping.

The first consideration must be the vessel's size and type of sail plan. Much depended on whether she was 'square' or 'fore and aft' rigged. There were basic differences in handling these two types of rig. The 'square riggers' include the full rigged ship, the barque, the brig, and the brigantine. In the nineteenth century the barquentine was added. The 'fore and afters' comprised the sloop, the cutter, the yawl, the ketch, the schooner, and the lugger, as well as vessels setting a spritsail. In many cases these vessels are further categorised by number of masts and by variations in the number and kinds of sail carried.

Thus there are two basic methods of spreading and supporting the canvas of the sails and presenting them to the wind. When moving the vessel forward the wind will normally always strike the after face of the square sail, whereas a fore and aft sail can have the wind blowing into it on either side, depending on the ship's aspect to the eye of the wind. Occasionally in manoeuvring the square sail can be arranged to have the wind strike the forward face, and thus drive the vessel astern or help in turning her, an important point in the handling of a square rigged vessel.

To understand shiphandling it is necessary to look at the sails and the limitations imposed by the masts and rigging in more detail. The square sail is 'bent' (secured) along its head (top edge) to a spar called a yard which is slung horizontally ahead of the mast, supported at its centre by a truss or halyard, and from the extreme ends (the yard arms) by 'lifts' (lengths of wire, chain or rope led to a position higher up the mast). The two lower corners of the sail (the clews) are controlled by lengths of rope, wire, or chain called sheets which are led via the yard below to the mast and then down to the deck. In the case of the sail hung from the lowest yard, often referred to as the 'course', these sheets lead directly to points on the hull. The yard and sail are free to swing around the mast in an arc of approximately 45 degrees in either direction from the arthwartships position. This limit is imposed by the standing rigging supporting the mast. The swing is controlled by lines, called 'braces', rigged between the yardarms and some convenient point in the vessel, either directly down to the hull, as was usual with the lowest yard, or to some place aloft and thence down to the deck.

The more the yards and square sails can be braced round, the better the vessel's windward performance. In its simplest form a single square sail on a mast with minimal standing rigging could have the yard lying almost fore and aft, allowing the craft to make good progress to windward – if she had a good hull form for sailing.

If we take the case of a larger vessel rigged with several square sails on each mast and having the yards braced round as far as they go, which we will assume to be 45 degrees to the fore and aft line (some vessels were able to brace them round even more), should the wind be the same angle on the bow, depending on which side it came from, it would either be blowing directly along the yard or at 90 degrees to it. In the first instance the 'weather leech' (edge of sail nearest the wind) would 'shiver' and the whole sail 'lift' or flap like washing on the line. In the second case the wind would blow directly into the forward face of the sail and it would be termed 'aback'. Assuming the vessel is lying with the yards pointing at the wind and she is now manoeuvred so that the eye of the wind is 50 degrees on the bow, the sails will fill, converting some of the wind's energy into a forward motive force, but at the same time a sideways thrust is experienced. This is to some

5.1 The full-rigged ship *Margaret*, built in Nova Scotia in 1826 and owned in Torquay, where she is seen lying in this photograph taken in the 1850s. *(Torquay Natural History Society)*

extent resisted by the underwater profile of the hull. The resulting track through the water will therefore not be the same as the direction in which she is heading. The difference between the two tracks is called 'leeway'. Changing her heading so that she now has the wind 60 degrees on the bow will greatly increase the forward thrust imparted to the vessel by the sails. In other words she will increase in speed and leeway will be much reduced. The average square rigged vessel would shape her course about 65 degrees from the eye of the wind if required to sail as close as possible to it. Her yards would be braced round as far as they could go and she would be termed sailing 'close hauled'. In addition to the sheet, the course, the lowest sail on each mast, has another line bent to the clew leading forward. This is called the 'tack', and in this situation the foot of the sail would be spread by the tack on the windward clew and the sheet to leeward. It follows that the windward sheet would be slack, as would the leeward tack. If the wind was on the port side she was said to be 'close hauled on the port tack'.

If her eventual destination lies directly in the eye of the wind, it is obvious that at some state the vessel will have to change her heading so as to put wind on the other bow, or, in other words, be on the starboard tack. This manoeuvre could be required several times, and thus the vessel would gain her objective with a zigzag course. Putting her bows through the eye of the wind requires each time a change in heading of at least 130 degrees. The yards have to be braced round through 90 degrees and the course reset by changing over the tack and sheet. It is this operation of changing over tack and sheet, much more significant in the fifteenth and sixteenth centuries when the main course comprised, perhaps, half the total sail area of the ship, which has given its name to the operation of going through the wind, which is still called 'tacking'.

The same terminology is used in fore and aft rigged craft that do not carry a course, and thus, strictly speaking, the word 'tacking' has no direct practical meaning in these vessels. Thus Devon seamen in schooners and ketches inclined to the use of the term 'going through the wind' for this manoeuvre, rather than 'tacking'. A vessel can also get from one tack to the other by turning away from the wind and going 'the long way round', through 230 degrees, and when halfway through the manoeuvre she is running down wind. This action is called 'wearing' the ship round, and is often the only option in heavy weather or with an unskilled crew.

There are many types of 'fore and aft' sails. Some, like 'jibs' and 'staysails', are triangular in shape and supported on their leading edge or luff by one of the forestays supporting the masts. The sail is bent on with metal hanks (or wooden hanks in earlier centuries) and is able to slide up and down the stay. It is hauled up by a halyard and pulled down by a downhaul. It was usual to have two sheets, one on each side, the sail being controlled or trimmed with the leeward one only. Other fore and aft sails like the gaff sail and spritsail were foursided and set abaft the mast, the most common in vessels which sailed offshore being the gaff sail. The name is perhaps derived from the Dutch word 'gaffel' which means a fork, and is an apt description of the inboard end of the spar supporting the head of the sail where the gaff 'jaws', as they are now called, embrace the mast. Sometimes the sail was loose footed, that is, it did not have a boom, the sheet being bent directly to the clew and lower part of the leech (the after edge of the sail). However, it was more common to have a boom extending the foot of the sail. In this case the sheet, usually in the form of a tackle, was worked from the outboard end, and the boom could be held in the fore and aft line if required.

These fore and aft sails allowed the vessel to lay much closer to the wind than a square rigged vessel, and the best craft in this respect were the sloops and cutters, both single masted and on the whole smaller than the square riggers. In the ideal conditions of a good breeze with no sea running, those with a fine hull shape, adequate draught, and a clean bottom could get to windward with the breeze only 45 degrees on the bow. The vast majority of the fore and afters would be close hauled with the true wind 50 degrees on the bow. In other words, they tacked through an angle of 100 degrees. All the square riggers carried a high proportion of their sail area in fore and aft canvas, stay sails, and boom sails, and in the case of a brigatine or barquentine this could be over 50 per cent of the total area.

All vessels of whatever type and class could maintain their optimum windward performance only in ideal conditions. Should the breeze freshen, becoming strong to gale force, and a head sea build up, or the wind die away, leaving only light airs but a heavy swell, or 'groundsea' as it was called in Devon, they would have to 'bear away', ie shape their course farther away from the eye of the wind. In the first case sail area would have to be reduced and in the second the vessel's motion could shake what little drive there was out of the sails. The object at all times was to keep moving, but at the same time still make some ground to windward if the destination of the passage was to windward, and in this respect bad weather had a greater adverse effect on the fore and afters than on the square riggers.

Many sailing ships could not attain these close hauled heading angles relative to the wind, and some square riggers, allowing for leeway, would not make better than 90 degrees to the wind. This poor performance could be caused by a combination of poor hull shape, inefficient rig, the vessel in ballast with the bottom heavily coated in weeds and barnacles, or in

5.2 The brig *Lord Ramsay* of Bideford, painted in Malta in 1838 by Cammillieri of Malta. *(Private Collection)*

5.3 The schooner *Lizzie Trenberth*, built by Samuel Moss at Par, Cornwall, in 1867 and employed in the Azores fruit trade. In this watercolour by Reuben Chappell of Goole, painted in the early years of this century, she is shown with a slightly reduced rig. Note that she has roller reefing on the main, points reefing on the fore. Note also the reefed staysail. *(Private collection)*

conditions of very strong winds and heavy seas. Such a vessel when sailing close to land and experiencing a sudden shift of wind blowing directly onshore would be in trouble, and if she was unable to get clear her anchors were the last resort.

The windward sailing ability, or how 'weatherly' a vessel was, must be considered as a prime safety factor, and it also conditioned the trades in which a vessel could be employed. Windward work, if the breeze was fresh to strong, was to be avoided if at all possible. This could mean a delay at the outset of a voyage, or, if already on passage and not far from shelter to leeward, could mean that the vessel had to be run off downwind and anchored to await a more favourable slant in the wind. However, a westward rounding of Cape Horn, for instance, required the vessel somehow to get to windward, sometimes a long and bitter struggle which could become an appalling feat of endurance.

Global voyages were planned to take advantage of the trade winds, monsoons, and ocean currents with a minimum of close hauled work. Winds on or abaft the beam (from the side or behind) were sought for and the voyage planned accordingly. This could mean a long and roundabout route, but was quicker for most vessels than trying to sail direct. Thus the classic sailing routes appear to the uninitiated to wander all over the oceans, rather than taking the shortest (great circle) route between two ports.

The Wind as a Source of Power

So far, when reference has been made to the wind, it has been the true wind that has been mentioned, but more important to the seaman is the relative or 'apparent' wind. Once a vessel gets under way and starts to move, the true wind seems to change in strength and direction. This is due to a combination of the observer's speed and direction and that of the true wind. For example, should the vessel be sailing close hauled, the wind direction as indicated by a flag at the masthead would appear to be finer on the bow than the true wind as suggested by the way in which the waves move. Furthermore, if having recently got under way from an anchorage, and on the same heading, the breeze will appear to have freshened. If, however, the vessel had been turned to run exactly downwind, the direction would still appear the same but the strength would be decreased by the speed of the vessel.

This prime motive force, or apparent wind, is harnessed by a large area of canvas supported by the masts and spars and is capable of developing great power.[1] It has been calculated that the sails of the huge German five-masted ship *Preussen*, built in 1907, developed over 6,000 horsepower from 60,000 square feet to move her at 17 knots, and for this to be achieved the wind would have to be near gale force, from just abaft the beam and with no sea running.

In 1805 the English naval officer Francis Beaufort devised the scale we know today for measuring wind speed. The graduations are from 0 (calm) to Force 12 (hurricane), ie 64 knots and over. Clear of land the wind velocity increases with height to a certain extent, so readings are measured at 33 feet above sea level. This means the relative wind will not be the same at the bottom of a tall mast as at the top and, depending on the vessel's aspect, the upper sails will be trimmed differently by a small amount from the lower. In the case of a large square rigger sailing with the true wind on, or just forward of, the beam, the lowest yard from which the course is set would be 'sharp

5.4 This photograph illustrates clearly two of the points made in this chapter. The yards and squaresails on the foremast are 'fanned', that is, the topsails are braced round hard to the wind while the topgallants and royal are progressively less braced round. The vessel is being sailed too close to the wind, with the result that the royal is almost empty of wind and the upper topgallant is also scarcely pulling. Although the photograph was taken in the 1930s on board the Finish barque *Penang*, it illustrates aspects of shiphandling which remained true from the 1500s. *(CS Cooper-Essex)*

up', at approximately 45 degrees to the fore and aft line of the vessel, but each yard above, working up the mast (and there could be five) would be braced slightly more 'square'. If one were to gaze aloft from the foot of the mast, this would appear as a slight spiral effect or twist, each successive sail being trimmed to the relative wind. This trimming of the yards and their sails is called 'fanning'. Furthermore, it was usual when sailing close hauled to have one of the uppermost square sails trimmed so that it would 'lift' or start to 'shiver' before the others when the vessel came too far up into the wind. If this sail, perhaps the mizzen royal, was kept just on the point of 'lifting', the helmsman knew that all the others would be drawing well and the vessel making her best course to windward.

The wind can also be expressed as a force measured in pounds per square foot for a given velocity. This force or pressure increases in proportion to the square of the wind speed, or in other words, double the wind speed and quadruple the pressure. For example, force 5 on the Beaufort Scale has a mean wind speed of 19 knots, exerting a pressure of about 1.3 lb per sq ft on a surface at right angles to it. Roughly double is force 8 at 37 knots, but the wind pressure has now risen to around 5.4 lb per sq ft, or nearly four times as much.

Imagine a full rigged ship (often referred to just as a 'ship') of average size under reduced canvas running before a gale at 10 knots. The wind is never constant in direction or force, but for the purposes of the exercise it is assumed steady at 37 knots. To those on board the relative wind direction would be from right astern, but blowing at only 27 knots. All the yards would be braced square so the pressure of about 3 lb per sq ft would be exerted on all surfaces at right angles to the wind. This would include not just the sails but hull, superstructure, masts, and rigging, which would all assist the ship's progress. In this case any sails set on the foremast would be to some extent blanketed by those on the main and mizzen masts. Therefore, in practice she would be under reduced canvas with the majority of sail set in the forward part of the vessel. The ship in fact has a higher potential speed with the wind on the quarter, or just abaft the beam, when all the sails would be drawing well.

If for some reason the ship was required to go to windward in these conditions, she would be rounded up close hauled, her yards braced sharp up, and some sail taken off her. The relative wind would probably be about 70 degrees on the bow at 40 knots and, because the vessel's speed would be reduced to around 4 knots, the relative wind would now be almost in the same direction as the true wind. The slower one goes, the closer are the relative and true winds. The wind pressure would be in the region of 6 lb per sq ft, but now striking the sails at an angle, and only a small fraction of this increased power would be converted into forward drive. Leeway would be considerable because of the windage of hull, masts, and spars.

The wind gave life to the sailing ship, but in its nature were also the seeds of her destruction. As mentioned earlier, a sudden wind shift could end up driving the vessel ashore, or perhaps a storm overwhelm her when far from land. Sometimes a vicious squall could strike her unawares on a calm sea with all her sails set, blow away some sails or, more seriously, force her over to such an angle that her cargo shifted over to one side of the hold. In this state, pinned down on her beam ends, her rudder would be almost horizontal and virtually useless. Unless she could re-stow her cargo and once more stand upright her position was serious. Normally there was some warning of wind shifts and squalls, and the appropriate action could be taken by those on board. Provided she had sea-room to leeward it was usual to run the ship off before the wind after taking in the upper sails. Alternatively she could be steered towards the wind so that all her square sails were shaking. In this situation her yards would be pointing at the relative wind, and great care was needed not to let the wind strike the forward face of these sails, lest she be caught aback and blown over. If the action was well judged, the fore and aft sails would keep her moving slowly ahead and therefore she would respond to the rudder. As before, the upper square sails would be taken in as quickly as possible. This course of action would only be attempted in a handy vessel.

Sometimes, of course, there was flat calm – no wind at all. But if the vessel was in an area subjected to strong tides, such as the English and Bristol Channels, all was not lost. Should the moon be new or full, rates of 3 knots tidal flow could be expected for two hours out of the six. Thus the vessel would be moving through still air at this speed and hence there would be a very light breeze created. For example, a vessel bound up Channel from a port in Devon and faced with a spring ebb of 3 knots would experience a light air from approximately the west-south-west. If she had a good spread of light weather canvas and her bottom clear of weed, this was enough to give steerage way and she could be worked diagonally across the tide, or do her best to maintain position until the next flood. To accomplish this there would have to be no groundsea, as the rolling and pitching would shake the sails and spill what little apparent breeze there was. In this situation, and in a reasonable depth of water (but losing ground), her position could be maintained with a light anchor lowered to the sea bed.

Should a vessel be required to proceed inland to the upper reaches of a harbour or even further up river, the state of the tide, which not only governs the depth of the water but also its direction of flow, may provide the only means of moving her. The very nature of the twists and turns in a river such as the Tamar deny the mariner a steady fair breeze, his heading constantly changing in relation to the true wind, and steep sided hills on either bank will further distort the airflow. Furthermore, as the river narrows there is less room to manoeuvre, making 'tacking' impossible. At this stage, should the tide be running in his favour, this alone can be utilised to carry the vessel towards her destination. The mariner can now drop the sails, and providing the stream is swift enough it will overcome a slight headwind. The vessel, drifting at virtually the same speed as the tide, is not under control, but providing there are no obstacles in her path she is in no danger. In smaller craft and barges some steerage can be established with the use of 'sweeps' (long oars) or long poles used to keep them off the shoals or banks. They may even be towed from ahead using the ship's boat, but a safer method was often resorted to on larger vessels. This was called 'drudging', the anchor being lowered to the river bed sufficient to retard the vessel's progress but not stop her. Now she was no longer just drifting with the current but swung round to stem the stream and travelling stern first.

The stronger the flow the more positive the control. For example, if the tide is running at 4 knots and she has now slowed down, moving at only 2 knots over the ground, a flow of 2 knots is established past the rudder and she will now react as if she has a slight amount of headway and can be sheered from one side of the river to the other as desired. As the river deepens or shallows, constant attention is required as to the amount of cable paid out. Too much will stop her, and in the deep patches the anchor could be off the bottom, the vessel once more drifting freely with the current at the same speed and no longer under command. Great care is needed not to run aground, as the rudder will strike first with the whole weight of the vessel behind it, and, should the wind become fair the vessel is of course facing the wrong way. Drudging was basically a safe way of travelling but local knowledge was vital, and thus it was used only by regular traders, or vessels with a pilot on board.

The handling characteristics of a vessel when light or loaded differed considerably, therefore draught was important in shiphandling. Not only was the depth to which she could be loaded important, but also her final fore and aft trim, which has a great influence on the vessel's handling characteristics, as does the distribution of the cargo, especially heavy parcels such as iron ore or railway track. Whatever types of goods were carried, great care was taken so that no damage occurred during the sea passage, the cargo being well secured against shifting.

This chapter has briefly covered some of the points, mostly of a technical nature, that affect the handling of a sailing vessel. It cannot conclude without mention of a human aspect. It may seem obvious, but is nonetheless worth stating that an experienced master with competent mates and a good crew who knew the vessel well would certainly handle her better and take more chances than if she were undermanned with less able seamen.

5.5 No-one will ever see again the sight recorded by a photographer who one day in the 1850s found some 300 sailing vessels lying windbound together in Plymouth Sound. Notice the absence of ketches at this period, and also how the square-rigged vessels lay outside, far offshore, where they could get to sea easily if the weather deteriorated and placed them on a lee shore. The handier schooners, which could beat out more easily, lie close inshore (B.G.). *(The late Captain F C Poyser)*

5: The Principles of Shiphandling

1 Alan Villiers, *The Way of a Ship* (1954), 19.

6 *The Marine Resources of Devon's Coastal Waters*

A J SOUTHWARD AND G T BOALCH

DEVON'S MANY AND VARIED COASTAL communities have sought to exploit the marine resources of the adjacent waters for centuries. This chapter provides a brief account of the resources available, their ecological basis, the extent to which they have changed in the past, and some thoughts about future prospects.

The coastlines of Devon lie close to a boundary between the shallow, turbid waters further up the English and Bristol Channels and the more open and deeper waters to the west, but there is a big difference in this respect between the north and south of the county (Fig. 6.1). In the English Channel the waters to the eastward tend to be vertically mixed, while west of Start Point and also in western Lyme Bay they are stratified in summer, with a layer of warm water overlying a layer of much colder water (Figs 6.2 and 6.3). This layering can separate warm-water life in the surface waters from colder-water life at the bottom. Tidal streams are stronger along the north coast, and as a consequence the water is well-mixed and the lines for equal salt content and temperature run perpendicular to the shoreline, so that the further east one travels up the Bristol Channel the less saline is the water and the colder it is in winter (Figs 6.4, 6.5, and 6.6). Along the English Channel coast the tidal streams are less fierce, except off Start Point, and lines of equal salt content and temperature tend to run parallel with the coast so that there is a tongue of high-salinity water, warm in winter, penetrating from the west.[1] Thus, with certain local exceptions, the North Devon seas are less oceanic and more 'northern' in character, compared with the softer, warmer and more 'southern' nature of the Channel coast.

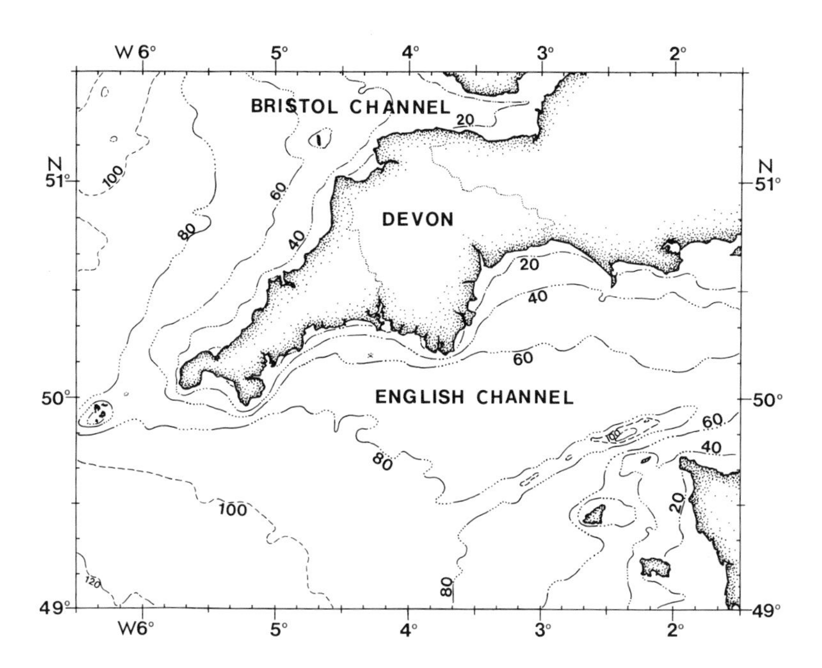

6.1 The seas adjacent to Devon, showing the depth of water in metres, according to the latest surveys (20 metres is approximately 11 fathoms or 66 feet, 100 metres approximately 55 fathoms or 330 feet). Note that deep water comes closer to the shore along the south coast.

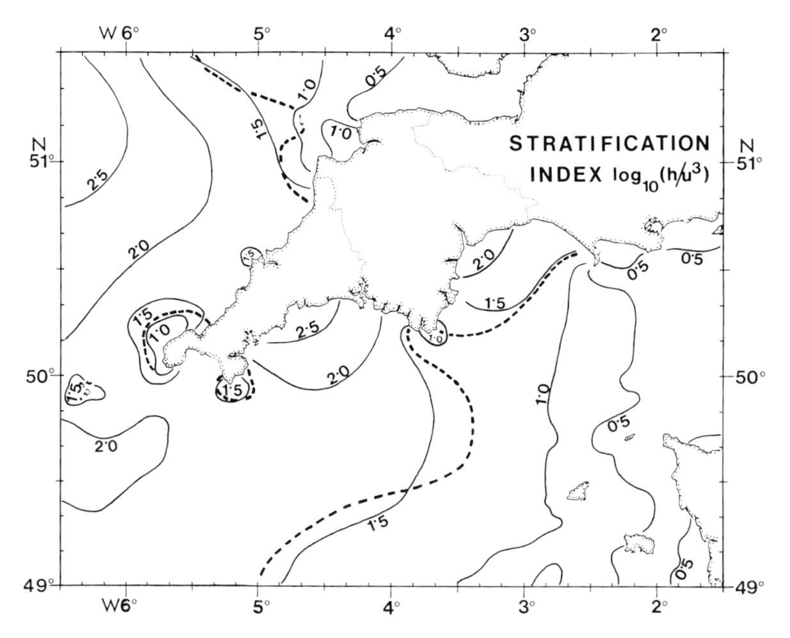

6.2 An index to the degree of stratification/mixing of the seas off southwest England, calculated from tidal forces and depth of water. Where the index is less than 1.5 the tidal streams are strong enough to produce almost complete mixing of the water down to the sea bed. At index values above 1.5 the water is often stratified in summer, when a layer of warm water lies over a bottom layer of colder water. The two layers are separated by a sharp discontinuity called the thermocline. The thick broken lines on the map, corresponding approximately to index values of 1.5, are places where 'fronts' are expected, marking the changes from stratified to mixed water. At such places there may be accumulations of microscopic plants sufficient to show as green patches at the surface and also lines of flotsam, including broken off pieces of coastal seaweed.

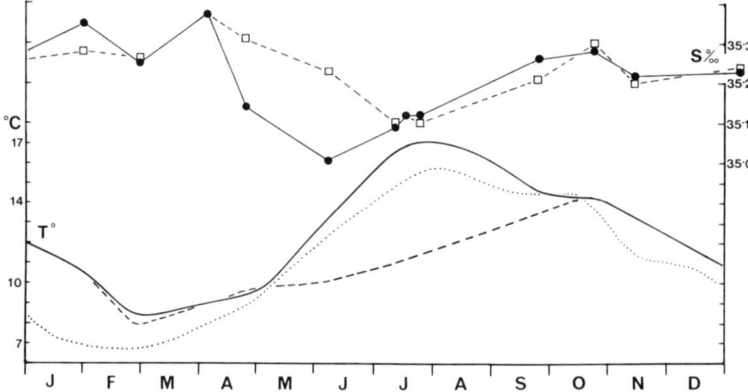

6.3 An example of the annual cycle of temperature (°C) and salinity (‰) of the sea 15 miles south of Plymouth in 1979, showing how the development of stratification in summer leads to the bottom water being colder than the surface. The solid line is surface temperature at this position, bottom temperature being shown as a broken line. For comparison, the dotted line shows the annual cycle of temperature inside Plymouth Sound where the water is mixed and is also much colder in winter.

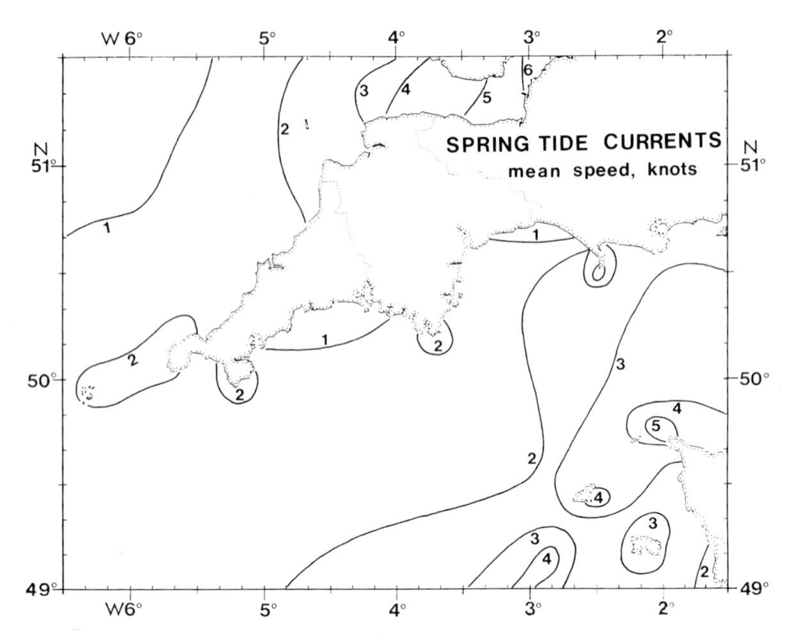

6.4 Tidal velocities at spring tides around Devon. Note the greater speed of the tidal currents on the north coast.

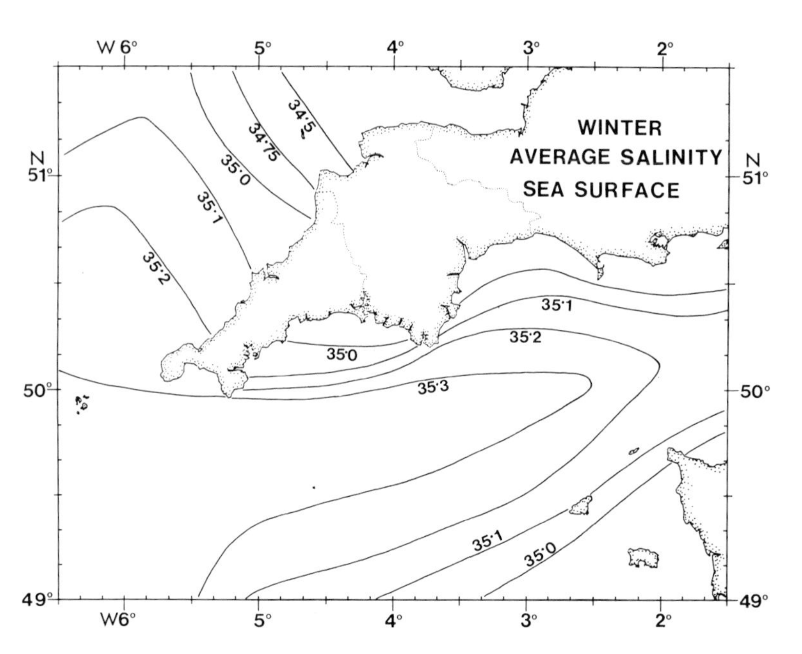

6.6 Average surface salinity (‰) of the seas around Devon in winter (February).

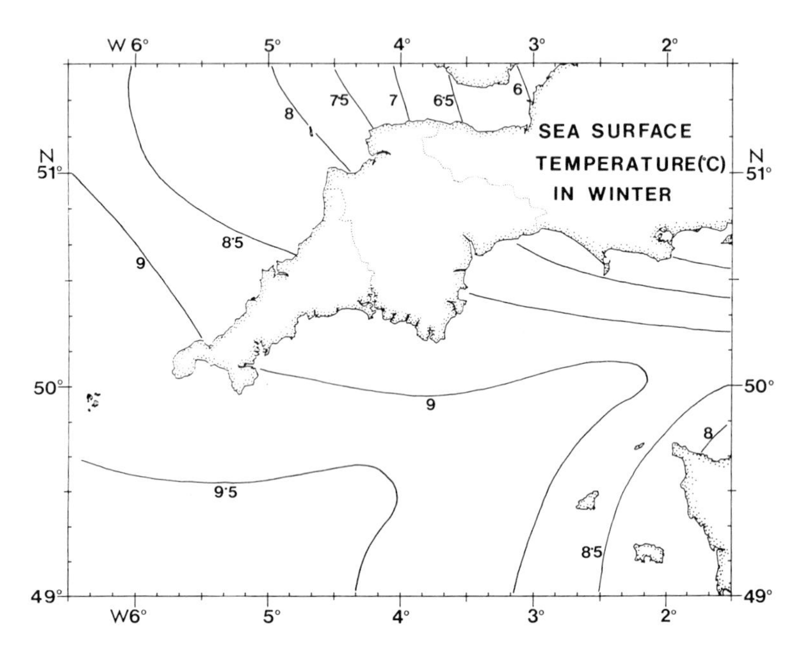

6.5 The average surface temperature (°C) of the seas around Devon in winter (February).

The seas off Devon are usually blue or blue/green except close inshore in rough weather or near estuaries. The clarity of the water allows marine plant life – both floating, microscopic algae and the large seaweeds fixed to the bottom – to grow as deep as 20, or even 25, metres (11 to 14 fathoms). These seas are open to winds over a wide arc to the west, and are generally rougher, with longer and higher waves, than those off the east coast of England. Depths greater than 75 metres (40 fathoms), the practical limit for bottom fishing before the days of mechanical help, occur within 20 nautical miles of both north and south coasts.

The differences in marine climate between Devon's north and south coasts, together with the east-west changes in the extent of mixing and the range of water depths, result in a great diversity of habitats for marine life and a corresponding richness in species. Proximity to the open ocean ensures comparatively high salinity and equable temperatures. The prevailing winds, allied to the effect of the earth's rotation (Corioli's force) and the distribution of tidal streams, produce a surface current system predominantly from the west or southwest (Fig. 6.7).[2] There appears to be a bottom flow tending in the opposite direction. The currents bring in western and oceanic species which cannot withstand extremes of salinity or temperature but which can extend into the deep sheltered 'rias' on the south coast. In contrast, the shallower estuaries, small coves, and beaches provide habitats for more typical coastal species that can better resist changing salinity and fluctuating temperatures. Offshore life is more varied off Devon than up Channel, where the bottom tends to be scoured more by the tides and currents.[3]

The southwest peninsula marks the geographical limit of various marine flora and fauna, a boundary zone where oceanic and warmer-water species meet and mix with inshore or colder-water species. A number of intertidal animals and plants reach their practical eastern limits in Devon, while the seas off the county are close to the southern limit of arctic/boreal or cold-water fish such as the herring and cod, and close to the normal northern limit of lusitanian or warm temperature species such as the pilchard and red

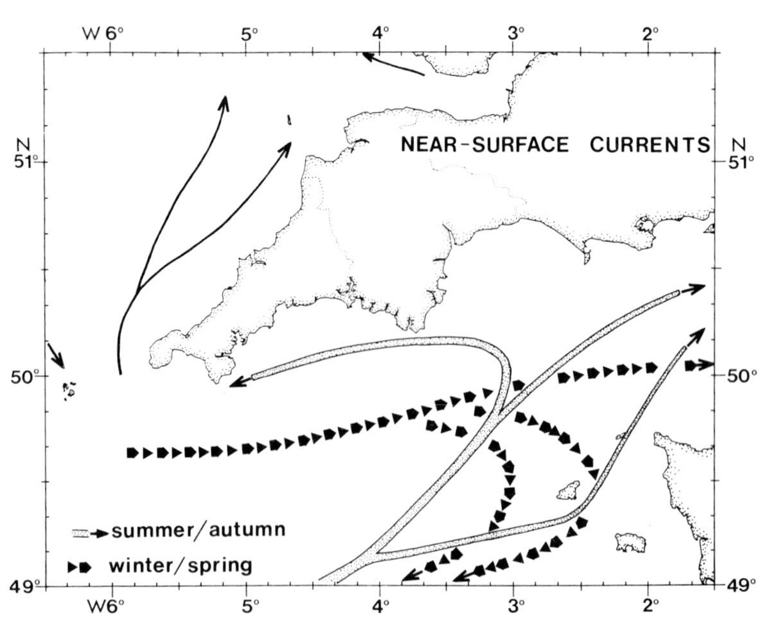

6.7 Surface water movements in the South West, deduced from annual changes in temperature. The currents shown off the north coast (thin arrows) are deduced from plankton movements.

mullet.[4] Mackerel are fish of intermediate distribution but are at home in local waters both as younger fish in summer and as mature adults in winter, waiting to go out to the Celtic Sea where spawning starts early in the spring. These and, to a lesser extent, sprat and horse-mackerel, are the main kinds of 'pelagic' fish, ie those that swim and feed in mid-water.

'Demersal' fish, those that live and feed close to the seabed, are common and diverse in the seas around Devon. On the inshore trawling grounds south of Plymouth, as Table 6.1 shows, up to 80 species of roundfish and flatfish can be taken, 31 of which are of marketable value; another species is processed for fish meal and three more are considered 'sport' fishes.[5] When estuarine and shore habitats are included, the total of fish species reaches 146.[6] Though some of these species do not occur off East Devon, the range of fish found here is still considerable, and flatfishes contribute particularly to the catch.

Shellfish are also diverse, and warmer-water forms such as the spiny lobster and the spider-crab occur in addition to the common lobster and edible crab.[7] Several of the south-coast estuaries have (or used to have) natural oyster beds and a potential for oyster cultivation, though only a few are in commercial production today.[8] All round Devon seaweed was once extensively used as fertilizer on arable land that lay close enough to the coast for carrying by horse or back-packing, but today only keen gardeners take the trouble to collect washed-up weed to add the valuable mineral it contains to their soil. On the North Devon coast there is a small harvest of the red seaweed *Porphyra*, or laver as it is called there, for human consumption.

Production In The Sea

Plant life

The basis of a marine ecosystem is the fixation of carbon dioxide by plant life and its conversion to organic matter by means of energy obtained from sunlight.[9] Outside the immediate coastal zone, marine plant life is solely comprised of minute floating phytoplankton. In clear water, solar radiation can penetrate deeply and plant production can occur some 25 metres below the surface.[10] In order to make the organic compounds that form the basis of all life, phytoplankton algae, like land plants, require large amounts of carbon dioxide and water (both more abundant in the sea than on land), and smaller amounts of other elements, chiefly nitrogen, phosphorus, and sulphur.[11] Plant production occurs every year in the sea, and most of it is consumed by small animals (zooplankton) living in the water. These small animals are in turn eaten by larger animals, including fish. Little fish are eaten by big fish and many of the big fish and some of the small fish are harvested by man. A proportion of the floating plants falls to the sea bed, as do waste products from the animals and their bodies when they die. This fall-out to the bottom provides food for many animals, including shellfish and fish that live on or in the sea bed.

How much of this plant production is transferred through the food chain in the sea and to the bottom is a topic for further research. Ultimately, however, the waste products of the plants and animals and their dead bodies are attacked by bacteria and 'mineralized', that is transformed back again to inorganic matter such as carbon dioxide, nitrate, and phosphate, ready to start a new cycle. In the seas off Devon an annual growth cycle of plant plankton, and then of animal plankton, is apparent.[12] In the stratified waters off the south coast the cycle shows two peaks of plant growth,[13] one in the spring and another smaller one in the autumn, with lesser amounts of phytoplankton during the summer (Fig. 6.8). The spring peak is chiefly comprised of the comparatively large diatoms that take advantage of the amount of nitrate, phosphate, and silicate then dissolved in the water. Their growth begins as soon as the sun is high enough in the sky for light to penetrate the sea surface, but this process can be delayed by stormy weather which prevents light penetration and also carries the plants too deep, below the well-lit zone where they can grow.[14] As the spring peak declines the place of the diatoms is taken by other plants, including dinoflagellates, which continue to dominate until the autumn peak, when diatoms appear again.[15] In some years certain species of diatoms flourish right through the winter months, but in others the seas become comparatively barren in winter. Where the waters are well-mixed – as, for example, near the eastern boundaries of Devon – there is a single peak of phytoplankton beginning in the spring, and diatoms may persist right through the summer.

Table 6.1

Fish commonly taken in the trawl off Plymouth by research vessels of the Plymouth Laboratory, 1919–1979.

The left column shows the species of commercial importance and gives their scientific names after the English name. The right-hand column shows fish of lesser or little commercial value, with the English name, where there is one, in parentheses. The list is in scientific systematic order, grouped into fish with characters in common, starting with the sharks and rays (cartilaginous fishes), then the herring-like (clupeid) fish, then the cod-like fish (gadoids) and ending with the flatfishes and angler fish.

IMPORTANT COMMERCIAL FISH		LITTLE OR NO COMMERCIAL VALUE IN DEVON
Dogfish	*Scyliorhinus canicula*	*Scyliorhinus stellaris* (Nursehound)
		Squalus acanthias (Spurdog)
		Prionace glauca (Blue shark)
		Galeorhinus galeus (Tope)
		Mustelus mustelus (Smooth hound)
		Mustelus asterias
		Squatina squatina (Angel fish)
Cuckoo Ray	*Raia naevus*	*Raia fullonica* (Shagreen ray)
Spotted Ray	*Raia montagui*	*Raia undulata* (Painted ray)
Thornback	*Raia clavata*	*Raia radiata*
Blonde Ray	*Raia brachyura*	*Raia microocellata*
Pilchard	*Sardina pilchardus*	*Engraulis encrasicolus* (Anchovy)
Sprat	*Sprattus sprattus*	*Alosa alosa* (Allis shad)
Herring	*Clupea harengus*	*Alosa fallax* (Twaite shad)
Conger Eel	*Conger conger*	*Syngnathus acus* (Pipe fish)
Whiting	*Merlangius merlangus*	*Micromesistius poutassou* (Blue whiting)
Pollack	*Pollachius pollachius*	*Trisopterus luscus* (Bib)
Cod	*Gadus morrhua*	*Trisopterus esmarkii* (Norway pout)
Hake	*Merluccius merluccius*	*Trisopterus minutus* (Poor cod)
Ling	*Molva molva*	*Pollachius virens* (Coal fish)
		Melanogrammus aeglefinus (Haddock)
		Brosme brosme (Torsk)
		Gaidropsaurus mediterraneus (Rockling)
		Gaidropsaurus vulgaris (Rockling)
		Rhinonemus cimbrius (Rockling)
John Dory	*Zeus faber*	*Capros aper* (Boar fish)
Bass	*Dicentrarchus labrax*	*Serranus cabrilla* (Comber)
Red Mullet	*Mullus surmuletus*	*Trachurus trachurus* (Horse mackerel)
Sea Bream	*Pagellus bogaraveo*	*Cepola rubescens* (Red band fish)
Black Bream	*Spondyliosoma cantharus*	*Labrus mixtus* (Cuckoo wrasse)
Mackerel	*Scomber scombrus*	*Labrus bergylta* (Ballan wrasse)
		Trachinus vipera (Weaver)
		Buenia jeffreysii (Goby)
		Callionymus reticulatus (Dragonet)
		Callionymus maculatus (Dragonet)
		Callionymus lyra (Dragonet)
		Blennius ocellaris (Blenny)
Grey Gurnard	*Eutrigla gurnardus*	*Trigloporus lastoviza* (Polperro Bull)
Red Gurnard	*Aspitrigla cuculus*	*Trigla lyra* (Piper)
Sapphirrine Gunard	*Trigla lucerna*	*Agonus cataphractus* (Pogge)
		Cyclopterus lumpus (Lump sucker)
Turbot	*Scophthalmus maximus*	*Zeugopterus punctatus* (Topknot)
Brill	*Scophthalmus rhombus*	*Phrynorhombus norvegicus* (Topknot)
Dab	*Limanda limanda*	*Lepidorhombus whiffiagonis* (Megrim)
Flounder	*Platichthys flesus*	*Arnoglossus laterna* (Scaldfish)
Plaice	*Pleuronectes platessa*	*Arnoglossus thori*
Lemon sole	*Microstomus kitt*	*Arnoglossus imperialis*
Sole	*Solea solea*	*Glyptocephalus cynoglossus* (Witch)
		Buglossideum luteum (Solenette)
		Microchirus variegatus (Thickback)
Angler fish	*Lophius piscatorius*	*Lophius budegassa*

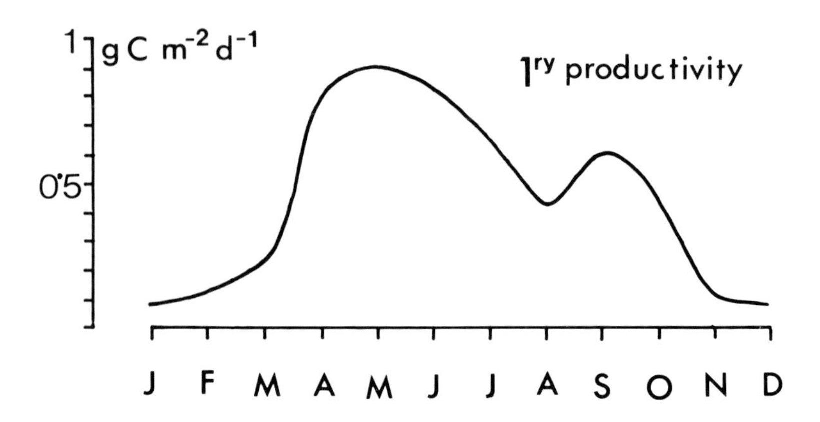

6.8 Average cycle of growth of microscopic plants (phytoplankton) in the sea off Plymouth. This shows the smoothed monthly values for primary productivity, estimated as the amount of carbon dioxide (labelled with the radioactive isotape ^{14}C) converted to plant tissue per day in the water below a square metre of sea surface.

Animal Plankton and Fish

The animals of the zooplankton that eat the phytoplankton are mostly very small copepods measuring a few millimetres in length. Slightly larger are the euphausids (krill) and mysids that eat detritus as well as phytoplankton. In spring and summer these little animals form dense swarms that are attractive to shoals of plankton-eating pelagic fish such as mackerel, herring, and pilchard.[16] These fish and the smaller sprats, which also feed mostly on zooplankton, combine in even larger shoals to breed. The eggs of mackerel, pilchard, and sprat are shed freely into the water, where they are fertilized and develop into tiny planktonic larvae. The eggs of herring are larger, with a sticky coating, and are laid in layers on the bottom, on rocks and stones, but also hatch into a planktonic larval stage. Practically all marine fish occurring around Devon, including those that live on the sea bed as well as those that swim in mid-water, have eggs that hatch into planktonic larvae that are often quite unlike the parent in appearance.[17] These larvae float for weeks, sometimes months, feeding on small zooplankton. Only when the larvae have grown to a size big enough to swim actively against the tides do they form up into shoals and metamorphose into juveniles that more closely resemble the adults.

Exploitation of Marine Resources

Shore and Shallow Sea

The falling tide exposes rocky reefs or stretches of sand inhabited by marine plants and animals that can withstand the twice-daily submergence in the sea and emergence into the air. Those on the rocks, such as seaweeds, limpets, and barnacles, are easily visible, but life in the sands and mud can only be detected by traces such as the burrows and coils of sand left by lugworms, pits that betray the presence of razor shells and heart urchins, the tracks of free-living worms and crustaceans, and the protruding ends of tubes inhabited by other worms. These beach animals can be exposed to view only by digging. Limpets and mussels on the rocks and the razor shells and clams in the sand have long been collected to bait fishing lines. In times of hardship, when fish were scarce inshore or the weather too rough, these animals were eaten by the poorer elements of society. There is evidence from neighbouring Cornwall that the families of pilchard fishermen eked out their meagre food supply with limpets when the fish disappeared from the coast in certain years at the end of the eighteenth century,[18] and nineteenth-century newspapers indicate that paupers were sometimes overwhelmed by the tide when collecting food on the ends of long reefs.

Today shore animals are still exploited as bait, but mostly for sport fishing, and are otherwise looked upon as wildlife to be conserved, or, as in Victorian days, natural history curiosities. Just at and below the lowest tides a wonderfully diverse marine life emerges, recently opened up to full view by SCUBA diving. Rare corals, first noted by Victorian naturalists, occur in this zone, particularly on stretches of rocks in Torbay and around Ilfracombe, while similar faunas have been described for Lundy, where human pressure is less intense and where they may still flourish in the future.[19]

Coastal Fisheries

Devon's fishing industry has attracted the attention of many an observer. Leland, referring to the time of Henry II (late twelfth century), described Sutton Prior as 'a mean thing as an inhabitation for fishers', though Plymouth, as it became, appeared much increased in importance during his visit in the 1540s. Brixham, at this point, seemed 'a pretty town of fishermen . . . a small pier by it . . . as a succour for fisher boats', while Kingswear and Salcombe were also described as fishing ports. Later commentators were more specific, Defoe, Maton, the Lysons and others identifying the types of fish taken; from these accounts it is clear that herring, pilchard and mackerel have long been commercially important, while 'bottom' fish and shellfish have formed useful supplementary catches. Historically, however, it is evident that stocks of the various species have fluctuated widely.[20]

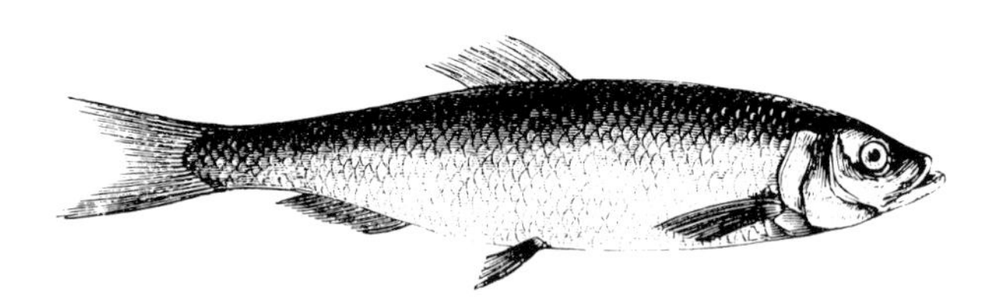

6.9 Wood engraving of herring, taken from William Yarrell, *British Fishes* (1833), vol. II.

Herring

Until the 1930s, herring was probably the most important of the species exploited by Devon fishermen (Fig. 6.9). Ample evidence attests to the harvesting of this species off the south coast, where the main fishery occurred in the autumn and winter, beginning earlier in Lyme Bay and reaching a climax in December and January off Plymouth. The grounds fished in winter included Start Point, Bolt Tail, Bigbury Bay, the Eddystone Reef, and off south-east Cornwall.[21] The fish taken from November to February were mostly 'ripe' (mature with fully developed roes) gathering together to spawn, or else spent fish that had just spawned and were beginning to feed and disperse. Before 1912 most of the catch was taken by drift nets operated from lugger-rigged 'drifters', some of which could alternatively be rigged for long-lining as 'hookers'.[22] In drift fishing, a long wall of netting, weighted at the lower end, is suspended from a headline fitted with floats; it hangs vertically in the water and the fish are caught in the meshes, behind their gills, when the shoals try to swim through. The drift net fleet was gradually motorised in the early twentieth century, and after 1918 was reinforced by steam drifters, most of which belonged to North Sea ports. Consequent upon the technological improvements, the south-coast catch of herrings increased remarkably in the 1920s, reaching a peak around 1929.[23] However, this intensive fishing effort, allied to a change in climate and in ecological conditions in the western Channel,[24] destroyed the large shoals and the fishery gradually petered out, lingering longest in the Lyme Bay area.[25]

A revival has taken place off Torbay in recent years, the herrings now being taken by mid-water trawling or purse-seining, along with the shoals of sprats which occur inshore about the same time of year, spawning from January to June. In former times sprats, and also mackerel in East Devon, were caught in seines, sometimes operated in the same way as the pilchard seines in Cornwall and South Devon, the nets being shot according to directions of a man on shore who could see the shoals (see below, chap 17). Seines and purse seines are basically ring-nets; thus, a wall of netting, similar to drift nets but usually deeper, is cast round a shoal of fish from a moving boat and the two ends brought together in a circle. The net may then be closed at the bottom by a draw string or the whole brought near shore into shallow water, and then the fish that are trapped are baled out in small nets.

Detailed, scientific, information about the herring fisheries of North Devon is sparse. In 1724, Defoe noted:[26]

> the herrings, about October, come driving up the Severn Sea . . . and beat all upon this coast as high as Bideford and Barnstaple . . . and are caught in great quantities by the fishermen, chiefly on account of the merchants of Falmouth, Fowey, Plymouth and other ports on the south.

He also referred to herrings on the coast at Hartland, presumably meaning Clovelly, and mentioned the Bideford practice of curing in salt dissolved in sea water – 'salt on salt'. However, seventy years later, Polwhele observed: 'within a few years herrings were very scarce at Ilfracombe and Clovelly [though] they now frequent the coast in great plenty'.[27] The Lysons, writing in 1822 but referring to material gathered earlier, identify herring fisheries at Clovelly, Ilfracombe, and Lynmouth, and note the export of white and red cured herrings from Ilfracombe.[28]

Bideford and Barnstaple also exported considerable quantities of pickled herrings in the seventeenth and eighteenth centuries.[29] For instance, in 1722/3 the Bideford Port Books indicate that shipments occurred almost weekly between November and March, confirming Defoe's suggestion that the fishery was conducted in the late autumn and winter. The figures show 23 barrels of red cure out of a recorded export total of only 825 barrels of herring, which may be converted to approximately 200 tonnes.[30] However, the Port Books give no indication as to where the herrings were caught, stating only that the catch was 'British taken and cured'. Thus, the figures may well include the returns of local boats fishing the herring shoals off southern Ireland and South Wales, rendering it difficult to gauge the abundance of herrings in North Devon waters. There remain sufficient stocks, nevertheless, to sustain a herring fishery at Clovelly to the present day. Noted for the 'perfection' of its product in the nineteenth century,[31] this small industry has suffered in recent years from the European Community's restrictions on the landing of herring, implemented to protect North Sea stocks.

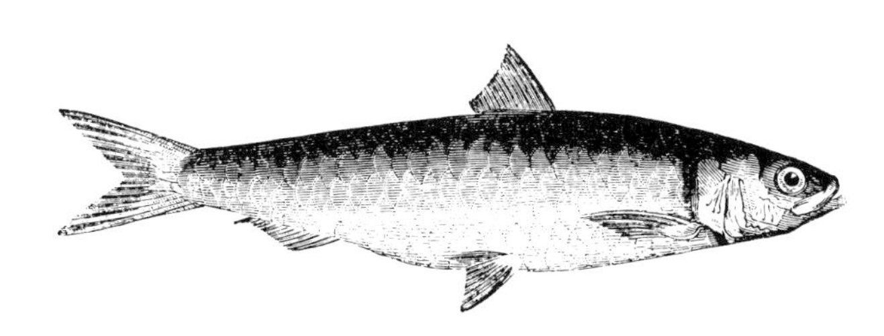

6.10 Wood engraving of pilchard, taken from W Yarrell, *British Fishes* (1833).

Pilchard

Devon's pilchard fishery has always been much less significant than that of Cornwall (Fig. 6.10). Confined to the south coast, the fishery has employed various techniques to secure its catch. In Elizabethan times, pilchard were generally captured in seine nets operated by small boats close inshore, a method which persisted in Cornwall into the present century.[32] In the eighteenth century, drift nets gradually replaced seining and persisted until the 1950s, when mid-water trawls or purse seines were deployed.

The south-coast pilchard fishery has apparently fluctuated according to long-term changes in the climate. In relatively warm periods, pilchards have been taken not only off Plymouth but in Bigbury Bay, Start Bay, and off Teignmouth, Sidmouth, and Beer.[33] Thus in the late-sixteenth century, a comparatively warm era, pilchard were cured and exported from Plymouth and Dartmouth, and much legislation was enacted to control the trade, as recorded in the Plymouth 'Black' and 'White' books.[34] In contrast, during the 'Little Ice Age' of the second half of the seventeenth century pilchard were no longer present off South Devon, and exports from Plymouth appear to have been few and in the nature of re-exports of Cornish pilchard, themselves scarce.[35] Curing and exportation of pilchard seems to have revived on a smaller scale at Dartmouth in the 1720s according to Defoe, a contention borne out by the Port Books,[36] but had ceased by the end of the eighteenth century, when there were periods of scarcity in Cornwall. In the early part of the nineteenth century pilchard seining took place in Bigbury Bay, but this ceased after the 1840s, when pilchard were also reported scarce off Plymouth.[37] In the present century, despite the very warm spell from the 1920s to 1960s, the traditional winter drift net fishery for pilchard failed, but large shoals are known to have been present in summer, though they were not exploited (Figs 6.11, 6.12 and 6.14).[38] Quite recently large catches of pilchards were made by purse-seiners fishing in winter for mackerel, but this brief bonanza has ended and pilchard now form only a small proportion of the fish landed in Devon.

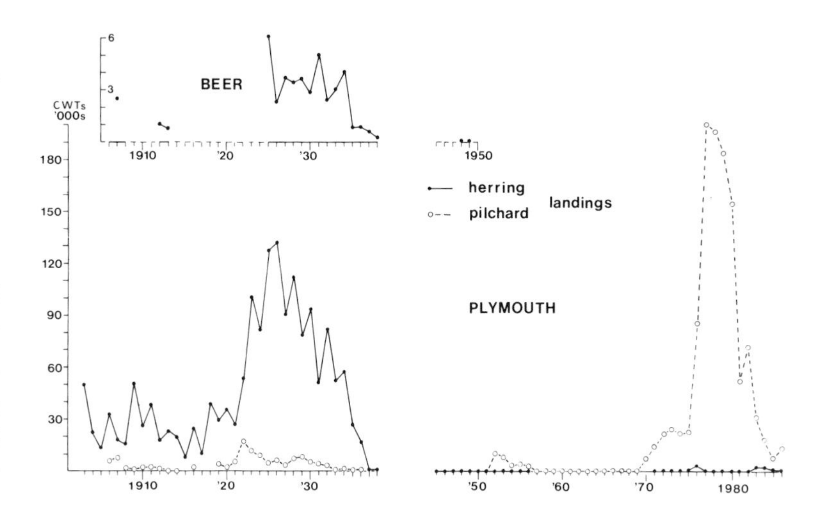

6.11 Changes in herring landings at Plymouth during the present century, and a comparison with Beer in east Devon, where only local boats were involved (note that a different scale is used for the Beer landings). The high catches in the 1920s at Plymouth were the result of landings of herrings by large numbers of steam drifters that visited Devon for the winter season. Landings of pilchards are also shown, the high catches in the 1970s being due to fishing by visiting purse seiners.

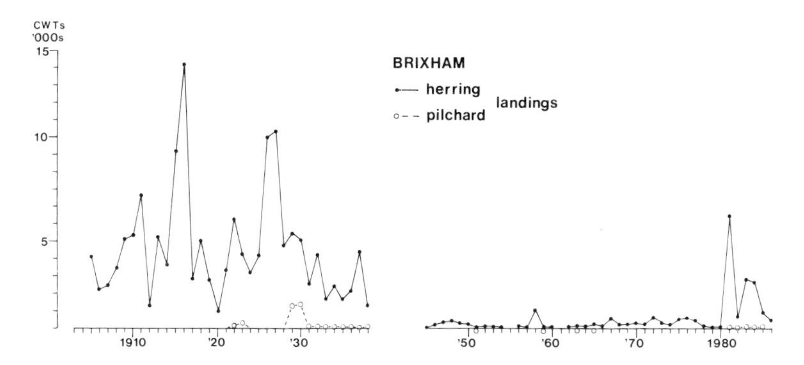

6.12 Changes in herring and pilchard landings at Brixham during the present century. Note that the scale is different from that used for Plymouth in Figure 6.11.

6.13 Wood engraving of mackerel taken from Yarrell, *British Fishes* (1833).

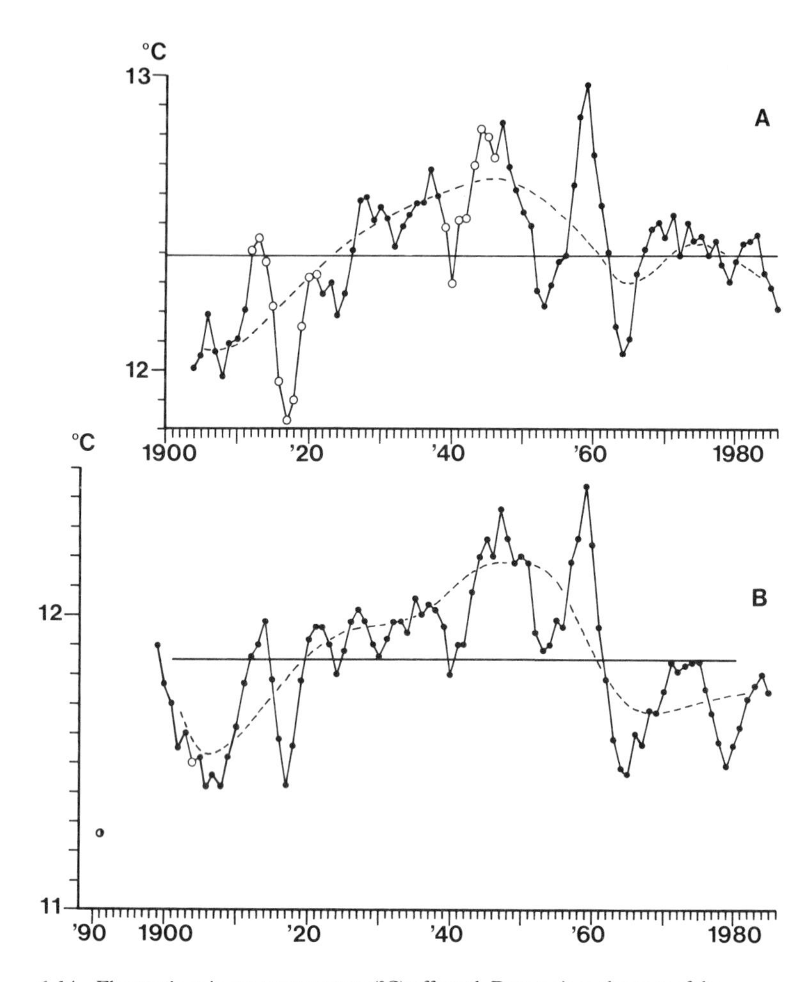

6.14 Fluctuations in sea temperature (°C) off south Devon since the turn of the century, comparing surface temperatures 15 miles offshore (A) with temperatures inside Plymouth Sound (B). The annual values (filled circles) have been smoothed by applying five-year running averages, and superimposed on these are long-term trends (dotted line) based on decade means. A few inshore temperatures taken in the 1890s are also shown (half-filled circle). The values shown as open circles represent years when the annual average is based on less than 12 months data owing to gaps in the records. It can be seen that from 1925 to 1961 there was a period of higher temperatures, both inshore and offshore.

Mackerel

Another commercially important pelagic fish in the South West is the mackerel (Fig. 6.13). In former times, mackerel were mostly locally caught and consumed, being too easily spoiled on keeping. They were caught on hand lines with spinners, mainly in summer, but at other times, especially in the spring, the sailing drifters and hookers would fish for mackerel, using drift nets with larger meshes than those designed to capture herring and pilchard, while in East Devon beach seines might be also used. The drift net fishery for mackerel expanded in the twentieth century as the advent of steam drifters, improved transportation links, and the wider availability of ice facilitated marketing in London and other big towns. Normally the steam drifters would turn to mackerel fishing after the close of the winter herring fishery. The drift fishery tended to decline after the Second World War, but there was a revival of fishing for mackerel with feathers in the 1960s, using lines with many hooks, operated by hydraulic line haulers.

At this time some very large fish, up to ten years old, were being caught on lines in the autumn off South Devon and south east Cornwall, an increasing catch rate which attracted larger boats, first using mid-water trawls, then purse seines, to the area. By the end of the 1970s mackerel from the South West had become the United Kingdom's largest fishery.[39] Most of the catch went for fish meal or to foreign freezer vessels for export, and the smaller boats, still using lines, found their catch diminished. After much scientific investigation quotas were enforced and the large vessels excluded from an inshore 'box'. Eventually the total catch dwindled, the fish having migrated north according to some analysts, though it is a local belief that the stock in the South West had been shattered by purse seining.[40]

By the late 1980s the fishery had largely reverted to local exploitation by lines, with few forays by larger vessels. As with the herring fishery, the ending of the short era of very high catches followed a combination of heavy fishing and environmental change (Fig. 6.15). In the period between the peaks in herring and mackerel fisheries, the pilchard was the predominant pelagic fish off South Devon, though the fishery was not exploited in the same way as those for herring and mackerel.

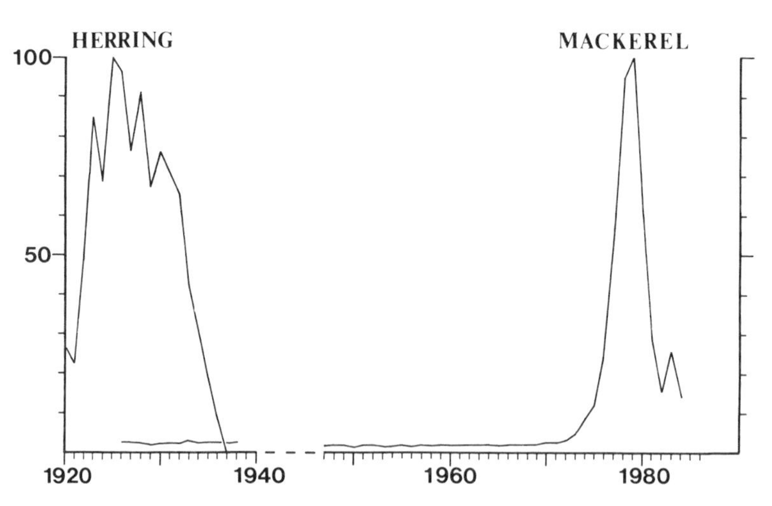

6.15 Comparison of changes in catches of mackerel and herrings in southwest England (mostly Devon and Cornwall) in the present century. For purposes of this comparison we take the year of maximum landings of each fish and allot it a value of 100, expressing the landings in other years as a percentage of this.

Bottom fish

Demersal fish living close to the sea bed used to be very abundant off Devon, and were at first caught mostly by baited hooks on long lines set out from 'hookers' (Fig. 6.16). The introduction of trawling was a technological breakthrough that obviated the need to collect bait and the laborious job of putting it on the long lines of hooks, but required the identification of a smooth sea bed to work over. Precisely when and where the first trawls were introduced is unclear, though it is known that beam trawling was well established at Brixham before 1790.[41] The beam trawl consists of a long conical bag with a purse-string at the tapered end, the other end being fastened to a heavy wooden beam raised off the bottom of the sea by iron or iron-shod runners. Steam-powered winches, or 'donkey engines', were introduced in the nineteenth century, a development which facilitated the utilisation of trawls with 48- and 56-foot beams.[42] Vessel size also tended to increase with the replacement of sail by steam power, though Devon fishermen were generally reluctant to adopt the new technology before the First World War (Fig. 6.17).[43] Further refinements in trawling techniques have occurred in the present century – principally the development of the otter trawl where the beam is replaced by two (otter) boards or doors which hold the mouth of the net open, giving it a wider gap than is possible with a beam. As a consequence, catches of species such as sole, plaice, and rays have increased to the extent that stocks of some, particularly the sole, have been seriously diminished (Figs 6.18 and 6.19). With average catches currently falling, European Community quotas have been enforced to protect individual species from overfishing, measures which have obliged trawl fishermen to remain in port for longer periods, change their techniques, or vary their fishing grounds.

'Bottom' fish are also taken by anchored gill nets and tangle nets worked close inshore from vessels of a relatively modest size. Indeed, recent data suggests that up to half the weight of fish landed in the South West may come from this source.[44] Technological advances have again played a

6.16 Engraving from C Spence Bate and J O Westwood, *British Sessile-eyed Crustacea* (1863), from a picture by Condy said to represent a Plymouth 'hooker'. As it is flying the pilot flag, this must be a fishing boat converted to a pilot cutter. Note the small mizzen mast that converts the vessel from cutter to yawl. The yawl rig was sometimes used in hookers.

6.17 The Plymouth sailing fishing fleet at the entrance to the Cattewater and Sutton harbour, photographed in October 1907 by E T Browne, a visiting scientist at the Plymouth Laboratory of the Marine Biological Association. Top: lugger-rigged drifters, mostly with Cornish registrations; middle, two ketch-rigged trawlers of the Brixham type, both registered in Plymouth and another lugger; bottom, a Plymouth 'hooker' between a Plymouth 'lugger' and a trawler.

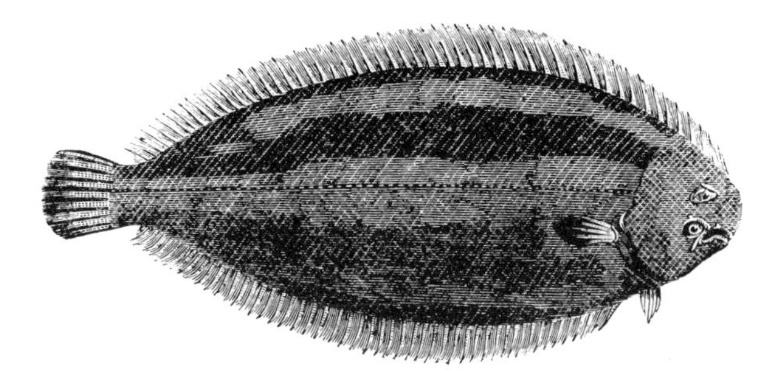

6.18 The common or Dover sole, a wood engraving from Yarrell, *British Fishes* (1833).

significant role in enhancing the efficiency of this fishing technique, notably the introduction of modern plastics into net-making, with rot-free, lightweight, monofilament nets, which are almost invisible to the fish, now widely used. This method is commonly utilised off South Devon, and there has been a big increase in landings of bass from monofilament nets laid close to reefs such as the Eddystone, where trawling is not possible. Large vessels are now deploying monofilament nets from powered drums, and fears have been expressed that the wider adoption of this technique will lead to a further and serious depletion of fish stocks.

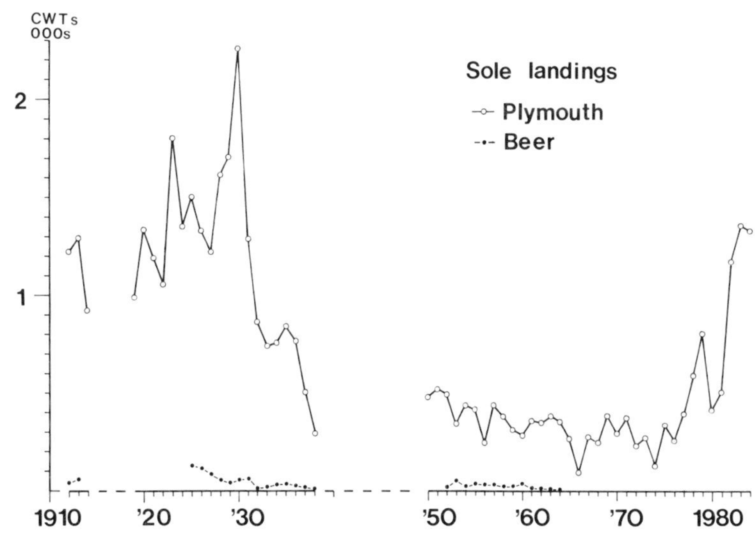

6.19 Landings of soles (*Solea solea* – the Dover sole) at Plymouth since the turn of the century. The increase after 1978 is due to improved methods, heavy beam trawls towed by powerful stern trawlers.

Shellfish

Commercially-important shellfish in Devon fall into three main categories: crabs and lobsters caught in traps ('pots'); scallops and the smaller queen scallops taken by dredging along the coast and offshore; and mussels, oysters, cockles, and shrimps, taken in estuaries.

The crab fishery is currently very important in Devon, with the common, edible crab of more commercial value than the spider-crab, *Maia squinado*, which is also common off South Devon. There are seasonal changes in the catch, related to migrations of the female crab, some of which appear to move west and southwest to breed in the autumn when they are most abundant in the pots, while spring and summer tend to be dominated by catches of male crab. In the 1970s Devon fishermen accounted for a large part of southern England's catch of crab, with 1,700 tonnes being landed at Dartmouth alone in 1975, nearly 500 tonnes at Salcombe, over 200 tonnes at Plymouth, and considerable amounts at smaller ports.[45] At this time there had been a big increase in effort, more crab pots being laid by large vessels of 60 foot or more that could fish in rough weather and travel farther out from land, some capable of producing one or two tons per day. It was thought that the exploitation rate of crabs was low, and stocks were not endangered, but in the 1980s it became apparent that fishermen, deploying still larger vessels, were having to venture 20 or 30 miles out to sustain the yield of the fishery. In 1987 over 5,000 tonnes of crab and lobster from the English Channel area were taken, though the catch landed at Plymouth had declined greatly compared with 1975, as Table 6.2 indicates.[46]

In recent years landings of lobsters at Plymouth have been very small, and it has been difficult to supply even local demand. The results of tagging in Cornwall suggest that the South West's stock of lobsters is very seriously over-fished, and an increase in the present legal minimum size for landing might well increase the yield of the fishery.[47] Lobsters moult their shells mainly in winter and early spring, the south-western stocks growing about 10 mm (2/5ths inch) at each moult. Very few lobsters now manage to reach their largest size, 6 to 7 inches tail length, at which they would be 15 to 20 years old. Crawfish, or spiny lobsters (*Palinurus vulgaris*), are warm-water shellfish, and are now much rarer around Plymouth than in the 1950s according to unpublished records of the Marine Biological Association. It is thought that they breed outside the immediate area and thus recruitment is dependent on climate and water movements; the distinctive larval stage, the Phyllosoma, can live a long time in the plankton. The eggs of crabs and lobsters are carried by the female 'in berry', to hatch into plankton-feeding larvae before undergoing further metamorphoses into young bottom-living adults.

Until recently, scallops were really a by-product of trawling, the relatively small fish taken off the south-west peninsula commanding a low market price. However, two intensive fisheries have developed in the last 30 years. In the 1960s a change in the region's plankton resulted in the increased settlement of young queen scallops off South Devon. This variety, half the size of the standard scallop, can swim off the sea bed by flapping its valves and is taken by trawling. Supplying overseas markets, fishermen exploited the stock of queen scallops for a decade or so, the fishery collapsing in the 1970s as few queen scallops were left on the formerly rich beds in Bigbury Bay and off south-east Cornwall. A further scallop fishery has developed in the 1980s, the yield being maintained, for the moment, by the exploitation of new beds. Based at Plymouth, Salcombe, Dartmouth, Brixham, Teignmouth, and Exmouth, vessels of up to 100 feet long are employed, with three or more dredges carried on each side, emptied and re-shot alternately. The dredges have to be heavy, with long teeth, to extract the scallops from depressions in the sea bed. In 1987, as Table 6.2 shows, over 2,000 tonnes of scallops were taken from the English Channel and landed mainly at South Devon ports. Unfortunately, future prospects for the species in Devon's coastal waters look bleak, as the recruitment rate of the young is probably too low to replace fishing captures.[48]

Mussels and oysters grow best in those parts of the estuaries where the salt content is less than 20‰, places where they are free of the predatory activities of the oyster drills and dog-whelks, small whelks that drill holes in the shells and suck out the meat. Almost all of Devon's estuaries are suitable for these shellfish, but harvesting for human consumption is now prohibited in rivers such as the Tamar, the Tavy, and the Lynher owing to pollution. Even where harvesting is allowed, it is essential for the shellfish to be placed in special tanks for a specified time to allow them to be cleansed of bacteria that would be harmful to the consumer. At present, mussels are not exploited commercially in Devon, the principal production sites being in Spain and Scotland, where settlement of young mussels is encouraged by provision of ropes suspended from floats. Fish farming is currently advancing in many areas, including Scotland, where scallops, too, are being kept for fattening, but so far Devon fishermen have not participated in this boom.

Cockles and shrimps are not much fished in Devon today, though they are sometimes taken and consumed locally. Natural stocks of native British oysters, *Ostrea edulis*, still occur in the Tamar and its tributaries, but cultivation is in abeyance owing to cases of enteritis when the fishery was re-opened briefly in the 1960s.[49] The Teign and the Exe are both suitable for cultivation, but at present are not commercially used. The Kingsbridge and Dart rivers are used for growing Pacific oysters, *Crassostrea gigas*, obtained as juveniles from hatcheries, and at one time some native oysters were relaid

Table 6.2
Landings of fish in 1987 at the larger Devon ports and for the whole Channel coast of south west England, in metric tonnes

Species	Plymouth	Brixham	English Channel (VIID & VIIE)
herring	226	91	424
pilchard	1042	15	1364
mackerel	4885	35	15,358
all pelagic fish	6349	1238	19,892
soles	129	228	1249
all demersal fish	1290	4640	15,263
crabs	3	120	4147
lobsters	<1	1	161
scallops	626	633	2058
all shellfish	680	1068	7219
value of all fish (£M)	3.82	10.41	47.84

Source: MAFF, Monthly Return of Sea Fisheries Statistics, England and Wales, provisional return for the period January–December 1987 (mimeographed 1987). Area VIID & VIIE refers to International Council defined regions used for statistical purposes, corresponding to most of the English Channel.

in the Dart. A well known oyster fishery has existed for a long time on the river Yealm, an area which was once used to fatten native oysters. Recently a private hatchery on the Yealm bred a clean stock of Pacific and other oysters for relaying in local estuaries. However, the commercial viability of oyster farming in Devon is precarious, and all oyster fisheries in southern England are now suffering from the pollution effects of organotin-based paints used by yachtsmen and fishermen to keep the bottoms of their boats free from growths of weed and barnacles.[50]

Fluctuations in Marine Resources

In the South West, the abundance of marine life and its species composition has changed over the centuries. Fluctuations in the relative numbers of herring and pilchard have been traced back to the sixteenth century,[51] with herring more abundant in periods of colder climate and pilchards commoner in warmer periods. More recently, as Table 6.3 indicates, changes have been seen in the abundance and proportion of the different bottom-living fish taken in the trawl.[52] In a comparison of this sort allowances have to be made for changes in fishing gear, even though the catches shown in Table 6.3 were made by research vessels and nets of a similar type and size. Thus, in the 1920s the trawl was a simple otter trawl, while in the 1950s it was rigged with long bridles, probably increasing its capacity for catching flatfish, and in the 1970s the net was more box-shaped, with floats on the headline, so that more of the fish that swim off the bottom were taken. These technical changes are reflected in the greater proportion of pelagic fish – herrings, sprats, pilchard, horse mackerel, and mackerel – caught in recent years.

Given these reservations, some conclusions about fluctuations in fish stocks can be drawn from the data. The increased catch of angler fish possibly indicates a disturbed ecosystem as a consequence of greater trawling activity. Other changes might also be due to fishing, either from the capture of too many fish,[53] or disruptions of the habitat such as the removal of 'weed' from the sea bed. For species like the spurdog, *Squalus acanthias*, and the various rays listed in Table 6.2, there is little doubt that human activity has been responsible for their depletion. These cartilaginous fishes produce very large young, the spurdog by live birth, the rays by hatching from large eggs

Table 6.3
Changes in Trawl Catches, 1919–79
The numbers of common species of fish, not all of commerical value, taken in the trawl by research vessels of the Plymouth Laboratory in three periods of survey of the grounds between Plymouth and the Eddystone Reef in 1919 to 1922, 1950 to 1952 and 1976 to 1979. The same marks were fished over at the same time of year with similar sized otter trawls. The catches have been converted to numbers of fish per hour the trawl was on the sea bed. The fish species are grouped into categories that showed the same trends in abundance over the period.

TYPE OF CHANGE	SPECIES	Number of fish per hour's fishing 1919–22	1950–52	1976–89
Decreasing since 1920s or 1930s; effect of fishing	*Scyliorhinus caniculus*	21.37	12.73	14.49
	Squalus acanthias	23.47	0.03	0.01
	Raia species	8.66	6.73	4.24
	Trigloporus lastoviza	2.58	0.80	0.11
	Scophthalmus maximus	0.36	0.11	0.10
	Arnoglossus species	13.52	14.16	0.14
Recent increases	*Trisopterus luscus*	4.47	3.63	15.20
	Trisopterus minutus	53.54	55.15	80.14
Increasing since 1920s; change in ecosystem or gear improvements	*Trachurus trachurus*	0.01	2.73	47.95
	Cepola rubescens	0.01	0.65	0.69
	Platicthys flesus	0.06	0.11	1.09
	Lophius piscatorius	0.86	1.71	2.01
Little or no change	*Aspitrigla cuculus*	41.07	42.58	44.74
	Callionymus lyra	83.97	97.42	77.16
Warm-water species that increased and then decreased in phase with climate change	*Scyliorhinus stellaris*	0.15	0.28	0.15
	Conger conger	0.24	0.57	0.08
	Merluccius merluccius	0.15	8.99	1.50
	Mullus surmuletus	0.06	1.19	0.10
	Pagellus bogaraveo	nil	0.79	0.03
	Scophthalmus rhombus	0.16	1.12	0.10
Cold-water species that decreased and then increased in phase with climate change	*Merlangius merlangus*	63.37	16.03	51.11
	Gadus morrhua	0.27	0.14	0.86
	Melanogrammus aeglefinus	0.03	nil	0.01
	Molva molva	0.16	nil	0.82
	Eutrigla gurnardus	46.62	0.84	1.46
	Limanda limanda	8.85	2.71	9.30
	Pleuronectes platessa	1.52	1.38	2.56
	Microstomus kitt	1.92	1.54	3.36
Warm-water species out of phase with climate	*Zeus faber*	7.28	2.20	8.14
	Solea solea	1.58	1.01	1.23
Total pelagic fish, including herring, sprat pilchard, mackerel and horse mackerel		2.14	3.39	94.84
Total all fish		394.10	280.78	394.07

laid on the sea bed, and the young are taken in trawl long before they reach maturity. Thus, even a modest amount of trawling reduces the rate of replacement of the adults, and the spurdog is now absent from South Devon waters, while all species of rays landed commercially are in decline.[54]

However, in spite of the impact of human activity, many of the fluctuations shown in Table 6.3 can be connected with long-term and short-term natural changes, especially with variations in sea temperature related to the climate of the northern hemisphere.[55] Some seven species are commoner in the warmer seas to the south of our area, and these fish increased in relative abundance during a period of warming climate between the 1920s and the 1950s and declined again when temperatures fell after 1961. A further eight species, more abundant in seas to the northward of Devon, became less abundant after the climate warmed up, but returned again in larger numbers after the climate began to cool. This latter group of fish comprises many of the marketable species most popular in England, and their scarcity in the 1940s and 1950s depressed Devon's fishing industry. The revival of fishing at many of the county's ports since 1960 is sometimes attributed to greater investment in boats and to the exclusion of foreign vessels from the inshore grounds within six or, latterly, 12 miles of the coast; however, it is probable that the effect of climatic change on species composition was the decisive factor.

Such natural forces conditioned some of Devon's fisheries before the twentieth century. However, the migration of Brixham fishermen, and the diffusion of their trawling techniques, to other parts of the British Isles, may well have stemmed from the decline in catches taken from local waters as a result of the technological improvement they introduced. At a number of public enquiries into the state of British fisheries during the nineteenth century,[56] many of those giving evidence described falling catches off South Devon. One fisherman who left Devon for Hull in 1846 noted the big increase in the fishing fleet in that town, from a few smacks in the 1840s to 300 sailing vessels and 150 steamers by 1890, yet there were still more young flatfish in parts of the North Sea than off Brixham. Scientific work around the turn of the century confirmed the greater abundance of young fish in parts of the North Sea.[57] Many other Brixham and Plymouth fishermen and merchants reported declines in some species of fish at these enquiries, though it sometimes appears that there were natural fluctuations, for losses of warm-water fish such as soles, red mullet, and hake were sometimes balanced by improvements in cold-water fish such as lemon soles, plaice, and cod. Nevertheless, very few of those giving evidence at the enquiries doubted that there had been a serious continuing decline in catch of soles in Devon's inshore waters; and this happened before the introduction of steam or motor power in the South West.

Recent improvements in technology have also influenced the structure

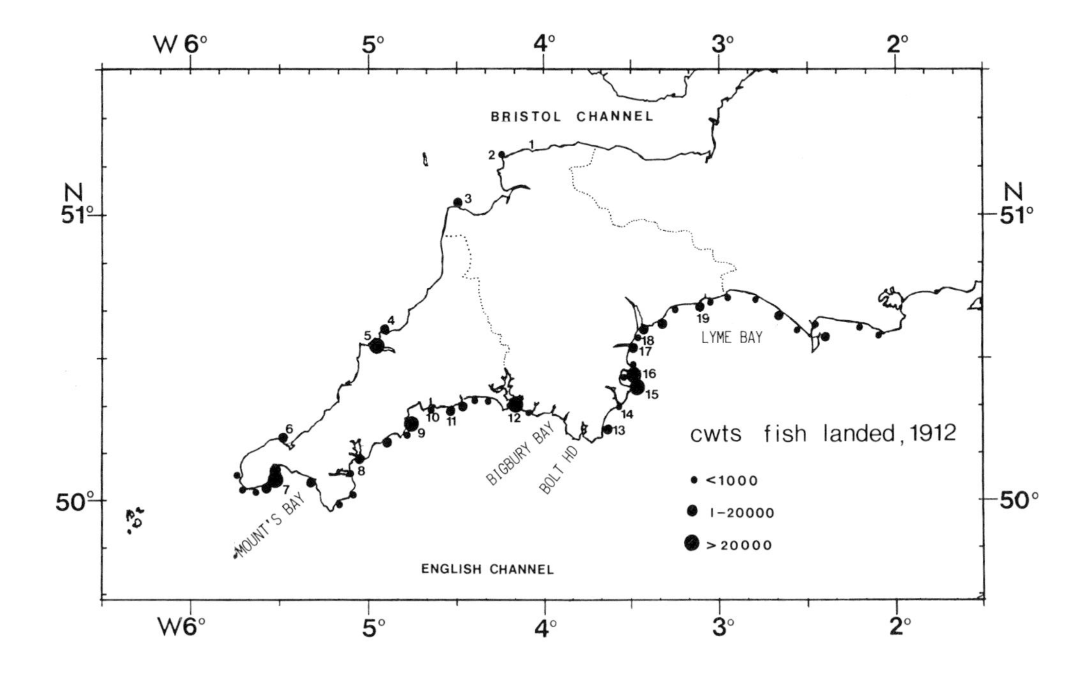

6.20 Ports in Devon and Cornwall quoted in *Annual Report of Proceedings under Acts relating to Sea Fisheries (England and Wales)* (1912), with the landings grouped into three categories of importance by weight. This year represents the heyday of the small ports and sailing vessels, before the onset of steam and motor power in the South West, and was the first time all the small port details for all fish species were printed in full. Today many of the smaller ports have ceased fishing or the landings are lumped with the larger ports.
1 Lynmouth, *2* Ilfracombe, *3* Clovelly, *4* Port Isaac, *5* Padstow, *6* St Ives, *7* Newlyn, *8* Falmouth, *9* Mevagissey, *10* Fowey, *11* Polperro, *12* Plymouth, *13* Start Bay, *14* Dartmouth, *15* Brixham, *16* Torquay, *17* Teignmouth, *18* Dawlish, *19* Beer.

and prosperity of Devon's fisheries. Echo-sounding, electronic navigation, and stern trawling have been introduced, while the adoption of the purse seine has constituted a technological advance as significant as that of trawling in the nineteenth century – an advance which threatens to wipe out local pelagic fish stocks.[58] These developments have fundamentally altered the character of Devon's fisheries, a change apparent if we compare the statistics relating to catches taken in 1912 (the year of best returns for small ports) and those returned in the 1970s. The 1912 fishery was mainly conducted in sailing vessels with much of the catch handled in a range of small harbours. In the 1970s landings were concentrated at the major ports, with much larger, capital-intensive vessels responsible for the bulk of a catch dominated by large quantities of pelagic fish destined for fishmeal conversion and by shellfish fetching high prices (Figs 6.20 and 6.21).

Whether Devon's fisheries have the capacity to sustain the present catch levels and marketing in the future is doubtful, given the rate of exploitation and the known trends in stocks. The present marketable catch is even less likely to be maintained in the face of predicted changes in species composition, notably declines in the abundance of popular cold-water fish such as herring, cod, lemon soles, and plaice, if the world's climate becomes warmer as a result of the 'greenhouse' effect.

Many friends and colleagues have helped us to prepare this chapter, and it is not possible to mention them all, but we would particularly like to thank Linda Maddock (Marine Biological Association), Libbie Stuart (West Devon Record Office), Alison Grant (North Devon Maritime Museum), the late Elizabeth Roberts (Information Officer, Marine Biological Association), and Stanley Jones and Michael Rolfe (Fisheries Laboratory, Lowestoft), for access to unpublished data; and Shirley Boalch and Eve Southward for assisting in research undertaken in Taunton and London. Thanks are also due to David Nicholson (Plymouth Marine Laboratory) for photographic help.

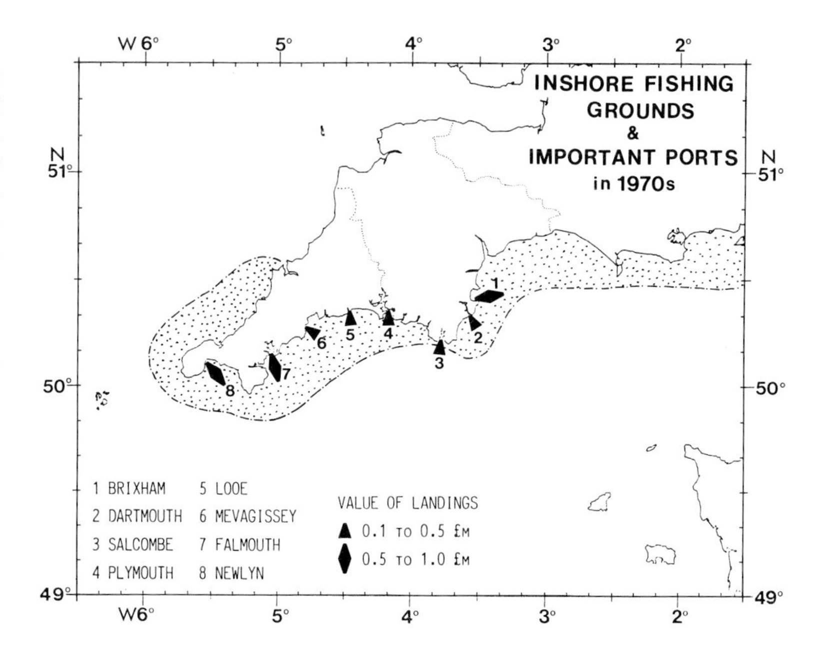

6.21 The important fishing ports in the 1970s, based on *Atlas of the Seas around the British Isles* (MAFF, HMSO, 1981), illustrating also the major area fished over. The increased importance (by value) of Dartmouth and Salcombe compared with 1912 (Fig. 6.20) reflects the proportion of shellfish landings. The lesser importance of Plymouth is due to the decline in herring and pilchard landings since 1912; the importance of Plymouth increased again briefly at the end of the 1970s, when mackerel and pilchard were landed in large quantities for conversion to fishmeal.

6: The Marine Resources of Devon's Coastal Waters

1 Ministry of Agriculture, Fisheries and Food (hereafter MAFF), *Atlas of the Seas Around the British Isles* (Southampton, 1981).
2 G Dietrich, 'Die anomale Jahresschwankung des Warmeinhalts im Englischen Kanal, ihre Ursachen und Auswirkungen', *Deutsche Hydrographische Zeitschrift* 3 (1950), 184–201; G Dietrich, 'Influences of Tidal Streams on Oceanographic and Climatic Conditions in the Sea as exemplified by the English Channel', *Nature*, 168 (1951), 811; SR Jones, 'Some results from Woodhead seabed drifter releases in the Western English Channel and Celtic Sea', MAFF, *Fisheries Laboratory Technical Report Series*, 10 (1974), 1–21.
3 NA Holme, 'The Bottom Fauna of the English Channel', *Journal of the Marine Biological Association of the United Kingdom* (hereafter *JMBA*), 41 (1961), 397–461; and *JMBA* 46 (1966), 401–93.
4 DJ Crisp and AJ Southward, 'The Distribution of Intertidal Organisms along the Coasts of the English Channel', *JMBA*, 37 (1958), 157–208; AJ Southward, 'The Distribution of some Plankton Animals in the English Channel and approaches. III. Theories about long term Biological Changes, including Fish', *JMBA*, 43 (1963), 1–29.
5 Southward, 'Distribution of Plankton Animals', III.
6 Marine Biological Association, *Plymouth Marine Fauna* (Plymouth, 1957).
7 *Plymouth Marine Fauna*.
8 P Davidson, 'Oyster Fisheries of England and Wales', MAFF, *Laboratory Leaflet*, 31 (1976), 1–15.
9 MJ Dring, *The Biology of Marine Plants* (1982).
10 Dring, *Biology of Marine Plants*; JTO Kirk, *Light and Photosynthesis in Aquatic Ecosystems* (Cambridge, 1983).
11 HW Harvey, *The Chemistry and Fertility of Sea Waters* (Cambridge, 1955).
12 HW Harvey *et al*, 'Plankton Production and its Control', *JMBA*, 20 (1935), 407–42.
13 AJ Southward and GT Boalch, 'Aspects of long term changes in the Ecosystem of the western English Channel in relation to Fish Populations' in T Wyatt and MG Larraneta, eds, *Long Term Changes in Fish Populations* (Vigo, 1988), 415–47.
14 Kirk, *Light & Photosynthesis*.
15 L Maddock, GT Boalch, and DS Harbour, 'Populations of Phytoplankton in the western English Channel between 1964 and 1974', *JMBA*, 61 (1981), 565–83; L Maddock, DS Harbour and GT Boalch, 'Seasonal and year-to-year Changes in the Phytoplankton from the Plymouth area, 1963–1986', *JMBA*, 69 (1989), 229–44.
16 DH Cushing, 'The Number of Pilchards in the Channel', *Fishery Investigations*, 2nd series, 21 (1957), 1–27.
17 FS Russell, *The Eggs and Planktonic Stages of British Marine Fishes* (1976).
18 WG Maton, in RP Chope, *Early Tours in Devon and Cornwall* (Exeter, 1918), 233–78.
19 PH Gosse, *A Naturalist's Rambles on the Devonshire Coast* (1853), *Sea and Land* (1865) and *A Year at the Shore* (1873); C Kingsley, *Glaucus; or the Wonders of the Shore* (1855).
20 See Chope, *Early Tours*, 53, 65–6 and passim.
21 JC Bellamy, *The Housekeepers Guide to the Fishmarket* (Plymouth, 1843); J Couch, *A History of the Fishes of the British Isles* (1865); W Heape, 'Notes on the Fishing Industry of Plymouth', *JMBA*, old series 1 (1887), 45–95; RN Worth, *History of Plymouth* (Plymouth, 1890); W Roach, 'Notes on the Herring, Long-Line, and Pilchard Fisheries of Plymouth', *JMBA*, new series 1 (1890), 382–90, and 2 (1891), 180–8; WL Calderwood, 'Monthly Reports on the Sea Fishing in the Neighbourhood of Plymouth', *JMBA*, 2 (1892), 277–8, 394–5; RN Worth, *Calendar of the Plymouth Municipal Records* (Plymouth, 1893); JT Cunningham, 'Fishes', in W Page, ed., *The Victoria History of the County of Devon* (1906), I; E Ford, 'An Account of the Herring Investigations Conducted at Plymouth during the years from 1924 to 1933', *JMBA*, 19 (1933), 305–84.
22 Heape, 'Notes on the Fishing Industry', 45–95; Calderwood, 'Monthly reports'; FG Aflalo, *The Sea Fishing Industry of England and Wales*, (1904).
23 *Annual Reports of Proceedings under Acts relating to Sea Fisheries (England and Wales)*, Board of Agriculture, 1903–18; *Sea Fisheries Statistical Tables (England and Wales)*, MAFF, 1919–66; *Monthly Returns of Sea Fisheries Statistics (England and Wales)*, MAFF, Fisheries Statistics Unit, 1967–86.
24 Southward, 'Distribution of Plankton Animals. III'.
25 AJ Southward, GT Boalch and L Maddock, 'Climatic Change and the Herring and

Pilchard Fisheries of Devon and Cornwall' in DJ Starkey, ed., *Devon's Coastline and Coastal Waters: Aspects of Man's Relationship with the Sea* (Exeter, 1988), 33–57.

26 Chope, *Early Tours*, 167.

27 R Polwhele, *Devonshire* (Exeter, 1797), I, 120.

28 D Lysons and S Lysons, *Magna Brittania, VI, Devonshire* (1822), ccxcv.

29 A Grant, 'Port Books as a Source for the Maritime History of Devon', in DJ Starkey ed, *Sources for A New Maritime History of Devon*, (Exeter, 1987), 57–9.

30 PRO, E 190, 905/8. Likewise, in the seventeenth century, the North Devon herring fishery was conducted in the autumn and winter months: ex inf. Alison Grant. However, as 3,441 barrels of salt were imported from France in the same year, the official returns must cover only a small part of the total cure.

31 E Parfitt, 'Fauna of Devon: Fishes', *DAT*, VII (1875).

32 M Culley, *The Pilchard: Biology and Exploitation* (Oxford, 1971).

33 Polwhele, *Devonshire*; Lysons, *Devonshire*; Southward *et al*, 'Climatic Change'.

34 Worth, *History of Plymouth* and *Plymouth Municipal Records*, passim.

35 JCA Whetter, *The Economic History of Cornwall in the Seventeenth Century* (Padstow, 1974); Southward *et al*, 'Climatic Change'.

36 Chope, *Early Tours*, 50–51; PRO, E 190, 996/1.

37 JC Bellamy, *Natural History of South Devon* (Plymouth, 1839); Southward *et al*, 'Climatic Change'.

38 J Bridger, 'The Cornish Pilchard and its Fishery', MAFF, *Laboratory Leaflet*, 9 (1965), 1–17.

39 S Lockwood, *The Mackerel. Its Biology, Assessment and the Management of a Fishery* (Farnham, 1988).

40 A Saville, 'The UK Mackerel Fishery in 1984 and the State of the Stocks', MAFF, *Fishing Prospects 1985*, 25–30; AJ Southward, GT Boalch and L Maddock, 'Fluctuations in the Herring and Pilchard Fisheries of Devon and Cornwall linked to Change in Climate since the 16th century', *JMBA*, 68 (1988), 423–45.

41 FM Davis, 'An Account of the Fishing Gear of England and Wales', *Fishing Investigations*, 2nd series, 21 (1958), 1–165; EWL Holt, 'An Examination of the Present State of the Grimsby Trawl fishery, with especial reference to the Destruction of Immature Fish', *JMBA*, 4 (1895), 339–48; Aflalo, *Sea Fishing Industry*; GL Alward, *The Sea Fisheries of Great Britain and Ireland* (Grimsby, 1932); H Wood, 'Fisheries of the United Kingdom' in M Graham, ed., *Sea Fisheries* (1956).

42 WC McIntosh, 'Remarks on Trawling', *JMBA*, 3 (1984), 307–34; Holt, 'Examination of the Grimsby Trawl Fishery'; Davis, 'Fishing Gear'.

43 Holt, 'Examination of the Grimsby Trawl Fishery'; Heape, 'Notes on the Fishing Industry'.

44 RS Millner, 'The use of Anchored Gill and Tangle Nets in the Sea Fisheries of England and Wales', MAFF, *Laboratory Leaflet*, 57 (1985), 1–27.

45 DB Bennett and GC Brown, 'The Crab Fishery of South West England', MAFF, *Laboratory Leaflet*, 33 (1975), 1–11; DB Bennett and GC Brown. 'Crab Migrations in the English Channel, 1968–75', MAFF, *Fisheries Notice*, 44 (1976), 1–12.

46 *Monthly Returns*, MAFF, 1967–86.

47 BT Hepper, 'Population Dynamics of the Lobster *Homarus gammarus* (L) off the Coast of England', MAFF, *Fisheries Technical Report*, 41 (1978), 1–29.

48 A Franklin, GD Pickett and PM Connor, 'The Scallop and its Fishery in England and Wales', MAFF, *Laboratory Leaflet*, 51 (1980), 1–19; A Franklin, GD Pickett, NA Holme and RL Barrett, 'Surveying Stocks of Scallops (*Pecten maximus*) and Queens (*Chlamys opercularis*) with Underwater Television', *JMBA*, 60 (1980), 181–91.

49 P Davidson, 'Oyster Fisheries', MAFF, *Laboratory Leaflet*, 31.

50 See MJ Waldock, and JE Thain, 'Shell Thickening in *Crassostrea gigas*: Organotin Antifouling or Sediment Induced?' *Marine Pollution Bulletin*, 14 (1983), 411–5; GW Bryan, PE Gibbs, GR Burt and LG Hummerstone, 'The Effects of Tributyltin (TBT) Accumulation on Adult Dog-Whelks, *Nucella lapillus*: Long-Term Field and Laboratory Experiments', *JMBA*, 67 (1987), 525–44.

51 Southward *et al*, 'Climatic Change'.

52 Southward, 'Distribution of Plankton Animals, III'.

53 ES Russell, *The Overfishing Problem* (Cambridge, 1942).

54 K Brander, 'Disappearance of Common Skate *Raia batis* from the Irish Sea', *Nature*, 290 (1981), 48–9.

55 Southward, 'Distribution of Plankton Animals. III'; Southward and Boalch, 'Aspects of Long Term Changes'; Southward *et al*, 'Climatic Change'.

56 *Select Committee on South Devon Fisheries* (BPP, 1817, 394); *Select Committee on British Channel Fisheries* (BPP, 1833, 676); *Report of the Commissioners appointed to Inquire into the Sea Fisheries of the United Kingdom* (BPP, 1865); *Select Committee on Sea Fisheries* (BPP, 1893).

57 E Ray Lankester, 'The scientific results of the International Fisheries Exhibition, London, 1883' in *The Advancement of Science; Occasional Essays and Addresses*, V (1890); EWL Holt, 'North Sea Investigations (continued). On the destruction of Immature Fish in the North Sea', *JMBA*, 3 (1894), 169–76; Holt, 'Grimsby Trawl Fishery'; W Garstang, 'The Impoverishment of the Sea', *JMBA*, 6 (1900), 1–69; HM Kyle, 'The Brixham Fishing Grounds and Fishery Statistics', *JMBA*, 6 (1903), 437–98; W Garstang, 'Report on Trawling and other investigations carried out in the Bays on the South East Coast of Devon during 1901 and 1902', *JMBA*, 6 (1903), 435–7 and 498–500.

58 Southward *et al*, 'Fluctuations in the Herring and Pilchard Fisheries'.

7 *The Port Towns of Fourteenth-Century Devon*

MARYANNE KOWALESKI

IN TERMS OF MEDIEVAL POPULATION, none of the Devon ports can be included among the first rank of English towns in the Middle Ages. Even Exeter, the largest of the Devon boroughs with a population of almost 3,100, ranked only 23rd in size among English boroughs in 1377. The other Devon ports were even smaller; in 1377 Plymouth's population was just over 2,700, while Barnstaple had almost 1,400 people and Dartmouth about 1,200.[1] Nor were these Devon ports particularly wealthy. In 1334 Exeter was assessed at £406, Plymouth at £400, Barnstaple at £187, and Dartmouth at £185. These low levels of wealth can hardly compare with the assessments of other provincial seaports such as Bristol, with a taxable wealth of £2,200, or Newcastle upon Tyne, assessed at £1,333.[2]

With the exception of Exeter at the end of the fifteenth century, the volume of overseas trade passing through Devon ports was also quite small. In the early fifteenth century, for example, the average annual value of goods paying poundage in the ports of Exeter and Dartmouth was only £1,935, for Plymouth and Fowey it was £1,863, but for London it was £70,342 and for Bristol £13,421.[3] The generally poor quality of wool in Devon and Cornwall meant that the south-western ports played a negligible role in the trade of England's most important export in the Middle Ages. Devon ports were to become more active in the export of cloth, but this prosperity came only at the very end of the Middle Ages; for most of this period Devon ports were not among the top five exporters of cloth.[4] Imports through Devon ports were also not impressive. Customs accounts show that, even combined, the Devon ports rarely ranked more than fifth or sixth in wine imports. Provincial headports like Bristol, Hull, and Southampton regularly imported two to three times as much wine as all the ports in Devon.[5]

The medieval port towns of Devon were, however, noteworthy in other ways. The county's two discrete coastlines gave her ports access to a wide variety of shipping routes and trading partners and promoted their role in the carrying trade. The ports on the south coast were particularly well placed because the quickest sea routes from England to south-western France and the Iberian peninsula began there, notably in the stretch of coastline from Dartmouth to Fowey. Ports on the more easterly portions of this coastline also took advantage of their location in the trade with Brittany and the Channel Islands.

The long coastline of Devon also contributed greatly to the economic diversity of the county. Rich fishing grounds lay off the Devon coast in the Middle Ages. Port towns and small villages alike profited from the plentiful hake, pilchard, and cod in nearby waters. Towns with good harbours, active markets, and accessible routes inland also gained from the services and trading facilities they offered to both mariners and traders. Lastly, shipping, whether for coastal trade, foreign commerce, or fishing, was a major source of income to many port town residents, especially those engaged in trade with Bordeaux, Brittany, and along the southern and south-western coasts of England.

Political events enhanced the geographical advantages of the south Devon ports. With the English acquisition of large areas in south-western France after the marriage of Henry II to Eleanor of Aquitaine in 1152, the south Devon ports were well placed to take advantage of the Bordeaux wine trade, as well as the Bay of Biscay salt trade. But perhaps the most important stimulus to the development of the southern ports came as a result of the Hundred Years War. Dartmouth and Plymouth became favourite embarkation points for royal travellers, pilgrims, troops, and supply ships to France and Iberia. Privateering and piracy profited many of the more adventurous Devon mariners. Despite the impressment of ships and mariners, the uncertainties of trade on dangerous wartime sea routes, and the threat of enemy attacks (Teignmouth, Dartmouth, and Plymouth all suffered from French raids), the fourteenth century was generally a prosperous period for the port towns of Devon, and particularly so for Dartmouth and Plymouth.

Borough and Port

While the size, wealth, and maritime activities of Exeter, Dartmouth, Plymouth, and Barnstaple distinguished them from other Devon boroughs, the differences between these four port towns were as significant as their similarities. Exeter and Plymouth, for example, were more than twice the size and over twice as wealthy as Barnstaple and Dartmouth. By the fifteenth century they had emerged as the two headports in the region, with Dartmouth and Barnstaple under the customs jurisdiction of Exeter, and all of Cornwall under Plymouth's authority.[6] But though similar in size and wealth, Exeter and Plymouth differed greatly from each other in terms of their political and economic development.

Exeter was the oldest and most prominent city in Devon. Used as a regional capital by the Romans, it was a prosperous city with an active mint in the Anglo-Saxon period.[7] From 1050, when it became the seat of a bishop who administered a diocese encompassing all of Devon and Cornwall, it served as the ecclesiastical centre of the south-western peninsula. Exeter also acted as the administrative and legal centre of the county; its castle, built by William the Conqueror after he had subdued the city, hosted the royal courts of the assizes and gaol deliveries. Exeter benefited from these economic, ecclesiastical, and administrative functions without the interference of an outside lord. From at least 1205 the city's burgesses elected their own mayor and governing officials.[8]

Although Exeter was located ten miles north of the sea on the Exe river, the city managed to establish an impressive level of jurisdictional control over the ports of the Exe estuary. Its right to collect town customs from owners of goods unloaded anywhere in the estuary dates from at least the late twelfth century, although one-third of the profitable wine custom was reserved for the lords of Topsham, the powerful earls of Devon.[9] For practical purposes, Topsham served as the port of Exeter since, with the construction of weirs by Topsham's lords in the thirteenth century, even the small boats which had carried cargo up the river were prevented from reaching Exeter. These weirs, set up primarily to garner greater profits from the Exe river fisheries for the earls of Devon, who owned both Topsham and Exminster, were part of a larger effort by the earls to promote the commercial growth of their property. This enraged the citizens of Exeter, who in 1263–4 tore down part of the weir and forcibly prevented merchants from landing and selling their goods at Topsham.[10]

Although Exeter did employ violence in this instance, and again at Littleham in the 1270s in an attempt to enforce its (ultimately unsuccessful) claim to wreck, the city more commonly used negotiations and litigation to extend its control over the estuarine ports. Thus agreements with the Abbot of Sherborne in the 1260s brought the ferry which crossed the lower Exe estuary and much of the fish trade at nearby Littleham under the control of the city. Throughout the fourteenth century the city was involved in many disputes and litigation with the Courtenay earls of Devon over Exeter's rights to collect port customs, make attachments and distraints on board ships at Topsham, and force merchants to sell their goods at Exeter. Some profits of the port at Topsham, such as anchorage, batellage, keelage, cranage, and one-third of the wine custom, were eventually siphoned off to the lords of Topsham.[11] But Exeter never lost its right to collect town customs (Fig. 7.1) on all goods unloaded at estuarine ports, and in general maintained its jurisdictional rights to distraint and attachment throughout the estuary.[12] By the fourteenth century, in fact, Exeter was insisting that all ships unload their cargoes at Topsham, and collecting considerable monies from those seeking licences to discharge elsewhere in the estuary and from those fined for failing to follow its directives concerning its customs jurisdiction.[13] The city's control of the port was evident, too, in the royal writs for naval levies or customs collection which, even if directed to the bailiffs of the port of Topsham, or what was called 'Exmouth' (which referred to all the ports of the estuary, including Exeter), were executed by Exeter officials, not the lords of Topsham or the other estuarine manors.

In contrast to Exeter's early prominence, Plymouth could hardly be called much more than a fishing village before the thirteenth century.[14] It was dominated, moreover, by its manorial lord, the Augustinian house of Plympton Priory, situated about four miles away on the other side of the river Plym.[15] With the phenomenal growth of Plymouth in the fourteenth century, however, its citizens increasingly sought self-rule from the priory. A Provost, probably elected by the burgesses, appeared around 1310, although he still worked under the Prior's authority, even when he began to be known as the Mayor around 1370.[16] But in 1384 some of Plymouth's citizens elected a rival Mayor who, with his supporters, forcibly prevented the Prior's Mayor from carrying out his duties. The Prior vigorously defended his liberties in the royal courts and the rival Mayor was eventually ousted, although disputes over the office of Mayor continued for decades.[17] The next generation of Plymouth burgesses, however, succeeded in 1439 in incorporating their own borough by capitalizing on the town's financial and naval contributions to the Crown during the Hundred Years War.[18]

While the Plymouth burgesses managed to obtain rights of self-government in the borough, they never exercised any control over the port of Plymouth. Conflicting claims between the local Valletort lords, the Prior of Plympton, and the Crown were eventually settled by official inquiries which determined that the harbour and quay belonged to the King.[19] The Crown made handsome profits from farming out Sutton Pool; from 1296 to 1334 the farm increased almost eightfold from about £2 10s to £17 10s.[20] In 1337 King Edward III included the port of Plymouth in the Duchy of Cornwall which he created for his son Edward, the Black Prince.[21] Henceforth the port of Plymouth was administered by the Duchy, which collected customs, appointed a water-bailiff, took the profits of wreck, and ran maritime courts there.[22] Medieval Plymouth, therefore, never possessed the direct financial or administrative control of its port that Exeter held over the entire Exe estuary.

Like Plymouth, Dartmouth's prosperity and maritime service to the Crown in the fourteenth century brought its burgesses new political privileges (such as the right in 1341 to elect a mayor, hold their own courts, and be free from local tolls and port customs).[23] But unlike Plymouth, Dartmouth's growth as a major seaport dates back to the early twelfth century. Large fleets of over 100 ships assembled at Dartmouth for the Second and Third Crusades and Dartmouth ships were active in the Bordeaux wine trade as early as the late twelfth century.[24] The lordship of Dartmouth belonged to the FitzStephens, who, early on, allowed the residents a good deal of self-government.[25] By 1327 the Crown had acquired Dartmouth's lordship; the King kept control of the port but eventually granted the manorial rights to his yeoman, Guy de Brian. De Brian, despite the extensive liberties granted to Dartmouth citizens in 1341, managed to retain many of the profits of lordship, along with the right to hold pleas jointly with the Mayor and to take the oath of the newly elected Mayor.[26]

The earliest claims to jurisdiction over the port of Dartmouth were made by the lords of Totnes, an ancient and wealthy borough eight miles north of Dartmouth on the navigable Dart river. Settled and fortified in Saxon times,

7.1 Exeter Town Customs Roll, temp. Edward I and Edward II, 1281–1323. This is the earliest record to survive of the collection of the Town Petty Custom, a local duty on incoming trade, from which only city freemen were exempt. *(Devon Record Office, Exeter City Records)*

Totnes was an important market town by the twelfth century, taking advantage of the navigability of the Dart, its position on one of the main roads of the South West, and its easy access to its hinterland (compared with Dartmouth).[27] Totnes's commercial success may have promoted the growth of Dartmouth in the twelfth century, but by the mid-thirteenth century the growing prominence of Dartmouth occasioned complaints from the lords of Totnes concerning their claims to market tolls in Dartmouth, as well as to wreck, fishing, and customs from all ships arriving anywhere in the Dart estuary.[28] These rights were acquired by the King's agent, Nicholas de Tewkesbury, about twelve years after he had purchased Dartmouth from the FitzStephens in 1293.[29] In 1327 he transferred the borough and port of Dartmouth to the Crown, which in 1337 granted the 'Water' of Dartmouth to the Black Prince as Duke of Cornwall.[30]

Thus the Duchy of Cornwall, closely linked to the Crown, came to control the two best harbours on the south coast of Devon. Its acquisition of these strategic ports just as the Hundred Years War broke out with France was surely no coincidence. Both were frequently used as embarkation points for

7.2 Exe Bridge, Exeter, one of eight arches, *c*1200. Note the use of Beer stone and local volcanic trap for the ribs. *(Royal Albert Memorial Museum, Archaeological Field Unit)*

7.3 The lower Dart estuary from the sea. The original settlement was at Townstall, a mile or so from the river (top left of picture) and in medieval times much of the present water front was tidal mudflats. *(J Saunders, Exeter University)*

troops, supplies, naval expeditions, pilgrims, and the wine fleets.[31] Plymouth, however, was favoured with such business more than Dartmouth, in large part because of its greater size, easier access to a larger hinterland, and, as suggested by Percy Russell, because Plympton Priory ensured a more 'pliable' borough administration and more generous hospitality than 'such magistrates-cum-privateers as the mayors of Dartmouth'.[32] It is important to remember, however, that the liberties of Dartmouth, as well as the eventual move to self-rule by the Plymouth burgesses, were all occasioned by royal grants in recognition of the maritime contributions of these two port towns in a time of national crisis.

Barnstaple was the only major port town on the north coast of Devon. Its geographic position meant that it was not as affected by trade or wars with France as the southern ports. Instead, its maritime trade was more orientated towards the Bristol Channel, Wales, and Ireland.[33] Like Exeter, Barnstaple was an Anglo-Saxon *burh* and a Domesday borough, though, unlike Exeter, its lordship did not devolve into the hands of its citizens. But this did not deter the burgesses of Barnstaple; in the 1340s they brazenly ignored the findings of two inquisitions and claimed that the rights of a free borough had been granted to them by a now lost charter of King Athelstan. Although occasionally challenged by subsequent lords of Barnstaple, the citizens seem to have enjoyed a degree of self-government unusual in a seigneurial borough. Their self-confidence was particularly evident in the forged charters of liberties they successfully passed off as genuine in the mid-fifteenth century.[34] The fairly rapid turnover of the town's largely absentee lords probably aided the burgesses' claims, but Barnstaple's prosperity in the late fourteenth century as the main centre of the county's internal cloth trade (see below) must also have promoted the townspeople's aspirations.

The control and profits of the port of Barnstaple remained in the hands of the lords of the town. They had the right to collect such port customs as keelage and a 1d tax from every tun of wine imported by unenfranchised merchants,[35] but there is no evidence that these town customs ever came close to equalling those collected by Exeter in the ports of 'Exmouth'. Indeed, Barnstaple's maritime profits were probably considerably less than those of the three major seaports on Devon's south coast. Not only did it lack the natural advantages enjoyed by the southern ports in trade and shipping with the Continent, but also its proximity to the rich and powerful port of Bristol precluded its emergence as a major port in the Bristol Channel.

Hinterland and Trade

The trade and prosperity of each port town was shaped in large part by the nature of its situation. Exeter possessed the largest, richest, and most populated hinterland. It stretched from Taunton in Somerset to the Dartmoor border town of Okehampton, encompassed all of east Devon, the eastern slopes of Dartmoor, and stretched as far south as Paignton.[36] As illustrated in Map 7.1, this region included the fertile valleys of the Otter, Exe, Creedy, and the Culm rivers, interspersed with sufficient upland grazing areas to support a prosperous pastoral economy. Although the rivers were not navigable, Exeter's inland position promoted better communications overland than those possessed by the other ports.

In contrast, the hinterlands of Dartmouth and Plymouth were much smaller, constrained by the granite mass of Dartmoor to their north. Dartmouth's commercial hinterland was particularly small, since it had to contend both with its own poor communications inland and with competition from its more powerful neighbour, Exeter. The only substantial town in its vicinity was Totnes, a centre of woollen cloth manufacture, although a fair amount of tin, much presumably from the stannary town of Ashburton on the edge of Dartmoor, passed through Dartmouth.[37] Plymouth's hinterland was slightly larger, extending from the fertile lands of the South Hams (part of which were also served by Dartmouth), up the Tamar and Tavy river valleys to include Tavistock and parts of eastern Cornwall.[38] Even so, the medieval inhabitants of Plymouth recognized the limitations of their inland links. In a petition to the King in 1396 concerning hindrances to their port trade, they argued that the surrounding countryside was so small and barren that they were forced to depend on foreign grain imports.[39]

Barnstaple's hinterland was almost as large as Exeter's, but much of it was sparsely populated and included some of the poorest land in Devon. Arable agriculture thrived only in the Taw and Torridge river valleys; elsewhere a subsistence level of arable agriculture prevailed alongside an increasing emphasis upon livestock husbandry.[40] This pastoral emphasis, however, helped foster a local cloth industry; for much of the late fourteenth and early fifteenth centuries north Devon was the most important centre of cloth production in Devon. As indicated in the first column of Table 7.1, 46 per cent of the cloth sold in Devon in 1395–7 was marketed in the towns of north Devon, with Barnstaple accounting for over 80 per cent of the sales. But

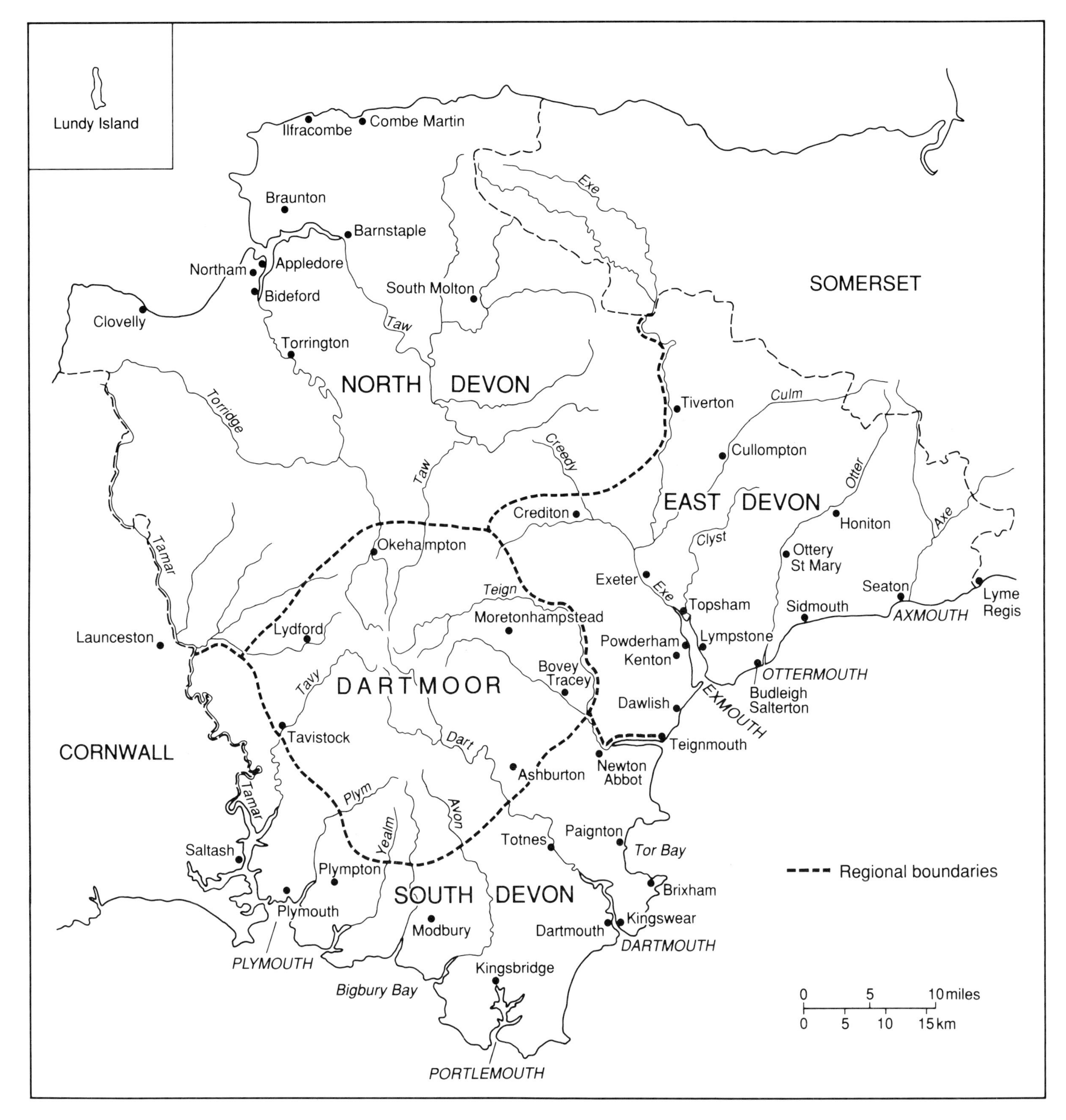

Map 7.1 Medieval Devon, showing the main regional divisions, ports and market towns. The names of river mouths shown in capital letters are those often used for groups of ports in the customs records.

north Devon's pre-eminence in cloth production did not last long; by the mid-fifteenth century Exeter and east Devon had emerged as the most important centres of both cloth production and sale.[41]

The most common cloths produced in fourteenth-century Devon were called 'dozens' or 'straits' because they were much narrower than the standard broadcloth. Narrow dozens measured only 12 × 1 yards, four being reckoned to equal one cloth of assize, while broad dozens, also manufactured in Devon, measured 12 × 2 yards. Dozens were coarse, rough woollens made of short wool, flocks, and lamb's wool. Primarily coloured russet, grey, or white, these cloths sold cheaply in the 1390s at about 4d per

Table 7.1
Percentage of cloth sales and exports by region in late medieval Devon

Region & Port	Cloths Sold 1395–7	Cloths Exported 1398–9	Cloths Exported 1383–99	Cloths Sold 1467–8
East Devon	41			51
Exeter	(23)	12	9	(20)
Teignmouth		1	1	
South Devon	10			36
Dartmouth		11	25	
Plymouth		47	37	
North Devon	46			13
Barnstaple		29	27	
Ilfracombe			1	
Dartmoor & Borders	3			0
Total	100	100	100	100
(Total No.	5582	960	£2871	940)

Source: 1395–7 figures based on PRO, Aulnage Accounts, E101/338/11, mm. 4–6d (two accounts covering 24 months). Exeter aulnage figures from PRO, Enrolled Customs Accounts, E358/8, mm. 2d, 4d (for 26 months from 1395–7 but here adjusted to a 24-month period); the figures in parantheses show the portion of east Devon cloths marketed in Exeter. Export figures for 1398–9 from PRO E122/40/23, 40/25. Export cloth values based on E122/102/14 (1383/4); 40/16, 40/26 (1391–2); 40/23 (1398–9). Aulnage figures for 1467–8 from PRO E101/338/14. Customs fraud at Barnstaple in the early 1390s (PRO E159/170 Mich. Recorda, mm. 3–6) means that its cloth exports for 1383–99 are underestimated. See Map 7.1 for the location of these regions.

yard. Since the main customers for these inexpensive cloths – wage-earners and other poorer people – possessed relatively greater earning power in the late Middle Ages, the market for these Devon cloths both at home and abroad, especially in Brittany and Gascony, remained relatively buoyant throughout the period.[42]

Table 7.1 also compares the regional distribution of cloth sales and exports in late fourteenth-century Devon. Although north and mid Devon produced almost half of Devon's cloth, the northern ports exported less than one-third of the county's cloth. Similarly, only about 10 per cent of the county's exported cloth passed through the ports of Exeter and east Devon, even though cloth sales in this region represented over 40 per cent of the total cloth marketed in Devon. This marketing pattern operated in reverse in south Devon. Dartmouth and Plymouth together exported well over half of all Devon cloth exports, yet south Devon produced only about 10 per cent of this commodity. Clearly the ports of Dartmouth and Plymouth managed to attract trade in local cloth from outside the normal bounds of their hinterlands. A variety of factors accounted for the remarkable pull of Dartmouth and Plymouth. Their excellent deep harbours were well suited to the larger ships on the overseas trade routes. Their easy access to French and Spanish ports, combined with the favour shown them by the Crown during the Hundred Years War, also encouraged use of these ports. Indeed, as their greater stake in the Devon shipping fleet indicates (see below, pp. 75–7), the economies of Plymouth, and particularly Dartmouth, were much more orientated to the sea in the fourteenth century than were those of the other Devon ports.

The greater maritime orientation of Dartmouth and Plymouth may also be seen in the volume of foreign trade which passed through these ports. Figures calculated from the late-fourteenth-century customs accounts (see Table 7.2) show that Plymouth accounted for 41 per cent and Dartmouth 25 per cent of the total value of goods involved in foreign trade in Devon ports. The value of Exeter's foreign trade did not lag far behind that of Dartmouth's, but this was due mainly to the value of its wine imports, since neither Exeter's exports (almost all cloth), nor its imports of other merchandise, ranked very high. Barnstaple was distinguished mainly by the value of its cloth exports; the low level of its imports reflected the poverty of much of the town's hinterland.

The fourteenth-century exports of both Barnstaple and Exeter were almost entirely restricted to cloth, but the other port towns, especially Plymouth, showed greater diversity. Tin exports appeared infrequently in the customs accounts, but fairly widespread smuggling and customs evasion probably resulted in an underestimation of the value of such exports.[43] Products derived from the profitable pastoral economy of Devon, such as hides, calf-skins, shoes, and cheese (usually from Plymouth) were regularly shipped from Devon ports, as were cider, ale, and mead.[44] Occasional exports (or re-exports) of salt were probably linked to the trade in fish; small vessels, like the *Stokfish* of Seaton, carried salt out of Devon ports and carried fish back in.[45] But salt imports were always more substantial than the exports because of the regular demand created by Devon's busy fishing industry and the higher quality of most imported salt.

Fish, particularly hake, was the most important export after cloth. In Plymouth these fish cargoes could be quite substantial, in some years approaching cloth exports in total value.[46] From an early date this trade in fish was linked to the Gascon wine trade. In 1202, for example, two Bayonne merchants farmed the Devon and Cornwall fisheries from the King, claiming purchase rights on whales, hake, and conger, whether salted or dried.[41] In the fourteenth century the dried fish of Devon and Cornwall represented one of the primary objectives of Gascon merchants, while Plymouth merchants often exported large quantities of hake overseas and imported wine on return trips.[48] The export records, however, show only a fraction of the total fish trade in medieval Devon because fish were frequently exempted from customs payments, and because the vast majority of fish was shipped by coast.[49]

Table 7.2
Percentage of foreign trade at Devon ports in the late fourteenth century

Ports	1383–4 Impts. Merc.*	1383–4 Impts. Wine	1383–4 Expts.	1391–2 Impts. Merc.	1391–2 Impts. Wine	1391–2 Expts.	1398–9 Impts. Merc.	1398–9 Impts. Wine	1398–9 Expts.	All Years Impts. Merc.	All Years Impts. Wine	All Years Expts.	All Years Combined Impts. & Expts.
Exeter	8	17	0	6	34	15	14	49	13	9	32	8	20
Teignmouth	0	6	1	7	4	1	5	2	2	1	4	1	3
Dartmouth	28	37	31	17	19	30	32	14	12	27	24	24	25
Plymouth	59	36	34	40	33	40	30	27	51	55	32	41	41
Barnstaple	5	4	32	27	10	14	19	8	22	8	8	25	11
Ilfracombe	0	0	2	3	0	0	–	–	–	0	0	1	–
Total	100	100	100	100	100	100	100	100	100	100	100	100	100
(Total, all trade	£4,448	706t	£1,410	£503	782t	£724	£549	541t	£1,106	£5,500	2029t	£3,240	£16,856)

Source: PRO E122/102/14 (1383/84); 40/16, 40/26 (1391–2); 40/23, 40/25 (1398–9); all accounts were for tunnage and poundage. In final column wine tun valued at £4 (see James, *Wine Trade*, p. 30). See also the note to Table 7.1 concerning customs fraud at Barnstaple.
*All merchandise other than wine.

Coastal trade, in fact, must have accounted for the bulk of all shipping activity through any one port. Since this trade went unrecorded in the national customs accounts, scholars have tended to ignore its significance, focussing instead on the more easily traceable overseas foreign trade. But the figures on foreign trade presented in Table 7.2 tell only part of the story. In Exeter, for example, where the survival of the local port customs accounts makes it possible to assess the scale of the incoming coastal trade, a comparison of national and local accounts show that fully 75 per cent of the shipping activity through the port came via coastal craft, not from overseas.[50] Only 20 per cent of the importers and 31 per cent of the ships discharging at Exeter during the 1380s–1410s employed direct overseas routes. Unfortunately, local port customs do not survive for other medieval Devon ports, so it is impossible to calculate the exact extent of coastal trade other than for the port of Exeter, but the coastal trade through Exeter must have been more active than elsewhere in Devon, given the town's large and populated hinterland, long-standing free borough status, industrial and commercial orientation, superior market facilities, and geographic position as a gateway to the south-western peninsula. Thus it appears that we must revise considerably upwards the total value of Exeter's maritime trade as shown in Table 7.2 – enough to show that Exeter, not Plymouth or Dartmouth, may have been the most commercially active port in medieval Devon.

The percentage of goods carried by coastal trade could vary greatly according to the commodity. Native English goods, such as coal, corn, fish, building stone, and roofing slates were transported solely by coastal craft passing to and from their sources of supply. For foreign goods, Exeter relied heavily on the re-export trade from the larger ports of Southampton and London.[51] In the 1390s, more than 90 per cent of the valuable trade in foreign dyestuffs, linen cloth, canvas, garlic, onions, and spices arrived by coast from such re-export centres.[52] On the other hand, 39 per cent of the wine imported at Exeter at about this time arrived on ships from overseas. But wine was the commodity most likely to arrive direct from a foreign port, and Exeter's demand for it was the single most important factor in the total valuation of the port's foreign trade (see Table 7.2).

Dartmouth, and probably Plymouth, also functioned as re-export centres; we must not assume that the impressive value of their foreign trade, shown in Table 7.2, was necessarily a reflection of the level of demand in these ports and their hinterlands. For instance, the sizable iron imports of Dartmouth during the late fourteenth century could not possibly have been destined exclusively for the inhabitants of Dartmouth and its tiny hinterland. In 1383/4 Dartmouth imported 378 tons of iron and in 1386/7 about 96 tons.[53] Yet in the decade from 1381–91, Exeter's annual iron imports, whether by coast or from overseas, averaged only 22 tons.[54] Dartmouth's considerable iron imports were probably a product of its regular shipping connections with Spain, the source of most of England's iron imports.[55] After they had been landed in Dartmouth and royal customs had been paid, it was likely that most of Dartmouth's iron imports were loaded on to coastal vessels and shipped elsewhere. Similarly, ships newly arrived from the Continent were known to stop first at Plymouth, pay custom, and unload part of their cargoes on to smaller vessels which then transported the goods, such as wine and fruit, to Southampton.[56]

The Smaller Ports

In the smaller Devon seaports, coastal trade and fishing represented the most important forms of commercial traffic. Some of the middling ports, such as Teignmouth on the south coast and Ilfracombe in north Devon, occasionally profited from foreign trade but this trade never rivalled that of the major ports (see Table 7.2). Teignmouth, though small, was in fact a quite prosperous port in the late thirteenth and early fourteenth century, frequently called upon to provide ships in naval levies.[57] But a destructive French raid in 1340 signalled a downturn in its fortunes, although it is likely that other factors, such as the insufficiency of its harbour, its ecclesiastical lordship (which did not pursue or encourage the necessary commercial investment), and competition from nearby Exeter and Dartmouth also prevented the port's growth in the later Middle Ages. Despite its occasional involvement in overseas trade, Teignmouth's shipping was probably employed most often on coastal routes, such as Adam Ganne of Teignmouth's transport of salt to Appledore, a small village on the north Devon coast, or the cargo of straw carried by the *Nau Dieu* of Teignmouth along the south Devon coast in the mid-fourteenth century.[58]

While the absence of smaller Devon ports in the national customs accounts probably means that the towns themselves carried on little direct foreign trade,[59] the presence of ships from such ports as Seaton, Sidmouth, Ottermouth, Paignton, Brixham, Kingswear, Kingsbridge, Bigbury, and Northam on overseas routes to Brittany, La Rochelle, Bordeaux, and Middelburg indicates that the ships of these ports were occasionally involved in the carrying trade overseas.[60] Ships from Paignton also carried pilgrims to Santiago, and in the early fifteenth century Brixham merchants were active in Rouen and Brittany.[61] Crayers and *naviculae* from Ilfracombe made regular voyages to Ireland, and to the Bay of Biscay for salt,[62] but most of the vessels based in these smaller ports more frequently engaged in coastal trade or in fishing. Such north Devon ports as Bideford, for example, sent *batelli* to Wales, while small coastal craft like the *Nicholas* of Budleigh and the *Welfare* of Kenton regularly shipped goods for Exeter.[63] Proximity to quarries promoted a specialized coastal trade in some ports. The limestone quarries at Beer and the slate quarries in south Devon stimulated coastal trade at Beer, Seaton, and Portlemouth in these building materials.[64] And the seven 'picards' (small vessels which served as lighters to fishing craft) of Ilfracombe, which (aided by men from Clovelly, Abbotsham, Northam, and Ilfracombe) plundered an Italian carrack off the coast near Mortehoe in 1418, suggests that smaller fishing boats were more common in these less prominent north Devon ports.[65]

The small villages which dotted the Devon coastline focussed on fishing above all else. The villeins of Stokenham, for example, were obliged by their lord to watch regularly for schools of fish from rocks on the shore, with their boats and tackle ready to set out to sea.[66] The lords of the manors of Stokenham and Stoke Fleming profited greatly from their tenants' catching mullet, plaice, bream, skate, conger, salmon, and porpoise.[67] Such fish were regularly sold in Exeter by men from Sidmouth, Exmouth, Topsham, Kennford, Slapton, and Brixham.[68] Residents of coastal villages were also involved in local seaborne trade. Stokenham villeins with boats were required to fetch wine from Totnes, Kingsbridge, and Dartmouth back to Stokenham.[69] Some of these rural residents also sailed further afield. When John Horyford was elected reeve of St Marychurch manor in 1422, for example, he was said to be *ultra mare*.[70] Mariners from Powderham and Pratteshide in the Exe estuary served on board Exeter ships which sailed to Scotland in the early fourteenth century on service to the Crown.[71] The involvement of Stoke Fleming inhabitants in cases before the Admiralty Court in 1430 also suggests maritime activity on the high seas.[72] Indeed, the attraction of the sea in Devon could extend well inland. In 1355 Thomas Knollyng, a villein of Ashburton manor on the edge of Dartmoor, was manumitted by his lord, the Bishop of Exeter, so that he could more freely practise his *ars navalis*.[73] Aged 50 and childless, he had been a sailor since youth, attesting to the influence and call of the sea even beyond the immediate coastal districts of medieval Devon.

Seafaring and Shipping

Just as the hinterland and trade of each port varied, so too did the degree of each port's maritime orientation, as seen in the occupational structure of each town. Few of Exeter's residents in the late-fourteenth century were directly employed in occupations related to the sea. In 1377 there was only one shipmaster and no mariners among the Exeter heads of household.[74] There were only 14 fishermen (who presumably sold fish caught in the Exe estuary) and 54 men (about 10 per cent of the householders) who at one time engaged in maritime trade, but only five of the householders owned ships and very few had actual experience at sea. Exeter's occupational structure reflected its position as the industrial and commercial centre of Devon; most of its residents worked in the victualling, cloth, leather/skin, or metal trades. The absence of purely maritime occupations in Exeter is not surprising, given its distance from the sea. The merchants of Exeter may have provided much capital and reaped a large share of the profits of the maritime trade in the Exe estuary, but they did not supply the manpower to run, build, or service the ships involved in this trade. Unfortunately, evidence of who did is not available.

Dartmouth's occupational structure in 1377 presents a startling contrast.[75] At least 25 per cent of this borough's householders took part in overseas commerce, 22 per cent were shipmasters, and at least 27 per cent are known to have travelled overseas as mariners, merchants, or in the service of the King. If our sources allowed us to identify common seamen, the proportion of Dartmouth residents with first-hand experience at sea would be even higher. Dartmouth was justifiably famous for the quantity and quality of its mariners; Chaucer's Shipman is said to have been modelled on John Hawley: ship owner, merchant, privateer, MP, and mayor of Dartmouth 14 times.[76]

An inquisition of 1394 concerning the alleged piracy in 1386 by Hawley's ships near Brest also shows the influence of the sea on Dartmouth occupations.[77] The inquisition's jury interviewed 82 men, all of whom had personal knowledge of the events since most had been on one of the ships involved in the dispute. Fully 65 of the men were from Dartmouth, and 41 gave their occupation as 'mariner'. The remaining 24 Dartmouth men came from other walks of life and included four tailors, two smiths, two barbers, a goldsmith, a baker, a carpenter, a mason, a cutler, an armourer, a labourer, a skinner, and several merchants. They were a remarkably mature lot as well. When interviewed eight years after the incident, there were only seven men in their twenties, 27 in their thirties, 23 in their forties, seven in their fifties (one saying he was over 55), and one, a carpenter, claimed to be 60 years old.

It is impossible to detail the occupational structure of Barnstaple or Plymouth, because no appropriate sources survive. Based on impressions received from the extant customs accounts, shipping records, and other maritime sources, however, it is fair to say that neither matched the extremes set by Exeter and Dartmouth. Barnstaple seems to have been more notable for its merchants than its mariners, although its ready access to the sea ensured that some mariners called it home. Plymouth's excellent harbour, involvement in overseas trade, and large shipping fleet (see Table 7.3) must also have promoted maritime occupations in that town. The size of its shipping fleet in the late fourteenth century lagged behind only Dartmouth's, and was twice as large as all the ships belonging to the ports of the Exe estuary, including Exeter.

But it was in Dartmouth that maritime matters exercised their greatest influence. The extraordinary emphasis upon the sea in Dartmouth is clearly reflected in the size of its shipping fleet in the fourteenth century. Table 7.3, drawn from a SHIPS database containing 4,461 references (90 per cent from 1345–1410) to ships in Devon[78] shows that Dartmouth (whose fleet included three ships from Kingswear and two from Totnes) contributed three times as many ships to the total Devon fleet in the late fourteenth century as the ports of the Exe estuary, despite the much greater wealth, size, and population of the latter region. The role of the north Devon ports (whose fleet in the 1390s included 12 ships from Barnstaple, four from Ilfracombe, three from Bideford and two from Northam) in the Bordeaux wine trade and in royal naval levies was predictably small, given their more northerly location off the Atlantic trade routes.[79] Plymouth's ocean-going fleet was about two-thirds the size of Dartmouth's, but its contribution to the Bordeaux wine fleet (see Table 7.4) was more substantial, an indication perhaps of the greater mercantile capital available in Plymouth. Whatever the home port, the average tunnage of the Bordeaux wine ships was almost identical, except for the smaller amounts carried by ships from lesser ports such as Seaton, Ottermouth, Brixham, and Portlemouth. Yet these smaller ports furnished Devon with a surprising number of ocean-going vessels; almost one-third of the ships in 1390–9 originated in such ports (Table 7.3), reflecting the widespread nature of maritime activity in medieval Devon.

Ships from these lesser ports, however, were not very prominent on the wine trade route to Bordeaux. Dartmouth and Plymouth alone accounted for 88 per cent of the Devon ships at Bordeaux in the late fourteenth century (Table 7.3). Most of the wine carried by these ships was not destined for Devon palates, since many Devon ships were engaged in the carrying trade to other English ports. Indeed, the role of Devon ships in this particular carrying trade became increasingly important in the fourteenth century, spurred on in part by the declining presence of ships from eastern England at Bordeaux during the Hundred Years War. Before the war began, Devon ships accounted for only 8 per cent of all vessels at Bordeaux, but by the second half of the fourteenth century their share had more than doubled to 18 per cent, and increased again in the first half of the fifteenth century to 22 per cent.[80] Their portion of the English fleet was even larger; in some years, such as 1372/3, Devon ships accounted for over 30 per cent of all English vessels exporting wine from Bordeaux.[81]

Ships from Devon also played an important role in the naval levies of the Crown during the fourteenth century. Dartmouth, in fact, provided more ships for the fourteenth-century war effort against the French than any other

Table 7.3
Devon's shipping fleet in the fourteenth century

Home Ports	1390–99 No. of Ships (No.)	%	1372–86: Wine Ships at Bordeaux (No.)	%	1324–1402: Ships in Royal Service (No.)	%
Axmouth	(10)	5	(1)	½	(6)	1
Sidmouth	(3)	2	–	–	(12)	2
Ottermouth	(11)	6	(1)	½	(5)	1
Exe Estuary	(18)	10	(10)	5	(34)	7
Teignmouth	(12)	6	(9)	5	(23)	5
Torbay	(6)	3	(1)	½	(6)	1
Dartmouth	(57)	31	(79)	40	(213)	45
Portlemouth	(9)	5	(1)	½	(14)	3
Plymouth	(40)	21	(96)	48	(137)	29
North Devon	(21)	11	(0)	–	(20)	4
Total	(187)	100%	(198)	100%	(470)	100%

Source: 1390–99 totals: based on 940 references to ships of Devon from 1390–9 drawn from SHIPS database (see note 78). Wine ships (each voyage counted once): PRO E101/179/10, 182/5–6, 183/11, 184/9. Ships in royal service (each incidence of service counted once): PRO E101/28/21, 29/1, 32/3, 32/6, 32/9, 32/22, 34/26, 36/20, 39/25, 40/19, 40/21, 40/40, 41/2, 41/27, 41/29, 41/30, 41/31, 41/32, 41/37, 41/38, 41/40, 42/5, 42/6, 42/7, 42/8, 42/18, 42/21, 42/22, 531/31, 676/32; BL Add. Ms. 26891; DRO Deeds M/196, 214; *CCR, 1341–43*, 629, 651, 664, 668–90, 700; *1343–46*, 84, 129–31; *1346–49*, 308; *1354–60*, 657; *1360–4*, 27, 416; *1381–5*, 523; *1396–9*, 330; *CPR, 1377–81*, 356, 405; *CIM*, v. 3, no. 421; Lyon et al., eds., *Wardrobe Book of William de Norwell*, 365–72; Watkin, ed., *Dartmouth*, 355, 374–5; Hewitt, *Organization of War*, 182–4.

Table 7.4
Tonnage of Devon ships in the fourteenth century

Home Ports	Wine Ships in Bordeaux 1372–86: Tuns of Wine	(No. of Ships)	Average Tunnage	Ships in Royal Service 1324–1402: (No. of Ships)	Average Tonnage
Axmouth, Sidmouth & Ottermouth	64	(2)	32	(9)	77
Exe Estuary	774	(10)	77	(18)	98
Teignmouth	691	(9)	77	(6)	83
Torbay	19	(1)	19	(3)	61
Dartmouth	6171	(79)	78	(80)	109
Portlemouth	26	(1)	26	(6)	64
Plymouth	6840	(96)	76	(60)	99
North Devon	0	(0)	–	(6)	47
Total	14,585	(198)		(188)	
(Average			74		98)

Source: Tunnage of wine ships (each voyage counted as one) drawn from Bordeaux wine accounts in PRO E101/179/10, 180/2, 182/5–6, 11, 183/11, 184/9; Plymouth figures include 95 tuns of honey. Tonnage of ships in royal service (each ship counted only once) based on figures drawn from documents listed in Source note to Table 7.3.

7.4a The only impression of the first Common Seal of the town of Dartmouth, 2 inches in diameter, affixed to a deed of 1281. The seal appears to depict a vessel in the northern clinker-built tradition, a single square sail and a steering oar. *(Devon Record Office, Dartmouth Corporation Documents, DD 60541, courtesy Dartmouth Town Council)*

7.4b The seal of the municipality of Dartmouth appended to a grant of the liberties of the borough of Dartmouth, 14 April 1341. The seal, 2 inches in diameter, has the King seated in a vessel with a stern rudder and raised poop, over which appears a crescent, and to the right a small forecastle over which there is a trident. *(Devon Record Office, Dartmouth Corporation Documents, DD 60653, courtesy Dartmouth Town Council)*

7.4c Seal attached to a conveyance of a toft in Dartmouth (Hardness) in 1278, 7/8 inch in diameter, bearing three anchors. *(Devon Record Office, Dartmouth Corporation documents, DD 60534, courtesy Dartmouth Town Council)*

single port in England.[82] As illustrated by Table 7.3, Dartmouth's contribution was particularly noteworthy since it represented almost half of all Devon ships called to serve the Crown at sea during this period. While the majority of these ships came from Dartmouth proper, the Crown did sometimes group towns together for the purpose of financing naval levies. At various times in the early fourteenth century, for example, Dartmouth was grouped with Brixham, Kingswear, Totnes, Portlemouth, and Kingsbridge, while Plymouth levies included contributions from Modbury, Plympton, Newton Ferrers, and the Yealm estuary, and Exeter levies drew upon the entire Exe estuary.[83] But this system of aid appears to have declined after the mid-fourteenth century, since such assistance was rarely mentioned in late-medieval levies. This decline paralleled a decrease in commercial traffic through the middling and smaller ports of Devon in the late-fourteenth century. A variety of factors was responsible for the growing prominence of the larger ports (often at the expense of the smaller ports). The fall in demand after the Black Death, the increasingly obvious deficiencies of the smaller harbours (aggravated by the increasing size of ships in the later Middle Ages), the costly dangers associated with sea travel and coastal locations during wartime, and the patronage the Crown consciously directed to larger ports like Dartmouth and Plymouth must all be taken into account.[84] Then, too, the smaller ports had less capital available to finance ventures and ships, as indicated by the smaller tonnages of the ships attached to these ports (see Table 7.4).

The concentration of capital and the greater maritime orientation of the larger ports of Dartmouth and Plymouth may also be seen in the number of active ship owners there. Table 7.5, based on information concerning 233 ship owners of Devon ships listed in extant records from 1340–1408, shows the distribution of ship owning amongst Devon ports. Ship owning, particularly ownership of more than one ship, was especially prevalent in Dartmouth, its neighbour Kingswear, and Plymouth. John Hawley of Dartmouth was the most substantial ship owner; he possessed at least twelve different ships during the period 1379–1406 and held only three of these in partnership. Other Dartmouth burgesses were also heavily involved in ship owning; William Smale, merchant, mayor, and MP for Dartmouth, owned at least five ships, and William Bacon and Thomas Asshelden, both merchants and one-time mayors of the borough, possessed four and five ships respectively. Plymouth also had its share of ship owners, although this activity was relatively less prevalent there, considering that Plymouth was more than twice the size of Dartmouth but had only half the number of ship owners of more than one ship. Thomas Fishacre and Robert Posbury, both merchants and prominent burgesses, were the major ship owners, possessing three ships each. In contrast, far fewer residents of Exeter owned ships, let alone more than one ship, despite the greater population and commercial orientation of the town. In 1377, for example, the population of Dartmouth included 25 ship owners but there were only seven resident in Exeter.

In general, ship owning was closely related to wealth, commercial success,

Table 7.5
Owners of Devon ships, 1340–1408

Owners' Residences	No. of Owners	No. of Ships	Owners of >1 Ship	Adjusted Figures* Owners
Seaton	1	1	0	4
Sidmouth	4	4	0	4
Budleigh	2	2	0	4
Exeter	7	8	1	7
Exe Estuary	5	5	0	8
Teignmouth	5	5	0	6
Brixham	2	2	0	2
Kingswear	9	13	3	12
Dartmouth	67	110	23	85
Kingsbridge	1	1	0	2
Plymouth	42	57	12	60
North Devon	3	2	0	6
Non-Devon	3	3	0	3
Gentry	7	7	3	7
Uncertain	76	76	0	23
Total	233		42	233

* Adjusted figures redistribute the uncertain ship owners by assuming that the ship owner's residence was the same as the ship's home port, or, in the case of Kingswear, by being able to rule out the possibility that ship owners of Dartmouth ships actually resided in Dartmouth.

Source: SHIPS database (see note 78). Plymouth figures include one ship from Bigbury. Gentry figures include three ships from Paignton, one each from Dartmouth and Plymouth, and two from unknown ports. The No. of Ships column is not totalled because ships were counted more than once in accounting for co-owners who resided in different places.

and political power. Five of the seven Exeter ship owners – Henry Aleyn, John Bole, Roger Plente, Adam Scut, and Robert Wilford – were deeply involved in overseas trade and served in one of the top two municipal posts (mayor and steward) of the city.[85] A similar pattern prevailed in Dartmouth; 13 of the ship owners had once been Mayor, another six had served as MP or in royal office in the county. Those ship owners who did not hold public office were still distinctly wealthy. John Cotte, for example, who probably named one of his four ships, *Constance*, after his wife, paid 10s in the 1332 Dartmouth lay subsidy, the second highest tax in the borough.[86] Richard de Whiteby of Kingswear, owner of at least three ships, was also taxed 10s in 1332 – ten times as much as any other taxpayer in Kingswear.[87] Nor was ship owning restricted to the urban rich; prominent members of the local gentry and aristocracy, such as Guy de Brian, lord of Dartmouth, Richard and William Gilbert of Compton Castle in Marldon, Otto Champernowne, whose father, Richard, had served the county as sheriff, Edward Courtenay, earl of Devon, and his uncle, Peter Courtenay, also owned ships.

But ship owning was not reserved exclusively for the most powerful and wealthy inhabitants of the county. In Dartmouth and Kingswear, in particular, less prosperous residents could pool their resources and own shares in a ship. Joan, daughter of Robert de Fowey of Dartmouth, was one such ship owner. She had a share, along with the wealthy William Smale and Richard de Whiteby, in the *Jonette* of Dartmouth. In a sheriff's inquisition concerning the preparedness of certain Devon ships for naval service, it was reported that, while William and Richard were able 'to make ready and munition that ship', Joan was 'insufficient'. Her inability was probably due to lack of funds; ten years earlier, in 1332, her father had been taxed only 8d in the lay subsidy, hardly comparable with the wealth possessed by her co-shipowners.[88] These partnerships could involve many owners, as was the case with the *Rose* of Dartmouth, co-owned by no fewer than nine Dartmouth men, three of whom were probably residents of Kingswear, and a burgess of Southampton.[89]

7.5 Medieval house in Higher Street, Dartmouth, now known as 'The Cherub', possibly *c*1380. *(J Youings)*

It is not surprising that a Southampton merchant owned part of a Dartmouth ship, given the strong trading connections between Southampton and the ports of South Devon. Nor is it surprising that his share was in a Dartmouth ship. Dartmouth's maritime focus, particularly its prominence in the carrying trade, meant that its mariners maintained a strong presence in an extraordinary number of other seaports. In the British Isles alone in the fourteenth century Dartmouth ships and mariners showed up in ports ranging from Ireland, Chester, Wales, every seaport in the West Country, Southampton, and Portsmouth, to more easterly ports in Sussex, Kent, and London, and as far north as Kingston-upon-Hull.[90] Their active presence (along with their fellows from Kingswear) in so many ports occasionally led to feuds with other maritime powers, such as the disputes they conducted with the Cinque Ports or Lyme.[91] Only in Dartmouth do we find, attached to an otherwise ordinary property lease, provision made for a contribution to the lessor's ransom if he (by occupation a mariner) happened to be captured at sea.[92] And it is only in Dartmouth that so many citizens had their personal seals decorated with pictures of ships, boats, anchors, masts, and sails. The common seal of Dartmouth itself depicted a ship with central mast and sail as early as 1281 (fig. 7.4a). Even in a county like Devon, noteworthy for its maritime orientation, Dartmouth's impressive activities in shipping and the carrying trade distinguish it from its neighbouring ports in the county. Indeed, the reputation and range of its mariners and ships must have set it apart from most English ports. Surely Chaucer, in his description of the Shipman from Dartmouth, recognized the ubiquity of its maritime presence when he wrote:

> Moons, harbours, pilots, he had such dispatch
> That none from Hull to Carthage was his match.
> Hardy he was, prudent in undertaking;
> His beard in many a tempest had its shaking,
> And he knew all the havens as they were
> From Gottland to the Cape of Finisterre,
> And every creek in Brittany and Spain . . .[93]

Conclusion

The differences noted here between port towns in medieval Devon should warn against any county-wide generalizations concerning the role of port towns in Devon's maritime history. This role could vary widely depending on a harbour's suitability, the port's location on particular trade routes, its agricultural and industrial hinterland, and even political circumstances. Royal patronage, occasioned by the Hundred Years War, was particularly important in promoting maritime activity in Dartmouth and Plymouth during the fourteenth century.

The fourteenth-century war effort also diverted a greater proportion of the relatively smaller manpower of coastal communities to the navy than inland towns and villages contributed to the army.[94] This burden, along with the diversion of shipping, fell heavily upon the port towns of Devon. When the king assembled a fleet to take him to Antwerp in 1338, 30 ships and 968 men represented Devon, even though the fleet assembled at the opposite end of the kingdom in Yarmouth.[95] The fleet involved in the siege of Calais in 1346 reportedly included 93 ships and 1,985 men from Devon.[96] Even the fishing village of Budleigh could claim in 1347 that continual maritime service to the king had cost its residents three ships, 12 boats, and 141 men.[97] The financial and psychological toll imposed by enemy raids and the expensive defensive measures they engendered must also be taken into account.

But the Hundred Years War also promoted economic development in fourteenth-century Devon.[98] The profits Dartmouth and Plymouth accrued from profiteering, the supply and outfitting of large military and diplomatic expeditions embarking from their ports, and the transport of troops and supplies, outweighed the damage to their local economies from the French raids and naval impressments. These endeavours also poured hard cash into the port towns, augmented by the lump sums paid to mariners on royal service because the Crown's rate of pay – 6d a day for shipmasters and 3d a day for mariners, plus bonuses – was fairly generous. The War may also have stimulated shipbuilding in the county, since port towns in Devon, as elsewhere in England, were called upon to provide vessels to the country's navy. Many towns, like Exeter, Dartmouth, and Plymouth, funded the building of new barges or the fortifying of old ships in response to the government's order,[99] but this burden may have fallen more heavily upon southwestern port towns because of their strategic importance during the Hundred Years War. Indeed, barges and balingers (oared sailing vessels whose speed and manoeuvrability made them most desirable during wartime) were more plentiful in Devon ports, particularly Dartmouth, than in other English seaports.[100] Devon carpenters for ships were also in demand outside the county, suggesting a long tradition of shipbuilding experience in Devon's port towns.[101]

The stimulus provided by the War to the development of port facilities, the expansion of borough liberties and economies, the recruitment of mariners, and the building of ships in fourteenth-century Devon built upon a long history of maritime activity in the county. These activities, which also included fishing and coastal and overseas trade, played an important role in the diversified economy which ameliorated to some degree in Devon the economic crises experienced by so many regions in England during the fourteenth and fifteenth centuries.[102] At the centre of the maritime economy were the county's four major port towns which provided the bulk of the investment, shipping, and manpower which linked Devon to the rest of England and Europe.

7: The Port Towns of Fourteenth-Century Devon

1 Figures are calculated from the 1377 poll tax returns and adjusted to allow for exemptions, evasions, and the clerical population; see PRO Exchequer Receipt Rolls E401/528 (Plymouth), PRO LTR Enrolled Accounts of Subsidies E359/8B/19d (Exeter), PRO Exchequer KR Subsidies E179/95/52/46 (Exe Island), E179/95/35 (Dartmouth), E179/95/42/2 (Southtown), and E179/95/49/41 (Barnstaple). The author gratefully acknowledges the financial support of the National Endowment of the Humanities and Fordham University for the research upon which this chapter is based.

2 RE Glasscock, *The Lay Subsidy of 1334* (1974), 52, 64–6. Exeter includes Exe Island and Dartmouth includes its suburb of Southtown. The Plymouth figure may be slightly inflated because of the inclusion of many rural residents in Sutton Vautort.

3 Average values calculated for the period 1415–20 from 'Tables of Enrolled Customs and Subsidy Accounts, 1399 to 1482', in E Power and MM Postan, eds, *Studies in English Trade in the Fifteenth Century* (New York, 1966), 330–60.

4 EM Carus-Wilson and O Coleman, *England's Export Trade 1275–1547* (Oxford, 1963); EM Carus-Wilson, *The Expansion of Exeter at the Close of the Middle Ages* (Exeter, 1963). See also below, chapters 9 and 11.

5 MK James, *Studies in the Medieval Wine Trade* (Oxford, 1971), 98, 107–16.

6 Carus-Wilson and Coleman, *Export Trade*, 175–93.

7 J Allan, C Henderson, and R Higham, 'Saxon Exeter', in J Haslam, ed., *Anglo-Saxon Towns of Southern England* (Chichester, 1984), 385–414.

8 B Wilkinson, *The Mediaeval Council of Exeter* (Manchester, 1931); MM Rowe and AM Jackson, 'Introduction', *Exeter Freemen, 1266–1967* (Exeter, 1973), xi-xx; M Kowaleski, 'The Commercial Dominance of a Medieval Provincial Oligarchy: Exeter in the Late Fourteenth Century', *Mediaeval Studies*, xlvi (1984), 355–84.

9 JH Round, ed., *The Great Roll of the Pipe for the Twenty-Fifth Year of the Reign of King Henry the Second, AD 1178–1179* (1907), 15; *CCR, 1216–25*, 248; AM Jackson, 'Medieval Exeter, the Exe and the Earldom of Devon', *DAT*, civ (1972), 60–1.

10 PRO Eyre and Assize Rolls JUST 1/178, m. 8d; Jackson, 'Medieval Exeter', 57–79.

11 PRO Ministers' Accounts SC6/827/39; BL Add. Ch. 64, 318–19; DRO WIZ 58M/G6/50. Topsham also benefited from payments for the storage of merchandise there; DRO Exeter Misc. Roll 3, no. 17; and PRO Exchequer Butlerage Accounts E101/78/18.

12 DRO Exeter Mayor's Court Roll (hereafter MCR) 1290/1 m. 15, 1302/3 m. 3d, 1409/10, m. 3; Jackson, 'Medieval Exeter', 67–9.

13 These licences and fines, enrolled on the dorses of the DRO MCR, are also listed in DRO Transcript 108.

14 Pottery finds confirm this picture. Imported pottery at Plymouth appeared in quantity only around 1300; JP Allan, 'Pottery', in C Gaskell-Brown, ed., *Plymouth Excavations: The Medieval Waterfront* (Plymouth, 1986), 15–18.

15 Plymouth also included a manor owned by the Valletort family and a mostly rural tithing known as Sutton Rauf; C Gill, *Plymouth: A New History* I (Newton Abbot, 1966), 97; RN Worth, 'Some Notes on the Earlier Municipal History of Plymouth,' *DAT* xvi (1884), 730–1; RN Worth, *Calendar of Plymouth Municipal Records* (Plymouth, 1893), 10–12, 37–9.

16 Worth, 'Some Notes', 737; Gill, *Plymouth*, 72, 86.

17 PRO Placita de Banco CP40/490 m. 229, 497 m. 292d; Chancery Common Law Pleadings C44/13/17; *Calendar of Inquisitions Miscellaneous* (hereafter *CIM*) 4, no. 279.

18 CE Welch, *Plymouth City Charters, 1439–1935* (Plymouth, 1962); Gill, *Plymouth*, 91–7.

19 Worth, *Municipal Records*, 10–11, 35–6; Gill, *Plymouth*, 50–75 passim.

20 Gill, *Plymouth*, 69.

21 The charter is printed in full in E Windeatt, 'Charter of Creation of the Duchy of Cornwall', *DCNQ*, x (1918–19), 135–44.

22 Duchy of Cornwall Record Office (hereafter DCO) Havener's Accounts passim; *CIM*, 7, no. 75; PRO Chancery Records C260/98/10, 110/16; SM Campbell, 'The Haveners of the Mediaeval Dukes of Cornwall and the Organisation of the Duchy Ports', *Journal of the Royal Institution of Cornwall*, n.s., iv (1962), 113–44.

23 *Cal. Charter Rolls, 1341–1417*, 3–4, 338–9; HR Watkin, ed., *Dartmouth. Vol. I – Pre-Reformation* (Exeter, 1935), 38–41; a copy was also included in the Exeter records in DRO Exeter Misc. Roll 2, no. 43.

24 Watkin, ed., *Dartmouth*, 353–54; P Russell, *Dartmouth: A History of the Port and Town* (1950), 4–10.

25 Russell, *Dartmouth*, 21–31.

26 *CPR, 1340–3*, 196, 199; JJ Alexander, 'The Lordship of Dartmouth Borough (1335–1537),' *DCNQ*, xix (1937), 247–54; Russell, *Dartmouth*, 31–2.

27 HR Watkin, *The History of Totnes Priory and Medieval Town* (Torquay, 1914), esp. 905–24; P Russell, *The Good Town of Totnes* (Exeter, 1964).

28 Watkin, *Totnes*, 146, 186–7, 201, 1050, 1056.

29 Watkin, ed., *Dartmouth*, 14; Watkin, *Totnes*, 201–2; Russell, *Dartmouth*, 29–31.

30 Windeatt, 'Charter of Creation of the Duchy of Cornwall', 138.

31 See, for example, *CCR, 1296–1302*, 121; *1307–13*, 417; *1341–3*, 597–8, 688; *1350–4*, 184–5, 486; *1354–8*, 137; *1369–74*, 65; *1377–81*, 195; *1381–5*, 259, 480–1; *1385–9*, 12, 257; *CPR 1361–4*, 317; *1381–5*, 225; *1396–9*, 432. For their participation in naval levies, see below.

32 Russell, *Dartmouth*, 14.

33 PRO Exchequer KR Customs Accounts E122/102/14, 40/16, 40/26, 40/25/1, 40/23, 1/1; Exchequer KR Memoranda Rolls E159/170 Michaelmas Recorda, mm. 3–6; E159/181 Easter Recorda, m. 20; PRO Assize Rolls JUST 1/195 mm. 2d, 4–4d; NDA Barnstaple Court Roll 441; DA Gardiner, ed., *Calendar of Early Chancery Proceedings Relating to West Country Shipping, 1388–1493* (Torquay, 1976), 56–7, 64, 66, 92–5; FM Mace, 'Devonshire Ports in the Fourteenth and Fifteenth Centuries', *TRHS*, 4th Ser., 8 (1925), 98–126; EM Carus-Wilson, ed., *The Overseas Trade of Bristol* (Bristol, 1937), 90, 118–19, 134–5, 205; JR Chanter and T Wainwright, *Barnstaple Records* (2 vols, Barnstaple, 1900), I, 150, 252.

34 S Reynolds, 'The Forged Charters of Barnstaple', *EHR*, 84 (1969), 699–720.

35 Chanter and Wainwright, *Barnstaple Records*, I, 119, 123.

36 M Kowaleski, *Local Markets and Regional Trade in Medieval Exeter* (Cambridge, forthcoming) Chapters 6 and 7.

37 In 1390 Dartmouth was granted a monopoly of tin exports for three years in recognition of the port's service to the King; *CPR, 1388–90*, 338. See also John Hatcher, *English Tin Production and Trade before 1550* (Oxford, 1973), 92, 110–15, 174.

38 See, for example, the evidence in DT Williams, 'Medieval Foreign Trade: Western Ports', in HC Darby, ed., *An Historical Geography of England before AD 1800* (Cambridge, 1951), 263.

39 PRO E159/172 Hilary Recorda, m. 5.

40 HSA Fox, 'Devon and Cornwall' in E Miller, ed. *The Agrarian History of England and Wales*, III, *1348–1500* (Cambridge, 1991), 157–8, 305–6, 316–18.

41 Percentages are used in Table 7.1 to give only a rough measure of the regional distribution of trade because of the unreliability of the absolute figures given in aulnage accounts; see EM Carus-Wilson, 'The Aulnage Accounts: A Criticism', in *Medieval Merchant Venturers* (1954; 2nd ed., 1967), 279–92. More recent studies have defended the accuracy of most aulnage accounts, particularly those for the late fourteenth century: AR Bridbury, *Medieval English Clothmaking* (1982), 47–59.

42 For more detail see Kowaleski, *Local Markets and Regional Trade*, Chapters 1 and 6.

43 Hatcher, *English Tin Production*, 112–15, 174–5; PRO E159/175 Hilary Recorda, m. 5.

44 PRO E122 passim.

45 PRO E122/102/14, 40/18, 1/1.
46 PRO E122/40/16 and 40/26, for example.
47 TD Hardy, ed., *Rotuli de Oblatis et Finibus in Turri Londinensi asservati, temp. Regis Johannis* (1835), 191.
48 *CPR, 1361–4*, 496; *1364–7*, 7, 11, 32, 50; *1370–4*, 181; PRO E122/40/7A, 102/14, 40/26, 40/16, 40/23.
49 Customs exemptions: *CPR, 1370–4*, 445; *CCR, 1374–7*, 30; *CCR, 1389–92*, 237, 348, 457, 474; H Touchard, *Le commerce maritime breton à la fin du moyen âge* (Paris, 1967), 129–30, n. 141. Coastal trade in fish: *CCR, 1313–18*, 488; PRO Exchequer Sheriffs' Administrative Accounts E101/555/1. DRO Exeter Port Customs Accounts (hereafter PCA) passim, show that the majority of fish imports arrived via the coasting trade.
50 This and following figures calculated by comparing extant particular national customs accounts from 1383–1411, PRO E122/40/26, 40/16, 40/18, 40/23, 40/30, 102/14A, with extant Exeter local port customs accounts, DRO PCA 1383/4, 1391/2, 1392/3, 1398/9, 1410/11. For similar estimates of coastal trade elsewhere, see RH Britnell, *Growth and Decline in Colchester, 1300–1525* (Cambridge, 1970), 70.
51 H Touchard, 'Le commerce maritime d'Exeter au début du XVe siècle', in *Économies et sociétés au moyen âge: Mélanges offerts à Edouard Perroy* (Paris, 1973), 533, 536; Williams, 'Western Ports', 269–82.
52 For this and the following, see note 50.
53 PRO E122 102/14, 177/16B.
54 DRO PCA 1381/2–1391/2.
55 For Dartmouth's involvement in Iberian trade during the late fourteenth century, see AH Thomas, ed., *Calendar of Select Pleas and Memoranda of the City of London, 1381–1412* (Cambridge, 1932), 194–7; *CCR, 1343–6*, 218–9; *1364–8*, 158; *1396–9*, 328–9; *CPR, 1377–81*, 631; *CIM*, 7, no. 220; WR Childs, *Anglo-Castilian Trade in the Later Middle Ages* (Manchester, 1978), 31, 45, 127, 156, 179.
56 *CCR, 1389–92*, 52, 423.
57 M Oppenheim, *The Maritime History of Devon* (Exeter, 1968), 6–17.
58 PRO JUST1/195 m. 2d.; PRO E101/555/20.
59 The national customs accounts probably underestimate the foreign trade in these smaller ports, however, because customs evasion was made easier by their inclusion under the customs jurisdiction of distant headports; see, for example, *CIM*, 7, no. 572 for the concealment of customs on the export of ale and victuals from Seaton, Sidmouth, and East Budleigh, and PRO E159/172 Trinity Recorda, m. 6d for an inquisition at Axminster concerning wool smuggling.
60 PRO Bordeaux Wine Accounts E101 passim; PRO E101/78/13, 79/5, 79/9, 80/25; PRO E122/16/21, 158/32; PRO Duchy of Cornwall Havener's Accounts SC6/817/1, 4, 6, 8, 818/8; DCO Duchy Havener's Accounts 2; *CCR, 1385–9*, 166; F Michel, *Histoire du commerce et de la navigation à Bordeaux* (2 vols, Bordeaux, 1867–70), I, 123–4.
61 ES Leadam and JF Balwin, eds. *Select Cases before the King's Council, 1243–1482*, (Selden Soc., 36, 1918), 118–19; *CPR, 1391–6*, 408; Touchard, *Le commerce maritime breton*, 242, 256.
62 PRO E159/170 Michaelmas Recorda, m. 3d.
63 PRO E159/181 Easter Recorda, m. 20; DRO PCA passim.
64 *CPR, 1348–50*, 474; *1358–61*, 519; *CCR, 1349–54*, 194; JP Allan, *Medieval and Post-Medieval Finds from Exeter, 1971–1980* (Exeter, 1984), 300–04; for local ships arriving at Exeter with these cargoes, see DRO PCA passim.
65 *CIM*, 7, nos. 553, 554. For picards, see D Burwash, *English Merchant Shipping, 1460–1540* (Toronto, 1947), 125–7.
66 HPR Finberg, 'The Customs of Stokenham', *DCNQ*, 24 (1950), 69–70.
67 Finberg, 'Customs', 70; DRO Stoke Fleming Court Roll, 1382–3, 902M/M2/2, mm. 1–2.
68 DRO Exeter South Quarter Mayor's Tourn passim; MCR 1379/80, m. 35; Kowaleski, *Local Markets and Regional Trade*, Chapter 7.
69 Finberg, 'Customs', 70.
70 DRO St Marychurch Court Rolls 4088M, Sept. 1422, m. 2d.
71 M Jones, 'Two Exeter Ship Agreements of 1303 and 1310', *MM*, 53 (1967), 315–17.
72 DRO Stoke Fleming Court Roll, 1430–1, 902M/M2/14.
73 FC Hingeston-Randolph, ed., *The Register of John de Grandison, 1327–69* (3 vols., 1894–9), 1159.
74 Survey based on DRO Exeter Misc. Roll 72 (1377 Murage Roll); see Kowaleski, *Local Markets and Regional Trade*, chapters 3 and 4 for this and the following.
75 The following is based on the 1377 Dartmouth poll tax in PRO E179/95/35, printed in M Kowaleski, 'The 1377 Dartmouth Poll Tax', *DCNQ*, xxxv (1985), 286–95, and supplemented with information concerning residents of Dartmouth's suburb, Southtown. Occupations were identified with the aid of information gathered from a wide variety of sources, many listed for the SHIPS database in note 78. For Dartmouth men serving as mariners, see especially PRO E101/39/25 and Chancery Miscellanea C47/6/4, Rolls 5 and 7.
76 DA Gardiner, 'John Hawley of Dartmouth', *DAT*, xcviii (1966), 173–205; SP Pistono, 'Henry IV and John Hawley, Privateer, 1399–1408', *DAT*, cxi (1979), 145–63. See below, chapter 10.
77 PRO C47/6/4, Rolls 5 and 7. Gardiner, 'John Hawley', 178–83, relates the complex story of this incident. See also chapter 10 below.
78 The SHIPS database contains 3,225 references to ships of Devon and 1,236 references to other ships at Devon ports. The sources for this database fall into three groups: 1) 1,811 references from DRO PCA 1345/6–1399/1400 of ships discharging cargoes at Exeter. The large number of references drawn from this source means that the tables based on SHIPS reflect fairly accurately the shipping stock of Exmouth and nearby ports such as Teignmouth and those in east Devon; 2) 947 references from all PRO E122 customs accounts for Devon and Cornwall from 1286 to 1406. These refer exclusively to ships involved in overseas trade. 3) 1,703 references from miscellaneous sources, the most important being: DCO Havener's Accounts; PRO E101 Navy Accounts (many listed in Source note to Table 3), Bordeaux Wine Accounts, and Butlerage Accounts; PRO E122 Customs Accounts; PRO SC6 Duchy Havener's Accounts; *CCR, 1337–9* through *CCR, 1396–9*; *CIM*, vols. 3–7; *CPR, 1348–50* through *CPR, 1396–9*; M Lyon et al, eds., *Wardrobe Book of William de Norwell, 1338–40* (Brussels, 1983), 365–72; HJ Hewitt, *The Organization of War under Edward III, 1338–62* (Manchester, 1966), 182–6. Since these sources refer almost exclusively to commercial or royal naval activity, the ships included in the database were largely ocean-going vessels.
79 The poor showing of north Devon ports in the Bordeaux wine trade and in naval levies means that their contribution to the total shipping fleet of Devon in Table 3 may be slightly underestimated.
80 Percentages calculated from figures in WR Childs, 'Devon's Overseas Trade', below, chapter 9, Table 9.1.
81 PRO E101/179/10; see also James, *Wine Trade*, 99–104.
82 TJ Runyan, 'Ships and Fleets in Anglo-French Warfare, 1337–1360', *American Neptune*, 46 (1986), 94–6.
83 *CCR, 1296–1302*, 612; Oppenheim, *Maritime History*, 10.
84 The smaller Cornish ports in the Duchy of Cornwall experienced a similar decline in business after the Black Death; see the DCO Havener's Accounts. Some of the Devon ports may have recovered and even grown by the second half of the fifteenth century: see below, p. 88.
85 DRO MCR election returns; DRO PCA passim.
86 AM Erskine, ed., *The Devonshire Lay Subsidy of 1332* (Exeter, 1969), 111; Watkin, ed., *Dartmouth*, 33, 283, 285, 356; CCR, 1341–3, 700.
87 Erskine, ed., *Lay Subsidy of 1332*, 4.
88 *CCR, 1341–3*, 700–1; Erskine, ed., *Lay Subsidy of 1332*, 111; Watkin, ed., *Dartmouth*, 25, 31, 32, 57.
89 *CPR, 1405–8*, 473.
90 *CCR, 1377–81*, 409; *CPR, 1374–7*, 145; James, *Wine Trade*, 152–3; KP Wilson, ed. *Chester Customs Accounts, 1301–1566* (Liverpool, 1969), 22–28; EA Lewis, 'A Contribution to the Commercial History of Mediaeval Wales', *Y Cymmrador*, xxiv (1913), 113, 128; RA Pelham, 'Some Further Aspects of Sussex Trade during the Fourteenth Century', *Sussex Archaeological Collections*, lxxi (1930), 184, 187; NSB Gras, *The Early English Customs System* (Cambridge, MA, 1918), 168, 179, 274, 282–99 passim; Thomas, ed., *Calendar*, 194–7; PRO E159/168 Easter Recorda, m. 3d., PRO E122/16/19, 16/21, 59/24, 59/8, 138/24, 138/25.
91 *CPR, 1258–66*, 421; *1348–50*, 133, 140.
92 Watkin, ed., *Dartmouth*, 105–6.
93 Geoffrey Chaucer, *The Canterbury Tales*, trans. Nevill Coghill (Baltimore, rev. edn, 1963), 28.
94 JW Sherborne, 'The Hundred Years War: The English Navy: Shipping and Manpower 1369–1389', *Past and Present*, 37 (1967), 163–75.
95 Lyon et al, eds. *Wardrobe Book of William de Norwell*, cii-civ, 363–86.
96 Watkin, ed. *Dartmouth*, 359. Watkin incorrectly includes ships and men from Lynn in his totals for Devon.
97 *Rotuli parliamentorum*, (1783) ii, 203.
98 This is argued at greater length in Kowaleski, *Local Markets and Regional Trade*, Chapter 1.
99 *CPR, 1354–8*, 221; *1377–81*, 298; PRO E101/41/2; PRO E101/555/8; Gill, *Plymouth*, 80. DRO Exeter Miscellaneous Roll 6, mm. 17, 25–28 contains an account of work on the town's barge.
100 Burwash, *English Merchant Shipping*, 107–8, 112–15, 190–200; JW Sherborne, 'English Barges and Balingers of the Late Fourteenth Century', *MM*, 63 (1977), 109–14.
101 PRO E101/555/8; *CPR, 1350–4*, 386; WJ Carpenter-Turner, 'The Building of the *Gracedieu*, *Valentine* and *Falconer* at Southampton, 1416–1420', *MM*, 40 (1954), 65.
102 Kowaleski, *Local Markets and Regional Trade*, Chapter 1.

8 *Devon Shipping from the Middle Ages to c1600*

IAN FRIEL

SCRATCHED INTO THE WALL PLASTER in one of the fifteenth-century lodgings of Dartington Hall, near Totnes, is perhaps the largest representation of a late medieval ship to be found in England. This graffito (Fig. 8.1) is some 10 feet long, and shows a three-masted vessel with prominent fore- and aftercastles and the great upcurving bow of a carrack. There is nothing specifically 'Devonian' about the ship. We can never know if the artist had seen such a vessel at sea, or was merely representing a ship then at anchor in Dartmouth harbour.[1] This ship-type was used by many countries in the later Middle Ages, and the graffito points up one of the problems encountered in writing the medieval and early modern maritime history of a single county. The subject is at once local, national, and international. General trends in ship construction and rig, changes in trade patterns, and issues of war and peace all impinged on shipping in Devon.

There is much documentary information about Devon ships and seafarers between the thirteenth and sixteenth centuries, but most of it is restricted to certain categories. For example, we know the names and types of many Devon ships, and have some idea of the trades in which they were engaged, but there is little first-hand information about their construction, rig, or equipment. The records of the construction and maintenance of royal vessels are of little help here, as the medieval and Tudor monarchs do not seem to have had any ships built in Devon. The only construction account known from medieval Devon relates to a small local barge built at Exeter.[2] Inventories of Devon ships are rare, depriving us of specific information regarding rigging and other equipment. The problem is not, however, insoluble.

Studies of documentary, pictorial, and archaeological evidence have made the general lines of the development of medieval and early modern ships fairly clear. From the sixth to the fifteenth centuries the main shipbuilding technique of Northern Europe was shell-first clinker construction. Single-masted square rig was in use from at least the early Middle Ages, and over the centuries both standing and running rigging became increasingly sophisticated. The fifteenth century was the period of greatest change. The Mediterranean two-masted rig, with a square mainsail and lateen mizzen, was introduced into England between about 1410 and 1420. Within the next twenty years a square-rigged foremast was added to the two-masted rig, creating the classic three-masted square rig which was to dominate European ship development for centuries. Skeleton construction – shipbuilding in which the strakes of the vessel were not joined together at the edges but linked only by the frames – was adopted in Northern Europe shortly afterwards, almost certainly initially in an intermediate form without continuous framing, and was in use in England by the 1460s. By the early sixteenth century the three-masted skeleton-built ship was the standard seagoing vessel type in Northern Europe.[3] Devon ships, like those from most other parts of England, will have shared in this general change.

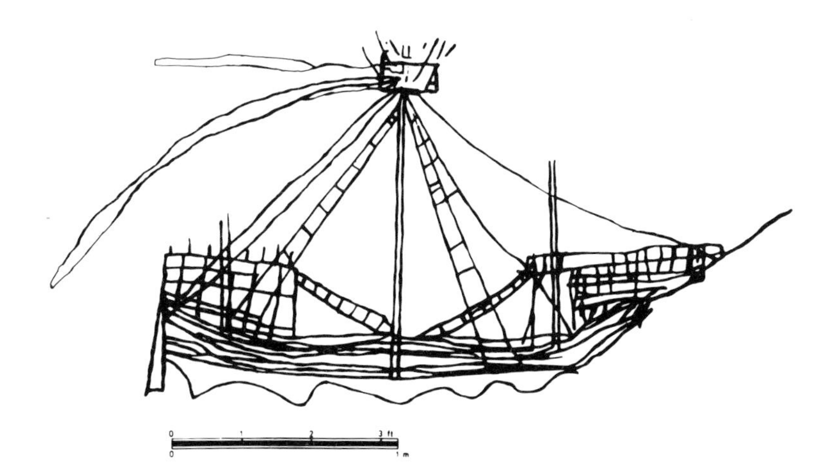

8.1 Graffito of a large, three-masted, sailing ship incised in some wall plaster at Dartington Hall, Devon. The ship has large fore- and aftercastles and resembles a late-medieval carrack. Probably between *c*1450 and *c*1530. Redrawn from a rubbing. *(National Maritime Museum)*

Underwater archaeology has so far produced only one major find in Devon waters for the period under discussion. This was a wreck found in the Cattewater at Plymouth in the early 1970s. This skeleton-built vessel sank in the first half of the sixteenth century, perhaps about 1530. It cannot be identified as a Devon-built ship, but may well have come from southwest England, as the majority of its ballast-stone originated in this region.[4]

The earlier Middle Ages

The evidence for shipping in Devon between *c*500 and *c*1200 is very limited (see above, chapter 4). In the *Anglo-Saxon Chronicle* references to shipping in Devon are almost entirely restricted to that of outsiders, particularly the Danes, who made use of the county's rivers to penetrate far inland with their raids. Exeter was destroyed on one occasion, and other evidence of seaborne attacks is to be found in Domesday Book, in references to a number of settlements destroyed by the Irish (probably during the expeditions from Ireland in 1068 and 1069, led by the sons of King Harold). We know virtually nothing of the people of Devon as seafarers at this period: only as the victims of seafarers. However, in the eleventh century Exeter, Totnes, Lydford, and Barnstaple all owed not only military but also naval duties to the Anglo-Saxon Crown. This presumably meant that, as with other parts of the country, they had to build, equip and man warships, or at least contribute money for them. There is no direct record of their vessels.[5]

No references to individual Devon ships have been found from the period before the thirteenth century, although it is clear that at least one Devon port, Dartmouth, was assuming some importance as a gathering place for overseas expeditions. Crusading fleets left Dartmouth in 1147 and 1190, and English royal expeditions set off from the port in 1205 and 1206. Ilfracombe also served as a mustering point in the early thirteenth century and, although no Devon ships are specifically mentioned as participating in these fleets, it is likely that some did. Also at this time, Exeter served as a base for two of the royal galleys.[6]

The Shipbuilding Industry

From the early thirteenth century onwards there are desultory references to shipbuilding activity in Devon, along with its ancillary trades. In 1205 a royal order was sent to Devon and other western counties to supply workmen to build and equip the king's ships. Twenty years later we find a mention of a ship of Romney being sent to Dartmouth to obtain timber and other necessaries for building royal ships. As Oppenheim suggested, these instances probably argue for the existence of an established local shipbuilding industry. Nevertheless, it should be remarked that medieval English governments often displayed a blithe ignorance of the maritime resources of their subjects.[7] The absence of any records of royal shipbuilding activity in Devon deprives us of the opportunity of studying how Devon shipwrights might have built large, sea-going vessels. The account for work on the Exeter barge in 1375–6 provides little information about the local industry or the vessel itself. However, it does not suggest that local work organisation or techniques were markedly different from those found elsewhere in England.[8]

There are later instances of the Crown impressing Devon shipwrights to work on the construction of royal vessels. Henry V had his massive 1,400-ton 'great ship' *Grace Dieu* built at Southampton between 1416 and about 1418. Although the origins of most of the shipwrights employed are not known, a document of the period lists 23 Devon men who were to be imprisoned for failing to obey the royal command to go to Southampton and work on the ship.[9]

Almost a century later, Henry VIII similarly brought men from different parts of the country to construct his ship *Henry Grace à Dieu* and three galleys at Woolwich. Conduct money was paid to a total of 252 named shipbuilding workers from places as far afield as Yorkshire and Cornwall, most of them probably shipwrights. Devon supplied 64, just over a quarter and more than any other single county. Twenty-three of these came from the Dartmouth area, whilst a further 17 came from Exeter and the Exe estuary. Plymouth contributed nine men, with six from Bideford, five from Otterton and others from smaller places. Three of the Exeter men were highly-specialised 'Topmakers', that is, they made topcastles for ships. The figures show that at least 11 Devon ports and coastal settlements were able to build ships (although it is unlikely that Plymouth's contribution reflected its true importance). The large proportion of Devon men in the draft suggests that the county's shipbuilding industry was recognised as having more than local importance (see also below, Chapter 14).[10]

If Devon shipbuilding is difficult to document, the evidence for its ancillary industries is even more fragmentary. The following examples offer no more than slight indications of the trades that once existed. In 1277 Plympton was receiving hemp from the great ropemaking centre at Bridport, and making it into rope. Unfortunately we do not know if the raw material was sent from Dorset because the industry there was unable to meet the demand for cordage, or if there was some other reason. It is not known if this was a regular practice or an isolated occurence: the 1277 reference arose from a dispute over payment. It is likely that most Devon ports of any size had at least one ropewalk. Four Dartmouth deeds dated from 1330 to 1389 mention a place in the town called 'le Ropetakele', suggesting the presence of a special location.

As in the early thirteenth century (see Chapter 7), later medieval Dartmouth seems to have been able to supply the Crown with ship's equipment. In 1396 two great masts with three anchors and some other items of ship's gear were supplied at Dartmouth for the King, and taken by sea to Greenwich. Over a century later, in 1516, Henry VIII's navy was supplied with masts from Dartmouth. Fourteen great masts were bound together with cordage to make a *raffe* (raft) and then towed by a ship from Dartmouth to the royal storehouse at Erith on the Thames. These references, and the fact that in about 1417 a Dartmouth ship was able to lade masts, may suggest the existence of a specialised mast-making industry in the port.[11]

The dearth of shipbuilding accounts for medieval Devon means that we cannot be certain of the sources for shipbuilding material. By analogy with other parts of the country, timber probably came from the region. Cordage was probably largely supplied by Bridport, but canvas was imported from France. Iron and iron nails were at times also imported, particularly from Spain.[12]

From the late fifteenth century onwards the English government tried to encourage private owners to construct vessels large enough to serve the Crown as warships. A bounty was paid on all ships of 100 tons burden or more, and Elizabethan records provide an indication of the output of the English shipbuilding industry for the first time in its history. Table 8.1 shows how the industries of Devon and London fared at this time. A modest demand for larger ships was created in the 1570s and 1580s by a growth in long-distance traffic to the Mediterranean and into Atlantic waters, and the privateering boom in the war against Spain from 1585 led to an unprecedented increase in the rate of construction. But London was still by far the largest shipbuilding centre in England, and was also the centre for privateering, so that it is not very surprising that the majority of these larger ships were built there. All other English regions, apart from the West Country, seem to have ceased building large ships in the years 1590–7. During this period, while Bristol built only five vessels of more than 100 tons, Devon produced nine, of which six came from the Exeter/Dartmouth area. Of the remainder, Barnstaple built two and Plymouth one. The Devon shipbuilding industry seems to have been relatively productive at the end of the Tudor period.

Table 8.1
Ship construction bounties paid, 1571–6 and 1580–97

Dates	National total		London total		Devon total	
	number	tons	number	tons	number	tons
1571–6	51	7,670+	17*	2,851	6	784
1580–94	46	10,493	25	5,363	8	1,980
1594–7	105	22,918	96	21,023	6	1,340

* including Leigh, in Essex

Sources: 1571–6, PRO, State Papers Domestic, Elizabeth, SP12/107/68; 1580–94, SP12/250/37; 1594–7, SP12/254/33 and SP12/262/126.

The Sizes of Devon Ships

The Bordeaux customs accounts show the maximum size of cargoes laded by ships in the port, and as such give a good idea of the sizes of ships used in the principal wine trade. The bulk cargoes and long distances were well suited to large ships, although, as Table 8.2 shows, many smaller vessels were also involved. Tables 8.2 and 8.3 have been compiled by means of identifying individual vessels in a selection of Bordeaux accounts. The danger of counting a vessel twice or more has been minimised by excluding all but one vessel from the same port with the same name and similar tunnages listed within the same account. The result is that these tables supply minimum numbers of vessels engaged. As some of the accounts do not cover whole years (e.g. the 1431 account covers only two months), the Tables are not intended to give a complete picture of the vessels involved in the Bordeaux trade, but rather to bring out changing trends in their sizes. The changes between the early fourteenth century and the early sixteenth century are very

Table 8.2
Tunnages of wine laded by Devon ships at Bordeaux, 1303/4–1520

Dates	200+	100–99	50–99	under 50	Total no.
1303/4–1307/8	–	30	47	27	104
1356/7	–	11	13	16	40
1409/10	–	2	25	18	45
1431	–	–	10	14	24
1435/6	–	6	12	14	32
1444/5	2	7	6	8	23
1494–1520	–	4	28	48	80

Sources: 1303/4–1307/8, PRO Exchequer, Accounts Various, E101/158/10, E101/160/3, E101/161/3, E101/162/1, E101/162/5; 1356/7, E101/173/4; 1409/10, E101/184/19; 1431, E101/191/3; 1435/6, E101/192/1; 1444/5, BL Add. MS 15524; 1494–1520, see note 15.

Table 8.3
English ships (excluding those from Devon) lading more than 100 tuns at Bordeaux, with Devon totals given underneath in brackets

Date	300+	200–99	100–99	Grand total
1356/7	–	–	26 (11)	37
1409/10	–	–	21 (2)	23
1431	–	3 (–)	20 (–)	23
1435/6	–	7 (–)	37 (6)	50
1444/5	1 (–)	5 (2)	27 (7)	42

Sources: see Table 8.2.

marked. In the years 1303/4 to 1307/8 just under 30 per cent of the Devon ships lading at Bordeaux could carry more than 100 tuns of wine. Two hundred years later, over a longer time-span and with the trade at a much lower level, we find that only 5 per cent of Devon ships at Bordeaux were able to do so. In the interim there had been an apparent decline in the numbers of larger ships, reaching something of a nadir in the early fifteenth century. This was counterbalanced by a trend, discernible in the 1431 account, towards building larger vessels. Ships of more than 200 tuns begin to appear, although Devon seems to have lagged behind other parts of the country. However, by the 1440s Devon was able to put forth vessels like the *Marie* of Dartmouth, which laded 236 tuns of wine at Bordeaux in 1444.

By the middle of the century Devon seems to have had some of the largest ships in the country. In 1449 and 1450, 69 of the total of 149 ships used in royal expeditions to Normandy and Gascony were of 100 tuns burden or more. Nineteen of these came from Devon, more than from any other county or major port. Dartmouth contributed thirteen of them, including the 400-ton *Trinitie*, one of only two vessels in the fleets to exceed 350 tons and perhaps one of the largest ships in England.[13] However, the English and European trend towards the construction of large vessels did not continue, and in the late fifteenth and early sixteenth centuries the larger ships were mostly supplanted by smaller vessels. A combination of economic and technical factors probably gave rise to this phenomenon, rather than any single overriding cause. A smaller ship is cheaper to build and run in absolute terms, but she is more expensive to operate per ton/mile and therefore less profitable. This development slightly post-dated the introduction of skeleton construction into northern Europe, and it is possible that the small size of the ships built was a reflection of shipwrights' difficulties in assimilating and applying the new constructional technique.[14] The Bordeaux records for the period 1494–1520 show that early Tudor Devon, like much of England and Europe, had for the time being largely abandoned the large sailing ship. It was the period described by Professor Bernard as 'the hey-day of the little coaster'.[15]

The great Elizabethan surveys of shipping (Table 8.4) show that there was some recovery by the third quarter of the sixteenth century. However, the figures quoted should be set against the overall evidence of the 1582 survey, which counted 1,634 ships in all. Vessels of more than 100 tons burden accounted for less than 11 per cent of these, and so were still comparatively rare. However, the decline in larger ships in Devon suggested by the 1582 survey is more apparent than real, for the survey unfortunately omitted the two largest ports, Dartmouth and Plymouth.

Table 8.4
Ships of more than 100 tons burden, 1560–82

Date	No. of Devon ships (and percentage of total)	Total no. for country
1560	18 (24%)	76
1577	15 (11.5%)	135
1582	7 (3.9%)	178

Sources: 1560, PRO, SP12/11/27; 1577, SP12/96/267 and SP12/111/30; 1582, SP12/156/45.

Despite the growing numbers and importance of ships of more than 100 tons burden in the later sixteenth century, it should not be forgotten that the vast majority of English ships were of small size. As noted above, the 1582 survey found that of the 1,634 vessels counted, 1,453 (89.1 per cent) were of less than 100 tons. The largest concentrations were in the Cinque Ports (210 vessels), Norfolk (152), Essex (147), Newcastle-upon-Tyne (121), and Devon (112, but excluding Plymouth and Dartmouth).[16] Thirty-seven of these last were based in seven north Devon ports and 75 in 16 south coast ports, the north apparently having proportionally slightly more vessels per port than the south. The inclusion of Plymouth's and Dartmouth's ships would, however, have tipped the balance decisively the other way.

The small ships of Elizabethan Devon were not merely coastal traders: they served as privateers, in royal fleets, and even regularly undertook transoceanic voyages. The ships from Barnstaple, Dartmouth, Exeter, and other western and southern ports which engaged in the Newfoundland trade between the 1580s and the early 1600s did not for the most part exceed 60 tons. In the case of Exeter ships their burden went as low as 40 tons.[17] At the end of the sixteenth century the Devon shipbuilding industry was evidently able to construct a wide range of sizes and types of vessels, suitable for work both in European waters and on the newer long-distance routes.

Ships and their Equipment

Details of the rig or equipment of Devon vessels in the Middle Ages or the sixteenth century are rare, but some examples are worth quoting. The balinger *Craccher*, which John Hawley of Dartmouth presented to Henry V in 1416, was a one-masted, square-rigged vessel of 56 tons burden, with approximately 48 oars. This vessel was typical of war balingers of the period, and was one of four bought from the Crown by Devon men in 1423. The *Craccher* returned to Dartmouth, with two others, and the fourth was sold to a Plymouth man.[18] A Devon merchantman of the time, the *Marie Welfare* of Dartmouth, was used to carry supplies for the King's ships. In about 1417 this ship carried some eight to ten large masts from London to Southampton inside her hull, which suggests that she was a fairly large vessel. The work of stowing and securing the masts in place required 23 pieces of timber with ironwork, and took at least three days.[19]

Over eighty years later, in 1502, we have evidence regarding another Devon ship. The *Marie Bricxam de Dartemue (sic)* was repaired at Bordeaux, and significantly the work was to include fitting 96 large *taules de carvelle* (carvel boards) to either side of the hull. The *Marie* was clearly skeleton-built.[20] Later still, we find another Devon ship typical of her time. This vessel, the *Heathe Henne (? Heathen)* of Topsham, was appraised for the High Court of Admiralty in 1586 or 1587. Her full value was estimated at just over £163, a high figure considering that her gear was incomplete and that she had evidently suffered some damage. The *Heathe Henne* was a three-masted square-rigger, and when fully rigged would have carried fore and main topmasts. This form of rig was very common in the late sixteenth century, and was found on many of the ships appraised between 1579 and 1590.[21]

More dramatic evidence of the equipment of Devon ships at this time is provided by the account of the fitting out of two Dartmouth ships to serve against the Spanish Armada in 1588. The *Crescent* (140 tons, 70 crew) and *Hart* (60 tons, 33 crew) of Dartmouth were financed by Dartmouth, Totnes and their surrounding villages. The account is mainly concerned with wages and the provision of victuals, weapons, and ammunition. Almost 18 cwt of gunpowder and 443 shot of various types (round, cross-bar, chain, and stone) were provided for the two ships, which were evidently armed with muzzle-loading minions (using four-pound shot) and falcons (two-and-a-half to three pounders) and the lighter breech-loading fowlers. The small arms supplied included 15 or more muskets, 42 calivers (light muskets), 64 pikes and nine swords. Items for the ships themselves comprised canvas (both for sails and for 'waist-cloths' to cover soldiers fighting from the waists of the ships), lanterns, platters, tankards, and items for their cook-rooms. Stocked with biscuit, beer, beef, pork, fish, butter and pease, these two vessels sailed off to join the fleet mustering at Plymouth.[22]

Ship Types

Many different ship-type names are encountered in the records of medieval and early modern Devon. The commonest are of course 'ship' and 'boat' in their Latin, Norman-French, and English forms, the former apparently denoting a large sailing vessel, and the latter a smaller craft, sometimes propelled by oars as well as sail. The problem is that one cannot always be sure if these names are being used to describe a specific vessel type or are merely generic descriptions. Another difficulty is that the same vessel might be described in two different ways. For example, in the Plymouth and Fowey customs accounts of 1437–9 a craft called the *Katerine* of Plymouth is once described as a barge and later twice, with the same master, as a balinger. In the same document a *Christofre* of Plymouth appears twice, with the same master, first as a scaff and later as a balinger.[23] It is not impossible that these were simply different ships, but the fundamental point remains: medieval and early modern descriptions of vessel types could be as fluid as those of later times.

Cogs, the archetypal bulk carriers of thirteenth and fourteenth-century Northern Europe, are encountered in medieval Devon. Eighteen of the 37 Devon ships in a royal fleet of 1345 (which comprised 148 vessels in total) have the word 'cog' as a prefix or suffix to their names. There were 23 other 'cog-named' ships in the fleet, from places as far afield as Tynemouth and Bayonne, although it is interesting that, of these, 13 were from Cornwall or Dorset. Perhaps this evidence indicates a concentration of cogs in the West Country, although we cannot be certain that the incorporation of the word 'cog' into a ship's name was not simply a fashion, and bore no relation to a vessel's type.[24]

On the other hand, there is massive archaeological and iconographic evidence of the evolution of the very clearly-defined cog type. She had an almost flat bottom, rockered fore, aft, and athwart-ships into a very shallow dish. The sides, joining the bottom of the sharp angle,were shell-constructed with the strakes laid clinker fashion. The stem and stern posts were straight and sloping. These constructional characteristics gave the cog a distinctive and instantly-recognisable appearance, to be seen in many north European town seals, in manuscript illustrations, and in graffiti. The most westerly iconographic evidence for the cog so far noted would appear to be its depiction in graffiti on a slate block found at Crane Godrevy, Gwithian, Cornwall (Fig. 8.2).[25] The presence of these casual graffiti in which cogs are carefully depicted would suggest that the use of the cog type in the far south west of Britain was common.[26]

In the earlier medieval period we encounter other ship-types. The prior of Plympton was granted a safe-conduct in 1234 for his ship called *Le Hulc* of St Mary to go overseas to lade wine, salt and other merchandise. 'Hulc' or 'hulk' was not an uncommon type-name in thirteenth-century England, and may in this case have denoted a double-ended hulk of the sort depicted on the New Shoreham seal of this period (see also above, fig. 7.4b, p. 69). It appears to have been associated with a distinct type of vessel construction for the existence of which there is massive iconographic evidence, but as yet no supporting archaeological data. She appears to have been curved both longitudinally and transversely, probably with a long, narrow flat keel curved up at the ends and usually without stem or stern posts. Most of the contemporary depictions of the hulc suggest clinker-laid planking running in a uniform curve parallel to the sheerline and ending in a horizontal line at the ends, or at one of the ends of the vessel, well above the water line.

8.2 Crane Godrevy, Gwithian, Cornwall. Late-medieval graffiti of cog-type vessels. *(Professor Charles Thomas)*

8.3 St Peter's Church, Tiverton. Oared and armed vessel among ships carved on the outer walls of the Greenway Chapel, *c*1517. Photographed earlier this century before deterioration and recent restoration. *(Devon Library Services, WCSL)*

The hulc type of construction seems to have become a predominant style in the fourteenth century, and its use in Devon is perhaps suggested by the fact that an early seal of Sutton (the later Plymouth), attached to a deed of 1368, shows a vessel with some of the characteristics associated with the hulc.[28]

It is possible to get a rough idea of the relative sizes and functions of different kinds of ship. Valuable work was undertaken in this area by Dorothy Burwash, although a great deal remains to be done.[29] From a study of the customs accounts and other sources of the period 1400–1513, she discovered that the small 'balinger', known to modern scholars as an oared fighting craft, was also extensively used for carrying cargo. She found that merchant balingers were most commonly found in Barnstaple, Ilfracombe, Exeter, and particularly Dartmouth. It is not known if the merchant balinger was an oared vessel: given the space requirement for cargo, this seems unlikely, but see Fig. 8.3. It is at least an example of a late medieval type used in England especially by Devon ports, although it was also used in Brittany and northern Spain, where it may have originated. Other small types of vessel, common in, although not exclusive to, late medieval Devon ports, were merchant barges and spinaces. Little is known of these craft, but the barges were usually slightly larger than balingers, ranging between 40 and 140 tuns burden, and spinaces were small, generally of less than 50 tons.[30] Crayers, small merchantmen of indeterminate type, were noted by Burwash as being more prominent in the Plymouth and Fowey customs accounts than elsewhere in the early fifteenth century. Nevertheless, even at this stage they were by no means confined to the west country. Out of 50 English crayers released from royal service in Normandy in 1417, only four came from Devon, and 39 of the other crayers came from Kent or the East Coast.[31]

The ship-type which spread skeleton construction around Northern Europe in the fifteenth century was the carvel, a development from the lateen-rigged Portuguese caravel (although northern carvels seem to have been square-rigged). Portuguese caravels are first found trading to England

8.4 St Peter's Church, Tiverton. Hulc-type ship on the outside of the Chapel of John Greenway (ob.1529), merchant and ship owner, *c*1517. *(Devon Library Services, WCSL)*

8.5 St Peter's Church, Tiverton. Four-masted ship and some of her crew carved on the outside of the Greenway Chapel, *c*1517. *(Devon Library Services, WCSL)*

in 1448, suffering capture by pirates off the Isle of Wight. In 1450 we have the first definite reference to an English-owned carvel, but there is also the intriguing possibility that a carvel was owned in Fowey between 1443 and 1450.[32] The arrival of a carvel of San Sebastian at Exeter in 1457 seems to be the first recorded instance of such a vessel touching at a Devon port. The Plymouth and Fowey customs accounts of 1461/2 record the movements of some ten or 13 carvels: some vessels of the same name and port are listed, but with different masters. Most were from Brittany or south-western France, but two or three belonged to Fowey, and one was a Devon ship, the *Jesus* of Stonehouse near Plymouth.[33] This vessel, with its six-ton cargo, was recorded arriving at Plymouth on 14 December 1461: it is perhaps the earliest-known Devon carvel. Twenty years later the Exeter and Dartmouth customs particulars note the movements of at least 15 Devon carvels: the manuscript has many lacunae, making it impossible to read all the entries. Ten or eleven of these belonged to Dartmouth, but there were also one or two of Barnstaple, one of Salcombe, one of Kingsbridge and one of Bideford.[34] It is apparent that the skeleton-built ship was established on both the south and north coasts of Devon by the 1480s.

Devon Shipping in the National Context

It is not easy to assess how important Devon shipping was, compared with other parts of the country, in the Middle Ages and sixteenth century. The participation of Devon ships in royal expeditions provides a crude index, although the extent to which a county's shipping might be involved naturally varied according to certain factors. These might include its proximity to the place of muster, or its ability to gain exemption. Nevertheless, the data in Table 8.5 provide some interesting information on the relative size of Devon's shipping fleet. Although the figures are from often widely separated dates, they do indicate that Devon shipping remained of considerable national importance between the fourteenth and sixteenth centuries. The apparent decline in the 1580s is accounted for by the omission of Dartmouth and Plymouth from the 1582 survey, and by the fact that the home ports of only about half of the ships in the English fleet in 1588 were recorded.

Table 8.5
Devon shipping listed in royal fleets or surveys, 1345–1588.

Date	Total no. of ships (excl. foreign)	No. of Devon ships (with percentage of total)
1345	143	37 (25.9%)
1346	690	97 (14.1%)
1417	118	13 (11.0%)
1449	88	18 (20.5%)
1450	61	16 (26.2%)
1560*	76	18 (23.7%)
1577*	791	104 (13.1%)
1582*	1634	119 (7.4%)^
1588	226	18+ (8.0%)~

* survey
^ excludes Plymouth and Dartmouth
~ total number of Devon ships not known

Sources: 1345, Hewitt, *Organisation of War*; 1346, Oppenheim, *Maritime History*, 14 and Watkin, *Dartmouth*, 359 (figures for this fleet are variable, and only provide an approximate guide to the total numbers of ships involved); 1417, Hardy, *Norman Rolls*, 325–9; 1449 and 1450, PRO E364/92, A m.1v–B m.2r, N m.1r–O m.1r; 1560, 1577 and 1582, see Table 4; 1588, JK Laughton, *The Defeat of the Spanish Armada*, II, 66, 181, 201, 257, 260, 287, 324–31.

Conclusion

From the later Middle Ages to the end of the sixteenth century the construction, rig, and equipment of Devon shipping seem to have been much like those found in other parts of England and northern Europe. This should occasion no great surprise, for the very mobility of ships means that technical innovation can be transmitted very rapidly. Devon also seems to have followed trends in the changing sizes of ships, as in the rise and decline of the large ship in the fifteenth century. The evidence is patchy and incomplete, but it does suggest that the shipbuilding and shipping industries of Devon of this time were well able to meet the challenges set by changing technology and the vagaries of international trade.

Within Devon itself over this period, it was almost always Dartmouth and Plymouth that were the leading ports, followed by the ports of the Exe estuary (sometimes loosely recorded as Exeter, Exmouth or Topsham) and Barnstaple. Individually, none of these ports attained the significance of places such as London, Bristol (but see below, chapter 11) or Newcastle-upon-Tyne, but together with the other ports of their county they ensured that Devon remained one of England's most important maritime regions.

8: Devon Shipping from the Middle Ages to c1600

1 This graffito and two others are discussed in A Emery, *Dartington Hall* (Oxford, 1970), 208–10 and n.10. The author would like to record his thanks to Dr Wendy Childs and Profesor Joyce Youings for their help and advice in the preparation of this paper.
2 DRO, Miscellaneous Rolls, G2/MR6, m.17r.
3 See general discussions of developments in construction and rig in B Greenhill, *Archaeology of the Boat* (1976); RW Unger, *The Ship in the Medieval Economy 600–1600* (London and Toronto, 1980); A McGowan, *Tiller and Whipstaff: the development of the sailing ship 1400–1700* (1981).
4 M Redknap, *The Cattewater Wreck: the investigation of an armed vessel of the early sixteenth century* (British Archaeological Reports, British Series 131, Oxford, 1984), 83–8, 95, 103.
5 GN Garmonsway, ed., *The Anglo-Saxon Chronicle* (1975), 74–7, 98–9, 124, 131–5, 203; HC Darby and RW Finn, eds, *The Domesday Geography of South-West England* (Cambridge, 1967), 274; M Oppenheim, *The Maritime History of Devon* (Exeter, 1968), 4; CW Hollister, *Anglo-Saxon Military Institutions on the Eve of the Norman Conquest* (Oxford, 1962), 103–26.
6 Oppenheim, *Maritime History*, 4–5; WL Warren, *King John* (1966), 128–9, 132–4; FW Brooks, *The English Naval Forces 1199–1272* (1933), 138–9.
7 Oppenheim, *Maritime History*, 5–6.
8 See note 2 above.
9 WJ Carpenter-Turner, 'The building of the *Gracedieu, Valentine* and *Falconer* at Southampton, 1416–1520', *MM*, 40 (1954), 65.
10 PRO, Exchequer, E36/5, ff.179r–188r.
11 JB Rowe, *A History of the Borough of Plympton Erle* (Exeter, 1906), 385; HR Watkin, *Dartmouth; Vol.I Pre-Reformation* (Devonshire Association: Parochial Histories of Devonshire, no. 5, 1935), 31, 46, 55, 71; PRO, E122/40/21 and E36/11, f.10r.
12 WR Childs, *Anglo-Castilian Trade in the Later Middle Ages* (Manchester, 1978), 115; see also above pp.
13 PRO, Exchequer, Lord Treasurer's Remembrancer, Foreign Accounts, E364/92, A 1v–2v and N 1r–2v.
14 GV Scammell, 'English merchant shipping at the end of the Middle Ages: some East Coast evidence', *EcHR* 2nd series, XIII (1961), 332–4; I Friel, 'The three-masted ship and Atlantic voyages', in J Youings, ed., *Raleigh in Exeter 1985: Privateering and Colonisation in the reign of Elizabeth I* (Exeter, 1985), 31.
15 J Bernard, *Navires at Gens de Mer à Bordeaux (vers 1400 – vers 1550)* (Paris, 1968), I, 310–7 and III, *Appendices: Mouvement de la navigation à Bordeux de 1445 a 1520, d'apres les archives notariales*, passim.
16 PRO, SP12/156/45, but see also below, chapters 11 and 12.
17 GT Cell, *English Enterprise in Newfoundland, 1577–1660* (Toronto and Buffalo, 1969), Table I.
18 PRO, E364 K m.1v; S Rose, ed., *The Navy of the Lancastrian Kings: Accounts and Inventories of William Soper, Keeper of the King's Ships, 1422–1427* (NRS, 1982), 66–7, 250.
19 Rose, *The Navy of the Lancastrian Kings*, 212–3.
20 Bernard, *Navires et Gens de Mer*, II, 841–2.
21 PRO, High Court of Admiralty, HCA 24/54, f.59r and HCA 24/50–57, passim.
22 E Windeatt, 'The fitting out of two vessels against the Spanish Armada at Dartmouth in 1588', *DAT*, 12, 1880, 312–21; JK Laughton (ed.), *State Papers relating to the Defeat of the Spanish Armada*, 2 vols, NRS i and ii (1894), ii, 329.
23 PRO, Exchequer, Kings Remembrancer, Customs Accounts, E122/113/55, mm.3r, 7v and 9r.
24 Unger, *The Ship in the Medieval Economy*, 136–54, 168–71; HJ Hewitt, *The Organisation of War under Edward III, 1338–62* (Manchester, 1966), 182–6.
25 Ex-inf. Professor Charles Thomas and Dr Basil Greenhill.
26 B Greenhill, *The Evolution of the Wooden Ship* (1988), 52–9.
27 *CPR 1232–47*, 66; H Ewe, *Schiffe auf Siegeln* (Berlin, 1972), 165.
28 RN Worth, *History of Plymouth* (Plymouth, 1890), 195.
29 D Burwash, *English Merchant Shipping 1460–1540* (Newton Abbott, 1969), 101–44, 186–200.
30 Burwash, *English Merchant Shipping*, 103–8, 115–6, 124–5.
31 Burwash, *English Merchant Shipping*, 121–3; TD Hardy, ed., *Norman Rolls; 1200–1205; 1417–1418* (1835), 325–9.
32 I Friel, 'England and the advent of the three-masted ship', *International Congress of Maritime Museums: 4th Conference Proceedings 1981* (Paris, 1983), 130–8; DM Gardiner, ed., *A Calendar of Early Chancery Proceedings relating to West Country Shipping 1388–1493* (DCRS, 1976), 67.
33 PRO, E122/114/1. mm 1r–8r, passim.
34 PRO, E122/41/6, mm 1v, 2r, 5r, 6v, 7r, 7v, 9r.

9 *Devon's Overseas Trade in the Late Middle Ages*

Wendy R Childs

The expansion of Devon's trade in the later fourteenth century was recognised at Westminster and prompted the reorganisation of the customs system in the South West. From the beginning of the fifteenth century, instead of appointing collectors to cope with the whole of Dorset, Devon, Cornwall, and parts of Somerset, as it had done in the fourteenth century, the government made Exeter and Dartmouth customs headports with jurisdiction over both north and south Devon coasts except for Plymouth, which itself was made the headport responsible for all Cornwall.

The different patterns of activity at Exeter, Dartmouth, Plymouth, and Barnstaple, established in the fourteenth century, continued into the fifteenth. Plymouth and Dartmouth were the busiest Devon ports in terms of international shipping movements as Table 9.4 (below, p. 86) shows, while Plymouth and Exeter were busiest in terms of the value of the cargoes handled by the ports. Exeter remained the greater consumer and industrial centre, but, as a river port, was less engaged in direct overseas voyages until the boom in the cloth industry at the end of the fifteenth century. Plymouth and Dartmouth continued to provide much of the greater shipping on the longer-distance routes, and these ports continued to be the main stopover for foreign and English vessels crossing the Channel in both directions. They remained intermittently naval mustering centres, and Plymouth was the official embarkation port for pilgrims to Corunna. Barnstaple, away from the busy Channel route, was always less busy and continued to reflect Bristol's trading pattern rather than that of the south Devon ports.

The Devon ports, with some ups and downs, flourished in a modest way for much of the century, generally handling more trade than neighbouring Dorset and Cornish ports, but still not coming near the trade levels of the great provincial ports such as Bristol, Southampton, and Hull. However, at the end of the century, with a trade boom especially at Exeter and with the east coast and Bristol in difficulties, the Devon ports for a short time became more important, rivalling and even surpassing Bristol and Hull, although remaining behind Southampton.[1]

Commodities

Exports

Devon had never played a major part in England's great wool trade, partly because of its distance from the main markets in Flanders, but mainly because of the poor quality of local wool. This had not even appeared on the government price-fixing lists of 1337 and 1454, and in 1343 had come right at the bottom with Cornish wool.[2] Nonetheless at times of great demand some had been exported, but even in the busiest year, 1357/8, this came to only 348 sacks, a mere one per cent of England's total trade. In the fifteenth century wool exports faded away entirely.[3]

Cloth, on the other hand, went from strength to strength. Devon had exported cloth at least from the early fourteenth century and, with local wool exports so meagre, the cloth exports must even then have been important locally. Russets, Mendips, and *grisancos* worth £120 exported from Exeter alone in 1323/4 had clearly been more valuable than exports of tin worth £61, and rivalled exports of less than 60 sacks of wool, worth about £200, for the whole coast from Weymouth to Plymouth.[4] In the second half of the fourteenth century cloth exports had risen in Devon as in the rest of England, and in the 1360s averaged just under 1,000 broadcloths or their equivalent a year. Expansion had not continued at this pace, but the fall to an average of some 300 broadcloths a year in the 1390s, recorded in the customs accounts, exaggerates the decline. Devon 'straits' were not included in this figure at this time, but when allowance is made for them, in 1398/9 for instance, exports were still running at the equivalent of 1,000 broadcloths a year.[5] In the fifteenth century exports rose again, especially after the 1420s with the greater stability in Anglo-French relations, and in 1447/8 Exeter, Dartmouth, Barnstaple, and Plymouth together handled some 4,500 cloths a year, 8 per cent of England's total exports. With the loss of Gascony and the trade crisis of the 1450s, cloth exports crashed to one third of their previous level, and Devon handled only 3 per cent of England's total cloth exports. Dramatic recovery came at the end of the fifteenth century, and in 1499/1500 exports at the four ports reached the unprecedented level of 8,000 cloths, well over 10 per cent of England's exports, and about double the level of exports at Bristol. This expansion was centred on Exeter. Plymouth, whose exports had faded especially fast in the 1450s, was thoroughly outpaced; whereas in the 1430s Plymouth had handled one third or more of southwestern cloth, now it exported one sixth.[6] Exeter's exports came from the expansion of her own industry and from the production of small country towns such as Tiverton and Cullompton, which also came to provide some of the richest merchants in Devon. These were joined, too, by Somerset merchants from Taunton, who transferred their trade from Bridgwater and Bristol to the better facilities at Exeter now that the Channel was safer than it had been during the Hundred Years War.[7]

Devon always exported some broadcloths, nominally two yards wide and twenty-four yards long, which were England's best-known export and on which the government lavished much quality legislation, but its main exports were a variety of lighter cloths like the russets and *grisancos* of 1323/4, the 'backes' sent to Spain in 1363,[8] and the straits, kerseys, and frieze cloth mentioned throughout the late fourteenth and fifteenth centuries. Strait cloths had formed between 73 and 83 per cent of exports in the 1390s, and this rose to over 90 per cent by the end of the fifteenth century.[9] Straits were narrow cloths one yard wide, and were often sold in lengths of 12 yards, or 'dozens'. Appraisals of Devon straits confiscated from smugglers in 1475 showed that in practice the cloths were woven to lengths between 9½ and 13 yards, and to widths between 27 and 32½ inches. Prices then varied between 3s 2d and 4s 4d a 'dozen' and clearly depended on quality and style, not simply on length.[10] Some local cloths were distinctive enough to carry their names with them: rolls of Exeter cloth were exported from Bristol in 1404; white (undyed) 'Barnstaples' were exported through Bridgwater between 1470 and 1483; and 'Tavistocks' were sold in Huelva in Southern Spain between 1480 and 1483.[11] English cloths were dyed many shades of red, pink, light and dark blues, turquoise, violet, light and dark greens, as well as the more sombre hues of brown, grey and black; they were also woven in stripes and medleys. Devon dyers certainly provided some of these shades, as imports of woad and madder testify to an active dyeing industry. Purchases for the Navarrese royal family included red and black as well as white cloth from Exeter.[12] The exact proportion of coloured (dyed) to white cloth is unclear, but possibly changed over time. Customs collectors' descriptions of strait cloths suggest that russets formed the majority of Devon exports in the early fifteenth century but steadily dropped thereafter; that coloured straits dropped after 1460 from between a quarter and a half of all exports to under a tenth, but grew again at Exeter at the end of the century; and that whites increased from under a tenth to between a third and a half of all exports. This change was reflected in the stagnation of dye imports in the fifteenth century.[13]

Tin was a Devon product much valued abroad, but Devon's early dominance in production gave way to that of Cornwall in the later middle ages. The main early markets for tin had been Flanders and France, through which much passed to the Mediterranean, but in the fourteenth century the French markets faded owing to the Hundred Years War, and also to the increasing Italian sea trade with England. Exports were also complicated by the lack of a free market, necessitating the obtaining of licences, and by the creation of the Staple at Calais. The main markets moved eastwards and most exports were sent through Southampton and London.[14] Few direct overseas exports are recorded from Devon, but Devon ships continued to transport tin to Southampton and London. Edward IV's greater liberality with export licences for English merchants returned 70 per cent of the legitimate export trade to Devon and Cornwall after 1495. Despite the greater Cornish tin production, about two thirds of this southwestern trade went through Devon ports: in the 1490s Exeter and Dartmouth together exported 200 to 300 thousandweights a year, worth £2,000 to £3,000, while Plymouth exported only 20 to 25 thousandweights. Fowey and the rest of Cornwall exported 143 to 163 hundredweights.[15] Tin was especially valued for making fine pewter, but most exports from Devon were in blocks or slabs of raw tin (see also below, p. 101).[16]

Devon also regularly exported hides, both tanned and untanned, sometimes from Cornwall, and sometimes dressed as shoe leather. Wheat, rye, beans, and peas were exported irregularly, according to harvests and in small quantities. Occasionally cheese or a horse was exported.

Fish was more important. Fishing must have been a major activity of local seamen, but beyond casual references to the dangers of war and seizure of fishing boats by enemy ships,[17] little evidence survives for the organisation and size of fleets. The fish trade, which was international, is better documented. Fish exports, mainly of hake, were always most important to Plymouth. In 1398/9, for instance, exports of 29½ tons of hake worth over £70 had formed 13 per cent of the value of Plymouth's total exports, while exports worth £11 had formed only 8 per cent of Dartmouth's trade, and exports had been negligible at Exeter and Barnstaple. A century later, in 1492/3, when the cloth trade was booming in east Devon, Dartmouth's much greater exports of hake, herring, rays, and pilchards worth £131 comprised only 3 per cent of the value of her total exports, while in 1498/9 at Plymouth, where the cloth trade was less vigorous, exports of hake worth £122 still represented 9 per cent of her trade.[18] The fish trade stimulated a small salt export trade. Boats of Stonehouse and Plymouth, and also of Kenton and Dittisham, regularly exported small amounts of up to six quarters of salt to Ireland and returned with fish (see also below, p. 102).[19] The fish exports from Devon probably included some of these Irish supplies, together with the fish caught and salted locally.

Imports

Imports were more varied: wine, foods of various kinds, and industrial raw materials always came, and increasing amounts of manufactured goods arrived as prosperity increased in the late fifteenth century. Imports came not only directly from abroad but also on coasting vessels, especially from Southampton and London.

Wine was the greatest import in bulk and value until the development of the linen trade in the late fifteenth century. Gascon wines and those of the upper Dordogne and Garonne predominated from the twelfth century, when England acquired Aquitaine, but wines from La Rochelle, Poitou, Biscay, Portugal and Adalusia were available in smaller quantities. No German wines and few Mediterranean sweet wines were directly imported. Imports of wine to Devon and Cornish ports together averaged about 640 tuns a year at the beginning of the fifteenth century and rose to over 1,200 tuns by mid-century, then accounting for between 10 and 14 per cent of all England's imports, but well behind the imports of Bristol, Southampton and Hull. The loss of Gascony in 1453 caused considerable short-term disruption to the wine trade, but the English market was too important for the French to ignore, and trade continued under licence. By the 1490s imports to Devon and Cornwall had recovered to 1,200 tuns again, and now, with the decline of the wine trade on the English east coast, this accounted for 18 per cent of England's total imports.[20] The loss of Gascony and then peace with France probably encouraged a search for other wines: in 1474/5 at least 150 tuns of La Rochelle wine, 60 tuns of Nantes, 78 tuns of Spanish, and 40 tuns of sweet wine were imported to Devon; and 240 of the 542 tuns imported at Exeter and Dartmouth in 1492/3 came on Spanish and Portuguese ships, but the most important source remained Bordeaux, where Spanish ships also picked up some of their cargoes.[21]

Imported food ranged from the mundane to the exotic. Corn had been imported in times of shortage in the fourteenth century, with peaks in 1323/4 and 1398/9,[22] but by the fifteenth century was more usually exported. Onions and garlic were steady imports, although not in such great quantities as on the east coast. Salt was steadily imported from the mid-fourteenth century, when the Bay of Bourgneuf became a major English supplier. Imports had been greatest at Dartmouth and Exeter, but Plymouth's imports increased in the later fifteenth century, reflecting her greater interest in the fish trade, and in 1498/9 reached 489 tons worth £161.[23] Fish imports, mainly from Ireland but also from the Channel Islands and Brittany, included herring, salmon, flatfish, hake, and congers. Figs, raisins, almonds, olive oil, and honey came from Iberia, and food became more exciting at the end of the fifteenth century with the arrival of fresh oranges, Madeira sugar, and Portuguese marmalade.[24] Sugar made suitable gifts, and Plymouth sent sugar loaves to Sir John Sapcote in 1491/2 and to Lord Broke in 1499/1500.[25]

More important for industrial prosperity were imports of raw materials, predominantly iron and dyes, but also cork from Portugal, pitch and rosin from Biscay and Gascony, wax from Iberia, and beech timber and glass from Normandy. England was a heavy importer of iron from Biscay, which was recognised as having 'mooste plentye of Iren of ony contrey of the worlde'.[26] The deposits were of the particularly malleable type most suitable for shipbuilding, architectural building, and decorative work. Devon's imports in 1383/4 had, exceptionally, reached over 400 tons, mostly through Dartmouth,[27] a level not reached again until the very end of the middle ages. After the mid-fifteenth-century slump, imports rose again to over 200 tons a year at Exeter, Dartmouth, and Barnstaple together, and Plymouth trade, although generally lower, reached 192 tons in 1497/8. This fifteenth-century rise was part of a marked increase in English iron imports in the southern and western ports with their access to Biscay, and is in considerable contrast to the stagnation in the eastern ports.[28] The imports seem high for local consumption, and some iron was undoubtedly sent on by coastal vessels.

Imported dyes included weld, orchel, litmus, and kermes, but the two most important were woad and madder. England's main woad supplier in the thirteenth century had been Picardy, to be replaced by Lombardy in the fourteenth and by Toulouse in the fifteenth centuries. The Devon cloth industry seems to have demanded as much woad in the early fourteenth century as it did in the later fifteenth. Direct imports to Exeter by aliens in 1323/4 had been worth at least £375. The volume of these direct imports is not given, but the total imports that year, including the coastal trade, came to 141 tons. It reached 196 tons in 1326/7.[29] In the later fourteenth century total imports including coastal trade were rarely over 50 tons, and in the fifteenth century they slackened further despite the modest cloth boom of the 1440s.[30] When they rose again at the end of the century, allowing for price inflation, they cannot have surpassed the level of the early fourteenth century: direct imports reached about 34 tons, valued at £340, in 1492/3 and total imports were still not much above 50 tons.[31] The stagnation may reflect a move towards the export of white cloth mentioned above, or a change in the shades used locally, as imports of madder for red and brown shades increased from the later fourteenth century. Direct imports of 20 to 30 bales of madder, worth £20 or £30, were low, but the main producers were in the Low Countries; these sent supplies to Southampton and London, whence it was sent on to Devon by coastal vessel. However, here too there was no increase: total imports reached 120 bales in 1423/4 and were still only 114 bales in 1492/3.[32] Mordants to fix the dyes appeared only in the coastal trade, and potash gave way to alum in the fourteenth century as the Genoese bulk trade in Mediterranean alum became fully established at Southampton. Cards, teasels, and smigmate soap were also imported for the cloth industry.

The most important manufactured goods were canvas and linen, mainly from Brittany and often brought on Channel Island ships. These included coarse canvas of Oleron and Pouldavid for sails or packing wool and cloth, and fine linens for sheets, napkins, and personal dress. Imports had been low in the fourteenth century, fluctuating from a value of £180 in Exeter and Dartmouth alone in 1383/4 to only £40 in all of Devon in 1398/9. Imports rose a little in the fifteenth century, then soared after 1480: at Exeter and Dartmouth in 1492/3 they reached a value of £3,955, representing some 400,000 ells, and in only six months in 1494 they reached £2,265. This now surpassed the value of wine imported to Exeter and Dartmouth and outstripped the imports of linens at Bristol and Southampton; only Poole and Lyme rivalled Devon in this trade. Devon and Dorset themselves did not have such great needs for sails, packing, or fine linen, and were playing a strong distributive role in this trade. Exeter merchants regularly sent linen overland to London.[33]

The import of small manufactured goods by Devon was tiny compared with that at Southampton. Devon was further from the northern European manufacturing centres and had a limited consumer market, and it was clearly not worthwhile for merchants to import large quantities directly, although some were brought by coastal vessels. From 1480 prosperity increased demand: ships of Dartmouth, Topsham, and Brixham brought typical Low Country cargoes of pottery, hats, laces, paper, cauldrons, pans, kettles, brushes, candlesticks, basins, featherbed ticks, and painted cloths, alongside madder and hops, while a few ships of Rouen brought the fruits of Norman and Paris industries – diaper cloth, camlet, more hats and paper, glass, bottles, trenchers, cups, tables, fine canvas, points, curtains, tablecloths, buckets, bellows, and daggers. Luxury cloths and furs rarely came by sea, but in January 1493 an exceptional ship of Bilbao probably caused a sensation at Dartmouth when it unloaded silk worth £572 and two parrots worth 13s 4d.[34]

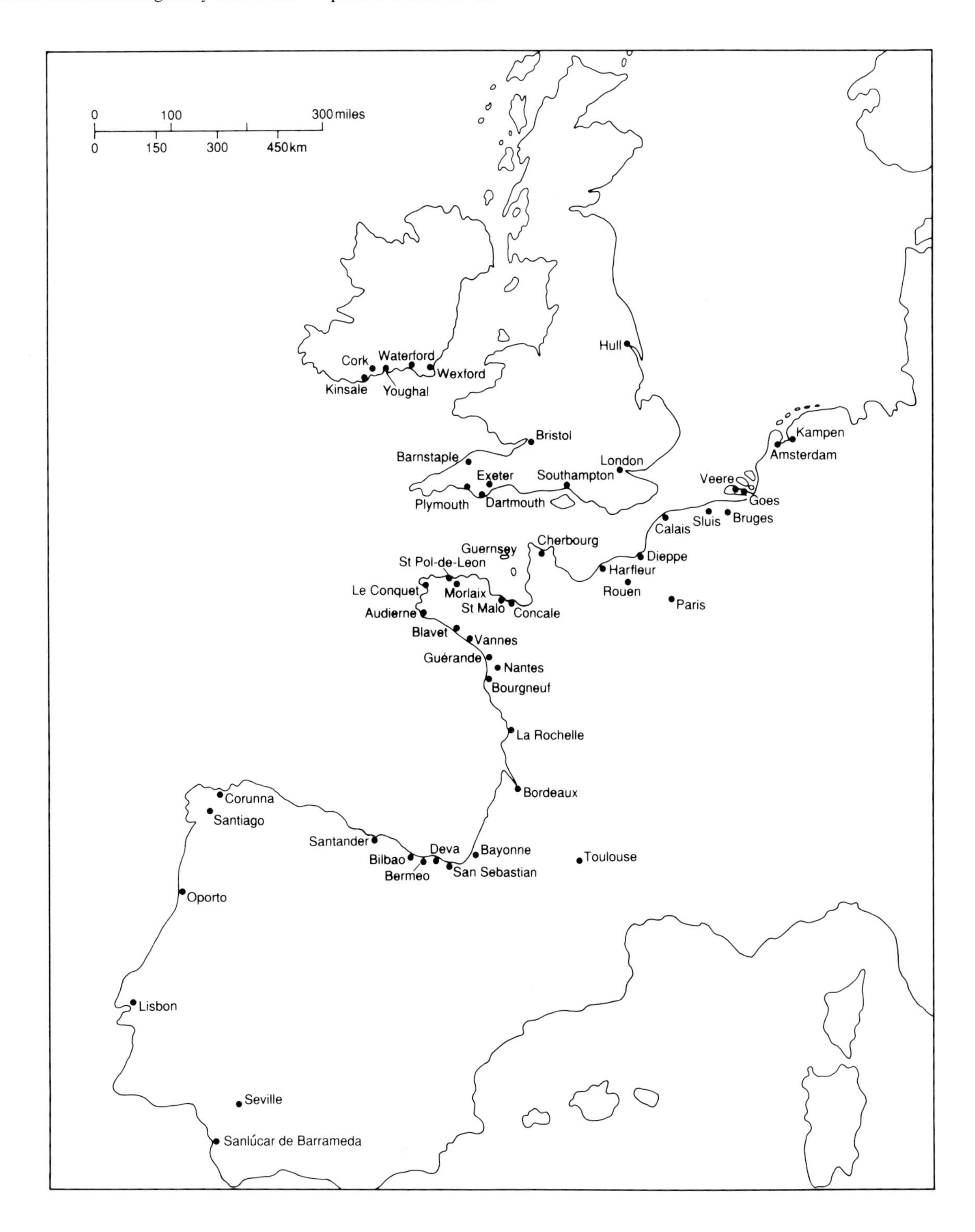

Map 9.1 Medieval England's European Trading Neighbours

Table 9.1
Devon ships at Bordeaux, 1303–1449

Date	Total no. of ships	No. of Devon ships	Devon % of all shipping	Total wine loaded (in tuns)	Wine loaded by Devon ships	Devon % of all wine
1303/4	905	62	7	55,393	4892	9
1304/5	1020	48	5	86,233	3648	4
1306/7	613	62	10	68,222	5362	8
1307/8	608	53	9	66,510	4772	7
1308/9	736	78	11	82,001	7311	9
1310/11	503	50	10	51,351	4388	9
1355/6	153	27	18	14,435	2435	17
1356/7	254	59	23	26,134	4234	16
1357/8*	220	37	17	18,161	3204	18
1359/60*	146	19	13	14,772	1650	11
1360/1	363	43	12	28,781	4179	15
1372/3	164	30	18	14,373	2068	14
1377/8	138	35	25	12,456	2537	20
1378/9	184	57	31	13,622	3664	27
1385/6	194	46	24	18,025	3523	19
1402/3	223	45	20	8,679	1760	20
1409/10	213	56	26	13,516	3199	24
1412/13	180	51	28	12,328	2981	24
1416/17	218	46	21	13,684	2683	20
1431/2	129	26	20	8,626	1212	14
1435/6	146	33	23	12,869	1997	16
1443/4	85	17	20	8,827	1599	18
1444/5	136	23	17	12,856	2117	16
1448/9	162	31	19	16,566	2655	16

* incomplete years

Source: PRO E101/158/10, 160/3, 161/3, 162/1,5,6, 163/1,4 173/4, 182/2, 179/10, 182/5,6, 183/11, 185/11, 184/19, 185/7,9, 188/12, 191/3, 192/1, 194/3, 195/19; BL Add MS 15,524. The figures used here are those for the main ladings at Bordeaux only, as the particular accounts for the minor ladings at outports do not regularly survive.

The Directions of Trade

Overseas Markets

Devon's exports were suitable for a range of markets, and her desire for imported goods led to contacts with much of western Europe, but inevitably her busiest connections were with her nearest western neighbours: France, Iberia, and Ireland. The French trade pattern was extremely complex because of the political structure and the intermittent Anglo-French wars. To the south-west Gascony was freely accessible between 1156 and 1453, while it was in English hands. Its hinterland was diminished during much of the Hundred Years War, but it still provided much wine, some honey, rosin, and iron, and (after the war) woad from Toulouse. Although a few ships of Bordeaux and Bayonne brought wine to Devon,[35] the bulk of Devon's Gascon trade was in Devon hands. Her ships had been deeply involved in the carrying trade from Bordeaux from an early date, as Table 9.1 shows. Although their cargoes had been modest, given Bordeaux's total level of exports in the early fourteenth century, Devon ships became more important during the Hundred Years War when many foreign ships withdrew, leaving almost all the trade to English shipping. Devon ships were also frequently employed in Bristol's Bordeaux trade.[36] As mentioned above, although the trade was temporarily disrupted with England's loss of Gascony in 1453, it was soon resumed under licence and then, like all French trade, stabilised by the Anglo-French treaty of 1475.

Further north, the coast around La Rochelle was firmly in French hands during the war and trade was necessarily intermittent and dependent on truces. Further north still, trade with Brittany was at first easier, because Anglo-Breton relations had always been close and England encouraged the Dukes in their independence from France. However, relations worsened in the fifteenth century when the dynasty changed. Bretons were involved in raids on Plymouth and Dartmouth in 1404 and 1405, and irritation increased when peacefully trading Bretons were arrested as Frenchmen.[37] Breton goods were always attractive – canvas, linen, salt, wine which came through Nantes, and some Iberian re-exports, since Breton ports were regular landfalls between the Atlantic and Flanders and became minor entrepots for such goods.[38]

To the east, Normandy, which England had lost in 1204, was also enemy territory, but was more freely accessible again when temporarily in English hands following Henry V's success in France. After the treaty of 1475 trade again increased. Most Norman activity was through Chichester, but Devon's tin and its increasing ability to absorb consumer goods from Rouen and Paris attracted some Norman traders to Devon in ships of Dieppe and Harfleur, but especially of Rouen.[39]

The Channel Islands, which remained in English hands after the loss of Normandy, were always open to Devon trade. They themselves acted as a conduit for North French trade. In the fourteenth century Channel Island activity had been frequent in all southern ports from Plymouth to Chichester, and cargoes had been mixed ones of linen, fish, and conger eels, but in the fifteenth century the pattern changed. Now Channel Island shipping concentrated in Dartmouth, Exeter and Poole, and Guernsey ships, which had become specialist carriers of Breton linen and canvas, predominated.[40]

Westwards, Iberian trade offered tremendous potential. The northern coast supplied iron, wine, rosin, beaver skins, and licorice, and Corunna attracted the pilgrim traffic for Santiago; in the south the *Reconquista* had opened up Portugal and Andalusia with their olive oil, figs, raisins, oranges, sweeter wines, soap, and dyes. Political relations had become close from 1251, when the future Edward I married Eleanor of Castile, and in the early fourteenth century ships of Santander, Castro Urdiales, Bermeo, San Sebastian, and Motrico had come regularly to Devon, although in small numbers, as Spanish merchants preferred the big commercial centres of Bristol, London, and Southampton.[41] The trade had been upset by the Hundred Years War, especially after 1369, when a change of dynasty brought Spain closer to France, and a Devon ship was among those which had immediate trouble: the *Margaret* of Plymouth had been seized as she sailed for Lisbon and Seville.[42] However, trade was resumed under licence and safe-conduct, and in the early fifteenth century Basque shipping again visited Devon before the re-opening of hostilities with France under Henry V.[43] Even then, Devon's Spanish interest was strong enough for the Crown to complain in 1418 that Devon and Plymouth men favoured the Spanish and let captured seamen go home without exacting ransom.[44] Following the Anglo-Spanish treaty of 1466, Basque shipping increased again, so that nearly 20 vessels a year might be found in north and south Devon ports.[45] Despite the higher number of Basque ships at Dartmouth, more serious Spanish trade was done at Exeter and Barnstaple, because Spaniards often used Dartmouth as a stopover between Spain and the eastern Channel, and dealt there only in small amounts in passing. Southern Spanish trade with England was carried mainly by Basque, English and Italian ships, although a vessel of Seville had brought wine to Plymouth in 1391.[46] Dartmouth and Plymouth ships were especially vigorous carriers in the Andalusian and Lisbon trade for Bristol and London from the late fourteenth century, and north Devon ships joined them on the Bristol route in the fifteenth century.[47] Relations with Portugal were always easier, although Portuguese men occasionally found themselves arrested as Spaniards.[48] The trade was encouraged by permanent alliance from 1388, and throughout the middle ages one or two ships a year from Oporto and Lisbon came to north and south Devon.

To the west, Irish trade was straightforward since Ireland was within the English king's dominions, but products were similar to Devon's. Irish traders were infrequent in south Devon, although occasionally ships of Youghal and Kinsale called at Exeter. More unexpectedly, evidence is slim for their activity on the north coast before the fifteenth century, when Wexford and Waterford ships became regular sights, and Cork, Kinsale, Drogheda, and Youghal ships were occasional visitors.[49] Devon's activity in Ireland was probably greater. Dartmouth and Plymouth ships carried goods between Bristol and Bridgwater, and Ireland, and many of the small shipments of fish imported to Plymouth and the Exe estuary were from Ireland. An enquiry in 1476 into Devon's trade showed voyages to Ireland in 1474/5 to be the next most frequent after those to Brittany, and one witness testified to Ilfracombe ships sailing in ballast to Ireland to carry fish from there to Bristol. This trade was clearly valuable, since in 1465/6 four Ilfracombe ships had imported fish worth £214 to Bristol.[50]

Flanders, England's main market, especially for wool, was inconvenient for Devon, but occasionally Devon ships visited and fetched Low Country cargoes.[51] Similarly, few Low Country ships came to Devon, but some of Bruges and Kampen had called in the late fourteenth century when war with Spain seems to have encouraged the use of neutral shipping in the western Channel, and again in the commercial expansion of the late fifteenth century some of Veere, Delft, Goes, and Amsterdam arrived.[52]

Elsewhere contact was slight. The Icelandic cod trade was dominated by Bristol and the east coast ports, but the *Christopher Courtenay* was licenced to go there in 1447; the *Mary* of Northam was forfeited for going without licence in 1448; and by 1481 links had encouraged at least one Icelander to settle in Exeter.[53] Baltic ships coming to the Bay of Bourgneuf for salt, and Italian vessels sailing to and from the eastern Channel, sometimes called in passing,[54] but there is no evidence that Devon ships tried to gain access to the Baltic or the Mediterranean.

The relative importance of markets changed with time and was distorted by war. Given the complexity of some voyages, and the lack of destinations recorded in the Devon customs accounts, it is difficult to obtain a clear picture, but the enquiry into concealments by the customs collectors does give more information for the number of voyages in 1474/5. At least 25 per cent of total movements then were for Brittany, and a further 15 per cent (for which information is less clear) were trading with either Brittany or the Channel Islands; Ireland also attracted 25 per cent of movements, and 11 per cent were for Spain and Portugal. A few ships went that year to La Rochelle and Normandy, and one went to Flanders.[55] The commodities passing through Devon ports, as recorded in the customs accounts, confirm this pattern, although the busiest routes were not necessarily the most valuable, and the emphasis varied in each port. Imports for the 1490s, as shown in Table 9.2, suggest probable peacetime proportions for the late fifteenth century. At Exeter and Dartmouth Brittany appears to supply the most valuable imports (canvas, linen, and wine), then Gascony (wine and Toulouse woad), then Iberia. Despite the high number of ship movements, Ireland's value was relatively unimportant. At Barnstaple Iberian cargoes were clearly the most valuable, and Irish cargo values outstripped Breton ones; while Gascony and Iberia were most important at Plymouth. Such figures are not precise because linen could come from Normandy and wine from Spain, but they suggest a possible order of importance for Devon's direct overseas suppliers.

Table 9.2
Import values at Devon ports in the late fifteenth century

Commodity	Value imported Exeter 1492/3 £	Value imported Dartmouth 1492/3 £	Value imported Barnstaple 1492/3 £	Value imported Plymouth 1497/8 £
Canvas and crestcloth	2892	1137	5	46*
Salt	152	107	36	102
Wine	1502	696	244	1428
Woad	320	15	5	144
Iron	280	49	174	251
Iberian foods etc.	139	594	164	228
Fish	77	171	44	85
Mixed Irish cargoes	–	–	17	–
Cordage, oakum, etc.	8	4	–	–
Mixed cargoes probably from Low Countries	160	–	–	–
Mixed cargoes probably from Brittany	–	–	–	145
Mixed cargoes probably from Normandy	84	36	–	–

* There were more shipments of crestcloth and canvas in Breton cargoes not separately valued.

Source: PRO E122/41/14, 201/1, 115/7.

Carrying and coasting

The pattern of international movements revealed in the customs accounts suggests that most voyages were simple journeys to a foreign market and back to Devon, with only minor landfalls en route, and the enquiry into trade in 1474/5 confirms that at least threequarters were of this type. Some ships specialised on Breton or Irish routes, making four or five round voyages a year.[56] However, some ships made more complex voyages. Devon ships, especially those of Dartmouth, were carriers for other ports. They had been particularly active in the wine trade from an early date as Table 9.1 shows, and at Bordeaux they often loaded double or treble the amount of wine which Devon itself imported. In 1409/10, for instance, Devon ships loaded 3,199 tuns at Bordeaux, but imports to all the Devon ports, including Plymouth with its Cornish dependencies, came to only 1,177 tuns.[57] These Devon ships can sometimes be traced in the fourteenth and fifteenth centuries carrying such wine to Bristol, Sandwich, London, and even Hull, where the *Trinity*, *Katherine*, *Mary Gale*, and *Christopher*, all of Dartmouth, unloaded large cargoes of wine between 1453 and 1467.[58] The loss of Gascony had disrupted but clearly not stopped this carrying trade. The English dominance in the transport of wine was never re-established, but 16 of the ships loading at Bordeaux in 1482/3 were again from Devon (ten from Dartmouth, five from Plymouth and one from Brixham). While still forming 29 per cent of the English convoy, however, they now formed only 5 per cent of total shipping movements there.[59] Dartmouth ships were busy carriers on other routes, too. John Hawley's barge had carried goods between Seville and London for Italians in 1392; the *Gracedieu* of Dartmouth carried goods between Flanders, Spain, and Ireland for Londoners in 1402; the *Mary Undercroft* of Dartmouth carried for merchants of Bridgwater between La Rochelle and Ireland in 1496.[60] Ships of Dartmouth and Plymouth had been particularly visible in the Bristol cloth trade, not only with Bayonne, but also with La Rochelle, Spain, Lisbon, and Ireland in the later fourteenth century. This activity shrank in the later fifteenth century as Devon's own cloth trade increased, but ships of Barnstaple, Bideford, and Northam moved in. Devon ships also carried Irish fish for Bridgwater and Bristol.[61]

The carriage of passengers to Corunna for Santiago, one of the major pilgrim centres after Rome and Jerusalem, was an additional source of income to Devon ship owners, and to Plymouth hostellers. The shrine's popularity in England became marked from the thirteenth century and continued despite the war with Spain.[62] In 1390 Plymouth had been designated the formal port of exit for pilgrims in the west,[63] and between then and 1485 about one third of the licensed crossings to Corunna were made by Devon ships, a far higher proportion than by those of any of the other counties or major ports. Cornish ships made one fifth of the voyages, and Dorset and Hampshire ships together only one tenth.[64] Jubilee years were busiest, when the feast of St James fell on a Sunday and increased indulgences were granted, and 1434, the busiest year of all, for which details are given in Table 9.3, was typical of the normal pattern. In that year the owners of the *Margaret* of Topsham found pilgrims profitable enough to buy three licences, and they had also sent the *Margaret* in 1428.[65] Most ships took 40 to 60 passengers, but large ships might take more: in 1445 the *Trinity Courtenay* was licensed to carry 200, and the *Mary Carew* and the *Nicholas* of Dartmouth 140 each.[66] Despite the discomfort of the longer sea journey, it was generally less arduous to go from Devon to Corunna than to go to Calais or even to Bordeaux and thence overland. William Wey, fellow of Eton and a Devon man, stayed a fortnight in Plymouth in 1456, waiting with other pilgrims for six ships to be filled and to sail together. His journey then took five days (three entirely at sea); the pilgrims were allowed three days for the visit to Santiago, and the return journey (after a delay of a week by bad weather) again took five days.[67] The relative importance of this carrying

Table 9.3
Licences granted to Devon ships for the transport of pilgrims in 1434

Home port	Ship	Petitioner/s	Date of licence	No. of passengers
Barnstaple	*Nicholas*	John Gobbe, master	13 Apr	50
Bideford	*Trinity*	Roger Cule, master	6 Feb	40
Plymouth	*Mary*	Henry Nynethank, master	1 May	60
Portlemouth	*John*	Roger Broke, master	3 Feb	60
″ ″	″	″ ″	18 May	40
Dartmouth	*Peter*	Richard Walter, master	3 Feb	60
″ ″	″	″ ″	13 May	60
″ ″	*Anthony*	John Lye, master	9 Feb	40
″ ″	*Thomas*	John Godyng, master	26 Feb	30
″ ″	*Katherine*	John Lysard, master	26 Feb	40
″ ″	″	″ ″	4 Mar*	40
″ ″	*Anthony*	John Rede, master	4 Mar	40
″ ″	*Laurence*	John Coleman, master	16 Apr	30
″ ″	*James*	John Heddon, master	20 May	70
Kingswear	″	″ ″	21 Jan	40
Brixham	*Mary*	Henry Hawekyn, master	4 Feb	30
″ ″	″	″ ″	8 Jun	30
Teignmouth	*John*	Richard Lindesey, master	26 Feb	30
Topsham	*Margaret*	Richard Pette, master (William Wenard and John Coyle, owners)	8 Feb	50
″ ″	″	William Wenard and John Coyle, owners	12 May	50
″ ″	″	Richard Pytte, master (William Wenard and John Coyle, owners)	2 Jul	50
Exmouth	*Trinity*	John Gerard, master	23 Mar	40

* This may be a correction of a faulty licence or a copyist's error.

Source: PRO, C76/116, mm. 9–14, printed (with some errors) in T Rymer, *Foedera, Conventiones, Litterae* . . . (The Hague, 1739–45), V, i, 1–4, 6. There were further licences to ships to transport another 2,140 pilgrims from other ports, including Bristol, 6 ships (330 pilgrims); Penzance 2 (50); Fowey 4 (210); Landulph 3 (170); Poole 3 (190), Winchelsea 2 (100); and London 2 (140). No other port received more than one licence.

trade in commodities and passengers in overseas trade cannot be precisely determined, but it was clearly profitable for a number of owners.

Coastal trade, apart from moving local goods, was also inextricably linked with overseas trade, both for moving English goods to the main ports for export and for distributing foreign goods once they had cleared customs. As shown above, Devon imported more iron and linen than it could use itself. Some merchants preferred land transport to the risks and delays of coastal trade, and sent goods between Devon and Bristol, Bridgwater, and even London, by cart or pack horse,[68] but much went by sea. At Southampton ships of Dartmouth, Ottermouth (East Budleigh), Kingsbridge, and Sidmouth unloaded tin, Devon slates, Irish salmon, herrings, linen, iron, and wine in return for woad, madder, and alum.[69] At Exeter such goods as well as figs, raisins, rice, almonds, timber, wick-yarn, and many foreign consumer goods were unloaded from local ships throughout the fifteenth century, alongside cartwheels, wheelbarrows, coal, stone, chalk from Beer, and thousands of local slates.[70] The relative importance of coastal and international trade varied in ports and over time. At Exeter in the late fourteenth century coastal trade in which 60 to 80 ships engaged had clearly been more important than direct international trade in which often only half a dozen ships had been active, but in the late fifteenth century this had changed: Exeter's foreign trade had grown and now probably half of Exeter's inward movements were engaged in international trade, and the values of the cargoes were much higher. Coastal movements at other Devon ports are not known, but at Dartmouth and Plymouth may have been quite high for the redistribution of foreign goods unloaded there.[71]

Shipping

Supply

Foreign shipping in Devon in the early fourteenth century had already included ships from the whole Biscay and Channel area, from Santander in the west to Sluys in the east, and these remained the main visitors in the fifteenth century. Widening horizons in the 1390s had added occasional ships from Seville and Danzig, and regular vessels from Lisbon and Oporto. At the end of the fifteenth century there appeared small ships from many more of the Breton harbours – St Pol, Ouessant, Guérande, Concale, and St Brieuc. The relative importance of this alien shipping varied between ports and over time, and reached its peak in the 1470s and 1480s. In the later fourteenth century it had accounted for well under half of Devon's international movements: then Barnstaple had seen virtually no foreign vessels, at Plymouth they had accounted for less than 30 per cent of movements, at Dartmouth for less than 40 per cent, and at Exeter for less than a half. In the 1470s and 1480s the proportion of alien movements fluctuated widely but clearly rose with the sharp expansion of Breton activity, and a lesser rise in that of Normans and Spaniards. In these decades it accounted for between 50 and 70 per cent of movements at Dartmouth and Exeter, between 40 and 80 per cent at Plymouth, and even 10 to 30 per cent at Barnstaple. However, by the 1490s alien activity had dropped back again to less than 40 per cent of movements at Dartmouth and Exeter, and around 25 per cent at Plymouth, although it continued to rise at Barnstaple, sometimes reaching 50 per cent.[72] The simple number of alien ships in ports exaggerates their role in trade, as many Breton ships were small and some other ships were simply using Plymouth and Dartmouth as stopovers. This in itself brought some profit to Devon suppliers and victuallers,[73] and undoubtedly for most of the time much of the profit from the carriage of Devon's trade remained with English, and usually Devon ship owners.

Much of the large Devon shipping used on the longer routes came from Dartmouth and Plymouth, where business and capital for shipping were greater, but minor ports contributed on all routes, as they had in the fourteenth century.[74] Some, such as Topsham and Barnstaple, like Teignmouth in the fourteenth century, had relatively large deep-sea fleets, but none could rival the hold of Dartmouth and Plymouth on the longer routes. The Bordeaux wine trade illustrates this well. In 1356/7 Dartmouth had sent 24 ships there, Plymouth 22, the Exe estuary seven, Teignmouth four, and Sidmouth two. Nearly a hundred years later, in 1448/9, the position was similar, although now a wider range of smaller ports, including those of the north coast, were engaged. Dartmouth sent 14, Plymouth eight, Barnstaple three, and Exeter, Topsham, Paignton, Salcombe, Kingswear, and Bideford one each.[75] Ships of Ottermouth, Dittisham, Brixham, Dawlish, and Tor(mohun) fetched cargoes from Brittany, Normandy, the Low Countries and Iberia, and the Irish trade attracted boats from many small harbours. The minor ports were much more important in coastal than in international trade, but even there Dartmouth was often strong, and in 1461/2 in the coastal trade at Exeter she provided 23 of the incoming ships, compared with 17 from the Exe estuary and 31 from eleven other Devon ports.[76] A most noticeable change in the late fifteenth century was the great rise in the numbers of ships engaged in international trade in Devon ports. This was partly due to the trend towards smaller ships at the end of the fifteenth century (see above, Chapter 8) but also to the boom in Devon's trade. The increase was particularly marked at Exeter, where a maximum of 20 international movements in the fourteenth century rose to 40 in the mid-fifteenth century, and to over 100 in the 1490s, when Exeter's movements came to rival Dartmouth's. Coastal arrivals did not increase at the same rate. The 80 or so arrivals of the late fourteenth century had reached 150 in the mid-fifteenth century, but the level did not pass that, and even dropped a little at the end of the century, no doubt because Exeter was now receiving so many of her supplies direct from overseas rather than through coastal redistribution. An even greater number of ships engaged in foreign trade in Plymouth and her Cornish harbours, but most of these were very small fishing boats, and the volume of trade did not rise at the same rate.[77]

Ship Owning

Ship owning was expensive and risky. Building and constant refitting were costly, but the English Crown, always worried about lack of shipping, sometimes allowed tax relief on the first voyage, as it did for Matthew Andrew when he built the 200-ton *James* of Topsham in 1482.[78] The shipowner also faced risks of total loss through wreck, piracy, or war seizure, and the burden of impressment for naval service, for which payment was often slow. Waiting at mustering ports, ships lost commercial voyages and masters and owners ran out of money trying to keep crews together. A few, like the three small ships of Dartmouth and Brixham in 1404, were released on grounds of imminent destitution.[79] Delay was a further problem. Ships had to wait for favourable winds, were blown off course, or ran for shelter only to find unsympathetic officials zealously checking ships' papers. Devon officials constantly provoked complaints of ignoring papers which were in good order, and of causing long delays as appeals were made to London courts.[80] Some recent research has suggested, too, that in the economic recession of the mid-fifteenth century, ship owning was not profitable anywhere in Europe, and certainly, even in the better times of the 1470s, the Cely family only just broke even on the *Margaret Cely*.[81]

To spread risk many held shares in more than one ship, and as shares were freely sold and bequeathed, non-merchants and women became owners. Dionisia Gabriell part-owned the *Juliane* of Dartmouth in 1402, and Johanna Langmead owned shares in the *Mary Carswell* with John Carswell in 1486.[82] Partnership might spread over distance, as when men of Barnstaple and Glamorgan invested together.[83] Most owners were merchants or shipmasters, and some judged the rewards promising enough even in the mid-fifteenth century to become multiple owners, as John Hawley had been in the fourteenth.[84] Thomas Gille of Dartmouth owned the *Anthony* and *Katherine* in 1436, built another ship in 1437, owned the *Christopher* which ran down the *George* of Wells off Start Point in 1440, and still owned a ship called the *Anthony* in 1451, when either he or his son also owned the *Young Gille*. About that time he sold the *George*, and in 1453 he bought the *St Mary* of St Andrews.[85] John Clerk was also an active ship owner, and in 1451 held the *New Trinity* and shares in four others.[86] None rivalled William Canynges of Bristol, but ship owning clearly absorbed a considerable amount of their invested capital.

Aristocratic and landed ship owners included the Carew family, Sir William Fitzwarin,[87] and the Courtenays. In 1384 the Earl of Devon had received the forfeited *St Marie Cog* of Bermeo, and in 1411 and 1413 three of his ships, the *Mary* of Dartmouth, the *Mary* of Kingswear, and the *Margaret* of Plymouth, held pilgrim licences. His son part-owned the *George*, which plundered a ship of Sluis in 1408, and his uncle owned a barge which carried pilgrims in 1395, and the *James* of Exmouth in 1398. The family tradition continued. Nearly fifty years later, in 1442, Sir Philip Courtenay's great ship, barge, and balinger were used in a sea-keeping force, and between 1444 and 1448 the *Trinity Courtenay*, *Mary Courtenay*, and *Christopher Courtenay* were active, variously carrying pilgrims to Spain, loading wine at Bordeaux, sailing to Iceland, and bringing cargoes into Exeter.[88]

Operation

Unless he was an active seaman himself, the owner left the regular operation of the ship in the hands of the master. The latter was therefore responsible for finding, keeping, paying, and disciplining crews, victualling the ship, carrying out running repairs, chartering, and navigation. The navigational skills of masters were emphasised by Chaucer: much was practical experience but, as described in chapter 2 above, rutters were available in the fifteenth century, and pilots were taken on for unfamiliar voyages and difficult havens. Often the masters were owners or part owners of the vessels, but many were employees, like Robert Pitte, who worked for at least seven years for William Wenard and John Coyle at Topsham, and John Lysard, who worked for Thomas Gille at Dartmouth.[89] Little is known about Devon crews at this time. In the fifteenth century ships of any size each regularly carried a purser, smith, carpenter, bo'sun, and ship's boys. Crews were often of mixed nationality, although likely to be predominantly of the nationality of the ship's home port. The treatment of crew members was governed by practices based on the Laws of Oleron, which ensured fair conditions, and they were paid in cash or by an allowance of cargo space which they could use or hire to merchants.

The agreement made by Thomas Lynne, master of John Hawley's barge the *St Mary* of Dartmouth, illuminates particularly well, as much for the fifteenth century as the late fourteenth, the responsibilities of the master, and also the carrying trade of Dartmouth ships. Genoese merchants chartered the *St Mary* at Seville on 1 March 1392 to carry 150 tons of goods to London. The freight was charged at 4½ gold francs the ton; the merchants were to pay the master 25 francs 'shoemoney'; all was payable in London within 25 days of arrival there. The merchants advanced the master 200 francs for provisions for the ship and crew which he would repay them from the freight due in London. The ship was to go to Sanlucar de Barrameda for the cargo, which was to be loaded within four weeks from 1 March. The ship would then sail direct to England, call at Southampton for four days to unload some cargo, and go on to London to unload the rest within 25 days of arrival. The merchants were to hire the long-distance pilot from Seville, and caulk the cabin (no doubt for their own greater comfort). The master was to arrange towage and petty pilotage in port, to provide a competent crew and adequate ship's gear, to provide a boat for use as a lighter, and to pay that boat's crew. He would also provide water, salt, firewood, and lighting for the merchants aboard. Any violation by either side incurred a penalty of 300 Spanish gold *doblas*.[90] Other agreements show similar precision, although few refer to Devon, the earliest surviving original charter party being for nearby Lyme, to take wine from Bordeaux to Newcastle in 1323.[91] Chartering in the coastal trade included similar stipulations on loading times. In 1474 Harry Denys failed to have the *James* of Ottermouth loaded in London within five days as agreed, so the master took the responsibility of finding an alternative charter and the ship's owner, Matthew Andrew, sued Denys.[92]

The emphasis on time is not surprising, as ships needed to be filled, and to be kept at sea, as much as possible to be profitable, if necessary in ballast. In 1474/5 at least 6 per cent of voyages out to Bordeaux, Spain, and Ireland were in ballast, as was the journey of the *James* of Ottermouth to London to pick up Denys' goods.[93] Ships were kept going in the winter in the fourteenth and fifteenth century. Wine was usually loaded at Bordeaux in the autumn and spring, but war sometimes made convoys late, and in 1360 22 Devon ships loaded in December.[94] Other goods were less seasonal and would be moved at any time. In 1378 John Hawley's barge had traded in and out of Dartmouth in December and January 1378/9, and winter trading continued throughout the fifteenth century.[95] Owners fitted in what they could. Some owners specialised: the *Margaret* of Topsham went three times to Corunna in the summer of 1434, and the *Trinity* of Kenton six times to Ireland in 1474/5. Others took what came: in 1474/5 the *Christopher* of Topsham made three voyages to Brittany, one to Flanders, and set off for Spain.[96] Sometimes they would fit between commercial voyages a period of sea keeping, which was the one naval activity which offered a good chance of reward, as well as being acknowledged as necessary to protect trade. Ship owners from Hawley to Gille and Courtenay were always willing to provide vessels for the western squadrons. Thus John Lysard, working for Thomas Gille, found himself in a short space of time in 1434–6 taking passengers to Corunna, loading wine at Bordeaux, and patrolling with a squadron in the Channel.[97] Sea keeping shaded into piracy, and piracy for some was a way of life,[98] but for most ship owners legitimate trade and sea keeping offered the steadiest profits. If all went well their ships could fit in two or three major voyages a year and twice that number on short routes. In that case, ship owning probably offered sound enough rewards even in the difficult times of the mid-fifteenth century.

Merchants

Alien merchants were generally less important in Devon than the alien shipping. Aliens had been very active in the early fourteenth century, but since English trade (apart from wool) was then untaxed, their precise share of the trade is unclear. In the later fourteenth century they had probably handled no more than 4 per cent of Devon's overseas trade by value. Their activity grew in the early fifteenth century, but probably remained under 10 per cent. There was similarly low alien activity in other western ports including Bristol, since many aliens were attracted to the bigger ports of Southampton and London. Their importance grew further in the later fifteenth century. After 1453 aliens, mostly Bretons with some Basques and Normans, handled over 50 per cent of Devon's wine imports, and at the peak of their activity in the 1480s they exported 46 per cent of Plymouth's cloth and 24 per cent at Exeter and Dartmouth. Their share of the value of general trade also rose from some 8 per cent in 1460 to nearly 30 per cent in the 1490s.[99] This increasing activity came partly from Devon's increasing attraction as a cloth supplier, and partly from the increasing safety of the western Channel in the peace following the Hundred Years War. Both Bristol (off the Channel) and the Dorset ports (with less cloth for sale) remained less patronised and less threatened by alien merchants. However, English merchants still dominated trade. They held back the alien surge in the cloth trade, and at the beginning of the sixteenth century again handled well over 90 per cent of the cloth themselves.

The English merchants handling the trade ranged from men with one small shipment a year (possibly seamen or merchants just branching into international trade) to substantial merchant figures, whose commodity investments ran into hundreds of pounds in the later fifteenth century. The customs account for Exeter and Dartmouth for 1492/3 illustrates the position.[100] At Exeter 123 English traders handled general trade valued at £3,700, exported 1,273 cloths, and imported 148 tuns of wine. Seventeen (14 per cent) were shipmasters, fourteen of whom dealt solely in fish, the greatest value of which was that of £11 13s 4d of John Wichehalse, master of the *James* of Dawlish. Of the other 106 merchants 43 (41 per cent) had moderate investments of under £20 and only seven had investments of over £200. At the extremes were John Trevale, who exported a barrel of shoes worth 15s on a Guernsey ship, and Thomas Moungoy, a Taunton man who became an Exeter freeman in 1492, whose general goods were valued at £438 18s 8d and who also exported 136 cloths. The total customs value of all his goods was probably over £600, and the market value would have been much higher. John Greenway of Tiverton came next in turnover, underlining the point made by Professor Carus-Wilson on the importance of the inland cloth merchants. John Ector, Thomas Fisher, Thomas Andrew, Richard Unday, and Robert Sherman were the others with investments of over £200. At Dartmouth the pattern was different. A larger number of traders handled fewer goods. One hundred and eighty-five traders handled goods worth £2,017, 1,428 cloths, and 55 tuns of wine. There were more shipmasters (37, making 20 per cent) and these had more substantial investments than those at Exeter. The largest was the £23 10s of William Stephen, master of the *Mary John* of Dartmouth. The 148 other traders were, on the other hand, less involved than those at Exeter. Seventy-eight (53 per cent) had investments of under £20, only five had investments over £100, and none over £200. The largest sum was that of Peter More, with general goods valued at £57 and 76 cloths. The number of shared cargoes was also higher at Dartmouth, suggesting less individual capital, although it may just reflect the continuation of a practice seen earlier in the Channel Island trade at Dartmouth. The pattern of trade in each port had changed from earlier decades, when not only the numbers of merchants and ships and the amount of cargo had been higher at Dartmouth than Exeter, but the wealthiest individual traders had also been found there. However, there was some similarity in that Dartmouth had always had a high proportion of small investors, possibly reflecting the easier openings in a coastal rather than a river port.[101]

A few women were active in international trade and formed partnerships, but, as at Bristol and Hull, they never accounted for more than 1 per cent of shippers. Most, like Alice Hoker who exported six cloths from Exeter in 1493, were probably widows closing their late husbands' businesses, but Margaret Brown handled several shipments in 1480/1, including one of fish in partnership with Richard Vincent. No widows in the fifteenth century continued long as independent traders as had Agnes Nymet, Magota Gold, and Elizabeth Wilford at Exeter in the different economic circumstances of the late fourteenth century.[102]

As in the fourteenth, so in the fifteenth century, town offices were dominated by merchants with strong interests in overseas trade.[103] Again as in the fourteenth century, their wealth did not come only from trade. Thomas Gille of Dartmouth was a major ship owner;[104] William Crugge of Exeter invested in industrial production;[105] and most invested in urban and country property for security, status, or retirement. John Attwill, merchant, deputy customs collector, and MP, not only traded, but owned a carvel, rented a wharf, ran a tavern, and owned livestock – at least six horses, two oxen, and 80 sheep in 1475;[106] and at the bottom of the scale, William Romant of Dartmouth, described as mariner and husbandman in 1498, may have had a fishing boat and a smallholding.[107]

The Trends of Trade

When King John had taxed trade in 1204 it was low in Devon – not surprisingly, as the main trade axes of the time were to the east, and Cornwall exported most of the tin. However, although detail is lacking, it is clear that during the thirteenth century Dartmouth, followed by Plymouth, had grown in wealth, and this continued as they gained independence from

Table 9.4
Comparative trade at the main Devon ports in the late fourteenth and late fifteenth centuries

		Exports			Imports		Total	Shipping
		cloth valued	other goods valued	tin valued	wine valued at £4 the tun	other goods valued	trade handled	Movements
		£	£	£	£	£	£	
1391/2	Dartmouth	199	42	–	604	95	950	41
(ten	Exeter	83	–	–	1056	33	1172	17
months	Barnstaple	100	–	–	320	140	560	10
only)	Teignmouth	11	1	–	20	33	65	9
	Plymouth	143	157	–	984	180	1464	44
1492/3	Dartmouth	2504 (1669)*	208	257	692	2113	5774	164
	Exeter	2654 (1769)*	213	956	1468	4025	9319	125
	Barnstaple	173 (115)*	18	–	136	371	698	40
	Teignmouth	(included with Exeter)						
1497/8	Plymouth	734 (489)*	392	239	1468	1029	3862	195

* To provide a rough comparison with 1391/2, when the collectors valued the cloth but did not count it, values are estimated at £1 10s a cloth. Numbers of cloths, as given in the accounts, are in brackets.

Source: PRO E122/40/15,16, 41/14, 201/1, 115/7. Plymouth accounted separately from Exeter and Dartmouth in the fifteenth century: 1497/8 is the nearest surviving account to that of 1492/3.

9.1 Cullompton Parish Church: Carvings of Ships etc on the outside of the aisle built in accordance with the will (1526) of John Lane, a local clothier and merchant. The lowest stone once showed John Lane's merchant mark with a teasel frame as in fig. 9.3. The vessel is a typical three-masted ship of the early sixteenth century. *(J Youings, courtesy of the Vicar and Churchwardens)*

9.2 Cloth Shears clasped by an angel high up inside the Lane Aisle in Cullompton Church. Lane will have profited from the industrial and commercial prosperity in Devon at the turn of the century. *(J Youings courtesy of the Vicar and Churchwardens)*

9.3 Cullompton Parish Church: Teasel Frame with Lane's merchant mark. Teasel heads were used for raising the nap on the newly woven cloth before it was sheared. John Lane was clearly both a maker and a dealer in woollen cloth. *(J Youings, by courtesy of the Vicar and Churchwardens)*

Totnes and Plympton respectively in the early fourteenth century. Their rise took place at a time of general European expansion, but it also reflected particular developments on the Atlantic coasts which in the end would shift the whole economic focus of Europe westwards. The intensification of international trade made economic specialisation possible. Gascony became overwhelmingly a wine producer and, a little later, the Bay of Bourgneuf became a major producer of salt. Both helped to attract more trade from east to west. The *Reconquista* opened up Iberia to Christian merchants in the thirteenth century, and the subsequent safe passage through the Straits of Gibraltar, together with northern European economic expansion, encouraged Catalans and Italians to use the sea route between the Mediterranean and the Channel, which in itself stimulated further western trade. Trade with Ireland also developed as the English hold there strengthened. Devon was well placed to take advantage of such trends.

In the early fourteenth century the western trade had still been very modest in national terms, but the ports of Devon were probably the busiest of the western counties in some aspects of trade. Devon ships had certainly been more evident at Bordeaux than those of Dorset, Cornwall, Somerset, or Bristol, and ships unloading wine in Devon had been more numerous than in the neighbouring counties and had rivalled those at Bristol. Alien imports worth £1,172 in Devon ports in 1323/4 had greatly surpassed those at Bristol worth £234, and exports worth £202 were certainly more valuable than the 6 cloths and 23 dickers of hides exported at Bristol that year.[108] However, this promising position in western trade was lost, partly due no doubt to Devon's traditional markets being disrupted by the Hundred Years War. Devon's trade continued to expand, but not fast enough: cloth exports formed a respectable 7 per cent of England's total exports in the 1360s, and Exeter's trade, including coastal trade, about doubled over the century, but by the beginning of the fifteenth century Bristol had drawn far ahead. Its natural advantages of a larger hinterland served by river transport and its relative safety during the Anglo-French war offset its geographical cul-de-sac off the busy Channel routes. Devon's trade, although still in excess of that of Dorset or Cornwall, was important locally rather than nationally.

In the early fifteenth century Devon's overseas trade slackened as exports adjusted to lower markets; and war, raids, and piracy brought further disruption. There was a good recovery with the greater stability in Anglo-French relations from the 1420s, but again trade nowhere near rivalled Bristol's, although it still exceeded that of Dorset. The severe blow of the loss of Gascony and the final rupture with France in 1453 coincided with both the lowest point of the general European recession and the deepest bullion crisis of the middle ages. Devon's trade suffered badly, with cloth exports crashing to one third of their previous level. Recovery began again, slowly at Plymouth, but with gathering speed in Exeter, and Devon did extremely well in the economic expansion and the peace of the late fifteenth century. Shipping movements increased; cloth exports rose to record heights; the wine trade recovered fully; and tin licences brought the export trade back to Devon ports. Poundage assessments of goods at Exeter and Dartmouth show a four-fold increase between the 1430s and 1490s.[109]

The expansion of the cloth trade in the fifteenth century meant that the balance of trade in Devon was also much better, as Table 9.4 shows. Whereas in the fourteenth century direct exports had been probably worth only one-fifth the value of imports, in the late fifteenth century they approached three-quarters. The rate of growth varied between ports, especially in exports. At Plymouth and Barnstaple import values about doubled, but at Exeter and Dartmouth they at least quadrupled. Export values were about six times greater at Plymouth, about 12 times greater at Dartmouth, and an exceptional 46 times greater at Exeter.

Compared with Bristol on one side and Southampton on the other, Devon ports had a much slower commercial life for most of the middle ages, but they came to rival Bristol for a while as it hit hard times at the end of the fifteenth century, although they could still not compare with Southampton's trade. Part of their increase was due to greater alien activity in the ports, but Devon men and ships held off the challenge and continued to handle the lion's share of trade.

Devon's fortunes at this time showed a marked variation from the rest of provincial England. England's overall trade expansion was centred on London, and eastern ports in particular proved unable to cope with London's competition as the Baltic trade declined. Even Hull, for long the fourth largest port or better for the wool, cloth, and wine trades, saw all these fall dramatically. The west and south did better. Bristol did not sink as far as Hull, and Southampton maintained a reasonable level of trade, but the Devon ports were the only real provincial growth areas. They were far enough away from London; the setbacks in the Gascon trade were more shortlived than those in the Baltic; the late-fifteenth-century treaties with France and Spain gave more encouragement to western trade than it had had for decades; peace in the Channel gave southern Devon ports an advantage over Bristol; Devon's traditionally lighter cloths could respond more quickly to changing demands; and Edward IV's change of policy boosted the direct overseas tin trade.

Neither the scale nor the extent of Devon's trade at this time should be overexaggerated. In 1500 Devon still exported only about 10 per cent of England's total cloth exports, none of England's now modest wool exports, and imported only some 11 per cent of England's wine. She was still operating within the traditional trade patterns: there were as yet no important new western markets, although the development of Madeira, and the voyages of exploration, especially from Bristol, were pointers to the future.[110] Within this traditional framework, however, with a steady amount of coastal trade, fishing, a role in naval forces, and a thriving though modest international trade, Devon's maritime life looked full of promise.

9: Devon's Overseas Trade in the late Middle Ages

1 My thanks are due to the British Academy for a grant which enabled me to complete research for this chapter at the Public Record Office.
2 TH Lloyd, *The Movement of Wool Prices in Medieval England*, EcHR Supplement, 6 (1973), 70–1.
3 EM Carus-Wilson and O Coleman, *England's Export Trade, 1275–1547* (Oxford, 1963),36–70, 122–3, 132–3.
4 PRO King's Remembrancer's Customs Accounts, E122/40/7a. The value of the wool is taken from Lloyd, *Wool Prices*, 70–1.
5 Carus-Wilson and Coleman, *Export Trade*, 75–87, 144–5; EM Carus-Wilson, 'Trends in the Export of English Woollens in the Fourteenth Century', in *Medieval Merchant Venturers*. (Oxford, 2nd edn, 1967), 253–7; PRO E122/40/23 shows exports of 3,337 'dozens' of strait cloths; for strait cloths see M Kowaleski, above, chapter 7.
6 Carus-Wilson and Coleman, *Export Trade*, 88–112, 138–9, 144–5, 154–5. It is reasonable to include Cornish cloth figures with Devon's, since particular customs accounts show that Plymouth accounted for 95 per cent and Fowey for only 5 per cent of cloth in the jurisdiction: PRO E122/114/1, 3, 115/7, 8.
7 EM Carus-Wilson, *The Expansion of Exeter at the Close of the Middle Ages*, Harte Memorial Lecture in Local History, 1961 (Exeter, 1963), 17–21.
8 *Calendar of Patent Rolls* [hereafter *CPR*], *1361–4*, 480, 492.
9 PRO E122 for Exeter, Dartmouth, Barnstaple, and Plymouth, passim.
10 PRO King's Remembrancer's Memoranda Roll, E159/253, Recorda, Mich. mm.27, 30.
11 PRO E122/26/2,8,10, 17/10b; Early Chancery Proceedings, C1/61/512.
12 J Castro y F Idoate, eds, *Archivo General de Navarra: Catalogo de la Seccion de Comptas: Documentos* (Pamplona, 1952 ff.), XXI no.931, XXIII no.962, XXVIII nos.627, 957, 1340, XXIX no.29. The editors took 'dacestre' to be Chester, but Exeter seems more likely for Anglo-Spanish trade at this time.
13 PRO E122 for Devon ports, passim; see also below.
14 J Hatcher, *English Tin Production and Trade before 1550* (Oxford, 1973), 18–19, 21–5, 59, 75–6, 91–110, App.A Table XVI, 155–9.
15 Hatcher, *Tin Trade*, App.A Fig.1, 162–3, App.B Tables XVII–XVIII, 170–81; PRO E122/115/7,8.
16 For the uses of tin, see Hatcher, *Tin Trade*, chap. 2, and App.B Table XVIII, 176–81.
17 PRO Ministers' Accounts, SC6/816/12; D Gardiner, ed, *A Calendar of Early Chancery Proceedings relating to West Country Shipping, 1388–1493*, Devon and Cornwall Record Society, new series 21 (1975), no.47.
18 PRO E122/40/23, 41/14, 201/1, 115/8.
19 PRO E122 for Exeter and Dartmouth, and Plymouth, passim. See Kowaleski, chapter 7.
20 MK James, *Studies in the Medieval Wine Trade* (Oxford, 1971), App.16, 108–16; at the end of the century just under half of the wine imported into the area under the jurisdiction of Plymouth was recorded in the particular customs accounts as through Plymouth itself, but earlier fluctuations had been wider, therefore Plymouth and Fowey have been included together here.
21 PRO E159/253, Recorda, Trin.m.25; E122/41/14, 201/1; see also Gardiner, *West Country Shipping*, no.94.
22 PRO E122/40/7a, 23.
23 PRO E122/115/8.
24 PRO E122/41/6 (oranges and sugar), 41/12 (sugar), 115/8 (marmalade); DRO Local cust. roll 8/9 Hen.VII; for the early history of marmalade, see C Anne Wilson, *The Book of Marmalade* (1985), 15–33.
25 WDRO, Plymouth Receivers' Accounts, W130, fos. 3v, 49v.
26 The Rev TO Payne, ed, *The Comodyties of England by Sir John Fortescue* (1863), 6–7. (The attribution to Fortescue is probably mistaken.)
27 PRO E122/102/14a.
28 WR Childs, 'England's Iron Trade in the Fifteenth Century', *EcHR*, 2nd series, XXXIV (1981), 28–9, 31–2.
29 PRO E122/40/7a; DRO Local customs rolls, 17/18 Ed.II, 20 Ed.II/1 Ed.III.
30 PRO E122 and DRO Local customs rolls, passim.
31 PRO E122/41/14, 201/1; DRO Local customs roll, 8/9 Hen. VII.
32 DRO Local customs rolls, 2/3 Hen. VI, 8/9 Hen. VII; for arrangements to ship from London, see Gardiner, *West Country Shipping*, no.89.

33 PRO E122/102/14a, 40/23,9, 41/6,8,14,18, 201/1; Carus-Wilson, *Exeter*, 27–8.
34 PRO E122/41/14.
35 PRO E122/40/23,35, 41/3,18, 201/2, 115/7,8; see Table 9.1.
36 PRO E122/15/8, 16/2,13,15,17–21,23, 40/17, 19/13,14, 20/5,9.
37 Gardiner, *West Country Shipping*, no.51.
38 PRO E122/40/10,15,16,23,30, 41/1–4,6,8,12,14,18, 201/1,2, 114/1, 115/7,8; H Touchard, *Le Commerce maritime breton à la fin du moyen âge*, Annales Littéraires de l'Université de Nantes, fasc. 1 (Paris, 1967), 111, 175–88, 224, 233–58.
39 PRO E122/40/11, 41/1–4,6,8,12,14,18, 201/1,2, 114/1, 115/7,8; M Mollat, *Le Commerce maritime normand à la fin du moyen âge*, (Paris, 1952), 144–56, 160–70.
40 WR Childs, 'Channel Island Shipping as recorded in the English Customs Accounts, 1300–1500', in AG Jamieson, ed, *A People of the Sea: The Maritime History of the Channel Islands* (1986), 44–58.
41 WR Childs, *Anglo-Castilian Trade in the Later Middle Ages* (Manchester, 1978), chaps. 1–2, provides the political background to the trade.
42 *Calendar of Close Rolls* [hereafter *CCR*], *1369–74*, 30,488.
43 *CCR,1396–9*, 367; *CPR,1413–16*, 36; PRO E122/40/15,23,30; DRO Local customs rolls 3–14 Hen.IV, 1–4 Hen.V.
44 *Calendar of Miscellaneous Inquisitions* [hereafter *CMI*], *1399–1422*, no.552.
45 PRO E122/41/6,12.
46 PRO E122/40/15.
47 *Calendar of Plea and Memoranda Rolls preserved among the archives of the Corporation of the City of London, 1323–1482*, ed. AH Thomas and PE Jones (Cambridge, 1926–61), III, 194–7; PRO E122/16/21,23, 40/17, 17/10, 19/4,7,8,11, 20/7.
48 *CCR, 1369–74*, 264, 270; *CCR,1374–7*,3,12,27,41; *CCR, 1377–81*, 268,292,318.
49 WR Childs, 'Ireland's Trade with England in the Later Middle Ages', *Irish Economic and Social History*, 9 (1982), 13–14,30; to these should be added ships of Wicklow and Waterford in 1462/3, of Wexford, Waterford, and Cork in 1480/1, of these three and Kinsale in 1492/3, of Youghal and Kinsale in 1498/9, PRO E122/40/10, 41/6,14, 201/1,2.
50 H Bush, *Bristol Town Duties* (Bristol, 1828), 17–25; PRO E122/16/19–21, 19/3,4,8,10,10a,11, 20/5,7, 26/2,7,13; E159/253, Recorda, Trin.m.25; see above, p. 80.
51 *CPR,1401–05*, 134,186–7; PRO E159/253, Recorda, Trin. mm.25–6; E122/41/6,8,14, 201/1; see above, p. 81, Map 9.1.
52 PRO E122/40/8, 102/14a, 40/23,35, 41/6,8,14, 201/1, 115/7; Gardiner, *West Country Shipping*, no.40.
53 PRO Treaty Roll, C76/129 m.3; *CPR,1446–52*, 156, 175; *CPR,1476–85*, 242.
54 PRO E122/40/16, 41/8; *CCR,1385–9*, 346–7; Gardiner, *West Country Shipping*, nos. 44, 71.
55 PRO E159/253, Recorda, Trin. m.25.
56 PRO E159/253, Recorda, Trin. m.25.
57 PRO King's Remembrancer, Accounts Various, E101/184/19; James, *Wine Trade*, App. 16, 109.
58 PRO E122/16/21, 19/13,14, 20/9; E101/80/5,25, 81/1; WR Childs, ed, *The Customs Accounts of Hull, 1453–1490*, Yorks. Arch. Soc. Record Series, CXLIV (1986), 2, 70, 80, 102.
59 *Registre de la comtablie de Bordeaux, 1482–3*, ed. MG Ducaunnes-Duval, Archives historiques du departement de la Gironde, L (1915), 1–166.
60 *Cal. Plea and Memo. Rolls, London*, III, 194–7; *CPR,1401–05*, 186–7; PRO E122/26/20.
61 See above, p. 80 and notes 35,47,49.
62 *CCR,1377–81*, 439.
63 *Statutes of the Realm*, ed. A Luders et al. (1810–28), II, 68 (13 Ric.II, stat.1, c.20). Not all pilgrims left from Plymouth: some were licensed elsewhere, as was the *Jonet* of Northam from Barnstaple in 1394 (*CPR,1391–6*, 393), and Margery Kempe certainly expected to sail from Bristol, *The Book of Margery Kempe*, ed. BA Windeatt (1985), 144–8.
64 PRO C76/74–221 passim; *CPR,1391–6*, 45, 246, 249, 251, 362, 393, 405, 408, 537–8, 565–6, 568, 572, 601, 602, 604, 708, 715; C Storrs, 'Jacobean pilgrims from England from the early twelfth to the late fifteenth century' (unpublished MA thesis, University of London, 1964).
65 PRO C76/110 m.11.
66 PRO C76/127 mm.4,10.
67 F Furnivall, ed, *The Stacions of Rome, and the Pilgrim's Sea-voyage, with Clene Maydenhod*, Early English Text Society, OS.25 (1867), 37–40; *The Itineraries of William Wey, Fellow of Eton College, to Jerusalem AD 1458 and AD 1462, and to St James of Compostella AD 1456* (Roxburgh Club, 1857, 1867), 153–60.
68 PRO C1/46/60; Carus-Wilson, *Exeter*, 26–8; PRO E122/41/6, 26/10.
69 B Foster, ed, *The Local Port Book of Southampton, 1435–36*, Southampton Record Series, 7 (Southampton, 1963), 11, 43, 47, 49; H Cobb, ed, *The Local Port Book of Southampton, 1439–40*, Southampton Record Series, 5 (Southampton, 1961), 35, 39, 46; DB Quinn and AA Ruddock, eds, *The Port Books or Local Customs Accounts of Southampton for the Reign of Edward IV*, Southampton Record Society, 37–38 (Southampton, 1937–8), I, 18, 75, 85–7, II, 149, 158–60, 172.
70 DRO Local customs rolls, passim.
71 See Kowaleski, above, p. 67.
72 PRO E122 passim for Exeter and Dartmouth, and for Plymouth and Fowey.
73 The *Margaret Cely* bought victuals, nails, and other gear at Plymouth en route for Bordeaux; A Hanham, *The Celys and their World* (Cambridge, 1985), 390.
74 See Kowaleski, above, chapter 7.
75 PRO E101/173/4, 195/19.
76 DRO Local customs roll 1/2 Ed.IV. For comparative roles in the navy see chapter 8.
77 PRO E122 passim; DRO Local customs rolls passim; see Table 9.4.
78 PRO C76, 165 m.1.
79 Gardiner, *West Country Shipping*, no.8; PRO C1/69/256.
80 Gardiner, *West Country Shipping*, nos.34, 46; *CCR, 1389–92*, 250; PRO C1/30/40.
81 Hanham, *Celys*, 396–7.
82 *CCR,1399–1402*, 446; HR Watkin, *Dartmouth*, I, *Pre-reformation*, Devonshire Association, Parochial Histories of Devonshire, 5 (1935), 409.
83 Gardiner, *West Country Shipping*, no.58.
84 See Kowaleski, above, chapter 7.
85 Gardiner *West Country Shipping*, nos.38, 39 and note, 45, 67 and note, 68 and note; *CPR, 1446–52*, 448.
86 *CPR, 1446–52*, 448.
87 PRO C76/110 m.7, 133 m.11; BL Add.MS 15,524; *CPR,1436–41*, 451.
88 *CPR,1381–5*, 398; *ibid. 1391–6*, 537; *CMI,1399–1422*, no.376; PRO C76/82 m.3, 94 m.25, 95 m.1, 96 m.37, 127 mm.4,10, 129 m.3; E101/195/19; BL Add. MS 15,524; DRO Local customs roll 24/25 Hen.VI; *Rotuli Parliamentorum* [hereafter *Rot.Parl.*] (1783), V, 59b. See also *CPR, 1452–61*, 612; Gardiner, *West Country Shipping*, no.73.
89 Pitte: PRO C76/110 m.11, 116 m.14; E101/192/1. Lysard: *CPR,1429–36*, 509; PRO C76/116 m.9,11, 127 m.4; E101/192/1, 194/3;DRO Local customs roll 24/25 Hen.VI; Lysard was working for the Duke of Exeter by 1451, *CPR,1446–52*, 447.
90 *Cal. Plea and Memo. Rolls, London*, III, 194–7. The *dobla* was worth perhaps 2s 8d. sterling (calculated from P Spufford, ed, *Handbook of Medieval Exchange* (1986), 158, 160, 201).
91 NMM AML/M/1 MS 58/038. In this case the merchants were responsible for towage and petty pilotage.
92 Gardiner, *West Country Shipping*, no.89.
93 PRO E159/253, Recorda, Trin. mm.25–6; Gardiner, *West Country Shipping* no.89.
94 PRO E101/182/2.
95 PRO E122/40/8.
96 Table 9.2; PRO E159/253, Recorda, Trin. mm.25–6.
97 PRO C76/116 mm.9, 11; E101/192/1; *CPR,1429–36*, 509.
98 See chapter 10.
99 PRO E122 for Exeter and Dartmouth, and Plymouth, passim.
100 PRO E122/41/14, 201/1. All valuations are at collectors' estimates; market prices were often double this.
101 See for instance 1460/1 and 1470/1, PRO E122/40/35, 41/1,3,4.
102 PRO E122/41/6, 201/1; M Kowaleski, 'Women's Work in a Market Town: Exeter in the Late Fourteenth Century', in B Hanawalt, ed, *Women and Work in Pre-Industrial Europe* (Bloomington, 1986), 155, and notes 5, 8, 58.
103 M Kowaleski, 'The Commercial Dominance of a Medieval Provincial Oligarchy: Exeter in the Late Fourteenth Century', *Medieval Studies*, 46 (1984), 355–84.
104 See note 85.
105 Carus-Wilson, *Exeter*, 23–5.
106 PRO E159/253, Recorda, Trin. mm.18-18v , 28-30v, 31v.
107 Watkins, *Dartmouth*, 410.
108 PRO E122/40/7a, 15/3.
109 Poundage figures, which included values for alien cloths exported, can be found in E Power and MM Postan, eds, *Studies in English Trade in the Fifteenth Century* (1933), 337–9, 352–4; PRO Lord Treasurer's Remembrancer's Enrolled Customs Accounts, E356/23 mm.15–20, 53–6.
110 KR Andrews, *Trade, Plunder and Settlement* (Cambridge, 1984), 41–50; GV Scammell, 'The English in the Atlantic Islands, c. 1450–1650', *MM* 72 (1986), 295–7.

10 *Devon Privateering from Early Times to 1688*

JOHN C APPLEBY

ALTHOUGH THERE WERE OCCASIONS when medieval English monarchs built up the royal navy, this period was marked by the absence of any continuous naval development, at least until the mid-seventeenth century. Indeed, by the later sixteenth century, when Elizabethan England was facing the challenge of Habsburg Spain, the Crown was forced into an uneasy partnership with privateering and piratical elements to fight the war, the consequence of which was reflected in growing disorder at sea during the 1580s and 1590s, and in a massive increase in English piracy in the early seventeenth century. In theory, of course, there was a world of difference between the lawfully commissioned privateer, seeking reparation for former wrongs from a specific community, and the uncommissioned pirate, who robbed and plundered indiscriminately. In practice, however, as the victims of English attacks affirmed, privateering and piracy were inextricably intertwined. This situation only began to change during the later seventeenth century, when the slow crystallization of an effective state navy ensured that the days of private entrepreneurs, who could slip easily from piracy into privateering, were numbered.[1]

It was within this general context that Devon privateering and piracy developed and flourished during this period. More specific local factors combined to produce a vigorous tradition of private maritime enterprise of varying shades of legality. The long medieval wars with France, followed by relatively shorter conflicts with Spain in the sixteenth and early seventeenth centuries, provided both a focus and an incentive for maritime activity in the South West, which was closely related to overseas commercial patterns, shipping resources and social attitudes. From an early date county society and culture favoured the development of organized, businesslike plunder at sea. This encouraged members of the landed classes, as well as merchants and shipowners, to forgo safer investments in land for riskier investments in privateering, and even piracy. This combination of landed and mercantile wealth gave Devon enterprise its strength, mobilizing wider resources of capital than would otherwise have been available, and spilt over into colonial enterprise in the later sixteenth and early seventeenth centuries. After the 1620s Devon enterprise tailed off to a very low ebb, and as the seventeenth century came to a close Devon privateering and piracy were in a transitional state, of which the full consequences were only to become clear in the succeeding century.

10.1 Lundy Island in the Bristol Channel, 11 miles from the north coast of Devon. An eighteenth-century drawing by Sparrow of the remains of the early-medieval Castle of the Marisco family, who in their time were notorious pirates. *(Devon and Exeter Institution, Exeter)*

The Medieval Experience: a Pattern Established

The middle ages were a time of general lawlessness at sea. For much of the period legitimate privateering, truce-breaking, and attacks on neutral shipping combined to turn the Channel into a treacherous strip of water infested with predators from Normandy, Brittany, Castile, Flanders, and England. All induced a wearying cycle of reprisal and counter-reprisal, setting a pattern which persisted well into the seventeenth century. Devon adventurers earned an unrivalled reputation for their activities during these years, one to which the author of the *Libel of English Policy* (1436) was to pay tribute when he linked Dartmouth and Plymouth with Fowey in Cornwall, another notorious west country nest of pirates and sea-rovers, as the three English towns which had been chosen by Edward III to make war on Brittany.[2]

Devon piracy and privateering in their very early days are shrouded in darkness. It may be assumed, however, that as soon as vessels ventured across, or up, the Channel either on fishing or trading voyages there would be men lying in wait, ready to seize the chance to acquire easy plunder. As FW Brooks suggested long ago, at this stage there was probably little distinction between fishing, trade, and piracy. Adventurers might engage in all three on the same voyage.[3] This type of activity, even when plunder became the sole or prime objective of a voyage, was essentially small-scale and opportunistic, involving small craft in short-distance raids into or across the Channel. It could encompass local feuds with other ports along the coast, such as the long-running dispute between Dartmouth and Lyme Regis, local raids by outlaw-pirates such as William de Marisco (*c*1240) based on Lundy Island in the Bristol Channel, or hit-and-run expeditions along the coasts of Normandy and Brittany.[4] The long-term consequences of the loss of Normandy in 1204 encouraged the development of more organized and sophisticated forms of raiding and plunder, and at certain times during the ensuing long conflict with France, piracy and privateering reached endemic proportions. The 1340s and 1370s witnessed near-anarchic conditions at sea during which precedents and patterns of enterprise were firmly established, combining a mixture of lawlessness, revenge, greed and what Ralph Griffiths calls 'rampant anti-foreignness'.[5]

For much of the fourteenth century, for which there is some written record, the typical form of enterprise was the seemingly random sacking of foreign vessels as they lay moored in Devon ports and harbours. Attacks on ships from Zealand, Spain, France and Italy lying in Plymouth and Dartmouth came to the King's attention in 1292, 1317, 1323, 1336, 1343 and beyond.[6] No doubt there were other cases which went unrecorded. Although a special commission of inquiry was issued in June 1327 to deal with piracies committed along the coast of Devon, its success seems to have been mixed. It may have done something to prevent outrageous attacks on foreign vessels in local ports, but it could do little to halt the growing number of piratical forays into the Channel by Dartmouth or Plymouth men.[7] From the late 1330s there are increasing complaints against the depredations of mariners from both ports, operating either in the approaches to the Channel or along the north-west coasts of France. The ships taken tended to be carrying miscellaneous cargoes of varying value, which were usually disposed of locally. Early in 1339 a number of merchants from Bruges and Lescluses in Flanders complained of the seizure of *La Godeyere*, of 200 tons, by Simon Feroun of Plymouth (and others from divers parts of the realm) off the coast of Brittany. Her cargo included 50 casks of copper, valued at £200; 100 lasts of herring, valued at £300; sea coals worth £10; and 1,500 boards valued at £10.[8] Two years later, in April 1341, William Gascoun, a merchant of Brittany, complained that some 'evildoers' in a barge of Dartmouth had seized *La Katerine* of Daurey, freighted with salt, cloth, and other goods, also off the Breton coast. Another ship taken in the same area at about the same time was brought into Plymouth, where her lading of salt was divided up between Thomas and John Austyn, Simon and John Begherewe (or Bonerewe), John Spert, Walter Hereward, and their accomplices, and subsequently sold.[9] On this occasion the lands and goods of the ringleaders, who included the Austyns, were ordered to be taken into the King's hands and the culprits brought before the King and Council. As in so many other cases during the period, however, the outcome is unknown.

Although these are random samples, selected from limited evidence, they underline the early importance of Dartmouth and Plymouth as centres for maritime activity of dubious legality. The other Devon ports seem to have been only intermittently active during these early years. The rise to prominence of Dartmouth was overtly recognised in December 1390, when a special grant was made to the port of the sole export of tin for three years. Dartmouth had earned this special privilege by becoming

> above other places in the realm . . . strong in shipping, and therewith has wrought great havoc on the King's enemies in time of war.[10]

It might have been added that the King's friends, too, had suffered at the hands of the men of Dartmouth, and in peacetime as well as war.

This predatory activity was in some ways a development of the shore-based attacks evident in the late-twelfth and early-thirteenth centuries. It was not highly organised, usually involving only one or two vessels, but in 1345 and 1346 a squadron of 13 private marauders from Dartmouth seized *La Seinte Marie Magdaleine* of Pleasaunce as she was bound for Flanders with a cargo of wines. In the course of a violent attack some of the Spanish ship's company were thrown overboard and the master was warned not to sue for restitution. Little is known about the pirate fleet's organisation, except that two vessels were owned by William Esmale of Dartmouth.[11]

The mounting disorder and increasing violence at sea are reflected in two separate incidents involving Plymouth and Dartmouth men in 1350 and 1361. The first concerned the seizure of the *Trinitie* of Fowey, laden with wheat and other victuals for the King's garrison at Bordeaux, by the *Nicholas* and the *Rodecoq* of Plymouth. The accomplices of the Plymouth men included men from Bristol and Chester, all of whom, it was reported after the attack, 'are now vagabonds in divers counties of England'.[12] Just over a decade later a partly English-owned vessel, bound from Nantes to Flanders, was seized by a small fleet of ships, some of which were owned by a William le Smale of Dartmouth, possibly one and the same as in 1345–6. Again this was a particularly violent attack during which, it was alleged, the master and 100 others of the ship's company were killed. Even allowing for contemporary exaggeration, there were clearly heavy casualties, reflecting, perhaps, the value of the prize – put at a staggering £20,500.[13]

The later-fourteenth and early-fifteenth centuries saw the culmination of these varying elements of maritime depredation, in which English privateering and piracy in general reached unprecedented heights. It is no coincidence that this period saw the emergence of one of the first privateering magnates in Devon, John Hawley, the wealthy merchant and ship owner of Dartmouth, whose ships terrorised the Channel for nearly thirty years, and whose son, also John, continued the business of plunder well into the 1430s.[14] Hawley senior's businesslike, entrepreneurial organisation, his ability to combine private enterprise with royal service, his combination of greed, godliness and patriotism, all make him a genuine forerunner of his more well-known Elizabethan successors, albeit within a European, rather than a transatlantic, context.

Hawley's involvement in privateering can be traced back to December 1379 when, together with Benedict de Bottessana and Thomas Ashenden of Dartmouth, he received a licence to set out a fleet of seven vessels against the King's enemies.[15] There is no evidence concerning the fate of the venture, but thereafter Hawley was regularly involved in privateering and sometimes piratical activity. In 1386 two of his ships captured a Genoese vessel which had sought shelter on the coast of Brittany; the following year one of his ships seized a vessel of Zealand; two years later, in 1389, he was in trouble again for the unwarranted capture of two more vessels. During the same year he was pardoned for taking 28 tuns of wine out of England without a licence.[16] Despite such mounting irregularities, Hawley's public career blossomed. In 1375 he served as Mayor of Dartmouth, as he was to do many times in the future. In 1388 he became one of the collectors of customs in the port, and along the way he was busy acquiring land in Devon, Cornwall, and the Scilly Isles, as well as a business interest in tinworks about Bodmin.[17]

Hawley's predatory activities continued into the reign of Henry IV when, in October 1403, with Thomas Norton of Bristol, he seized seven Spanish vessels in the Channel laden with goods owned by Spanish, Italian and Flemish merchants. The seizure aroused a storm of controversy, forcing the King to take unusually strong measures against both Hawley and his son. Although Hawley senior evaded a command to attend the King in person, claiming to be 'not able to ride, and not well able to walk', his son suffered a brief period of imprisonment towards the end of 1406.[18] Even so, there were always limits to what the crown could do to discipline privateering 'barons' like the two Hawleys. Both were dominant figures in the local community; both also played a leading role in the organisation of local defence and naval services. Although the Hawleys indulged in piratical activity, their raids into the Channel helped keep the enemy at a safe distance, and could sometimes be used as a card in the game of high diplomacy.[19] The elder Hawley died in 1408 (Fig. 10.2), but his son maintained the family business, attacking English and other vessels intermittently until his own death in 1436.

The Lancastrian monarchy certainly made some effort to deal with the rising tide of lawlessness at sea. In 1414, for example, Henry V introduced an anti-piracy law which would have turned some of the activities of the Hawleys, and those who maintained them on land, into acts of high treason.[20] However, the legislation soon proved unworkable, essentially because no medieval government could deal effectively with the broader challenge to order that piracy (or illegal privateering) posed. The problem was graphically underlined in Devon in the very year that the anti-piracy legislation was enacted. Following the appointment of a commission of oyer and terminer for the county to investigate charges of piracy as well as of counterfeiting coin, in what has been described as an 'extraordinary act of defiance' most of the local juries simply refused to make any returns to the visiting justices.[21] Such attitudes were to hamper government attempts to deal with piracy through to the early seventeenth century.

It was partly for this reason that Devon privateering and piracy persisted during the 1420s and 1430s, although at a lower level than during the days of John Hawley the elder. The breakdown in political authority during the middle decades of the fifteenth century encouraged a revival of maritime lawlessness and disorder on a large scale. One of the more prominent figures in the business at this time was Thomas Gylle, merchant and ship owner of Kingsbridge near Dartmouth, whose ships were at sea from the mid-1430s through to the 1450s, plundering friend and foe alike. In January 1440 one of his vessels, the *Christopher* of Dartmouth, of 320 tons, attacked an English ship, the *George* of Wells (Norfolk), of 120 tons, at Start Point, sinking the vessel after plundering it of goods valued at £600.[22] In May 1449 there occurred Robert Winnington's spectacular privateering assault on the Hanseatic salt fleet. More than 100 vessels were captured by this Dartmouth seaman in an attack which revealed the vulnerability of Hanse shipping in the Channel.[23] In some ways this was a real harbinger of change, not just in the example it provided of the capabilities of organized privateering, but also in the connections it revealed between the leaders of the privateering fleet and some of the members of the King's Council. In this situation, as Postan

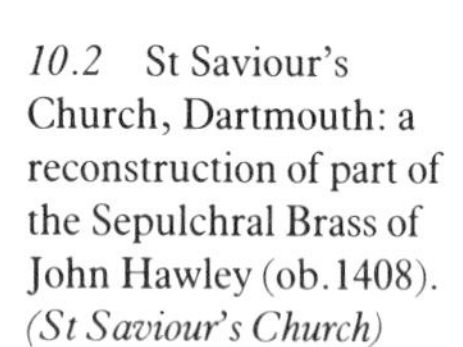

10.2 St Saviour's Church, Dartmouth: a reconstruction of part of the Sepulchral Brass of John Hawley (ob.1408). *(St Saviour's Church)*

10.3 East Budleigh Parish Church: a Bench-End with a carving of a three-masted sailing ship, her boat and an anchor. Note the seaman standing on the main yard. Undated but almost certainly contemporary with another bench-end dated 1537 and linked with Walter Raleigh esquire, who lived nearby at Hayes. He and his elder sons were actively involved in privateering in the 1540s. *(J Youings, courtesy of the Vicar and Churchwardens)*

argued, matters of state policy 'were made to serve the predatory aims of powerful men',[24] a pattern of enterprise full of prescience for the future. That it did not come to immediate fruition in the later fifteenth century was partly due to the revival of monarchical authority under Edward IV, which helped bring this bout of maritime lawlessness to an end. At the same time the ending in 1475 of the long conflict with France, and the consequent improvement in overseas trade, attracted merchants and ship owners back into more peaceful business, weakening the predatory drive of the 1450s before it could get into full gear.[25]

This, then, was a formative period, when merchants, masters, and mariners began to acquire experience and expertise in the business of plunder. In general, privateering and piracy were restricted to the ports of the south coast of the county, especially Dartmouth and Plymouth, and there is little evidence that Devon men sailed beyond the straits of Dover or beyond Ushant to the south-west.[26] They preyed mostly on French shipping, but there were many occasions when their attacks became indiscriminate and increasingly violent, most noticeably during the period from about 1300 to 1450. The scale of local enterprise is impossible to estimate, although it is evident that there were certain periods of intense activity at sea. Evidence of the size, build, or armament of the vessels used is also scant, but as Thomas Gylle's *Christopher*, of 320 tons, suggests, they were not all of small tonnage. Where local shipping is described it indicates that 'barges' were more commonly in use for most of the fourteenth century, but were replaced thereafter by 'balingers', faster, more manouverable vessels.[27]

Finally, it is worth emphasising that privateering and plunder were increasingly organized along businesslike lines during this period, and tended to be dominated by local merchants and ship owners. Landed families were also engaged in privateering, and even piracy, especially when they already had shipping interests of some kind. During the 1450s and 1460s members of the Courtenay family, whose head was the Earl of Devon, were regularly at sea on voyages of plunder. In the 1460s Sir Hugh Courtenay and his followers, in the *Peter Courtenay*, plundered the *Marie* of Dordrecht, laden with wines belonging to John Jay and other merchants of Bristol.[28] Moreover, the emergent business structure, of privateering in particular, encouraged a fairly broad cross-section of county society to participate in local maritime enterprise, ranging from yeoman farmers to craftsmen such as goldsmiths, and even priests. The *Galyot*, involved in the capture of the *Marie*, was partly owned by John Fennell, chaplain; the victuallers of the *Christopher* of Exmouth included Richard Duke, a yeoman of Exeter; and certain Dartmouth ships at sea during the mid-1460s were set out by a large syndicate including Sir Philip Courtenay and Sir John Gardener, priest.[29]

The Long Sixteenth Century: a Golden Age of Plunder

During the period from the 1540s through to the 1620s privateering and piracy flourished as never before. So great was the maritime disorder, in which Devon adventurers played a leading part, that by the close of the sixteenth century the English had earned for themselves in Europe the reputation of being a nation of pirates. Under the early Tudors government policy, combined with the expansion of Anglo-Iberian trade, kept piracy at a low level. However, Henry VIII's wars with France, in 1512–1513, 1522 and especially in 1545, encouraged the revival of privateering, again largely in Dartmouth and Plymouth. These wars left a legacy of robbery at sea which persisted, in varying forms, through to the late 1570s, often with official sponsorship or encouragement.[30]

Alongside the persistence of enmity towards France, the period also witnessed the growth of a deep and abiding hostility towards Spain, which was to affect local maritime enterprise profoundly. With the accession of Queen Elizabeth, England once more embraced Protestantism, and under Philip II Spain was more firmly entrenched than ever in the New World. Religious and commercial rivalry were thus to become entangled, especially from about 1569 with the failure of John Hawkins's attempt to penetrate the Spanish colonial market. Thereafter, piratical attacks against Spanish shipping in the Atlantic and the Caribbean, often in conjunction with French Huguenot adventurers, steadily mounted.[31] The rise of long-distance oceanic adventuring thus took place against a potentially explosive background, in which older forms of patriotism and greed were buttressed by ideological hatred. In the eyes of the leaders of this movement, Hawkins and Drake, pillage and plunder, reprisal and revenge, godliness and gratuitous violence formed part of a view of the world which identified England with true religion and what John Hawkins called 'God's own cause'.[32] All these varying elements were to flourish during the long war with Spain from 1585 to 1604, and for some adventurers, especially in Devon, that war never really ended. English piracy, sometimes masquerading under a debased patriotism, reached new heights in the early seventeenth century. The return of war with Spain in 1625 also saw the revival of large-scale privateering in all of the leading Devon ports. For many, the real end of the Elizabethan age came in the later 1620s.

The survival of the rich documentary material of the High Court of Admiralty provides much more detailed evidence of Devon maritime enterprise during this period than exists for the middle ages. As the work of Kenneth Andrews on Elizabethan privateering or Clive Senior on Jacobean piracy has shown, it is possible to derive from this material some rough estimates of the scale of maritime predation, to describe the type of vessels involved in privateering or piracy, including some indication of their manning and ordnance, and to make some analysis of the way the business of plunder was organised.[33]

Such details as are available of the number of Devon vessels engaged in privateering are provided in Table 10.1. These should be used with some caution. They are based on incomplete source material, the identification of individual vessels often being extremely difficult, so much so that it is impossible to provide a single estimate for the 1620s. Instead, the figures provided are maximum and minimum totals. Moreover, no realistic estimate can be made of unrecorded, or illegitimate, privateering by adventurers who put to sea without any formal commission. This is a serious problem, particularly from 1585 to 1604, when the formal administration of

Table 10.1
Devon privateering ships, 1544 to 1625–30

	1544	1558	1589–91	1598	1625–30
Total (Devon)	12–16*	22	42	10	175–230
Overall Total	na	na	236	86	663–950

* The 'west parts' in general.
na: No data available.

Sources: *Letters and Papers of the Reign of Henry VIII*, XIX, Part 2, 337; Oppenheim, *Maritime History*, 31; Andrews, *Elizabethan Privateering*, 32–3; Appleby, 'English Privateering', II, 98–137, 141–5, 304.

privateering was slowly being established, and when the Lord Admiral, Lord Howard of Effingham, was prepared, at a price, to turn a blind eye to irregularities.[34] For this reason the figures for 1589–91 and 1598 are probably underestimates when compared with those for the shorter, and better regulated, war of the 1620s.

Nevertheless the data in Table 10.1 clearly underline the growing significance of privateering within the local economy, and especially its fundamental importance for the shipping industry and ship owners. Devon was usually the leading non-metropolitan county involved in privateering although London, which dominated the business more than any other port, usually set out more privateers each year than all of the Devon ports combined.[35] By the 1620s, indeed, the Devon ports – of which Plymouth and Dartmouth were still easily the most important, with Exeter not far behind – accounted for about one quarter of the English privateering effort.[36] Even allowing for the problem of unrecorded activity, there was clearly a significant increase in Devon privateering from the later 1590s to the wars of the 1620s. In part this merely reflects a decline in Devon privateering, especially during the 1590s, when London adventurers came to dominate the business in an unprecedented way. It is ironic that, as local enterprise tailed off, complaints against the depredations of Dunkirk privateers mounted. In March 1602 the magistrates and merchants of Dartmouth, Exeter, and Totnes, as well as those of Lyme Regis and Taunton, complained that their

> trade exceedingly decayeth, the strength of shipping in those parts is much impaired, her Majesty's Customs diminished, and the country thereabouts greatly impoverished,

all because of 'great and grievous losses' at sea at the hands of the Dunkirkers.[37] By contrast with the Elizabethan conflict, the wars of the 1620s were short and came at the end of a period of peace during which Devon's overseas trade and shipping had flourished. This economic buoyancy enabled Devon adventurers to set out more privateers after 1625, to which the outbreak of war with France in 1627 was an added imperative.

In addition to these broad economic differences, however, the period separating the 1590s from the 1620s saw an important shift in sea-politics at court. During the long Elizabethan war with Spain many of the leading promoters of privateering ventures – Drake, Hawkins, and Raleigh – became engaged in semi-official expeditions in which the Queen herself had a large interest. Such ventures, which included Devon men and capital, usually had a wider purpose than mere plunder.[38] By the 1620s, however, this partnership between public and private enterprise had broken down. The government of Charles I was certainly prepared to encourage privateering, but neither the King nor his leading ministers were willing to participate in the type of joint-stock enterprise engaged in by Elizabeth and many of her ministers. With the benefit of hindsight it is possible to connect this with the slow crystallization of a state navy, a development deserving more attention than it can be given here, but its immediate impact in Devon was that, during the 1620s, men and capital resources were no longer being attracted into large semi-public enterprises based in London.[39] In the short run this seems to have contributed to the flourishing state of privateering from 1625 to 1630, enabling merchants, ship owners, gentry, and local officials to build up extensive interests in the business. Allan Penny, an Exeter merchant, had interests in at least six vessels set out with letters of marque; Sir Edward Seymour, formerly Vice-Admiral of the county, had an interest in four vessels set out from Dartmouth; and Edward Eastman, a merchant of Barnstaple, had interests in five vessels.[40]

Privateering was clearly an important activity in Devon during this period. Probably more than half of the region's shipping resources were engaged in the business during the early years of the Elizabethan war with Spain, and the proportion for the 1620s was certainly higher. Yet most of these vessels, as Table 10.2 indicates, were fairly small. Although these figures reveal a generally upward trend in the tonnage of privateers, even in the 1620s more than half of the Devon vessels engaged in privateering were below 100 tons burden. Moreover, all of the larger vessels, those of 200 tons and above, were of Plymouth, Dartmouth, and Exeter.[41] Most of them were well-manned and well-armed. The range of armaments included heavy ordnance, capable of holing an enemy vessel, but used sparingly so as not to damage a potential prize seriously; smaller pieces such as 'murderers', used more often to disable and kill the crew of an enemy vessel; and a miscellany of smaller hand weapons such as muskets and pistols and even pikes, clubs, crossbows, and darts. Despite the arsenal of weapons carried by many privateers, successful plunder usually depended on having a large number of men, not only to board and win a prize by hand-to-hand fighting, but also to man any captured vessels. Consequently, privateers were usually very heavily manned. The *Swallow* of Barnstaple, of 80 tons, was set out against Spain in August 1626 with a crew of 70 men. As a purely merchant vessel she would have had barely half that number. Even aboard larger vessels, where conditions were generally not so cramped, men were still forced to live and work in what must have been stifling proximity.[42]

Table 10.2
Tonnage variation of Devon privateers 1589–91 and 1625–30

Tons	0–99	100–199	200–299	300+	Unknown	Total
1589–91	18	2	2	0	20	42
1625–30	97–130*	61–80	14–17	2	1	175–230

* Minimum–maximum figures.

Sources: Andrews, *Elizabethan Privateering*, 32–3; Appleby, 'English Privateering', II, 98–137, 142–5.

Most of these recruits were mariners or from marine-related occupations. However, the lure of prize and profit at sea also attracted a wide range of landsmen into service aboard privateers, as well as providing casual employment for underemployed craftsmen and artisans. The company of the *Katherine* of Stonehouse, at sea against the French from 1563 to 1564, included Richard Martin, farmer, from Stoke Damerell, and Ralph Janson, a yeoman from Plymouth.[43] The shortage of surviving crew lists for Devon privateers in the sixteenth and early-seventeenth centuries makes any statistical analysis of privateering crews impossible, but it is clear that men of all degrees, except the very highest or very lowest, and of many occupations, served aboard Devon privateers during this period. They were of all ages: by the standards of the day Thomas Saunders, aged 60, John Raw, aged 62, and John of Meale *alias* Teague, aged 67, the three oldest members of the company of the *Samaritan* of Dartmouth in 1626, were all well advanced in years. The core of her crew of 140 came from the highly localized hinterland of her home port, 31 being resident in the parishes and towns of south Devon, and only three of them had actually been born outside the county.[44] However, some of the mariners who served aboard other Devon privateers came from a much wider geographical background, including Weymouth, Aldborough, Lincoln, and London.[45]

There was usually no problem in finding recruits to serve aboard privateering ships in this period. Towards the end of 1601 one official in Plymouth complained that most of 'the best men for sea service in these parts will shift themselves to the sea in men-of-war', to the detriment of the Queen's service.[46] The lure of private service, which attracted such a diverse range of recruits, was essentially financial. According to custom the crew, like the owners of the vessel and her victuallers, received one third of all prizes taken and adjudged as lawful by the High Court of Admiralty. The crew's third was divided up on a share system according to rank and position. Although the system could vary from ship to ship, the captain and his officers usually received the lion's share. Thus the captain of the *Willing Mind* of Exeter received 12 shares, his lieutenant 9, and the ordinary mariners 2½. Of course the value of the crew's third was related to the type of prize taken. One share in a French vessel taken by the *Edward* of Topsham in 1629 was worth £2 10s: by comparison, a single share in a Portuguese ship taken by the *Willing Mind* of Exeter in 1626 was worth at least £10. In the latter case the captain's share amounted to £120 and that of the ordinary sailor came to £25, for a voyage that lasted little more than several months.[47] But the prize taken by the *Willing Mind*, a rich 'Brazilman' laden with sugar and other goods valued at £14,000, was a rare catch. More typical was the French vessel taken by the *Edward*, where the common sailor's share was £7 10s, or the prize taken by the *Indeavour* of Topsham in 1631, out of which William Peirce, mariner, expected only £2 or £2 10s.[48] In addition to these shares, however, the crew of a privateering vessel were entitled to 'pillage', an ill-defined custom which some crews exploited to ransack prize ships of their furniture and cargoes. The *Madre de Dios*, one of the richest prizes ever brought into a Devon harbour, was stripped of the better part of her rich cargo of jewels, silks, and spices within hours of her capture by a small fleet of English privateers in 1592. Indeed, it was the prospect of pillage that drove men on at sea, regardless of the dangers. In February 1629 the *Dolphin* of Dartmouth finally caught up with a rich 'Brazilman' after a long chase at sea lasting from four o'clock in the morning until nine or ten in the evening. As some of the *Dolphin*'s company later recounted, they

> hoised out their boat to go aboard the prize . . . *for desire of pillage* . . . [but] so many men pressed and leapt into the boat that she was overturned and two men lost or drowned.[49]

Ironically, the Portuguese had surrendered without offering any resistance to the English.

Tonnage, manning, and armament could decisively affect the tactical choices open to privateers. Commenting in 1545 on the small size of the west country privateers, John Lord Russell pointed out that 'their usage . . . [was] to keep along the shore and meddle only with merchants'. These tactical disadvantages could be offset by consorts at sea between two or more vessels – as some Dartmouth privateers showed to good effect in the 1540s.[50] But in general Devon privateers hunted alone, or occasionally in conjunction with a small auxiliary vessel known as a pinnace. In March 1588 Drake warned the Privy Council of the dangers of this practice, arguing that the 'smaller sort of . . . shipping' was especially vulnerable on the coast of Spain to

> those Flemish flyboats, which go in fleets, by the least five, seven, and nine in company, which will not leave one English man of war untaken upon that coast, and I doubt lest some are taken already.[51]

Despite the warning, the almost anarchic individualism of Devon, and English, privateering captains persisted. And when privateers did consort together at sea the result was often a bitter dispute concerning the ownership of a prize, leading to lengthy and horrendously complex legal cases before the High Court of Admiralty in London.[52]

With such constraints Devon privateering tended to be focussed on short or middle-distance targets. Only a handful of Devon adventurers was seriously interested in long-distance plunder in the Caribbean and elsewhere in the New World, although their activities, as recounted by Hakluyt and Purchas, have diverted attention away from the more typical small adventurer who plundered in western European waters. Sir Francis Drake or his successor, Captain William Parker of Plymouth, both of whom carried out a series of spectacular raids in the West Indies,[53] were the princes among privateers, but for most others it was a small-scale business, albeit one with high risks, based on a private war at sea of small actions and petty conflicts. During 1626, for example, the *John and Margaret* of Topsham, under the command of Andrew Fulford, spent about ten weeks sailing along the coasts of Spain and Portugal fruitlessly seeking a prize. A quick foray to the Azores proved equally unrewarding. However, on their return voyage the company sighted a vessel off Cape Finisterre which they captured after a lengthy chase. The crew of the vessel, the *Golden Sun* of Hamburg, put up a stout resistance. In the ensuing fight, which lasted for nearly two hours, seven of the *John and Margaret*'s company were killed, including Fulford's son, and another eight were wounded. All this was for a prize which turned out to be laden with fish, whose value could not have been much greater than £1,000.[54]

Privateering was thus for most of its participants an unglamorous and very risky business. As a business, however, it could be readily combined with other types of enterprise such as overseas trade or colonial venturing. Indeed, as in the sixteenth century, all three might be combined in the same speculative venture. In 1627, for example, the *Thunder* of Topsham, set out by Allan Penny and others of Exeter on a reprisal voyage, was also furnished for a trading voyage to Virginia, 'in case she should not have lighted upon either Spaniard or Frenchman to make prize of'.[55] Ventures which combined trade and privateering were especially common on voyages to the Mediterranean or Africa. Most Devon vessels departing for, or returning from, southern voyages in the 1620s seem to have carried letters of marque, enabling them to indulge in speculative plunder off the Iberian coasts on the voyage home.[56] But the practice had a long history, not the least of its adherents having been Sir Richard Grenville when engaged with Sir Walter Raleigh in establishing English colonists on the eastern seaboard of North America in the 1580s.[57]

Unfortunately the speculative element in privateering always threatened to reduce the business to disorder. Both at sea and on land this was a world of lies, deceit, betrayal, and sharp practice. In 1618 Sir Lewis Stukeley, then Vice-Admiral of Devon, alleged that his father had been deceived by Raleigh out of a £10,000 share due to him for an adventure in the *Tyger* in 1585. The story rings true even if Stukeley had his reasons to blacken Raleigh's posthumous reputation.[58] Sir Walter was certainly involved in the collapse of a privateering syndicate, headed by Sir John Gilbert, amid a welter of accusations of embezzlement following the capture in 1602 of a rich Venetian prize. Six other English captains were involved in the seizure of the *St Mark*, and all were determined to get their share of the plunder. Captain Doggett, commander of one of the privateer ships, pursued a legal vendetta against Gilbert lasting several years, even though to meet the costs he was forced to sell off house and home, reducing his wife and nine children to near penury.[59]

Despite the disorder and the disputes, privateering continued to attract adventurers from a broad cross-section of Devon society. Members of well-established county families, especially younger sons, as well as the less-wealthy parish gentry, were all attracted in varying degrees to the business of plunder. According to Andrews it was the gentlemen who did most to transform the petty marauding in the Channel of the 1560s and 1570s into the oceanic campaign of plunder in the 1580s and 1590s.[60] Yet the importance of their considerable investment should not blind us to the extent to which privateering also rested on petty contributions from a host of smaller investors such as fishermen, bakers, inn-keepers, rope-makers, or gentlemen of small fortune who were willing to gamble their few savings in the victualling of a privateer.[61] The victualling of the *Samaritan* of Dartmouth, set out in 1626 by Sir Edward Seymour, illuminates this pattern of investment. The total cost of provisioning the ship came to £476 15s 8d. Edward Hart, Captain of the *Samaritan*, was responsible for the victualling arrangements. Instead of taking sole responsibility for what was a large investment, Hart spread the costs of provisioning among a wide range of small adventurers. In return for small quantities of provisions friends or associates received bills of adventure which promised them a share in any prizes taken at sea in proportion to the value of their original investment. Table 10.3 summarizes details of the known victuallers of the ship. Although incomplete, it provides some insight into the type of investors attracted to the business of privateering, ranging from Thomas Woodward, a young gentleman who 'depends upon his father', to Walter Diamond, an elderly rope-maker who 'is little worth'. Among the other victuallers Henry Turpin possessed a total estate valued at £300, that of Christopher Searle was worth

Table 10.3
Known victuallers of the *Samaritan* of Dartmouth, 1626

Name	Age	Occupation or description	Adventure	Value £ s d
Thomas Woodward	25	Gentleman	A shallop, drum &c.*	62 0 0
Walter Diamond	56	Rope-maker	Pork, powder, match, &c.	33 2 2
George Plumley	29	Gentleman	Bread and beer	25 5 0
Aldred Staplehill	48	Merchant	Irish beef, pork, shot, a gilt lantern &c.	25 0 0
William Sames	–	Baker	Bread	18 15 0
Richard Smyth	34	Merchant	Beef	14 0 0
Andrew Sames	40	Fisherman	2 Barrels of powder	10 0 0
Christopher Searle	40	Merchant	Fish and a flag	7 0 0
Henry Turpin^	30	Gentleman	Not stated	unknown
Nicholas Fortescue~	32	Gentleman	Not stated	unknown

* And other provisions. Hart claimed that Seymour had not fully furnished the ship.
^ Of Thorverton.
~ Of Totnes. Apart from these two, the rest were of Dartmouth.

Source: PRO, HCA 13/232, Part 3.

£5, and that of Richard Smyth apparently was valued at only 2½d, after his debts were paid.

Did the gamble pay off? Was privateering a profitable business? Details of costs are exceedingly scant for this period; and while those relating to prizes are more plentiful, they, too, are limited and need to be used with caution. Despite its limitations, the material in Table 10.4 suggests that privateering was by no means an easy pathway to wealth and profit.[62] Certainly Devon privateers were responsible for the capture of an impressive number of prizes. Totals of 39 for 1589–91 and 194 for 1625–30 indicate that the number taken was at least roughly equal to the number of privateers set out during these years. The aggregate total value of these captures is equally impressive. Based on contemporary estimates, prizes valued at nearly £130,000 were taken during the 1620s, and if account is taken of the prizes of unknown value the total may be nearer £200,000 – or between one fifth and one quarter of the value of prizes taken by English privateers overall. However, the individual value of these prizes varied considerably. As Table 10.4 shows, in the 1620s no less than three-quarters of the prizes of known value taken by Devon privateers were valued at under £1,000. Many of them were small French fishing or coasting vessels, often not worth more than £300 to £400, but easy to plunder in fairly large numbers. By contrast, the richer Spanish prizes proved more elusive; and while the lonely Portuguese 'Brazilman' laden with sugar, tobacco, and hides was an easier target, Devon privateers faced stiff competition in their capture from other English, as well as Dutch, men-of-war.[63]

When it was organised as a business, privateering could be highly profitable. Drake, for example, made a fortune from his privateering voyages, but he was an experienced and skilful sea captain who paid close attention to the organisation of his voyages, especially his earlier ones. He knew how to control large numbers of unruly mariners during long, often frustrating, cruises at sea, and he had the professional's eye for the best hunting grounds for prize.[64] Luck could be a decisive variable in the successful outcome of a venture, and privateering remained a volatile enterprise in which profit in one year might easily turn into loss in another. At the level below the large-scale, semi-public ventures of Drake and Hawkins, the fortunes of most Devon adventurers during this period were very mixed. Unlike the professional operators in London, most provincial privateers never quite made it into the big league of plunder and prize.

Table 10.4
Valuations of prizes taken by Devon Privateers, 1589–91 and 1625–30

Range of values £	1589–91* Number	1589–91* Value £	1625–30** Number	1625–30** Value £
1–999	6	1,135	92	29,293
999–4999	4	7,195	20	44,843
5000+	2	26,000	8	54,570
Total known	12	34,330	120	128,706
Unknown	27	–	74	–
Total Prizes	39	–	194	–

* Includes a share of one prize claimed by a Weymouth privateer.
** Includes 26 prizes taken by Devon privateers in consort with other men-of-war.

Sources: Andrews, *Elizabethan Privateering*, 254–8; Appleby, 'English Privateering', II, 237–62, 265, 289–94.

If this conclusion raises a question mark over the description of these years as a 'golden age' of plunder, it must also be admitted that there was a darker side to the period. Privateering acted as a spawning-ground for piracy, especially as it became increasingly difficult to integrate large numbers of mariners who had served aboard privateers back into peacetime occupations. By the early Jacobean period the link between piracy and unemployment was openly affirmed by Hakluyt and other commentators. In July 1611 Sir Ferdinando Gorges, governor of Plymouth Fort, warned the earl of Salisbury that the problem was likely to get worse because

> these peaceable times affords no means of employments to the multitude of people that daily do increase, and many are enforced (by necessity) to seek some ways to sustain themselves.[65]

Yet there were many different paths into piracy, and by no means all of those taking them were unemployed mariners. In a society such as that of Devon, where under-employment was as serious a problem as unemployment, coastal piracy was a useful part-time occupation. Moreover, even among deep-sea rovers piracy was not usually a permanent occupation. It was more a temporary activity pursued by men who expected to return to homes ashore after a couple of voyages at sea.

Aiders and abettors ashore were to be found at all levels of society. Support also came from local admiralty officials who were responsible for dealing with the menace. From Sergeant Gilbert Peppit in the 1570s through to Richard Hawkins in the early seventeenth century, accusations were levelled against officials who sheltered and protected pirates.[66] Early Stuart Plymouth was a hotbed of illegal activity, whose corrupting influence dragged the city authorities and local admiralty officers into a dangerous game of judicial rivalry. In 1605 Richard Hawkins, Vice-Admiral of the county, alleged that neither the Mayor nor his officers would do anything against the pirates living in the town. Instead, he averred, they spent their time publicly reporting that Hawkins was in the pay of the pirates, and 'excluded [him] from their fellowship' for trying to uphold the jurisdiction of the admiralty. But, he added, only one pirate had been apprehended by the town authorities, and then, after payment of a 'composition', he had been set free. Moreover,

10.4 Buckland Abbey, Devon, the property bought by Sir Francis Drake in 1581 from his profits from his great voyage of circumnavigation, which certainly made him, in the eyes of the Spaniards, the greatest pirate of his age. By T Allom, 1832, engraved by E Challis. *(Devon and Exeter Institution)*

In the absence of Sir Richard they meet the pirates and see them daily . . . Alleging that it is cruelty in Sir Richard for prosecuting pirates.

In fact, none of the principals to the dispute had clean hands: James Bagg, the Mayor, was a regular purchaser of pirate booty (see below, chapter 13), while Hawkins was eventually dismissed from his post in 1610 for similar dealings with pirates.[67]

Seventeenth-century Recessional: Decline and Transition

The early seventeenth century was the heyday of organised piracy in Devon. Thereafter the problem all but disappeared from local shores. The reasons for this are complex, and are part of broader developments in the character of piracy itself, of the state response to it, and of changing social attitudes to the pirate community. Although this was to be a lengthy process, the signs are evident in the early seventeenth century with the emergence of a new breed of pirate such as Thomas Norton or Captain Salkeld, the pirate king of Lundy Island, whose deliberate plunder of local shipping undermined community support and sympathy for piratical activity.[68] Thomas Norton, a Devon mariner who was captured by Algerian pirates in 1620, escaped to Sallee from where, it was reported, he 'goes to sea on his own account, and is accounted . . . to exceed the Turk's cruelty to his own countrymen'.[69] The net result of these developments was the gradual physical, social, and cultural marginalisation of pirates during the seventeenth century, turning them into outlaws of the sea, living tenuously on the peripheries of empire in North America, the Caribbean, or Africa. It was left to Defoe to save the lives of such men from complete oblivion, but by then pirates were on the verge of becoming popular entertainment for the reading public of Georgian England.[70]

The decline in locally-organized piracy during the seventeenth century was accompanied by a serious decline in privateering after the 1620s. During the Dutch wars of 1652–4 and 1664–7, for example, less than a handful of Devon privateers seem to have been active, and of these the majority were small vessels under 100 tons burden.[71] Essentially this was because, after the 1620s, the general environment began to change in a number of fundamental ways. In particular, the rise of a large state navy, especially in the 1650s, almost inevitably reduced the importance of privateering. From being what Andrews has called the 'characteristic form of maritime warfare' during the reign of Elizabeth it was now on the way to becoming more of an incidental by-product of war. The private adventurer was in danger of becoming a hindrance to the effective performance of the navy, competing for the same scarce resources, especially manpower.[72] In March 1653 the Council of State empowered naval officers to take men out of privateers to make up their numbers.[73] By the 1660s many privateering commissions contained a special clause limiting the number of Englishmen serving aboard ship. When he received a letter of marque against the Dutch in April 1665, George Sparke, owner and captain of the *Barbara* of Dartmouth, had to give 'security not to employ any English in the said ship except four persons'.[74] It is clear that by the second half of the seventeenth century the government no longer gave the same encouragement to private enterprise as it had done in the past.

The impact of these naval developments on Devon was accentuated by a broad change in the privateering target areas. With the exception of the Spanish War of 1655–60, the very end of this period saw a switch away from southern targets such as Spain and Portugal to the United Provinces. The three Dutch wars of 1652–54, 1664–67 and 1672–74 (see below, Chapter 24) certainly witnessed a revival of privateering, if not on the scale of the 1620s, but it was focussed predominantly on the North Sea and the eastern Channel. The major privateering ports were thus to be found along the east and south-east coasts: the South West was peripheral to a conflict which remained restricted to a fairly narrowly-defined area.[75] Nor had local merchants and ship owners, who had formed the core of the privateering interest in Devon in the past, the same need to turn to the business of plunder. The county's overseas trade, especially the export of woollen cloth, was approaching its heyday. During the 1660s and 1670s merchants were more concerned about government convoys for trade and shipping than they were with setting out men-of-war.[76] However, the decline in local alternative activity during these decades was not terminal. With the renewal of the long rivalry with France at the end of the seventeenth century there was a revival of privateering in all of the Devon ports. But the naval developments over the period from 1588 to 1688 ensured that there would be no return to the days of Hawley or Drake.

10: Devon Privateering from early times to 1688

1 See PM Kennedy, *The Rise and Fall of British Naval Mastery* (1976), especially 33, 38–9, 47, 64, 66–7; and KR Andrews, *Elizabethan Privateering: English Privateering during the Spanish War, 1585–1603* (Cambridge, 1964). I am indebted to Professor Kenneth Andrews and Professor Joyce Youings for reading and commenting on this chapter.
2 T Wright, ed., *Political Poems and Songs Relating to English History*, 2 vols (1859–61), II, 166–7.
3 FW Brooks, *The English Naval Forces. 1199–1272* (n.d.), 119–120.
4 M Oppenheim, *The Maritime History of Devon* (Exeter, 1968), 6–7; FM Powicke, 'The Murder of Henry Clement and the Pirates of Lundy Island', in *Ways of Medieval Life and Thought* (1953), 38–68; *Calendar of Patent Rolls, 1321–24*, 151 (hereafter *CPR*); *CPR, 1334–38*, 293, 297, 355, 377, 578–9.
5 FA Mace, 'Devonshire Ports in the Fourteenth and Fifteenth Centuries', *Transactions of the Royal Historical Society*, 4th series, VIII (1925), 114–5, 123–4; RA Griffiths, *The Reign of King Henry VI: The Exercise of Royal Authority. 1422–1461* (1981), 170, 201–2, 551–3; A Beardwood, *Alien Merchants in England, 1350 to 1377: Their Legal and Economic Position* (Cambridge, Mass., 1931), 60–1.
6 Oppenheim, *Maritime History*, 8–9; *CPR, 1281–92*, 522; *CPR, 1313–17*, 699; *CPR, 1334–38*, 578–9; *CPR, 1340–43*, 451; *Calendar of Fine Rolls, 1337–47*, 448.
7 *CPR, 1327–30*, 153; Oppenheim, *Maritime History*, 9.
8 *CPR, 1338–40*, 280.
9 *CPR, 1340–43*, 210, 448, 540–1, 552.
10 *CPR, 1388–92*, 338; Mace, 'Devonshire Ports', 101; Percy Russell, *Dartmouth: a History of the Port and Town* (1950), 15.
11 *CPR, 1343–45*, 100.
12 *CPR, 1348–50*, 593; *CPR, 1350–54*, 24.
13 *CPR, 1358–61*, 584–5.
14 For John Hawley see also WR Childs, *Anglo-Castilian Trade in the Later Middle Ages* (Manchester, 1978), 164, 169; SP Pistono, 'Henry IV and John Hawley, Privateer, 1399–1408', *DAT*, CXI (1979), 145–63; CJ Ford, 'Piracy or Policy: The Crisis in the Channel, 1400–1403', *Transactions of the Royal Historical Society*, 5th series, 29 (1979), 63–77; CL Kingsford, 'West Country Piracy: The School of English Seamen', in *Prejudice and Promise in Fifteenth-Century England* (Oxford, 1925), 78–106, 177–203.
15 *CPR, 1377–81*, 405
16 *CPR, 1385–89*, 165; *CPR, 1388–92*, 147, 159.
17 Pistono, 'Henry IV and John Hawley', 147–8; *CPR, 1385–89*, 497, 500–1, 508; *CPR, 1388–92*, 100, 126, 156, 247; *CPR, 1391–96*, 359–60; Hawley's activities also extended to shipbuilding, *CPR, 1385–89*, 428.
18 Pistono, 'Henry IV and John Hawley', 145–7; FC Hingeston, ed., *Royal and Historical Letters during the Reign of Henry the Fourth*, 2 vols (1860), I, 270–3.
19 Ford, 'Piracy or Policy', 63–77. For the Hawleys' involvement in a variety of naval activities see S Rose, ed., *The Navy of the Lancastrian Kings: Accounts and Inventories of William Soper, Keeper of the King's Ships, 1422–1427* (NRS, CXXIII, 1982), 50. On their later activities, see DM Gardiner, ed., *A Calendar of Early Chancery Proceedings relating to West Country Shipping, 1388–1493* (DCRS, new series, 21, 1976), 8–9, 12–13, 15, 16–18, 25–6.
20 Gardiner, *Early Chancery Proceedings*, xiv–v; Oppenheim, *Maritime History*, 18–19.
21 E Powell, 'The Restoration of Law and Order', in GL Harriss, ed., *Henry V, The Practice of Kingship* (Oxford, 1985), 62–3; Kingsford, 'West Country Piracy', 80.
22 Gardiner, *Early Chancery Proceedings*, 41–2, 47–9, 72–5, 76–7.
23 Gardiner, *Early Chancery Proceedings*, xvii; Griffiths, *Henry VI*, 442, 554; MM Postan, 'The Economic and Political Relations of England and the Hanse from 1400 to 1475', reprinted in *Medieval Trade and Finance* (Cambridge, 1973), 273–4.
24 MM Postan, 'The Trade of Medieval Europe: The North', reprinted in *Medieval*

Trade, 216. Griffiths (*Henry VI*, 201–2) argues that in this period English skippers were able 'to recoup their losses in true Elizabethan fashion'.

25 C Ross, *Edward IV*, (1974), 219, 366–8. The change is reflected in a falling-off in complaints before the court of Chancery. See Gardiner, *Early Chancery Proceedings*, 101–19; Kingsford, 'West Country Piracy', 105.

26 But see Hingeston, *Royal and Historical Letters*, II, 63–6, for the capture of a Danzig vessel off Cape Finisterre, in 1405, by men-of-war from Plymouth, Dartmouth, and Barnstaple.

27 Gardiner, *Early Chancery Proceedings*, 47–9. For types of ships see chapter 8.

28 Gardiner, *Early Chancery Proceedings*, 90–1; JAF Thomson, 'The Courtenay Family in the Yorkist Period', *Bulletin of the Institute of Historical Research*, XLV (1972), 233–4.

29 Gardiner, *Early Chancery Proceedings*, 57–8, 69, 80–4, 90–1, 95–6, 109–12. See also Mace, 'Devonshire Ports', 115.

30 Oppenheim, *Maritime History*, 22–33; KR Andrews, 'The Expansion of English Privateering and Piracy in the Atlantic, c.1540–1625'. I am indebted to Professor Andrews for allowing me to make use of this unpublished paper. See also RG Marsden, ed., *Select Pleas in the Court of Admiralty*, 2 vols, (Selden Society, 1892–1895), 31–4 for a fairly typical example involving John and George Raleigh.

31 For the link between Devon enterprise and Huguenot, or Dutch Calvinist, privateering, see IA Wright, ed., *Documents concerning English Voyages to the Spanish Main, 1569–1580* (Hakluyt Society, 2nd series, LXXI, 1932), xvi, xxii–xxiii, for the Caribbean, and B Dietz, 'Privateering in North West European Waters, 1568–1572' (unpublished PhD thesis, University of London, 1959) for the general context.

32 G Connell-Smith, *Forerunners of Drake: A study of English Trade with Spain in the early Tudor period* (1954), gives the background. On the religious dynamic, see especially JK Laughton, ed., *State Papers relating to the Defeat of the Spanish Armada. Anno 1588*, 2 vols, (NRS, I & II, 1895–1900), I, 58–62, 147–9.

33 Andrews, *Elizabethan Privateering*; CM Senior, *A Nation of Pirates: English Piracy in its Heyday* (Newton Abbot, 1976); CM Senior, 'An Investigation into the Activities and Importance of English Pirates, 1603–1640' (unpublished PhD thesis, University of Bristol, 1972).

34 Andrews, *Elizabethan Privateering*, 22–4.

35 Andrews, *Elizabethan Privateering*, 120, 121–2, 140–4; JC Appleby, 'English Privateering during the Spanish and French Wars, 1625–1630', 2 vols (unpublished PhD thesis, University of Hull, 1983), II, app. 1, and 304.

36 Appleby, 'English Privateering', I, 207–14.

37 BL, Lansdowne MS 142, ff 123–4; *HMC, Salisbury MSS*, 10, 350–1. Plymouth seems to have done much better: JA Williamson, *Hawkins of Plymouth* (1969 edn), 196–200.

38 For this reason, and because of their different organisation, they are not included in the figures in Table 10.2.

39 For the Elizabethan background, see Andrews, *Elizabethan Privateering*. For the 1620s, see Appleby, 'English Privateering'.

40 Appleby, 'English Privateering', II, 98–121, 142–5, 175.

41 Appleby, 'English Privateering', II, 308.

42 On manning and armament in general see Andrews, *Elizabethan Privateering*, 37–45, and Appleby, 'English Privateering', I, 222–38, and II, 118, 144.

43 PRO, HCA 13/224.

44 PRO, HCA/13/230(1). See the evidence for the crew of the *Willing Mind* of Exeter, HCA 13/230 (2); or that for the crew of the *Dolphin* of Dartmouth, HCA 13/232 (1), for a similar pattern.

45 Namely, Portland Bun of Weymouth, captain, and John Petty of London, surgeon, of the *Willing Mind* of Topsham: PRO, HCA 13/232 (2); Stephen Garland of Aldborough, master of the *George* of Dartmouth, PRO, HCA 13/232 (1); and William Booth of Lincoln, captain of the *Dolphin* of Dartmouth, PRO, HCA 13/232 (1).

46 *HMC Salisbury MSS*, 11, 533–4.

47 PRO, HCA 13/232, parts 1 & 3; 13/234. William Drake, a local collector of tenths in Devon, and the captain of the *Willing Mind*, subsequently bought up the crew's shares at £10 per share.

48 PRO, HCA 13/234.

49 PRO, HCA 13/230, part 3; 13/232, part 1. On the *Madre de Dios* see Andrews, *Elizabethan Privateering*, 73.

50 *Letters and Papers of the Reign of Henry VIII*, XX, pt 1, 622; RMS Tugwood, 'Piracy and Privateering from Dartmouth and Kingswear, 1540–1558' (unpublished MA thesis, University of London, 1953), 34–5, 140–8.

51 Laughton, *State Papers relating to the Defeat of the Armada*, I, 94.

52 For example, see the case below involving Sir John Gilbert.

53 KR Andrews, ed., *English Privateering Voyages to the West Indies, 1588–95* (Hakluyt Society, 2nd series, CXI, 1959), 19–20, 59–85, 219–24, 308–25; S Purchas, *Hakluytus* Posthumus or Purchas His Pilgrimes, 20 vols (Glasgow, 1906), XVI, 113–31, 292–7.

54 PRO, HCA 13/230 (2), no. 164.

55 PRO, HCA 13/230 (3), no. 162. The close connection between privateering and colonisation is also discussed in Andrews, *Elizabethan Privateering*, chapter 9.

56 R Davis, *The Rise of the English Shipping Industry in the Seventeenth and Eighteenth Centuries* (1962), 331–2, 381. Both of the ships which entered Exeter from ports in Italy in 1628 were issued with letters of marque, as was the *John and Margaret* of Topsham, which was engaged in voyages to Barbary and the Canary Islands: PRO, E190/947/3; Appleby, 'English Privateering', I, 102, 104, 108.

57 D B Quinn, *Set Fair for Roanoke* (1985), 145–6.

58 'The Humble Petition and Information of Sir Lewis Stukeley', *The Harleian Miscellany*, III (1809), 65.

59 KR Andrews, 'Sir Robert Cecil and Mediterranean Plunder', *EHR*, LXXXVII (1972), 523, 528–9; BL, Lansdowne MS 142, ff.157–8, 247–8, 332; PRO, HCA 13/225; *HMC Salisbury MSS*, 11, 446–7, 457–8, 480–7, 527–8; 12, 98–9, 102–3, 117–9.

60 Andrews, *Elizabethan Privateering*, 15. For one such family see AL Rowse, *Sir Richard Grenville of the 'Revenge'* (1937), 39–40, 97, 116–8, 216–7, 248–9, 332, 347; Williamson, *Hawkins of Plymouth*, 34–8, 41, 164–7, 173–5, 194ff. As the survey of Devon ships of July 1570 makes clear, the Hawkins family was by far the largest ship owning group in Plymouth, with a fleet of 13 vessels totalling more than 2,000 tons: PRO, SP 12/71/75. I owe this reference to Professor RL Pollitt.

61 See, for example, the range of victuallers for Sir Edward Seymour's ship, the *Samaritan*, in 1626: PRO, HCA 13/232 (3), no. 171, and the backers of Bernard Drake's venture in 1586: PRO, HCA 13/27, ff 243, 260, 269v, 272v.

62 Davis, *Shipping Industry*, 331–2; Andrews, *Elizabethan Privateering*, 145 ff.

63 Appleby, 'English Privateering', chapter 4.

64 KR Andrews, *Drake's Voyages: A reassessment of their place in Elizabethan Maritime Expansion* (1967). Raleigh, too, seems to have made privateering pay: see VT Harlow, ed., *The Discoverie of the Large and Bewtiful Empire of Guiana by Sir Walter Ralegh* (1928), xxvi–xxix.

65 See the comments of Joseph May to Cecil, 8 June 1603, *HMC Salisbury MSS*, 15, 127; and of John Martyn, Mayor of Plymouth, in June 1603, *HMC Salisbury MSS*, 15, 151; KR Andrews, 'Elizabethan Privateering', in JA Youings, ed., *Raleigh in Exeter: Privateering and Colonisation in the reign of Elizabeth I* (Exeter, 1985), 4–5; PRO, SP14/65/16.

66 PRO, SP12/123/40, 122/32 & 58; JA Williamson, ed., *The Observations of Sir Richard Hawkins* (1933), lxxxiv–vi; PRO, HCA 1/43, f.84–84v; *HMC Salisbury MSS*, 18, 237, 257–9, 309–13.

67 BL, Lansdowne MSS 142, ff 340–1; Senior, 'Investigation of English Pirates', 274–7, 281–2; C Gill, *Plymouth: A New History*, 2 vols (2nd edn, Newton Abbot, 1979), II, 14–16; see also JC Appleby, 'Settlers and Pirates in Early Seventeenth-Century Ireland: a Profile of Sir William Hull', *Studia Hibernica* XXV (1989–90), 76–104.

68 On Salkeld, see *HMC Salisbury MSS*, 21, 209–10, 212–3, 214–5; and JC Appleby, 'A Nursery of Pirates: The English Pirate Community in Ireland in the Early Seventeenth Century', *International Journal of Maritime History* II (1990), 1–27.

69 Oppenheim, *Maritime History*, 51–5; PRO, SP16/370/12. PRO, HCA 1/47 contains many examples of Devon pirates. See also Todd Gray, 'Turkish Piracy and early Stuart Devon', *DAT* 121 (1989), 159–171.

70 For some of these later developments see RC Ritchie, *Captain Kidd and the War against the Pirates* (Cambridge, Mass., 1986), 18–19, 20–5, 140–59; P Earle, *The World of Defoe* (1976), 60–4; JS Bromley, 'Outlaws at Sea, 1660–1720: Liberty, Equality and Fraternity among the Caribbean Freebooters', in F Katz, ed., *History from Below: Studies in Popular Protest and Popular Ideology in Honour of George Rudé* (Montreal, 1985), 301–20; Daniel Defoe, *A General History of the Pyrates*, ed. M Schonhorn (Columbia, South Carolina, 1972); and Marcus Rediker, *Between the Devil and the Deep Blue Sea: Merchant Seamen, Pirates and the Anglo-American Maritime World, 1700–1750* (Cambridge, 1987).

71 Devon privateers were also active during the English Civil War, but the impact of this conflict on local merchants and shipowners was ambivalent: see JR Powell and EK Timings, eds., *Documents relating to the Civil War, 1642–1648* (NRS, CV, 1965), 76–7, 99, 100–01, 105, 121, 147–8, 208, 314–5.

72 Andrews, *Elizabethan Privateering*, 6, 19–21; Kennedy, *British Naval Mastery*, 45–6, 66; R Davis, *English Merchant Shipping and Anglo-Dutch Rivalry in the Seventeenth Century* (1975), 18; Davis, *Shipping Industry*, 304–5, 321, 323.

73 SR Gardiner and CT Atkinson, eds., *Letters and Papers Relating to the First Dutch War, 1652–1654*, 6 vols (NRS, 1898–1930), IV, 202.

74 PRO, HCA 25/10.

75 Oppenheim, *Maritime History*, 73; JR Jones, *Britain and the World, 1649–1815* (Brighton, 1980), chapter 4.

76 See, for example, *Calendar of State Papers Domestic, 1666–67*, 202; *CSPD, 1672*, 184–5; *CSPD, 1673*, 268. Also relevant is WB Stephens, *Seventeenth-Century Exeter: A Study of Industrial and Commercial Development, 1625–1688* (Exeter, 1958).

11 *Seafaring and Maritime Trade in Sixteenth-Century Devon*

JOYCE YOUINGS WITH PETER W CORNFORD

LIKE THEIR MEDIEVAL FOREBEARS most of the people of sixteenth-century Devon viewed the sea from dry land, and those who journeyed across the county usually kept closer to Dartmoor than to the coast. But John Leland, who came to the South West in the early 1540s in search of things likely to interest his royal patron, took considerable note of the region's maritime connections. Dropping down into north Devon (Fig. 11.1) from Exmoor, he found the ancient port of Barnstaple on the river Taw somewhat decayed, although he noticed that small coastal craft could proceed from the 'haven' up a tributary, the river Yeo, right up to the bridge leading to Pilton, a place 'maintained by cloth making'. At Bideford on the river Torridge he spotted a whole street of 'smiths and other occupiers for shipcraft', and in the parish of Northam on the spit of land between the two rivers a 'good village' called Appledore, already no doubt a community of seafarers.[1]

Returning from Cornwall, Leland crossed the Tamar by the ferry at Saltash, whose people 'use both merchandise and fish[ing]', and to seaward he observed Millbrook, 'a rich fisher town' and other small creeks in which lay a constellation of maritime communities centred on the town of Plymouth (Fig. 11.2). Here he saw merchants' houses built of stone, including the one in which the mayor, Thomas Painter, had entertained the princess Katherine of Aragon in 1501, the time being far distant when Plymouth men would see all Spaniards as their mortal enemies. As he traversed the coast eastwards, crossing south Devon's many rivers, Leland noted how many of what had formerly been navigable estuaries had, in what he was assured were recent times, become choked with debris from the Dartmoor tinworks, or, especially in east Devon, had had their entries barred by silt and pebbles. Salcombe, Kingswear, Brixham, and Exmouth he dismissed as mere 'fisher towns', but at Dartmouth he found not only fishermen but also many merchants and a creek above the town which seemed to him 'a place meet to make ships in'. In the city of Exeter itself he was more concerned with matters military and ecclesiastical, but below the city he found 'Apsham', as Topsham was usually called in the sixteenth century, 'a pretty townlet on the shore . . . [where is] great trade and road for ships that useth this haven and especially for the ships and merchantmen's goods of Exeter'. He heard how the citizens 'contend to make the haven to come to Exeter', that is to make the river navigable right up to the city walls.[2]

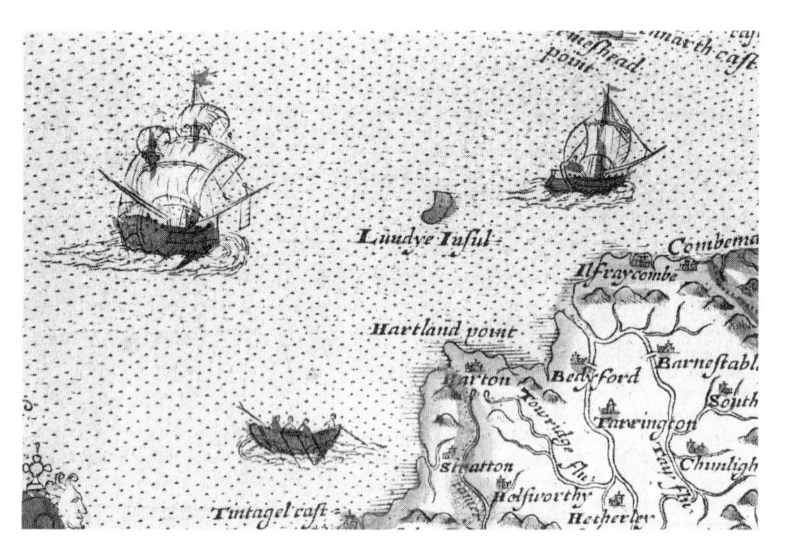

11.1 From Christopher Saxton's Map of Devon, 1579: the coast of north Devon with a variety of vessels offshore. From an original copy in Exeter University Library.

Havens and Quays

For many centuries the county's administrative centre, both lay and

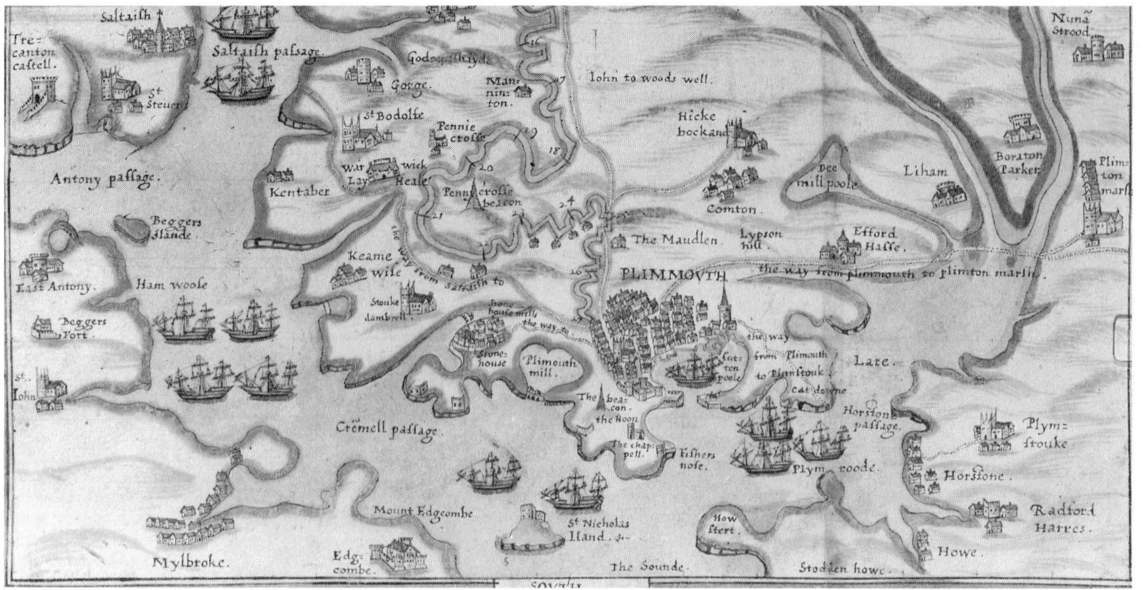

11.2 Tudor Plymouth and her maritime neighbours. Part of a Map drawn in about 1591 to show the course of the Conduit or Leat constructed under the direction of Sir Francis Drake to provide fresh water for the citizens of Plymouth and ships' crews, and to power the mills of which he was the city's tenant. It is a copy of a more elaborate map now at Hatfield House made by Robert Spry of Plymouth, 'painter'. It shows, better than any description, how varied and yet how compact was the chief port and its satellite creeks, including Saltash on the Cornish side of the Tamar. BL Cotton MS Augustus, I,i.41, selected and annotated by Dr Helen Wallis. *(British Library)*

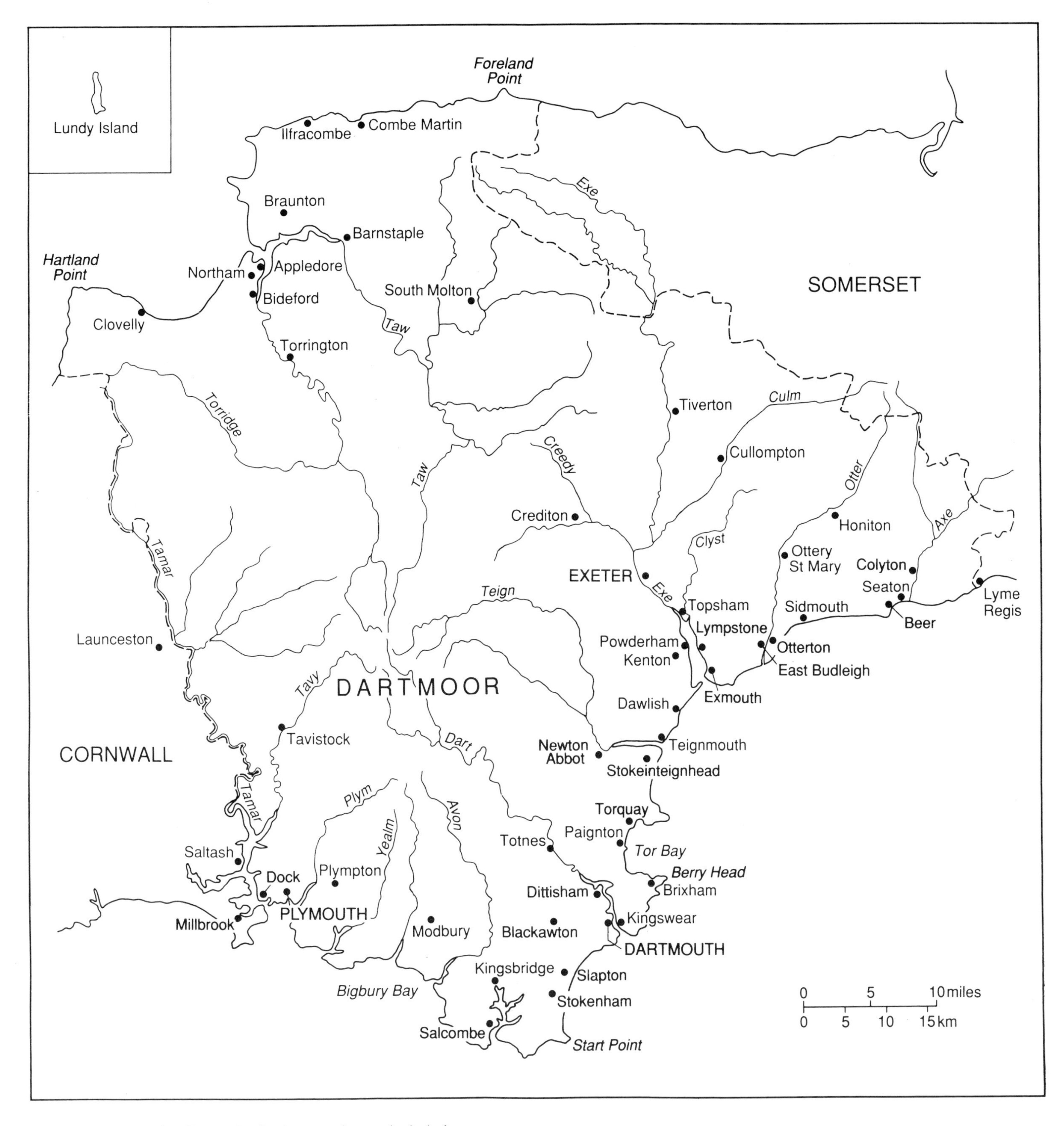

Map 11.1 Early-modern Devon, showing its ports, rivers and principal towns

ecclesiastical, and its chief emporium (Map 11.1), Exeter had been inaccessible for merchant ships since the fourteenth century, largely due, it was believed, to the machinations of the Courtenay family who owned most of the land on either side of the river below the city. The execution of the marquis of Exeter in 1538 raised great hopes, but it was not until the 1560s that some progress was made with the cutting of the first stage of the Ship Canal parallel to the west bank. This was the first pound lock waterway to be built in England, its engineer being Robert Trew, a Welshman, but even with its later extensions it was never really navigable by ocean-going vessels. Goods continued to be unladen and laden at Topsham and transported to and from the city either by land or in the lighters which the city built for the purpose.[3] Recent excavations on the Quay at Exeter have, however, revealed once more part of the massive stone wharf reported in 1577 as being 150 feet long and 80 feet broad, 'all of ashlar work . . . [and] with a convenient crane thereupon builded'.[4] By dint of such expenditure the city ensured its continuing status as one of the county's two head ports for customs purposes. What was described in 1566 as a 'commodious' Customs House in Southgate Street was rented from the Dean and Chapter for 40 shillings a year, and here the early Elizabethan Customer, John Peter, himself one of the city's most active merchants, collected the Queen's dues from the owners of all goods entering and leaving not only Topsham and the other creeks in the Exe estuary, but all the seaside landing places from Teignmouth to Seaton.[5]

At Dartmouth, which for customs purposes remained a member of the port of Exeter, John Peter had as his deputy one John Plomleigh, also a leading local merchant, who actually lived in a Customs House on the waterfront leased from Mr Carew of Haccombe. To him came perforce the owners, or their agents, of all goods passing into or out of anywhere along the coast from Torbay to the river Yealm.[6] Peter also had a deputy in north Devon, technically at Barnstaple, but Anthony Honey seems to have lived in Bideford.[7] Plymouth continued to be a head port with members all around the coasts of Cornwall.

Little could be done about the sandbanks which seemed increasingly to bar all Devon's shipping havens except Dartmouth, but strenuous efforts were made from time to time to reopen formerly navigable estuaries. John Leland saw the Otter estuary 'clean barred', though he was told that less than a hundred years before great ships had used the haven and that the village of Salterton 'had been in times past a thing of some estimation'. In 1553 it was reported that the parish of East Budleigh had sold a silver cross for the considerable sum of £45, of which they had given Mr Duke (the purchaser of much former monastic land on either bank of the river) £25, as well as one of the church bells, towards the cost of making a haven at 'Ottermouth'. A plan among the papers of Lord Burghley (Fig. 11.3) shows an Elizabethan scheme for a massive stone-walled channel protruding from the river mouth, providing access for ships to a haven large enough to dwarf that of the Exe.[8] Lack of the necessary engineering skill or of capital resources no doubt put paid to any progress. Yet further towards the Dorset border the men of Colyton, a particularly lively industrial and market town at the head of the former estuary of the river Axe, based their case for the restoration of their haven on the discovery of old ships' anchors and other gear below the surface of their fields. They made no secret of their main purpose, which was to attract to their waterway the trade of a hinterland stretching as far away as Wellington, Ilminster, and Crewkerne. But not even a nationwide appeal for funds backed by a royal proclamation, and powers to impress both labour and raw materials, resulted in more than a few false starts to this Elizabethan scheme for a great port on the Devon/Dorset border.[9]

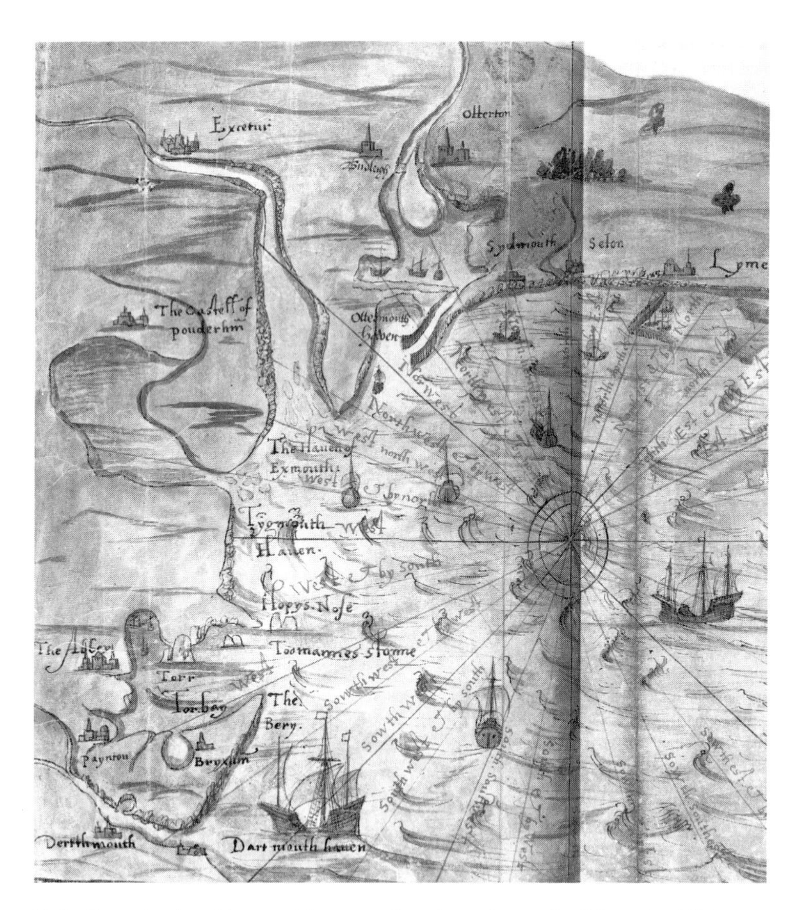

11.3 Part of a pictorial map of the coast of southeast Devon (and Dorset), *c*1540, with later additions, including some by Lord Burghley, from whose collection it comes. There are contemporary notes pointing out the advantages of constructing two jetties (shown) at the mouth of the river Otter to provide an alternative haven to the barred Exe and the decayed Teign mouth, which suggests that it may have been prepared for one of the Duke family of Otterton. BL, Royal MS, 18, D III, fos 9r–10. *(British Library)*

For those ports which retained their seaways, wharves, like town walls, were in need of constant repair, and major improvements were not easily afforded. Elizabethan Plymouth merely extended her fish quays and improved Sutton Pool, the old inner harbour, but the most ambitious and successful scheme was put into effect at Dartmouth, where, beginning in about 1584, a small inlet was reclaimed and the whole quay area extended. Nothing could be done about the wind currents caused by the contours of the hills which enclosed the river all the way to the sea, but at the very end of the century there was uproar about a quarry which was opened up on the cliff below Kingswear, causing gravel and even large rocks to fall into the narrow channel. There were, however, seamen ready to testify in court that the spot was a useful source of ballast.[10]

At Barnstaple in the early 1550s, as a means of protecting the town from flooding, the burgesses built a new quay all of 'five hundred clothyards' in length, at a cost, they claimed, of no less than 500 marks. It was the beginning of much greater improvements to the 'Strand' effected towards the end of the century. Meanwhile, one of the most enduring, if not most important, projects was that of Mr Robert Cary, lord of the manor of Clovelly, way out towards Hartland Point. Here, before his death in 1601 and at a cost of £2,000, he constructed at sea level cellars, warehouses, and the massive quay which virtually created the small fishing port and which still survives as a promenade for today's visitors.[11]

The Coastal Trade

Although few details are available, there must have been a good deal of very local traffic by water, both of passengers and goods. In a county so intersected by rivers there were many ferries, those ancient combinations of private rights and public duties, but there seem to have been no regular sea communications between, say, Exeter and Dartmouth or Plymouth such as there were for official messengers on land. There is at least one contemporary reference to special sand barges,[12] and agricultural communities already very well versed in the use of lime and marl as artificial fertilisers, to say nothing of seaweed, must have had a use for all kinds of water transport, if only in the tidal reaches. According to John Hooker what he called 'slimy', i.e sand dug at low water, was incomparable as dung.[13]

Fortunately for historians – insofar as the records have survived – all merchant vessels coming from or bound for another English port were required to register their movements. In 1554, the first year for which anything approximating to a complete record survives for Plymouth, the Customer, William Amadas, noted the arrival from London on 3 March of the *Adrian John*, from which were unloaded three lasts of pitch and tar, two chaldrons of grindstones, a poke of hops, two kilderkins of soap and three tuns of beer, all of these the property of one John Comer. This was presumably not the whole of her cargo: she would have had other ports of call. Very shortly the *Mary* of Bideford arrived from Bristol with three weys of wheat, and a small 'scaffa' came from Gloucester carrying malt, wheat, barley, peas and, on a subsequent visit, 200 horseshoes. Mid-Tudor Plymouth evidently had much need of food supplies, either for home consumption or for export, and they came from all directions. She herself sent cheeses to Bristol, but she also received from other English ports all kinds of hardware. In January 1553 the balinger *Leswallo* of Truro had brought from London hops, pitch, tar, malt, a case of Normandy glass, and a barrel of gunpowder, and the *Leonard*, also from Truro, brought from London hops, nails, soap, and four dozen bows and 'timber for arrows'. But the greater part of Plymouth's coastal trade was with other ports of the South West and was equally specialised. On 1 February 1554 the *Jesus* of Bridport brought in ten packs of rope, a quantity of hemp and one hundredweight of oakum. Outgoing cargoes were largely of fish, a large consignment of hake, congers and dried fish leaving for Topsham on 20 January 1554, although on 8 February 43 barrels of white herring, three of whiting and 16 of pilchards arrived from Dartmouth.[14]

The coastal trade of Dartmouth followed a similar pattern, even to the sending of pilchards to Plymouth, but Dartmouth sent away much larger quantities of Dartmoor tin, some of it to Southampton but mostly to London, and distributed Biscay salt all along the coast eastwards. Her incoming cargoes included grain from Norfolk and Kent, and from London she, too, derived a continuous supply of imported soap, dyestuffs, hops, and the pitch, tar, and cordage needed by her shipbuilders and repairers.[15]

Exeter's coastal trade was substantially greater in volume than that of either Plymouth or Dartmouth, no doubt because she had a larger local market and better inland communications. She received all kinds of specialised wares from other parts of the kingdom, including, as with Plymouth and Dartmouth, foreign goods coming via other entrepôts, which she in turn sent on to other southwestern ports, especially Dartmouth. It is impossible to exaggerate the extent to which the coastal trade of the Devon ports, including those of north Devon, was locked in with that of other counties as they functioned both as feeders to and redistributors of England's trade with her European neighbours.[16] The merchandise included many bulky goods, the price of which, even without allowing for the state of Devon's roads, would have been prohibitive if they had been brought overland.[17] As in medieval times, those people in Devon who lived within fairly easy reach of her ports enjoyed great advantages over their hill-farming cousins.

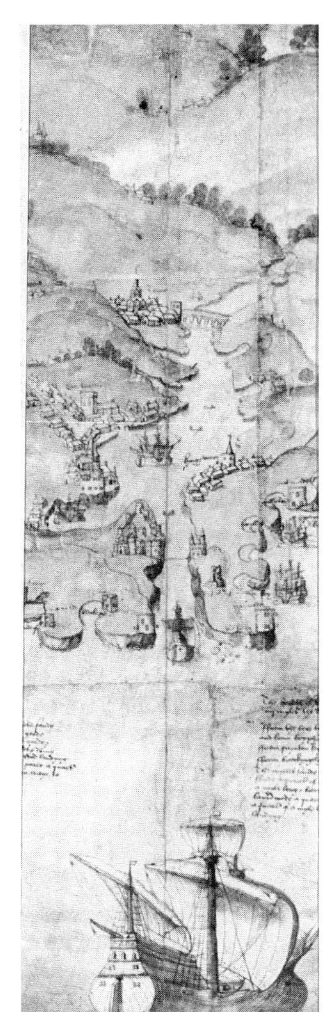

11.4 The Ports on the river Dart: part of a pictorial map drawn in about 1539, showing the relationship between Totnes and Dartmouth. Note the contemporary three-masted ship. BL, Cotton MS Augustus I, i, 39. *(British Library)*

Overseas Trade to 1550

It is far easier to describe the overseas trade of the Devon ports in the sixteenth century than to quantify it or to determine long-term trends. The summarised Enrolled Customs Accounts, which are fairly complete for the first half of the century, obscure local details, especially in failing to distinguish between Plymouth and her Cornish member ports, and the local Particular Accounts survive for only isolated and often incomplete years.

As in medieval times, Devon had two valuable commodities to offer to other nations. One was woollen cloth, the product of many local specialist craftsmen and women from woolcombers to dyers, and including spinners, weavers, and fullers, not forgetting sheep farmers. Although many of these, especially those who were country-based, had other occupations, principally farming, the standard of living of many thousands of Devonians depended on the ability of the county's merchants to sell the cloth overseas. The other principal commodity was tin, which, although extracted from the ground with much manual toil and skilfully refined and cast into blocks, was still essentially a raw material when laden aboard ship. It, too, employed many hands, many also part-time but nonetheless dependent on the health of the overseas market. Neither product was unique to Devon, woollen cloth being made in far greater quantity in many other parts of the country, and tin production, especially in the sixteenth century, being much greater in Cornwall. But together Devon's own cloth and tin went far to ensure that the county's balance of trade was favourable.

Even compared with the tremendous upswing in national trade from about 1475, Exeter's commercial growth towards the end of the fifteenth century was quite phenomenal. By the decade 1501–10 she was exporting, with her member ports, an average of 8,600 cloths a year, over ten per cent of the national total. The peak year was 1501–2, when very nearly 11,000 cloths were sent overseas, only 473 of these by alien merchants. After 1510 the annual total settled down at around 5,000 a year until the middle of the century.[18] From such detailed local customs accounts as are available it would appear that Dartmouth's share of the 'Exeter' total crept up from about one third in 1509–10 to a half in 1523–4, to fall back in the 1530s and then to rise to over 60 per cent in 1533–4, but these figures are to a certain extent inflated by the use made of her port facilities by Exeter merchants,[19] a practice which did not stop with the cutting of the Exeter Ship Canal. In fact, while most of the ships which used Dartmouth were owned by local residents, most of the goods they carried were the property of the merchants of Totnes (Fig. 11.4), a situation reflected in the taxation assessments of the two towns in 1523–5.[20] Exeter's buoyancy in the early decades of the sixteenth century compared very favourably with Bristol's trade, which, after peaking at over 8,000 cloths in 1495–6, drifted steadily down to barely 3,000 by the 1540s.[21] Plymouth at no time in the sixteenth century exported as many as 1,000 cloths, and in 1532–3 just topped 100, only doing so then and in the early 1540s with the help of alien merchants.[22] North Devon's share was by comparison very small indeed, probably rarely exceeding 500 cloths a year,[23] but some Barnstaple merchants found it convenient to send cloths to Exeter for shipment. No outport, of course, compared with London, whose cloth exports moved inexorably upwards from around 40,000 a year in 1500 to over 100,000 by the early 1540s.[24] But the Hanseatic (or German) merchants who handled so much of London's early-sixteenth-century trade did not penetrate the western ports, nor indeed did any aliens play more than a minor role in sixteenth-century Devon's overseas trade. Of the 9,979 woollen cloths which were exported by Exeter and her member ports in 1502–3, no fewer than 7,782 (over 75 per cent) were laden on English-owned ships, 1,785 on those of the Channel Islands and only 312 in foreign-owned vessels. That remained the pattern until the late 1530s and early 1540s, when even in Exeter there was some increase in alien involvement, the reason for which is not easily discovered.[25]

The pattern of the export trade in tin from Devon in the early sixteenth century at first followed very closely that in woollen cloth, except that Plymouth and her Cornish member ports played the major part and, indeed, a great deal of Cornish tin was sent abroad (or to London) through Plymouth. Exeter and its associated ports reached a peak of over 500 thousandweight (1 mwt = 1,200 lb) in 1503–4 and then dropped to an average of around 200 mwt until the middle of the century, considerably less than half of this usually being shipped through Dartmouth, which, however, practically captured the market in 1542–4.[26] Plymouth and the Cornish ports reached over 700 mwt in the later 1530s and early 1540s, after which the annual total plummeted to barely 100 thousandweight in 1542–3. Of this, Plymouth probably handled under 20 per cent, which put her well behind Dartmouth and Exeter. Alien merchants made no inroads on the tin trade even in the 1540s, but the merchants of the Devon ports were more successful than those of Cornwall in keeping the London merchants at bay.[27] Besides woollen cloth and tin, Devon had little to sell abroad except hides and sheepskins, and the monotony of her outward cargoes was relieved only by the re-export of foreign goods, especially French and Spanish wines and dried fruit from southern Spain.

Compared with her exports, Devon's imports were varied and exotic. At the beginning of the sixteenth century Exeter was importing over 600 tuns of wine a year (Fig. 11.5), amounting to about 160,000 gallons if the casks were full, Dartmouth nearly 200 tuns, and even the north Devon ports some 75 tuns. Plymouth at this time was importing about 260 tuns, about half of these being brought in from France by alien merchants. By 1511–12 the total had increased quite considerably, and alien involvement was down to one-sixth, a trend which continued.[28] As in the later fifteenth century, imports ranged from utilitarian merchandise such as Normandy canvas and linen, Spanish iron and Biscayan salt for the fisheries, and cloth dyes, especially the Toulouse woad and alum used as a mordant, to Spanish oil and luxurious comestibles such as Spanish prunes, marmalade, honey and sugar. There was also the occasional consignment of soap, both white for domestic use and the black or 'smigmate', used for washing wool. In 1531–2 Dartmouth imported 55 barrels of black soap, valued for customs at £215, more than the total value put on 67 tons of iron and 500 tons of salt. Pots and pans, nails, and even quilts and bed ticks, came packed in barrels to enable them to survive rough treatment on the slipways, and Exeter imported ladies' hats made in Paris.[29] In fact in all the Devon ports the total *ad valorem* duty of 12 pence in the pound rose fairly steadily throughout the first half of the century, most of it levied on imports.

All the ports, but particularly Dartmouth and Plymouth, imported very large quantities of salted fish, mostly hake, which were bought from the fishermen of southern Ireland. At Plymouth, including her circle of near neighbours, especially Stonehouse and Millbrook, a sizeable fleet of small

11.5 St Peter's Church, Tiverton: a very fine carving (probably early sixteenth century) of wine casks high up on the external string course. *(RA Erskine, by courtesy of the Vicar and Churchwardens)*

batillae was regularly involved, each one sailing two and even three times a year laden with four to six quarters of salt and returning after several weeks' absence with hundreds, and sometimes thousands, of fish. In the year 1535–6 we can follow the *Kateryn* of Yealm as she sailed on 9 October under her master, John Russyn, with two quarters of salt, returning on 21 December with 2,000 hake ('*dentrices*'), only to sail again on 1 February with twice as much salt. Altogether that year there were over 60 vessels involved, about half of them based at Stonehouse and a quarter at Millbrook. On one day, 20 December 1535, 13 boats came into Plymouth Sound carrying between them 23,000 fish, and by Christmas a further 7,400 had been landed. Over the whole year, from Michaelmas to Michaelmas, these small craft supplied Plymouth and her neighbours with over 65,000 of these quite large fish. At a total valuation for customs of rather over £100, this brought in about £5 in customs revenue, barely sufficient to pay the wages of one of the Customs House waiters.[30]

From the port Searchers' records, which for many decades survive in greater numbers than the actual customs accounts, it is possible to follow the unlading of goods from single ships (Fig. 11.6), often over a period of several days and even weeks, presumably awaiting the arrival of the owners of the merchandise, or their agents, and the entering of their elaborate merchant marks and signatures. In fact it is instructive to descend from the Customs House to the quayside and consider the actual number of shipping movements. For example, in Plymouth, although this varied considerably from year to year, a rough average during the early sixteenth century – ignoring years in which there were temporary embargoes – was a little over 170, of which half were inward. At Dartmouth the average total was rather more, but it varied between 126 and 270.[31] The sea lanes, then, if not the harbours, were never crowded.

Ship Owning

Information about the ownership of ships is very difficult to come by (see above, Chapter 8), and seems to have been the last thing the government wanted to know about. A shipping survey of 1570 (Table 12.1, below, p. 110) reveals the existence at that time of a fleet of no fewer than 13 ships of various sizes belonging to 'Hawkins of Plymouth', but the only other fleet mentioned is that comprising the three vessels belonging to John Prowse of Kingswear. Otherwise the ships in this list were owned singly.[32] Aristocratic fleets, of course, had gone the way of private armies, and there were in any case very few noblemen in sixteenth-century Devon. John Lord Russell, later earl of Bedford, who stepped into the void left by the Courtenays in 1539, owned a ship called the *Mawdelyn* which he used in the 1540s as a privateer under the captaincy of Thomas Wyndham, and in 1545 his *Marlin*, with a crew of 60, was at Saltash being made ready for the King's service.[33] There is no evidence that his son, the second earl, had any maritime interests.

Of the county's far more numerous knights and gentlemen Sir Walter Raleigh is thought, at one time or another, to have owned about eight ships, as almost certainly his father and half brothers had done before him.[34] But, like Sir Francis Drake, he owned nothing which could be called a fleet and only used his own ships along with those of his fellow-investors. The Gilberts probably always had a ship or two on the Dart below their house at Greenway, and may have done a little trading. In July 1588 Sir John, the head of the family, was able to provide the *Commande*, alias the *Gabriel*, 120 tons, to augment Drake's fleet at Plymouth, and his brother Adrian the *Elizabeth*, 70 tons. Mr Gawen Champernowne supplied the *Phoenix*, also 70 tons.[35] Such vessels were mostly used by their owners for what they called 'keeping the seas', a mixture of not-unrewarding public service and private enterprise, for which purpose Sir Peter Carew claimed in 1565 to have 'furnished' the *Bowes*, 200 tons, the *Baxter*, 160 tons, and the *Peter* of Dartmouth, 70 tons. In Henry VIII's reign Sir John Fulford hired out the *Dorothy Fulford* for 4s 2d per day.[36] The lesser gentry were more often only part-owners. In about 1550 John Parker, esquire, of North Molton, the son of a wool merchant, was joint owner, with Robert Gilbert of Powderham on the Exe, of the *Clement*, a 40-ton bark, 'fresh and new . . . strong and well-builded . . . with masts, sails, anchors, cables, ropes, poles' etc., as well as four guns and other 'artillery', as Parker described her when he took his partner to court for failing to share the profit, 'as other joint owners of ships in trust use to do'.[37] Multiple ownership was also not uncommon among the merchants. For the owners of many of the coastal and cross-Channel vessels of under 50 tons it is probably not necessary to look beyond their own masters.

Seamen

A survey of the number of mariners in Devon, made in 1570 (Table 12.2, below, p. 110) came up with a total of 1,250, with a further 311 expected home shortly. Presumably there were others whose return was less certain and many more who had managed to escape notice. The main interest of the list is the number of locations mentioned which were not seaports. For north Devon only Bideford (nine mariners), Northam (38), and Fremington (33) were included, Ilfracombe and, more oddly, Barnstaple, being omitted. The largest concentration was in the Dartmouth area, 28 in the town itself, 35 in Kingswear, 29 up the river in Dittisham, and no fewer than 76 in Brixham, Churston Ferrers and Galmpton. Barely a day's walk westwards the enumerator found 55 mariners in the parish of Blackawton, 42 in Slapton and no fewer than 123 in Stokenham – a grand total of 415 within easy reach of the river Dart. Plymouth, including her neighbouring maritime communities, was credited with only 196. In the other direction, from Paignton north-eastwards as far as Teignmouth, there were rather fewer, only 223, but this was more than three times as many as those found living in the Exe estuary. Only two, if we may believe the record, lived in Topsham. The coastal parishes of east Devon could muster rather over 100, including 33 in Sidmouth.[38]

A more elaborate parish survey carried out in 1582 is rather more illuminating, as it lists ships' masters by name, but it is deficient in omitting both Dartmouth and Plymouth. Even so, the county's tally of master mariners is, at 169, over ten per cent of that of the country as a whole, being larger than that of London and exceeded only by the county of Norfolk. Figures taken from Customs records, including those of Plymouth and Dartmouth, raise the total number of Devon masters active in 1582 to about 250. Comparable figures for other counties are not yet available. According to the survey Devon's ordinary mariners made up some 16 per cent of the national total, and there were over twice as many as in the port of London. The use of the 1570 figures to cover the lack of returns for Dartmouth and Plymouth indicates a total number of seamen in Devon in the early 1580s of around 3,000, but this is almost certainly a conservative estimate.[39] Nevertheless, whenever a national emergency occurred the cry locally was of a shortage of skilled men. In 1545 John Lord Russell informed the Council from Plymouth that the 'greatest need is of mariners', and the very same day the mayor of Saltash told Russell that, although some newly-built ships were almost ready, he was 'unable to set forth any ships for lack of mariners'. The situation was no better forty years later in 1588, when Sir Francis Drake had the greatest difficulty in finding suitable men to replace the great losses by sickness on the ships which Lord Admiral Howard had brought from London.[40] In 1590 Sir John Hawkins and William Borough expected to be able to impress 800 mariners, sailors, gunners and sea-carpenters in Devon, a quarter of these in the north of the county, compared with 300 each in Cornwall and Dorset, but in 1597 the earl of Essex had to explain to Westminster from Plymouth that although he was desperate for mariners he had had to discharge many of those taken by the pressmasters because, although they were wearing mariners' clothing, they 'know not one rope in the ship'.[41]

The 1582 survey included more parishes in north Devon than that of 1570, Ilfracombe now being credited with as many as 71 mariners, of whom four were named as masters. Northam's total, which encompassed Appledore, was now 115 to Bideford's 39. The greatest concentration was now along the coast immediately west of the Exe estuary, where nine parishes contained the homes of over 500 mariners, including 134 in Stokeinteignhead and 77 in the larger parish of Paignton, all of these well placed, of course, to find ships either in the Dart or the Exe estuaries. But the largest single parish total was still that of Stokenham (146) which, with Blackawton

11.6 St Peter's Church, Tiverton: a carving of a clinker-built ship shown in harbour with goods being discharged into or loaded from a boat. *(Photograph, c1929, in possession of the Vicar and Churchwardens)*

(55) and Slapton (51), was no doubt the chief source of mariners for the ships of Dartmouth (see also below, chapter 14).

The fact that so many of the mariners lived in what were essentially rural communities suggests that a great many of them went to sea as a secondary occupation and, like the tinners and many of those who made woollen cloth, were firmly rooted in agriculture, as farm labourers, farmers' sons, tenant farmers or even small freeholders.[42]

The Mid-century Commercial Crisis

In theory, the Devon ports should have been comparatively immune from the depression which hit the nation's trade in the 1550s, especially that of London with Antwerp, and which continued well into the reign of Queen Elizabeth.[43] In practice, however, the county was bound to suffer a knock-on effect from recession elsewhere, so closely was her trade, both coastal and overseas, interlocked with that of the rest of the country. In the South West in particular the French wars of the 1540s tempted many of the more lively spirits, including William Hawkins of Plymouth, into privateering, and the early years of Elizabeth's reign were dogged by international tension, there being a total embargo on trade with Spain in 1563–4 and again from 1569 to 1573.

However, some official figures for cloth exports and wine imports for the years 1559 to 1563 show that Exeter and its member ports were then handling more trade in these commodities than Poole (with Weymouth) and even Southampton. Plymouth (and the Cornish ports) was still trailing, collecting in wine tonnage on average only £184 per annum, compared with Exeter's £301, but as the latter figure included Dartmouth it is possible that Plymouth proper was holding her own.[44] In terms of shipping movements, however, it is possible to say that in the half-year Michaelmas to Easter 1559–60 Dartmouth was actually ahead with 89, with only 55 at Exeter and a mere 29 in as well as out of the north Devon ports.[45] For the whole year 1565–6 over 200 movements each way are on record for Dartmouth, the great majority being English vessels carrying goods belonging to native merchants, including the usual preponderance of Totnes names.[46]

One of the first ports to show signs of real recovery was Barnstaple (including Bideford, which made no separate customs returns). During the half-year Easter to Michaelmas 1565 the total revenue for 11 ships entering and 22 leaving amounted to well over £100. Using the home ports of the ships as a guide, it appears that the trade was about equally divided between the Taw and Torridge. Most of the imports were useful goods such as iron and salt, but on 21 July the *Trinity* of Northam arrived from Biscay with 1,000 oranges and another ship brought in 10,000 prunes, valued for custom at £50. During the same period some 23 coastal ships came in, about half of them setting off again with goods bound for destinations as far apart as Port Isaac in Cornwall and the city of Gloucester. The Torridge ports, including Instow and Fremington, seem to have been more involved in the coastal trade than was Barnstaple, but some of their ships were only four tons burden.[47]

It was, perhaps, a sign of their comparative buoyancy that the outports of Devon were to become increasingly antagonistic towards the London merchant companies with their fierce protectionism. In 1571 even the merchants of Exeter, who had their own closed shop,[48] joined with those of Bristol, Barnstaple, Totnes, and Dartmouth in petitioning for the Portuguese trade to be open to all comers.[49] The absence of Plymouth may have been due to the fact that the breakdown in England's longstanding commercial relations with Portugal was largely due to English penetration of Portuguese preserves in Africa, not least by John Hawkins. When a new Spanish Company was formed in London in 1577 only Exeter joined initially, providing no fewer than 29 of the named members and having two representatives on its Council. Plymouth and Barnstaple subsequently joined, but the merchants of Dartmouth remained aloof, one of the many signs of its growing vitality as a port in the later sixteenth century.[50]

The Later Years of Queen Elizabeth

The restoration of normal trade between England and the Iberian peninsula in the mid 1570s brought new hope to those Devon merchants and shipping interests, probably the great majority, intent on the pursuit of lawful business. The fragmentary survival of the port books (as they are called from 1565) makes it difficult to discern the exact extent to which trade improved during the last years of what Burghley liked to think of as 'the long peace', but fortunately at Westminster the chief concern was that the Queen's customs revenue should be maximised. To that end various 'views' of the situation were taken. One of these shows that, in the years of greatest normality, from 1578 to 1583, the port of Exeter consistently more than held her own against both Bristol and Poole. Plymouth, in terms of customs revenue, still had a long way to go, averaging £168 p.a. compared with over twice that amount collected at each of her eastern neighbours.[51]

Exeter and her member ports

The seaborne trade of the Exe and Dart estuaries in this period continued to be about evenly balanced, any marginal differences being obscured as far as their individual merchants were concerned by the extent to which they continued to avail themselves of each other's facilities. What appears to be a reliable analysis made in 1584, the last year of peace, shows that during the half-year from Easter to Michaelmas the total customs revenue of the head port and its members was as follows: Exeter, 44 per cent; Dartmouth, 40 per cent; and Barnstaple, 16 per cent, proportionately much the same as half a century earlier.[52]

In 1581 the more substantial residents of the county were assessed for tax. Using the somewhat arbitrary notional figure of £10 in goods as a dividing line, predictably the greatest number of wealthy persons, 33, was in Exeter, most of those named appearing regularly in the customs accounts, the rest being engaged in industrial occupations, primarily the manufacture of woollen cloth and therefore largely dependent on the state of the city's seaborne trade. There were, however, no fewer than 21 of these comparatively wealthy individuals in Tiverton and ten in Cullompton, most of them also frequent exporters of cloth through Exeter, although some of them, like Peter Blundell, probably also sent some cloth by land to London. Over on the Dart the situation still reflected very noticeably the use of Dartmouth as the port of Totnes, there being only three well-to-do residents of Dartmouth compared with as many as 15 in Totnes. In north Devon, however, the situation had altered quite dramatically since the 1520s, Barnstaple having in 1581 no fewer than 22 residents assessed at £10 or more, Torrington 12, and Bideford still only three.[53] Such figures should not, of course, be taken too literally. There was much evasion and the wealth of Torrington may have been largely rural. But Barnstaple was a very compact and almost totally urban community. At any rate it is clear that there had been growth in the economy of north Devon proportionately greater than in the south of the county, and greater than would appear from the record of customs paid. Were official suspicions about customs revenue perhaps well-founded in north Devon? Was there perhaps more smuggling?

One of the few complete customs Searchers' returns for Exeter during the early 1580s, that of 1582–3, shows some 160 overseas movements of shipping, somewhat fewer than had been the tally early in the century. Few vessels entering or leaving the estuary were over 50 tons and some, like the *Trinity* of Topsham, were only 14 tons burden. They plied very regularly to and from the ports of western France, especially La Rochelle. There was also, in greater proportion to the whole than earlier in the century, a considerable direct trade with Spain and Portugal, especially in such luxury goods as soap, wine, and dried fruit, especially the old favourite, prunes. But there were still also considerable quantities of woad and other dyestuffs and, as always, salt. There was the occasional ship based in Jersey, but the great majority were English, alien ships being few and alien merchants' goods very rare indeed. There were, however, the occasional visitors from the Low Countries and Germany, especially Middleburg, a sign of things to come, but as yet little sign of any disposition among Exeter's own merchant fraternity to explore the Dutch market. The Exeter merchant establishment had clearly achieved a monopoly only within its own community, for those frequenting the quays at Topsham included a fair number of merchants from Tiverton and Cullompton and also some from Taunton and even Chard in Somerset. There was even the occasional merchant from Bristol.[54]

In 1585 England and Spain finally entered on a period of war which was to last until the end of the century and beyond. In 1585 the number of recorded shipping movements in and out of Exeter dropped to 152 and the Merchants Company considered 'of the dangerous time that now is and how it is like to be worse and worse daily for the trade of us merchants'.[55] But Exeter was to a certain extent protected by her ongoing trade with France and the Channel Islands, and when the veil is lifted by a surviving customs account for the third quarter of 1590 nothing very much seems to have changed. Mr Thomas Spicer was in a position on 4 September to send eight tons of Spanish iron, valued at £32, to La Rochelle in the *John Drake* of Topsham. It was perhaps part of a load of 48 tons which William Braylie and his partners had imported on the *Gift* of Exeter from St Jean de Luz near the Spanish border on 25 June.[56] Any shortfall in normal customs revenue was now to some extent being made up by duties levied on prize cargoes. On 28 July Captain Batten, a man well known to the officials of the High Court of Admiralty, and his ship's company brought in the *Anthony* of Portugal, now, of course, fair game and laden, *inter alia*, with nine chests containing four hundredweight of sugar. The 'composition' paid to the Queen's Customer was only £6 18s 6d, but in 1594–5 the total customs revenue for Exeter and its members was the highest for any single provincial port of England.[57] It is perhaps worth noting that admissions to the freedom of Exeter by those calling themselves merchants, which had averaged less than one a year in the 1550s, rose to just over three in the following three decades and to nearly five in the 1590s.[58] Clearly Exeter's young men saw a future for themselves in 'adventuring', preferably of the more legitimate kind.

At Dartmouth in the 1590s (Fig. 11.7) the actual number of shipping movements, even excluding the fishing fleets, was now considerably in excess of that of the Exe estuary. Merchandise, too, was more varied, especially exports. In 1591–2, besides despatching 34,000 'Newland' fish in the *Hopewell* of Amsterdam for Leghorn in Italy, the new quay saw the

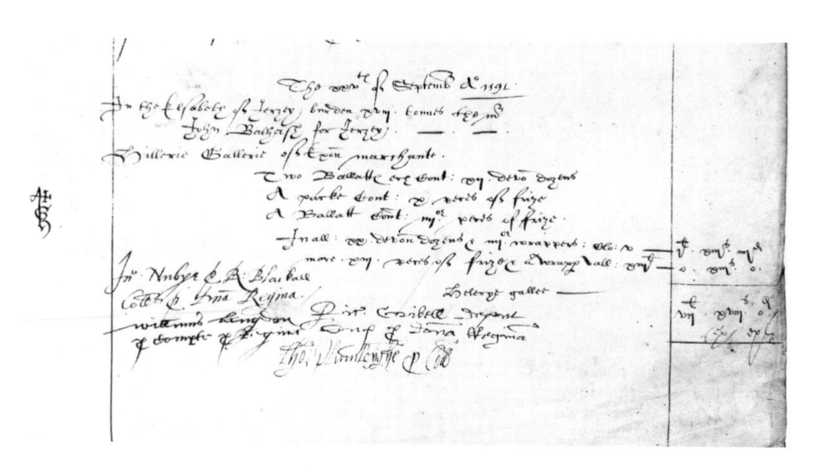

11.7 Dartmouth, Port Searcher's Book, 1590–91, PRO, E122/201/16. The *Elisabeth* of Jersey, 18 tons, John Balhash master, is sailing with cloth belonging to Hilary Gallerie, merchant, of Exeter, whose mark is entered in the left-hand margin. Signatures include that of the Deputy-Customer, Thomas Plumleigh. *(Crown Copyright)*

lading of enormous quantities of 'shingle stones', presumably quarried locally and used for roofing. In 1596–7 individual shipments of a few thousand at a time in the whole year made up a total of nearly 200,000. By 1598–9 Dartmouth was sending cider to Rouen, now one of the town's chief trading partners. Where imports were concerned there were still fewer luxury goods than reached Exeter, Dartmouth having few opportunities for marketing such wares, the local market apparently calling rather for the traditional imports of canvas and linen, especially that speciality of Brittany, lockram, the supply of which was unending. There were also the occasional consignments of glass, brown paper, and white soap.[59]

There were rather more foreign ships calling at Dartmouth in the closing years of the century. In 1596, a year of particularly disastrous harvests in Devon, the people of Dartmouth and their near neighbours must have welcomed the arrival of the *Seahorse* of Emden in Germany, carrying 80 quarters of rye and 36 of wheat – not a great deal, of course, but indicative of the ability of the county's seaports to stave off the effects of famine more easily than the inland towns.[60] It was hardly likely that such foreign shipments would reach north Devon in the course of normal trading, and that same year the people of Barnstaple – many of whom could well afford to do so from their privateering profits – collected the sum of £100, as a result of which, the following June, three ships returned from Dantzig laden with rye.[61] One hopes that some of it found its way over the bridge and along the causeway for the relief of the poor weavers of Pilton.

The Trade of Elizabethan Plymouth (Contributed by Peter Cornford)

In terms of shipping, Plymouth's Elizabethan port books suggest that, at least until 1585, the total annual tonnage entering the port was approximately balanced by that which left it. William Hawkins II played a major role, but others such as Abraham Colmer, Anthony Goddard, Humphrey Fownes, and John Gayer were continuously trading in and out of Plymouth. Unfortunately, few books survive from 1585 to 1610, the period when it would appear that the town's fortunes really soared. In 1610 some 350 shipments were recorded entering or leaving the port, twice as many as in the early 1580s.[62]

Imported goods were much as before, but there was now a considerable trade in wines and other exotic foods such as figs, prunes, dates, and spices for cooking. Sugar in particular formed the bulk of many cargoes and, on occasion, a ship's cargo consisted entirely of brown unrefined cane sugar originating from Brazil and the West Indies. Manufactured goods for a wealthy consumer market, such as writing paper, glass, and fine cloths from the Continent, together with items of good furniture, musical instruments, trinkets, and various other finery, were increasingly imported towards the end of Elizabeth's reign. Less exciting cargoes of cereals and vegetables from northern France were also unloaded regularly on Plymouth's quays.

The principal region exporting to Plymouth was the Bay of Biscay. La Rochelle and Bordeaux, together with the Breton ports, particularly those along the northern coast, supplied Plymouth merchants with some 90 per cent of their overseas cargoes during the first half of Elizabeth's reign. Other than the trade with Newfoundland, no ships are recorded from further afield than the Atlantic Islands before the turn of the century. Where port books have survived before 1585 they suggest that the merchants of Plymouth received very few shipments direct from Spain, and this being so they had less cause than other ports to deplore the outbreak of hostilities.[63]

The importance to Plymouth merchants of La Rochelle and Bordeaux in terms of imports was matched by the quantity of goods shipped to those ports. The most noticeable development in Plymouth's overseas markets, however, was the growth in Mediterranean demand for her goods. Some 20 per cent of shipments were destined for Italian ports by the early seventeenth century. The commodities exported were much as before. Although Plymouth's contribution to the cloth trade was still not so great as that of Exeter or even Barnstaple, its continuing importance as the chief outlet for Tavistock's main industry should not be underestimated. Together with Helston and Truro, Plymouth also still provided the main outlet for Cornish tin bound for the Mediterranean. The one commodity which seems to have shown a dramatic increase in importance in terms of the bulk exported was hellingstones, that is, roofing slates. In the early 1590s about 100,000 were exported annually, as at Dartmouth, mainly to northern France, and by the early years of James I's reign the quantity had risen eight-fold.[64] The extent to which Plymouth's economy in the Elizabethan period was based on fishing cannot be assessed, since, although it was undoubtedly of great significance, as the continuous importing of salt testifies, custom was no longer paid on fish. The Newfoundland trade did not take off in Plymouth until the last years of the sixteenth century.[65]

The coasting trade continued to form a vital part of the local economy. Not surprisingly, the greatest trade was with London and other south coast ports, particularly Exeter and Dartmouth. Ships unloaded raw materials such as provisions, particularly pulses, and household utensils and other manufactured goods, especially ordnance and furniture. Plymouth's role as a distribution centre is clear in that most types of product imported from overseas were re-shipped along the coast, with the notable exceptions of dyestuffs and metals, which were used largely in the town and its immediate hinterland.

The picture painted thus far is of an increasingly active port, and one would expect to discover an expanding body of wealthy merchants. Yet in the county tax assessment of 1581 only two men from the town were assessed at more than £10 in goods: William Hawkins at £20 and Gregory Cock at £10. In the same assessment no fewer than seven Tavistock men were assessed for goods at £10 and more. Forty Plymouth men were thought to be worth between £3 and £8 in goods (and a further eight were assessed at more than £4 in lands), but the apparent comparative poverty of the Plymouth merchant community is striking.[66] Was Elizabethan Plymouth a mere outport for Tavistock, or were its merchants particularly adept at concealing their wealth?

New Horizons

It is easier to identify those Devon ships' captains and their sponsors who led the sixteenth-century penetration of the New World beyond Europe than to determine the extent to which the county's ordinary seamen, or indeed her merchants, were committed to such ventures. As far as is known there was no early Devon interest in North America, no involvement in the Cabot enterprises based on Bristol, and from the late 1530s until the early 1570s the only Devon actors on the new stage were the Hawkinses of Plymouth and John Davis of Stoke Gabriel on the Dart.[67] It was William Hawkins, a native of Tavistock, who first appears in the Plymouth customs records in the early 1520s, who first sent a ship into the south Atlantic in or about 1530, perhaps sailing himself, first to the Guinea coast of West Africa and then across to Brazil. His younger son, John, made an honest if optimistic effort to trade in the Spanish colonies, culminating in the near-disastrous episode at San Juan in Mexico in 1568, an experience which may have set the seal on the future exploits of his young cousin, Francis Drake, who sailed with him.[68]

The rest of Drake's career in non-European waters was a mixture of a genuine mission to discover a legitimate place for Englishmen in the new world dominated by the imperial powers of Spain and Portugal, and a determination to make sea ventures pay, if necessary by bare-faced robbery on the high seas. As was supremely demonstrated by his voyage of circumnavigation of the world in 1577–80, he was an explorer probably without rival in sixteenth-century England, and it must not be forgotten that, but for a near-disaster which necessitated jettisoning her least-valuable cargo, the *Golden Hind* would have returned to Plymouth laden not only with precious metals but also with a large quantity of cloves.[69] Setting out, as they so often did, from Plymouth, though using ships from London and other south coast ports, the Hawkinses and Francis Drake must have been the means whereby many Devon mariners first saw the potentialities of the New World, for plunder, for trade, and even for permanent settlement.

But for dreams of colonisation, either by discovery or by conquest, we have to consider those of more ancient lineage, the gentlemen, and theirs was rather a story of thwarted ambition. The three knights, Richard Grenville, Humphrey Gilbert, and Walter Raleigh, were all by training and experience professional soldiers and, although coming of landed families, the last two were younger sons. They therefore went, or sent others, not primarily as navigators but as entrepreneurs, en route to where they hoped to find both wealth for the taking and also dominion. Grenville's hopes lay in the southern hemisphere, but the Queen decided otherwise, and although he did on several occasions partake in maritime enterprises his service, especially in 1588, was primarily on land. It is ironic that the crisis at home that year frustrated what might have been his greatest achievement, the relief of the colonists whom he had previously conducted to the eastern seaboard of north America for Sir Walter Raleigh.[70]

Sir Humphrey Gilbert certainly saw the Atlantic as a highway on which Englishmen might travel in search of new lands, and the wealth and prestige which they would bring to him and his descendants. His birth at Greenway above Dartmouth was no doubt one of his main inspirations, but in fact most of his expeditions were actually mounted from Southampton, and there is no evidence that he had much concern for the development of the Newfoundland fisheries. His untimely death put an end, not to the cod fishery, but to the founding of a new and almost feudal overseas kingdom.[71] Whether he would have found takers in his native county for his projected land grants we shall never know.

Raleigh is still an enigma. Apart from one very brief adventure with Humphrey Gilbert in 1578 he saw very little of the sea before 1600. His greatest inspiration as far as Devon was concerned was perhaps his choice in 1584 of the two young ships' captains, Philip Amadas of Plymouth and Arthur Barlow of his own native East Budleigh, to command his initial investigatory expedition to what is now the coast of North Carolina, even though their natural desire to give satisfaction led them to exaggerate the region's attractions. Raleigh certainly had a way with seamen, but more likely with those of London than with his fellow-Devonians. He was more popular in the South West with the tinners, and if he ever had a private army it was one based on land rather than on sea. He was too much of a courtier for his fellow gentry and was unable to raise much financial support either among the merchant fraternity in Exeter or in Plymouth, where he was always upstaged by Drake. In spite of extensive research it has not been possible to identify more than a handful of Raleigh's 'Lost Colonists' as Devonians, and it is difficult to imagine why sixteenth-century Devonians should have shown any interest in north America, except, of course, as a place to go fishing.[72] Raleigh's other great interest, and indeed one which at times took priority over his transatlantic project, was the conquest and plantation of Ireland. He and other Devon gentlemen were instrumental in transporting more Devonians to Ireland, both as soldiers and as potential settlers, than to the New World proper, but here, too, by 1600, very little had been achieved.[73]

Other Devonians with wider horizons were all essentially individualists. John Davis of Stoke Gabriel strove unremittingly to find a passage to the East round the north of North America, but his most immediate achievement was the invention of the navigator's quadrant (see above, Chapter 3).[74] Perhaps the saddest story of all is that of the young Devonshire gentleman, John Chudleigh of Ashton, who, after some early achievements at sea, followed by a brief career as the county's representative in Parliament, set off in 1589 on a treasure hunt to Peru and foundered in the Magellan Straits.[75] By the 1590s the New World had become what Hawkins and Drake had for so long made it, the place in which, if at all, the might of Spain might be challenged, but with too little thought of what kind of society Englishmen, including Devonians, would put in its place should they be successful.

11: Seafaring and Maritime Trade in Sixteenth-Century Devon

1 *The Itinerary of John Leland*, ed. L Toulmin Smith, 5 Vols (1907), i, 169–72.
2 *Itinerary* i, 210–44.
3 WB Stephens, 'The Exeter Lighter Canal, 1566–1698', *Journal of Transport History*, III, i (1957), 1–11.
4 CG Henderson *et al.*, 'Archaeological Investigations at Exeter Quay', *Exeter Archaeology 1985/6* (Exeter 1987), 1–19; BL, Lansdowne Ms 25, fo.4.
5 PRO, Exchequer, Special Commissions, E178/2880.
6 PRO, E178/2880.
7 TL Stoate, ed., *Devon Taxes, 1581–1660* (Bristol, 1988), 19.
8 *Itinerary* i, 241; *Exeter Diocesan Architectural Society Transactions*, Series II, ii, 275.
9 *Itinerary* i, 242–3; PL Hughes and JF Larkin, eds, *Tudor Royal Proclamations*, 3 vols (1964–9), ii, 387–9; *Calendar of Patent Rolls, Elizabeth I*, VI, 463 and VII, 57–8; DRO, DD 37597; PRO, State Papers Domestic, Queen Elizabeth, SP12/209/77.
10 P Russell, *Dartmouth* (1950), 95–7; PRO, E178/8 James I/Hilary 23.
11 Joyce Youings, 'Tudor Barnstaple: New Life for an Ancient Borough', *DAT* 121 (1989); PRO, Wills, Prob. 11/99/40.
12 PRO, Chancery Proceedings, Queen Elizabeth, C3/87/69.
13 DRO, Z19/18/9, p.25.
14 PRO, Exchequer, King's Remembrancer, Customs Accounts, E122/118/38, 117/12, and 118/39. For the Devon trade in fish see also above, pp. 80, 83 and for the fisheries, below, chapter 17.
15 Laura M Nicholls, 'The Trading Communities of Totnes and Dartmouth in the late-fifteenth and early-sixteenth centuries' (unpublished MA thesis, University of Exeter, 1960), 100–108. My debt to this is far greater than can be indicated by specific references.
16 PRO, E122, passim, and Exchequer, King's Remembrancer, Port Books, E190, passim. The most detailed account of Elizabethan coastal trade will be found in TS Willan, *The Inland Trade* (Manchester, 1976), 26–41, and see also JA Chartres, *Internal Trade in England, 1500–1700* (1977).
17 Willan, *Inland Trade*, 1–14.
18 EM Carus-Wilson and Olive Coleman, *England's Export Trade, 1275–1547* (Oxford, 1963), 105–19 and 144–5. See also EM Carus-Wilson, *The Expansion of Exeter at the Close of the Middle Ages* (Exeter, 1963).
19 *England's Export Trade*, 113–19, RMS Tugwood, 'Piracy and Privateering from Dartmouth and Kingswear, 1540–58' (Unpublished MA thesis, University of London, 1953), Appendix A, and Nicholls, 'Trading Communities', 103.
20 Laura M Nicholls, 'The Lay Subsidy of 1523', *University of Birmingham Historical Journal*, IX (1963–4), 116, 120, and 124–5.
21 *England's Export Trade*, 105–19 and 143.
22 *England's Export Trade*, 105–19 and 153.
23 PRO, E122/41/25, 201/3, 42/1, 201/4,5, 201/9, 43/11, 201/10,11, 43/14, and 201/12.
24 *England's Export Trade*, 112–19 and 141.

25 PRO, E122/41/25 and *England's Export Trade*, 118 and 145.
26 J Hatcher, *English Tin Production and Trade before 1550* (Oxford 1973), 181–93, 197 and Tugwood, 'Piracy and Privateering', 13.
27 Hatcher, *English Tin Production*, 198, 127, and 141.
28 PRO, E122/41/25, 115/7, 206/1 and passim.
29 Tugwood, 'Piracy and Privateering', Appendix A, xvi–xx and Carus-Wilson, *Expansion of Exeter*, 13.
30 PRO, E122/206/6.
31 PRO, E122/201/4, 42/7, 43/4, 43/7, 43/14, and 43/15.
32 For Devon ships in the sixteenth century see above, chapter 8 and below, Table 12.3, p. 110.
33 G Connell-Smith, *Forerunners of Drake* (1954), 134, 181–2; *Letters and Papers, Foreign and Domestic, of Henry VIII*, xx, ii, 17.
34 G Scammell, 'Shipowning in the Economy and Politics of early modern England', *Historical Journal*, XV, 3 (1972), 390 and MG Stanford, 'The Raleghs take to the Sea', *MM*, 48 (1962), 18–35.
35 PRO, SP12/222/30.
36 PRO, SP12/36/38 and DRO, Dartmouth Court Book, f. 205.
37 PRO, Early Chancery Proceedings, C1/1150/40.
38 PRO, SP12/71/75.
39 PRO, SP12/156/45 and 46 (identical copies). For a more detailed analysis see Joyce Youings, 'Raleigh's Country and the Sea', *Proceedings of the British Academy*, LXXV, 1989, 267–90.
40 *Letters and Papers of Henry VIII*, XX, i, 635 and JK Laughton, ed., *State Papers relating to the Defeat of the Spanish Armada*, 2 vols, NRS i and ii (1894), i, 218, 258 and 276.
41 PRO, SP12/231/19 and 264/11.
42 This theme is elaborated in Youings, 'Raleigh's country', 285–9.
43 For London's dependence on the Netherlands market see R Davis, *England's Overseas Trade, 1500–1700* (1973), 11–19.
44 PRO, SP12/30/8.
45 PRO, E122/201/15.
46 Russell, *Dartmouth*, 61.
47 PRO, E190/925/10. Cf TS Willan, *Studies in Elizabethan Trade* (Manchester 1959), 82–3 where the magnitude of Barnstaple's early Elizabethan commercial expansion is exaggerated by attributing to her the total customs revenue of Exeter and its member ports.
48 For the establishment of the Exeter Company of Merchants trading to France see WT MacCaffrey, *Exeter 1540–1640* (Harvard 1958), 136–59.
49 J Vanes, ed., *The Overseas Trade of Bristol in the Sixteenth Century*, Bristol Record Society, XXXI (1979), 156–7.
50 P Croft, ed., *The Spanish Company*, London Record Society, IX (1973), xvii.
51 BL, Harl. Ms 1878, ff 45–48, summarised in WB Stephens, 'The Foreign Trade of Plymouth and the Cornish Ports in the early seventeenth century', *DAT*, 101 (1969), 126.
52 PRO, SP12/173/38.
53 Stoate, *Devon Taxes*, 2–110 passim.
54 PRO, E190/934/4.
55 PRO, E190/935/5 and W Cotton, *An Elizabethan Guild of the city of Exeter* (Exeter 1873), 136–7.
56 PRO, E122/46/43. For the continuance of English trade with Spain after 1585 see P Croft, 'Trading with the Enemy; 1585–1604', *Historical Journal*, 32 (1989), 281–302.
57 Willan, *Studies in Elizabethan Trade*, 80.
58 Margery M Rowe and Andrew M Jackson, eds, *Exeter Freemen, 1266–1967*, Devon and Cornwall Record Society (Exeter 1973), 78–109.
59 PRO, E190/935/15, 936/1, 935/7 and 935/6.
60 Duchy of Cornwall Records, Dartmouth Water Bailiffs' Accounts, no. 23 (1595–6).
61 'The Diary of Philip Wyott', in JR Chanter, ed., *Striking Incidents in the History of Barnstaple* (Barnstaple, 1865), 104–5.
62 PRO, E190/1010/7, 1016/11.
63 PRO, E190/1023/16.
64 PRO, E190/1023/16 and 18.
65 See below, chapters 17 and 22.
66 Stoate, *Devon Taxes*, 2 and 8.
67 The latest and most comprehensive treatment of this vast subject is KR Andrews, *Trade, Plunder and Settlement: Maritime Enterprise and the Genesis of the British Empire, 1480–1630* (Cambridge, 1984), and of the many great works of David Quinn perhaps the most relevant here is his *England and the Discovery of America, 1481–1620* (1974). For Davis see above, chapter 3.
68 JA Williamson, *Hawkins of Plymouth* (1949). The best of the many works which deal with Drake's maritime exploits are listed in Andrews (note 67), to which may be added John Sugden, *Sir Francis Drake* (1990).
69 For a succinct commentary on this voyage see David B Quinn, *Drake's Circumnavigation of the World: a Review* (Exeter, 1981).
70 AL Rowse, *Sir Richard Grenville* (1937)
71 David B Quinn, *Raleigh and The British Empire* (1947) and ed., *The Voyages and Colonising Enterprises of Sir Humphrey Gilbert*, 2 vols, Hakluyt Society, Series 2, 83–4 (1940).
72 David B Quinn, *Set Fair for Roanoke: Voyages and Colonies, 1584–1606* (Chapel Hill, 1985); Joyce Youings, *Raleigh's Country: The South West of England in the Reign of Queen Elizabeth I* (Raleigh, 1986) and William S Powell, 'Who were the Roanoke Colonists?', in HG Jones ed., *Raleigh and Quinn: The Explorer and his Boswell* (Chapel Hill, 1987).
73 The most recent study of this still obscure subject is M MacCarthy-Morrogh, *The Munster Plantation: English Migration to Southern Ireland, 1583–1641* (Oxford, 1986), but see also D Quinn, *The Elizabethans and the Irish* (1966).
74 Andrews, *Trade, Plunder and Settlement*, 179–82.
75 PW Hasler, *The House of Commons, 1558–1603* (3 vols. 1981), I, 608 and Andrews, *Trade, Plunder and Settlement*, 256–7.

12 *Devon and the French and Spanish Wars*

RONALD POLLITT

WHEN THE FIRST HENRY TUDOR came to the throne in 1485 the nation was in no condition to contemplate, much less to embark upon, foreign adventures. The new king's policies consequently reflected England's relative impotence, and the quarter of a century ending in his death in 1509 was a relatively quiet time, punctuated by domestic unrest early in the reign and a modest assertion in the Breton war that neither served English national interests nor saved Britanny from the expansive plans of Charles VIII. The South West now for the first time faced a cross-Channel coast in the occupation of a single power. Among Henry VII's more positive achievements were the foundation of a modern navy and a grasp of the significance of sea power. His son was less prudent, only a few years elapsing before he let himself be drawn into hostilities with France that served England little purpose but provided the young king with a lesson in the realities of war.[1] The French war of 1512–14 set a bench mark indicating how Devon would be drawn into national affairs in the years ahead.

In essence, the conflict was another phase of the Hundred Years War, but circumstances made it impossible for Henry to wage the war of Edward II or the Black Prince or even of Henry V. What really mattered happened at sea, but for England it was maritime trial and error, either by the king himself or by Edward Howard, his Lord Admiral, who succeeded the earl of Oxford in August 1512. The plan for the war was simple but flawed. It included a scheme to attack French shipping as well as dispatching an army by sea to support Henry's father-in-law, King Ferdinand of Spain. As far as Ferdinand was concerned, England's role was to attract enough French attention around Bayonne to tie down the Valois forces that might otherwise thwart his designs on Navarre. The English losses were part of Henry VIII's first lessons in statecraft, but the disaster that befell the army presented the navy with an opportunity to demonstrate the importance of sea power to an island kingdom, and began that process of elevating Devon from a provincial outpost into the spearhead of England's maritime power.[2]

For Howard, Devon was a conventional staging area for military adventure against the French. His plans were thwarted, however, by the French, who, anticipating an English thrust against their Channel coast, had begun in the Autumn of 1512 to prepare a fleet to counter any such attack. Commanded by Pregent de Bidoux, whose reputation and skill equalled or exceeded those of Howard, the French naval force was sufficiently powerful by the spring of 1513 to raise fears of an invasion of the South West at or near Plymouth or Falmouth.[3] The prospect acted as a spur to Howard's preparation of the English fleet in the Thames, and by the end of March he was ready in his flagship, the *Mary Rose*, to lead a squadron down Channel. Although the invasion alarm proved false, Howard's arrival in Plymouth by 5 April set the stage for a more creditable war, from England's point of view. Writing to Wolsey on his arrival in Devon, Howard lamented the state of his force. Supplies were short and victuals spoilt, and he clearly counted very little on local resources to make good the shortcomings of his fleet: 'I have sent to Plymouth on mine own head to get some victuals if it be possible. I trust you will allow for it. I would I had never a groat in England that I might keep these west parts till they and I meet.'[4] Clearly the Lord Admiral did not expect Devon to provide much, least of all ships, men, supplies, and leadership, in support of his efforts to protect the South West from French attack.

Howard led his fleet out of Plymouth to engage the French in actions which did redeem English martial pride but cost him his life. He personally led a force of four small craft against Bidoux's galleys in an effort to lure the French out of their secure haven for a combat conforming to the dictates of medieval warfare, and was either lost overboard or killed in the affray. His fleet returned to Plymouth and Howard's place was taken by his brother, Thomas. He, too, did not perceive Devon as a source of power, nor could he think of any other course than retreat. Informing Wolsey of his brother's death in a letter dated 7 May 1513, he lamented the state of the fleet and absolved himself from running any risks. He also reinforced the notion that the South West was only incidental to war, capable only of furnishing supplies and amusements for the soldiers and seamen who went ashore. He certainly had no desire to be isolated in a remote Devon harbour.[5] English honour was only salvaged by land battles. Meanwhile, Henry VIII continued, albeit fitfully, to lay the groundwork for his daughter's later successes at sea, although a state paper of 1522 merely specified that ships would be appointed 'to guard the sea for the transport of victuals and men, and to prevent the enemy from annoying the realm'.[6] It seems not to have occurred to him to supplement the naval forces of the Crown with local armed merchantmen (Fig.12.1). Devon was virtually untouched by the second of Henry VIII's French wars, that of 1522–5, not even being used as a staging area, for the focus of the conflict was the Pas de Calais, and the emphasis was on traditional land warfare.[7]

Before Henry unsheathed his sword against the French for the third time, one minor event constituted a turning point in the transformation of Devon from a secondary to a primary force in the shaping of national affairs. This took place in 1530, at the beginning of Henry's struggle with the Roman Church, when the Plymouth merchant and ship owner, William Hawkins, decided to open up a trade between England, Africa, and the New World. Fitting out a ship, the *Paul* or *Pole* of Plymouth, Hawkins transported English merchandise to Guinea, traded it for African goods such as 'oliphants' teeth', and sailed westwards to Brazil, where he exchanged those commodities for the produce of the New World. He not only made a goodly profit, but he carried a Brazilian king back to England, where Henry VIII and his Court did 'not a little marvel' at the sight of the holes in the king's cheeks 'made according to their savage manner'.[8] It was the first of a succession of voyages which were eventually to inspire Hawkins's younger son, John, and other Devonians, to look beyond the confines of Europe and to take the lead in England's challenge to the worldwide dominion of Iberia.

Meanwhile, Henry VIII's principal concern was the country's relationship with his immediate neighbours in Europe, and by the mid-1540s he was involved in a war, again with France, which was to present him once again with the spectre of foreign invasion. However, with more ships and his new Navy Board, Henry expected to meet the French in home waters on more than equal terms. In spite of the setback of the sinking of the *Mary Rose* off Portsmouth, Henry did thwart the French design and firmly established a significant English naval presence in the Channel that had to be taken into account by all European powers.[9]

Devon and the Spanish War

Several forces combined to produce the national predominance of Devon during the last half of the Tudor century, of which a search for trade was

12.1 St Peter's Church, Tiverton, Greenway Chapel. Carving of a merchant ship, probably one of John Greenway's (ob.1529) own trading fleet, with guns and armed soldiers and, at the head of the main mast, a fighting 'top' stacked with weapons. The proportions of the masts and spars are more reminiscent of the fifteenth century. *(From a photograph, c1929, in possession of the Vicar and Churchwardens)*

certainly one. Hawkins's unique adventures had demonstrated that profit was to be had outside the traditional limits of European trade, but it was not until William's son John established a powerful link between the seafaring merchants of Devon and the national leaders at Elizabeth's Court in the 1560s that Devonian expansionism and national policy began to combine, although commercial rivalry soon gave way to a military, or naval, trial of strength fought out in the long struggle with the empire of Philip II.[10]

It would be absurd to explain the conflict between Elizabeth and her brother-in-law as the achievement of a handful of Devonian adventurers organized and led by John Hawkins. The war evolved slowly and was shaped by elements as disparate as religion and maritime technology. Yet there can be no disputing that John Hawkins and his backers, who undertook three voyages during the 1560s in violation of Spanish and Portuguese prohibitions on trade with their overseas territories, did much to crystallize the conflicting interests of England and Spain (with Portugal). In the 1570s Hawkins was more than happy to direct England's resources and energy in the war which he had done so much to start. Through his London connections, particularly his father-in-law, Benjamin Gonson, Treasurer of the Navy Board, he was able to associate himself with the most influential men at Court, and by succeeding Gonson as Treasurer in 1577, to advocate revolutionary warship design, as well as framing strategy and personally leading fleets against Spain. John Hawkins personified the rise of Devon to national prominence during the Elizabethan era. It was a rapid transformation that followed directly from his slaving voyages of the 1560s.

It was, in fact, John Hawkins's third and last slaving voyage which, in conjunction with other events, precipitated the rupture of Anglo-Spanish relations and a poisoning of the atmosphere between the two powers which was to survive the century. Encountering a seasonal hurricane on his way home to England in 1568, Hawkins took refuge in San Juan de Uloa, the port of Mexico City, where, despite a solemn agreement to the contrary, he and his men were attacked by a Spanish fleet commanded by the recently-appointed Viceroy of New Spain. Only two of his ships survived, the tiny *Judith* commanded by one Francis Drake, and the badly-damaged royal vessel, the *Minion*, under Hawkins.[11] English reaction to the news was more explosive than would have been the case less than a decade earlier, and the Queen's own shipping loss gave a special vividness to William Hawkins's newsletter from Plymouth reporting his brother's probable fate (he actually crept home after Drake).

> . . . this present hour there is come to Plymouth one of the small barques of my brother's fleet, and for that I have neither writing nor anything else from him I thought it right and most my duty to send you the Captain of the same barque, being my kinsman called Francis Drake, for that he shall thoroughly inform your honour of the whole proceeding of these affairs. . . . and for that it doth plainly appear of these manifest injuries from time to time offered and our losses only in this voyage two thousand pounds at least, besides my brother's absence, which unto me is more grief than any other thing in this world, whom I trust, as God has preserved, will likewise preserve and send well home in safety . . .[12]

Family ties and business interests were closely linked in the Hawkins scheme of things.

But in 1568 the Hawkinses were not the only victims. By a remarkable coincidence a Spanish squadron carrying specie to pay the Duke of Alva's troops in the Netherlands was intercepted and chased by French privateers shortly before the return of the remnants of the Hawkins fleet, and fortuitously took refuge in English ports, including Plymouth. When the English, on the Queen's instructions, impounded the treasure, technically borrowing it from the Genoese bankers from whom it had been borrowed by the Spaniards, the Spanish, too, were outraged. (The people of Saltash, where the treasure was temporarily stored, must have been driven almost crazy with excitement.) The Duke of Alva unwisely followed the advice of Guerreau de Spes, Philip's ambassador in England, and seized all English goods in the Netherlands, whereupon Elizabeth retaliated in kind. Men of Devon, including those who took charge of the Spanish treasure on the Tamar, were now clearly at the front of the national stage.[13]

The period beginning in December 1568 and ending with the exposure of the Ridolphi Plot in September 1571 has long been recognised as a turning point in Elizabeth's reign in all sorts of ways, including, of course, the religious issue, but how it affected the country's maritime affairs has not been explained in any detail. It can be argued that events during this period both alerted the Queen and her councillors to the dangers posed by Spanish power and led them, slowly but steadily, to formulate policies which prepared England for the challenge which came in 1588.[14] Indeed, some responses were immediate. The assembly of a large and powerful fleet in 1570 to escort Philip's new queen, Anne of Austria, through the Channel, and the suspicions that it aroused of a threat of invasion, led to a hasty survey being made of all available shipping and mariners, and the very comprehensive returns, especially of manpower, for the county of Devon, point to the importance placed on the county both as the strategic linchpin and a primary repository of maritime strength. In the Spring of 1570 Devon, at least theoretically, could supply the Crown with 42 ships ranging in capacity from 30 to 500 tons (Table 12.1), together (Table 12.2) with 1,561 mariners. It is especially noteworthy that 'Hawkins' of Plymouth, presumably the two brothers in partnership, was perceived at county level as meriting an individual entry for fleet ownership. They were credited with 13 vessels, four of which were 'at the seas', these including the unusually large *Christopher*, of no less than 500 tons. The smallest were three of 60 tons.[15]

Early in 1572 Thomas Colshill, Surveyor of the port of London, submitted a report in response to a Crown directive of the previous year. He found a total of 93 ships based in the port of Exeter (Table 12.3), including

Table 12.1
Shipping in Devon Ports, 1570

	100 tons and over	60–100 tons	Under 60 tons
Exmouth		2	2
Teignmouth			1
Brixham			1
Kingswear	1	1	1
Dartmouth	1	6	1
[strangers]	[4]		
Plymouth			
'Hawkins'	*9	4	
others			3
[strangers)			[2/4]
Saltash (Cornwall)	1		4
Northam		1	1
Fremington			1
Bideford			1
Total [excluding strangers]	12	14	16

* including 4 at sea

Source: PRO, SP12/71/75. The figures for tonnage are likely to be very approximate, and only at Plymouth is there mention of ships at sea.
Note: the above and Table 12.2 were compiled by Joyce Youings largely from material supplied by the author.

Table 12.2
Mariners mustered in Devon, July 1570 (places in order as returned)

Seaton	21	Churston	28
Axmouth	7	Cockington	20
Beer	21	Brixham	43
Branscombe	3	Kingswear	35
Sidmouth	33	Dartmouth	28
Budleigh	16	Dittisham	29
Exmouth	21	Stoke Fleming	25
Lympstone	8	Blackawton	55
Woodbury	11	Slapton	42
Topsham	2	Stokenham	123
[strangers	10]	Chivelstone	18
Dawlish	23	Portlemouth	12
East Teignmouth	10	Salcombe	56
Kenton	23	Charleton	10
Bishopsteignton	7	South Milton	7
Powderham	5	South Huish	23
West Teignmouth	40	Bigbury	7
Mamhead	3	Kingston	8
Stokeinteignhead	25	Newton Ferrers	23
Combeinteignhead	12	Plymstock	51
St Marychurch	25	Plymouth and Stonehouse	86
Ringmore	13	Saltash (Cornwall)	36
*'Teignharvey'	4	Bideford	9
Tormohun	14	Northam	38
Paignton	43	Fremington	33
Galmpton	5		

Total 1,264 (actually 1,250: Ringmore is entered twice)
'. . . at the seas at Scarborough and elsewhere, daily looked for home:-311'.
* in parish of Stokeinteignhead.

Source: PRO, SP12/71/75.

Dartmouth and north Devon, 11 of these being rated at 60 tons and over, and 89 in the port of Plymouth, which included Cornwall, of which six were of 60 tons and over.[16] The national tally was 1,383 ships, of which 86 were of 100 tons and more and a further 234 of 60 tons and over. Devon's merchant vessels were small by national standards.

By 1574 trade relations between England and Spain had been more or less restored, but throughout the rest of the decade Devon's leadership in the slowly-unfolding struggle with Spain became apparent. It was now the turn of Francis Drake, based largely on his home port of Plymouth, to take the lead. He it was who returned to the New World to avenge the attack in Mexico, his two somewhat mysterious voyages of 1570 and 1571 being followed by his daring raid on the treasure train in Panama in 1573.[17] His spectacular circumnavigation of the globe in 1577–80, to say nothing of his stupendous profits, secured his reputation and by association that of his native county.[18] He had virtually invited Spanish retaliation, though an actual state of war was still some five years away. Meanwhile, John Hawkins in his work for the Navy Board was supported in his efforts by the most influential man in Elizabeth's government, Lord Burghley,[19] an early investor in Hawkins's slaving voyages, and more recently in Francis Drake's 'Famous Voyage'. He can have had no doubt where leadership in maritime matters was to be found.

Six years before the Spanish Armada set sail, the Lord Admiral submitted to Burghley a 'Brief Report containing the names and number of such ships' as might be used by the Crown in an emergency. The report is no less than a mustering of the private maritime strength of the realm, and it demonstrates how much that of Devon had grown over a decade, in terms not only of ships capable of supplementing those of the Royal Navy, but also in terms of maritime population. Both categories had more than doubled, even without allowing for the absence in 1582 of any returns for Plymouth and Dartmouth and their immediate neighbours.[20] Within two years, and while England was still technically at peace, Burghley was giving much thought to naval matters. All great ships of the realm, in the event of an emergency, would be 'stayed' from their voyages to join with the Queen's ships, all being divided into three companies, one of which would 'lie about the Isles of Scilly'.[21] In time the notion of a fleet standing off the Scillies was abandoned, no doubt because of a realisation that the task was beyond the capabilities of Elizabeth's ships. Instead, following Drake's advice, protection of the

Table 12.3
Thomas Colshill's Survey of Devon's Merchant Ships, 1572 (order as returned)

Port of Exeter	Over 100 tons	60–100 tons	Under 60 tons	Total tonnage
Topsham			14	343
Kingswear			3	50
Barnstaple		2	10	435
Salcombe			5	150
Dartmouth		8	24	1,015
Ilfracombe			3	56
*Millbrook (Cornwall)			13	295
Powderham			4	75
Kenton			6	125
Exmouth			5	145
Teignmouth			5	100
Torbay			5	145
*Mounts Bay (Cornwall)			3	70
Northam			3	90
Bideford		1	5	220
*Oreston			4	66
'Exwater'			1	20
* 'Creeks' of the port of Plymouth				
Total (including *)		11	113	3,400
Port of Plymouth				
Plymouth	1	2	23	890
Cornish ports		3	40	1,079
Total	1	5	63	1,969
Total (Devon only)	1	13	120	3,925

Source: PRO, SP15/22. For a summary of the national totals see *Calendar of State Papers, Addenda, Elizabeth*. p.441.
Note: Table 12.3 was compiled by Joyce Youings.

Western Approaches by a fleet stationed at Plymouth was adopted, and it was thus that Devon assumed its central role in the defeat of the Armada, but only just as the crisis materialised. The fortifying of Plymouth Sound against a possible enemy landing was very much a last-minute precaution and was left largely to local initiative (Fig. 12.2 and below, p. 121). Indeed, up to the last moment Drake was almost alone in his conviction that the Armada would sail up the English Channel and not attempt a landing somewhere else in western Britain. But Devon ships and Devon sailors had already served in the front line with Drake's raid on the Spanish Caribbean possessions in 1586 and in his attack on the nascent Armada itself in 1587.

The Defeat of the Spanish Armada

Modern scholarship since the Second World War has reduced somewhat the importance of England's triumph over Spain in 1588. As part of the effort to scale down the Armada clash, historians have revised their estimate of what gave England the victory.[22] Some have found diplomacy, the gathering of intelligence, and governmental administration the keys to their understanding. Others have preferred to credit heretofore ignored individuals or attributed the outcome to tactical niceties and strategic subtlety. But regardless of their particular theses nearly all recent authors to a greater or lesser degree have diminished the stature of the traditionally-acclaimed leaders of the English fleet, Drake and Hawkins. The courage and perseverance of the two men became less important than the storm damage to Philip's fleet, or the frustrating of Parma's assembling of the barges by the Dutch rebels. As the standing in Armada scholarship of Drake and Hawkins diminished, so too did the significance of Devon. Yet Devon's leadership in maritime affairs was never higher than it was in 1588.

A glance at the list of ships and commanders who faced the Armada leaves no doubt about Devon's prominence: no fewer than 25 of the Queen's ships in the English fleet were constructed during the Hawkins era at the Navy Board, and 16 of those, including the *Rainbow* and *Vanguard*, each of 500 tons, were built between 1585 and 1587. In all, nearly 75 per cent of the Queen's ships which disputed the Armada's passage were the product of John Hawkins's leadership. Great reliance was placed on privately-owned ships to supplement these: of the three squadrons which originally constituted England's naval defence, commanded respectively by Lord Admiral Howard, Sir Henry Seymour, and Sir Francis Drake, the ships of Drake's fleet, stationed at Plymouth (to be joined by that of Howard) were mostly armed merchantmen. Virtually all of the 43 ships that served in

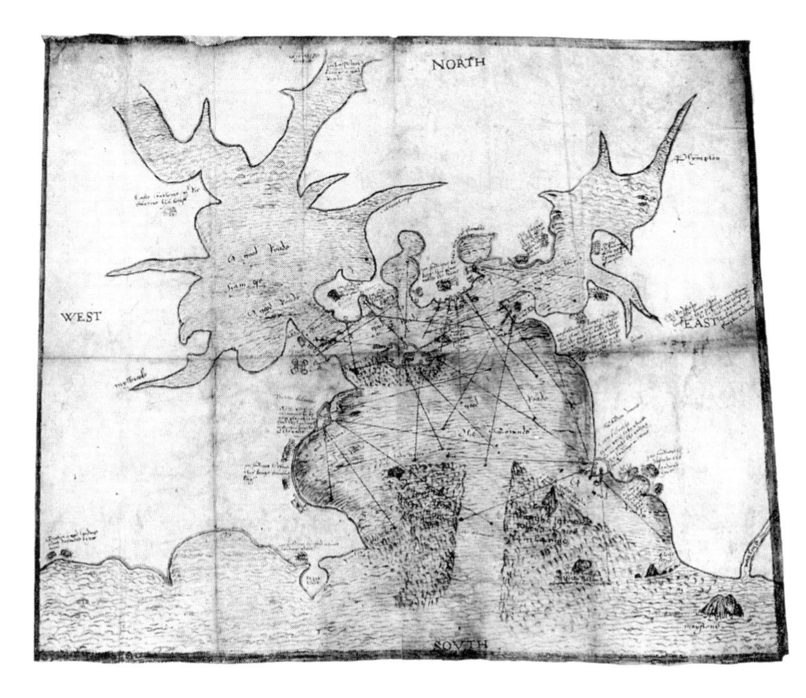

12.2 Plymouth Artillery Defences, PRO, SP46/36/4: a Plan, probably drawn up by Sir Richard Grenville in 1587/8 and not fully implemented. Besides guns, it also provided for detachments of soldiers at strategic points. Note the narrow channel through which ships had to pass, there being very little draught of water on either side of the entry to the Sound. *(Crown Copyright)*

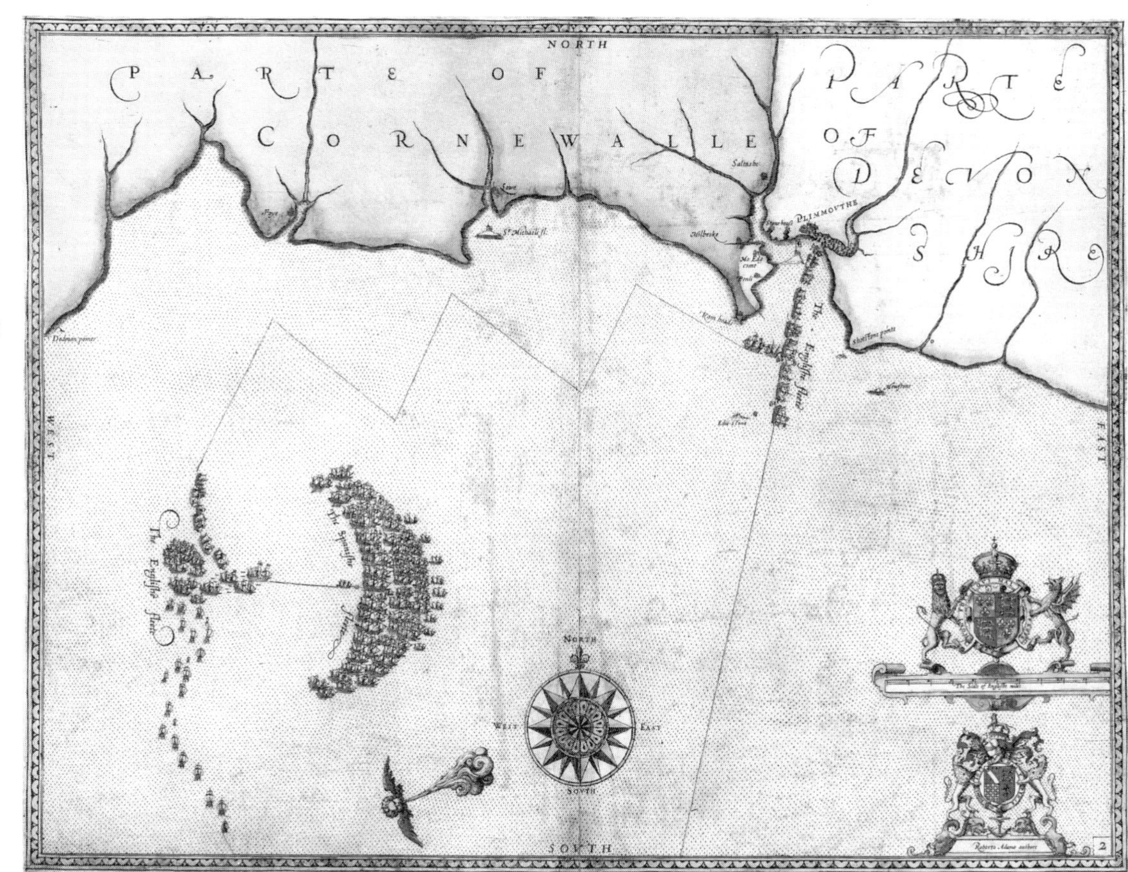

12.3 Adams Chart no. 2, one of a series commissioned by the Lord Admiral, Charles Lord Howard, soon after the Spaniards had sailed for home. *(National Maritime Museum)*

The Spanish fleet had been sighted off the Scillies on the morning of 19 July 1588 (OS) by Thomas Fleming, captain of the bark *Golden Hind*, who had sped to Plymouth and reported to Howard and Drake the same afternoon. The English fleet had only returned to port on 12 July, but was ready to sail on the ebb tide. By the morning of 20 July the main fleet of some 54 ships, led by Howard in the *Ark Royal* and John Hawkins in the *Victory*, had crossed to a position windward of the advancing enemy, while a smaller squadron under Drake in the *Revenge* tacked westward near the shore and joined the rest of the fleet early the same morning. The chart shows the 80-ton English bark *Disdain* firing the Lord Admiral's medieval style 'defiance' into the enemy's rear. The Spanish fleet held to its appointed course, a feat of considerable seamanship, its battle array spanning at least two miles from flank to flank. Its progress up the Channel was watched from the clifftops by many of the people of Devon, and from Plymouth the Mayor, William Hawkins, John's elder brother, reported having had 'plain view' of the action.

12.4 The 'Spanish Barn' at Torquay. Almost on the shore, this former property of nearby Torre Abbey was used in 1588 as a temporary prison for the crew of the Spanish ship *Nuestra Senora del Rosario*, which was taken on the night of 21 July by Sir Francis Drake. Her military commander, Don Pedro de Valdés, and some of her officers, remained with Drake on the *Revenge*, but the ship and the rest of her crew were removed to Dartmouth in the custody of Sir John Gilbert. *(J Youings)*

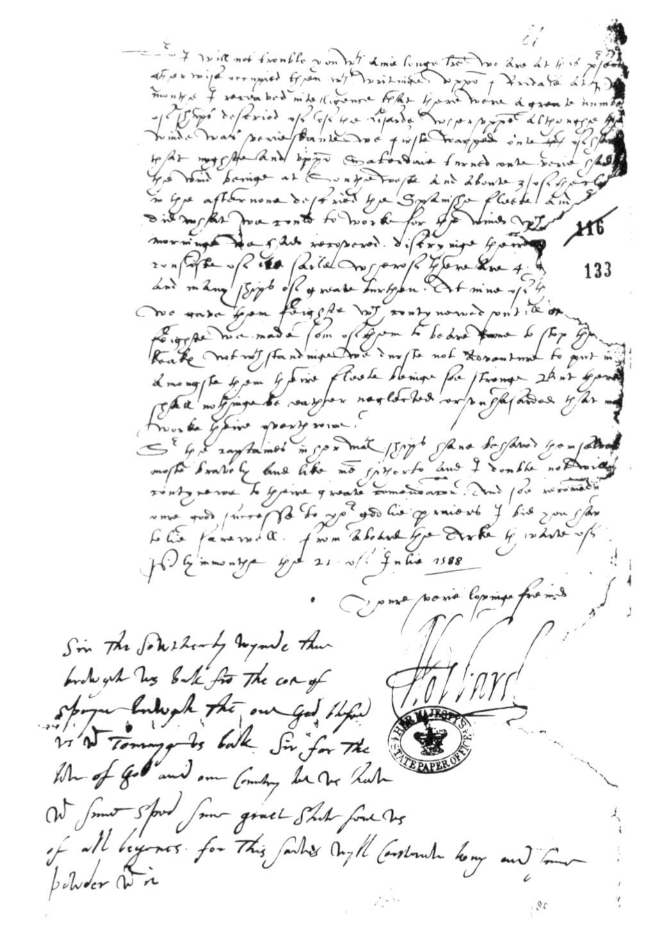

12.5 Lord Howard's letter to Walsingham, 21 July 1588 (OS), reporting on the arrival of the Spanish Armada and the ensuing action off the coast of Devon. PRO, SP12/212/80. *(Crown Copyright)*

Drake's fleet, totalling 5,220 tons and manned by 2,334 mariners, were privately-owned. Many were Devon ships, such as the 200-ton *Hope* of Plymouth commanded by John Rivers or the 60-ton *Elizabeth Drake* captained by Thomas Seely.[23] Moreover, Plymouth was not chosen as the station for the Western squadron merely because of its protected anchorage, strategic considerations, and the fact that it was Drake's home port. It was regarded as the heart of the nation's maritime strength. In 1577, for instance, the government had drafted 3,870 mariners and gunners out of the maritime counties, the largest single draft, of 600 men, being levied on Devon.[24] That number and more were required in the summer of 1588 to replace those lost by sickness from the ships which had come from London.[25]

Details of the Armada battles in the Narrow Seas up Channel, and the disastrous homeward voyage of the Spanish fleet, are too well known to need recounting here. What is unlikely ever to be known for certain is the extent to which Devon rose to the demands made upon it for supplies of all-important victuals. Lord Admiral Howard's despatches to Westminster, the few letters of Drake, and the frantic appeals for assistance, both financial and material, of the local Assistant Surveyor of Victuals, Marmaduke Darell, suggest that Devon's farmers were not very forthcoming in furnishing this particular market.[26] On 13 June 1588 Howard declared in a letter to Walsingham that never again would he go to 'such a place of service but I will carry my victuals with me'. His only consolation was that there was 'good fishing in the seas'. In a postscript to his letter Howard gave his frustrations full play:

> Sir, you would not believe what a wonderful thing it is to victual an army as this in such a narrow corner of the realm, where a man would think that neither victuals were to be had, nor cask to put them in.

A week later he reported to the Privy Council in London that both Hawkins and Drake had advanced cash for victuals and impressment of mariners, suggesting that lack of this commodity was at the root of their difficulties. Burghley's response was to express amazement that the death of so many men at sea had not led to economies! Only the combined charisma of the English admirals ensured that their ships were adequately manned.

With the passage of the Spanish Armada Devon's leadership in the war changed, beginning to descend from its apogée as the conflict began to lose its intensity during the last years of the Queen's reign. Ironically this coincided with the post-Armada blaze of adventure and martial activity which brought to full circle the course plotted by Hawkins and Drake almost a generation earlier. First, Drake's 'counter-Armada' of 1589 managed both to disappoint the financial hopes of its backers, private as well as official, and to fail to take advantage of Philip of Spain's weakness in the aftermath of his fleet's disaster.[27] Sir Francis's poor showing was followed by the expedition to the Azores in 1591 commanded by Lord Thomas Howard, with Sir Richard Grenville as his Vice Admiral. The courage and defiance shown by Grenville (Fig. 12.6), his subsequent death, and the sinking of the *Revenge* (Drake's flagship in 1588), served both to ensure Grenville's place in history and to remind the country of Devon's record of defiance of Spain.[28] But in retrospect the futility of his gesture seems to sound the death knell of provincial leadership in the conflict rather than to confirm it. A few years later it was the turn of the two who had really started the conflict with Spain, Hawkins and Drake (Figs 12.7, 8, 9), to perish pointlessly in a vain enterprise. Aiming to carry the war into enemy territory, as well as to enrich themselves and the Queen, they failed as dramatically as in earlier days they had succeeded.[29]

The Early-Stuart Wars at Sea

The peace that settled over England and Spain after 1604 was grudgingly accepted by most of James I's subjects, whether or not they agreed with Sir Edward Coke that 'England never prospered as much as when she was at war with Spain'.[30] Some, indeed, were forced to shift from privateering to outright piracy.[31] Occasionally an event occurred, such as William Hawkins junior's voyage as captain of the *Hector* to the East Indies from Plymouth in 1607, which harked back to the time when Devonians had held centre stage in matters maritime.[32] But circumstances had changed with the succession of James I, and when the wheel turned yet again Devon reverted only to the position held under Elizabeth's father. Indeed, it was not until the last few years of his reign, when King James was under the influence of the Duke of Buckingham, that he began to move away from the pro-Spanish policy that had led him to execute Sir Walter Raleigh, towards a foreign policy which

12.6 Sir Richard Grenville as a young man *c*1571. *(National Portrait Gallery)*

12.7 Sir John Hawkins, 1591, aged 58, a portrait by Hieronymo Custodis at Buckland Abbey, almost certainly a true likeness. *(City of Plymouth Museums and Art Gallery)*

12.8 Sir Francis Drake, aged 52, a portrait by M Gheeraerts at Buckland Abbey. Painted a decade after the miniature by Nicholas Hilliard, this is almost certainly a true likeness. *(City of Plymouth Museums and Art Gallery)*

had the general approval of his subjects, especially those in Devon. Prince Charles and Buckingham, especially after the former's accession to the throne in 1625, envisioned war against Spain on a grand scale, including even a descent on the Spanish mainland. Parliament favoured a modest naval war which would largely pay for itself, an opinion firmly held by Sir John Eliot, the Cornishman who was Vice-Admiral of Devon from December 1622 to October 1626, when he was suspended from the post.[33] The penchant of Charles and Buckingham to reach far beyond their grasp was never more evident than in the episode which directly involved Devon in the revival of war with Spain, the Cadiz expedition of October 1625. But the role of the county proved to be rather different to what it had been in the days of Queen Elizabeth, merely that of a staging area whose main contribution would be the provision of manpower and military supplies. The parallels between the French War of 1512–13 and Charles I's Spanish and French wars of 1625–8 are quite striking.

Preparations for the Cadiz campaign were well under way by the late spring of 1625, and the role of Devon can perhaps best be seen in the activities of Sir James Bagg, who held the post of Chief Victualler and 'prester' for the South West.[34] Since virtually everything provided for the fleet, including (unlike in 1588) most of its manpower, had to be procured in Devon, a great strain was placed on the region. Seizure of food and other resources (on a scale which Elizabeth would never have contemplated) caused many hardships, as did local taxation, impressment of men, and especially the billeting of pressed troops in private homes for months while the fleet was slowly and painfully assembled and equipped. Much disorder, violence, and abuse were visited on the residents of Devon by pressed soldiers and mariners who were bored, largely unpaid, and strong enough to take whatever they wanted.[35] Corruption became commonplace, with many cases of pressers lining their own pockets by releasing individuals who could afford to bribe them.

When ready, or as ready as could be, the expeditionary force included nearly 100 ships, 5,000 seamen, and an army of 10,000 land soldiers.[36] On 15 September the King and Buckingham came down to Plymouth to inspect the fleet and army. The ignominious return to Plymouth and elsewhere signalled a great diminution in the prestige of both king and favourite, and Devon provided no leadership in easing Buckingham's pain. Indeed, the county was now more than ever a reluctant provider of resources for new adventures. It also afforded a proving ground for those who were soon to gather evidence against the Duke. Sir John Eliot was able to tell Parliament

12.9 Drake's Drum, now at Buckland Abbey. Cherished by Drake's heirs, this has been pronounced a genuine item of ship's furniture (see Frontispiece). *(City of Plymouth Museums and Art Gallery)*

at first hand how the impressed soldiers and mariners of Devon had suffered.[37]

Once again, in the French war of 1627–8, Devon became a mere supplier of goods and service, with none of the satisfaction of success to make the pressures worthwhile. As before, many soldiers and mariners were quartered in Devon households, becoming more of a menace to their fellow countrymen than to the enemy. There was also the fear, probably quite unrealistic, of a French attack across the Channel. The corporation of Dartmouth was invited by the Privy Council to prepare for 'any foreign attempt'. In fact, as it turned out, once again the French were not strong enough to carry the war to England.[38] As late as the end of September Sir James Bagg was still trying to obey a royal command for the levying of 2,000 men to reinforce Buckingham at La Rochelle.

Over the century and more that began with Henry VIII's first French war and ended with Charles I's Spanish and French wars, Devon felt the impact of the far-reaching changes affecting Tudor and Stuart England perhaps more than any other English county. At the height of the nation's foreign conflict in Elizabeth's reign, Devon was transformed by war, but by the time Charles I had decided to rule without parliaments the county had returned to the position it had held before Elizabeth's accession. The support for the Crown of Hawkins and Drake, and indeed the awe which both of these otherwise fearless men felt for the Queen, was transformed into the bitter condemnation of his monarch by Sir John Eliot. Throughout the period, however, Devon remained, as a maritime county, of vital importance to the nation as a whole, a harbinger of the time when Plymouth would provide the foremost naval establishment of the realm.

12: Devon and the French and Spanish Wars

1 SB Chrimes, *Henry VII* (1972); JJ Scarisbrick, *Henry VIII* (1968); and for a broader sweep, RB Wernham, *England before the Armada* (1966).
2 For an earlier view of Henry VIII's youthful foreign relations see JD Mackie, *The Earlier Tudors* (Oxford, 1962), chapter VIII.
3 BL, Cotton MSS, vol. 40, fo. 40r.
4 H Ellis, *Original Letters illustrative of English History*, series 3, vol.1 (1846), 145–51.
5 BL, Cotton MSS, Caligula D vi, fos 107–10; A Spont, ed., *Letters and Papers relating to the War with France, 1512–13*, Navy Records Society 10 (1897), 159–61.
6 *Letters and Papers, Foreign and Domestic, of the reign of Henry VIII* (hereinafter *LP*), III ii, 2012.
7 *LP* V ii, 2013.
8 CR Markham (ed.), *The Hawkins Voyages*, Hakluyt Society LVII (1878), 3–4.
9 M Oppenheim, *History of the Administration of the Royal Navy* (1896), 52 and CSL Davies, 'The Administration of the Royal Navy under Henry VIII: the Origins of the Navy Board', *EHR* LXXX (1965), 268–86.
10 JA Williamson, *Hawkins of Plymouth* (1949), chapters III–VIII; R Pollitt, 'John Hawkins' Troublesome Voyages: Merchants, Bureaucrats and the Origins of the Slave Trade', *Journal of British Studies*, XII (1973), 26–40; DB Quinn and A Ryan, *England's Sea Empire, 1550–1642* (1983), 28–9 and KR Andrews, *Trade, Plunder and Settlement* (1984), chapter 6.
11 R Unwin, *The Defeat of John Hawkins* (1960), passim and PRO, State Papers Domestic, Elizabeth, SP12/53.
12 PRO, SP12/49/36.
13 C Read, 'Queen Elizabeth's Seizure of the Duke of Alva's Pay Ships', *Journal of Modern History* V (1933), 443–64.
14 R Pollitt, 'The Mobilization of English Resources, 1570–85', in W Cogar, ed., *New Interpretations in Naval History* (Annapolis, 1989).
15 For the national figures see Oppenheim, *History of the Administration of the Navy*, 120. For orders to stay shipping see PRO, SP12/71 and 73, and for the Devon report, SP12/71/75.
16 PRO, SP15/22. These are corrected figures. Sixty tons was the minimum size acceptable for auxiliary vessels requested from the coastal towns in 1588.
17 JA Williamson, *The Age of Drake* (1952) does not differ significantly from J Corbett, *Drake and the Tudor Navy* (1898), vol.1.
18 For the fruits of the most recent research see Norman J Thrower, ed., *Sir Francis Drake and the Famous Voyage, 1577–80* (Los Angeles, 1984).
19 R Pollitt, 'Bureaucracy and the Armada', *MM* 60 (1974), 119–32.
20 PRO, SP12/156/45. But see also above, p. 107, n.39 and for the mustering of the county militia, Joyce Youings, 'Bowmen, Billmen and Hackbutters: the Elizabethan Militia in the South West', in Robert Higham, ed., *Security and Defence in South-West England before 1800* (Exeter, 1987), 51–68.
21 PRO, SP12/168/3.
22 The most recent and highly acclaimed work is C Martin and G Parker, *The Spanish Armada* (1988). For new light on Drake's involvement see Paula Martin, *Spanish Armada Prisoners* (Exeter, 1988).
23 BL, Harl. MSS, 168, fos 176r–178v.
24 PRO, E351/2374.
25 J Laughton, ed., *State Papers relating to the Defeat of the Spanish Armada*, Navy Records Society, I (1894), 218, 258, 276.
26 Laughton, *State Papers*, I, 198, 199, 284.
27 KR Andrews, *Drake's Voyages* (1967), 156–68.
28 AL Rowse, *Sir Richard Grenville of the Revenge* (1937) should serve to send readers back to Sir Walter Raleigh's *Report of the Truth of the Fight about the Isles of Azores* (1591).
29 P Hoffman, *The Spanish Crown and the Defense of the Caribbean, 1535–85* (Baton Rouge, 1980), and for greater detail and an explanation of the implications of the expedition, KR Andrews, *The Last Voyage of Drake and Hawkins*, Hakluyt Society, Series II, 142 (1972).
30 M Lee, *James I and Henri IV: an Essay in English Foreign Policy, 1603–10* (Urbana, 1956) and W McElwee, *The Wisest Fool in Christendom* (1958).
31 See above, chapter 10.
32 BL, Egerton MSS, 2100, which is somewhat damaged.
33 H Hulme, *Life of Sir John Eliot* (1940), 94 and the same author's *Sir John Eliot and the Vice-Admiralty of Devon*, Camden Miscellany, 17 (1940).
34 see below, chapter 13.
35 PRO, SP16/6/3 and 18/7 leave no doubt about the ordeals inflicted on south Devon residents by the largely uncontrolled soldiers and mariners.
36 A Grosart, ed., *The Voyage to Cadiz in 1625*, Camden Society, Series 2 (1883), 3, but in spite of its Whiggish slant recourse should also be had to SR Gardiner, *History of England*. VI (1896), 17–20.
37 For Buckingham's attempts to exculpate himself see R Lockyer, *Buckingham: the Life and Political Career . . . 1592–1628* (1981) and H Williams, *George Villiers* (1940), 211, for the sufferings of his troops and seamen.
38 *Acts of the Privy Council, Charles I* (1940), 37.

13 *The Bottomless Bagg? Sir James Bagg and the Navy, 1623–8*

ANDREW THRUSH

FEW EARLY STUART OFFICIALS have been more vilified by historians and contemporaries alike than Sir James Bagg. For Conrad Russell he was 'one of the most corrupt of Buckingham's agents', while to Richard Cust he 'represented the worst type of corrupt, court-backed local tyrants'.[1] In the 1630s the west country peer Lord Mohun alleged in Star Chamber that Bagg, the Navy's wartime victualler at Plymouth, had defrauded the King of thousands of pounds. It was a measure of the opprobrium he incurred in some quarters that, from at least 1628, Sir James enjoyed the unenviable nickname 'the bottomless Bagg'.[2]

Bagg was the eldest son of James Bagg of Saltram, a minor Plymouth dignitary. Born in 1592, he first seems to have achieved local office in 1614, when his father surrendered to him his grant of the Comptrollership of the Customs at Plymouth and Fowey. In 1620 he was added to the Commission of Oyer and Terminer in Piracy Causes in Devon. It was not only in Devon that Bagg achieved local prominence, however. By the early 1620s he had become Vice-Admiral of south Cornwall, a job which entailed little more than gathering the Lord Admiral's share of the proceeds in the county's Admiralty Court cases, but one in which he evidently excelled.[3]

Bagg was not content to remain a mere Vice-Admiral, but instead decided to bring himself to the notice of the Lord High Admiral, the Duke of Buckingham. In June 1623 he made direct overtures to the Duke, who was then in Spain with Prince Charles, offering to provide victuals for the Earl of Rutland, the commander of the fleet which was to be sent to fetch Buckingham and the Prince. 'If your honour pleases to command oft that way, or to esteem me as your servant in this place,' he remarked, 'I shall by the performance of your commands give a true testimony.' The willingness with which this gesture of service was received delighted Bagg, who reciprocated the favour by baking some meats 'for the Duke my Master'.[4]

The preparations for war with Spain at the beginning of 1625 soon afforded Bagg the opportunity to serve Buckingham on a grand scale. He was also furnished with the means to do so, for at the beginning of the year he had inherited nearly all of his father's estate. By March he was engaged in preparing victuals worth £10,000 at Plymouth for the use of the fleet, apparently on the Duke's orders. So busy was Bagg in his new capacity that he had no time to take his seat as an MP.[5] In addition, Bagg was approached by the head of the Navy Commission, Sir John Coke, to undertake the impressment of mariners in Devon and Cornwall that year. He had already served the Commissioners as a pressmaster in 1622, and again in April 1623, a business which he found 'fuller of trouble than I did imagine'.[6] Now he was to find his task even more difficult. The extension of Bagg's authority into Devon brought him into conflict with Sir John Eliot, the county's Vice-Admiral. The death of King James in March afforded Eliot the opportunity to express his disgruntlement by dismissing the seamen gathered at Exeter for impressment.[7] This marked the beginning of Eliot's disenchantment with Buckingham, which culminated in Eliot being stripped of his Vice-Admiralty in November 1626, an office which was then bestowed on Bagg and Sir John Drake jointly.[8]

Over and above the problems created by the rivalry with Eliot, the government's heavy demand for mariners was translated locally into a hatred of Bagg. In December 1625 he told Coke that he had asked one captain to press men himself, 'for this country cries out and thinks ill of me'.[9] But if Bagg was unpopular because he did the Navy's bidding, he was criticised in other quarters for supposedly not doing it well enough. Earlier in the year he defended himself against allegations of pressing many who were not seamen. 'Such men as we take were the best,' he affirmed, 'only let me advise that their own reports carry no credit for they will, in hope to avoid the service, disparage themselves.' It is impossible to be sure whether this was true, but Bagg was undoubtedly right to observe that 'business of this nature hath few friends, and less tongues to speak well of the actor's care or service'.[10]

Bagg continued to act as both a victualler and pressmaster until shortly after Buckingham's assassination in August 1628. During that time he showed that he was not one to hide his light under a bushel. In December 1627 he stressed the central role he had played in salvaging two of the King's ships after they were nearly wrecked at Plymouth, 'which service I have done without the help of any from London'.[11] In trumpeting his achievements Bagg wanted to create the impression that he was indispensable, so he took great offence when he was made to take a back seat. He took umbrage when the King ordered Sir Henry Mainwaring to assist in the preparation of ships at Plymouth to transport reinforcements to Buckingham at the Ile de Ré, complaining to Coke that: 'the service was and should have been done without Sir H Mainwaring's coming to Plymouth, whom I desire to be a spectator, and not to perform the duties of James Bagg to his sovereign'.[12]

The vigour with which Bagg claimed to pursue his naval employments is amply confirmed in the correspondence of other naval officials of the period. In January 1626 Captain John Pennington described Bagg as 'wondrous industrious to do all things for his Majesty's and my Lord Duke's benefit'.[13] Pennington's rival, Sir Henry Mervyn, shared this view. 'His care to expedite your Grace's desires,' he told Buckingham, 'easily complies to anything that may tend thereto.' Mainwaring, too, thought Bagg 'most dexterous in his undertakings', describing him as 'sine qua non'.[14] In March 1627 one of the Victualler of the Navy's deputies contrasted the assistance he had received from Sir James, who had been forthcoming 'both in money and credit', with the backwardness of Sir John Drake.[15]

Bagg's widely acknowledged devotion to duty stands in stark contrast to the charge of corruption levelled against him by Lord Mohun in the 1630s. Yet not merely did Bagg win the case, but no fewer than 13 of the 16 judges found in his favour in June 1637. Part of the reason for this may have been the King's known sympathy for Bagg.[16] However, there were clearly those among the judges who felt strongly about their decision to acquit. Lord Cottington described one of Mohun's witnesses as 'a mere rogue and counterfeit', while the Earl of Manchester reminded Mohun, Bagg's former associate, that he himself had once said that 'no prince in Christendom had better subject, nor Duke better servant, than Bagg'. For Chief Justice Bramston the deciding factor was the impossibility of pinning the responsibility for rotten victuals on Bagg, whose major role as a victualler had been as a distributor and not a provider.[17] As Bagg himself had complained in August 1627, although he was then simply responsible for assisting the Victualler's deputy and disbursing his own money, 'whilst I am reputed a victualler, the faults of others are made mine'.[18]

Bagg's fingers were caught firmly in the till only once. In January 1628 Portsmouth's deputy victualler, Henry Holt, complained that Bagg had confiscated and sold a cargo of salt aboard the *Costly* of Dover, which had been sent from the Ile de Ré for the salting of naval victuals. Although Bagg claimed Buckingham's authorisaton, he had refused to show Holt his warrant. This was unsurprising, since Buckingham had earlier heard of Bagg's detention of the ship and ordered her release.[19]

Bagg's embezzlement of the salt was probably not the product of greed, but the inevitable consequence of his financial commitment to the King's service, and of the Exchequer's inability to reimburse him. A few weeks later Bagg pleaded with Buckingham to preserve his credit with the Customs farmers, from whom he had borrowed heavily for the war effort.[20] The immediate upshot of the episode was that the Victualler, Sir Allen Apsley, became thoroughly distrustful of Bagg; it may also have given rise to Bagg's nickname. That Buckingham apparently accepted Bagg's apology for his offence suggests he may have felt sympathy for his plight.[21] Right up until his death he recognised the extent to which Bagg had put himself in debt on behalf of the Navy, and he endeavoured to ensure that Bagg's finances were not permitted to collapse. The scale of Bagg's commitment to the Navy was impressive. In 1630 he calculated that he had disbursed more than £51,609 during the war years, of which he was still owed more than £26,491.[22] This figure may not have been exactly accurate, but this matters less than the fact that the heaviness of Bagg's expenditure on the Navy can be demonstrably proved.

Perhaps Bagg's most serious failing was that he omitted to keep adequate records of his financial activity, thus laying himself open to the charge of corruption. During the early 1630s he was prosecuted in the Exchequer Court of Pleas by Margaret and Thomas Bespitch of Plymouth, two of his suppliers in 1627 and 1628, who claimed they had been underpaid. Bagg retorted that he had actually overpaid them by £188, but confessed that he could not 'precisely prove payment', presumably for lack of a written record. Consequently he sought permission to have the suit heard as an equity case.[23] The outcome of the affair is uncertain, but it is probably significant that the Bespitches were still trying to get their money in 1637. At any rate, it would be unwise to assume that Bagg was guilty of shortchanging the Bespitches because he did not have the documentation to prove otherwise. Many litigants were obliged to resort to equity for similar reasons.[24] Nor is it plausible to suggest that the charge against Bagg makes little sense if it was untrue. According to Bagg, the Bespitches fabricated their story to avoid repaying the money they owed him.

In the hectic war years of the 1620s, the documentation necessary to provide proof of expenditure was sometimes the last thing on the mind of an overworked Sir James Bagg, whose distance from London made it impossible to reconcile immediate naval requirements with the need to receive proper authorisation. Typical of the man was a letter to Buckingham's naval secretary, Edward Nicholas, which explained that he had furnished two ships with stores 'without estimate, warrant or money, for which I hope rather to receive a reward than chiding'.[25] On another occasion Bagg implicitly criticised the Navy Commissioners for requiring him to produce authorisation for having disbursed money to save two naval warships which were nearly wrecked. Of course Bagg did not have any authority, except 'my heart's duty to preserve his Majesty's ships'.[26] Both Buckingham and Charles appreciated loyalty which, in a crisis, dispensed with niceties of form. When it came to settling Bagg's account, Charles waived the Exchequer's normal accounting procedure on the grounds that Bagg had 'had an eye rather to the . . . good of the service than delayed the same for want of warrants or taking care . . . for his own formal discharge'.[27]

It is difficult to avoid the conclusion that Sir James Bagg has been harshly treated by posterity. It is true that he was excessively sycophantic towards Buckingham, but sycophancy is not in itself a mark of dishonesty. In Bagg it may demonstrate nothing more than his extreme loyalty, as well as showing that he knew on which side his bread was buttered. Far from being one of the most corrupt characters of his day, Bagg was probably one of the most capable. His diligence and industry inspired the admiration of his fellow naval officers, and his preparedness to employ his own financial resources to bolster a failing Exchequer, even though this took him to the point of bankruptcy, was astounding. In the immediate aftermath of the affair involving the *Costly* of Dover, Admiral Sir Thomas Button, who found himself at the centre of a remarkably similar case the following year, confessed to having heard 'strange reports' of Bagg. But, seeing him at work, his doubts vanished: 'I say he is as fit a man to be cherished as any man I have ever known, and as far forth as either his purse or credit will give him leave, he is the first to do it that ever I knew'.[28] Few of Bagg's contemporaries in naval administration were ever accorded quite such an accolade.

13: The Bottomless Bagg? Sir James Bagg and the Navy, 1623–8

1 Conrad Russell, *The Crisis of Parliaments, 1509–1660* (Oxford, 1971), 288; Richard Cust, *The Forced Loan and English Politics, 1626–28* (Oxford, 1987), 202. I am grateful to Miss Anne Richmond for commenting on an earlier draft of this paper.
2 John Rushworth, *Historical Collections* (1721), I, 519.
3 *C(alendar) of S(tate) P(apers) D(omestic), 1611–18*, 235; PRO, C181/3, fo.2, commission dated 5 April 1620; PRO, SP 14/185/80, 19 March 1625, commissioners of Buckingham's estate to Buckingham.
4 PRO, SP14/147/3, Bagg to Buckingham, 17 June 1623; SP14/147/83. Bagg to Coke, 28 June 1623.
5 PRO, SP14/185/89, Bagg to Buckingham, 21 March 1625; PROB11/145, fos 252v–253; SP16/5/6, Bagg to Buckingham, 2 August 1625.
6 BL, Coke MSS, C12/19 (old piece numbers), Bagg to Coke, 10 April 1623; C95/33, notes by Coke.
7 BL, Coke MSS, C18/6, Bridgeman to Bagg, 1 April 1625; C18/8, Bagg to Coke, 2 April 1625; C18/13, Bagg to Coke, 18 April 1625.
8 BL, Add. MS 37816, fo. 183v. He was also granted the reversion of the Captaincy of St Nicholas Island in February and the Collectorship of Impositions, with his servant Abraham Bigges, in December (PRO, SO3/8).
9 *HMC Twelfth Report* (1888), appdx 1 (hereafter *HMC Coke*), 234, Bagg to Coke, 6 Dec. 1625.
10 BL, Coke MSS, C18/24, Bagg to Navy Commissioners, 6 May.
11 PRO, SP16/86/85, Bagg to Nicholas, 16 Dec. 1627.
12 PRO, SP16/78/50, Charles I to Mainwaring, 18 Sept. 1627; *HMC Coke*, I, 324, Bagg to Coke, 24 Sept. 1627.
13 BL, Coke MSS, C24/20, Pennington to Coke, 17 Jan. 1626.
14 PRO, SP16/87/29, 22 Dec. 1627; SP16/79/62, Mainwaring to Nicholas, 29 Sept. 1627; SP16/96/2, Mainwaring to Buckingham, 23 March 1628.
15 PRO, SP16/98/94, Buxton to Nicholas, 31 March 1628.
16 PRO, SP16/361/55, Rossingham newsletter, 15 June 1637; PRO, C115/N4/8615, Burgh to Scudamore, 17 May 1637.
17 Bodleian Library, Rawlinson MSS, C827, fos. 76v–85v, 80v–81.
18 For a rather different interpretation of the verdicts, however, see W Hawkins to Leicester, 8 June 1637, *HMC De L'Isle and Dudley*, VI, 111; BL, Coke MSS, C30/48, Bagg to Coke, 17 Aug. 1627.
19 PRO, SP16/90/6, Holt to Nicholas, 2 Jan. 1628; BL, Add. MS 37817, fo. 161v, Buckingham to Bagg.
20 PRO, SP16/90/122, Bagg to Nicholas, 18 Jan. 1628; SP16/91/35, Bagg to Buckingham, 23 Jan. 1628; SP16/96/38, Bagg to Nicholas, 17 March 1628.
21 PRO, SP16/94/42, Apsley to Nicholas, 25 Feb. 1628; SP16/91/54, Bagg to Buckingham, 25 Jan. 1628.
22 PRO, SP16/113/3, Buckingham to Pye, 16 Aug. 1628; SP16/172/109, Charles I to Exchequer, 31 Aug. 1630.
23 PRO, E112/170/65: I am grateful to Dr Todd Gray for this reference.
24 Bodleian Lib., Rawlinson MS C827, fo. 61; GE Aylmer, *The King's Servants, 1625–42* (Oxford 1974), 47.
25 PRO, SP16/84/47, Bagg to Nicholas, 9 Nov. 1627.
26 PRO, SP16/110/50, Bagg to Buckingham, 22 July 1628.
27 PRO, SP16/170/50, Charles I to Weston and Cottington, 12 July 1630. Bagg's accounts were audited in November 1631: PRO, AO1/1798/372.
28 PRO, SP16/93/16, Button to Nicholas, 12 Feb. 1628. For a more detailed discussion of the charges against Bagg see my University of London PhD dissertation, 'The Navy under Charles I, 1625–40' (1990).

14 *The Duke of Buckingham's Survey of South Devon Mariners and Shipping, 1619*

TODD GRAY

IN 1619 THE DUKE OF BUCKINGHAM, as Lord High Admiral, ordered a report of all shipping and mariners in south Devon. This survey, which bears the signatures of Sir William Courtenay and Jasper Swift, was subsequently 'acquired' by Samuel Pepys.[1] The report is particularly important to the study of maritime Devon, in part due to the incomplete and unreliable nature of the other and hitherto better-known early Stuart surveys of the county.[2] In 1626 not only were a great number of seamen involved in the war with France and Spain, either serving with the Royal Navy or more likely on privateers, but also the survey of that year covered only a small portion of the county's two coasts. Buckingham's survey is unusually detailed in its listings of both men and ships and neatly encapsulates the character of the whole of maritime south Devon at this time. Unfortunately it does not cover north Devon.

Mariners

Altogether in the survey of 1619 there are 102 parochial and other locations and the resident seamen are recorded by name, age, and occupation. In many instances it was specified whether at the time of the survey they were at home or were abroad, and occasionally it was noted in which country. There were nine occupations given: 'mariner', 'sailor', 'fisherman', 'seineman', 'cooper', 'surgeon', 'bargeman', 'sounder',[3] and 'shipwright'. A 'sailor' referred to a member of a ship's company below the rank of officer, while 'mariner', could be applied to all men aboard a ship, in the same sense as the term 'seaman'. But 'mariner' was also used to describe the most senior rank of seaman, the ship's master, who was responsible for the running of the vessel. In all, there were 3,653 seamen listed: a great difference from the 567 men recorded in 1626. The overwhelming majority, 3,189 men, or 87 per cent of the total, were described as mariners or sailors. Of the remainder 250 (7 per cent) were fishermen, 168 (5 per cent) shipwrights, with 41 bargemen, 16 coopers, 5 sounders, and 4 surgeons accounting for the remaining one per cent.

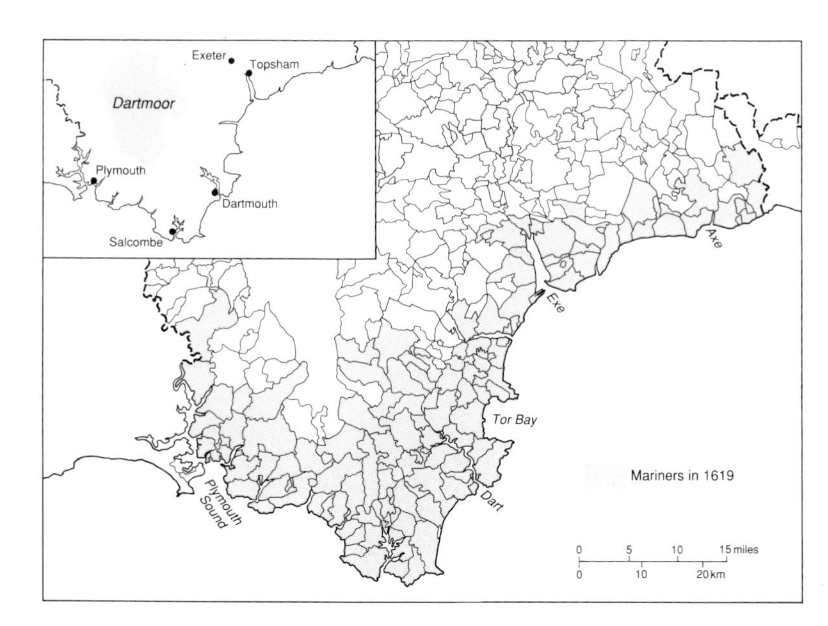

Map 14.1 Parish Locations of south Devon's Mariners, 1619

Nearly all parishes had some mariners or sailors. The 250 men identified as fishermen were distributed along the length of the coast: Sidmouth had the single greatest number with 73, and Dawlish had the only men listed as seinemen. The remainder were Beer and Seaton (32), Blackawton (29), Brixham (12), Churston Ferrers (3), Holbeton (9), Paignton (14), Stonehouse (34), and Thurlestone (25). These 250 men were clearly only a portion of the Devon men involved in fishing: a large number of the men listed as mariners and sailors will also have served aboard fishing boats. The 168 shipwrights were likewise located across the county, but there were three main concentrations; in and around Dartmouth, Plymouth, and surprisingly, Otterton in east Devon. In a county not thought to have had much in the way of shipbuilding it is significant to find shipwrights as follows: Blackawton (10), Chivelstone (3), Colaton Raleigh (5), Dartmouth (40), Kingswear (5), Malborough (5), Otterton (21), Paignton (2), Plymouth (23), Plymstock (10), Ringmore (4), Stoke Fleming (15), Stokenham (13), West Teignmouth (3), Withycombe Raleigh (2), and Woodleigh (7). Some of these probably built only small fishing boats and mainly did repairs.

Not only were all of the coastal parishes recorded as having mariners, but many inland ones were as well, including most of those on the southern border of Dartmoor (Map 14.1). Dartmouth had the highest individual total listed (428), but there were several parishes, such as Charleton, which had only one. Table 14.1 shows the distribution across the county. The greatest number were in Dartmouth and Torbay, while the Exe estuary and east Devon had comparatively few. Plymouth with its neighbouring parishes had the second highest number, but this does not include the large population of mariners on the west side of the river Tamar in Cornwall. Their inclusion would no doubt substantially inflate Plymouth's number of seamen and thus its standing among the ports.

Table 14.1
South Devon seamen in 1619

Area	number	per cent
Plymouth	604	17
Salcombe	427	12
Dartmouth and Torbay	1,538	42
Teignmouth	489	13
Exe estuary	306	8
East Devon	289	8
Total	3,653	100

The number of seamen in south Devon compares favourably with one estimated national total. In a reappraisal made in 1635 of the earlier maritime surveys of the 1620s it was calculated that, throughout England, there was a total of 15,905 seamen. This included 3,080 fishermen and 2,520 watermen.[4] Although this figure was based on a lower total for Devon (and not Buckingham's survey), it nevertheless underlines the significance of south Devon's 3,653 mariners.

14.1 Pictorial map of Dartmouth signed by Nicholas Townsend, 1619. He was paid 21s by the Corporation for drawing four 'platts'. *(Devon Record Office, Dartmouth Corporation Documents, reproduced by permission of Dartmouth Town Council)*

Table 14.2
South Devon shipping in 1619

Port	number	per cent	tonnage	per cent
Plymouth area	57	23	3,052	31
Salcombe area	20	8	670	7
Dartmouth and Torbay	93	38	3,916	39
Teignmouth area	7	2	247	2
Exe estuary	53	22	1,887	19
Beer and Seaton	17	7	176	2
Total	247	100	9,948	100

Shipping

South Devon's shipping in 1619 was located in six areas: Plymouth, Salcombe, Dartmouth (with Torbay), West Teignmouth, the Exe estuary, and Beer and Seaton. Table 14.2 shows a distribution very similar to that of seamen. A comparison of tonnage also shows Dartmouth to have been the leading port, with Plymouth in second place, although again this excludes the shipping on the west side of the Tamar river but includes vessels in Stonehouse and Oreston. The Exe estuary included ships of Powderham, Kenton, Topsham, Lympstone, and Exmouth, but significantly none based in Exeter itself, the city being virtually inaccessible to anything other than lighters. The shipping in and around Dartmouth (Fig. 14.1) was more complicated: besides the 58 ships listed as of Dartmouth, there were five ships recorded as 'in the harbour of Dartmouth, the owners of Totnes' and there were similar headings for the four Dittisham ships, the five Kingswear ships, the three ships of Churston Ferrers and also the nine ships of Torbay.[5]

In comparison with the rest of England, south Devon's shipping appears to have been considerable. It was calculated in 1635 that in 1629 there was a national total of 509 ships (of which 95 had been recently built and 52 repaired).[6] Although the south Devon total included some small boats, the overall figure of 245 compares favourably with this national estimate.

The poorer standing of Beer and Seaton, Teignmouth, Salcombe, and even the Exe estuary was doubtless a result of those ports' problems with access and anchorage. All suffered from a mixture of silting and sand bars which had continued from the late middle ages.[7] Beer and Seaton's ships were listed simply as '12 boats of between 5 and 10 tons', and were most probably dragged up on to the shingle as they still are today. There were only 15 vessels in south Devon which had tonnage of over one hundred tons; Plymouth and Dartmouth had six each, Topsham had two, and there was one at Salcombe.

Incidental details can also be gleaned on such matters as the age of shipping, location, and ordnance. A total of 193 of the 245 ships had their age recorded. The oldest ships were in Dartmouth: the *John Baptist*, the *Mayflower*, and the *Swiftsure* were all listed as being 40 years old. The average age was 12 years. For the Exe estuary and Teignmouth the location of the ships was recorded: the majority of them were either at home or at Newfoundland, with the remainder at the Atlantic islands, Spain, Wales, and St Malo. The ordnance which was recorded shows that a minority of the vessels were armed, only 50 out of the 245.

14: The Duke of Buckingham's Survey of South Devon Mariners and Shipping, 1619

1 PL 2122, Pepys Library, Magdalene College, Cambridge. I would like to thank Dr Andrew Thrush, who first alerted me to the existence of this survey, and also the Master and Fellows of Magdalene College for their permission to use this material.
2 Oppenheim, 61–2; PRO, SP16/34/98–103, 155/31. For a more extensive description see Todd Gray (ed.), *Early-Stuart Mariners and Shipping: the Maritime Surveys of Devon and Cornwall, 1619–35*, Devon and Cornwall Record Society, New Series 33 (1990).
3 Five only, all in the parish of Blackawton, perhaps an error for 'seiners'.
4 PRO, SP16/282/135.
5 In another survey of Dartmouth's ships (DRO, DD 61940), contemporary with Buckingham's survey, the Churston Ferrers ships were listed as of Brixham. The nine Torbay ships in Buckingham's survey were recorded twice: in the second listing they appear as from Cockington and Tor Mohun, and it is uncertain whether, unlike the Totnes, Kingswear, and Churston Ferrers ships, these were actually moored in Dartmouth harbour.
6 PRO, SP16/283/120.
7 See above, p. 100.

15 *The Military Coast Defences of Devon, 1500–1956*

R A Erskine

The coasts of medieval Devon were more often the resort of foreign and domestic marauders than of invading armies. The reason was less the distance from London than the fact that for most of the period Brittany was a small but independent duchy, most of southwestern France was ruled by the kings of England, and the Iberian peninsula was friendly territory. Booty was usually the main attraction, especially as recompense for English depredations, but there was the occasional destructive raid. Appeals for royal grants towards the cost of coastal defences were seldom successful, and permanent fortifications were rare. In any case, the prevention of seaborne landings by the use of shore-based artillery was not practicable until the end of the medieval period. The outcome of all attempts at landings depended very largely on the amount of support or resistance offered by local residents.

By 1500 France had regained all the English territories in France (except Calais) and had absorbed Brittany. The potential western invasion bases of Le Havre, Cherbourg, St Malo, and Brest were all in French hands. A technical revolution had also taken place. By the 1520s–30s developments in cannon design and improvements in gunpowder had made the smooth-bore, muzzle-loading, wheeled cannon an effective weapon. Medieval military architecture had already been modified during the fifteenth century to counter siege artillery, producing the low, thick-walled, flat-roofed artillery tower.

Henry VII avoided war, but Henry VIII's aggressive policy towards France, plus the expected strong reaction of the Empire against Henry's anti-papal policy, led to the isolation of England in the late 1530s, and to a new threat of invasion which materialized in the French landings in the Isle of Wight in 1545. The confiscation of monastic property enabled Henry to finance a comprehensive system of permanent coastal defences, with special attention to the east and south coasts. The system thus created, which was administered by the Office of the Ordnance, was to last with improvements until the mid-nineteenth century. These Henrician castles were the ultimate development of the late-medieval artillery towers; an entirely new style was now emerging in Italy, based on the pointed, four-sided bastion. From 1545 onwards English engineers began to build likewise, for example at Portsmouth.[1] The scale of the system is illustrated by the 'Brief Declaration' of military and naval expenditure for 1539–1552, totalling £3,491,472. Of this sum, new coastal defences had cost £216,408 plus £74,254 for 12 years' garrison wages.[2]

In 1539 the defence of the four south-western counties was entrusted to a commission of 12 local knights, led by Sir John (later Lord) Russell. They surveyed the coasts, encouraged the local urban authorities to defend their areas, and reported to London. In the South West provision of permanent fortifications financed by the Crown was restricted in the early 1540s to Weymouth Bay and Falmouth Haven; between 1548 and 1552 the Scillies were fortified. But other areas were considered. The well-known 'great pictorial map' of 1540 (probably made for the commissioners) shows that forts had been proposed for potential enemy landing places in Tor Bay, Start Bay, and Cawsand Bay. (Fig. 15.1) Thomas Cromwell's 'Remembrances' of 1539, and the Draft Act of Subsidy, 1540, show concern for the adequate defence of Plymouth, Dartmouth, and Tor Bay.[3]

Plymouth

In the fifteenth century, Plymouth was concerned only to defend its own harbours, Sutton Pool and the Cattewater. Although it was formerly

15.1 Pictorial Chart of Plymouth, *c*1539, part of a larger chart from Lands End to Exmouth *(BL, Augustus, I, i, 38)*. The deer park at Mount Edgcumbe was granted in 1539 and 'platts of the towne and port' are mentioned in the Plymouth records for 1538–9. Note that possible enemy landing places are drawn on a larger scale than the intervening coast (Helen Wallis). *(The British Library)*

15.2a Dartmouth Castle and the Old Battery, the former built in 1481 on the west bank of the lower Dart estuary, the latter in 1861 to replace the old Maiden Fort. The early-sixteenth century Bayard's Cove Castle lies at the water's edge in the centre top of the picture. *(English Heritage)*

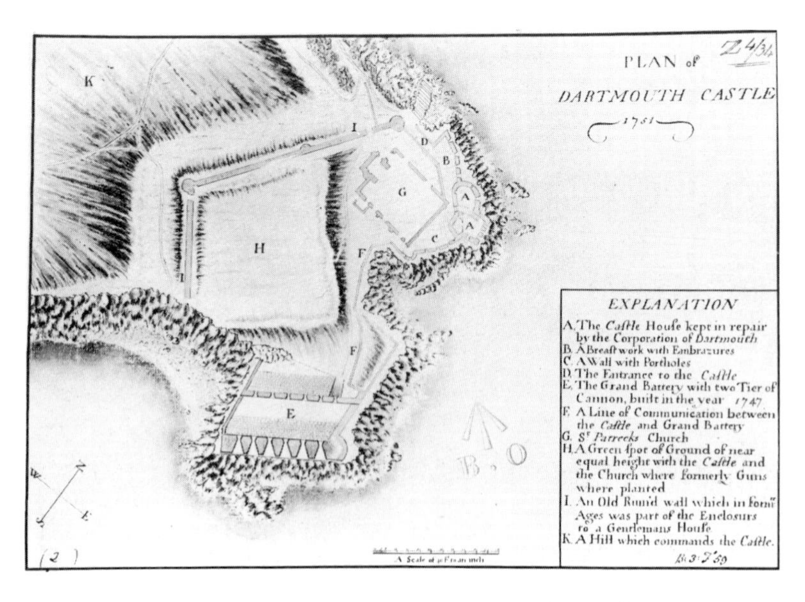

15.2b Dartmouth Castle: Plan of 1751, present location unknown, from *Archaeologia*, vol. 85 (1935), p. 142.

believed to have been a walled town, recent studies indicate that its only medieval fortification was a small castle built soon after French attacks in 1403–4, protecting Sutton Pool. This was maintained by the town until 1660. In design a quartet of two-storied, flat-roofed towers, it was armed with light guns.[4] By 1540 the seaward defence of the town had been extended to include five blockhouses – small, stone-built, one- or two-storied works of various shapes from square to octagonal. They are shown on the 'great pictorial map' of 1540 as existing buildings, but no definite date of construction can be assigned to any of them. However, the town's records show expenditure at least from 1486 onwards on the building, repair, modernizing with gunports, and equipping with cannon of 'bulwarks', and a very early sixteenth-century date is quite possible. From east to west they were sited at Fisher's Nose (part surviving), Millbay (two), Firestone Bay (surviving), and Devil's Point (surviving). A sixth, which also survives, was built, probably in 1545, by Sir Peter Edgcumbe on his land at Wilderness Point, across the Tamar opposite Devil's Point.[5] Not major forts of the Henrician 'castle' type, these blockhouses were perhaps comparable with those built in the Thames estuary in the 1540s.

In May 1545 the Privy Council urged the town to fortify the vital sea passage between St Nicholas Island and Stonehouse. Nothing happened until 1548/9, when Sir Francis Fleming, the Lieutenant-General of the Ordnance, surveyed the Island at the town's expense. Later, the town reported that a turf wall had been built, and was thought to be sufficient in view of the natural strength of the site. It seems, however, that a tower was built in a walled enclosure, the work being directed by William Hawkins of Plymouth, the Crown contributing £175. The town formally agreed to maintain the new fort, and to pay four gunners in peace, and 12 in war. The development of the Island into a fortress had begun.[6]

Dartmouth

The mouth of this safe, commodious harbour was originally defended by a fourteenth-century castle on its west side. On this site the town built Dartmouth Castle (surviving) in 1481 (Fig. 15.2a and b), securing an annual royal grant towards its maintenance. The new castle was a double artillery tower with square and round sections, two-storied above a basement bedded on rock, and very advanced for its date. The basement walls were pierced by gunports of an early type, adequate only for the crude breech-loading cannon mounted on flatbeds, which preceded muzzle-loaders. The castle was complemented across the river by Kingswear Castle (surviving), a square artillery tower built in 1491. The two castles protected the ends of a cross-river chain.

Dartmouth Castle's site was cramped; neither the tower itself nor its small, stone, flanking platforms could accommodate a substantial battery of large muzzle-loaders. Possibly for this reason the town built Bayard's Cove Castle (surviving) in about 1510 (or perhaps in 1537) as an open riverside battery within the town, opposite Kingswear. An important development was the construction in 1545 of a battery called Lamberd's Bulwark, on the cliff top next to Dartmouth Castle, which served as its magazine and store. This battery became the principal seaward battery; in the 1590s it was described as a simple earthwork with six to eight cannon.[7]

Tor Bay

Despite official concern, no permanent fortifications were built to defend the bay. The Earl of Surrey, writing enthusiastically in 1522 about Dartmouth's potential as a fleet anchorage, recommended blockhouses for Tor Bay, to prevent a landing and an overland attack on the Dart two miles away. Nothing was done, apparently, then or later. Thomas Cary, a local landowner, petitioned in 1545 for the keepership of one of the blockhouses, 'which was supposed to have been made' in Tor Bay, but he was disappointed.[8]

The Exe Estuary

The Exe led to one of England's most important cities, ten miles up river, which was itself defended by strong medieval walls, towers, gates, and a castle, all of them well maintained, according to Leland. Its port was Topsham, well within the estuary. Russell was so concerned about Exeter's safety in 1545 that he personally supervised the construction of a bulwark at Exmouth. This supplemented Powderham Castle on the west bank, which, again according to Leland, was 'strong, and hath a barbican or bulwark to bete the haven'.[9]

Salcombe

Though not mentioned in any contemporary source, Salcombe, at the mouth of the Kingsbridge estuary, is credited with an Henrician blockhouse, built on a sea rock by the town. Part of a half-round tower, and 'the foundation of a larger D-shaped bastion with 6 or 7 gunports facing seawards', has been identified. The bastion has been regarded as comparable with St Catherine's Castle, Fowey, mentioned by Leland and dated by O'Neil to about 1522–3.[10]

The Armada and its Aftermath

Between 1552 and 1583 the only major new coast defence work anywhere in England was Upnor Castle in Kent, to protect the Medway anchorage. The prospect of war with Spain led to a review in 1583, and £8,950 was spent by the Exchequer on repairs at selected forts from Essex to Cornwall, including Pendennis Castle, and forts in Dorset. Nothing was done for Devon. Between 1583 and 1588 the Crown concentrated on modernizing fortifications at Portsmouth and at Carisbrooke Castle on the Isle of Wight. After the passage of the Armada, the Spanish War continued until 1604, and fresh Spanish expeditions were expected in the 1590s, directed at the South West. In 1595 Spanish troops actually landed in Mount's Bay and burnt Newlyn, Mousehole and Penzance; a smaller force fired houses in Cawsand. At last the Crown decided to build a fort at Plymouth and to develop St Nicholas Island, as well as adding an extensive enceinte to Pendennis Castle and building Star Castle in the Scillies.[11]

Plymouth

Left to their own devices, the townsmen maintained their meagre defences and from 1580–1 onwards increased expenditure on ordnance, the Castle, the blockhouses and the Island, spending nearly £900 over the four years, 1585–6 to 1588–89. As many as 29 cannon (mainly of the culverin type) and two mortars, including 12 new pieces, may have been placed round the Sound by 1588 (Fig. 12.2, above, p. 111). Existing cannon and three new ones were distributed to support the blockhouses, with eight cannon and two mortars on the Island. Nine new cannon were emplaced in new locations: three on Hoo Stert (Mount Batten), and three each in earthwork redoubts at Picklecombe Point and Staddon Point. Thus the defensive system was extended to the commanding headlands of the Sound.[12]

Panic in Plymouth in 1590 for fear of a new Armada was checked by Drake, who had been made responsible by the Privy Council for the town's defence. With the mayor he petitioned the Crown for a new fort to seaward of the old castle on the site of the present Citadel (Fig. 15.3, below), and a wall round the town with three gates and nine bastions, in the Italianate style. Robert Adams, sent by the Privy Council to inspect, recommended the fort, but reported the proposed town wall to be too expensive. He suggested a ten-foot wall as security against a *coup de main*, and stressed the importance of the Island. The Crown, concerned to defend the anchorage rather than the town, agreed to the fort, and between 1592 and 1598 was forced to meet most of the cost, about £2,500. Plymouth Fort was substantial. It was nearly 500 yards in circumference, built in the new style with two bastions, facing west and north, the stone walls being 13 feet high and 4 feet 8 inches thick at the base, protected by a ditch 20 feet deep and wide, cut in the rock. The southern face of the Fort followed the line of the Hoe cliffs overlooking the strip of low ground curling round the south-eastern corner of the Fort, including Fisher's Nose blockhouse and adjacent batteries. This area was designated the Lower Fort (see below, Fig. 15.3), and it was here that the heaviest guns were placed.[13]

The Fort and Island now became a joint fortress under an experienced royal Captain, Sir Ferdinando Gorges, the town being left to maintain its ordnance, castle, and blockhouses, and to contribute to the Island defence, and possibly to build the town wall. St Nicholas Island seems to have acquired a perimeter wall by 1590; on Gorges' recommendation the works

15.3 The Royal Citadel, Plymouth, begun in 1665, incorporating the Elizabethan Plymouth Fort on its south-east perimeter, where the open space marks the site of the former Lower Fort. This photograph was taken on 16 February 1988. *(Frances Griffith, Devon County Council)*

were developed, and barracks and a governor's house were built. The wartime garrison was increased to 68, of whom only 28 were paid by the Crown. A Spanish report of 1598 notes 40–50 cannon and 100 men in the Island, 30 cannon and 100 men in the Fort, and 6–7 cannon in the Castle. It is however improbable that the Island ever held 40–50 cannon; the 14 shown on Robert Adams's plan of 1592 is a more likely number.[14]

In spite of the long Spanish war, the new defence works were not tested. From the end of the war in 1604 to 1642 the south-western coast continued to be vulnerable. The widespread depredations of corsairs and pirates went largely unchecked by the King's ships, and the fears of local communities were increased when England again went to war with Spain (1625) and France (1627). But complaints about the decay of coastal fortifications and requests for guns were largely disregarded. The Privy Council showed some concern for the permanent forts; in 1617 it replenished the ordnance supplies of Plymouth Fort, and in 1622–3 there was a survey of forts of the South West which recommended renovations. The forts at Dartmouth were actually repaired, but Gorges' complaints in 1624, 1627 and 1628 about the Crown's failure to maintain the works at Plymouth, and to pay the garrison, went unheeded.[15]

The Civil War, 1642–46

Oppenheim observes, and the following account illustrates, that:

> The military fortune of the Devon ports is extremely instructive to the student of maritime history. The Royalists could not take Plymouth because the Parliament had command of the sea, and always, when success seemed in the hand of the Royalist generals, threw in reinforcements and supplies; equally, they could not hold Exeter and Dartmouth because they could not succour these places from the sea, and Salcombe fell for the same reason as soon as attention was turned to it in earnest. Experience shows that to take a well-defended port when the garrison can receive assistance from the sea is one of the most costly operations in warfare.[16]

Plymouth

Increasingly in the course of the seventeenth century the government's main defensive efforts concentrated on Plymouth, whose potential as the major strategic port and harbour of the region became more and more apparent. The conditions for an adequate defence were established in the Civil War. Town and garrison declared for Parliament and withstood a prolonged siege between December 1642 and January 1646. An inner 'Town Line' was constructed or repaired, being an earth rampart linking the town gates, strengthened with redoubts and armed with guns. More important, a four-mile chain of triangular earth forts, revetted with timber or stone and armed with cannon, was built along a ridge from Stonehouse Creek to the head of Lipson Creek and connected by a continuous entrenchment. The line was prolonged at each end by detached works, westward to Devil's Point and eastwards to Laira Point, Prince Rock and Cattedown. The Hooe Peninsula was secured by Fort Stamford. The Royalists' siege was a blockade punctuated by skirmishes, and by serious land-based assaults on the outer line of landward forts in December 1643 and January 1645, neither of which reached the town or the sea. In 1642 the Cornish Royalists seized Mount Edgcumbe and prevented the garrison from using the Hamoaze and Stonehouse Creek. In October 1643, after a bitter 17-day struggle, Royalist forces took Fort Stamford and then Hoo Stert; they bombarded Plymouth, but ineffectively. Nevertheless, resupply was restricted to Millbay until Hoo Stert and Fort Stamford were recovered in July 1644. The latter was again taken by the Royalists, who had to be ejected by an amphibious expedition supported by the fire of the sea forts and Vice-Admiral Batten's ships. (The tip of the peninsula became known as Mount Batten). The siege demonstrated the conditions for the all-round defence of Plymouth: extensive landward fortifications to keep an enemy out of cannon range of vital areas, and occupation of the points round the Sound which controlled access to the harbours. A substantial garrison was needed. In 1643 up to 9,000 were serving; in April 1646, 7,500 men plus the town militia were under arms. This force, and the civilian population, had to be supplied and reinforced by sea.[17] Given a large garrison, Plymouth was defensible against land or sea attack, but if the enemy commanded the supply routes the town's situation would become desperate.

Dartmouth

The permanent seaward defences, reinforced with temporary batteries near Kingswear Castle and at One Gun Point, were never challenged, but it proved to be impossible to defend the town and harbour from a strong attack overland. In 1642–3 the Parliamentarians established a line of earthworks and converted buildings from Dartmouth Castle via Tunstall Church to Mount Boone, covering the approach roads from the west. These could not keep Prince Maurice's artillery out of range, and the town surrendered. The Royalists added two substantial earth forts, described by O'Neil as 'particularly fine examples of their kind', viz. the five-bastioned Gallant's Bower above Dartmouth Castle, and Mount Ridley Fort above Kingswear. Despite a garrison of 800 men and about 100 cannon, the Royalists quickly succumbed to a fierce attack by the New Model infantry from the West. Only a sizeable army could hold a perimeter of such length, on two sides of an unbridged river. In May 1650 the Parliamentary Council of State decided to keep only 'two blockhouses' in commission, presumably Dartmouth and Kingswear Castles.[18]

Exeter and the Exe Estuary

Held for Parliament initially, the town's medieval fortifications were repaired and earthwork fortifications were made beyond the walls, protecting the medieval gates and landward approaches. Isolated by the Royalist armies, the city's hope of relief was by sea, via the Exe estuary. In July 1643 Admiral Warwick's six ships, with soldiers on board, had first to overcome small batteries at Starcross, at Guncliff, Exmouth, and at Powderham. Having secured Exmouth Bight, he sent ships up river which destroyed by gunfire Topsham Castle (a temporary fort, probably built below Mount Howe), but these were in turn bombarded and damaged by a new Royalist half-moon battery. The landing force was repelled by Royalist troops, and Warwick withdrew from the river with the loss of three ships. Never again was any attempt made to attack Exeter from the sea. After the surrender to the Royalists in September 1643, they secured the river mouth by building or restoring a fort on Dawlish Warren. This was complemented by 'Exmouth Castle', probably the name given to the Guncliff battery. (There was a reference in 1568 to both fort and castle, and either may date back to Russell's bulwark of 1545). These secured the river, and it required serious operations by the Parliamentary army to retake them, the castle in December 1645, and the fort in March 1646 after a six-week siege, 12 cannon being taken. In May 1650 the Parliamentary Council of State ordered 'the fort in the island at Exmouth' (i.e. the Warren Fort) to be garrisoned for defence of the coast.[19]

Salcombe

By 1642 its Henrician blockhouse had decayed and was known as the 'Old Bullwarke'. The site was refortified by Sir Edmund Fortescue to protect the harbour, which was used as a base for Royalist privateers who defied Admiral Batten's attempts to suppress them. Named Fort Charles, it cost £1,356 to build, and £3,197 in total including arms for its garrison of 66 men. It was reduced at the end of the war by a regular four-month siege, capitulating on 7 May 1646. It was then dismantled.[20]

Barnstaple and Taw and Torridge Estuaries

Held originally for Parliament, Barnstaple was taken by the Royalists (with Appledore and Bideford) in the summer of 1643. Briefly lost in 1644, it was again held until April 1646. Situated well within the estuary system which reaches the sea at Appledore, the town was made into a strong fortress in 1642–3. Ultimately armed with 44 light guns, the town was described by Sir Edward Hyde in 1645 as 'the most miraculously fortified place I know'. It was indeed the principal Royalist stronghold in North Devon, and was supplied from Royalist Wales across the Bristol Channel. The possession of Appledore, where a fort was built on Staddon Hill commanding the estuary, enabled the Royalists to prevent the Parliamentary navy from resupplying the town when it successfully revolted in 1644, ships with munitions having been sent round from Lyme Regis. The Parliamentarians unsuccessfully attacked Appledore in July 1644, and it is evident that its fort was an important factor in the struggle for possession of both Barnstaple and Bideford. It was not until October 1645 that the Parliamentary navy appeared in sufficient strength in the Bristol Channel to be able to cut off Royalist supplies to Barnstaple from Wales.[21]

Lundy

The Island was never a serious factor in coastal defence; it was easy to defend, with its high cliffs, and the only landing place was overlooked by the medieval Marisco Castle (Fig. 10.1, above, p. 90). Queen Elizabeth's Privy Council urged its owner, Barnard Grenville, to defend it against the Spaniards, and Brazen Ward Battery may date from this period. Held for the King in the Civil War, it subsequently received a small Parliamentary garrison. The bastion and battery of the Castle, and probably some open batteries on the north and north-east coasts of the island, are of seventeenth-century date. With the Restoration, Lundy reverted to its customary lawlessness until the late eighteenth century.[22]

1660–1815

The disaster to the English fleet laid up in the Medway in 1667, owing to the lack of adequate coastal defences, was followed by de Ruyter's unopposed Channel cruise, while a brief period of French naval dominance followed de Tourville's victory off Beachy Head in 1690. Neither of the victorious admirals felt able to attack fortified ports in Devon, although in 1667 small undefended Torquay, and in 1690 Teignmouth, were raided.[23] Otherwise Devon escaped fairly lightly. When a successful major invasion did take place through Brixham in 1688 it was with almost unanimous, if largely tacit, local support, and no shots were fired, even on the beaches. The Dutch artillery was landed at Topsham.

The renewal of rivalry with Britain's nearest neighbour in 1688 produced frequent invasion scares right up to 1859 at least. For much of the period British naval ascendancy was fairly tenuous. French expeditions reached Ireland on four occasions between 1689 and 1789, and Jersey was attacked in 1779 and 1781. De Tourville's raid of 1690 revealed Devon's exposed position, and the development of a naval dockyard at Plymouth from the 1690s was no guarantee of immunity. Indeed, it made an attack more attractive, a nightmare that came close to reality during the American War, 1775–83, when the British fleet, reduced by its American commitments, was outnumbered in the Channel by the Combined Fleet of France and Spain. However, though invasion was many times feared, the only actual landing in the county after 1690 was that by a small raiding party near Ilfracombe in February 1797, which then sailed off to Fishguard and eventually surrendered.

Plymouth 1660–1755

After the great siege and under Charles II, the permanent defences were strengthened by one major and one minor addition: the Royal Citadel and the Mount Batten Tower (both surviving). In 1660 the Fort mounted 67 cannon, the Island 38, and the old Castle four. The Tudor blockhouses were no longer operational, while a survey in 1661 estimated that £2,198 was needed for repairs to the Fort alone.[24]

To what extent a wish to improve the seaward defences led to a decision to build the Citadel on the site of the Fort, and how far the Stuart government's distrust of the erstwhile rebel population of Plymouth was influential, it is impossible to say. Begun in 1665 and built to the design of Sir Bernard de Gomme, the chief royal engineer, it has been described by O'Neil as 'a product of the policy which relied more on coastal defences than efficiency at sea' and 'the best of the very few fortifications of its period in this country, to be set beside the masterpieces of Vauban in France' (Fig. 15.3). Three regular bastions faced landward, while three-and-a-half bastions conform to the line of the old Fort, i.e. the cliff edge of the east Hoe, facing south and east, with the Lower Fort retained below, dominating the entrances to Sutton Pool and Cattewater and flanking the channel to the east of the Island. The ramparts, with their rock-cut ditch, encompass 41 acres. The main defences took five years to build. Barracks for a regular garrison of 500 were ready by 1670, and magazines, stores and a residence for the governor were added. The old Castle and Fort were demolished. The Citadel had guns mounted when the Dutch arrived off the Sound in 1667, which helped to deter them from attacking.[25] In 1679 there were 113 guns in the Citadel and 40 in the Lower Fort. Considered strictly as a defence against enemy ships, the Lower Fort was more important, the heaviest guns being placed in its rock-based open batteries close to the sea edge. The Citadel, though important as a fortified barracks for the general security of the area (it could eventually house 1,000 men) was not strictly necessary as a heavy coast battery.[26]

The Mount Batten Tower is a two-storied, flat-roofed stone building, which mounted ten light guns. It has been variously dated to the Commonwealth period and the reign of Charles II. It was not a significant fortification, perhaps being most useful as an observation post, and as a barracks and magazine for nearby batteries.[27]

The accession of William III was closely followed by the arrival off the Devon coast of Admiral Tourville in 1690. The town promptly contributed £100 towards the cost of two batteries, one on Mount Batten, and one at Pigg's Point in Coxside, the latter to be known to later generations as Queen Anne's Battery. Across the Sound a 'Bowling Green Battery' was built at Cremyll (possibly near the Tudor blockhouse at Wilderness Point), and a battery at Cawsand, possibly an Elizabethan or Civil War survival, was strengthened.[28] Although ordered to attack Plymouth, the French admiral considered the town too well defended for his available resources.

The development of the Navy in the Civil War, the three Dutch Wars, and wars with France, with the need to protect seaborne trade to the Mediterranean and Americas, led to the establishment of naval repair, victualling and hospital facilities at Plymouth, first by Sutton Pool and the Cattewater, and then, additionally, from 1691, in the Hamoaze, where a major dockyard comparable to Portsmouth quickly developed.[29]

One of the advantages of the Hamoaze site for the new dockyard was that its entrance from the Sound was easy to defend, since enemy ships of any force would be obliged to follow the channel to the east and north of St Nicholas Island and its batteries, pass Stonehouse and navigate the narrow turn into the Hamoaze. The defence of the dockyard was the new priority. In 1701 the Ordnance provided four new batteries, two on the Island, and one 11-gun battery for Stonehouse. A fourth, of 24 guns for Mount Edgcumbe, was perhaps the arming of the 'Bowling Green Battery' mentioned above.[30]

At the end of the War of the Spanish Succession in 1713 there was a Board of Ordnance review of the forts and their cannon by Colonel Christian Lilly, recently appointed chief engineer for the Plymouth Division (Devon, Cornwall, Dorset). He noted that in addition to general dilapidations at the Citadel and the Island, Mount Batten Tower was useless, and recommended that its guns and those at Pigg's Point should be removed. Lilly's views on the Lower Fort are instructive: 'being low and close to the sea side is a very good battery towards the Sound, and the chief security for the entrance to the Cattewater'. Lilly recommended that the 318 guns on the defences be reduced to 190, distributed between the Citadel (71), Lower Fort (38), the Island (57), Stonehouse Point (20), and Cawsand Bay (4). The Ordnance view, which prevailed, was that 70 were enough, and in 1725, 69 were in place: sixteen 42-pounders, sixteen 18-pounders, twenty 9-pounders, ten 6-pounders and seven 4-pounders. The specific mention of 42-pounders, the largest guns to be used up to 1815, reflects the need to respond to the growing size and armament of warships.[31]

There were invasion scares in 1744–5, but no developments in the defences between 1713 and 1756 other than the not unimportant adaptations of the Citadel's ramparts and bastions to accommodate fewer and heavier cannon. The platforms and parapets of the Lower Fort, which by 1725 formed a continuous line westwards from Fisher's Nose, were strengthened by the construction between 1753 and 1755 of Ligonier's, Earle's, and Frederick's Batteries, together mounting 32 guns.[32]

Devonport Lines and the Seven Years War, 1756–63

It had been expected before 1756 that war might bring invasion. At

Plymouth the dockyard and its satellite town of Plymouth Dock (renamed Devonport in 1823), which were separated from Stonehouse by a creek and from Plymouth by undeveloped land, were thought to be vulnerable to a sudden attack from the land side. Work on the Devonport Lines began in 1756, anticipating the Crown's purchase of 195 acres of land in 1758, when an Act of Parliament provided £25,159 for land and works. This land stretched in an arc from Morice Town to Mount Wise, enclosing the dockyard, gunwharf and Devonport. The Lines, designed by Mr Leonard Smelt, Royal Engineer, were about 2,100 yards long and occupied 77 acres. They are well delineated in Benjamin Donn's map of Devon, 1765, and in John Manson's plan (Fig. 29.2, below). They comprised a rampart, with variously-shaped bastions, faced by a ditch cut in solid rock, and followed an irregular trace. The excavation work was very arduous, and the fortification produced by 1763 was not strong, though armed with 30 guns. Work was resumed in 1779, again from 1810 to 1816, and was completed in the 1850s. In front of the ditch was the glacis or 'killing-ground', now represented by the open spaces of Devonport Park, the Recreation Ground and the United Services Cricket Ground. Although less elaborate than the works built at Portsmouth, these developments illustrate the importance of Plymouth.[33]

Plymouth during the War of American Independence, 1775–83

The long-matured French invasion plans featured Plymouth as the secondary or reserve target to Portsmouth, and in 1779 it was regarded by the French as unprepared and open to attack. This was partly true; the local command was divided and indecisive, but measures were being taken to improve the defences. It had been realized that the dockyard could be bombarded from the far side of the Tamar and that the Devonport Lines were overlooked by Mount Pleasant (Stoke), only 800 yards away. In 1779 the Board of Ordnance sent down Lt Col. Dixon RE to advise the Governor. He found 61 heavy pieces (18-pounders upwards) in position in the Citadel, Mount Wise, Western King (Stonehouse), and St Nicholas Island. Dixon reinforced the approaches to the Hamoaze and dockyard by six new batteries: Eastern King, four 18-pounders; West Hoe, six 12-pounders; Passage Point (Devil's Point), four 18-pounders; Stonehouse Bridge (Bluff Battery), six 12-pounders; Cavalier Battery (at the north end of the Lines),

Map 15.1 Plymouth's Military Defences

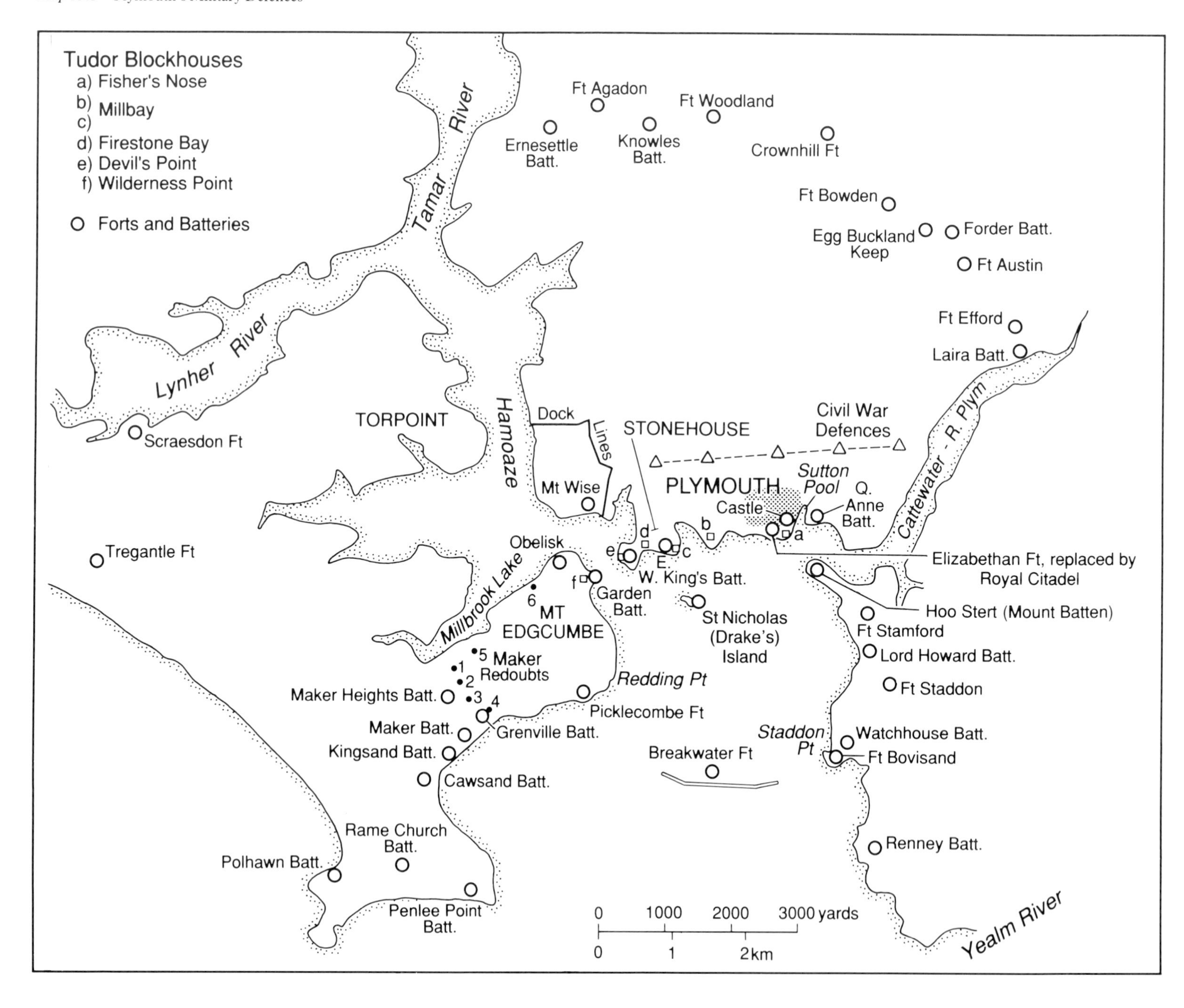

15.4 The Berry Head Forts, begun in 1794 to protect the Navy's Torbay anchorage and the advanced fleet base at Brixham. They were dismantled in 1817. Photographed on 23 December 1986. *(Frances Griffith, Devon County Council)*

six 9-pounders; and Lower Mount Wise, six 24-pounders.

To counter a possible landing in Cawsand Bay, with access to the Maker Heights overlooking the dockyard, three redoubts were built to cover the foreshore, armed with sixteen 12-pounders. These supplemented batteries in existence on the west side of the Sound since 1770 at the latest: at Kingsand (the Amherst Battery of twelve 18-pounders) and at Redding Point, together with the Mount Edgcumbe Battery. A redoubt was also built at Obelisk Hill, close to Cremyll, opposite Mount Wise. At this time Staddon Heights Battery of ten 12-pounders was established on the east side of the Sound above Bovisand Bay. To secure Mount Pleasant, a redoubt (a small square earthwork) was built there, enclosing a blockhouse which may have been erected in the Seven Years War. In 1781 the Crown retrospectively purchased the land for Mount Pleasant Redoubt, Stonehouse Redoubt, Western King Redoubt, and Staddon Heights Battery.

The situation of Plymouth in August 1779 was not perhaps as desperate as some accounts have suggested. Four battalions of infantry, including two of regulars, were in garrison, plus artillerymen. Four hundred dockyard workers were trained to man the batteries, reinforced by naval crews from ships in port and the crews of a convoy of 70 merchantmen which took refuge in Plymouth on 17 August. Three old battleships were moored to defend the Hamoaze, and 630 Cornish miners were brought in to deepen the ditch of the Lines and build the Retreat Battery (incorporating Obelisk Redoubt).[34]

The Duke of Richmond was critical of the Plymouth defences before his appointment in 1780 as Master-General of the Ordnance. A keen advocate of additional fortifications, he proposed to protect Plymouth dockyard from overland attack by building a system of detached forts on the Maker Heights and at Torpoint. There was professional and political support in principle for some additional defences, but the difficulty of getting large Ordnance estimates through Parliament for peacetime expenditure was fatally compounded by the Duke's personal unpopularity, his lack of political finesse, the objections of some senior naval men (who saw no need of forts), the vested interests of some large landowners, and revived fears of standing armies (the new forts would need large garrisons). Despite Prime Minister Pitt's strong support, the estimates failed to pass the House of Commons in 1785 and 1786. Richmond pruned his scheme at Plymouth to what could be achieved with ordinary Ordnance funds. In 1782 the earthworks for a chain of five redoubts were completed, running in an arc some 3,000 yards from the Hamoaze entrance, from above Cawsand Bay to Millbrook Lake. After the war, work on casing these works with permanent masonry and building their garrison accommodation, magazines, etc. went on slowly. About 103 acres of land on Maker for these works were bought in 1784 for £13,945. Two of the five were completed by 1791 with casemates and all-round defences; the other three were completed as batteries. They were armed with six to eight 18-pounders each. A sixth redoubt was built at Empacombe in 1806–7. In the wars of 1793–1815 the redoubts were armed and manned; the redoubt system included the Cawsand shore batteries previously mentioned, whose 16 cannon were stored in peacetime in the redoubts.[35]

Plymouth during the Revolutionary and Napoleonic Wars

Apart from the continued work on the Maker defences and the Lines, mentioned above, there were only minor additions to the fixed Plymouth defences during this period. A five-gun redoubt was built on Stonehouse Hill to protect the road between the Citadel and the Lines, and a four-gun battery was made at Devil's Point. Ordnance records for 1805 show 255 cannon and carronades, mainly in the 18-pounder to 42-pounder sizes, at Plymouth, distributed as follows: Citadel 65, Dockyard 100, Western King 10, Island 28, Staddon heights 10, and Maker Heights 42. The Citadel and St Nicholas Island mounted most of the heaviest cannon, the 42- and 32-pounders.[36]

At about this time the Mount Edgcumbe Battery at Wilderness Point was rearmed with 21 long 8-pounders. Despite this battery's tactical importance, the Crown allowed the site to remain in the possession of the Edgcumbe family (as a private saluting battery in peacetime) until 1862.[37]

Tor Bay, 1688–1815

From 1688 to 1815 Tor Bay claimed a degree of the government's attention second only to Plymouth. It provided the Navy with an advanced base, protected from westerly winds, to support operations against the French. A fleet-watering facility was established at Brixham in about 1700, and the Privy Council authorised a 14-gun battery there in 1691. In 1745 the Board of Ordnance issued five 12-pounders to Brixham. The close blockade of

Brest, first systematically applied in the Seven Years War, emphasised the role of Tor Bay. Early in the American War, i.e. 1779–80, the Board of Ordnance installed a substantial armament, mainly of 20 or 24-pounders, distributed between four batteries: ten at the tip of Berry Head (the promontory flanking the south side of the anchorage), three each at the Danish Castle and Hardy's Head batteries (on the north side of the Berry Head promontory), and five at Fishcombe (on the north-west side of Brixham). The importance of the Tor Bay anchorage was underlined when, in 1781, the outnumbered British fleet took up a defensive formation there.[38]

During the wars of 1793–1815 a considerable war establishment was built up at Brixham, comprising a stone quay, store houses and naval and military hospitals. The permanent fortification of Berry Head was begun in 1794, when 132 acres of land were purchased. The batteries of 1779–80 were re-established, but for their protection two forts were built. The main fort, in which twelve 42-pounders faced seawards (in the half-moon battery) occupied the tip of the Head (Fig. 15.4). Its principal defence was a limestone-faced rampart running from cliff-edge to cliff-edge across the peninsula, about 200 yards long, earth-filled, 56 feet thick at the base and 12 feet at the top, and provided with gun platforms for 12-pounders behind stone embrasures. The rampart, designed to protect the main batteries from an attack overland, was fronted by a dry moat 26 feet wide and 8 feet deep. On the south side of Berry Head was built the South Fort, its rampart built round from cliff to cliff on one side of the peninsula, designed as an advanced work to protect the main batteries. Both forts were provided with magazines, stores, barracks, kitchens, etc., for a force of gunners and a garrison of a militia battalion, in all about 1,000 men. These forts were supported by two small batteries north-west and west of the main fort, overlooking Brixham; Hardy's Head Battery, and the Round Top or Castle Battery, for four and three guns respectively, together with a five-gun battery at Fishcombe. This strong coast defence station, of which a great deal survives, was dismantled in 1817 and not re-established.[39]

Dartmouth, 1660–1815

Dartmouth Castle, the town's chief fortress since the later middle ages, with the linked Lamberd's Bulwark, was maintained by the Board of Ordnance until the nineteenth century, with a master gunner in residence. However, since the town continued to receive Edward IV's grant of £40 p.a. from the Customs, the Ordnance insisted, e.g. in 1685 and 1715, on the town repairing the fabric. Bayard's Cove and Kingswear Castles were no longer used, the latter being described in Colonel Lilly's report of 1715 as 'useless and irreparable'. In 1667 a merchant convoy from the Mediterranean sheltered from de Ruyter in the river, their guns and seamen reinforcing the militia and fixed defences. The Dutch retired to attack the easier target of Torquay. In the crisis of 1690 Lamberd's Bulwark was rebuilt in stone and armed with eight culverins, and temporary seaward batteries were built which were sufficient to deter Admiral Tourville's reconnaissance party. Renamed Maiden Fort, the Bulwark was again rebuilt in 1747 as a two-tiered battery for 12 guns. The Castle and Fort provided the fixed defence of the harbour during the wars of 1793–1815, the Castle serving as headquarters of the militia and volunteer gunners. Their armament was steadily upgraded. In 1715 Lilly reported 48 miscellaneous cannon; by about 1725 this collection was reduced to six 12-pounders, six 6- and six 3-pounders. Finally, by 1805, the main battery was changed to ten 18-pounders, with only two 3-pounders.[40]

The Minor Ports to 1815

Dartmouth and Torbay were significant exceptions to the general Crown policy, exercised through the Ordnance, of relying upon local initiative to build emergency batteries and raise volunteer artillerymen to protect minor ports and estuaries. Normally only cannon and ammunition were provided by the Ordnance, but during the great crisis of 1779 it built batteries in the South West at Weymouth, Swanage, Poole, Lyme Regis, Torbay, Mevagissey, Looe and Fowey. During the wars of 1793–1815 a very extensive system of emergency coastal batteries was built to protect every anchorage and likely landing place from the Firth of Forth round to Liverpool. In Devon, other than Tor Bay, Dartmouth and Plymouth, the Ordnance list for 1805 also included Seaton (four 18-pounders) and Ilfracombe (five 18-pounders). There were certainly others, probably owing little to Ordnance initiative, as evidenced by a list of volunteer artillery corps formed, viz. in 1797 at Beer and Seaton; in 1801 at Appledore, Brixham, Dartmouth, Exmouth and Sidmouth, Maker, and Stonehouse; and in 1805 at Barnstaple, Haytor, and Plymouth.[41] While some contingents served in the main fortresses, others served in local batteries, of which Exmouth, Sidmouth, Teignmouth, and Yealm are examples. Charts of 1743 and 1761 show a fort still in existence opposite Exmouth on the Warren; a battery here was being operated by the Preventative Service in 1855. In Exmouth itself a battery was built (or rebuilt) at the riverside in 1794, following, it is said, a visit by the Duke of Richmond.[42] At Sidmouth, Fortfield and Fort Cottage recall the battery of four 12-pounders built by 1793 and dismantled in 1815. A view of the beach painted in 1820 shows the Fort as a platform fronting the sea, with a magazine building.[43]

At Teignmouth, the memory of the destructive French raid of 1690 prompted a local petition in 1744 for permission to build a small battery on the beach at East Teignmouth, i.e. on the north side of the harbour entrance, and to secure cannon from the Ordnance. Twelve 12-pounders were authorized. This work soon decayed; Donn's map of 1765 marks the 'ruins

15.5 Fort Bovisand, begun in 1861 and covering the channel between the eastern end of Plymouth Breakwater and the shore, received its first main armament by 1872. *(John Saunders, Exeter University)*

of a fort'. A petition for a new fort in 1774 was unsuccessful, but to one sent in 1793 the Duke of Richmond responded favourably. He inspected, and provided six (or four) 12-pounders and ammunition. The sum of £200 was raised locally to rebuild the earthwork battery, described as a segment of a circle about 110 feet in diameter, eight feet above ground level. The guns were served by a Teignmouth volunteer artillery corps of 65 members formed in 1795, uniformed in blue jackets and red trousers.[44]

The river Yealm, the first estuary and landing place east of Plymouth Sound, was a potential back door to Plymouth. A battery built there in 1803 at the river mouth was manned by the East Devon Militia, supported by a blockship.[45]

1815–1870

After 1815 Britain had overwhelming naval superiority. The army was drastically reduced and mainly deployed overseas. The Parliamentary Select Committee on Finance was critical, in the post-war years, of previous Ordnance expenditure on fortifications, promoting the view that a strong fleet and a patriotic militia would suffice for security. The Ordnance dismantled all temporary batteries, retaining only the permanent works, but rivalry with France continued, eventually creating fears in some military and political circles about the weakness of the army at home and of the coastal defences.[46] From the 1840s, moreover, technical and scientific advances produced steam-powered, iron-hulled, warships, and led to the development of ever-larger, longer-ranged guns and more powerful explosives. The Crimean War demonstrated that the ships, guns, and fortifications of the Napoleonic Wars were now obsolete.

In the late 1840s Peel's government began to pay attention to coastal defences, influenced by that powerful advocate of rearmament Sir John Burgoyne RE (appointed Inspector-General of Fortifications in 1845). In a memorandum of 1846, circulated to the Cabinet and supported by Palmerston, Burgoyne called for more regulars, a new militia, and the refortification of key dockyards and arsenals. Ordnance expenditure on defence works rose from £87,210 to £294,842 p.a. over the period 1843–7. A powerful stimulus to refortification was given by the military adventurism of Napoleon III, which created alarm throughout the 1850s and produced in 1859 a public atmosphere of near-panic about a possible French invasion.[47]

Plymouth

Some work was carried on in the 1830s and 1840s. At St Nicholas Island the still existing barrack block for 100 or more men and a new commanding officer's house were built in 1830–5. In 1849 the strong, stone Prince of Wales Redoubt was built at Eastern King. Two nine-gun batteries were built between 1848 and 1850 at Picklecombe Point and Staddon Point, to cover the entrance to the Sound round the ends of the great Breakwater which had been built between 1812 and 1848. In the late 1850s work to complete Devonport Lines was started, and, more importantly, the large forts, Scraesdon and Tregantle to the west of Antony, 7,000 yards from the Hamoaze, were started as the main elements in a defence line from the Lynher River to Whitsand Bay. At Cawsand, a new battery was begun in 1858 to replace the three redoubts of 1779.[48]

The *Report of the Royal Commission on the Defences of the United Kingdom*, published in 1860, recommended fortifications for nine naval bases including Plymouth. The government approved the *Report* in principle, but cut the cost by reducing the number of proposed works, including 15 of various kinds in Plymouth. The cheaper scheme was approved by Parliament.[49]

The Royal Commission provided for two possible modes of attack: a direct frontal assault by water and an indirect approach from the landward side following a landing elsewhere. At the entrance to the Sound, convex-fronted casemated works were built at Picklecombe, Bovisand (by Staddon Point) and St Nicholas Island. An oval iron-armoured fort was built in the sea behind the breakwater. The inner seaward defence was secured by a casemated battery (the 'Garden Battery'), replacing the Mount Edgcumbe saluting battery; the Eastern and Western King's Batteries and the Citadel were rearmed and a new small battery was made at Devil's Point. At Whitsand Bay, outside the Sound, Polhawn Battery was built, near Rame church. Conscious of the continual development of more powerful guns, the engineers of the 1860s allowed for the future fitting of armoured shields to the gunports of the casemates of the seaward forts.

Plymouth's Landward Defences

The original plan was for an arc of forts, interrupted only by the rivers Lynher, Tamar and Plym, from Tregantle on Whitsand Bay, round Saltash, across the Tamar to Ernesettle, east to Laira via Crownhill, across the Plym to Staddon Heights. The Saltash sector was deleted; perhaps it was calculated that the Tamar, and the distance of this sector from the sea over difficult country bisected by the Lynher and extensive mud flats, would deter an attack. Otherwise the scheme was implemented: on the west, Tregantle and Scraesdon Forts (already begun); on the north, Ernesettle Battery, Agaton Fort, Knowles Battery, Woodland Fort, Crownhill Fort, Bowden Fort, Egg Buckland Keep, Forder Battery, Fort Austin, Fort Efford and Laira Battery – all (except the Keep) sited to command the country beyond them. Across the Plym, on Staddon Heights, Fort Stamford and Fort Staddon dominated the high ground. The line was well out; Ernesettle was two miles from the dockyard, Laira four miles.[50]

The military architecture of the new landward forts was a radical departure from the bastion and curtain-wall style current in Europe since the sixteenth century. A simple polygonal trace, with no outworks, was now employed. The land works were intended to dominate the ground between them with cannon and mortar fire, keeping siege guns beyond bombardment range and breaking up large formations of enemy troops. The garrison was intended to include a mobile force able to counterattack in any threatened sector. For Plymouth, the Commission had recommended fort garrisons totalling 7,000 men with 742 guns, to be reinforced to 15,000 men of all arms in wartime.[51] In effect, a ring fortress on a Continental scale had been created. The late-nineteenth-century defences of Plymouth, like those of Portsmouth and Chatham, were as modern and as strong as any maritime defences in Europe.

In the event, the British navy rapidly outbuilt the French, and the catastrophic defeat of France by Prussia in 1870 gave the new French Republic another national enemy, and a new eastern frontier to fortify.

Dartmouth and the Minor Ports to 1914

After 1815 Dartmouth remained the only coast defence station in Devon other than Plymouth maintained by the Board of Ordnance, the Castle and Maiden Fort being kept in repair. As a sequel to the panic of 1859 Maiden Fort was replaced in 1861 by a new two-storied battery. A rectangular stone structure, it was finally armed in the 1890s with five rifled muzzle-loading 64-pounder guns; two mounted on the open platform which formed the roof of the battery, and three in the casemate below. Behind the gun position were magazines and some gunners' accommodation, though the Castle continued to be used. The battery was manned by a unit of the Devon Volunteer Artillery. The Castle became an ancient monument in 1907; the Battery was rearmed in 1940.[52]

War fears during the 1850s produced a new mass Volunteer movement. In coastal districts which felt threatened, Volunteer Artillery Corps were formed and demanded guns. The government had plenty of naval muzzle-loaders made surplus by rearmament and, perhaps reluctantly, distributed them when local patriots could not be denied. At Torquay, for example, a volunteer corps raised in 1852 became the 4th Devon Volunteer Battery in 1859 and in May 1860 secured two ex-naval 24-pounders to mount at Corbyn's Head, a site abandoned in 1884. In 1876 a two-gun battery was established at Walls Hill. Similarly, at Brixham, a volunteer corps was given two heavy guns in July 1860. The two units survived until absorbed into the Territorial Force in 1908.[53] At Sidmouth in 1859 a Volunteer Artillery and Rifle Corps was formed and two 24-pounders were mounted on the old fort.[54] At Exmouth a corps was formed in 1860, and guns were mounted at an old battery site near the present Lifeboat Museum. In 1862 the battery was rebuilt, described as of 'a quadrate form, with three embrasures, and enclosing a bomb-proof magazine and a battery keeper's dwelling'. It was armed with three 32-pounders and an eight-inch mortar. A smaller battery built on the Maer in 1864 was demolished in 1908.[55]

Coastal Guns, 1860s to 1956

After the 1850s guns ceased to be the simple, smooth-bore (SB) muzzle-loading (ML) weapons of the previous 300 years. Apart from a great increase in size, they first became rifled (R), though still muzzle-loading, because the early breech-loaders (BL) proved unsatisfactory. In 1856 the regular coastal defences were mainly armed with large numbers of SBML guns, many of which were then converted to rifled barrels. In Plymouth, in 1867, there were four RML, 128 SB and 10 carronades. In 1881 there were 81 RML, 103 SB converted to RML, and 90 SB. Thirty-eight-ton 12.5-inch, 25-ton 10-inch, and 12-ton 9-inch RML guns were mounted on the heavy batteries in the 1870s and 1880s.[56]

In the late 1870s the breech-loading problem was solved, and in the early 1880s, after fierce arguments amongst the experts, the principle was conceded; all ML guns were made obsolete and rearmament began. The Navy was given priority; coastal defence did not start receiving the new heavy breech-loaders until about 1890. There were two results. First, a very limited range of guns were installed by 1914 in the defences at Plymouth as elsewhere: 9.2-inch and 6-inch, and two quick-firers, 4.7-inch and 12-pounder. Second, there was a complete change of policy regarding actual fortifications. Armoured and masonry all-round defences were abandoned, and land guns were dispersed. Ranges increased: in the 1860s ships and forts were expected to engage at about 2,000 yards; by 1914 the 9.2-inch had a range of 17,400 yards. Harbour defences had to cope with very fast-moving light craft and submarines; they were aided by greatly improved range-finders, torpedo tubes, nets and searchlights.[57]

The emergence of Germany as Great Britain's naval rival from 1900 had consequences for the defence of naval bases hardly appreciated in time. Even the new main fleet base at Scapa Flow was inadequately defended by 1914. Nevertheless, the southern dockyards and bases were still of great importance, and powerful new guns were installed, the heaviest in new locations on outer headlands to give the greatest range seawards. At Plymouth, the reorganization of the 1890s and up to 1914 produced a World War One armament of eight 9.2-inch, 13 6-inch, three 4.7-inch, and 15 twelve-pounders. The 9.2-inch guns were in new batteries built in the 1890s: Rame Church (two), Penlee Point (three), Renney (three). The six-inch were at the Watchhouse Battery (Staddon Point, 1895), Maker Heights (about 1892), Lord Howard (Jennycliff Bay), Picklecombe Fort and St Nicholas Island. The lighter guns were at Grenville (above Cawsand), Picklecombe, Bovisand, Lord Howard, St Nicholas Island, Western King and Devil's Point. (St Nicholas Island became known as Drake's Island in the second half of the nineteenth century).[58]

Between the two world wars the coast batteries at Plymouth were reduced somewhat. The two 9.2-inch guns at Rame Church were removed, and batteries at Grenville, Maker Heights, Devil's Point and the Lord Howard were dismantled; otherwise the system was maintained, with the addition of a 12-pounder battery at Mount Batten.[59]

The Second World War brought with it a real invasion threat, especially in 1940, when the German forces occupied the European coast from Norway to France. The Navy's freedom of action was hampered by German air power, and while the main threat was seen to be to the South East, measures were taken to rearm the whole coast. Fortunately, the great demand for guns could be met from the large numbers of 6-inch, 5.5-inch, 4.7-inch and 4-inch guns saved from ships scrapped after World War One. These were quickly mounted and provided with concrete gunhouses against air attack. In Devon, pairs of 4.7-inch or 4-inch guns were allocated as follows: Dartmouth, Exmouth, Brixham, Torquay, Salcombe, Seaton, Sidmouth, Dawlish, Teignmouth, Appledore, Barnstaple, and Ilfracombe. Some batteries on the south coast saw action. The Dover batteries were particularly busy, and others, such as that at Falmouth, were occasionally employed against E boats. In January 1943 the emergency was deemed to be over.[60]

In 1956 the Ministry of Defence decided that expenditure on coast defence batteries was no longer justified. The coast artillery was abolished from 31 December 1956, and there ended an era in Devon's maritime history extending over five hundred years.

15: The Military Coast Defences of Devon, 1500–1956

1 C Duffy, *Siege Warfare: The Fortress in the Early Modern World, 1494–1660* (1979), 1–4, 25–34; JR Hale, 'The Defence of the Realm, 1485–1558', in HM Colvin, ed., *The History of the King's Works*, IV (1982) (hereafter *King's Works*), 367–401; and especially A Saunders, *Fortress Britain* (1989), 34–52.

2 PRO, State Papers Domestic, Edward VI, SP 10/15/11.

3 *Letters and Papers of Henry VIII* (hereafter *L & P*), XIV i, 398, 400, 426, 655, 685, XV, 502, XX i, 1055, 1104, 1254; BM Cotton MS Augustus I i, 35–6, 38–9 (great pictorial map); M Biddle, HM Colvin and J Summerson, 'The Defences in Detail', in *King's Works*, 587–602.

4 J Barber, 'New Light on Old Plymouth', *Proceedings of the Plymouth Athenaeum* IV (1973–9), 55–66; RA Preston, *Gorges of Plymouth Fort* (Toronto, 1953), 90; RN Worth, *History of Plymouth* (Plymouth, 1890), 402–4, 411–15.

5 M Brayshay, 'Tudor Artillery Towers and their Role in the Defence of Plymouth in 1588', *Devon Historian* 35 (1987), 3–14; CW Bracken, *A History of Plymouth and her Neighbours* (Plymouth, 1931), 68; BH St J O'Neil, *Castles and Cannon* (Oxford, 1960), 47; JR Kenyon, 'Early Artillery Fortifications in England and Wales', *Archaeological Journal* 138 (1981), 218–19; RN Worth, *Calendar of the Plymouth Municipal Records* (Plymouth, 1893), 89–114; *King's Works*, 484, note 8 (sixth blockhouse).

6 *King's Works*, 484–5; Worth, *Calendar*, 116.

7 O'Neil, *Castles and Cannon*, 38, 39, 45; BH St J O'Neil, 'Dartmouth Castle and other Defences of Dartmouth Haven', *Archaeologia* LXXXV (1935), 133–45; AD Saunders, *Dartmouth Castle*, English Heritage Guide (1983), 1–9, 12–18; AC Carpenter, *The Cannon of Dartmouth Castle, Devon*, (Plymouth, undated), 1–5.

8 *L & P III* ii, 2355, Addenda I ii, end of 1545.

9 *L & P* XX ii, 242; L Toulmin Smith, ed., *The Itinerary of John Leland* (1907), 227–8, 232.

10 *King's Works*, 595; O'Neil, *Castles and Cannon*, 45.

11 *King's Works*, 403–7; M Oppenheim, in *Victoria County History of Cornwall* I (1906), 494.

12 M Brayshay, 'Plymouth's Coastal Defences in the Year of the Spanish Armada', *DAT*, 119 (1987), 169–96, especially 176–87; Preston, *Gorges of Plymouth Fort*, 456–7 (maps of Sound, 1588); P Sheppard, 'A Note on the Post-Medieval Fortifications', in C Thomas, ed., *Archaeological Survey of the Rame Peninsula*, Institute of Cornish Studies Special Report No.2 (Truro, 1974), 30.

13 Preston, *Gorges of Plymouth Fort*, 56–65, plan of fort and maps of Sound, 459–61; *King's Works*, 485–8.

14 Preston, *Gorges of Plymouth Fort*, 58–9, 61, 65, 98, 124–5; *King's Works*, 487; Worth, *History of Plymouth*, 414. See FW Woodward, *Drake's Island* (Exeter 1991), 3, 5 for Adams's plans.

15 Oppenheim, *Maritime History of Devon*, 52–64; Preston, *Gorges of Plymouth Fort*, 127, 130–1, 246–7, 255–6, 263; *Acts of the Privy Council of England, 1616–17*, 161–4.

16 Oppenheim, 65.

17 EA Andriette, *Devon and Exeter in the Civil War* (Newton Abbot, 1971), 98–101, 123–34; Oppenheim, 65; Worth, *History of Plymouth*, 92–129, 416–17; Worth, *Calendar*, 159–61; Worth, 'The Siege Accounts of Plymouth', *DAT*, 17 (1885), 215–39.

18 Andriette, *Civil War*, 95, 97, 115, 159–60; O'Neil, *Castles and Cannon*, 108–10; P Russell, *Dartmouth* (1950), 41, 111–18; *Calendar of State Papers Domestic, 1650* (1876), 144. Maps and plans: Andriette, *Civil War*, 96; O'Neil, *Castles and Cannon*, fig.9; Russell, *Dartmouth*, 9, 24, 25, 59; Saunders, *Guide*, 6.

19 M Stoyle, *Exeter City Defences Project: Documentary Evidence for the Civil War Defences of Exeter, 1642–3* (Exeter Museums, Report No 88.12, 1988), iii–iv, ix–x, xiv–xv; RW Cotton, 'Naval Attack on Topsham', *Devon and Cornwall Notes & Gleanings* I (1888), 153–4; H Stone, *DCNQ* 11 (1921–2), 96; W Wilson Holman,

DCNQ 11 (1921–2), 143; R Bush, *The Book of Exmouth* (Buckingham, 1978), 89–90; ER Delderfield, *Exmouth Milestones* (Exmouth, 1948), 32–3; W Cotton and H Woollcombe, *Gleanings from the Municipal and Cathedral Records relating to the History of the City of Exeter* (Exeter, 1877), 106; *Calendar of State Papers Domestic, 1650*, 144.

20 PQ Karkeek, 'Sir Edmund Fortescue and the Siege of Fort Charles', *DAT* 9 (1877), 336–50; Oppenheim, 64, 66.

21 RW Cotton, *Barnstaple and the Northern Part of Devonshire during the Great Civil War, 1642–1646* (1889), 49, 51–4, 72, 75, 110–21, 162–3, 218, 227–8, 262–3, 336, 352–3, 367, 387, 431, 506; Appledore Fort, 206, 297–9; ships from Lyme, 322.

22 J Thomas, 'A History of Lundy from 1390 to 1775', *DAT* 110 (1978), 113, 115, 118–20, 122–3, 129–30, 139; KS Gardner, 'The Archaeology of Lundy', in A and M Langham, *Lundy* (Newton Abbot, 1970), 129, 132–3, 140–1; Oppenheim, 66.

23 R Ollard, *Pepys; A Biography* (Oxford, 1984), 159–64; Oppenheim, 70–1

24 Oppenheim, 71–2; FW Woodward, *A History of the Royal Citadel, Plymouth* (Exeter, 1987) 21–2.

25 Woodward, *Citadel*, gives a full account. For the design and construction see Chapters 7–10; O'Neil, *Castles and Cannon*, 114–15.

26 Woodward, *Citadel*, 52–8

27 Oppenheim, 71–2; AD Saunders, 'The Coastal Defences of Cornwall', *Archaeological Journal* (1973), 234.

28 Woodward, *Citadel*, 133; Worth, *Calendar*, 170; Sheppard, *Rame Survey*, 30; Bracken, *History of Plymouth*, 198. See also chapter 27 below.

29 Oppenheim, 66–70, 77 ff. See also below, chap. 28.

30 Oppenheim, 75, 92.

31 Oppenheim, 92–3; Woodward, *Citadel*, 59–61; Woodward, *Drake's Island*, 10–11; KW Maurice-Jones, *The History of Coast Artillery in the British Army* (Chatham, 1959), 19, 20, 25.

32 Woodward, *Citadel*, 61–6.

33 Oppenheim, 93; Worth, *History of the Town and Borough of Devonport* (Plymouth, 1870), 14, 15, 50; Benjamin Donn, *A Map of the County of Devon 1765* (Devon and Cornwall Record Society, New Series 9, 1965), sheet 12b.

34 A Temple Patterson, *The Other Armada* (Manchester, 1960), 6–19, 46–7, 70–2, 100, 117, 124, 133, 138–50, 181–93, 222–3; Oppenheim, 94, 113–15; Maurice-Jones, *Coast Artillery*, 52–3; Sheppard, *Rame Survey*, 31; Sheppard, 'The Amherst Battery', *Cornish Archaeology* (1973), 75–6; Mount Pleasant Blockhouse: Worth, *History of Devonport*, 15.

35 Temple Patterson, *The Other Armada*, 218–22; AG Olson, *The Radical Duke* (Oxford, 1961), 3, 5, 9, 46, 74–5, 79, 81; *The Annual Register* 28 (1788), 95–108; C Ross, ed., *Correspondence of Charles, First Marquis of Cornwallis* (1859), 195–6; Sheila Lambert, ed., *House of Commons Sessional Papers of the Eighteenth Century* (Wilmington, USA, 1975), 36 (1781–4), 364, 369–73, 385–6; 50 (1784–7, 37–42; D Evans, 'The Duke of Richmond, James Glenie, Maker and the Fortifications Bill', *Fort*, 16 (1988), 73–82 and 'The Duke of Richmond as Designer' *Fort*, 18 (1990), 83–93; Sheppard, *Rame Survey*, 14, 23–4, 31; Maurice-Jones, *Coast Artillery*, 97.

36 S Rowe, *The Panorama of Plymouth* (Plymouth, 1821), 112; GA Cooke, *Topography of Great Britain* I (early 1820s), 191–3; Oppenheim, 95; Maurice-Jones, *Coast Artillery*, 97; W Camden, *Britannia* I (2nd edn., 1806), 45–6.

37 Cooke, *Topography*, 206; R Brindley, *Plymouth, Stonehouse and Devonport Directory* (Devonport, 1830), 72; IV Hogg, *Coast Defences of England and Wales 1856–1956*, (Newton Abbot, 1974), 185.

38 P Russell, *A History of Torquay and the Famous Anchorage of Torbay* (Torquay, 1960), 39–40, 45; Oppenheim, 95; for Brixham guns, 1691 and 1745, Privy Council data from Mr CJN Trollope, Fortress Study Group; AR Pye, *Berry Head Fort Brixham* (Exeter 1989), 4–5.

39 P Russell, *History of Torquay*, 73; Pye, *Berry Head Fort*, 6–11, 32–4 and figures; *House of Commons Sessional Papers of the Eighteenth Century* (BPP, 1794, 93), 63.

40 Oppenheim, 71–2, 93–4; Maurice-Jones, *Coast Artillery*, 25, 50, 53, 97; Saunders, *Guide*, 11–12. For Dartmouth guns, 1690, Privy Council data from Mr CNJ Trollope.

41 Maurice-Jones, *Coast Artillery*, 32–3, 50–2, 55, 75, 93–4, 97, 103–4; Saunders, *Fortress Britain*, 114–6; Seaton: W Stukeley, *Itinerarium Curiosum* (1774) in R Pearse Chope, ed., *Early Tours in Devon and Cornwall* (Newton Abbot, 1967), 143; Camden, *Britannia*, I, 59.

42 JF Chanter, *DCNQ*, 13, (1924–5), 32–3; WJ Harte, *DCNQ*, 22 (1942–6), 254; Bush, *Exmouth*, 89–90.

43 PO Hutchinson, *New Guide to Sidmouth and Its Neighbourhood*, (Sidmouth, 1857), 21; G Holmes, ed., *Sidmouth: A History* (Sidmouth, 1987), 41–2.

44 G Griffith, *History of Teignmouth* (Bradford on Avon, 1973), 55, 61; for 1744 guns, Privy Council data from Mr Trollope.

45 WCSL, H Woollcombe, MS History of Plymouth, 1803; JW Lee, 'Devon on Guard, 1759–1815', *DAT* 40 (1908), 238.

46 EL Woodward, *The Age of Reform, 1815–1870* (Oxford, 1938), 157–8, 186–229; H Strachan, *The Reform of the British Army, 1830–54* (Manchester, 1984), 6–11, 14, 197.

47 Strachan, *Reform of the British Army*, 198–202 and *From Waterloo to Balaclava* (Cambridge, 1985), 101–2, 126–9; PM Kennedy, *The Rise and Fall of British Naval Mastery* (1976), 172–3; Whitworth Porter, *History of the Corps of Royal Engineers*, II (Chatham, 1951), 212–17.

48 *Report of the Commissioners appointed to consider the Defences of the United Kingdom* (BPP, 1860, 23), (hereafter *Royal Commission*), xxxiii–xxxv, 72, 74, 76; Hogg, *Coastal Defences*, 182, 184, 190–1, 195–6; Sheppard, *Rame Survey*, 31; Woodward, *Drake's Island*, 13–14.

49 *Royal Commission*, xxxii–xxxviii and Appendix 5; Hogg, *Coast Defences*, 19–26, 176–8; Maurice-Jones, *Coast Artillery*, 178.

50 Hogg, *Coast Defences*, 50, 177–204; Whitworth Porter, *History of the Corps of Royal Engineers*, II, 219–23; L Jewitt, *A History of Plymouth* (Plymouth, 1873), 655–62 and FW Woodward, *Plymouth Defences* (Ivybridge, Devon, 1990), 15–29, which is useful for the whole period 1500–1956.

51 Hogg, *Coast Defences*, 45–9, 174–6; Maurice-Jones, *Coast Artillery*, 141–6.

52 Saunders, *Guide*, 12–13; Carpenter, *Cannon*, 10–11.

53 AC Ellis, *An Historical Survey of Torquay* (Torquay, 1930), 391–4; O/S Map 1891, Devonshire Sheet CXVI, shows battery.

54 G Holmes, *Sidmouth*, 82–3.

55 Bush, *Exmouth*, 90–1; Delderfield, *Exmouth Milestones*, 34, 110; W Webb, *Memorials of Exmouth* (Exmouth, 1872), 104.

56 Maurice-Jones, *Coast Artillery*, 167–70.

57 Hogg, *Coast Defences*, 76–89; Maurice-Jones, *Coast Artillery*, 169–74, 180; W Baker Brown, *History of the Corps of Royal Engineers* IV (Chatham, 1952), 222–30, 241–2; George Sydenham Clarke, *Fortification* (1907) chapters XIII and XIV.

58 Maurice-Jones, *Coast Artillery*, 187, 195–6; Hogg, *Coast Defences*, 178–95; Woodward, *Citadel*, 82–4; Woodward, *Drake's Island*, 23–32.

59 Maurice-Jones, *Coast Artillery*, 218, 220; Woodward, *Citadel*, 85–6 and plate 33; Hogg, *Coast Defences*, 178–95.

60 Maurice-Jones, *Coast Artillery*, 219, 226–30, 232–40, 276–7.

16 *Devon Shipping, Trade, and Ports, 1600–1689*

ALISON GRANT

IN SPITE OF WARS AND POLITICAL UPHEAVALS, England's trade, shipping, and general economy expanded over the period 1600–1689. After peace with Spain in 1604 old trades were quickly re-established, but soon a crisis in the cloth trade showed the need for new markets and products. The short but disastrous wars of the late 1620s, the Civil War, and the foreign wars of the next two decades caused heavy losses to many ports and merchants, and trade was slow to recover, even after 1660. Subsequently, however, as governments protected and promoted commerce and colonies, England's shipping and trade reached levels never before achieved. Devon merchants, having been among the first to exploit new sources of supply and open up markets across the Atlantic, played a notable part in making this expansion possible. Although some ports fell victim to changing circumstances, the county was in a good position for new trades, and throughout this period men with enterprise, judgment, and the courage to exploit new opportunities became rich and successful.

Ports and Merchants

The seventeenth century was a period of mixed fortunes for Devon ports. Silt or shingle had already caused the decline of Teignmouth, Seaton and Sidmouth, and as vessels increased in size the old river-ports became difficult to reach. Exeter was only a port by virtue of its canal, and when this was neglected, as in the middle years of the century, there was little waterborne trade. Most vessels discharged at Topsham, but the city successfully resisted attempts to wrest from it the status of head port. Owing to silting of the Dart, large ships could not reach Totnes, so most trade was handled downstream at Dartmouth, where the water was deeper. At Barnstaple, sand in the Taw made the 'haven but shallow, so that it hardly beareth small vessels', and many goods had to be lightered seven miles to and from Appledore, which flourished in this period as never before.[1] Barnstaple's main rival, however, was Bideford, only three miles up the straighter, deeper, faster-flowing Torridge. Here, as at Plymouth, the best harbour in the county, there was no separation of ancient town and deep-water port.

16.1 Customs Chest from Bideford, probably seventeenth century, now in North Devon Maritime Museum, Appledore. The elaborate pierced and engraved plate inside the lid conceals a locking device. *(Alison Grant)*

Devon's ports were long-established communities where knowledge of commodities, markets, trade routes and shipping had been built up over many generations. In 1600, with the prospect of peace and expanding trade, confidence was high; waterside sites were being developed at Dartmouth, a new quay 'was begun to be builded' at Barnstaple, and a quay 'at John Smart's door' cost Plymouth corporation £58 1s 5d. By 1620, Exeter, having earlier repaired the 'ruinated' quay at Topsham, had become the third port of the kingdom in terms of customs revenue, and Totnes maintained a significant export of cloth to France.[2] An unstable economic climate, however, made the seventeenth century a testing time, and before 1689 Totnes, and to some extent Dartmouth, were in decline. Although Barnstaple secured the title of head port in 1671, it was saved only by its coastal trade, and 'overflow' from Bideford, which was now realising the full potential of its position. Meanwhile, Exeter overcame the decline in trade with France by opening up profitable new markets in the Netherlands, and Plymouth forged ahead in transatlantic trade.

After the peace of 1604, Devon merchants resumed and expanded traditional trades, and initiated colonial settlements and commerce. They dominated corporations and had a strong voice in parliament, as their fortunes, like those of their towns, depended on safeguarding and extending trade. Leading merchant families were already very rich. The goods of William Spicer of Exeter, for example, were valued at £3,822 14s 8d when he died in 1604. Among his possessions were imported luxuries such as a 'little Rouen chair', a Turkey carpet, and a silk Naples girdle. The 'great rebuilding' in Devon ports continued apace in the early seventeenth century, and many merchants' houses with the magnificent moulded plasterwork ceilings and carved panelling of the period are still to be seen. In Dartmouth the merchant Mark Hawkings spent nearly £2,500 on the houses of the Butterwalk (Fig. 16.2), completed in 1635. The poor were not forgotten; the Orphans' Aid and the Hospital of Poor's Portion were founded in Plymouth, and the Horwood and Penrose almshouses and school for poor maids in Barnstaple typify other charitable endowments of the time. New public buildings included the merchants' walk at Totnes, built in 1616 by Richard Lee, three times mayor there. At Dartmouth John Plumleigh built the Great Conduit to bring water to the quay, and Plymouth merchants subscribed to a new guildhall and a new church.[3]

Some leading Devon merchants, like Roger Mallock of Exeter and the Trelawnys of Plymouth, were the younger sons of landed gentry. They tended to be royalist, whereas many 'merchants born' were puritanical and parliamentary in outlook. In Exeter and Totnes, which had their own merchant companies, sons often followed fathers into the cloth trade, but there was no bar to outsiders. Trading opportunities in the ports often attracted men from inland towns, like Richard Dodderidge, originally from South Molton, who was one of Barnstaple's wealthiest merchants by 1600. A few came from farther afield. Abraham Colmer, a leading Plymouth merchant who died in 1631, was born in Birmingham. Large ports attracted merchants from smaller ones; Justinian Peard, from Goodleigh near

Barnstaple, was drawn to Plymouth, where he twice served as Mayor. There was no check on mobility, so men like William Shapleigh of Clovelly, whose father was a yeoman, could also establish themselves in trade. Shapleigh became a merchant in Barnstaple where, as in most of the older ports, substantial fortunes could still be made in the cloth trade. As the Newfoundland fishery and colonial ventures expanded, master mariners used to conducting trade in distant places often joined the ranks of merchants, and even masters of coasting vessels, and men starting with small amounts of capital, could, with good fortune and hard work, become traders, or enable their sons to do so.[4]

Some men simply became merchants; others were formally apprenticed. In 1680 Alice Brooking, widow of an Exeter merchant, left £200 for her grandson to be 'bound out an apprentice to some able merchant as soon as he is fit'. Youngsters might also be sent abroad. In 1680 John Pym, a member of Exeter's merchant élite, left £600 to settle his son, Clement, 'as a factor in Rotterdam (beside what he has cost me and I have already promised and given him)'.[5] The system was not rigid, however. Less affluent parents sent sons to grammar school, then abroad by arrangement with relations and friends. No money changed hands, when, early in the century, John Peard of Barnstaple arranged for four fellow-merchants to employ his son as a factor in La Rochelle on a commission of '£1 in the £100 on all goods there and back . . . usually . . . allowed unto such factors in that place'. The young man, 'receiving little or no maintenance from his father or anyone else for three years', got into debt on his meagre commission, and fled with money due to his employers. Although there had been no written agreement, they sued his father, saying he had undertaken 'to see them duly paid'.[6]

Although some proved unreliable, many young men sent abroad by their families were invaluable in maintaining trade. In 1668, for example, Richard Ackland of Barnstaple, a factor in Bilbao for his elder brother, shipped 'sempiternes, cloth wools, felt wools, and Segovia wool', bought fish from 'John Hellman's mariners' and others, paid a Spanish merchant for wax and sugar, and handled all kinds of currency.[7] He was among the factors who eventually returned home and became leading merchants. Some remained abroad all their lives, others travelled as 'supercargoes' on board ship, transacting their masters' business in a number of ports, and all were part of the intricate network of connections on which Devon's overseas trade was based in the seventeenth century.

Merchant dynasties rose and fell with some speed in this period, few families surviving longer than two or three generations in trade. Many bought land for their heirs if not themselves, like John Adams of Exeter, who wished to save his wife 'the trouble of looking after my estate [assets] which lyeth abroad in other men's hands and beyond the Sea, and God only knows how or when if ever it may be had'.[8] Marriage into the gentry often completed the change of status, with subsequent loss of mercantile experience and capital. The Civil War impoverished many merchants and reduced their numbers, setbacks from which Totnes, Dartmouth, and Barnstaple did not fully recover. Expanding ports, however, were able to draw in new generations of merchants to rival the old in numbers, successful trade, and munificence. Plymouth merchants repaired and extended quays and rebuilt their guildhall in 1666, and John Lanyon, naval agent as well as merchant, left the poor £2,000, some said ill-gotten, which was used to found a school. Bideford merchants refounded the grammar school, twice lengthened the quay, and built magnificent houses in the newly laid-out Bridgeland Street. Great personal fortunes continued to be made in Exeter. In 1680, having bequeathed 'manors, lands, messuages, tenements, and hereditaments' to his son, John Mayne could still leave £6,000 to his daughter. At this time, too, the City Chamber improved the canal, extended the quays, added a new warehouse alongside the rebuilt lighter dock, and built the fine Custom House which still stands (Fig. 16.3) as an appropriate reminder of the greatest days of Exeter's merchants.[9]

Trade and the Struggle with London, 1600–42

In 1600 Devon's overseas trade, like the country's in general, was depressed, although south Devon merchants had retained their markets in northern France. La Rochelle, the chief French market for north Devon goods, had not recovered from the wars of religion, while campaigns in Ireland brought trade there to a virtual standstill and affected other commerce as ships were pressed for troop transport. Trade with Spain, long dislocated by war, was now subject to a high tariff. In 1604 William Palmer, factor in St Jean de Luz, obtained official permission to send Barnstaple bayes into Spain, only to have them 'embargoed for the 30 per ciento in San Sebastian'. Like most traders he longed for the promised peace, 'until which time (when we shall have free liberty for the bringing of all sorts of English goods into Spain), myself, neither the rest of my friends will not send any more goods into Spain'.[10]

After the peace of 1604, Devon merchants' 'free liberty' was threatened by proposals to restrict Spanish and French trade to members of London-based companies, thereby virtually excluding the outports. The Lord Chief Justice, Sir John Popham, who supported western enterprise, wrote: ' . . . I fear me it will overthrow all the towns, shipping, and mariners of the West parts'. Devon MPs therefore raised a storm of protest when the new Spanish Company was set up in 1605. They claimed that prices would rise and trade fall, because 'whatsoever the Londoners conclude, all must obey, though it be to the cutting of their own throats'. Condemning the system which gave

16.2 The Butterwalk at Dartmouth, 1628–40. T Allom 1830, engraved by FJ Havill. *(Devon and Exeter Institution)*

16.3 Custom House, the Quay, Exeter, 1680–81, architect Richard Allen. The ground-floor arches were originally open. The upstairs rooms contain magnificent contemporary plaster ceilings by John Abbot of Frithelstock. *(Royal Albert Memorial Museum, Archaeological Field Unit)*

London six times as much trade as the rest of the kingdom, Sir Edwin Sandys, leader of the free trade lobby, put the case for giving all merchants the right to trade wherever they could find markets. The campaign succeeded, and in 1606 parliament established this right, thereby putting an end to the Spanish Company.[11]

These moves ensured the rapid expansion of Devon's Iberian trade, and in 1615 25 outward voyages were made from Dartmouth, for example, compared with seven in the twelve months ending at Michaelmas 1600. Although some were by 'passing' vessels from other ports, most carried Totnes cloth to southern Spain and the Atlantic islands, returning with such things as raisins, wine, dyewoods, and goods from the 'Indies'. Exeter also sent cloth; in 1617 two vessels left for Portugal, three for nothern Spain, one for Cadiz, and seven for St Lucar, the port for Seville. Plymouth merchants likewise favoured southern Spain; in 1620 Abraham Jennings traded with Cadiz, Lisbon, Alicante, and Barcelona, but he also sent four cargoes to Bilbao. This was the most popular market for north Devon merchants, who, with 12 vessels out to Spain and Portugal in 1615, had resumed the trade in Barnstaple bayes, with return cargoes of iron and wool. Spanish wool was at first used mainly for felt, but after about 1620 was mixed with other wools to make medley, also known in Devon as Spanish cloth.[12]

Although Iberian trade expanded, Devon's chief markets were still in France. Older types of woollen cloth, Devonshire dozens, for example, and narrow pinwhites, made in or around Totnes, were the main export in 1600, but cheaper cloths such as Barnstaple bayes and colourful lightweight serges became more important as demand changed abroad. Most of south Devon's export went to the great cloth mart at Rouen and the Breton ports of St Malo and Morlaix, which all sent back canvas and coarse linen. La Rochelle took the greater part of north Devon's cloth exports, and substantial quantities from Plymouth and Totnes, supplying in exchange salt, and goods collected through its entrepôt trade. When London interests set up a French Company in 1611, Devon merchants, fearing interference in these valuable markets, reacted strongly.

16.4 Plaster ceiling, dated 1620, formerly on the first floor of 62 Boutport Street, Barnstaple. The inclusion of the arms of the Spanish Company of London suggests that this was a house of one of the many Barnstaple merchants engaged in the Spanish trade at this time. *(Devon County Council, courtesy the Woolwich Building Society)*

The new French Company sought to lessen opposition by enrolling outport merchants, publishing their names with its charter. Exeter, with its own French company, was not involved, but Totnes, with 57 of the 126 Devon merchants named, claimed that this had been done without their knowledge. They broke away and joined Plymouth, Dartmouth, and Barnstaple in a protest against a monopoly that would, they said, 'utterly overthrow their whole trade, to the undoing of themselves and many thousand handicraftsmen and others that depend on the same'. In 1613 the Privy Council, after hearing both sides, agreed to 'liberty of free trade without restriction or limitation' for western merchants, exempting them from control by the French Company. This 'temporary' compromise, which was never revoked, suited all but Exeter. Although the city had supported free trade with Spain in its own interests, it did not accept the principle, and later sought to control the French trade of the other Devon ports through its own French Company. When this produced the usual outcry, Exeter even sought an alliance with the London French Company against the rest. Although this failed, lack of unity weakened outport interests, and added to the difficulties of trade with France. A ban on English imports imposed in 1627, after the outbreak of war, was not officially removed until 1639, and at Rouen there was frequent hostility to English traders. La Rochelle suffered in the renewed religious wars, and took many years to recover from the terrible siege of 1627–8. These problems forced many merchants to turn to other markets.[13]

Newfoundland fish enabled Devon ports to extend their trading interests, for the salt cod, like the pilchards caught off south Devon, was sold in Mediterranean ports. In 1617 a decree that only members of the London-based Levant Company could ship certain goods home through the Straits of Gibraltar brought a strong protest from Dartmouth, which then refused to contribute to a London-led expedition against pirates. Plymouth, also smarting from the restrictions, grumbled that Londoners were worse for trade than pirates. This was not far wrong, for during these years the Cockayne project, by which a group of London merchants attempted to supplant the old-established Merchant Adventurers' Company, seriously affected the cloth trade. Depression spread westward, Devon's worst year being 1621. Plymouth blamed the 'restraint of trade to certain companies of merchants of London', and Exeter, after the failure of the Cockayne project, complained at the renewal of the Merchant Adventurers' monopoly of markets in Germany and the Netherlands. Dartmouth's doughty merchant MP, William Neale, agreed, proclaiming that engrossing the cloth trade into a few hands was 'very prejudicious' and 'the principal cause of the decay of trade'. In 1624 the free traders in parliament carried the day, forcing the Merchant Adventurers to admit all who wished to join their company, and to allow outport merchants to deal in almost all types of cloth.[14]

By 1624 Devon ports were recovering from the depression, but war with Spain and France soon dealt them an even harder blow. All ports suffered, with Plymouth almost ruined by badly-organised expeditions and plague brought back by survivors. The 1630s saw only a slow recovery, with some trades failing to regain prewar levels. Trade with northern Europe was an exception, Norwegian ships regularly bringing cargoes of deals (soft wood planks). Some Dutch ships brought Baltic timber, some was shipped coastwise from Southampton and Portsmouth, and Devon vessels also went to Rotterdam and Amsterdam to collect it, along with Swedish iron and all kinds of manufactured goods. Although cargoes of slates were sent from Plymouth and Dartmouth, trade with the Netherlands was import-led until three Exeter merchants successfully tested the market for cloth. In 1634 the Merchant Adventurers' Company of London had regained their monopoly, but Thomas Ford, Thomas Knott, and Richard Ford found that outport merchants could become members for £25. They joined, and were thus entitled to export all kinds of cloth to the Netherlands. London members tried to restrict the trade of these 'young and inexperienced' merchants, but the Privy Council ruled that any Devon-made cloth could be exported from Devon ports to Germany and the Netherlands.[15] Adapting to the demands of this new market, Exeter, with its wealthy hinterland and broad commercial base, increasingly manufactured and exported serges, but Totnes, unable to adapt to new demands, and in competition with Dartmouth for the trade of a limited hinterland, began to decline. The cloth trade of Plymouth and Barnstaple also gradually fell away, but these ports, like Dartmouth, increasingly looked westward.

Devon gentry, merchants, and mariners were among the pioneers in colonial exploration and trade. The Council for New England grew out of the Plymouth Company of 1606, and Plymouth merchants were soon involved in fishing and trade on the coast of Maine. Good returns were to be expected. In 1624 John Fownes made bequests totalling £400 out of his 'five-eighth parts of a ship called the *Eagle* of Plymouth and her voyage for Virginia or New England if please God to send her and her proceeds safely to return'. Dartmouth and Topsham vessels also traded to New England, but north Devon ships were the most numerous – nine out to New England and Virginia in 1631, for instance, with livestock and goods for settlers and fishermen. Return cargoes included furs; in 1636 the *Golden Lion* of Barnstaple brought home 1,219 beaver and 26 otter skins, valued by customs at 5s and 2s each, but probably worth more. Tobacco, another valuable commodity, was now grown in Virginia, Bermuda, and the West Indies. John Delbridge, a leading Barnstaple merchant, pioneered its import into Devon, taking out shares in the London Virginia Company and the associated Somers Islands (Bermuda) Company, and shipping cargoes to Barnstaple. His success prompted London merchants to get the import of tobacco restricted to London, but Devon traders were not easily deterred, and in the 1630s West Indian tobacco, mainly from St Christopher, was shipped into Dartmouth, Plymouth and Barnstaple. Some tobacco, with other colonial goods such as cotton and dyewoods from Barbados, was absorbed locally, some was sent inland, from Barnstaple to Exeter and Taunton, for example, and the rest was re-exported, sometimes to Europe but more frequently in this period to Ireland, or coastwise to other English ports.[16]

After the end of Tyrone's rebellion, Devon merchants re-established trade with Ireland, re-exporting tobacco and other colonial goods and opening up trade with the new plantations in Ulster. Irish farm produce, wool, hides, and barrel staves were in demand at home, but merchants of Dartmouth and Exeter, concerned with more profitable trades, generally left the masters of a few small Irish vessels to bring in and sell their own goods. Plymouth, in constant need of meat, butter, and other ships' provisions, also employed a number of its own ships, while the Irish trade was the mainstay of many small ships of Bideford and Northam. In 1618 60 brought Irish goods in, and although only 26 took cargo out direct, many of the rest probably went via south Wales to load coal.[17]

Small Devon vessels not only carried Welsh coal elsewhere, but brought it home: in 1605, about 250 tons came in to Dartmouth, 280 to north Devon, and 300 to Exeter. Dartmouth, however, with another 100 tons from Newcastle via London, imported the greatest quantity overall. In 1611 Plymouth received five or six cargoes from Newcastle direct, one or two others by way of other ports, and about 20 from south Wales. As coal increasingly replaced wood for fuel, and industrial and domestic demand grew, the coal trade expanded dramatically, with a consequent increase in the number of ships and mariners in the coastal trade. North Devon, through its position, benefited most, and in 1651 imported over 5,000 tons in only six months, compared with less than 1,000 tons for Plymouth at that time. North Devon was also in a good position to open up other rewarding trades, particularly with Bristol, 'the metropolis of the west', which absorbed local and Irish produce, Newfoundland train oil, and other imports, and provided metals, glassware, groceries, haberdashery, and household wares. South Devon, almost cut off from this honeypot by the length and potential dangers of the voyage around Lands End, conducted the same kind of trade with London, in spite of distance, contrary winds, and pirates in the Channel. The south coast was also able to supply good cargoes; grain, hops, and malt from Kent, Sussex iron, and ships' supplies from Portsmouth and Southampton.[18]

The coastal trade in this period was import-led. In 1605 76 vessels brought cargo into Dartmouth and 49 took goods out. Their average tonnage was 22, and 52 per cent were owned outside the port, for Dartmouth was well-placed for passing trade. In the same year the port of Barnstaple had 90 coastal ships in and 44 out, but average tonnage was only 13, as the majority did not venture outside the Bristol Channel. Small ships of Northam (including Appledore) predominated, a few larger vessels were of Barnstaple, and only 11 per cent were owned outside the port. Plymouth's coastal trade cannot be directly compared, for no record survives for 1605. In 1611, a much better year, something like 112 vessels brought in, and 45 took out cargo, but about 80 per cent were owned outside the port. Abraham Jennings had a large interest in the London trade, but most Plymouth merchants, like those of Exeter, were more concerned with overseas trade. In 1605 61 vessels brought cargo coastwise to Exeter and ten took it out; they averaged 22 tons, and 77 per cent were owned outside the port. The city's expansion brought increased consumption and in 1637, although only 13 cargoes were sent out, 139 came in.[19] Although all ports suffered from the wars of the late 1620s, Devon's trade, both coastal and overseas, expanded overall in the period before the Civil War.

Ships and Seamen

Shipbuilding

Shipbuilding in Devon in the seventeenth century remained, in all but the largest ports, a simply organised craft, requiring little more than a waterside site, family labour, and tools made by a local smith. Timber, which had to be seasoned, tied up a certain amount of capital, but for building and repairing small vessels this was not excessive, and even coastal villages had shipwrights to serve local needs.

As was common practice among seventeenth-century artisans, a smallholding formed part of the family economy of William Smyth *alias* Bayley of East Budleigh, a shipwright who died in 1623. To his son, John, he bequeathed 'a hook and a hatchet, a mattock and a shovel', and four sheep, together with two saws and his working tools, while a daughter received 'the herbgarden before the foredoor' and the part of the house she occupied with her husband, another shipwright. William Smyth's estate was appraised at £22 0s 3d; his lifestyle is likely to have been frugal, and the vessels he built small. He may have been related to William Bayley, a more prosperous shipwright of nearby Otterton, whose assets, including farm stock and land, were valued at £107 14s 8d when he died in 1613. Three of his sons were shipwrights, and at least one man worked for him for wages. He left most of his estate in trust for his youngest son, 'my Babe, William Bayley . . . for the godly education and bringing up of the said William in learning and fear of God at school . . .'. Surviving documents show that some shipwrights could not write their names, but at this time an increasing number of artisans like William Bayley were seeking education for their sons.[20]

John Bayley of Otterton, one of Devon's leading shipbuilders in the early seventeenth century, was probably William Bayley's brother. In 1626 he was named as builder of the 140-ton *Resolution* of Exeter, and the *Merchant Royal* of Dartmouth, 120 tons. He died in 1638, but Bayleys of Otterton continued to build ships until the 1650s. Farther west, at Teignmouth, Peter Martyn and Vincent Hillman were building ships in the 1630s. There were also shipwrights at places like Lympstone, but the busiest shipyards in the port of Exeter in the seventeenth century were those along Topsham Strand. One shipwright there was John Hillman, whose assets at his death in 1674 were valued at £99 0s 2½d. Repair and maintenance provided plenty of work as numbers of ships increased, and much new construction also went on, William Green, for example, building 'near 100 ships and 400 boats' at Topsham between 1666 and 1711.[21]

In north Devon the main shipbuilding centres lay within the Taw-Torridge estuary. John Curtis, shipwright, was recorded in Barnstaple in 1617, and 'a garden sometime Curtises' mentioned in later corporation records had a slip down to the river Yeo. After the Restoration John Prideaux, a shipwright who leased similar property beside the Taw, flourished, eventually becoming a member of the corporation. Good sites by deep water were not cheap. In 1652 a Bideford shipwright, John Symons, paid £32 for the lease of 'houses and rooms' a herbgarden and an orchard, 'on the East side of the River of Torridge', where shipbuilding had probably been continuous since John Leland had described East the Water as a lively street for 'ship craft' over 100 years before. Another north Devon shipwright, Philip Cocke of Northam, left assets valued at £335 11s 8d in 1633, but he may also have invested in ships and voyages, as he had two sons who were master mariners. Cocke and his other son, Abraham, a shipwright, probably built at Appledore, then part of Northam, and a James Cocke worked there in 1651.[22] They were probably not the first, and certainly not the last of that name to build and own ships there, and sail them out over the Bar.

Devon's maritime community included anchorsmiths, coopers, and block-, rope-, and sailmakers, working in conjunction with shipwrights like Roger Spark of Dartmouth, who leased property 'next the river' at Hardness for a total of £32 in the 1650s. Some became prosperous, like Emmanuel Woolley, a ropemaker who supplied cordage for the navy in the Second Dutch War, then became a shipowner, and was twice mayor of Dartmouth. Edward Wren, another prosperous roper, became mayor of Bideford, where, by 1691, he had built a fine new house and expanded his premises to include storehouses, a large garden, and a rope path, with a yarnhouse, a tarhouse, a 'hatchell' house where fibres were teased out, and a number of lofts, workshops, and chambers. Hemp was grown at Combe Martin, but there is no evidence that at this time it was used for anything other than twine. Ropers got most of their raw materials abroad. In 1647, for example, one of Edward Wren's predecessors, Thomas Wren, imported 40 rolls of cable yarn, 13 bundles of hemp, and 4½ lasts of tar from Rotterdam.[23]

Men like Edward Wren, who inherited a business, often had the advantages of education and family connections, but it was hard for poor artisans to get to the top. In Plymouth, such was the pressure on suitable shipbuilding sites that it cost Ambrose Collins £140 to lease one by Sutton Pool in 1657. He was a shipwright with capital and connections, but many who had neither remained wage-earners, like the 14 pressed for government service in 1666 and sent to Portsmouth with 13s 6d each for press and conduct money. Only nine arrived! In peacetime men could work where they chose if they owned their own tools. In December 1635 some Plymouth shipwrights returning home from Catte Down wielded a three-foot rule, axes, adzes, and a sledgehammer in a brawl with Dutch seamen. The incident occurred between six and seven in the evening; workers' hours were much longer in summer. In 1630 shipwrights could earn 20d a day or 12d with meat and drink, twice as much as agricultural labourers, but not enough to set up on their own in Plymouth. Hercules Hunking, one of the shipwrights mixed up in the brawl, went to sea for a time and became a master mariner, but later, like Arthur Gill, another of them, he went to Richmond Island in New England and became an independent shipbuilder.[24]

Surviving correspondence between Gill and Robert Trelawny, the Plymouth merchant for whom he built a 100-ton vessel in New England, gives a rare insight into methods used by Devon shipwrights at this time. A letter of 1638 shows that Gill was used to working from plans, but did not think much of the one Trelawny had sent him:

> . . . there is no scale upon it whereby to have the proportions of anything, nor no shape of the mould, which is the greatest point of all; and for the upper work it is not proportionable nor ship shapen . . . if you will trust me with building of her, you may far better trust me with drawing of the draft.

A year later the shipwright reported the frame almost complete, 'the outside of as good a oak in my judgment as any you can have in England.' Trelawny's agent wrote independently with details:

> The ship is framed up to the top timbers, 10 or 12 a side; all the growed timbers [knees], stiddell timbers [ribs] and naval timbers are in her, and her two bends. Plank I want, but sawing still . . . Our plank must have most of the next summer's dryeth to season it . . . She is very well timbered for a ship of her burden.

At last, in 1641:

> . . . our new ship was launched . . . She swimmed as upright as might be . . . and very stiff of her side . . . much work to do on her; both decks to caulk, the hatches to make, her head to set up, and our masts to make, and her boat to build.[25]

Colonially-built ships made use of plentiful supplies of cheap timber, but at home scarcity drove up prices, and estate owners opposed anyone who threatened their virtual monopoly. The Earl of Bath wrote to the King in 1604 to complain of a 'woodmonger', Philip Bushen of Tiverton, who had obtained a licence to float timber from High Bickington ten miles down the River Taw to 'Barnstaple and the ports near unto the same, where there is great want thereof for the uses of shipping and building'. The Earl claimed that his weirs and banks at Tawstock were being damaged, as no doubt they were, with strong tides swirling the rafts of timber. Bushen, however, leased a yard at Barnstaple Quay, and 'ceased not to put his wood in the water'. No doubt he got a good price for it. In south Devon, with competition from the navy, timber shortage was critical, particularly in wartime, when imports of Baltic plank and masts were also vulnerable. Other ships' supplies, like French sailcloth, also became scarce at times of crisis or embargo. Some sailmakers turned to Dorset linen, which, in Barnstaple at least, came to be 'esteemed . . . far before the French'.[26]

Ship Owning

In 1626 returns of ships and mariners were made to the vice-admiral of Devon. Although incomplete, they provide useful information. The list of ships for Braunton Hundred, which included Barnstaple, shows most of the smaller craft owned outside the main port by men who worked them with their families. George Somer, for example, the owner of the *Elizabeth* of Watermouth, 20 tons, was a seaman of 46 from Berrynarbor, and Nicholas and Humphrey Somer, in their 20s and another Nicholas Somer, aged 30, were fishermen; Philip and John Bustinge of Braunton, both seamen in their 20s, presumably manned the 15-ton *Mary*, owned by Walter Bustinge. They were typical of many Devon families who ran a small vessel to make or augment a living by fishing or short-haul trading, and some who did well moved to the main port and up the social scale.[27]

Small craft needing relatively little capital often had only one owner, and at the opposite end of the scale some rich men ventured large sums in sole ownership. Their investment paid off if the ship made a successful trading voyage, or, like the *Delight* of Barnstaple, the merchant Edward Eastman's sole property, brought back a prize in war. Thomas Newman of Dartmouth, on the other hand, suffered heavy losses in 1615 when his new 120-ton ship was taken, as so many were, by pirates. In spite of the risks, the 1626 list for Plymouth and Stonehouse shows 53 per cent of the total tonnage of 3,500 in sole ownership. Such lists are not completely reliable, for names of partners may have been omitted, but other sources show that sole ownership was not rare. Wills of Plymouth merchants, for example, show that in 1628 Leonard Pomeroy owned the *Providence*, 80 tons, and twenty years later Abraham Jennings had the *Jacob*, 35 tons, and the *Grace*, 80 tons. In 1626 he had been listed as sole owner of five vessels of 35, 50, 80, 100, and 160 tons. The Civil War caused losses for such owners. Roger Mallock of Exeter was among merchants who lost ships they owned. After the Civil War sole ownership was less common, but in periods of heady expansion men were still prepared to ignore the risks involved. In Bideford, for example, a number of merchants became sole owners of tobacco ships.[28]

Ships were a popular form of investment in the seventeenth century, for risks could be spread by shareholding. Some of the gentry, Sir Arthur Champernowne for instance, set out privateers and expeditions to the colonies in the Elizabethan tradition, but most had little interest in trade. The lists of 1626 show that most shareholders were merchants, but there were a few professional men, like Francis Facey, a lawyer, who was part-owner of the *Phoenix* of Barnstaple, with Nicholas Delbridge, a merchant, and Mary Jenning. It was not unusual for women of means, particularly merchants' widows, to invest in ships and voyages. Small partnerships of relatively well-to-do people were common in the South West at this time, but the upheavals of the 1640s and 1650s helped cause a gradual change to larger groups of shareholders. With an increase in the number and size of ships, and therefore in the amount of capital required, eighths and sixteenths became commoner, and some 'shopkeepers and inland traders' were drawn in.[29] Many of these, however, were men of substance, and, like merchants, often owned multiple shares. In Devon, the day of the really small investor was yet to come.

Devon ship owners with large sums at stake, or at times of unusual risk, occasionally took out insurance. Andrew Voysey of Dartmouth insured £1,000 of his £1,800 interest in the *Charles* of Dartmouth, 300 tons, and her voyage to New England in 1641 through the Royal Exchange, London. The growth of shipping also stimulated local financial services. In 1656 Malachy Pyne and Nicholas Isaac of Exeter insured the *White Angel* of Dartmouth, 180 tons, at the high wartime premium of 14 per cent for a voyage to Virginia. Where more ships were employed it was commoner for merchants to spread their risks by shipping cloth and other valuable cargo in small amounts on a number of vessels. Some owners may also have deliberately avoided using their own ships, but some preferred them. In 1624 Lewis Downe, owner of the *George* of Barnstaple, used her to ship his cargoes to and from Ireland, and Edward Eastman brought Newfoundland train oil home in his own ship, *Delight*.[30] Although they risked both vessel and cargo, these owners were able to take all profits and save freight costs.

Freight charges were not usually high, for owners did not wish to discourage trade. Outward goods were often taken freight-free, to gain more profitable inward cargo. Charges depended on the amount of cargo, taking value, volume, and distance into account; 1d on a pound of Bermuda tobacco in the 1620s, for example, and 3d or 4d on an 18-pound 'great stone' of wool from Dublin to north Devon 50 years later. Vessels, or space in them could also be hired by the voyage. In 1641 Barnstaple owners hired out the *Speedwell* 'for the Newfoundland, Bilboa, Rochelle and from thence home . . . at £16 15s per month for the bare ship, and [the hirer] obliged to keep her six months'. No tonnage was recorded in the account, but if she was the 50-ton Barnstaple vessel of the same name trading in 1636, the owners would have received about £2 per ton, with no expenses apart from fitting out, the cost of which would depend on the age and condition of the ship. The *Speedwell*'s owners probably hoped for a profit of at least £1 10s a ton.[31]

Unless the vessel was hired out as above, ship owners were responsible for provisions and wages. For men shipped from Barnstaple to Ireland in 1601, victuallers charged 7d–8d per man per day, the equivalent of 17s 6d or £1 per month, but these 'government' prices are unlikely to have been paid in normal times. Food and labour were both cheap in Devon, and provisions cost even less in Irish ports where many ships victualled for transatlantic voyages. Crew numbers and wages were kept as low as possible. On a crew list for the *Abraham* from Barnstaple to La Rochelle in 1656 the lowest monthly rate was 15s, probably for a boy; the rest varied from £1 to £1 11s for seamen, £2 for the carpenter, £2 3s for the bo's'n and £2 15s for the mate. This was wartime, and as the vessel carried an unusually large company of master and 21 men, including a gunner at £1 17s a month, she was probably on a privateering voyage. Peacetime wages were lower. Foremastmen were paid 24 or 25 shillings a month in the 1680s, and bo's'ns 3 or 4 shillings more.[32]

At the highest rates exemplified or estimated above, including fitting out at £1 per ton, provisions, wages, and 5 or 10 per cent added for miscellaneous items, total costs for a seven-month voyage to Newfoundland and Bilbao in 1664 by a vessel like the 60-ton *True Dealing* of Topsham, with master and seven men, would have amounted to just over £200. If victuals and repairs cost 25 per cent less, the total would have been reduced by about £30. The owners of this vessel let 30 tons of freight at £4 10s a ton; provided they let the rest, they would have cleared between £70 and £100 in profit, about the same as the *Speedwell*'s owners got for hiring out the whole vessel. However, delays, default on payments, legal costs, or lack of cargo or customers could turn modest profit to loss, to say nothing of storm damage or the complete loss of a vessel. Ship owning, therefore, was seen by some not as an end in itself, but as a means to trade, which was usually more profitable. A gentleman who paid £37 in all for one sixteenth of a new ship of 70 tons, the *Margaret* of Topsham, launched in 1674, sold it for £18 to be 'put out onto an Adventure of the said ship in a voyage'. The purchaser and agent was the ship's master.[33]

Master Mariners

A good master could be worth his weight in gold to the ship's owners, and to himself, for opportunities usually matched responsibilities. John Roope, master of the *True Dealing* of Topsham on the voyage mentioned above, had an interest in the vessel, for owners 'seldom suffer any to go Skipper or Master, but he that hath a share or part in her'. The master's salary of something like £4 a month represented only a small proportion of his potential gain. He would expect to trade on his own account, it being:

> usual for Owners of Ships to allow their Masters and Mariners the Storage of a small quantity of goods of their own freight-free if the merchants or owners . . . find [them] careful and honest . . .[34]

Masters could claim expenses and certain exemptions from duties, and earn commission and 'presents' when negotiating for fitting out, freight, and insurance, and acting as middlemen in buying and selling cargoes. Established masters might also gain from training future ones, for prosperous fathers were willing to pay for their sons to learn a good trade, and it was no shame for merchants' sons to serve family interests in this way.

In the coastal, Irish, and Channel trades a master needed enough skill to recognize the coast and get in to port, but the wide wastes of the Atlantic presented different problems. A vessel sailing from Barnstaple to Bermuda in 1626, 'after seven months and 20 days at sea returned in great misery, not finding the Island, and never saw land before their return'. Training in navigation became more usual as the century progressed. In Bideford in 1625 a teacher was appointed 'for the instructing and teaching the children and 'prentices of the inhabitants' especially in 'the Art of Arithmetic, very fit and necessary to teach in this our town . . . being a town of navigation'. In a crisis a great deal depended on the master's judgment; if the sky was obscured his 'asterlaby instrument' and other aids to navigation were of little use. If a storm forced the vessel on to her beam ends he might have to 'stave several vessels of water to ease her', or 'throw the windlass and several other things overboard', or 'wear the ship' and alter course. These were the measures taken by a Bideford master returning from Newfoundland in a severe storm that prevented him reaching his home port. He eventually brought his ship safely to Topsham.[35]

Masters of ocean-going vessels enjoyed high status, and many became merchants. Steady work in humbler vessels could also bring rewards. Joseph Comer of Appledore, master of ships in the Irish trade for about 40 years after 1660, left 'a shop of goods' worth at least £300, two houses, a quarter share in a vessel, the *Swan Pink*, and a considerable sum of money. For those with no reserves to combat losses the story was different. Huguenots who settled at Stonehouse after 1685, with no assets but their own small vessels, were forced out of foreign trade by heavy duties and other problems. Some joined the fleet of colliers plying to South Wales, but many, described as '*dans la dernière nécessité*', had to depend on charity.[36]

Seamen

On small vessels where a couple of seamen or a man and boy served under a father, uncle, or friend of the family, there was reasonable hope of eventual command, and no great gulf between master and crew. On larger ocean-going vessels an able man might become a bo's'n or mate, and even save enough to buy a share in a vessel, but would find it hard to obtain command without connections. Most foremast hands remained seamen, on wages which, although higher than labourers', scarcely allowed for risks and discomfort. Their duties, which included cargo-handling, were often arduous, dangerous and unpleasant, and their quarters cramped and wet. Their diet, in spite of quantities of fish, was often 'insufficient for the good health of the human body'. Lacking anti-scorbutics, the mariners returned 'all sick and weak' from the abortive seven-month voyage to Bermuda already mentioned, although they still had 'victuals enough, for they brought home 11 hogshead of beer; store of bread, beef, butter, cheese . . .'. Dried and heavily salted provisions were hardly appetising when fresh, and before the end of the voyage, as a Plymouth merchant claimed in a court case against a victualler, even hard 'ship's bread' could become 'mouldy and putrid'.[37]

Many seamen were from the poorest levels of society; labourers seeking work, or, occasionally, boys apprenticed by the parish. An indenture of 1637 for Richard Verchill, son of a Barnstaple mason, shows, in the usual form, that the master, Simon Amery, a merchant, undertook, in return for the apprentice's good service until the age of 24, to provide:

> meat, drink, lodging, apparel, linen-woollen hose, shoes . . . and bring up and teach . . . his said apprentice to be a sailor or seafaring man, and also in the art, mystery, or science of Navigation as much as he . . . shall be capable of . . .

Not all seamen received such training, and a number were illiterate: Thomas Heyward of Northam could only make his mark at the end of his will in 1633. He left the residue of his estate to his wife, Suzan, after bequests of 5s to the poor of Northam, and 3s 6d to the parish church. He also left a bed 'performed' (with bedding) to his elder son Thomas, and his wearing apparel equally between his two sons. His daughter Anne and younger son Emmanuel received the 'quarter part of the good bark or vessel called the *William* of Northam of the burthen of 18 tons or thereabouts'. Their father had perhaps also been her master.[38]

The Civil War and its Effects

To Devon merchants who agreed with John Delbridge, when he declared in the parliament of 1628 that Devon's trade had been killed by government exactions, ship money in the 1630s was the last straw. Exeter was assessed at £350, Plymouth at £190, Barnstaple, bitterly complaining, at £150, Totnes at £120, Dartmouth £80, and Bideford £40. Although the ports wanted piracy suppressed, they were unwilling to pay this unparliamentary tax regularly. In 1637 Delbridge, now over 70, was among those who refused to pay. In the Short Parliament, George Peard, another outspoken Barnstaple MP, attacked ship money as 'an abomination', and in 1642 Devon ports declared against the king. Exeter spent £4,374, and Barnstaple £2,230 on fortifications, only to see them dismantled when, like the other ports apart from Plymouth, they were captured by the royalists.[39] The parliamentary blockade now stifled trade, and many ships were commandeered or lost. John Budley of Dartmouth declared that he had lost:

> a ship called the *Vineyard*, burthen 80 tons, laden with fish and train, being within the port of Dartmouth at the time of surrendering the Town, much of the goods taken away by the enemy, and the Ship utterly spoiled, with other losses in my personal estate. The said Budley being at that time the unhappy mayor of the town, and known constant well-wisher to Parliament, was imprisoned thirteen weeks at Exon gaol and other places.

The clerk added a marginal note: 'beside the loss of his eldest son in the Parliamentary Service'. Budley was one of many merchants who suffered as each side called for financial sacrifice from supporters, while imprisoning and fining opponents.[40]

In 1646, with Exeter in debt to the tune of £14,000 and Plymouth even more, impoverished ports and merchants needed to return to trade, in spite of a shortage of ships. Dartmouth's recovery in 1647 was helped by ships of the Netherlands and north Europe, which brought in goods and took back large cargoes of slates. Vessels from London and the south-east acted as carriers for the major part of the 1,720 hogsheads and 16 tons of pilchards exported, for in troubled times bigger ships armed against pirates were needed for Spanish and Mediterranean voyages. Smaller local ships resumed cloth export to France for Totnes merchants. Into Dartmouth that year came the usual cargoes of French canvas and salt, deals from Norway, 144 hogsheads and 45 tons of Newfoundland train oil, and tobacco from Barbados and North America. Dutch vessels brought Baltic supplies both to Dartmouth and Exeter, but Devon vessels carried most of the city's large export of serges and perpetuanas (a hard-wearing type of serge) to Rotterdam. Quarrels and confiscations still disrupted the export of English cloth to Rouen, but fortunately St Malo and Morlaix took a great deal. Exeter's cloth industry, having survived Civil War, depression and plague, still had enormous potential to expand.[41]

Plymouth had suffered badly from siege and epidemics, and a partial record of 1644 shows a mere trickle of overseas trade. Even so, goods arrived from Spain, the Netherlands, and France, and one Plymouth vessel came in from St Christopher, no doubt with tobacco. There is no Plymouth record for 1647, but it was a good pilchard year, and the port probably shared in the local and national revival. Barnstaple and Bideford, recently devastated by plague, were slower to recover. Trade with Spain was at a low ebb, perhaps because few large armed vessels were owned in the port. Thomas Horwood, who exported Barnstaple bayes to Spain through Exeter, and William Palmer, who used Dartmouth, were among merchants who overcame this problem. Others sent bayes to La Rochelle, which, now re-established as an entrepôt, was able to provide return cargoes of Spanish iron and wool, and St Christopher tobacco as well as French wines and salt. Twenty-five north Devon ships traded there in 1647, some taking out coal, which indicates that the coastal trade was alive again. Without this lifeline north Devon's trade would have been more depressed than it was, for Ireland had not recovered since the rebellion of 1641, and although 15 outward cargoes were sent there in 1647, only four came in.[42]

The revival was short-lived. The king's execution set off a spate of anti-English privateering, and shook European markets, France taking the opportunity to exclude English cloth for a time, then readmitting it with greatly increased duties. Retaliatory embargoes on French wine and other goods further depressed trade. Devon ships suffered as Rupert's fleet harassed merchant vessels on both sides of the Atlantic, and ships and seamen were pressed into parliament's service for renewed campaigning in Ireland, which again shattered trade. During the Dutch War of 1652–4 Exeter and Topsham apparently lost the important Dutch market, but much of the increased export of cloth to the Spanish Netherlands and Dieppe was probably for Holland. Blake's expedition to Tunis in 1655 brought welcome relief from pirates, but war with Spain then put a 'great stop' to trade. Barnstaple mariners and merchants were soon complaining of 'losses by seizure and imprisonment at Lisbon', and, in one action off Portugal in 1657, four Dartmouth and two Plymouth vessels were taken, which 'made many of sad heart in those parts'.[43] In spite of intervals of partial recovery, Devon traders, suffering from wars, taxation, and uncertain trade, if not 'utter ruin', could only hope that the change of government in 1660 would bring about the restoration of prosperity as well as the king.

Trade 1660–89

After a slow start and, in spite of periods of war and depression, the years 1660 to 1689 saw considerable commercial expansion. Outport merchants benefited from the Navigation Acts, which protected not just London traders but the shipping and commerce of the whole nation. As the Merchant Adventurers lost the monopoly of markets in the Netherlands, Exeter, despite dislocation of trade during the Dutch Wars, built up the export of perpetuanas there to 67,000 pieces in 1676, and over 100,000 in 1680, stimulating useful return cargoes of goods garnered by the Dutch. This was a fortunate change in the direction of trade, as prohibitive French duties on English cloth, and retaliatory English tariffs, diminished trade with France in this period and a total embargo was placed on French imports between 1678 and 1685. Wine, salt, canvas, and linen were now obtained from Spain and Portugal, which increased sales of Exeter cloth in those markets. The end of the embargo stimulated trade as French goods again poured in, but the events of 1688–9, culminating in war with France, pricked the bubble, bringing a sharp decline at the end of the period.[44]

At Dartmouth, customs duties, payable on exports as well as imports, fell sharply from £2,217 in 1672, to £837 in 1679, recovering only slightly before falling again towards the end of the period. This decline was mainly due to the prolonged tariff war with France, which closed Morlaix to English ships on occasion. This killed Totnes's cloth trade, which, unlike Exeter's, had no alternative markets. Plymouth, where customs receipts also fell, had similar problems marketing older-style cloth; in 1683, 'Tavistocks' exported to Barbados had to be brought home 'for want of sale'. In both ports, however, much of the fall in customs duties must have been due to the embargo on imports from France, for French canvas and linens had previously paid 45 per cent. Plymouth made a good recovery, and in 1683 almost 60 vessels, presumably including returning Newfoundland ships, brought in goods from the Mediterranean, Spain, Portugal, and the Atlantic Islands, over 30 entered from northern Europe and the Netherlands, and 24 from Virginia and the Caribbean. In the same year about 100 ships took cargo overseas, and many others must have victualled in Plymouth. As at Dartmouth, the decline in actual trade was not as great as falling customs duties indicate, for fish 'English taken' was duty free for Englishmen, and both ports continued to send many vessels to Newfoundland, and quantities of pilchards and other fish to southern Europe.[45]

In this period the export of Barnstaple bayes declined until, in 1683, Bilbao took only 237 pieces, and La Rochelle, owing to the tariff war, none. Barnstaple now had fewer merchants, but their other trade was buoyant that year, with six vessels out to Maryland and Virginia, and one to Barbados. Large vessels re-exported colonial goods to northern Europe and the Netherlands, and small ones had resumed trade with Ireland. After the Restoration all north Devon ports began to import Irish livestock, a trade which briefly transformed Ilfracombe, which in 1637 had had only £16 in customs revenue. In 1666 126 pigs, 3,815 cattle, and 17,957 sheep were brought in, generating over £800 in customs dues. Of the vessels engaged in this trade, 17, averaging 27 tons, were owned in Ilfracombe itself. Cattle Acts, to protect the interests of English farmers, banned the trade from 1667–79, and again after 1681. Ilfracombe ships continued to trade where they could, but a drop in customs duties to £118 in 1683 shows the adverse effect of government policy. The trade in animal products which replaced the livestock trade was largely captured by Bideford.[46]

The import of Irish long-staple wool, which was used for a proportion of the yarn in bayes and serges, was well-established before the Civil War, and increased after the Restoration as serge manufacture in and around Exeter grew. Exeter imported increasing amounts direct, but many Irish merchants, like one who wrote to a ship's master in 1673, were against 'venturing to Exeter or any place beyond the Land's End while war and winter lasts. The venture is too great upon both accounts for the small matter gotten by wool to run the hazard of'. Greater quantities were therefore sent via north Devon – 15,000 stone in 1665. In 1683 Barnstaple imported 19,124 stone, and Bideford 41,501. Customs officers 'allowed 18 lbs to the stone . . . called the great stone', so north Devon imported over one million pounds in 1683, about one-third of England's annual wool import from Ireland at this time, with Exeter's own import of 675,530 lb bringing Devon's proportion to well over half. Irish trade was now big business, and high interest rates and limited capital in Ireland prompted a number of Irish traders to settle in Bideford. Hartwell Buck, for example, who married the daughter of a leading Bideford merchant, became the founder of a merchant dynasty, which like the town of Bideford itself grew rich on the Irish and tobacco trades. The two were linked, for business partners in Ireland (usually relations or friends of Bideford's new merchants) provisioned ships for colonial voyages, and distributed and sold tobacco re-exported from Bideford.[47]

The late seventeenth century was a favourable time for outport tobacco trade, for small vessels could take much-needed goods direct to the scattered plantations beside the rivers of Virginia and Maryland, then load fresh early tobacco without delay or middlemen. Bideford's trade developed rapidly, and in 1676 over 300,000 lb came in, most of it for local merchants. By 1683 566,700 lb was brought into Bideford and 155,600 lb to Barnstaple, as ship owners there joined the profitable trade. More was carried by north Devon ships, for, although obliged to declare cargoes in England, they did not have to return to their home port, and some with tobacco for Europe touched at Falmouth, for example. The majority seem to have come home, however, and in 1683, after putting in to Bideford, the tobacco ships *Henrietta* and *Exchange* went to Norway, and the *Hopewell* to Amsterdam, returning with timber and other goods. As the trade of the port expanded, more vessels went to the Caribbean for sugar, molasses and rum, and an increasing number joined the Newfoundland fleet.[48]

The growth of overseas trade stimulated north Devon's coastal trade, with surplus imports from Ireland and the colonies absorbed, as before, by Bristol. Local resources were also exploited, with the export to Bristol and Gloucester of tobacco-pipe clay dug at Peter's Marland near Torrington rising from 91 tons in 1654 to an average of over 300 tons in the early 1680s. This was a more lucrative export than the pipes themselves, which, however, were also made in Devon and sent to Ireland and the colonies. In this period the export of north Devon earthenware also rose, until in the early 1680s the number of 'parcels' shipped coastally each year averaged over a quarter of a million. A parcel consisted of one or two large pieces or more small ones; one

16.5 North Devon sgraffito-ware dish *c*1660, excavated at Jamestown, Virginia. Diameter about 11 inches. *(Colonial National Historical Park, Jamestown, and the University of Exeter)*

large pitcher or four one-pint jugs, for instance. In the same period overseas exports of almost 140,000 parcels brought average annual shipments to 367,000. This trade added to the prosperity of the ports by enabling traders to fill cargo space outward and make a profit both ways.[49]

While pottery brought in the pennies for north Devon's coastal traders, perpetuanas earned pounds for Exeter's. By 1683 coastal cargoes equalled those overseas, with 37 vessels taking cloth to London, 14 to Plymouth, and 23 to other ports for reshipment overseas, or for the growing home market. Goods of all kinds came back from London, and Exeter's expansion stimulated the coastal trade of the other Devon ports. Sugar, paper, and tobacco, for example, were received from Dartmouth, and particularly from Plymouth, which was an important distribution centre for foreign produce. Topsham and Plymouth ships, which even before the Civil War had not carried many coastal cargoes, could not handle all the trade of their ports, so vessels from London and the south and east coasts predominated. Dartmouth and north Devon also provided one or two carriers, mainly in the trade with south Wales, which employed more local ships. In 1683, for example, Topsham vessels brought in 67 cargoes of coal and culm (anthracite) out of a total of 140, but no local vessels were among those carrying a further 44 coal cargoes from Newcastle and Sunderland. North Devon's small ships, which continued to handle almost all their own coastal trade, made more voyages – 328 in 1682 – to bring home about the same amount of coal and culm from south Wales. Three years later 5,570 tons of culm were sent to north Devon from Milford alone, while Exeter, having recently improved its canal, took 14,666 tons of coal and culm from all sources in 1688. This remarkable increase in the import of coal contributed not only to domestic comfort, but to industrial growth, which in its turn promoted the expansion of trade, ports, and shipping.[50]

Between 1600 and 1689 Devon's maritime communities kept pace with opportunities, and overcame most disadvantages. At the beginning of the period, corporations successfully campaigned against central control of outport trade, and merchants, self-interested, but usually shrewd, used old-established contacts to maintain traditional markets. As magistrates, they controlled the workforce, fixed wages and maintained the apprenticeship system, ensuring adequate local skills and keeping down the cost of labour. Population grew during the period, and people attracted to the ports in search of work provided the extra workers and seamen needed as trade and shipping increased. Devon's traders, exploiting favourable geographical and economic circumstances, were among the first to open up the New World, and by the end of the period were using more and bigger vessels in profitable Atlantic trades. On the whole, however, small vessels still predominated, providing the frequent returns needed by provincial traders without tying up capital for long periods. In the seventeenth century, although there were signs of change, ships had not yet outgrown provincial quays and anchorages, large ports had not put all the small ones out of business, individual merchants had not been crowded out by large companies, and Devon was still an important feature of England's maritime map.

16: Devon Shipping, Trade, and Ports, 1600–1689

1 DRO, Z/19/18/9, J Hooker, 'Synopsis Chorographical' (unpub. ms.), 256; T Risdon, *Survey of Devon* (1811), 327.
2 'The Diary of Philip Wyot, 1586–1606', in JR Chanter, *Sketches of Some Striking Incidents in the History of Barnstaple* (Barnstaple, 1865), 108; RN Worth, *Calendar of the Plymouth Municipal Records* (Plymouth, 1895), 22, 143; WB Stephens, *Seventeenth-Century Exeter* (Exeter, 1958), 8.
3 D Portman, *Exeter Houses 1400–1700* (Exeter, 1966), 101; Percy Russell, *The Good Town of Totnes* (Exeter, 1964, rpt. 1984), 62–3; Ray Freeman, *Dartmouth: a New History of the Port and its People* (Dartmouth, 1983), 58–61; C Gill, *Plymouth: a New History* (Newton Abbot, 1979), II, 19–21.
4 WB Stephens, 'Roger Mallock, Merchant and Royalist', *DAT*, 92 (1960), 279; SE Dodderidge, and HG Hastings Shaddick, *The Dodderidges of Devon* (Exeter, 1909), 10; WDRO, 745/36, Will of Abraham Colmer; *DCNQ*, 22 (1942–6), I, 10; WSL, Will of N Shapleigh, in Olive Moger, 'Copies of Transcripts and Extracts from Wills' (hereafter Moger Wills).
5 Frances Wood, 'Merchants and Class: The Social Identification of Merchants in Exeter 1680–1760' (unpublished MA thesis, Monash University, 1977), 78–9, 83.
6 PRO, Chancery Proceedings, Series II, bundle 306 (1617–21), no. 81.
7 DRO, Acland papers, 1142/B/EA/94.
8 PRO, Will of J Adams, PCC, PROB 11/483/164, cited in Wood, 'Merchants and Class', 69.
9 Gill, *Plymouth*, II, 43; A Grant and P Christie, *The Book of Bideford* (Buckingham, 1987), 27, 103; Wood, 'Merchants and Class', 66; C Henderson, 'An Early Warehouse on Exeter Quay', *Devon Buildings Group Newsletter*, 1 (1986), 5.
10 *HMC Reports* 9, Salisbury, XVI, 136.
11 *HMC Reports* 9, Salisbury, XVII, 418; R Ashton, *The City and the Court* (Cambridge, 1979), 85.
12 PRO, Exchequer, King's Remembrancer Port Books, E190/942/12, /937/8, /943/10, /1029/19, /942/13; PJ Bowden, *The Wool Trade in Tudor and Stuart England* (1971), 47–8.
13 WB Stephens, 'Merchant Companies and Commercial Policy in Exeter 1625–88', *DAT*, 86 (1954), 143; E Windeatt, 'The Constitutions of the Merchants' Company in Totnes', *DAT*, 10 (1908), 170; *Acts of the Privy Council* (hereafter *APC*), *1613–14*, 247–8; Stephens, 'Merchant Companies', 143–5.
14 DRO, Dartmouth Documents, DD 61927; RN Worth, *History of Plymouth* (Plymouth, 1890), 89; SD White, *Sir Edward Coke and the Grievances of the Commonwealth* (Manchester, 1979), 108–9.
15 Stephens, 'Merchant Companies', 145–8.
16 WDRO, 745/51, Will of John Fownes; James Phinney Baxter, ed., *The Trelawny Papers* (Portland, Me., 1884), 154, 222, and below, chapter 18; PRO, E190/947/3, /947/8, /949/10; JH Lefroy, *Memorials of the Bermudas or Somers Islands, 1515–1685* (1882) I, 444–7.
17 PRO, E190/944/1.
18 PRO, E190/939/2, /939/6, 939/10, 939/8, 939/11, /1024/15; JU Nef, *The Rise of the British Coal Industry* (1952), 90.
19 PRO, E190/939/2, /939/6, /939/10, /939/8, /939/11, /1024/15; EAG Clark, 'The Estuary Ports of the Exe and Teign, with special reference to the period 1660–1860' (unpublished PhD thesis, University of London, 1957), 933.
20 WSL, Moger Wills, W Bayley, W Smythe.
21 PRO, SP 16/16/43; 16/16/89; PRO, Will of R Bayley, PCC, PROB 11/233/3; DRO, DD 62366; WSL, Wills of P Martyn, J and V Hillman, in 'Copies of wills collected by Sir Oswyn Murray'; PRO E134/9 and Clark, 'Estuary Ports', 199.
22 T Wainwright, ed., *Barnstaple Parish Register 1538–1812* (Exeter, 1903), Baptisms, 59; NDRO, B3971, B360, B3985; DRO 3896 (additional); J Leland, 'The Itinerary of John Leland the Antiquary, 1534–43', in R Pearse Chope, ed., *DCNQ*, IX, II, *Early Tours in Devon and Cornwall* (Exeter, 1918), 5; WSL, Moger Wills, Cocke; DRO, Admiralty Court Proceedings, Chanter 780b, f.101.
23 DRO, DD 62800, 62820, 63519; *CSPD 1666–7*, 486; NDRO, Bideford Bridge Trust, A1/78; PRO, E190/952/4.
24 *CSPD 1665–6*, 191, 203; *CSPD 1634–5*, 583–6; DRO, DD 62257A; PRO, E190/1036/18; William G Saltonstall, *Ports of Piscataqua* (New York, 1941, rpt. 1968), 13; Baxter, *Trelawny Papers*, 133.
25 Baxter, *Trelawny Papers*, 133, 157, 161, 165, 257. See also below, chapter 18.
26 *APC 1601–4*, 7; *HMC Reports* 9, Salisbury, XVI, 150, 362; *CSPD 1656–7*, 575.
27 PRO, SP 16/34/103 and Todd Gray (ed.), *Early Stuart Mariners and Shipping*, Devon and Cornwall Record Society, vol. 33 (Exeter 1990), 92–4.
28 DRO, DD 61927; WDRO, 745/107, Will of L Pomeroy, WDRO, 745/84, Will of Abraham Jennings; *CSPD 1641–3*, 449; PRO, SP 23/183/488, cited in Stephens, 'Roger Mallock', 289–90; PRO, Lists of ships in plantation trade, CO5/749.
29 PRO, SP 16/34/103; R Davis, *The Rise of the English Shipping Industry* (1962), 100.
30 *CSPD 1641–3*, 2; DRO, Basket D/17/27; PRO, E190/945/7.
31 Davis, *English Shipping Industry*, 287, 365–9; Lefroy, *Memorials of the Bermudas* I, 446; LM Cullen, *Insights into Irish History 1660–1830* (Dublin 1971), 5; NDRO, B3987.
32 *HMC Reports* 9, Salisbury, 11, 444; NDRO, B3987; DRO, ADM 1–3, Chanter 780d, Act Book 1670–82, fos. 93*d*, 108–9, 115*r*.
33 DRO, DD 63416; DRO ADM. 1–3, Chanter 780d Act Book 1670–82, fos. 128–129
34 C Molloy, *De Jure Maritimo et Navali* (1676), 203, cited in Davis, *English Shipping Industry*, 127; DRO, Diocesan Records, Admiralty papers, CC/181/18/8.
35 Lefroy, *Memorials of the Bermudas* I, 444; DRO, Schoolmasters' Licences, Moger PR, 510–510a. PRO, Will of R Sherman, PCC, PROB 11/219/248; DRO, CC/181/18/13/2.
36 PRO, Will of J Comer, PCC, PROB 11/455/45; A Grant and R Gwynn, 'The Huguenots of Devon', *DAT*, 117 (1985), 175–6.
37 Lefroy, *Memorials of the Bermudas* I, 449; WDRO, Jennings v. Searle, W356.
38 NDRO, B1185; DRO, ADM. 1–3, Chanter 780d Act Book 1670–82, fos. 44, 137–8; NDRO, B617.
39 *CSPD 1635*, 376; *Privy Council Registers* IV (HMSO 1968), 612; *Dictionary of National Biography*, George Peard; *DCNQ*, 18 (1934–5), 340–1; RW Cotton, *Barnstaple and the Northern Part of Devonshire during the Great Civil War 1642–6* (Chilworth and London 1889), 79, 115. See also chapter 15 above.
40 DRO, DD 62701.
41 *DCNQ*, 18 (1934–5), 340–1; Gill, *Plymouth*, II, 32; PRO, E190/952/1, /952/3; Stephens, *Exeter*, 67.
42 PRO, E190/1036/23, /952/4.
43 Davis, *English Shipping Industry*, 11; Stephens, *Exeter*, 69–71; *CSPD 1655–6*, 148, 276; *CSPD 1657–8*, 466.
44 Stephens, *Exeter*, 85–104; PRO E190/956/14, /961/5.
45 Stephens, *Exeter*, 162; PRO E190/1047/13. See also chapter 22 below.
46 PRO, E190/950/2, /954/98, /961/1, /962/8; D Woodward, 'The Anglo-Irish Livestock Trade of the Seventeenth Century' *Irish Historical Studies*, XVIII (1972–3), 513.
47 Cullen, *Insights*, 5; PRO E190/954/6, /961/1; Stephens, *Exeter*, 123; LM Cullen, *Anglo-Irish Trade 1660–1800* (Manchester 1968), 20; A Grant, *North Devon Pottery: The Seventeenth Century* (Exeter, 1983), 121.
48 PRO, E190/956/7, 961/1.
49 A Grant and D Jemmet, 'Pipes and Pipemaking in Barnstaple, Devon', *British Archaeological Reports* (1985), 459–60, 485; Grant, *North Devon Pottery*, 72–5.
50 PRO, E190/962/6, /960/13; Stephens, *Exeter*, 117–25; TS Willan, *The English Coasting Trade 1600–1750* (Manchester, 1938), 65.

17 *Devon's Fisheries and Early-Stuart Northern New England*

TODD GRAY

IN TERMS OF COLONIZATION THE English were relative latecomers to the New World. Unlike the Spanish, who had rich native cities and kingdoms to sack in the southern half of the Americas, the English in North America had to identify, or introduce, suitable commodities which would be lucrative enough to guarantee continued investment and thus finance colonies. In Virginia the adventurers grew South American tobacco, and in the West Indies sugar was raised as a cash crop. At the beginning of the seventeenth century the pace of colonization of these areas remained slow and erratic, and the character of Devon's involvement was much like that of other counties: its merchants, gentry, and seafarers played a role that was neither insignificant nor exceptional.[1] However, from the beginning Devonians had a unique part in the development of New England, where it had quickly become apparent that the most obvious commercial possibilities lay in the exploitation of fishing resources. For Devon men the discovery of New England continued from the previous generation's development of Newfoundland, where its dried codfish may have been an 'unglamorous, every-day commodity' but it was 'the fulfilment of the mercantilist dream'.[2] Once the extent of the resources became known, Devon merchants became involved not only in the exploration but also in the subsequent settlement of New England. This chapter is concerned with why the discovery of New England fishing resources was particularly attractive and also necessary to continue the prosperity already gained by the Newfoundland fisheries. It will be shown that Devon's fishermen were interested in a number of fisheries. Their ships were not just in local waters or across the Atlantic, but also sailed far to the east in search of fish. New England became an essential part of a great network, and it also proved to be the last new source of fish.

Fishing was important to the county for several reasons, one being that it was a source of cheap food. In 1630 Thomas Westcote noted that Plymouth was well supplied with fish which 'ease[d] the price of victuals in the market'.[3] Part of a boat's catch would be sold directly upon being brought to shore and the rest, if not exported, was carried inland by what were called in Devon and Cornwall 'jowters'. One of these was John Lyle of East Teignmouth, who in 1614 carried fish from that haven to inland parts.[4] Fish was obviously a sought-after commodity: in 1635 Hugh Upington of Rackenford travelled thirty miles to Dawlish with his horses laden with five fish pots, just to collect pilchards.[5]

Fish was seen by John Hooker in the late sixteenth century as Devon's third most valuable commodity: he thought that only the cloth and tin industries were more substantial.[6] Tristram Risdon, in his survey of the county written between 1605 and 1630, recorded that Devon was:

> well stocked with fish of all sorts . . . for the good of the country at home and abroad: for by traffic of them . . . commodities are transported into this land from foreign nations.

and Westcote noted that the amount of fish brought to Plymouth was sufficient to:

> entertain and furnish the wants of such of our country or foreign friends that arrive here, where you may very often number a hundred sails sometimes, often double the number.

An Italian merchant's letters of the 1580s and 1590s show that there was aggressive competition between him and French and Dutch merchants for fish in Devon.[7] Great quantities of fish were transported to Catholic Europe, but a good portion of this was shipped directly from the overseas fisheries. Because of this, and also because fish was excluded from import duties from 1563, a precise assessment of the total value of the fish trade is not possible. Nevertheless, some glimpses of its worth can be found. It was estimated in Parliament in 1621 that from Newfoundland alone came fish worth £120,000 per year[8] and, although few port books have survived, it can be seen that in 1617 almost £10,000 of fish was exported from Plymouth and at Dartmouth in 1624 fish worth £17,000 was exported.[9]

In 1580 Robert Hitchcock included in his *Pollitique Platt* a description of Britain's fisheries.[10] His account shows the seasonal nature of a network of fisheries all around the British coast, and also the importance of Ireland as a source of fish. John Hooker wrote a few years later that Devon was:

> inhabited and replenished with great households and families of seafaring men, which do travel far and near as well in merchandise as in fishing in all places both far and near in deeps and places of the best fishing.[11]

This differentiation between the two types of fishing was an important one. In Brixham there was a distinction between the fishing in local waters, which was known as their 'home' voyages, that is the local inshore or coastal fisheries (which in Brixham were generally completed within one day and night), and those migratory fisheries in the 'deep' sea, whether offshore or further abroad, which could involve journeys of six months or more.[12]

Local fishing

In an early version of his *Pollitique Platt* Robert Hitchcock omitted reference to a number of fisheries, including that for pilchards in the South West, but these were nevertheless noted on a later copy.[13] There was, however, a great variety of fish caught off Devon. John Hooker wrote that whiting were always in season and that there were also haddock, colefish, cod, 'millwell' (also cod), ling, hake, mackerel, gurnard, piper, millet, bass, plaice of many kinds, sole, and others, among which he named 'holy book flounders' and 'millers' thumbs'. Last, but by no means least, there were herrings and pilchards, 'which of all others be most beneficial to the good of this country at home and to the like of all foreign nations abroad'.[14] The range of fish which Hooker found in Tudor Devon continued into the seventeenth century: both Risdon and Westcote likewise enthused about the variety of local fish.

In 1566 Hooker himself, on behalf of Sir Arthur Champernowne, Vice-Admiral of Devon, licensed 84 fishing nets in South Devon. Table 17.1 shows how the seine, tuck, and hake nets, and thus the fishermen who owned them, were scattered along the length of the coastline. In 1619 there was still a wide distribution: the Duke of Buckingham's survey of south Devon in that year recorded fishermen in the parishes of Beer and Seaton, Sidmouth, Paignton, Dawlish, Brixham, Churston Ferrers, Blackawton, Thurlestone, Bigbury, Holbeton, and East Stonehouse, while a survey of 1626 shows them also in Moreleigh, Diptford, Loddiswell, South Milton, Yealmpton, Plympton St Maurice, and Plympton St Mary. The men specifically identified as fishermen were only a portion of the overall labour force involved: many of the several thousand men who were listed as mariners and sailors also certainly worked in the various fisheries. In fact,

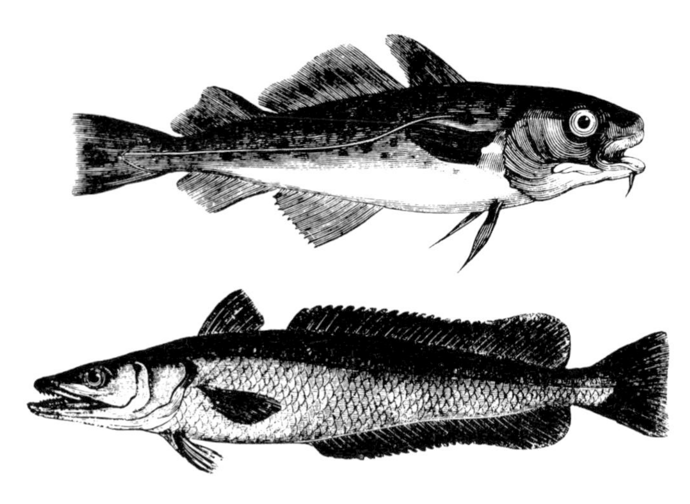

17.1 The Common Cod and the Common Hake, from Yarrell, *British Fishes* (1833). For Herring and Pilchard see above, Figs. 6.9, 10.

Buckingham's survey noted only two places as having fishing craft: two fishing boats, each of twenty tons, were listed at Exmouth and 12 fishing boats of between 5 and 10 tons were at Beer and Seaton.[15] There was obviously a considerable amount of fishing in east Devon. Risdon wrote that Sidmouth was 'one of the especialist fisher towns of this shire, and serveth much provision into the east parts, whereupon her principal maintenance consisteth'.[16] But there were many other parishes where fishing was an important activity, as will be seen below.

As mentioned above, there were two principal coastal fisheries in Elizabethan and early Stuart Devon: for pilchards along the south coast and for herring in the north. Risdon wrote in 1630 of Lynmouth that it was:

> of late years notable for the marvellous plenty of herrings there taken, a kind of fish which in our fore-fathers' day kept, as it were, their station about Norway, but in our time . . . take their course round about this isle of Great Britain by shoals in great numbers. And from September until Christide offer themselves to the fisher[men]s' nets, to the no little benefit of this land.[17]

Westcote noted that herring, which he called the 'king of fishes', was caught at Clovelly as well as Lynmouth.[18] Little more is known about the Lynmouth fishery except that a number of smoked-herring houses were destroyed in a great flood at Lynmouth in 1607.[19] However, Risdon's observation that the herring was unknown two generations previously was acutely observed: the proceedings of several church court cases, particularly the testimony of one old man, confirm that herring first appeared off north Devon in the 1580s and shows it to have been even then a considerable fishery. John Kale had his great grand-daughter testify on his behalf (as he was too ill to leave his bed) that the herring arrived in Lynmouth in 1583 and that the season lasted approximately from Michaelmas to Christmas. The Lynmouth fishery attracted men from the length of the Bristol Channel, including such places as Minehead and Northam, who actually rented cottages for the three-month season. In this particular case it was reported that six Northam men took over 1,200 meazes of herring which were variously valued at between £180 and £240.[20] Another sign of the importance of this fishery appears in a second case, in which it was disclosed that, during the fishing season, a clergyman read divine service at the mouth of the river Lyn (Fig. 17.2) specifically for herring fishermen. He alternated morning and evening prayers between the east and west sides of the river and testified he was employed in that task because the distance between the river and the parish churches of Lynton and Countisbury (a mile and a half) was too far for the incumbent to travel on a Sunday.[21] The apparent need for such additional services implies that there was a considerable number of fishermen.

Although there was a decline of pilchards in Devon waters in the middle of the seventeenth century,[22] there was earlier a considerable industry along the length of the south Devon coast and probably into Dorset. Both Risdon and Westcote noted that Hope Cove was an important place for pilchard fishing, and it was claimed in 1583 that 900,000 pilchards were caught there by only five men.[23] The coast between the mouths of the Teign and the Exe was also a centre for pilchards. Both Dawlish, of which Westcote wrote: 'here is plenty of fish taken, which is the greatest benefit it hath', and Teignmouth, of which Risdon wrote: 'their greatest benefit is abundance of sea fish there taken, whereof the county is from thence plentifully served', were clearly important. As seen in Table 17.1, almost a third of south Devon's fishing nets licensed in 1566 were located around the mouth of the Teign.[24] The 15 seinemen recorded at Dawlish in the Duke of Buckingham's survey in 1619 must have been employed in the pilchard fishery. There are also records showing fishing for pilchards from such parishes as West Alvington, Thurlestone, Cockington, and Beer and Seaton, and it is most likely that pilchards were caught from all the coastal parishes.[25] It was reported in 1622 that pilchards were one of the three native commodities exported to the continent from Dartmouth and Plymouth, but a great number were also brought from Cornwall to Plymouth.[26]

Table 17.1
South Devon seine, tuck, and hake nets, 1566

Locality	Seines	Tuck nets
Seaton	3	
Branscombe	3	
Budleigh	4	1
Sidmouth	3	
Woodbury & Lympstone	2	
Kingsteignton and Bishopsteignton	2	
Dawlish & East Teignmouth	8	5
West Teignmouth	8	
Cockington & Tor [Bay]	5	
St Marychurch, Stokeinteignhead and Combinteignhead	6	
Churston Ferrers, Galmpton, Brixham, and Woodleigh	1	5
Kingswear	5	
Dartmouth	1	
Slapton & Blackawton	9	7
Charleton, South Poole, East Portlemouth and Dodbrooke	4 (and 2 hake nets)	
Thurlestone, Kingston and Kingsbridge	1	
Salcombe	11	
Ringmore	3	
Bigbury, South Huish and Milton	3	
Plymouth	1	
Stonehouse	1	
Newton Ferrers	(1 hake net)	
Total	84	18 (and 3 hake nets)

The following places were mentioned without reference to nets: Salcombe Regis, Topsham, Powderham, Exmouth, Dittisham, Wembury, Maker, St Budeaux, Plymstock, Halberton, and Noss Mayo.

Source: DRO, Exeter City Archives, Book 57, fos. 158–71.

Offshore fishing

Fishermen throughout the county, on both coasts, were obviously highly mobile. In the 1580s fishermen from Salcombe in south Devon annually visited the fishery at the north Cornish port of Padstow for up to ten weeks and rented 'cellars' (storehouses) there in which to keep their tackle and victuals. These included such men as Malborough resident Robert Reynolds, who was master of the *Margaret* of Batson (Salcombe), and Henry Evans, master of an East Portlemouth vessel. Both men also visited the parish church while at Padstow.[27] Parishioners of Stoke Gabriel, just above Dartmouth, fished on the Dart river, in Tor Bay, and also in Newfoundland.[28] At Paignton in 1540 seamen fished with seines upon the coast, 'hawked, hucked and tucked' in Tor Bay, and fished at Mounts Bay in

Cornwall, in the Scillies, off Winchelsea in Sussex, and in Ireland.[29] Likewise, men from Newton Ferrers, near Plymouth, fished in Ireland (from 1624 to 1626 and again in 1631), at Newfoundland (in 1617 as well as from 1619 to 1621 and in 1633 and 1634), and northern New England (in 1622 and 1623). Philip Crope of Kenton fished not only at Great Yarmouth and Scarborough, but also in Ireland.[30]

The enthusiasm with which Hooker, Risdon, and Westcote wrote concerning the availability of local fish stocks overshadowed their references to the fish brought great distances from Devon. All three did admit that there was a great deal of 'foreign' fishing, but not one fully expressed its extent: for, considerable as the supply of local fish was, the county also imported vast amounts of fish, probably more than it harvested in its own waters.

The reasons for seeking supplementary fish supplies were many. One consistent characteristic of the fisheries is that the size of the fish stocks regularly fluctuates. Not only are there continually alternating periods of shortages, sufficiency, and plenty, but there are times when the stocks disappear altogether. As was seen earlier, herring suddenly arrived off the north Devon coast in the 1580s, and pilchards, which may have reappeared in Devon in the early part of the sixteenth century, disappeared from south Devon in the middle of the seventeenth century. In the late sixteenth century there was a period in which pilchards were particularly scarce in Devon and Cornwall: from 1587 to 1597 there were at least four years of shortages.[31] There were also scarcities in the Newfoundland fishery in 1592 and 1621, as well as in the Irish fisheries in 1592 and 1597.[32] It is with the response to such shortages that the link between the fisheries becomes apparent. At Plymouth in 1587 an Italian merchant was advised to buy Newfoundland fish because of the scarcity of pilchards. His factor failed in an attempt to buy hake as a substitute because French merchants had purchased the lot and five days later sought herring because it was cheapest.[33] In 1621 Bristol merchants sought information about the New England fishery because that at Newfoundland had 'failed'.[34] It is clear that, when one stock became unavailable, merchants substituted fish from other sources, and it was this need for a constant source of fish that required Devon's merchants to search further afield.

Englishmen are known to have been fishing for Irish herring, cod, hake, and ling from at least the fifteenth century. In the 1530s a veritable fleet of Devon boats brought considerable quantities of Irish hake into Plymouth and in 1600 Devonians were still fishing off Ireland.[35] Irish herring became less available during the early seventeenth century, and pilchards may have been new to Ireland around the turn of the seventeenth century. They had arrived by 1611 at the latest and English fishermen followed the pilchards there, introduced seine fishing, and established communities around the fishery, particularly in the southwest of Ireland. As many as 2,000 English migrants worked in the Munster fisheries. One of the entrepreneurs was William Hull, an Exeter ship's captain who settled in Munster and became the Vice-Admiral there. He was knighted in 1621. Another leader in the Irish fishery was Sir Richard Boyle, later Earl of Cork, who was buying land in Devon and had ties with Sir Edward Seymour of Berry Pomeroy and Mr George Cary of Cockington. One of Boyle's three partners in establishing the fishery at Ardmoor was William Waymouth, also of Cockington, whose family had a long history of involvement in the Newfoundland fishery. There are many other references to Devon fishermen in Ireland. For instance, in both 1606 and 1607 Stoke Gabriel fishing boats caught £200 worth of fish.[36] Humphrey Burrow of Beer sent his ship the *Jonas* to Ireland in 1617, and anticipated that each man's share would be worth five pounds.[37] Two sources in particular reveal more substantial details of the fishery. First, there is an undated petition from Salcombe and Sidmouth fishermen engaged in the Irish herring fishery. Each of their boats carried six men and cost £16 for the salt, nets, and victuals. Once in Ireland the fishermen hired a drover, a small boat used for trawling nets. They had to pay custom as well as tithe (of one twentieth of the fish) in Ireland. It was also noted that in the previous two years 60 men and 15 barks had been lost there.[38] Secondly there is another petition, of 1623, which claimed that a total of 400 Devon ships annually fished for Irish herring.[39] If this was accurate and each ship carried the full crew of six, as claimed in the Salcombe and Sidmouth petition, then as many as 2,400 Devon fishermen were in Ireland each year in the 1620s just for herring.

In the sixteenth century Devon fishermen were also involved in the fisheries in the eastern part of the Channel and in the North Sea. In 1540 Paignton fishermen were fishing at Winchelsea in Sussex, as were fishermen from Stokeinteignhead in the 1560s. The Stokeinteignhead men also fished

17.2 Lynmouth, north Devon, as depicted in a drawing by GB Campion, engraved by James Bingley and published in 1831, but probably little changed in two hundred years. *(Devon and Exeter Institution)*

in the North Sea at Scarborough for 'buckhorn' – whiting which was 'gutted, split, powdered, and dried'. Brixham seamen, too, were fishing at Scarborough in 1563.[40] Perhaps the fishing experience of Philip Crope of Kenton, mentioned earlier, most clearly illustrates the nature of this North Sea fishing. In the summers of 1559 and 1560 he fished (with hooks) for millwell, pollack, and ling at Scarborough, and in the winter of 1559/60 travelled to Great Yarmouth in Norfolk where he fished for herring (with nets) in an Exmouth boat. Crope claimed that in total each year he and his servants caught 40 ling and 100 millwell, as well as 300 each of plaice, whiting, tub gurnard, rochet (red gurnard), bream, haddock, sole, thornback, ray, and 'hound' dogfish. He also caught 10,000 each of herring and pilchards. All of this was salted.[41] Crope's case in the church court is the only surviving one of its kind, but it is unlikely that his experiences were unique. Most conclusively of all, a survey of Devon mariners made in 1570 noted that, while there were 1,264 seamen then in the county, there were a further 311, almost a fifth of the total, 'at the seas at Scarborough and elsewhere daily looked for [at] home'.[42]

Newfoundland

Devon's involvement in the North Sea seems to have contracted in the late sixteenth century, when the county's involvement in the New World fisheries expanded. English fishermen, almost certainly including men from Devon, also had a long tradition of fishing off Iceland, but it is said to have been a steadily declining fishery throughout Elizabeth's reign.[43] Some time in the early to mid-sixteenth century, however, English fishermen looked even further to the west and began visiting the Newfoundland fishery. It was a Devon man, Sir Humphrey Gilbert, half-brother to Sir Walter Raleigh, who claimed Newfoundland for the Queen as the first English colony, but this was not until 1583.[44] It is known that ships were returning to Plymouth from Newfoundland as early as 1544,[45] but it seems most likely that the fishery started to expand only in the 1560s. In 1563 tithes were requested at Brixham for fish brought in the *Charity* of Kingswear which, it was alleged, had been to Newfoundland 'diverse and sundry times', but it was also said in evidence that: 'the fishing into the Newfoundland hath been used but within these four years'. One old man testified that he could supply information about the Irish fishery but not about Newfoundland because vessels only recently went there.[46] Furthermore, the earliest that men from Tor Mohun in Torbay claimed to have been in Newfoundland was 1565, from Stoke Gabriel 1568 and from St Marychurch (also in Torbay) 1570.[47] That the fishery only really began to be more frequently visited at this time is also supported by a statement in 1578 that, within the previous four years, the Newfoundland fleet had grown from 30 to 50 ships. By the 1630s it was claimed that over 10,000 seamen were there every year.[48]

Devon men were not, of course, the only Englishmen at Newfoundland. There were a great number of men from throughout the west country and there was some participation of London merchants. However, Plymouth and Dartmouth almost certainly were the two leading ports involved during the early seventeenth century, and Dartmouth was probably the more important. Fishing was of greater importance to its economy than it was to Plymouth, Exeter, or even Barnstaple.[49] The mayor of Dartmouth explained in 1609 that the port's involvement with, and dependence on, fishing stemmed from a longstanding lack of natural commodities to trade. He claimed that, to rectify this, Dartmouth's merchants had to participate in the offshore fishing.[50] Dartmouth was able to do this partly because the harbour was free of sandbars or shingle and could offer one of the best anchorages in the South West. In the early seventeenth century, and probably before, it was Devon's greatest port in terms of the number of its ships as well as in overall tonnage. It was also the centre for south Devon's mariner population.[51] Dartmouth's accelerated, if not spectacular, growth from the late sixteenth century was very largely a result of these fishing voyages. One visible sign remaining of this prosperity is the collection of merchant town houses known as the Butterwalk (Fig. 16.2, above p. 131).[52]

New England

It was from Dartmouth that the first recorded voyage of exploration to New England set out. According to a corporation petition of 1620 a Dartmouth ship had explored that coast in 1597, five years earlier than any other known journey.[53] There were three principal English expeditions to the new England coast from 1602 to 1608, including that of George Waymouth of Cockington in 1605. The accounts of all three ventures were published, and this began to familiarize Englishmen with the new England.[54] Regulation followed very quickly, official interest being concerned with colonial settlement. The administration of the more than 2,000 miles of coastline claimed by the English was divided in 1606 between the two halves of the Virginia Company. The southern area, which in 1584 had become known as Virginia, was run by the South Virginia Company, which was composed of a collection of Londoners. The northern region, which was initially known as Norumbega, then as north Virginia, and finally from 1616 as New England, was administered by the North Virginia Company, which was based in Plymouth and comprised almost exclusively westcountrymen. Their leaders were Sir John Popham of Somerset, Lord Chief Justice of England, Raleigh Gilbert of Greenway near Dartmouth, and Sir Ferdinando Gorges, the governor of Plymouth Fort.[55]

It was under the North Virginia Company's auspices that the first settlement of New England was attempted. In May 1607 two ships left Plymouth and attempted to establish a colony on the banks of the Sagadahoc river in the north of the region. Partly owing to an unusually cold winter, but also because of the deaths of several leading men, including George Popham at the colony and John Gilbert in Devon, the colony failed and the settlers returned to Devon. There was, however, a legacy of this first venture, as well as of the earlier exploratory journeys. This was the establishment of a seasonal fishery in the richest fishing area, which proved to be in the north of the region. The *Gift of God* of Topsham, which brought the colonists home from Sagadahoc in the autumn of 1608, returned the following fishing season to 'Virginia' (as it was still called) and arrived back in Topsham on 4 November 1609 with a cargo of fish and train oil. This vessel was perhaps the first of the Devon ships to capitalize on the findings of the journeys to New England from 1602 to 1608: all three expeditions publicized the fishing resources and compared them favourably with the Newfoundland fishery. Some stated that the New England fishery was even better than that of Newfoundland. John Brereton's account of the 1602 voyage claimed that the cod were 'more large and vendible for England and France than the New[found]land fish', and Martin Pring reported from his 1603 journey: 'we found an excellent fishing for cod, which are better than those of Newfoundland'. Finally, James Rosier wrote in 1605 that he had discovered that it would be possible in

> a short voyage with few good fishers to make a more profitable return from hence than from Newfoundland: the fish being so much greater, better fed, and abundant with train [oil].[56]

Islands such as Monhegan became popular for the drying of fish.

The North Virginia Company was superseded in 1620 by the New England Council, which was also based in Plymouth and had Sir Ferdinando Gorges once again as its leader. The members included Mathew Sutcliffe, Dean of Exeter, and the Cathedral's legal Chancellor, Barnaby Gooche.[57] In the 1620s the Council attempted to finance its colonization plans by taxing the fishing industry, which had by now expanded considerably. The Council proposed the establishment of joint-stock companies in the ports and environs of Bristol, Exeter, Dartmouth, Plymouth, and Barnstaple. It was suggested that these ports would send representatives twice-yearly to a central body at Tiverton, chosen for its central position in the south-west peninsula, which would co-ordinate the fishery. The number of delegates reflected the relative importance of the ports. Exeter and Bristol were each to have 18 representatives and Dartmouth, Plymouth, and Barnstaple were to have 12 each. The scheme failed, largely because of the hostile reception it received from merchants and fishermen.[58] The New England Council was unable to control the pattern of settlement, and after the establishment of the separatist colony at New Plymouth, but more so with the 'Puritans' of Massachusetts Bay, the southern half of the region fell outside its jurisdiction. However, Gorges managed to retain his control of the most northerly part of New England until the Civil War, and it is with the settlement of northern New England that Devon has been largely identified.[59] The county's involvement led one nineteenth-century historian to conclude that, in the early seventeenth century, 'more persons originating in Devon and Cornwall, and perhaps Somerset, were living on the seacoast of Maine and New Hampshire, and on the adjacent islands, than from all other counties in England'.[60] This may well have been so, but not all who made the voyage to northern New England took up residence.

There was a mixture of motivation bringing men to northern New England. Such Devon men as Thomas Gorges, nephew of Sir Ferdinando Gorges, who later returned and settled at Heavitree near Exeter,[61] became involved in the administration of the region, and Francis Champernowne, his father's sixth son, emigrated to establish an estate of 1,000 acres around Portsmouth harbour. Champernowne grew up on the large family estate of Dartington and named the town of Kittery in southern Maine after his family's house in Kingswear. Although Champernowne himself appears to have been more concerned with land prospects, his family's interests in New England were not divorced from fishing. His father had been sending his boats fishing to New England since at least 1622.[62] The character of the northern area was overwhelmingly dominated by fishing. Although there were 1,000 emigrants, i.e. settlers, in the region by 1650, there were probably as many as several thousand fishermen who migrated, i.e. travelled, to the Gulf of Maine fishery each year.[63] An investigation of the social backgrounds of the Devon emigrants to, i.e. settlers in, New England has shown that they were overwhelmingly from the coastal parishes, underlining the part fishing played in New England's colonial development.[64] Some Devon merchants bought coastal land and established fishing 'stations' where fishing could easily be engaged in. Proximity to the fisheries was the prime consideration: the corporation of Exeter decided that it would consider the purchase of land only if it was convenient for fishing. Likewise, several Barnstaple merchants enquired into land for fishing and in 1623 the Dorset town of Dorchester established a fishing station at Cape Anne, named after Anne of Denmark, the wife of James I.[65]

The Plymouth merchant Robert Trelawny established the best-known of these fishing stations in 1630. He employed a company of up to 60 men from Devon and Cornwall at his plantation at Richmond Island in southern Maine, and hired a Plymouth man, John Winter, as the manager. He preferred that the fishermen served for three years. Most men returned to England at the end of their contracts, but others remained and established themselves as settlers.[66]

Conclusion

The distances which men travelled (500 miles at least to Scarborough, over 3,000 miles to Newfoundland, and even more to northern New England) reflect not only the need to secure supplies of fish, but also an ability to adapt to changing conditions and situations within the fishing industry. The industry was clearly inconstant: disruptions were commonplace, whether caused by political forces, as in the case of the Iceland fishery, or by natural conditions, such as the scarcities of pilchards in the 1580s and 1590s. Devon merchants and fishermen not only survived these changes but clearly were able to overcome them and actually prosper, possibly increasingly so at the beginning of the seventeenth century. This could not have been an easy accomplishment. It demanded a certain level of initiative and enterprise and the loss of many lives as the small boats, some of just 20 tons, navigated through unknown waters for what were often uncertain gains. It is difficult to judge which is more impressive, that these mariners established fisheries off uninhabited shores such as New England and Newfoundland, or that they had already successfully competed with native fishermen in Ireland, in the Channel, and in the North Sea. Clearly there was a marked degree of commercial shrewdness in identifying fishing resources and adeptness in exploiting them. The building of new fish markets at Plymouth in 1602 and Dartmouth in 1623 is a reflection not only of past prosperity, but also of the industry's buoyancy.[67] Ultimately, Dartmouth became so successful at the seasonal fishing that it was largely dependent upon it. The movement of these seamen to the fisheries and back again to Devon was an integral and essential part of the emigration and colonization process in Ireland, Newfoundland, and New England. But it was not an unusual activity. Devon fishermen had been on the move for many years, and seasonal migration was simply a commonplace activity for many residents of Devon's maritime communities.

17: Devon's Fisheries and Early-Stuart Northern New England

1 KR Andrews, NP Canny, and PEH Hair (eds.), *The Westward Enterprise, English Activities in Ireland, the Atlantic and America 1480–1650*, (Liverpool, 1978) and KR Andrews, *Trade, Plunder and Settlement, Maritime Enterprise and the Genesis of the British Empire, 1480–1630* (Cambridge, 1984). See also below, chapter 19. I would like to thank Professor Joyce Youings for her many comments made during the preparation of this paper.
2 Gillian Cell (ed.), *English Attempts at Colonisation, 1610–1638* (Hakluyt Society, 2nd series, CLX, 1982), 29.
3 Thomas Westcote, *A View of Devonshire in 1630* (Exeter, 1845), 378.
4 Joyce Youings, *Ralegh's Country, The South-West of England in the Reign of Queen Elizabeth I* (Raleigh, 1986), 29–30; DRO, Chanter 867, f.7.
5 DRO, Devon Quarter Sessions (hereafter DQS), Bundle Box 5b, Mich. 1635, f.20.
6 William J Blake, 'Hooker's Synopsis Chorographical of Devonshire' *DAT* 47 (1915), 348.
7 Tristram Risdon, *The Chorographical Description or Survey of the County of Devon* (1811), 8; Westcote, *View of Devonshire*, 378; DRO, 4366 Add. (Corsini Papers photocopies), 975/1.
8 Wallace Notestein, *Commons Debates 1621* (New Haven, 1935), 6:218, 357.
9 Gillian Cell, *English Enterprise in Newfoundland* (Toronto, 1969), 137.
10 RH Tawney & Eileen Power (eds.), *Tudor Economic Documents* (1951 edn), III, 245–6.
11 Blake, 'Hooker's Synopsis', 348.
12 DRO, Consistory Court (hereafter CC), 3C, 1.
13 BL, Harleian MSS, 6238, f.211.
14 DRO, Z19/18/9, 14–15.
15 DRO, Exeter City Archives, Book 57, fos 158–71; PRO, SP16/34/98–103, and below, Fig. 35.1.
16 Risdon, *Chorographical Description*, 34.
17 Risdon, *Chorographical Description*, 351–2.
18 Westcote, *View of Devonshire*, 67–8.
19 JF Chanter, *A History of the parishes of Lynton and Countisbury* (Exeter, 1907), 25–6, 187.
20 DRO, CC 93, CC 89, f.295. A meaze was a measure of herring.
21 DRO, CC 89, Box 98, f.185.
22 See above, chapter 6.
23 Risdon, *Chorographical Description*, 177; Westcote, *View of Devonshire*, 393; DRO, Chanter 861, fos 283r–285v.
24 Westcote, *View of Devonshire*, 444; Risdon, *Chorographical Description*, 145.
25 DRO, CC 6B/15; 48/13/2/3/2, fos 145–6; CC 20A/140.
26 PRO, SP16/522/130; AL Rowse, 'The dispute concerning the Plymouth pilchard fishery, 1584–91', *Economic History*, 7 (1932), 461–72.
27 DRO, CC 84, 29 May 1583.
28 DRO, CC 3C, Box 9, testimony of Alan Reach.
29 DRO, Chanter 854b, fos 288r–288v.
30 WDRO, Newton Ferrers Overseers of the Poor Account Book; DRO, Chanter 855, fos 494r–494v. See also below, chapter 18.
31 DRO, 4366 Add., 975/1, 1082/4, James Bagg to Philip Corsini (17 Sept. 1595), 1082/12, 1020.
32 BL, Hargrave MSS, 321, fos 103, 133–4; Miller Christy, 'Attempts toward

colonisation: The Council for New England and the Merchant Venturers of Bristol, 1621–1623', *AHR* IV (1898/99), 693; BL, Harleian MSS, fos 16–17, *CSP Ireland 1596–97*, 210/80.

33 DRO, 4366 Add., 1082/1, 19 October, 1587.

34 Miller Christy, 'Attempts toward colonisation', 693.

35 See above, p. 102; DRO, DQS, OB 1/1, f.317.

36 Aiden Clarke, 'The Irish economy, 1600–1660', in TW Moody, FX Martin, FJ Byrne, eds, *A New History of Ireland* (Oxford, 1976), III, 181; Michael MacCarthy-Morrogh, *The Munster Plantation: English Migration to southern Ireland, 1583–1641* (Oxford, 1986), 155–8, 223–4; Pamela Bradley, 'Sir William Hull of Exeter', *DCNQ* 35 pt.1, 1982, 41; AB Grosart, *Lismore Papers* (1886–8), I, 153, 170, 172; DRO, 48/13/2/3/2, fos 3, 52–3; DRO, CC 3C Box 9.

37 WSL, Moger will abstracts, 462.

38 DRO, DD 67829. Almost certainly this was Salcombe Regis near Sidmouth rather than Salcombe in the parish of Malborough, as the former is so near to Sidmouth.

39 PRO, SP14/157/24.

40 DRO, Chanter 854b, fos 288r–288v; Chanter 856, fos 376–7; FE Haliday, *Richard Carew of Antony* (1953), 120 for more on buckhorn; DRO, Chanter 855b, fos 69v–69r.

41 DRO, Chanter 855, fos 520r–522r.

42 PRO, SP12/71/75.

43 Oppenheim, 27, 35. See also above, p. 83 and EM Carus Wilson, 'The Iceland Trade', in E Power and MM Postan (eds), *Studies in English Trade in the Fifteenth Century* (1933), 168–9, 174.

44 DB Quinn (ed.), *The Voyages and Colonising Enterprises of Sir Humphrey Gilbert* (Hakluyt Soc., 2nd series, LXXXIII, 1938).

45 John J Beckerlegge, 'Plymouth muniments and Newfoundland', *Transactions of the Plymouth Institution*, XVIII (1936–7), 3.

46 DRO, Chanter 855b, fos 13r–14v, Chanter 855a, fos 478v–479r.

47 DRO, Chanter 864, f.117v, CC 3C, Box 9, CC 19, 77.

48 Oppenheim, 35, 37.

49 For views on the importance of the Newfoundland fishery to the Devon ports see Cell, *English Enterprise*, 101, passim; WB Stephens, 'The Westcountry Ports and the struggle for the Newfoundland fisheries in the Seventeenth Century', *DAT* 88 (1956), 90–101; and below, chapter 22.

50 DRO, SM 1989.

51 See above, chapter 14.

52 P Russell, 'The Building of the New Quay, 1584–1640', *DAT* 82 (1950), 281–90.

53 DRO, DD 61616.

54 DB Quinn & A Quinn (eds), *The English New England Voyages, 1602–1608* (Hakluyt Soc., 2nd series, CLXI, 1983), 1–12.

55 Charles Andrews, *The Colonial Period of American History* (New Haven, 1934) I, 80–83.

56 Quinn, *English New England Voyages*, 1–12, 171, 216, 301, 335; DRO, Exeter Town Customs Roll 1608–1610, overseas.

57 Charles Deane (ed.), 'Records of the Council for New England', *American Antiquarian Society Procs* (1867), 59, 75.

58 Richard Preston, *A Life of Sir Ferdinando Gorges* (Toronto, 1953), 187.

59 Andrews, *The Colonial Period*, I, 320–43, 400–29.

60 CW Tuttle, *Captain Francis Champernowne* (Boston, 1889), 81.

61 RE Moody, *The Letters of Thomas Gorges* (Portland, Maine, 1978).

62 CE Champernowne, *The Champernowne Family* (1954, typed Ms, WSL), 256–64; Tuttle, *Captain Francis Champernowne*, 81. He also named one large tract of land 'Dartington', after the family home of that name, and another tract 'Godmeracke', after a dwelling at the mouth of the River Dart.

63 Douglass R MacManis, *Colonial New England: A Historical Geography* (London & New York, 1975), 65.

64 Richard Brown, 'Devonians and New England settlement before 1650' *DAT* 95 (1963), 221.

65 Preston, *A life of Sir Ferdinando Gorges*, 249–50, 229; Frances Rose-Troup, *John White, the Patriarch of Dorchester and the Founder of Massachusetts* (London and New York, 1930), 49–56.

66 See also below, chapter 18.

67 WDRO, Widey Court Book, f.140; DRO, DD 62109.

18 *Richmond Island: an Early-Stuart Devon fishing station in the Gulf of Maine*

TODD GRAY

ENGLISH FISHERMEN, INCLUDING MANY from Devon, seized upon the many small islands in the Gulf of Maine as the location for their seasonal land bases. Such islands as Monhegan, Damariscove (Fig. 18.1), and the Isles of Shoals, including Appledore, a small rocky island which was almost certainly named by men from north Devon, were popular spots for the fishing stations. Another of these was Richmond Island (Fig. 18.2), situated a few miles to the south of Portland, Maine. It is particularly notable on account of the survival of the Trelawny Papers, a collection of early Stuart financial accounts and letters from John Winter, a Plymouth man and manager of the station, to Robert Trelawny, his employer, who was a Plymouth merchant, ship owner, and MP.[1]

Together with one Moses Goodyear, another Plymouth merchant, and other associates, Trelawny obtained a land grant in 1631 and established a prosperous 'plantation' on Richmond Island which lasted until his death in 1643/4.[2] John Winter, too, had been resident in Plymouth: in 1619 he was listed as a Plymouth mariner of 53 years, and two years later he appears as a ratepayer in Loo Street Ward.[3] He was described as a 'grave and discreet man'.[4] He claimed to have been fishing in Maine as early as 1627, and the Plymouth port book for that year records him as master of the *Consent* of Plymouth, 100 tons, which arrived on 10 August with train oil and beaver skins.[5] The following year, when the French and Spanish markets were closed owing to war, he served as the *Consent*'s captain on a privateering journey financed by John Jope, a Plymouth merchant, who also had a land grant in northern New England.[6] It may have been Jope who introduced Winter to Trelawny, who was also involved in privateering. It was in 1633 that Winter was first employed at the Island. He brought over his wife and daughter in 1636 and remained there until his death.[7]

Many of the 60 or so men whom Trelawny employed came from the parishes on or near the river Yealm, east of Plymouth, an area with which John Winter had ties, his wife Joan (Bauden) coming from Holbeton. Andrew Algar of Yealmpton served on the island from 1635 to 1639, and there were other members of the family, a brother Arthur and Thomas and Tristram Algar from Newton Ferrers, next door.[8] Trelawny also employed men from Plymouth, Millbrook, and Saltash, as well as a great many others for whom no parish origin is known. Many were married and, while serving their three-year contracts at the island, arranged for Trelawny to provide their wives with a portion of their wages.

The brothers Charles and Philip Hatch from Newton Ferrers, both of them younger sons, fished for Winter at Richmond Island on three-year contracts while apprenticed to residents at home, Charles's master being Mr Clement Penwill, a fisherman. Charles was first employed by Trelawny in 1633 at the age of 20. He returned to Devon in 1638 to marry, then went back to the island accompanied by his brother but leaving his wife behind, having arranged for Trelawny to supply her not only with money but also with grain. In 1640 he wrote to Trelawny, requesting that she not be supplied with any further money because she had not written to him. Hatch earned £2 9s 9¾d in 1637, £7 12s 11½d in 1638, and £8 4s 7¾d in 1639. In 1639 he spent, at the station, £2 16s 4d on wine, 16s 1½d on aqua vitae (brandy), £2 6s 1½d on tobacco, and 3d on cider. In 1643 Clement Penwill and his son fished off Richmond Island aboard the *Margery*. Her master was Ambrose Bowden of Holbeton, who had been Winter's apprentice in Plymouth in 1627 and was now his brother-in-law. He, too, had been employed on the island and later hired many other men from the Yealm area. The Hatch brothers and Bowden all eventually settled in Maine.[9]

18.1 Damariscove Island, Maine. Archaeological work has revealed evidence of an early-seventeenth century fishing station in the bay in the foreground, in line with the copse. *(Basil Greenhill, 1989)*

18.2 Richmond Island, New England, from the mainland. *(Todd Gray, 1988)*

Trelawny employed two women at the island. Priscilla Bickford complained that she had to sleep on goatskins, and that Winter's wife beat her, but Mistress Winter claimed that Priscilla 'was so fat and soggy she can hardly do any work', and that she had to be locked in at night to stop her from running away. A second woman was drowned as a result of slipping into the sea while trying to retrieve her hat as she was bringing the cows across the sand bar.

A great variety of fish was caught at the island, to be salted and exported directly to the continent of Europe. Cod was the main catch, but there was also haddock, pollock, whiting, and bass. Pilchards were brought from Devon or Cornwall for use as bait. To his chief interest, fishing, Trelawny added attempts to trade with the native Americans, but although he obtained some beaver and otter skins, he had little success. Winter was instructed to grow crops and to raise cattle, goats, and pigs, at which he was more successful, in spite of the depredations of wolves and poachers. Trelawny's other interest was in timber. He exported clapboard and pipe (cask) staves, which were destined for the Atlantic Islands, Spain, or England, and he was also interested in shipbuilding. He employed a number of house and ships' carpenters, including Plymouth shipwright Sampson Jope, who were continuously involved in building ships at the island. The *Richmond* was built in 1636, and two years later Arthur Gill, from Cattedown in Plymouth, constructed another vessel to Trelawny's specifications. The ship was built 'betwixt 49 and 50ft by the keel, 18½ft to the beam . . . 2 decks with a forecastle and a quarterdeck, 9ft in [the] hold and 4½ft betwixt the decks'.[10] In 1643 Trelawny's ships the *Richmond*, the *Little Richmond* and the *Tiger* were seized by Parliament off Mount's Bay in Cornwall.[11]

Following the deaths of both Trelawny and Winter, but also because of the disruption caused by the Civil War, the island's management was taken over by Winter's son-in-law. The link with Devon weakened as the region became increasingly more independent, and the county never regained the influence it formerly had in the New England fisheries. But during the first half of the seventeenth century, with the great number of its fishermen crossing the Atlantic every year, Richmond Island was a Devon outpost in the heart of the New World.

18: Richmond Island: an Early-Stuart Devon fishing station in the Gulf of Maine

1 James Phinney Baxter, *The Trelawny Papers* (Portland, Maine, 1884), a reasonably reliable edition of the collection which is now in the custody of the Maine Historical Society in Portland. My thanks are due to Mr Stephen Seames for help with these papers.
2 Baxter, *Trelawny Papers*. xxv. Trelawny, while serving as an MP, was arrested at the start of the Civil War and died in prison at Winchester House in London between 24 August 1643 and 19 November 1644.
3 Pepys Library, Cambridge, PL 2122; WDRO, W138, 68. In 1626, however, he was listed as a Plymouth mariner, aged 36: SP16/34/98.
4 Baxter, *Trelawny Papers*, xx.
5 PRO, E190/1031/5,6. The Port Books do not record imported fish.
6 PRO, HCA25/6; E190/1033/5.
7 Baxter, *Trelawny Papers*, xxvii.
8 Baxter, *Trelawny Papers*, 250. Baxter states that Andrew and Arthur came from Dunster in Somerset, but he was apparently unaware of the hamlet of Dunstone on the edge of the parish of Newton Ferrers.
9 Baxter, *Trelawny Papers*, 41, 140, 182, 186, 194, 220–1, 280–1, 293, 300, 250, 360–1. Charles and Philip Hatch were baptised on 5 September 1613 and 28 December 1616, respectively: WDRO, Newton Ferrers Parish Register.
10 Baxter, *Trelawny Papers*, 165–9.
11 PRO, SP16/497/43.

19 *Emigration from Devon in the Seventeenth Century*

Alison Grant

During the seventeenth century thousands of people from Devon left their homes, some to settle in Ireland, others to undertake long, dangerous voyages and face hardship and privation in unknown lands. Some went willingly, from religious convictions, or in the hope of gain. Others were driven by adversity or necessity to seek a change of circumstance. Many of these, and others who thought they were going of their own free will, were manipulated, not to say bought, by those who could make money from shipping them to grow the cash crops necessary for more profit. Colonization was supported by merchants, and increasingly backed by governments as an integral part of English trade in the seventeenth century, but for most of the ordinary folk who left Devon's towns and villages in the hope of a brave new world, a hard voyage was usually the prelude to an even harsher reality.

Early Emigration

Ireland

In the seventeenth century the scale of emigration to Ireland increased as rebellions and reprisals depopulated huge tracts of land. London interests did not take up all options to 'plant' protestant settlers, so the field was open for provincial entrepreneurs, many of whom came from Devon. Gentlemen saw the chance of providing land for their heirs, following the recent example of Sir Walter Raleigh, who had 'sought a princely patrimony in Ireland', and Sir Richard Grenville, who had settled a younger son on his estates in Munster. Although these early plantations collapsed in the insurrection of 1598, the Elizabethan tradition of planting Irish lands was continued by two Devon knights, Arthur Chichester, who became Lord Deputy of Ireland in 1605, and Thomas Ridgeway. Such men usually looked to their own localities for settlers to work these estates, for ships to transport them, and for the goods needed for new settlements. Ridgeway was from Torbay but, although emigrants may well have embarked from south Devon, the long and often dangerous voyage round Land's End prevented regular contacts developing. Chichester, who acquired over 4,000 acres in Ulster, was from north Devon, which was better placed, and by 1615 north Devon ships were making regular voyages to Londonderry, Coleraine, and Carrickfergus with mixed cargoes, including a good deal of earthenware. Archaeologists frequently find sherds of seventeenth-century north Devon pottery in Ulster, and clay floor-tiles made in north Devon and stamped 'CARICFARGUS 1615' are likely to have been made for Sir Arthur's mansion at Carrickfergus, built at this time. Thus Irish settlement could stimulate shipping, trade, and industry, and, as contacts developed, further emigration.[1]

Virginia

In the early days of colonization the name Virginia was often used for all English settlements in North America, but here it will be used for the lands south of latitude 38° N which were granted to the Virginia Company of London in 1606. Writers of pamphlets promoting emigration described it in glowing terms. According to a tract of 1609, it had

> air and climate most sweet and wholesome, much warmer than England . . . rosin, turpentine, pitch and tar; sassafras, mulberry trees, and silkworms; many skins and rich furs; many sweet woods and dyers' woods and other costly dyes; plenty of sturgeon; timber for shipping – mast, plank, and deal; soap ashes; caviar; and what else we know not yet because our days are young . . .[2]

Nothing was said of hard winters, or of the 'starving time' and the low fevers already experienced by the first settlers. When the natives, portrayed as 'generally very loving and gentle', massacred one-third of the population of the colony in a surprise attack in 1622, the 347 victims included some of the earliest emigrants from Devon. The Virginia Company, a joint-stock venture, set out to attract capital not only from London, but from small investors among provincial gentry and merchants. Having failed to raise as much as it needed, the Company tried lotteries, and was grateful for Exeter's 'bountiful return' of £97 in 1615. Agents were soon touring the provinces offering large prizes, and donations to local charities. There was considerable participation in Devon, for 'upon the shutting up of the lottery for Virginia', Totnes charities received £35, Tiverton's £30, Great Torrington's £10, and similar donations were probably made to other towns. Lotteries, which aroused great excitement among ordinary people as well as investors, were suspended in 1621, as 'demoralizing' to trade and industry, but they had promoted interest in emigration, and made Virginia a household word.[3]

Emigrant ships from London often called at Plymouth, and no doubt picked up a few local passengers, but the *Swan* of Barnstaple, 100 tons, was the first Devon ship to carry emigrants for the Virginia Company. John Delbridge, the merchant who despatched her in 1620, had been MP for Barnstaple in 1610 and 1614, and was probably influenced by the enthusiasm for colonial ventures amongst his fellow members, especially Sir Edwin Sandys, one of the directors of the Company, who had family connections with Devon. Although London finance dominated the Company, many great merchants did not wish to set up plantations or send out emigrants, and this left room for provincial gentry and merchants. After 1612, the year when Delbridge joined the Company, tobacco transformed the economy of the colony, and in 1616 each purchaser of a £12 10s share was allotted 50 acres of land. This was soon increased to 100 acres, with an extra 50 for every emigrant transported to work the shareholder's estate. In 1619 Delbridge obtained a patent for a 'particular plantation', and permission to transport 200 men. A few months later the *Swan* sailed with 71 'choice men . . . out of Devonshire . . . brought up to Husbandry'. All survived the voyage, and the Company resolved that 'some other ships might be sent out of Barnstaple by the help of Mr Delbridge'. In 1621 he became a member of His Majesty's Council for Virginia, a unique achievement for an outport trader.[4]

Bermuda

In 1609 Sir George Somers's flagship, *Sea Venture*, was separated in a tempest from a fleet sailing for Virginia, and driven aground on Bermuda. The Virginia Company claimed the island, but in 1612 sold its rights to the Somers Islands Company, which allocated land to shareholders on condition they sent out settlers. In 1619 John Delbridge, one of the original members, undertook to find 30 or 40 hardworking Devon emigrants for Sir Edwin Sandys and other prominent men in the company, and to arrange their passages at £5 a head on the Barnstaple ship he was sending with his own settlers. In 1620 he sent another ship 'freighted mainly with passengers', most of them 'well-chosen labouring boys for apprentices'. In 1621 another 'small ship' of Barnstaple 'came into the town's harbour and was very well conditioned . . .'. She brought 'some few more inhabitants, as likewise single women . . . for wives, and young boys for apprentices'. In spite of Delbridge's services to the Company, the promoters tried to cut him out when tobacco began to bring in profits, saying all trade must be conducted through London. When that failed they demanded a payment of £2 for every passenger he landed, then in 1627 forbade him to send any ship without their express permission. Delbridge protested that, as he felt responsible for the

> poor planters there, where there is as I think at least a hundred poor souls that I have sent thither . . . I will send to them and the rest until by authority I be restrained, though I be not suffered to bring home one pound of tobacco.

He continued to despatch small vessels to Bermuda, and the settlers took his side, maintaining that he

> supplied at reasonable rates necessaries of which there was great dearth, and dealt fairly with the colonists who ventured a few pounds of tobacco with him.

Delbridge, who became known as 'the free trader' on both sides of the Atlantic, thus played a large part in establishing early settlement in Bermuda, and ensuring the continued existence of the colony.[5]

The West Indies

English settlement of West Indian islands was mainly financed by London interests, but Devon's position meant that its ports and merchants were involved in shipping and providing emigrants. In 1631, a few years after the settlement of St Christopher, one of the Leeward Islands, the island's proprietor, the Earl of Carlisle, commissioned Robert Trelawny, owner of the Plymouth ship *Robert Bonaventure*, of 150 tons: 'to lade and transport victuals, beer and other provisions to serve for 50 men, besides the ship's company for a whole year,' as 'planters to the Island called St Christopher's or any of the other Caribe Islands within his Lordship's plantations'. The *Robert Bonaventure* made regular voyages to St Christopher in the years that followed, probably taking emigrants each time, for a record survives of 35 people, nine from Devon, and most of the rest from Cornwall, who took the oath of allegiance in Plymouth before going aboard this vessel in 1634. Another 30 were sent out at the same time in the *Margaret* of Plymouth, 60 tons. In 1635 the two ships again sailed to the island, but on the return voyage the *Robert Bonaventure* was seized by pirates. A west-country bridgehead had, however, been established in St Christopher, and Devon merchants increased their import of tobacco. For example, three Plymouth vessels, including the *Margaret*, brought home cargoes in 1638. At least the same number probably sailed each year with settlers out and tobacco home; the *Margaret* was still in the St Christopher trade in 1643. North Devon ships, which occasionally brought in tobacco from St Christopher, could also have taken out emigrants, who, by this time, were becoming an integral part of the economy of transatlantic voyages.[6]

In February 1634 there were 25 Devonians listed among the 31 'persons bound for St Christopher' who took the oath of allegiance at Dartmouth. They could have emigrated in a Dartmouth ship in company with the *Robert Bonaventure* and the *Margaret*, which sailed at the same time, or might have transferred to those or other ships at Plymouth. Lists of early emigrants from Devon are extremely rare, and this one, which gives each emigrant's place of origin, occupation, and approximate age, is worth detailed examination.[7]

William Haukins of Exeter, glover, aged 25
James Courtney of Exeter, blacksmith, aged 23
Richard Skose of Newton Abbot, seafaring man, aged 37
Francis Boyce of London, buttonhole maker, aged 25
William Carkille of Plymouth, sailmaker, aged 21
William Gurge of Exeter, shoemaker, aged 20
Alice Whitmore of Honiton, spinster, aged 25
Philipp[a] Stephens of Ashburton, spinster, aged 28
Sara Coose of Exeter, spinster, aged 18
Judith Stevens of Exeter, spinster, aged 19
Margaret Harwood of Stoke Gabriel, spinster, aged 22
Edward Morris of Exeter, 'locker', aged 21
Thomas Bryant of Bampton, husbandman, aged 23
William May of 'Myniard', Somerset, seaman, aged 32
Hutinne Oweth of St Stephens, Cornwall, husbandman, aged 24
John Wills of Barnstaple, feltmaker, aged 35
Simon Weeks of Exeter, worsted weaver, aged 16
Thomas Germayne of Exeter, ostler, aged 30
John French of Waterford, Ireland, seaman, aged 26
William Hill of Great Torrington, husbandman, aged 28
John Hocksley of Stoke Canon, tailor, aged 28
James Rosman of London, husbandman, aged 21
Elizabeth Reed of Exeter, spinster, aged 19
Mary Harte of Lyme, spinster, aged 18
Mary Hoppine of Exminster, spinster, aged 20
Mary Harries of Stockleigh Pomeroy, aged 23
Elizabeth Quicke of Barnstaple, aged 18
Elizabeth Hill of Brixham, aged 24
Joan Short of Exeter, aged 20
Joan Laners [Lavers?] of Modbury, aged 19
Jane Gouldinge of St Thomas, Exeter, aged 16

In the absence of other lists, it is difficult to say whether these people were typical of emigrants from Devon. 'Honest painful labour men', sent by John Delbridge were more welcome in Bermuda than the paupers and prisoners sent from London, but there may have come a point when suitable workers were hard to find even in Devon. There are signs that towns and parishes helped some of their poor to emigrate. In 1633–4, for example, Barnstaple Corporation paid out 10s 4d for 'shoes for three poor boys sent to Virginia'. All the men listed above claimed to have a trade, and, to judge by their ages, some would have just finished apprenticeships, and these at least, even if poor, are unlikely to have been rogues or vagabonds. There were, however, few of the useful trades usually sought by emigration agents:

> Carpenters, Shipwrights, and Wheelwrights, Brickmakers, Bricklayers, Potters, some to clean lath and pate, and make Pipestaves, Joiners, Coopers, Sawyers, Smiths, Cutlers, Millers, Leatherdressers, Fishermen and Gardeners Etc., [and] able labouring men.

Able or not, the glover, tailor, feltmaker, and the rest on the Dartmouth list, like the 65 emigrants who sailed out of Plymouth at the same time, were probably all bound to husbandry.[8] Female emigrants, too, were often bound to fieldwork, or taken as 'maids for wives', but the girls listed above were not necessarily on the parish, on the streets, or even from poor backgrounds. Elizabeth Quicke, baptised in Barnstaple in July 1614, was the daughter of a goldsmith who had inherited a substantial business from his father, and probably the latter's house in one of the most prosperous streets of the town. The other emigrants are harder to track down. A James Courtney was baptised in 1609 in the parish of St Paul, Exeter, and there were Whitmores in Honiton, Harwoods in Stoke Gabriel, and Lavers in Modbury.[9] The majority of the other emigrants listed do not seem to have been baptised in the parishes named, but as it was not uncommon for people to move from their native parishes in the seventeenth century, this does not necessarily mean that emigrants were more itinerant than others. On the other hand, a move overseas may have been the last of several. Few, if any, of the emigrants listed would have possessed the means to make their individual ways to Dartmouth and maintain themselves there while waiting for a ship. They are therefore likely to have been among the thousands rounded up in this period by emigration agents on behalf of proprietors, ship owners, and other interested parties, for by this time there was much money to be made by shipping servants.

Emigrants soon discovered that work was hard and mortality high in the West Indies. Unless they signed new indentures, those who survived their time were usually replaced by others newly shipped. Very few got the hoped-for smallholding, for by 1640 something like 20,000 people were living on St Christopher and the neighbouring island of Nevis, the two together being scarcely bigger than the Isle of Wight. Nevis had been settled after a party from a Barnstaple ship on its way to Virginia landed on St Christopher. Anthony Hilton, a Durham man employed by Barnstaple merchants, returned to start a plantation but, finding problems with the natives, moved to Nevis in 1628. In the 1630s Sir Thomas Warner, the governor of these two islands, sent surplus settlers to plant other islands belonging to the Earl of Carlisle. Thus Devon people would have been among those who settled in Antigua and Montserrat, while others moved to Barbados, a fertile island where again settlers soon outstripped the land available and many lost the struggle for existence. Devonians were also among the unfortunate people recruited by Sir Nathaniel Rich, and John Pym who had been MP for Tavistock, to plant Old Providence (Santa Catalina). The venture was a failure from the start, and the island, which soon fell prey to raiders, was eventually taken by the Spaniards in 1641.[10]

The English Civil War

Many English ports suffered in the Civil War, and the Commonwealth's wars with the Netherlands and Spain caused losses and delays to shipping, yet colonial populations grew between 1640 and 1660. One reason was the number of 'extraordinary emigrations' of political refugees and captured rebels. Westcountrymen taken in Penruddock's Rising of 1655, for instance, were imprisoned at Exeter, then sent to Plymouth to be shipped to Barbados.[11] Irish rebels were also transported, and others fled, leaving land that the government was anxious to plant with loyal protestants.

Ireland

In 1641 Parliament, seeking money with which to put down the Irish rebellion, passed an act inviting adventurers to buy and eventually plant the land of dispossessed rebels. Many people from Devon subscribed. The 'adventure of the Town of Dartmouth for purchasing of rebels' lands in Ireland', for example, attracted 143 subscribers who paid a total of £2,668 7s 6d. The list was opened with £50 from a Mr William Cary, who later returned with £25 2s 6d 'by assignment from 20 persons', and then another £57 10s 'by assignment from 39 persons'. Some of the gentry still planned to set up family estates in Ireland, and as Cary's assignments were the smallest *per capita* contributions, they could have been for tenants attracted by an acre or two for themselves to move to Ireland to work on Cary's lands. Mistress Lucy Cary contributed another £26 10s, but the total Cary investment was not the largest, for Roger Matthew, one of Dartmouth's MPs, paid £300, and four other rich merchants ventured £100 each. There were many smaller payments; Roger Spark, shipwright, paid £12 10s for 13 Irish acres, and Clement Palmer, ropemaker, £25 for 26. Years of conflict delayed the allocation of land until 1653, when William Cary drew 220 acres for himself and the 59 others for whom he had paid. Some of the other Dartmouth adventurers were dead, but their heirs, like the survivors, drew shares in the Westmeath barony of Rathconrath. Some may have emigrated, but after the Restoration there was no noticeable increase in Dartmouth's trade with Dublin, the nearest port. If a group did go out, however, it would, as the historian of this venture has said, be 'interesting to know to what extent that barony remained a preserve of Dartmouth men, and whether they generally held on to what on average were quite small holdings.[12]

Some Devon investors in Irish lands already had experience of promoting emigration. The Plymouth merchant and MP Robert Trelawny, who owned a plantation in New England, probably intended to establish one nearer home when he subscribed £450, but he was dead by the time his 1,000 acres were allocated in Tipperary. John Delbridge had died in 1639, but his interest in emigration schemes was maintained by his daughter, Elizabeth Blake, his brother-in-law or nephew of the same name, John Hanmer, and his granddaughter's husband, the merchant Thomas Mathew, who subscribed £10, £26, and £150 respectively. They did not themselves emigrate to Ireland, and, like the Exeter merchants Samuel Clarke MP, Philip and Thomas Crossing, and Richard Sweet, who all subscribed £100 or more, were probably investing spare capital. A total of £15,000 was paid in from Exeter, but the 'phenomenon of small investment' there was partly due to people who, although they were listed under Exeter, came from elsewhere in Devon. Places with a strong maritime connection with Ireland showed much interest. Bideford's nonconformist lecturer, William Bartlett, put £10 into the scheme, perhaps inspiring others from that puritanical port to follow his example. Other Bideford men listed under Exeter included the merchants John Strange, Anthony Dennis, and Thomas Wadland, who invested £50, £40, and £30 respectively, and William Greening (£5) and George Luxon (£6), who were both master mariners. They, or their heirs, were eventually allotted land at Portnahinch, Queen's County, and John Boole and Abraham Johns, two more Bideford merchants who invested £10 each, drew 13 acres in County Limerick. All were already connected with Irish trade, an interest which appears to have been cause rather than effect of any settlement on these lands.[13]

In 1651, even before the land scheme was drawn, government agents were appointed at Exeter, Plymouth, Barnstaple, Bideford and Ilfracombe to recruit settlers for Ireland, and these ports were ordered to make sure that they were transported at reasonable rates, and to help hire vessels and treat with shipmasters. North Devon ports probably handled most of the emigration from Devon, for many people preferred not to voyage round Lands End, especially in wartime. Thomas Pitt, an intending emigrant for New Ross, wrote from Exeter in 1658 that he would embark from Barnstaple for the greater security of himself and his children. Emigration from Devon to Ireland continued after the Restoration, when some leading families established branches there. Samuel Rolle, for instance, emigrated to Castletown, King's County, to take up 1,666 Irish acres (equal to 2,699 English ones) for which his father had subscribed £1,000 to the land scheme. Before the family sold it for £10,000 in 1752, this estate was bringing in rents of £400 a year.[14]

Post-Restoration

After the Restoration the emigration of useful citizens was discouraged, for England was no longer regarded as over-populated, the argument being that a larger labour force would increase the country's wealth. In spite of this, and although emigration was checked from time to time by economic and political considerations, a considerable number of people still went overseas from Devon in the later seventeenth century.

The West Indies

In 1647 thousands of servants and smallholders in Barbados, St Christopher, and other West Indian islands died in a terrible plague, perhaps the same infection which had devastated Devon ports the previous year. These workers were mainly succeeded by African slaves, who, unlike time-expired white servants, did not have to be freed, and were thought more suitable for work on the sugar plantations which were replacing tobacco smallholdings after 1640. A small amount of emigration from Devon was, however, generated by merchants who invested capital in plantations and sent out people to run them. Justinian Peard of Plymouth was an absentee proprietor whose emigrant associate, Richard Evans, appears never to have paid him or his heirs a debt of £1,500 due from his Barbados plantation. Such problems made some owners go out themselves. John Paige, from Plymouth, was described in 1680 as 'of Barbados, merchant'. Other merchants sent trusted relatives to manage their plantations and trade. It could be a hard life; a younger John Delbridge, great-nephew of the Barnstaple merchant, 'died in the Barbados unmarried'.[15]

After 1670 island governments, alarmed at the low proportion of white settlers, made it compulsory for planters to have one white servant for a given number of blacks. Antigua added the inducement of 2,000lb of sugar for anyone bringing a good English, Scots, or Welsh servant, and Barbados guaranteed a minimum price, £12 10s, in 1682. Thus the trade in servants was revived; in 1685 William Croppin of Brixham, 'being a lusty young man about 26 year old and very desirous to go overseas', signed on to serve for three years in Antigua. He was one of a handful of young people from Devon recorded as sailing from London in the years 1682–92.[16] Although no such lists survive for Devon ports, all sent vessels to the islands for sugar, no doubt providing passages for many more emigrants and profits for those who shipped them.

Virginia and Maryland

Servants continued to form the majority of white emigrants to the colonies. In this period most were not shipped for particular plantations, but as a speculation on the part of Devon shipowners, merchants, agents, and master mariners, who competed to offer free passages to people who would sign indentures. These legally binding documents could be sold for £15–£30 in the colonies, ensuring a profit of 200 per cent or more on the cost of the passage, and making servants virtual slaves until their term expired. By the end of the century over half the vessels in Bideford's tobacco trade, for example, were taking out a few servants as a matter of course, some from Devon and others from Irish ports, where, when they called in for provisions, ships' captains could ship servants rounded up by unscrupulous agents. A dozen servants could add £100 or more to the profits of a voyage, so the trade continued well into the eighteenth century.[17]

Merchants and master mariners had another great inducement to ship people to the colonies in North America. Early emigrants to Virginia received a grant of land on completing their service, but after 1620 the land could be claimed on arrival. This 'headright' system was also adopted in Maryland and other colonies, as a way to recruit cheap labour. In practice poor emigrants got no land, for they had to assign their entitlement to whoever bore the cost of their passages, then bind themselves to work for several years as servants. In February 1667 John Best, newly arrived in Virginia, went to a court in Isle of Wight County to claim 50 acres each for himself, his wife Mary, son John, daughter Jane, and another man, Joseph Rudd. Humphrey Barnes, likewise, claimed 50 acres apiece for himself, his wife, and son, but these land grants were assigned at the same court to a man called William Cook. The people named had probably arrived on the 100-ton *Fellowship* of Barnstaple, aboard which Rudd had consigned goods when she sailed from her home port the previous November. In Virginia he was soon acting as agent for a Barnstaple merchant. The Bests can be traced in Barnstaple parish registers, and Barnes and Cook had also been baptised in Barnstaple. Cook was neither the ship's master nor apparently a merchant; he may have been acting on his own behalf or for Hugh Mathews, the man to whom he assigned 850 acres four months later. The emigrants probably made good. By 1705 William Best and John Barnes, who may well have been their descendants, were respectively renting 100 and 200 acres of land in Isle of Wight County.[18]

The headright system also encouraged independent emigrants. Younger sons of small gentry, and others with little hope of patrimony, were among land-hungry settlers who made their own way to Virginia. One such was Hugo Yeo, son of a Hartland landowner, who was in Virginia by 1649. He added to his original estate by transporting 13 persons in 1655, and another seven, including a cousin and other people from north Devon, in 1668. After his death without issue in 1680, his elder brother in England made over the 1,000-acre estate on the eastern shore of Chesapeake Bay to a younger brother, Justinian, who, after living there for a time, leased it to his sister, Deborah, and her husband, William Cleverdon. Families like this, and groups of friends, neighbours, and co-religionists, made an important contribution to emigration by drawing others to join them overseas. Many maintained links with home, which stimulated trade, shipping and shipbuilding, production, and employment on both sides of the ocean. The Smith family of Bideford set up one of their members, Joseph, on a plantation in Virginia. There he grew tobacco for his brother Benjamin, a ship's master, to carry home for another brother, John, a Bideford merchant, to sell. Their father, Thomas, owned ships like the *Virginia Dove*, 100 tons, built cheaply in the colonies. She was soon carrying servants out to Virginia – 13, for instance, in 1702. The family may have sent out shipwrights to the Potomac, where she was built in 1699, or to the Chester River in Maryland, where they also had ships built. A further link in this family chain of trade and emigration was provided by another brother, James, who, living near Waterford, was in a good position to provision outgoing ships and drum up Irish servants.[19]

Ireland

Although servants were shipped out of Ireland, skilled workers were being enticed to go there. Rent-free houses and other inducements attracted a number of cloth workers from Exeter and rural districts nearby, but in 1675 emigrant weavers' looms awaiting shipment were destroyed in the king's warehouse at Topsham by fellow-workers, roused by their employers' prophecies of imminent ruin if Irish manufactures were allowed to compete with theirs. In 1698 120 'persons lately removed to Ireland from the serge manufacture of the city and neighbourhood' were listed by Exeter merchants and manufacturers, when, supported by Tiverton, Barnstaple, and other Devon towns, they petitioned parliament that the 'woollen manufactures of Ireland should not prejudice those of England'. They were successful, and restrictions subsequently placed on Irish cloth manufacture stopped the emigration of skilled workers.[20]

Huguenots

Many Huguenot refugees, having come initially to Devon, made their way to Ireland, some staying there after fighting in William III's forces. Some went farther, for in this period, when there was little encouragement for English people to emigrate, Huguenots were among those who could be 'spared' to settle new colonies, like Carolina, with which the great Devonian George Monck, Duke of Albemarle, was associated. In May 1687 the ship *King David*, belonging to David Delacombe, a Huguenot merchant who had settled at Stonehouse, returned to Plymouth laden with 57,000lb of tobacco from Virginia. She had not gone there direct, but had sailed to Carolina, almost certainly with emigrants, for the small amount of cargo on board was more suitable for settlers' use than for profitable sale. Delacombe, who must have made a large profit on the tobacco, may have shipped his fellow Huguenots free or at cost, and Huguenot charities paid for others. In 1687, for example, John Warren of Plymouth was reimbursed for shipping 'several persons that went to Carolina'. These emigrants, therefore, would not have had to surrender headrights or indentures in exchange for passages, and probably gained through leaving Devon. They had little or nothing to lose.[21]

Monmouth Rebels

After the Monmouth rebellion, prisoners convicted by Judge Jeffreys at Exeter and elsewhere were granted to contractors and royal favourites, who made a profit from transporting them. Although they were not actually shipped from the county's ports, many Devon men were among these unwilling emigrants, who were sold into virtual slavery on arrival in the West Indies. About seven months after his arrival in Barbados, one of them, Thomas Franklin, a yeoman from Luppitt, east Devon, wrote to his wife that he was well, although about 60 of the men transported had died. He gave no details of his life in the island, and complained only that he had received no letters from home, although:

> Peter Bagwell and John Whicker have had a letter each of them, John from his father, and Peter from Sarah Thompson . . . and . . . I did understand from Peter Bagwell's letter that there was some hope of deliverance . . .

Franklin was referring to efforts being made to secure pardons for the rebels and bring them home, and begged his wife to do her utmost to enable him to enjoy again the presence of his 'wife and children, friends and relations in poor old England'.[22] It is doubtful whether Franklin got his wish, for although the rebels were pardoned early in the next reign, employers would not free them before their time expired, and few if any could then find transport home. Franklin's friends, Peter Bagwell and John Whicker, both from Colyton, did not wait for a pardon, however, but made a daring escape in a small boat with a few others. They survived storms, shipwreck, semi-starvation, malaria, attacks by privateers, capture by Spanish pirates, and six months slavery in Cuba. Eventually, the arrival of the Duke of Albemarle in Jamaica made the Spaniards release their English prisoners, who arrived home to a heroes' welcome in the summer of 1688. Whicker's own account of their adventures was published in 1689, and in the same year, at Seaton, Peter Bagwell married Sarah Thompson, who had written to him in his exile.[23]

Conditions on Board Ship

Most emigrants suffered discomfort, if not actual hardship, on board ship, but conditions for convicts and political prisoners could be appalling. On one of the vessels carrying Monmouth rebels, 99 men were shut

> under deck in a very small room, where we could not lay ourselves down without lying one upon another . . . we were not suffered to go above deck for air or easement, but a vessel was set in the midst to receive the excrement, by which means the ship was soon infected with grievous and contagious diseases, as the smallpox, fever, calenture, and the plague, with frightful blotches. Of each of these diseases several died, and we lost of our company 22 men. This was the straitest prison that ever I was in, full of crying and dying.[24]

There was no need to inflict such restrictions on free emigrants, but their quarters were often cramped and there was always the risk of infection. In 1620, on a voyage from London to Bermuda, 20 or 30 emigrants died of an infection attributed to 'ten persons . . . taken out of Newgate'.[25] Conditions were usually better for Devon emigrants. John Delbridge chose his with care, and provisioned his ships well. In 1627 he lost three passengers, but a letter he wrote shortly afterwards reveals his previous good record:

> I have found it by experience that having sent divers times small ships both to Virginia and Bermuda, and that full of people, I never lost man woman or child going or coming before this last voyage.[26]

Most of Delbridge's ships were 30–40 tons, so the *Pelican* of Barnstaple, described by him as 80 tons but sometimes listed as 100, was large by comparison. It is possible to discover a little about conditions on board by comparing her with Robert Trelawny of Plymouth's 100-ton *Richmond*, which was 50ft by the keel, 18½ in the beam, and had 4½ feet between her two decks. Vessels of this size could carry 60–70 passengers, most of them in the ''tween decks', in which adults could not stand upright, yet in a letter to the London associates for whom he had agreed to ship emigrants to Bermuda on board the *Pelican*, Delbridge described her as 'a ship most fit for passage of people'. He also intended to put four heifers and a bull on board, and extra provisions for settlers after arrival. He asked his correspondents to:

> send each of you a man or two or more to see that such men and boys as shall be appointed for each of you from hence may be provided with apparel and other things necessary. I thought it also not impertinent to advise you to be at the charges that every man and boy may have some quantity of meal and bread to land with them for fear of wanting corn. All which or any other provisions whatsoever is here to be had as good and cheap as in London.[27]

Provisioning local emigrant ships probably brought some modest profit to ports like Barnstaple in this period. For Plymouth, where many London ships called, it became an important business.

Emigrants and mariners alike lacked fresh food on long voyages, but Delbridge at least put plenty of other stores on board. When one of his ships put back to Barnstaple without landing her emigrants, plenty of bread, beef, beer, butter, and cheese remained, although the state of these provisions after more than seven months at sea was not recorded.[28] Some emigrants, though, were short of food. A young Huguenot, John Fontaine, who paid for his own passage and those of four servants on the *Virginia Dove* of Bideford early in the eighteenth century, described his Christmas fare:

> . . . pease as hard as shot for breakfast. Two fowls killed by the bad weather for dinner and stirabout for supper.

Seven weeks after setting out for Virginia, he wrote in his journal:

> Everybody was put upon allowance of a bottle water for 24 hours and a biscuit. The servants and people suffered. This saved the salt beef.

The *Dove* was another six weeks at sea and, although some fish were caught, there were probably other days on short commons.[29]

The *Dove*, which had earlier been forced to return to Bideford after a storm, took about a month longer than usual to reach Virginia after she set out again. By this time most vessels used the direct northern route, but in earlier years, when ocean navigation presented problems, many ships went south via Portugal, the Canary Islands, and the West Indies, which provided more landmarks. Thus, in 1623, a Barnstaple ship for Virginia was recorded as 'passing by St Christopher as they knew no other way'. On this long southern route emigrants often suffered from tropical heat and delays caused by unpredictable winds, but the northern route was subject to storms, especially in winter. A passenger in a Bideford vessel homeward-bound from New England in November 1639 saw, after a severe storm, 'many dead bodies of men and women floating by us'. The presence of women's bodies as well as men's indicates the loss of an emigrant ship.[30] Seventy-five years later, John Fontaine and his fellow-emigrants in the *Dove* narrowly escaped the same fate:

> . . . the wind blew so terribly in the rigging that it clapped one side of the ship under water to that degree that the sea water from the steerage door came in in such abundance that had it continued long it would have filled the ship. The sailors was for cutting away the main mast, but two went up and cut away the main top mast, then the ship righted . . . the wind blowing most dreadfully and the night dark as it could be, the wind drove the water out of the sea, and the foam and water was mixed together 7 feet above the deck, so that the air seemed to be all on fire. The sea was a continual flame and foamed upon our deck ready to tear us to pieces. One wave came on board which tore away our bowsprit close to the foot of the foremast and the shock was so terrible that we thought the ship must stove in pieces. What a terrible cry the people gave expecting to go down any minute . . .[31]

Fontaine's account of the storm was interspersed with long and heartfelt prayers, and when the ship eventually arrived he wrote thankfully: 'God was pleased to preserve us as at other times'.[32] Then, like the thousands of other emigrants from Devon in this period, he set off to face the unknown.

19: Emigration from Devon in the Seventeenth Century

1 AL Rowse, *Sir Richard Grenville of the Revenge* (1937), 267–70; P Robinson, *The Plantation of Ulster* (Dublin, 1984), 72; PRO, Exchequer, King's Remembrancer Port Books, E190/942/13; A Grant, *North Devon Pottery: The Seventeenth Century* (Exeter, 1983), 101.

2 Robert Johnson, 'Nova Britannia. Offering Most Excellent Fruits by Planting in Virginia' (1609), in LB Wright and EW Fowler, eds, *English Colonization of North America: Documents of Modern History* (1968), 29. For New England see above, chapter 18.

3 WM Billings, JE Selby, and TW Tate, *Colonial Virginia: A History* (New York, 1986), 44; *Historical Manuscripts Commission* (hereafter *HMC*), 73, *Report on the Records of the City of Exeter* (1916), 99; C Andrews, *The Colonial Period of American History* I (New Haven, 1934), 137–8; *The Report of the Commissioners concerning Charities: County of Devon* (Exeter, 1828), II, 45, 202; W Harding, *The History of Tiverton in the County of Devon* (1847), II, 269; JJ Alexander and WR Hooper, *The History of Great Torrington in the County of Devon* (Sutton, 1948), 73.

4 WR Scott, *The Constitution and Finance of English, Scottish and Irish Joint-Stock Companies to 1720* (Cambridge, 1912) II, 246–85 *passim*; SM Kingsbury, ed., *The Records of the Virginia Company of London* (Washington DC, 1906–1935), I, 259, 351, 409–10, 473; III, 309; IV, 157 and A Grant, 'John Delbridge, Barnstaple Merchant, 1564–1639' in S Fisher (ed.), *Innovation in Shipping and Trade*, Exeter Maritime Studies, 6 (1989), 99–100.

5 AJ Wingood, '*Sea Venture*. An Interim Report on an Early Seventeenth Century Shipwreck lost in 1609', *The International Journal of Nautical Archaeology and Underwater Exploration*, 11, 4 (1982), 333; *HMC*, Duke of Manchester's MSS., J Delbridge to Sir E Sandys, 243. JH Lefroy, ed., *Memorials of the Bermudas or Somers Islands, 1515–1685* (1882) I, 445–9 and A Grant, 'Bermuda Adventurer: John Delbridge of Barnstaple, 1564–1639', *Bermuda Journal of Archaeology and Maritime History*, 3 (1991), 3–6, 11–12.

6 *Acts of the Privy Council, Colonial Series* (hereafter *APC Col.*) 1613–80, VI, 162. AP Newton, 'The Great Emigration 1618–48', *Cambridge History of the British*

Empire (hereafter *CHBE*), I, 143–6; JC Hotten, *The Original Lists of . . . Emigrants . . . to the American Plantations 1600–1700* (1874), 151–4; *Calendar of State Papers Domestic* (hereafter *CSPD*) *1631–3*, 251; PRO, E190/1035/10, E190/1036/18.

7 From Hotten, *Original Lists*, 151–2. Spelling, except for surnames, has been modernised.

8 *HMC*, Duke of Manchester's MSS., 243; NDRO, B1, 3972, 228/2; *HMC Reports* 73, 204.

9 JF Chanter, 'The Barnstaple Goldsmiths' Guild', *DAT*, 49 (1917), 179–80; DRO, Registers of parishes named.

10 AP Newton, 'Great Emigration', *CHBE* I, 172–4; VT Harlow, ed., *Colonising Expeditions to the West Indies and Guiana, 1623–7*, Hakluyt Society, 2nd Ser. LVI (1924), 4. CM Andrews, *The Colonial Period of American History: The Settlements* (New Haven, 1934), I, 497.

11 WW Ravenhill, *Records of the Rising in the West, AD 1655* (Devizes, 1875), 154.

12 DRO, Dartmouth Corporation Documents, DD 68452, 62700A, 62712; KS Bottigheimer, *English Money and Irish Land* (Oxford, 1971), 158.

13 Bottigheimer, *English Money*, 65–6, 175–213.

14 *CSPD 1651*, 120; *CSPD 1658–9*, 406; DRO, Rolle manuscripts, 96M, Box 9, 1C.

15 WSL, Wills transcribed by Olive Moger, Peard family; DRO, Lease of 1680, 56/8/7/4; JJ Howard, ed., *Miscellanea Genealogica and Heraldica* 3rd series, I (1896), 200.

16 AE Smith, *Colonists in Bondage* (Chapel Hill, 1947), 31; M Ghirelli, *A List of Emigrants from England to America, 1682–92* (Baltimore, Md., 1968), 20.

17 Smith, *Colonists in Bondage*, 15; PRO, Colonial Office Records, CO5/1441, *fos.* 195, 181.

18 JB Brodie, *Isle of Wight County, Virginia* (Baltimore, Md., 1973), 449, 559; PRO, E190/954/9; TJ Wertenbaker, *The Planters of Colonial Virginia* (Princeton, 1922), Appendix.

19 NM Nugent, *Cavaliers and Pioneers. Abstracts of Virginia Land Patents and Grants*, II (Richmond, Va., 1977), 158, 204; RT Whitelaw, *Virginia's Eastern Shore: A History of Northampton and Accomack Counties* (Richmond, Va., 1951), 720–1; Grant, *North Devon Pottery*, 105, 116, 119.

20 WG Hoskins, *Industry, Trade and People in Exeter, 1688–1800* (Manchester, 1935), 33–5; Joyce Youings, *Tuckers Hall Exeter* (Exeter 1968), 103–5.

21 A Grant and R Gwynn, 'The Huguenots of Devon', *DAT*, 117 (1985), 172–3.

22 DRO, Letter from Barbados, 146B Add/E1.

23 CH Firth, *Stuart Tracts* (1903), 468–76; W MacDonald Wigfield, *The Monmouth Rebellion, a Social History* (Bradford on Avon, 1980), 111; DRO, Seaton and Beer marriage register. See also below, chapter 20.

24 John Coad, *A Memorandum of the Wonderful Providences of God to a poor unworthy creature during the time of the Monmouth Rebellion* (1849), cited in Wigfield, *Monmouth Rebellion*, 100.

25 JH Lefroy (ed.), *History of the Bermudas* (1882), 188.

26 Lefroy, *Memorials of the Bermudas* I, 446.

27 *HMC*, Duke of Manchester's MSS., 243; PRO E190/943/9; JP Baxter, *The Trelawny Papers* (Portland Me., 1884), 165.

28 Lefroy, *Memorials of the Bermudas* I, 449.

29 EP Alexander, ed., *The Journal of John Fontaine* (Williamsburg, 1972), 49, 75.

30 Harlow, *Colonising Expeditions*, 4; AP Middleton, *Tobacco Coast. A Maritime History of Chesapeake Bay in the Colonial Era* (Newport News, 1953), 5–7; J Josselyn, *A Relation of Two Voyages to New England* (1674), 30–2.

31 Alexander, ed., *Journal of John Fontaine*, 49–50.

32 Alexander, ed., *Journal of John Fontaine*, 81.

20 *Convict Transportation from Devon to America*

KENNETH MORGAN

A SIGNIFICANT NEW FEATURE of Devon's maritime history in the late seventeenth and eighteenth centuries was the transportation of convicts to America. This form of enforced migration began modestly. Approximately 4,500 English convicts were sentenced to banishment before 1700, and only 151 were dispatched from Devon to the colonies between 1664 and 1717.[1] In 1718, however, a parliamentary statute was passed which applied transportation to the largest group of offenders tried in the courts: grand larcenists and petty larcenists (or those convicted respectively of stealing goods worth more than a shilling or less than a shilling).[2] The Transportation Act was intended to deter criminals and to supply the colonies with labour. Probably 50,000 convicts, including at least 1,139 from Devon, were shipped from the British Isles under this legislation until the traffic was cut off by the American Revolution. Nearly all of the transported convicts ended up in Virginia and Maryland, where there was always a demand for cheap, white, bonded labour.

Most British convicts in the eighteenth century were young, male, and poor. They were usually people who had resorted to theft during hard times, rather than habitual criminals. Between 1718 and 1775 some 535 (63 per cent) of the Devon convicts whose length of service is known received seven-year sentences, which was the usual term prescribed for those found guilty of non-capital offences against property. Among this group were people convicted of crimes such as perjury, counterfeiting a pass, and obtaining money by false pretences.[3] A further 304 (36 per cent) were given fourteen-year sentences, which was the usual term for those pardoned by the monarch after conviction on capital charges. This group included those found guilty of arson, burglary, stealing livestock, and receiving stolen goods.[4] Only nine (1 per cent) in the sample were sentenced to life servitude, a penalty reserved for serious crimes such as rape and murder.

Transportation sentences were meted out at quarter sessions and assize courts held throughout Devon. In the period 1 November 1769–1 November 1776, for instance, some 105 convicts were ordered for transportation by judges at the Western circuit assizes in Exeter, and a further 40 received the same sentence from justices of the peace at Devon quarter sessions.[5] Once felons had been convicted they were kept in gaols until the time came to put them on board ship. The conditions they experienced while imprisoned were often very miserable. When the philanthropist John Howard visited Plymouth Town Gaol in the 1770s he came across three men who had been confined for nearly two months while waiting to be transported. He peered in through the door of the clink to see 'a pale inhabitant' who 'had been there ten weeks under sentence of transportation, and [who] said he had much rather have been hanged than confined in that noisome cell'.[6] The generally poor conditions in gaols often led to convicts coming aboard ship in imperfect health, an especially severe form of typhus known as 'gaol fever' being the most common infectious disease present on convict vessels.[7]

Conveyance of convicts across the Atlantic was carried out by merchants who contracted with the courts for batches of felons. Merchant firms received £5 from the county of Devon for each convict taken.[8] Gaolers were also paid fees for delivering convicts to their ports of departure. By the 1760s and 1770s this usually amounted to one or two guineas per convict.[9] Devon merchants in ports such as Exmouth, Bideford, Sidmouth, Plymouth, and Teignmouth were involved in transportation.[10] The most favoured port was Bideford, where George Buck alone dealt with 16 shiploads of convicts between 1726 and 1743.[11] Buck's participation in the traffic undoubtedly arose from his prior trading connections with Virginia, for he was the leading Devon merchant engaged in the Anglo-Chesapeake tobacco trade at this time.[12]

From the mid-1750s convicts sentenced in Devon were invariably taken overland to Bristol for shipment: 30 shiploads of these convicts were handled by Bristol merchants in the period 1756–1773, but only 11 by shippers from Devon.[13] This changing practice stemmed from the declining role of Bideford and Barnstaple in the tobacco trade, and from vigorous efforts made by two Bristol firms to monopolise the supply of convicts from south-west England.[14] The more important of the two firms – Stevenson, Randolph & Cheston – secured a transportation contract by guaranteeing to carry off their human cargoes within two months of the spring and fall assizes.[15] This arrangement suited justices in Exeter because it helped to cut down the expense of keeping criminals in gaols for extended periods,[16] but surviving correspondence reveals that serious disagreements arose between Stevenson & Randolph and the Treasurer for Devon over the fees due to the firm for conveying convicts to Bristol.[17]

It is virtually impossible to trace the fortunes of Devon convicts once they reached the western shores of the Atlantic. In general, convicts were sold to purchasers in Virginia and Maryland, where they were employed in agricultural, industrial, craft, service, and construction work. Some served out their terms and became free men and women, but others tried to escape bondage by absconding from their owners and attempting to jump ship back to Britain. One such runaway was the notorious Bampfylde-Moore Carew, who had been sentenced as 'an incorrigible rogue' to seven years' transportation at the Exeter Quarter sessions in 1739.[18] Carew escaped twice from Maryland and became famous for more than a century because he left a printed account of his adventures which went through various editions.[19] When Carew arrived back in Exeter after his second sojourn in America, he proudly told his friends, who asked whether he had been sold, that he 'took care to get out of the way before they had struck a Bargain for me'.[20] Most transported convicts were not so lucky, however, for they experienced terms of involuntary servitude in America until 1776 and in Australia from 1787 onwards.[21]

20: *Convict Transportation from Devon to America*

1 General comments in this chapter are based on RB Morris, *Government and Labor in Early America* (New York, 1946), 323–37; AE Smith, *Colonists in Bondage: White Servitude and Convict Labor in America, 1607–1776* (Chapel Hill, North Carolina, 1947), 89–135; AGL Shaw, *Convicts and the Colonies: A Study of Penal Transportation from Great Britain and Ireland to Australia and other parts of the British Empire* (1966); JM Beattie, *Crime and the Courts in England, 1660–1800* (Princeton, NJ, 1986), 470–83, 500–19, 538–48, 560–5; and AR Ekirch, *Bound for America: The Transportation of British Convicts to the Colonies, 1718–1775* (Oxford,

1987). Figures for Devon convicts are calculated from PW Coldham, *Bonded Passengers to America V: Western Circuit, 1664–1775* (Baltimore, 1983), 9–34, which is based on a thorough examination of quarter sessions and assize court records.

2 4 Geo. I, c. 11. For additional statutes that buttressed this legislation see Morris, *Government and Labor*, 324, n.40

3 Coldham, *Bonded Passengers, Vol. V*, 14–5, 20–1, 24.

4 PRO, ASSI 21/6, n.p.; Maryland Hall of Records, Annapolis, Baltimore County Convict Entry Book, 1770–1774.

5 J Howard, *An Account of the Principal Lazarettos in Europe . . .* (Warrington, 1789), 247.

6 J Howard, *The State of the Prisons in England and Wales . . .* (Warrington, 2nd edn, 1784), 389.

7 K Morgan, 'The Organization of the Convict Trade to Maryland: Stevenson, Randolph & Cheston, 1768–1775', *William and Mary Quarterly*, 3rd series, XLII (1985), 213–15

8 Howard, *State of the Prisons*, 383; DRO, QS 1/18, 79 (Easter 1738) makes it clear that merchants could be prosecuted for subcontracting the transportation of convicts without authorization from magistrates.

9 Howard, *State of the Prisons*, 383; DRO, QS 1/20, 48, 134 (Easter 1760 and Michaelmas 1762).

10 Based on examination of 93 contracts spanning 1726–1776 in DRO, QS 129/1–10. The names of merchant contractors for convicts sentenced on the Western Circuit are listed in Coldham, *Bonded Passengers, Vol. V*, ix–x.

11 DRO, QS 129/1–10. Additional bonds with George Buck for the transportation of felons are to be found in NDRO, Administration Legal Papers, nos. 2032, 2204–2211.

12 JM Price, *France and the Chesapeake: A History of the French Tobacco Monopoly, 1647–1791, and of its relationship to the British and American Tobacco Trades* (2 vols., Ann Arbor, Michigan, 1973), 563, 593–4.

13 DRO, QS 129/1–10.

14 See Smith, *Colonists in Bondage*, 115, and Morgan, 'The Organization of the Convict Trade to Maryland', 201–27.

15 DRO, QS 129/94/4: Articles of Agreement for the Transportation of Convicts between Stevenson & Randolph and JPs for Devon, 1769.

16 DRO, QS 129/94/6: William Stevenson to Adam Pierce, 11 Nov. 1768.

17 DRO, QS 129/94/8, 10, 19, 25: Adam Pierce to William Stevenson & Co., 1 March 1769; William Randolph to Adam Pierce, 21 April 1769 and 1 May 1770; Stevenson & Randolph to Adam Pierce, 25 Feb. 1771.

18 DRO, QS 1/18, p. 105 (Easter 1739).

19 See *An Apology for the Life of Bampfylde-Moore Carew . . .* (n.d.) This has been convincingly dated to 1749 by CH Wilkinson, ed., *The King of the Beggars: Bampfylde-Moore Carew* (Oxford, 1931), vii.

20 *An Apology for the Life of Bampfylde-Moore Carew*, 133–4.

21 LL Robson's 5 per cent sample of all British convicts transported to New South Wales and Van Diemen's Land suggests that about 1,980 convicts from Devon were sent to these destinations between 1787 and 1852: *The Convict Settlers of Australia* (Melbourne, 1965), 176, 178, 186.

21 *The Marine Cartography of South-West England from Elizabethan to Modern Times*

William Ravenhill

Whether it be land space or sea space, space is best expressed by space itself, reduced to human scale of course, to make it manageable. Hydrography and cartography should therefore be inseparable twins. In Elizabethan times[1] the good father to such twins was John Dee, the intellectual giant of the age, the Ptolemy of the Elizabethan period. In his *General and Rare Memorials pertayning to the Perfecte Arte of Navigation*, published in 1577, he indicated clearly and pointedly how Dutch marine surveying and charting was in advance of the British even in our own waters.

> And, of these sort of people they be, which (other whiles) by colours and pretence of coming about their feat of fishing, do subtly and secretly use soundings, and searching, of our channels, deeps, shoals, banks or bars, along the sea coasts, and in our haven mouths also, and up in our creeks, sometimes in our bays, and sometimes in our roads, &c. Taking good marks, for avoiding of the dangers: And also trying good landings. And (so, making perfect charts of all our coasts, round about England and Ireland) . . .[2]

What John Dee was deploring, however, led to an outstanding late-sixteenth-century achievement in nautical cartographic synthesis by the Dutch. Lucas Janszoon Waghenaer codified and presented the then current nautical knowledge of western Europe in his *De Spieghel der Zeevaerdt*,[3] printed in Leiden in 1584–5. It was a major advance in the evolution of hydrographic publication. Within the covers of one volume the seaman was provided with a manual of practical navigation, a set of printed charts drawn to a common scale, sailing directions, and numerous tables. The charts were on a scale large enough for pilotage, with offshore detail of vital consequence to mariners, such as soundings, shallows, sea-marks, anchorages, and channels. On shore he provided coastal views, vertically projected as seen from the sea. His charts were clearly intended for pilotage, not so much for navigation, because there is deliberate distortion of the coastline by the enlargement of the entrances to rivers and havens (Fig. 21.1). Drawings of ships served a dual function; they were decorative and also useful, since they depicted the type of vessel met with off various stretches of coast. This facilitated position finding. The English Lord High Admiral was so impressed with *De Speighel* that he laid it before the Privy Council for authorization to translate and publish it in England. When it appeared in 1588 with the title *The Mariners Mirrovr*,[4] a significant difference between the Dutch and English versions was the treatment of the sea surfaces. In the latter they were deliberately left blank to facilitate additions and amendments to the information – a ploy clearly expressive of the enquiring scientifically-oriented spirit of the times.

John Dee was also involved in the highly innovative national mapping undertaken by Christopher Saxton in the years 1574–83. Saxton produced two masterpieces, the so-called *Atlas* of county maps and, more significantly in the present context, the large general map published in 1583, wherein Britain, by a most sophisticated treatment of the geographical co-ordinates, has been placed in its global setting by means of the Donis projection.[5]

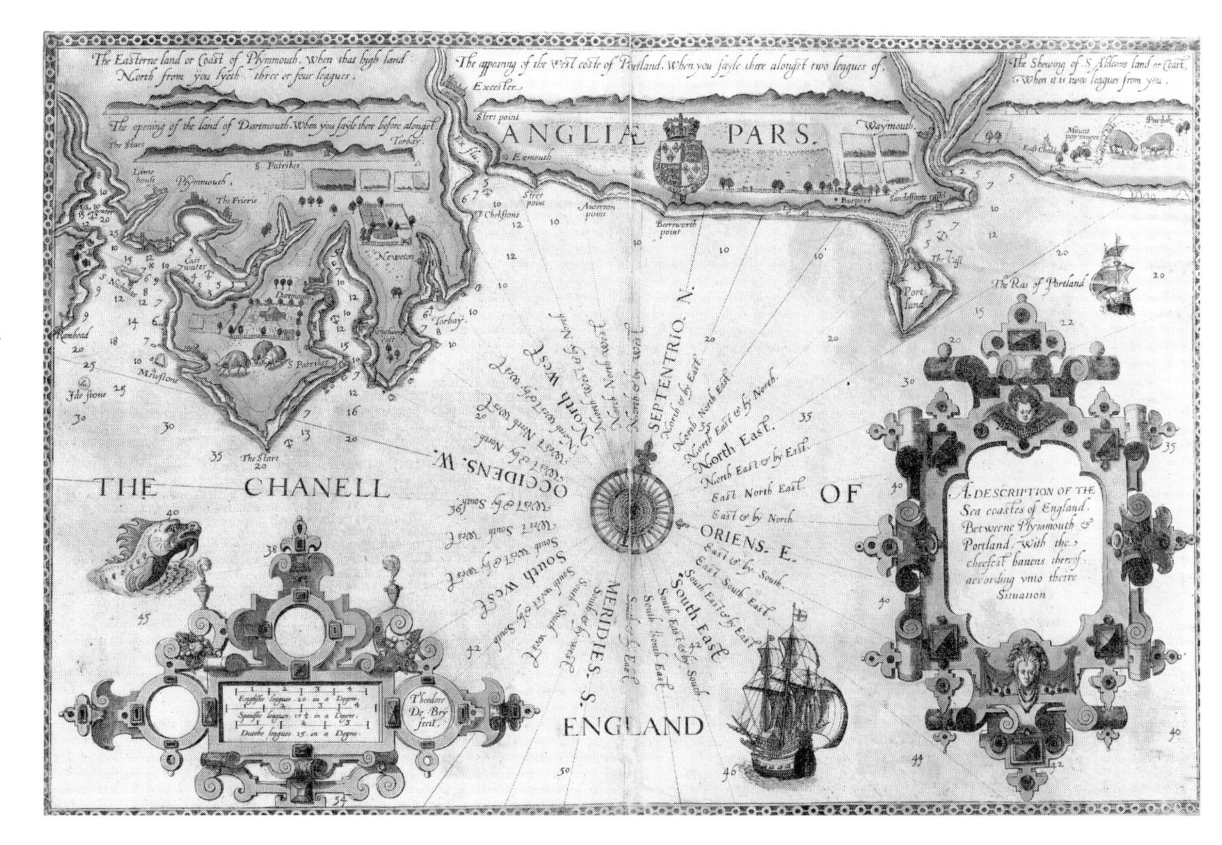

21.1 The 'Waggoner' chart of the coast between Plymouth and Portland, first printed in *The Mariners Mirrour* by Lucas Jansz. Waghenaer at Leiden in 1584–5, and reissued in London, with English translation, by Anthony Ashley in 1588. The first printed sea-atlas, it was made for pilotage and depicts estuaries and harbour approaches on a larger scale to permit inclusion of hydrographical data. Cliffs are shown in elevation (Helen Wallis). *(British Library)*

21.2 Part of Christopher Saxton's Map of England, 1579: the south-west peninsula. *(From an original copy in Exeter University Library)*

While Saxton must be praised for his overall accuracy, he seriously misaligned the most important part of the country as far as contemporary marine navigation was concerned. The peninsula of south-west England (Fig. 21.2) appears with an orientation too pointedly in an east-to-west direction.[6] Saxton's overall delineation of the British coastline was far superior to that of any previous map-maker but, surprisingly, chartmakers for a long time to come ignored his excellence and continued to depict the country crudely. Cross-fertilization between cartography and hydrography seemed for a time to be lacking, a loss being deplored as late as 1717:

> Tis observable, that not only the sea coasts, in two several maps of the same parts commonly differ strangely from each other, but also rarely ever any agree in that respect with the sea charts which happens for want of consulting the Waggoners, either through their little concern for exactness, or imagining a map is to be drawn only by a map, and a chart from a chart.[7]

The merit of printed charts was that they tended to eliminate copying errors and to standardize hydrographical information. In Britain, however, it was the manuscript chartmakers who flourished, particularly as regards ocean-going charts. A noteworthy early example was produced by Thomas Hood in 1596 (Fig. 21.3). It merits notice since it is one of the earliest, possibly the earliest, to show soundings out to sea as far as the 100-fathom line and to have a latitude scale.[8] These two items of hydrographical information could be combined to good effect, particularly on approaching the entrance to the English Channel. A ship's navigator, by taking the altitude of the sun at noon or the pole star at dusk to obtain the required key latitude and then 'running down this latitude', could subsequently take deep soundings until the seabed was encountered at the 100-fathom line. A position line for the latitude of entry could then be intersected with a position for the sounding, thus providing a fix, though the sixteenth-century seaman would not have been familiar with such modern terms.

Hood's chart was a manuscript plane chart but, almost contemporaneously in 1599, Edward Wright had constructed his table of Meridional Parts by a continuous summation of secants and produced a chart of roughly the same area on a Mercator's projection.[9] Wright's chart was printed and included another important feature, namely information about magnetic variation. Such innovations express, at least in some quarters, the application of scientific and mathematical principles to navigation which, during the reign of Elizabeth, brought England abreast, and in some respects ahead, of her continental rivals in marine cartography. Alongside this innovative, imaginative, and intellectual thrust there was, of course, conservatism and suspicion of new-fangled techniques and instruments. William Bourne could justifiably grumble about 'ancient masters of ships' who 'derided and mocked them that have occupied their cards and plats . . . saying: that they cared not for their sheeps skins'.[10] Even these 'sheeps skins', still for the most part plane charts, had now been superseded by Edward Wright's Mercator-chart sailing. Many seamen were, however, unable to make use of these advances and loath to give up old practices and well-tried procedures even though they were known to be inefficient and hazardous. There was something to be said for their point of view. The charts, though of considerable use, could not claim to be accurate and reliable. They needed to be used with extreme caution. After all, how many of them could possibly have been based on good surveys, and for how many places on the surface of the whole globe had geographical co-ordinates been determined to a high order of accuracy? It was a century before Mercator charts and Mercator sailing replaced the plane charts and, as far as Britain was concerned, before printed charts replaced the manuscript 'sheeps skins'.

A school of manuscript chartmakers in the portolan tradition and mould emerged and flourished throughout the seventeenth century in England. They plied their trade in shops lining the streets and alleys that led down to the waterfront on the north bank of the Thames down river from the Tower of London. These chartmakers were linked in a master-apprentice relationship in the Drapers' Company.[11] One of their number, Joel Gascoyne (1650–1705), features prominently not only in a national but also in a regional context.[12] In the 1670s the English cartographer John Seller tried to break the Dutch monopoly of publishing atlases of printed maps. Samuel Pepys, as Secretary to the Navy, consulted Joel Gascoyne in October 1680 on the accuracy and quality of Seller's products as compared with those of the Dutch. From what happened shortly afterwards, Gascoyne's report must have been very damning.[13] Although they were printed in England, some of Seller's charts were pulled off old Dutch copper plates touched up in places to give them the appearance of being new. The sequel was that, after nearly one hundred years of reliance on printed Dutch charts, Pepys issued an

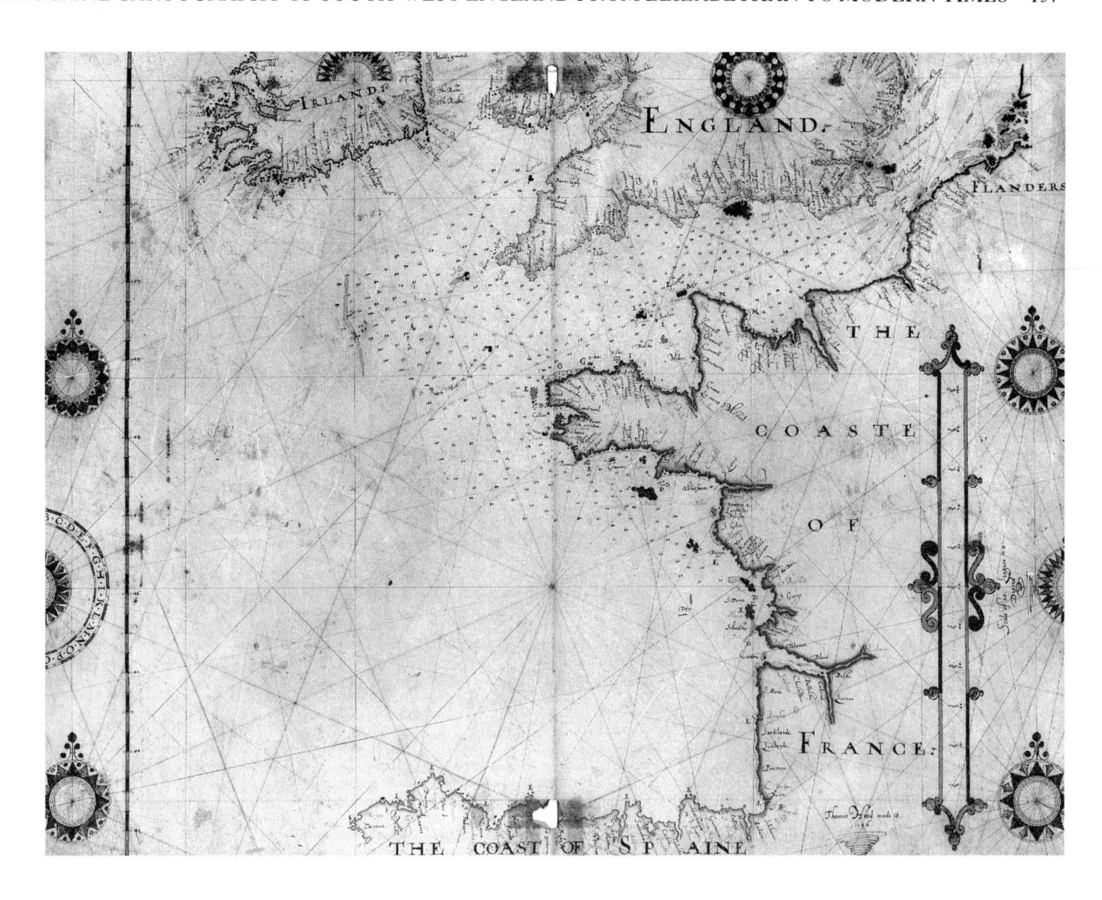

21.3 Thomas Hood's manuscript plane chart of the Bay of Biscay and the English Channel, 1596. *(National Maritime Museum)*

Admiralty Order, in June 1681, assigning a naval officer, Captain Greenvile Collins, to the task of surveying the coasts and harbours. A significant practical advance was made on 23 June 1681, when Charles II issued a proclamation announcing the appointment of Collins to the command of the yacht *Merlin*:

> to make a survey of the sea coasts of the kingdom by measuring all the sea coasts with a chain and taking all the bearings of all the headlands with their exact latitudes . . .[14]

The work of survey took place between 1681 and 1688, and culminated in 1693 in the publication of *Great Britain's Coasting Pilot*.[15] One would have expected the outcome of this government-sponsored survey to have been published by a government agency, but this was not the case, and the work was left to a private printer. It was the first systematic survey of Britain's coastal waters, and the first marine atlas to be engraved and printed in London from original surveys (Fig. 21.4). Some of the charts first became available in the mid 1680s and almost immediately began to receive critical comment, not least by some of the Fellows of the Royal Society. This is not surprising. If one examines the chart for the Lizard, the important contemporary landfall, the peninsula is crudely delineated and the latitude determination of 50° is too far north by 2′ 28″. Technically, the surveying principles applied by Collins were right, but the methods he employed left much to be desired and the support he received was woefully inadequate. Marine surveying should be based on a previously-conducted land survey of the coastline, but to do so by open traverses with chain and compass with little or no overall control will inevitably give rise to cumulative errors. Doubt has even been expressed whether Collins actually used this method everywhere, and not the older running surveys of sailed traverses, and indeed whether in some parts he did not use previous land maps to help him draw the coastline. Furthermore, the whole work was completed in a remarkably short period of time; for instance, he had surveyed the Channel from Dover to Land's End in Cornwall by 1682! This is incredibly swift progress for such an intricate and complex undertaking, especially when the meagre resources in terms of manpower and facilities are taken into account. At the time, those who commissioned the work must have had but little conception of the magnitude of the task. Later they did. 'And then', Pepys reflected, 'it is meet to consider how far a single man is to be trusted alone on a business of this weight and nature.'[16]

On a less extensive geographical scale some, more local, work was being undertaken or commissioned. First among these may be noted the output of Edmund Dummer (fl.1677–1713), who in 1692 was appointed Surveyor to the Navy at Portsmouth. This was one occasion when chart-making was organised as a combined effort between the Navy Board and Trinity House. In 1689 he, together with another 'Commissioner of His Majesty's Navy and two Masters of Trinity House at Deptford', conducted 'A survey of the Ports on the South-West Coast of England from Dover to the Lands-End'.[17] It was no coincidence that a new threat of war with France was looming and so only two months were allotted for the work. Among the 17 plans that were 'delineated in July and August 1698' were 'The River of Exmouth', 'The Harbour of Dartmouth' (Fig. 27.1, below, p. 183), 'The Harbour of Fowey', and 'The Harbour of Falmouth'. These sketches bear all the signs of a hasty and superficial survey, their main aim being to explore possible sites for dockyards rather than the making of charts. Nine copies only of the report and charts were made and since, as far as the South West was concerned, most of these estuaries had already appeared in Collins's *Coasting Pilot*, no substantial input of new data had been acquired by this joint enterprise.

It could have been expected that an immediate reaction to the publication of Greenvile Collins's *Coasting Pilot* would have been a thorough reappraisal of what was needed for hydrographical surveying. Neither the Admiralty nor the Royal Society after Robert Hooke's death showed the required interest and enthusiasm for such practical matters. It was clear that, in addition to ships and sailors, a great deal more finance was required, as well as better instrumentation and technique. Since the precursor of successful marine survey was an accurate land survey, these two aspects of national mapping needed to be co-ordinated. For this to happen, not only were appropriate institutional structures required to be initiated, but they also had to be set up in such a way that they would work in close harmony. Nothing so collaborative, however, occurred in the whole of the eighteenth century, and both these aspects of mapping proceeded along different unco-ordinated pathways in the domain of individuals and enterprises not closely related to one another, and certainly without a national body responsible for an overview of their activities. The outcome was predictable; the surveys of

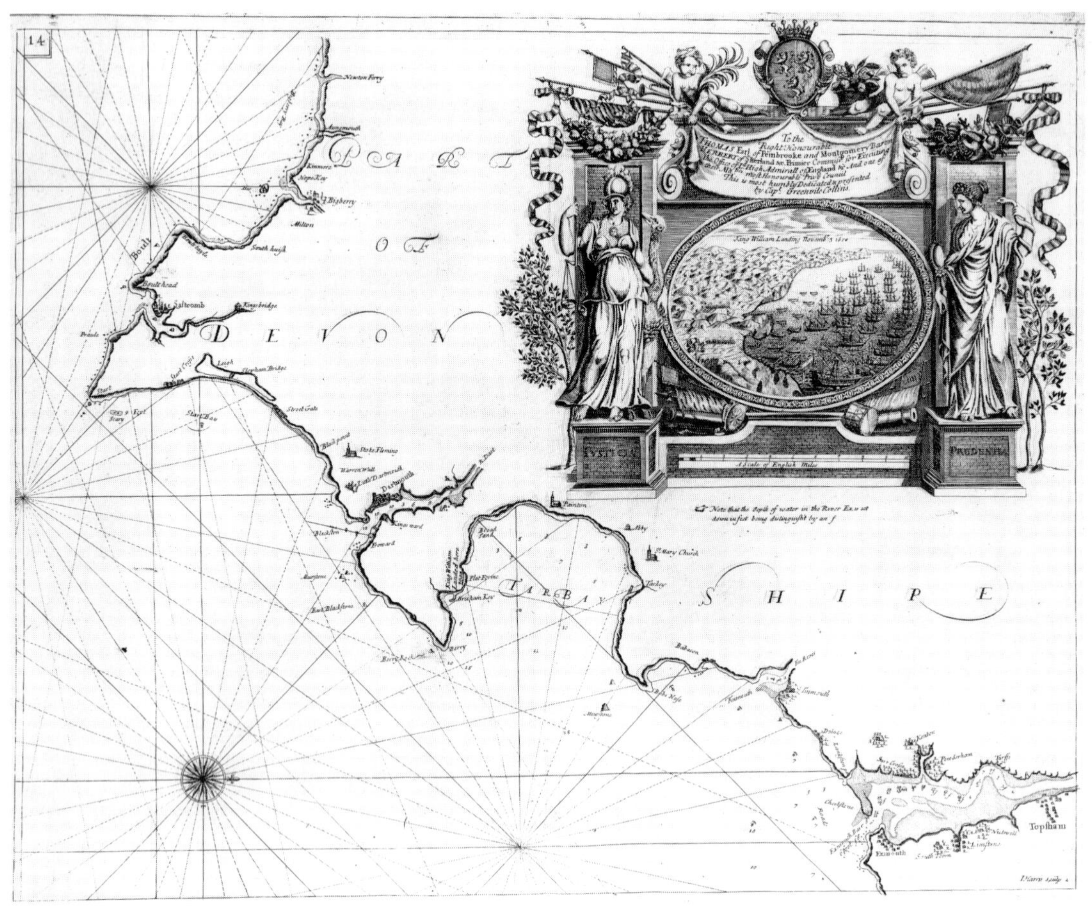

21.4 Greenvile Collins's chart of the South Coast of Devon, printed in his *Great Britain's Coasting Pilot*, 1693. With a ship and crew provided by the Admiralty, Captain Collins was appointed by Charles II in 1681 to make the first systematic survey of the British coasts, a task he completed by 1688. The engraving was done at the expense of Trinity House (Helen Wallis). For an enlargement of the cartouche see below, Fig. 26.1. *(National Maritime Museum)*

Collins remained unchallenged as the only systematic extensive treatment of British coastal waters for more than a century – indeed, until the third decade of the nineteenth century. In the meantime a sporadic and piecemeal accumulation of information slowly found its way on to charts, and these continued to be engraved and sold by private dealers. The quality of their products ultimately depended on new work being done at sea and on the land.

With regard to the latter, a major step forward occurred in 1699 with the publication of Joel Gascoyne's near one-inch-to-the-mile map of Cornwall.[18] For the first time for over a hundred years a significantly-improved outline of this important peninsula, commanding the entrance to the English Channel, had been achieved. Moreover, Joel Gascoyne had determined a latitude for the vital landfall of the Lizard only 1′ 34″ south of its modern determined value.[19] Contemporary with this mapping on land was the pioneering work being undertaken at sea by Edmond Halley, financed by the public purse. In 1698, while in command of the *Paramour*, he investigated the variation of the magnetic needle over the North Atlantic Ocean, and in 1701, with the same ship, he carried out a comprehensive survey of the tidal currents on both sides of the English Channel. Almost immediately the results of these three activities were conflated in the production of *A Large Chart of the Channel between England and France done from the Newest and Best Surveys of the flowing of the Tydes and the Setting of the Current as they were Observed in the Year 1701 By Capt. Edmund Halley By His Majesties Command.*[20] The chart was actually drawn by Joel Gascoyne and engraved by John Harris. It has been described as 'one of the most important maps ever made' and the parent 'of a most numerous progeny'.[21] It quickly became the standard chart for the English Channel, appearing in *The English Pilot Part One* in the year 1702 and again in *The English Pilot, The Third Book*, published by John Thornton in 1703, covering the 'Oriental Navigation'[22] for which there are a number of circumstances to suggest that it was produced with the official patronage of the East India Company since Thornton dedicated the volume to their Honourable Court of Managers. Alongside the new data regarding magnetic variation and tides, the other significant new addition was the coastal configuration of Cornwall, which greatly improved the navigation into the mouth of the Channel. The further influence of Gascoyne can be clearly detected insofar that Lizard Point as read from the marginal graduations is placed at latitude 49° 56′ 30″, only a minute south of its modern determination. Also, there is an inset chart of the Fal estuary which, in terms of soundings, differs so markedly from that of Collins to suggest that this is a new survey. Furthermore, the explicit note on the right-hand side speaks eloquently of the author's familiarity with contemporary science:

> The Variation was observed in all parts of the Channel to be about seaven Degrees and half, from the North, Westerly or two-thirds of a point. In the Year 1701, and so much must be allowed in all courses on this chart wherein the Meridians are the true.

In a modified form the chart took a place of priority in being used as the first entry in Collins's *Coasting Pilot* in editions published after 1723, and continued to be included in the volume for the next 20 editions,[23] the last of which appeared in 1792. Ironically, the title still claims this to be *A New and Correct Chart of the Channel between England & France with considerable Improvements not extant in any Draughts hitherto Published . . . with ye flowing of the Tydes, and setting of the Current; as they were observed by the Learned Dr. Halley*. Although the coastal outlines in the two charts are recognisably similar, the marginal graduations for latitude have been moved southwards relative to the land, giving Lizard Point the value of 50° 02′ 15″, or just under 5 minutes too far north, an error in a direction which increases the danger to ships attempting to enter the Channel 'running down the latitude'. Additionally, it introduces an inconsistency between two values for Lizard Point in the same volume, the larger scale chart No.19 placing Lizard Point at latitude 50°. Even more insidious is the omission of the 'Anno 1701' originally inscribed under the variation of the compass, thus rendering these values not only useless but hazardous as the years of the eighteenth century rolled on. For instance, in the 1753 edition of the *Coasting Pilot* the variation off Start Point is still being given the same value as in 1701, when in truth the variation had been increasing westward; it was 20° by 1765. This is but one of the many instances of inertia under the management of Mount and Page both as far as *The English Pilot* and *The Coasting Pilot* were concerned. They did little to keep either of these publications up to date, neither with respect to the text nor the charts. After nearly a century of use both volumes remained not that much different from the last input of expertise provided by John Thornton, the most notable and least acknowledged of the contributors to hydrographic advancement in the early part of the century. Mount and Page, on the other hand, reaped benefits from the expertise of others, and, being concerned more with profit than the quality of the product, they did little to enhance the reliability of either of the *Pilots* during their long ownership of them. What was in the van of progress at the time of John Thornton was hardly likely to be good enough half a century and more later. No wonder, then, that the British institution most conscious of such matters, the East India Company, made moves to remedy the position from French sources after mid-century, particularly with charts made by Jean Baptiste Nicolas Denis d'Après de Manvillette. An English version, *The East India Pilot or Oriental Navigator on one Hundred and fourteen plates Improved, and chiefly composed from the last work of M. D'Après de Mannevillette; with considerable additions from private manuscripts of the Dutch, and from Draughts and Actual Surveys communicated by Officers of the East India Company*, was published by Robert Sayer and John Bennet of No 53 Fleet Street, London c.1775. In the same year this firm became noted for producing charts of the south coast of England. This activity culminated in the appearance in 1779 of *A Complete Channel Pilot: comprehending the English and French Coasts from the Thames Mouth to the Bay of Biscay From Actual Surveys and Observations of Experienced Navigators Engraved on Twenty-eight Copper-Plates*.[24]

Among these were charts providing almost complete coverage of the south coasts of Devon and Cornwall. This collection starts with *A New Hydrographical Survey of the British Channel* improved from a large chart of the late but much renowned Thomas Jeffreys. He, with two others,[25] first produced this chart in 1759, and in its updated issue it has seven inset port maps, among which are *Mevagizey Bay, Mounts Bay, Plymouth,* and *Falmouth*. Equally important are the larger-scale charts, the first of which is *An Hydrographical Survey of the Coast of Devonshire from Exmouth Bar to Stoke Point* . . . with an inset map of *The River, Harbour and Road of Dartmouth*. Although no source is quoted on the 1779 copy, the later issue dated 1786 describes it as 'from Donn's Survey, &c.'[26] It should be recalled here that a survey of similar magnitude and extent to that of Cornwall by Gascoyne did not occur for Devon until 66 years later, when Benjamin Donn published his one-inch-to-the-mile map of the county. In so doing particular attention was paid 'to have its Sea Coasts accurately laid down, together with the Latitudes and Longitudes of the principal Harbours, Capes, or Headlands'.[27] Wholesale copying without acknowledgement was common practice, but in this case Benjamin Donn possibly complained. The trade links, however, are readily established insofar that Donn's Devon was engraved by Thomas Jefferys and in the following year, 1766, the latter was declared bankrupt.[28] Among those who came to his rescue was Robert Sayer, who acquired many of Jefferys's copper plates. As with Gascoyne so with Donn, their land mapping was quickly used to update charts, the south coast of Devon being much in need of improvement from the way in which it was drawn on the 1759 chart. *Plymouth Sound, Hamoaze* and *Catwater* from surveys undertaken in 1770, completes the coverage for Devon. For Cornwall there is *A Plan of the Road and Harbour of Fowey* surveyed by Lieutanant James Cook of the Royal Navy; a *Plan of the Bays of Polkerris and Megavizey; Falmouth and Carreg Road with Helford Sound; A New Chart of Mounts Bay with the Adjacent Coast from Cape Lizard to Cape Cornwall* surveyed by John Thomas and William Denys; *A Chart of the Entrance into the Channel and Scilly Islands with all the Soundings*; and finally *A New Chart of the Islands of Scilly with their Soundings, Channels and Sailing Marks* by A Tovey and N Ginver.

Robert Sayer and John Bennet were but one of a number of private chart sellers, William Heather 'At the Sign of the Little Midshipman' in the City of London being another who sold charts of the South West. It was in such hands that lay the entire responsibility for the issue of charts. Indeed, it had become a recognised practice for serving officers in the Royal Navy to have their surveys engraved and published privately for their own gain. In fairness it can be said that some of these private firms did promote and finance surveys, but naturally of those areas where the potential demand for the resulting charts would be high. From the above account it can be seen how unsatisfactory the situation was, with the chart dealers being dependent upon foreign sources, the unpredictable reporting of sea captains, and *ad hoc* surveys. With no offical surveying service it was impossible to provide a reliable and up-to-date supply of charts for merchantmen.[29] In 1779 the East India Company was persuaded by Alexander Dalrymple of the need for a more systematic collection, verification, and issue of charts for the use of captains of their ships, and to this end appointed him their official hydrographer. Dalrymple had been in the Company's employ since 1752, when, at the tender age of 15, he had been sent out as a writer to Madras. In 1759 he secured an appointment in the Secret Service of the Company, and was assigned the task of exploring the eastern passages. In the course of these voyages he made running surveys of the coasts, annotating them with sketches of the coastline as seen from seaward and other pieces of information and intelligence which came to hand by way of discourse with others who sailed those seas. It was therefore no surprise that, in 1779, when he became the Company's official hydrographer, he was assigned the specific task of preparing charts for the use of the Company's vessels and arranging for them to be printed. Dalrymple, who, incidentally, was a personal friend of Mannevillette, lost no time in setting up the necessary machinery for the speedy production and printing of engraved charts, updating as required when new data from ships' captains was received. The charts were compiled in folios covering geographical areas. Modestly titled and well designed, they are fine examples of the cartographers' and engravers' art. The Royal Navy also relied on the efforts of the private chart sellers for the supply of their charts. Their ships' captains were, if anything, even worse off, as the examples available were intended to suit the needs of the merchant fleet, while the Royal Navy ships could be called upon to perform a much greater variety of tasks. One far-seeing individual in the West Country had long since perceived the need for an official organisation to be set up to map and chart the British Isles. William Borlase in 1765 had declared: 'It is not an affair in the reach of a private purse, or a single person'.[30] True though this was, the English did not heed this good advice until the closing years of the eighteenth century. In this respect England was lagging behind her continental rivals, France having established a hydrographic office in 1720.

When, belatedly, in 1795 the Admiralty finally decided to establish an official chart-making service, they conferred the title of Hydrographer of the Navy on a civilian. He was none other than Alexander Dalrymple, who thus became Hydrographer both to the Board of the Admiralty and to the East India Company. Since Britain was fighting a particularly difficult war with France, the appointment of Dalrymple came none too soon. The Order in Council commanded their new Hydrographer:

> to take charge of such plans and charts as are now or may hereafter be deposited in this office belonging to the Public, and to be charged with the duty of selecting and compiling all the existing information as may appear to be requisite for the purpose of improving the Navigation, and for the guidance and direction of the Commanders of Your Majesty's Ships.[31]

Reference was clearly being made here to the numerous drawings, sketch surveys, and other maritime data which had accumulated and lain unused, gathering dust, on the crowded shelves of the Admiralty. Somewhere in this neglected pile would have reposed, awaiting resurrection by Dalrymple, the valuable original surveys undertaken by Murdoch Mackenzie Junior. He was the nephew of Murdoch Mackenzie Senior, who had not only evolved appropriate and much-improved methods of surveying the coast by triangulation, but had also carried out in a private capacity the charting of the Orkney and Lewis Islands. After this, and now with the support of the Admiralty, Mackenzie Senior surveyed the whole of the Irish coasts and the west coast of Britain as far as Carmarthen Bay.[32] When he retired as official Maritime Surveyor to the Admiralty, in 1771, his place was taken by his nephew, who continued where his uncle had left off, surveying in the Bristol Channel. By 1773 he had worked his way round the southwest peninsula to Plymouth Sound:[33] after measuring a new base line and fixing his trigonometrical stations, and thus being all prepared to start sounding in 1774, the Admiralty posted him to duties in eastern England, where he was joined by his cousin, Graeme Spence. They both returned to the West Country to resume their work in 1777, surveying Plymouth, Falmouth, Torbay and the coast westward. By 1783 Lieutenant Mackenzie's eyesight began to fail, but he continued as head nautical surveyor until 1788, when the Admiralty ceased to employ him and his assistant, Spence. The latter was re-engaged in August 1789 to survey the Scillies, a task which took until 1793 to complete, but this, fortunately, did involve linking the Scillies by triangulation to the mainland.[34] In this way the islands could be plotted in relation to the survey of the mainland carried out by Mackenzie and referred to above as taking place in 1773. This new material again found its way on to the shelves of the Admiralty, even though the Scillies lay close to a much frequented shipping route and their true position was known to be in doubt.

The year 1795 is memorable not only for the appointment of the first Hydrographer to the Navy, but also for the removal of one of the main obstacles to successful charting, namely the existence of an accurate land survey. The date 10 July 1791 may be taken as an appropriate one to mark the official constitution of the Ordnance Survey. By 1795 a chain of triangulated stations extended from east to west through southern England to Lands End, and from there angles to points on the Scillies were observed in 1797. The detailed land mapping of Devon and Cornwall proceeded in the ensuing years. It must be recognised, however, the the Trigonometrical Survey had wider scientific and practical applications than just providing a framework for the one-inch topographical maps of the country. Latitude values were computed for the principal stations and their intersections, together with differences of longitude from the Greenwich meridian. General William Mudge FRS, the Director of the Trigonometrical Survey from 1798 to 1820, explained how in the 'early stage of the survey, the first object in view' was 'to determine the situations of the principal points on the sea coast, and those objects which are near to it'.[35] In so doing he went on to claim that 'the position of many remarkable objects in terms of their latitudes and longitudes were now verified'. They were, as a result, of considerable value to navigators and to the Admiralty for the correction of its marine charts.

This was the quarter century of turmoil and conflict with France following the French Revolution and its Napoleonic sequel. For most of these years the British were principally involved with encounters and blockades at sea, with, at times, a direct threat of invasion somewhere along the Channel coast. It was then that the making and acquiring of maps and charts by both sides in the conflict reached explosive proportions. Never, it seems, were the cartographic demands of either the navy or the army adequately satisfied during this war, and the question of which command held what maps and charts was not without its incongruous and fascinating features. One such incongruity emerges from the correspondence between General John Graves Simcoe and the Lords Commissioners of the Admiralty in 1804. General Simcoe, who by this date had been placed in command not only of the Western Division but also of Plymouth, was, like Napoleon, one of the new breed of soldiers who fought their wars from maps and charts. In Simcoe's possession was a survey of the coast of Cornwall by a Captain Lane, a copy of which was eagerly being sought by the Admiralty. How Simcoe acquired it is not known, but it had been commissioned by the Admiralty, as its title makes clear:

> Report on a Survey of the Coast of Cornwall, commenced on the 22nd of August, and ending the 30th of September 1796 persuant to an Order from the Right Honorable the Lords Commissioners of the Admiralty, by C: H: Lane.

It must have been a rapidly conducted survey 'taken in a coasting voyage' under a threat of impending enemy action, but this is as far as interpretation can proceed as, unfortunately, a copy of it seems not to have survived. No trace of it can be found either in the Hydrographic Department's archive or in the Simcoe or Clifford collections.[36]

Graeme Spence terminated his active surveying in 1803, and until shortly before his death in 1812 was employed in the Admiralty writing up both his own and Mackenzie's surveys, and endeavouring to reconcile them with the new coastlines and geographical positions emanating from the fieldwork being undertaken by the Ordnance Survey. It is to this period that belongs his lengthy annotation on the manuscript 'A Trigonometrical Plain Chart showing the relative Situations of Scilly, the Landsend and the Lizard'.[37] He notes its compilation from Mackenzie's survey of 1773 and his own of 1793 and, now in 1807 'wishes that Mr Dalrymple would Compare the Whole with the Grand Trigonometrical Survey, and correct them where necessary'.[38] That same year the Admiralty began to feel impatient at the slow productivity of the Department, and ordered their Hydrographer to hasten the supply of charts at once both from his own Department and by purchase from private firms. A tangible expression of the Navy's predicament was the fact that, in 1805, the flagship of the British Fleet, Lord Nelson's *Victory*, was still using a 40-year-old French chart to navigate in the western Mediterranean basin. With a small staff and only one copper-plate printing press Dalrymple was clearly being overstretched; his being a perfectionist by nature did not help matters, and little published material actually reached the Fleet. Under such pressure he realised that it would be necessary to procure charts from the commercial chart-sellers, and in this respect freely admitted that he was handicapped by his lack of knowledge, particularly of the coasts of Europe. To overcome this deficiency he suggested that a Charting Committee of naval officers be established to advise him on the selection of suitable charts.

Their Lordships appointed such a committee in 1808, one member of which was a Captain Thomas Hurd. He it was who, after the brief peace of Amiens, secured the use of a revenue cutter from Falmouth to survey in 1805 the approaches to Brest, but when weather conditions were unsuitable for such work on the enemy's doorstep he surveyed Falmouth Harbour and the coast as far as the Manacles.[39] Although they were first suggested by Dalrymple, the Charting Committee's far-reaching proposals of how best to supply the navy with charts efficiently and quickly led to friction between him and the committee. Their Lordships broke the news gently to Dalrymple that the new arrangements required the exertions of one much younger. Dalrymple died within a few weeks of being supplanted in 1808 by Captain Hurd, who became the first naval officer hydrographer. He saw his calling in a less scientific and more entrepreneurial manner than Dalrymple, and set about carrying out the recommendations of the Charting Committee with vigour and determination. They were to provide sets of charts for each naval station, to attempt to buy back the copyright of the many charts made by naval officers then currently being produced and sold by the private chart-sellers, and to expedite, as far as was possible, a speedy despatch of a comprehensive supply of charts to the naval stations for a Navy which was at war. Among the first list of charts to be obtained from the private sector were 169 issued by, among others, Arrowsmith, Dalrymple, Faden, Heather, Laurie & Whittle, Mount & Davidson, and Steel.[40] Captain Hurd vigorously pursued every piece of hydrographical information that came to his knowledge and was concerned about the surveying of home waters which, since Spence had retired in 1803, had not been actively pursued. In this respect, however, considerable help was forthcoming through the Board of Ordnance as a result of Colonel Mudge's survey of south-west England. Maps of the whole of Devon and a good deal of Cornwall had been engraved by 1807, the remainder following by 1811. It was, however, as early as 1 November 1808, only two months after his appointment, that Hurd suggested to their Lordships:

> the necessity of an application being made to the Board of Ordnance that this office be allowed to have a copy of such parts of Colonel Mudge's military survey of England as respects the sea coast thereof together with all remarkable objects in the vicinity, as may be judged useful to navigation.[41]

These new official maps were of immense help to hydrographers in so far as they provided a first essential requisite, but they were not above reproach, and criticism of their inaccuracies was fully justified. The crew of the survey ship *Hasty*, working off Lundy Island in September 1820, found the direction of the island as given by the Ordnance Survey to be quite inaccurate.[42] When this complaint was investigated it was found that the original survey of Lundy had not been tied into the general triangulation. There were difficulties also in adjusting the earlier surveys of Mackenzie and Spence with the newer ones and with the Ordnance Survey maps. Surveys associated with the construction of Plymouth Breakwater, for example, failed so severely to be reconciled with former ones that Commander Martin White in the *Shamrock* was sent there to make new theodolite observations from the Breakwater terminals so that this new feature could be laid down correctly on the charts.[43] The correction of imperfect work on the coastlines of Devon and Cornwall had to be put in hand in the 1830s. This quite unacceptable state of affairs chiefly stemmed from the practice of paying the surveyors by the completed square mile, a system of remuneration which was modified after 1834.

From 1808, however, Hydrographic Office charts of the South West were regularly made available to the Fleet, and means existed to update them as new information came in. The following title is an interesting example of the new regime.

> A Survey of the Coast of Cornwall from the Lizard Point to St Agnes Head, By Lieutenant Mackenzie 1772 and the Scilly Islands by Mr. Graeme Spence, 1792. Hydrographical Office. Published according to Act of Parliament Sepr. 19 1808. by Capt. Hurd R.N. Hydrographer to the Admiralty. The Writing by T Harman.[44]

This, however, was but one chart, and three years later appeared Hurd's large folio atlas *Charts of the English Channel*,[45] which contained no fewer than 31 charts, some his own, others by colleagues in the Hydrographic Office, and a few of them printed from privately published plates. Some were endorsed 'Approved by the Chart Committee of the Admiralty', and some merely rubber-stamped 'Hydrographical Office'. Hurd re-established the post of Head Maritime Surveyor, which had been in abeyance since the retirement of Graeme Spence in 1803, and it was given to George Thomas. His early surveys in home waters were, for the most part, isolated examinations of harbours, one such being of Fowey in 1811.

Reference has already been made to the chart-making and vending carried on by private entrepreneurs, and the purchase by the chart committee of some of their printed sheets and copper plates in circumstances when the small staff of the Department could not satisfy the demands of the Fleet. This dichotomy in the provision of charts continued, with naval personnel entering into relationships with commercial firms. One such relationship developed between William Faden and Lieutenant Joseph Foss Dessiou, resulting in a *Chart of Part of the Coast of Devonshire from Rame Head to Exmouth*, published on 13 June 1811. Similar relationships existed between William Heather, Dessiou, and Trinity House, again with naval officers providing the appropriate surveys. In an attempt to rationalize this situation and to concentrate effort Hurd, in 1816, suggested that Admiralty charts should be placed on sale to the public, so that the revenue obtained could enable his department to become self-supporting and expand to meet the demand existing both in the Navy and in the mercantile market. Their Lordships opposed any such scheme until 1820 when, much to Hurd's surprise, they referred to him just such a plan sent in by William Faden who, not surprisingly, proposed that he alone should become the sole agent for the sale of Admiralty charts to the public. Hurd, in grasping the opportunity to put into practice his long-cherished scheme, insisted that other commercial chart sellers who had been more co-operative than Faden in relinquishing their copyrights formerly published on behalf of naval officers should also be offered agencies. This proposal was duly accepted, and Hurd was instructed to compile a catalogue which was forwarded to their Lordships on 28 June 1821.[46] No copy of this catalogue has yet been found, but the charts were available for sale soon afterwards, as this announcement in the *Western Luminary* for Tuesday 10 July 1821 makes clear:

> NAVAL CHARTS
> Admiralty-Office, 30th June, 1821
> The Lords Commissioners of the Admiralty having caused various Charts to be Engraved in this Office, for the use of His Majesty's Ships, and being desirous of extending the benefit thereof to Navigation in general; – *This is to give Notice*, That the said Charts may be had both Wholesale and Retail, at moderate prices, at Mr. FADEN'S, Charing Cross, and at Mr. ARROWSMITH'S, Soho-square, from whom may also be had Catalogues of the said Charts, shewing the *retail price* of each Article.
> As more Charts were, during the course of the late war, mounted on Canvas, for the use of the Navy, than His Majesty's Service at present requires, a large Assortment of such mounted Charts, marked with their respective prices, will be found at the Shops of the before-mentioned Agents.
> JW CROKER[47]

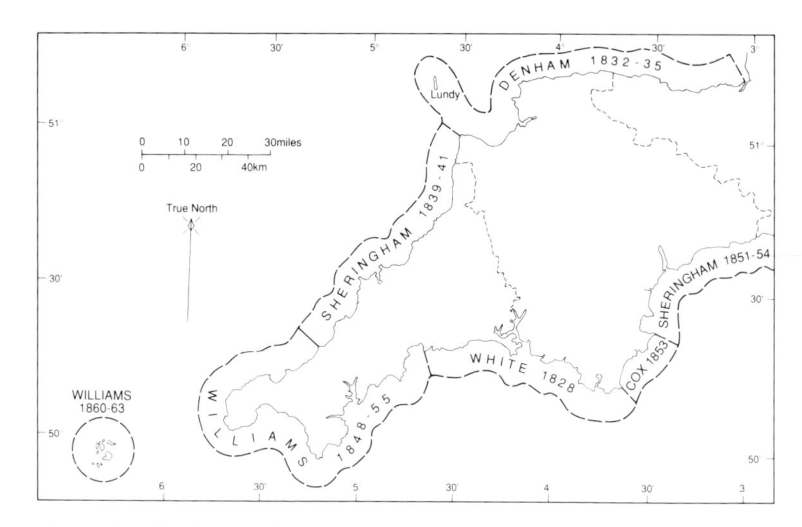

Map 21.1 The Charting of the South-west peninsula

The signatory was the Right Honourable John Wilson Croker, LLD, FRS, who had been appointed Secretary to the Board of the Admiralty in 1809. He held the post for the next 21 years; from 1812 to 1817 he was particularly noted for his severe economy measures.

Although official Admiralty Charts had been made available by purchase to the public since 1821, this did not sound the death knell for the private chart-sellers, who remained in business compiling charts from information derived from naval officers and Admiralty sources. In 1823 the Admiralty reached the conclusion that their official charts were used by the agents only to improve their own charts for sale, and so decided to appoint forthwith just one agent who was to be kept under strict surveillance. Thus it was that the name of RB Bate became synonymous with Admiralty Charts, as did that of JD Potter of the Minories after 1850. Nevertheless, some individuals remained in business, but their sales continued to dwindle, particularly as the Hydrographic Department grew both in actual survey operations and its publication of charts.

A chart is never complete. The full appreciation of this truism occupied the mind of Captain Francis Beaufort who, at the age of 55, became the new Hydrographer to the Navy in 1829 and remained in the post for the next 26 years. Soon after taking up his post he had plotted on a world map those parts covered by surveys: the voids appalled him so much that he resolved to fill them. With regard to home waters, save for one exception, he considered the surveys which were available totally inadequate for the safety of shipping, and set about planning how so much that needed to be done could be achieved. What became known as Beaufort's *Grand Survey of the British Isles* was his successful attempt to re-chart practically the whole of the coasts and inshore waters of our islands. As far as the South West was concerned there was only one stretch of coast, from Start Point to Gribbin Head, which Beaufort was prepared to accept as accurate enough from the surveys of the earlier period.[48] It had been charted by Martin White in the *Shamrock* in 1828. The remainder of the coast was surveyed in the ensuing years. Interestingly, one of the results of this new hydrographic survey was to bring to view inaccuracies in the Ordnance Survey mapping, making it necessary in the 1830s to re-engrave a number of sheets of south-west England. The sheets most in need of coastline revision were those of north Devon and north Cornwall, the inaccuracies being exposed by the hydrographic surveying carried out by Captain HM Denham in the years 1832–35. His surveys covered the whole coast of north Devon from the mouth of the River Parret round to Hartland Point, including Lundy. The coast from Hartland Point southwestwards was surveyed in the years 1839–41 by Captain W Sheringham. When he had completed his work as far as St Agnes Head he was posted to Portsmouth. From there, in the following years, he moved westwards, and in 1851 was off the Dorset and south Devon coast, reaching Berry Head by 1854. Adjacent to him, surveying the coastal stretch between Berry Head and Start Point, was Commander HL Cox who, when he finished his task in 1853, had filled the gap remaining between Sheringham's work and that of Martin White. All the coastlines of Devon were in this way surveyed to the satisfaction of Beaufort by 1854. Farther west, the stretch of coast between St Agnes Head around the Penwith peninsula to Gribbin Head, where the link with Martin White's work could be made, was being actively pursued contemporaneously. Commander G Williams undertook the survey of this very difficult southwestern stretch of coastline, a task which took him the seven years from 1848 to 1855.

Commander Beaufort died in 1855, which may be regarded as a memorable year in the annals of British Hydrography. The charting of the long and intricate coastline of Britain to Beaufort's high standards had almost been completed. Interestingly, the one remaining unfinished piece in the jigsaw was southwest England. In the years 1857 to 1859 Commander Williams was doing more work around the vital landfall of Lizard and, finally, the Isles of Scilly in the period 1860 to 1863. It is on this great survey, undertaken in the main during the tenure of Admiral Sir Francis Beaufort as Hydrographer, that all subsequent charts of Britain's coastlines have been based.

21: The Marine Cartography of South-West England from Elizabethan to Modern Times

1 For a discussion of the pre-Elizabethan period of charting the waters of the South West see William Ravenhill, 'The Marine Cartography of Devon in the Context of South-West England' in David J Starkey, ed., *Devon's Coastline and Coastal Waters: Aspects of Man's relationship with the Sea*, Exeter, 1988. See also above, chapter 3.

2 John Dee, *General and Rare Memorials pertayning to the Perfecte Arte of Navigation*, (1577), 7.

3 Lucas Janszoon Waghenaer, *De Spieghel der Zeevaerdt* (Leyden, 1584–1585). Reproduced in facsimile with an Introduction by RA Skelton, Theatrum Orbis Terrarum First Series IV (Amsterdam, 1964).

4 Anthony Ashley, *The Mariners Mirrour* (1588). Reproduced in facsimile with an Introduction by RA Skelton, Theatrum Orbis Terrarum Third Series II (Amsterdam, 1966).

5 William Ravenhill, 'Christopher Saxton's Surveying: An Enigma', in Sarah Tyacke, ed., *English Map Making 1500–1650* (1983), 112–9.

6 William Ravenhill, 'As to its Position in respect to the Heavens', *Imago Mundi* 28 (1976), 83.

7 John Green, *The Construction of Maps and Globes* (1717), 137.

8 Derek Howse and Michael Sanderson, *The Sea Chart* (Newton Abbot, 1973), 47.

9 Edward Wright, *Certaine Errors in Navigation* (1599).

10 William Bourne, *An Almanacke and prognostication for three yeares . . . 1571. and 1572. & 1573* (1571). It can conveniently be consulted in EGR Taylor, ed., *A Regiment for the Sea and other Writings by William Bourne of Gravesend*, Hakluyt Society (Cambridge, 1963), Preface to the Reader.

11 Tony Campbell, 'The Drapers' Company and its School of Seventeenth Century Chart-makers', in Helen Wallis and Sarah Tyacke, eds., *My Head is a Map* (1973), 81–106. See also Thomas R Smith, 'Manuscript and Printed Sea Charts in Seventeenth Century London: The Case of the Thames School', in Norman JW Thrower, ed., *The Compleat Plattmaker* (Berkeley, Los Angeles, London, 1978), 45–100.

12 William Ravenhill, 'Joel Gascoyne, Cartographer', *Geographical Magazine* (1972), 335–41.

13 JR Tanner, ed., *Samuel Pepys Naval Minutes*, NRS, 60 (1926), 42, 237.

14 FH Blackburne Daniell, ed., *Calendar of State Papers Domestic Series, 1680–1681* (HMSO 1921); see also BL, Harleian MS 5946, f.202.

15 Greenvile Collins, *Great Britain's Coasting Pilot* (1693).

16 JR Tanner, ed., *Pepys Naval Minutes*, 188–9.

17 A manuscript copy of the Report and Charts is in BL, K.Mar.III 67; further copies are in the NMM and the Royal Geographical Society Map Library.

18 W Ravenhill, 'Joel Gascoyne, A Pioneer of Large-Scale County Mapping', *Imago Mundi* XXVI (1972), 60–70.

19 William Ravenhill, 'Mapping the Lizard', *The Map Collector* 13 (1980), 29–36: 'The Lizard as a Landfall', *The Journal of Navigation* 35, No.1, (1982), 75–89; Herman Moll, *A New Description of England and Wales* (1724), 1.

20 BL, Maps 189.a.16.

21 Arthur H Robinson, 'The Genealogy of the Isopleth', *Cartographic Journal* 8, No.1 (June, 1971), 51; S Chapman, 'Edmund Halley as a Physical Geographer and the Story of his Charts', Occasional Notes, *Royal Astronomical Society*, 9 (1941), 122.

22 Can be conveniently consulted in the facsimile published by Theatrum Orbis Terrarum (Amsterdam, 1970).

23 Coolie Verner, 'Captain Collins' Coasting Pilot: A Carto-Bibliographic Analysis', *The Map Collectors' Circle* 6, No.58 (1969), 1–56; Coolie Verner and RA Skelton, Introduction to the facsimile copy of John Thornton's *The English Pilot, The Third Book*, Theatrum Orbis Terrarum (Amsterdam, 1970), XI–XIII.

24 Royal Geographical Society, 14.B.84. In the 1789 edition the ascription was changed to 'From Observations and Actual Surveys by John Stephenson and George Burn Masters in the Royal Navy, and other Experienced Navigators'.

25 BL, Maps 1068.(15). This chart was 'Printed for & Sold by' Tho. Jefferys, Robert Sayer and Henry Parker.

26 Royal Geographical Society, 14.B.87.

27 Benjamin Donn, *A Map of the County of Devon 1765* reprinted in Facsimile with an Introduction by WLD Ravenhill (Devon and Cornwall Record Society and the University of Exeter, 1965).

28 JB Harley, 'The Bankruptcy of Thomas Jefferys: an Episode in the Economic History of Eighteenth Century Map-making', *Imago Mundi* XX (Amsterdam, 1966), 27–48.

29 GS Ritchie, *The Admiralty Chart: British Naval Hydrography in the Nineteenth Century* (1967), 10–20.

30 Letter from William Borlase to Charles Lyttleton, 3 May 1756, BL, Stowe MS 752, f.176. The author is indebted to Peter Pool FSA for calling his attention to this correspondence. See William Ravenhill, 'The Marine Cartography of Devon in the Context of South-West England', in Starkey, *Devon's Coastline & Coastal Waters*, 5–23.

31 *Charting the Seas in Peace and War: The Story of the Hydrographic Department . . .* (HMSO, 1947), 6.

32 AHW Robinson, *Marine Cartography in Britain* (Leicester, 1962); Murdoch Mackenzie, *A Treatise of Maritim Surveying* (1774), XII.

33 Hydrographic Office, Taunton, HD 703 Di.

34 Hydrographic Office, Taunton, HD 674 15E: A Maritime Survey of Scilly taken by order of the Right Honourable the Lords Commissioners of the Admiralty at the Request of the Corporation of Trinity House by Graeme Spence 1792.

35 William Mudge, *An Account of the Operations Carried on For Accomplishing a Trigonometrical Survey of England and Wales* II (1801), 177; JB Harley and Yolande O'Donoghue, *The Old Series Ordnance Survey Map of England and Wales* II (Lympne Castle, 1977), XII.

36 John Graves Simcoe Papers, Archives of Ontario, Series A-4-1, Loose Correspondence, Letter 2 July, 1804, Simcoe to Admiralty; William Ravenhill, 'The Honourable Robert Edward Clifford: A Georgian Military Map-Collector', forthcoming.

37 Hydrographic Office, Taunton, HD 702 Shelf Dc.

38 Howse and Sanderson, *The Sea Chart*, 91.

39 BL, Sec.1.(32), *Survey of Falmouth Harbour and the Coast to the Manacles . . .* Admiralty Chart, 1808.

40 Andrew David and Tony Campbell, 'Bibliographical Notes on Nineteenth Century British Admiralty Charts', *The Map Collector* 26 (1984), 13.

41 PRO, Admiralty 1/3523.

42 WA Seymour, ed., *A History of the Ordnance Survey* (Folkestone, 1980), 101–3.

43 GS Ritchie, *The Admiralty Chart*, 103.

44 Cornwall Record Office, DDJ 1640.

45 Thomas Hurd, *Charts of the English Channel* (1811).

46 Andrew David and Tony Campbell, 'Bibliographical Notes . . .', 14; GS Ritchie, *The Admiralty Chart*, 161.

47 Royal Institution of Cornwall, Truro, *Western Luminary*, 1821.

48 Tony Campbell, 'Episodes from the Early History of British Admiralty Charting', *The Map Collector*, No.25 (1983), 33.

22 *Devonians and the Newfoundland Trade*

David J Starkey

The waters off the seaboard of northeastern America form an ideal environment for the cod. Here, in the coastal reaches of New England and the Maritime Provinces of Canada, and further offshore in the relatively shallow seas covering the extensive continental shelf known as the Banks, this adaptable member of the *Gadus* family proliferates in highly favourable climatic, biological, and oceanographic conditions (see Map 22.1).[1] Europeans happened upon this abundance of fish during the great age of discovery and exploration in the late fifteenth century, and attempts were soon being made to relate a plentiful New World supply of protein-rich food with the rising demand of an Old World experiencing the beginnings of a demographic surge. Inevitably, the island of Newfoundland, the most easterly point of the North American continent and the nearest land mass to the Banks, became the focal point of the fishery which developed. The consequent extraction, processing, and marketing of 'Newland' cod constituted a significant industry in which many of the nations fringing the North Atlantic engaged at different times and to varying degrees.

Englishmen were among the first to investigate the potential of Newfoundland's fishing grounds, though a limited domestic market, already supplied with fish taken from home, Irish, and Icelandic waters, restricted the development of an English fishery during the first half of the sixteenth century.[2] In contrast, extensive home demand encouraged the French – who were afforded the further advantage of a ready supply of salt – and, in the mid-sixteenth century, the Spaniards and the Portuguese, to expand their transatlantic cod-fishing interests. From the 1560s, however, developments in the internal affairs and international relations of the European maritime states conspired to alter this market situation, precipitating a marked growth in the English fishery at Newfoundland. While religious strife seriously hindered France's fishing industry, the onset of the Anglo-Spanish War in 1585 provided the impetus for a concerted attack on Iberian fishing interests in the North Atlantic.[3] Accordingly, in the last quarter of the sixteenth century, English fishermen exploited a situation in which a rising domestic demand for cod coincided with successive crises of supply in the French and Iberian markets. By the end of the Elizabethan era the English had assumed a dominant role in the Newfoundland fishery, a primacy that was to last for some two hundred years.

Two vital features of the fishery remained constant. First, it was a seasonal business with a strong migratory character. Much of the equipment and the labour necessary to produce the commodity at the heart of the English trade – the lightly-salted, dried cod – was conveyed across the Atlantic to fish the shoals which normally appeared in Newfoundland's inshore waters in the summer months. Once secured, the cod was processed by the transient workforce on the island's shores, the marketable product, and most of the productive factors, being carried to Europe in the autumn. Second, from its inception this fishery was conducted largely from the ports of south-west England. A favourable westerly location, together with the failure of local fisheries,[4] perhaps explains the initial interest of Westcountrymen in the Newfoundland grounds. It seems that they quickly established a lead in the industry, a hold that was consolidated as regularity of operation led to the accumulation of capital and managerial expertise by the region's merchants, and the acquisition of seafaring and fishing skills by the local labour force.

Westcountrymen continued to dominate this business until the closing years of the eighteenth century, when the migratory fishery was finally eclipsed by the sedentary industry of Newfoundland's growing resident population. By this time, however, exploitation of the fish resource was not the only facet of the so-called 'Newfoundland trade', for the carriage of supplies to sustain the island's inhabitants – many of whom had emigrated from the West Country[5] – and the transportation of their cod to market had long since emerged as an important adjunct to the fishery. Devon played a

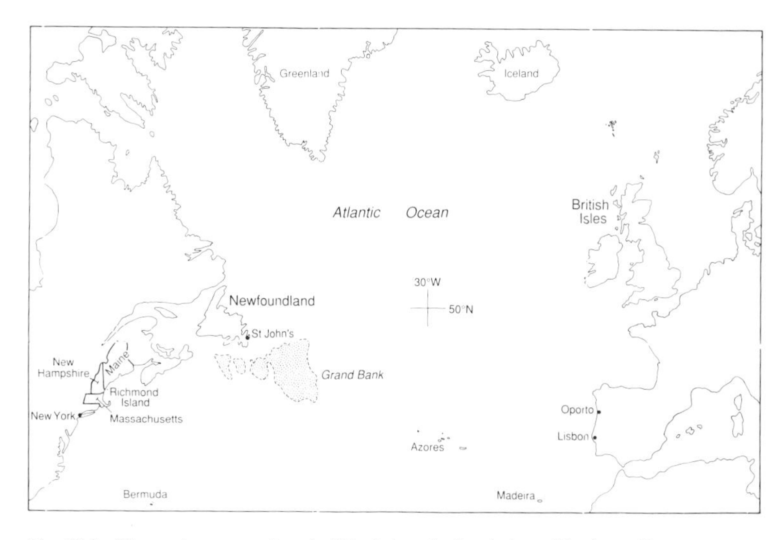

Map 22.1 The northeastern seaboard of North America in relation to Northwest Europe

22.1 Newfoundland: a typical 'tickle', a stretch of water between the mainland and a sheltering island, in 'a land that is infinitely silent, motionless, poor in vegetation, above all poor in its variety of living creatures, and a sea which harbours every form of life'. From R Perret, *La Géographie de Terre-Neuve* (Paris, 1913), 172. *(Public Archives of Canada)*

leading part in both the fishery and commerce of Newfoundland throughout the migratory era. While most of the county's maritime communities participated in some aspect of the business during its long course, the ports of south Devon, together with Poole in Dorset, emerged as the principal foci of the trade in the eighteenth century. Countless Devonians invested their capital and deployed their labour in a business which linked the fishing grounds of the North Atlantic, the shores of Newfoundland, and the marts of southern Europe but was organised from the counting houses and quays of their home county. It was here that the annual fishing and trading ventures were launched, and it was in Devon that most of the merchants, fishermen, and seamen continued to live. Thus, in examining this enterprise and its significance to the county's economy, this chapter concentrates on the Devon

> merchants and mariners who for centuries went annually to Newfoundland to win a living which would enable them to remain still in England.[6]

Long-term Fluctuations and Adaptations

The Newfoundland trade was a complex business. At base it was a fishery, though in time it developed into a broader branch of commerce involving the transportation and exchange of goods other than dried cod. While the fishery was essentially Eurocentric, in that it was largely conducted by English migrants whose product was consumed in Catholic Europe, it entailed an important island-based or 'sedentary' dimension, for the fish was invariably processed on Newfoundland's shores. Moreoever, from the early seventeenth century, part of the catch was taken by inhabitants of the island; though inconsequential for many decades, the output of the residents' fishery increased as Newfoundland's population expanded over the eighteenth century, surpassing the production of migrants during wartime and eclipsing it finally in the 1790s (see Table 22.1). As the basis of the fishery altered from the migratory to the sedentary, so the interest of migrants shifted from harvesting cod to servicing the island-based producers. Such transitions were by no means gradual, however, for the pace and direction of change was ultimately conditioned by the general prosperity of the fishery – a precarious determinant which itself fluctuated according to a wide array of influences.

Table 22.1
Output of the Migratory Fishery in War and Peace, 1698–1826

Years		Total Output	Migratory Output	Proportion Migratory
		(Quintals p.a.)		%
1698–1701	P	342,150	206,600	60.4
1702–1712	W	104,637	44,039	42.1
1713–1738	P	187,566	130,396	69.5
1739–1748	W	322,616	174,713	54.2
1749–1755	P	420,277	232,111	55.2
1756–1763	W	374,061	141,171	37.7
1764–1775	P	628,530	338,589	53.9
1776–1783	W	428,966	218,840	51
1784–1792	P	648,667	348,233	53.6
1793–1801	W	412,977	123,076	29.8
1802	P	n.a.	n.a.	–
1803–1815	W	678,032	34,641	5.1
1816–1826	P	745,964	47,715	6.4

P = Peacetime
W = Wartime
n.a. = not available

Source: S Ryan, 'Newfoundland Consolidated Census Returns, 1698–1833. Abstract of CO 194 Statistics' (unpublished typescript, Memorial University of Newfoundland, 1969).

In the mid-sixteenth century perhaps four or five vessels sailed from England for Newfoundland's fishing grounds each year.[7] As market factors turned in its favour, however, the infant English industry prospered to the extent that a 30-strong fleet known to have been operating in 1574 had expanded to 50 vessels in 1578, and to 250 'fishing' ships, producing 300,000 quintals (1 quintal = approximately 112lb) of dried cod in 1615.[8] Five years later, it was estimated that 300 craft made the outward passage to Newfoundland, a fleet which engaged the services of no fewer than 10,000 men.[9] This probably represented the high-water mark of the 'ship' fishery, the organisational system prevalent in the late sixteenth and early seventeenth centuries. 'Fishing' ships were fundamental to this operational system, being deployed to convey large numbers of fishermen from England to Newfoundland each year. On reaching the island a base, or fishing 'room', was established where the ship was laid up while the men fished the inshore waters in small boats; the catch was returned daily for curing on wooden stages and 'flakes' (drying platforms) erected at the shore base. At the end of the season the room was abandoned and the dried cod was transported to European markets in the fishing ship or else in a 'sack' ship, a carrying vessel despatched to Newfoundland (often with a consignment of salt) to lade cargoes which were surplus to the capacity of the fishing fleet. The profits generated by these fishing enterprises were divided; thus, 'to excite their industry, and reward their labour', fishermen held

> a certain share or shares in the fish and oil that was taken and made during the voyages and upon their return the whole cargo was sold, and the proceeds divided, two-thirds to the owners, and one-third to the ship's company . . . which made it their interest to attend diligently to their employment, and raised an emulation among them to outvie one another.[10]

Labour-intensive and essentially migratory – characteristics which appealed to governments obsessed by the notion that trade should serve as a 'nursery of seamen'[11] – the ship fishery was a high-risk system critically dependent on buoyant markets and an abundant labour supply. Its vulnerability was clearly demonstrated in the 1625–30 war with Spain and France, as the Navy claimed a large portion of the workforce and the Spanish market was closed, causing a commercial crisis in the fishing ports.[12] Subsequently, its viability was undermined as a long stretch of predominantly poor fishing seasons, exacerbated by civil strife in England and successive conflicts with Spain and the Dutch, led to a prolonged depression in which the fishing fleet declined erratically from a zenith of 270 ships in 1644 to a nadir of 32 vessels in 1682.[13] Increasingly untenable, the 'ancient' system was gradually transformed as entrepreneurial elements within the workforce began to 'fish out their own account', employing five or six wage-earning fishermen to work the inshore waters in small shallops left 'bye' on Newfoundland during the winter.[14] While this practice eroded the cod-catching function of the traditional fishing ship, it added to her carrying role, for she now conveyed the 'bye-boatkeepers', together with their men and materials, across the Atlantic at the start and end of the season. As paying passengers and cargoes, these productive resources formed a stable and increasingly important part of the income generated by the fishing ship, encouraging vessel owners to curtail their fishing operations and reduce their crews to an average of 15 to 20 wage-earning men – a third of the size of the traditional, shareholding complement.[15]

The development of the 'bye-boat' fishery therefore modified the established order, ushering in functional and organisational changes which effectively reduced risks, stabilised costs, and introduced wage labour into the fishery. Moreover, this innovation signalled the future course of the Newfoundland trade. Though it took hold only slowly, and in certain areas, during the second half of the seventeenth century, the emergent system augmented the sedentary dimension of the fishery without disturbing its migratory pattern, for the capital employed by the bye-boatkeepers was based on the island but worked by labour and other factors transported annually from Britain. In due course, as Table 22.2 indicates, a growing proportion of the fishery was undertaken in boats kept permanently in Newfoundland – owned by resident or migratory boatkeepers – as the transatlantic fishing ships were increasingly deployed in servicing the island-based producers. Accordingly, as the eighteenth century progressed,

Table 22.2
Vessels Employed in the Newfoundland Fishery in War and Peace, 1698–1833

(Average Number of Vessels p.a.)

		British Ships		Boats		
		'Sack' Ships	'Fishing' Ships*	'Fishing' Ship Boats	'Bye-Boats'	Inhabitants' Boats
1698–1701	P	54	137	585	101	522
1702–1712	W	37	44	129	57	283
1713–1738	P	54	116	283	267	354
1739–1748	W	72	80	182	319	449
1749–1755	P	84	160	308	434	748
1756–1763	W	77	95	183	253	927
1764–1775	P	116	275	452	462	1,245
1776–1783	W	108	217 (86)	336	567	990
1784–1792	P	140	277 (168)	353	446	1,448
1793–1801	W	109	66 (54)	75	133	1,290
1802	P	170	58 (58)	n.a.	0	n.a.
1803–1815	W	349	33 (19)	52	0	2,331
1816–1833	P	443	20 (20)	n.a.	0	3,461

P = Peacetime
W = Wartime
n.a. = not available
* number of 'bankers' in brackets

Source: S Ryan, 'Newfoundland Consolidated Census Returns, 1698–1833. Abstract of CO 194 Statistics' (unpublished typescript, Memorial University of Newfoundland, 1969).

a relative decline was apparent in the number of boats working from fishing ships. In absolute terms the number operational varied with conditions of peace and war, but never again reached the level attained in 1698–1701.

That the fishing fleet increased in size – and the migratory contribution to total output remained fairly stable – in times of peace until the 1790s was due to a further refinement in the migratory fishery. In fact, many of the fishing ships enumerated in official returns before 1769 were engaged in taking catches of inferior quality fish on the Banks. Like the bye-boat fishery, this offshore operation was essentially a response to conditions which adversely affected the business. Thus, when the cod failed to appear in its usual abundance in Newfoundland's inshore waters for nearly 20 years after the 1710 season, migratory fishermen directed their attentions to more distant and productive grounds. Here, comparatively small sloops and shalloways, worked by just six or seven men, made three or four sorties a season, mooring for up to a month at a time before returning their heavily-salted catches to Newfoundland for drying. So successful did the adaptation prove that 'bankers' were despatched from England even after the inshore fish stocks revived in the 1730s, forming the mainstay of the migratory fishing fleet, as Table 22.2 suggests, for a further hundred years.[16]

While depression thus fostered new methods of prosecuting the fishery, it served to retard settlement in Newfoundland. The first concerted attempt to colonise the island, stimulated by the fishery's prosperity, was made by the Newfoundland Company in 1610. Though this and other proprietary efforts failed,[17] individuals settled in various parts of Newfoundland's 'English Shore' as the seventeenth century proceeded, surviving by fishing the inshore waters. These 'planters' and their contracted labourers, or 'servants', rarely remained on the island for long, returning to England after two or three winters or else moving on to New England.[18] Such ebbs and flows were largely conditioned by the state of the fishery. Accordingly, with recession regularly afflicting the business during the century following the 1630s, Newfoundland's population remained small, peaking at about 3,700 inhabitants in successful fishing seasons like that of 1700. It was not until the fishery experienced a period of sustained prosperity from the 1740s onwards that the island's population began to grow as a result of natural increase rather than temporary migration, at last developing the secondary employments, the administrative institutions, and the social infrastructure commensurate with a permanent settlement rather than a string of fishing stations. With the number of residents rising from under 5,000 in 1748 to over 20,000 in 1804,[19] the output of the sedentary fishery accelerated, accounting for much of the expansion in total production apparent in Table 22.1. This growth did not occur independently of the migratory sector, however, for the planters, like their seventeenth-century forebears, relied heavily on fishing and sack ships for supplies of materials and servants as well as for the carriage of their product to market. Therefore, as the island's population and its fishery became ever more established, so the interest of British merchants shifted away from cod production towards the supply trade.

The Seven Years' War (1756–1763) and the American Revolutionary War (1776–1783) interrupted the long-term expansion of the fishery as enemy naval and privateering operations, market closures, and the depletion of the labour force rendered transatlantic commerce both dangerous and costly. These conflicts also served to expedite the shift in the balance of the industry from the migratory to the sedentary, for the transportation problems of wartime were particularly acute for the owners of fishing ships and fishermen based in Britain. Consequently, the contribution of Newfoundland residents to total output increased, reaching 65.9 per cent in 1781,[20] and though migratory production revived with the onset of peace in 1764 and again in 1784, the absolute growth of the sedentary fishery continued. Under the stimuli of expanding markets and an abundance of fish, the peacetime periods of 1764–75 and 1784–88 witnessed marked upturns in both the resident and migratory elements of the industry. However, when the propitious market conditions evaporated in 1789, exposing the hollow, speculative nature of the postwar boom, it was the migratory fishery – by now the marginal, fluctuating arm of the business – which contracted sharply and irreversibly.[21] Within a decade the fishing fleet despatched from Britain had declined from an historic peak of 389 vessels in 1788 to just 47 craft in 1797.[22] Though 'bankers' accounted for roughly 6 per cent of the total catch in the early nineteenth century, the climacteric of the late 1780s effectively marked the end of the migratory fishery, an activity which had taken root over the previous two hundred years. Henceforth, the exchange of supplies for island-produced fish, a business which had its origins in the late seventeenth century and had grown rapidly as settlement proceeded from the 1750s, was to be the sole constituent of Britain's Newfoundland trade.

Devon's Significance in the Newfoundland Trade

'First settled by merchants and other adventurers inhabiting the western parts' of England,[23] the Newfoundland fishery (and the supply trades it spawned) was largely based in the West Country throughout the migratory era. Most of the ports between Bristol and Southampton engaged in the business at some stage during this long span, though the distribution of activity varied considerably over time, as the extent and prosperity of the fishery fluctuated, rival trades developed or declined, and entrepreneurial responses differed from place to place.[24] The largest and most populous southwestern county, Devon was conspicuously and consistently involved in this enterprise; while various of its ports emerged as focal points of the business, the county's merchants, seamen, and fishermen supplied many of

22.2 'The Old House Shipyard and Outhouses at Trinity, Newfoundland', probably painted by Michael Corne (1752–1845). Note the 'flakes' (drying platforms) at bottom left and the covered 'stages' to the right. *(Dorset Natural History and Archaeological Society)*

the productive resources which sustained the South West's deep-seated relationship with England's 'oldest colony'.

This involvement is clear in various sources relating to different phases of the trade's development. Thus, in its infancy, the fishery was largely undertaken by Bristol men,[25] though incidental evidence like the record of a payment of 8d to the watchman at Rame Head for lighting beacons to guide the 'Newfoundlandmen' into Plymouth in 1543 suggests that Devonians were even then involved.[26] This interest developed as the fishery expanded in the final quarter of the sixteenth century, the port books indicating that Plymouth and Dartmouth were by now 'predominant in the trade'.[27] By 1620, when the ship fishery was at its height, these two south Devon ports each accounted for 80 fishing ships in an English fleet of 300 sail.[28] As the golden age of the ship fishery passed and the long depression of the mid-seventeenth century set in, so Devonians retained their stake in the Newfoundland trade. This is evident in the source of many of the petitions which the fishing interest submitted to government throughout the period, like the aggrieved 800 Newfoundland fishermen who dwelt in the Torbay area in 1635,[29] the 'Gentry, Merchants, Owners of Ships, and other subscribed citizens' of Exeter, Dartmouth, Totnes, and Plymouth in 1670,[30] and those 'most humble servants', the mayors of Barnstaple and Bideford in 1675.[31]

The five censuses of the fishery undertaken between 1675 and 1684 indicate more precisely the interest of Devonians in the Newfoundland trade.[32] By this time the shortage of locally-owned carrying tonnage – which had led their predecessors to fear the monopolistic aspirations of London sack ship owners in the 1610s and 1620s[33] – had been remedied somewhat; thus, as Table 22.3 shows, London vessels were still engaged in the trade, but the shipping resources of Westcountrymen now constituted a substantial proportion of the carrying tonnage, with over 60 per cent of the sack ships that set forth in 1684 belonging to Devon ports. The county's preponderance was still more marked in terms of fishing ships, with almost 70 per cent of the fleet despatched in 1675 sailing from the county's havens, a proportion which increased to over 80 per cent in the 1680s. Dartmouth was the leading port in the ship fishery at this juncture, with Plymouth maintaining a relatively strong interest along with the north Devon bases of Barnstaple and, more especially, Bideford. Fishing ships belonging to at least 17 other British ports embarked for the Newfoundland grounds in the 1670s and 1680s, with Bristol, Fowey, Poole, Southampton, and Weymouth reinforcing the West Country basis of the industry. Significantly, these places, with the exception of Poole, withdrew from the business in the depressed season of 1684, an indication that the bedrock of the fishery lay in south Devon (especially Dartmouth), north Devon, and Poole.

The decline of the ship fishery and the innovation of the bye-boat and 'bank' modes of operation did not diminish Devon's role in the migratory fishery, but it did alter the pattern of the business within the county. As many of the bye-boatkeepers and bye-boatmen had learned their craft in fishing ships, merely changing their status from shareholder to passenger in the vessels which conveyed them to Newfoundland, the bye-boat system tended to reflect the pre-existing spatial distribution of activity. However, the enhanced sedentary dimension of the new system determined that it originated in the source areas which had established firm footholds in the more convenient harbours of Newfoundland. In this respect, as Map 22.2 shows, the fishing interests of Dartmouth, Teignmouth, and Topsham held the advantage, for their vessels had regularly frequented the coast between St John's and Cape Broyle, acquiring a strong familiarity with the most easterly and settled of the island's shores. The bye-boat fishery therefore developed in south Devon, consolidating the area's migratory links with St John's and its environs. A survey of 440 bye-boatmen working in St John's in 1680 revealed that 50 per cent were employed by boatkeepers from Teignmouth, 34 per cent were engaged by Dartmouth masters, while the others worked

Table 22.3
'Fishing' and 'Sack' Ships at Newfoundland by Port of Origin, 1675–84

Port	1675		1681		1684	
	F	S	F	S	F	S
Barnstaple	4	2	11	0	1	2
Bideford	23	3	14	2	6	4
Brixham	1	0	0	0	0	0
Dartmouth	29	8	33	6	15	14
Plymouth	12	10	6	6	4	6
Teignmouth	3	0	8	0	5	0
Topsham	0	10	0	5	0	11
Devon Total	72	33	72	19	31	37
Bristol	1	8	0	1	0	4
Channel Islands	5	0	6	1	0	1
London	8	16	0	21	0	4
Poole	8	0	8	0	6	6
Southampton	4	2	0	3	0	1
Weymouth	5	3	0	3	0	3
Others	1	3	2	7	0	3
Total	104	65	88	55	37	59
% Devon	69.2	50.8	81.8	34.5	83.8	62.7

F = 'Fishing' ships
S = 'Sack' ships

Source: K Matthews, 'A History of the West of England–Newfoundland Fishery' (unpublished D.Phil thesis, University of Oxford, 1968) 181.

for employers hailing from parishes between Stokeinteignhead and Brixham.[34]

In the eighteenth century the failure of the inshore fishery brought differing responses from the principal West Country fishing ports. The merchants and fishermen of north Devon, having exhibited little interest in the bye-boat system, persisted with a ship fishery that survived until the Seven Years' War, one of the 'minor mysteries' of the trade.[35] Entrepreneurs from Poole were less conservative, investigating inshore waters to the north and south of the extant English shore and, in time, developing an expansive supply trade with the settlements thereby established.[36] In contrast, south Devon's fishing interest, increasingly concentrated in the ports and creeks from the Dart to the Exe, exploited the relative proximity of its Newfoundland base to the offshore fishing grounds and invested in the 'bank' fishery. With the earnings of 'bankers' supplemented by the carriage of men and supplies for the bye-boatkeepers, a certain interdependence was apparent between the various strands of south Devon's fishing industry. Such integration heightened the area's significance as the Newfoundland trade expanded and diversified from the mid-eighteenth century. Thus, as Table 22.4 indicates, Dartmouth and Exeter, including its member ports of Teignmouth and Topsham, clearly dominated Devon's stake in the business by the 1770s, with Plymouth and north Devon having all but shed their interest. In national terms, moreover, Poole was the only centre to approach the south Devon bases in terms of the number of vessels despatched to Newfoundland.

However, the figures presented in Table 22.4 do not distinguish betwen craft licensed to engage in fishing and those deployed in the transportation of supplies and fish to and from the island – between fishing ships and sack ships in the anachronistic classifications still utilised by the Board of Trade[37] – while vessels calling at ports *en route* to Newfoundland are excluded. As Devon's prominence had always been more pronounced in terms of fishing ships, and as many of these craft sailed to Europe to pick up salt before crossing the Atlantic, it seems likely that the proportion of Newfoundland-bound vessels belonging to the county's ports, which ranged between 52.7 and 60.3 per cent in the 1770–92 period, underestimates the contribution of Devonians to the fishing fleet. Thus, when the migratory fishery collapsed in the 1790s, one anonymous observer remarked that

> all the decked vessels, and the greater part of the boats, which have been withdrawn from the fishery, are owned by merchants and boatkeepers usually residing in Great Britain, and chiefly in the county of Devon.[38]

Although this signalled the virtual end of the county's direct interest in the cod fishery, its economic ties with Newfoundland remained strong, for the migratory fishing merchants had long since cultivated the growing demand for goods and labour from the island's residents. Mirroring the spatial pattern of the fishery from which it derived, the commercial facet of the Newfoundland trade was based in south Devon and Poole. Thus, in 1785, a list of the 44 'most powerful traders in Newfoundland' included 22 Devon-based firms – 15 in Dartmouth, five in Topsham, and one each in Newton Abbot and Teignmouth – together with 14 merchant houses established in Poole.[39] In the same year Lieutenant-Governor Elford acknowledged the foci of the trade in suggesting that

> Poole and Dartmouth are the principal support of this country . . . they are the props which support Newfoundland and when both or either of these fails Newfoundland will be shaken to the core.[40]

Though it is somewhat exaggerated (merchants from Glasgow, Waterford,

Map 22.2 The English Shore of Newfoundland in the later seventeenth century

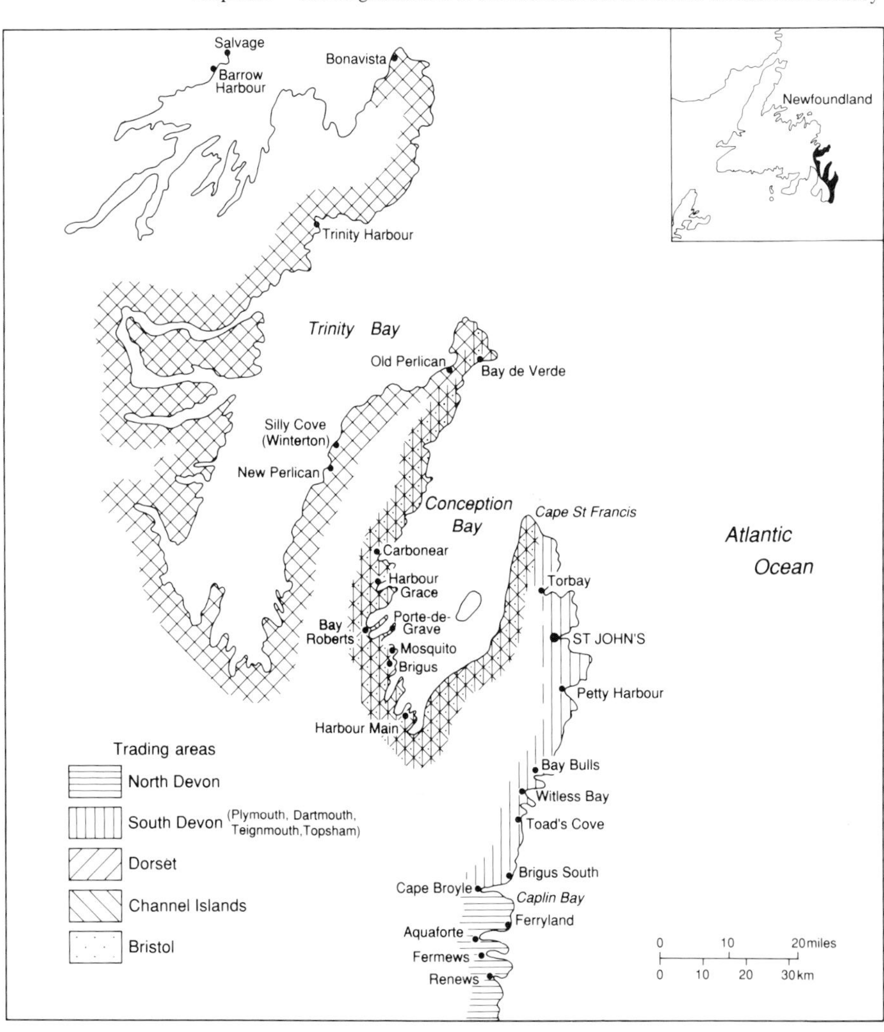

Table 22.4
Ships Clearing for Newfoundland from English Ports, 1770–92

Port	1770	1772	1774	1788	1790	1792
Barnstaple	0	2	2	0	0	0
Bideford	6	3	4	1	1	1
Dartmouth	61	65	74	118	90	85
Exeter	67	58	56	55	41	43
Plymouth	0	0	0	8	3	1
Devon Total	134	128	136	182	135	130
Liverpool	6	8	8	11	12	11
London	19	19	7	17	18	19
Poole	81	68	66	80	84	65
Southampton	7	7	5	2	1	2
Weymouth	6	5	2	0	0	0
Other	0	1	4	10	6	3
Total	253	236	228	302	256	230
% Devon	53	54.2	59.6	60.3	52.7	56.5

Source: Second Report of the Committee Appointed to Enquire into the State of the Trade to Newfoundland, 1793. Appendix 6(A). Reprinted in S Lambert, ed., *House of Commons Sessional Papers of the Eighteenth Century* (Wilmington, Delaware, 1975), vol. 90, 227.

and Liverpool had already begun to penetrate the trade), Elford's assertion implies that the business 'first settled' by adventurers from the 'Western Parts' in the sixteenth century was still centred in the South West on the eve of the nineteenth century.

Devon's Comparative Advantage in the Newfoundland Trade

Much of the quantitative evidence pointing to Devon's significance in the Newfoundland trade relates to the shipping requirement. Devonians owned a large proportion of the transatlantic vessels deployed in the business at various times – at least 55, 80, and 60 per cent of the fishing fleet in 1620, 1681, and 1788, respectively – and therefore controlled the major part of the industry's capital stock, for other fixed costs, notably the stages and flakes used for processing the cod, were relatively minor. Yet the capital assets at the core of the trade were decidedly unremarkable. By all accounts, a modest investment could secure entry into the industry, as fishing and carrying vessels were limited in size throughout the migratory era. Thus, Elizabethan and Jacobean commentators such as Hitchcock and Whitbourne concurred that the ideal fishing vessel should be between 70 and 100 tons.[41] In 1644 the average tonnage of the ships forming the fishing fleet was held to be 80 tons;[42] Dartmouth craft such as the *Byron* and the *Good Intent*, both of 90 tons burthen, embarked for 'Newfoundland and a market' with 'fishing craft, bread and flour' in their holds;[43] while Peter Ougier of Dartmouth informed the Enquiry of 1793 that 'bankers' ranged between 40 and 100 tons, and required 'only a moderate capital'.[44] Sack ships, too, were small compared with other transatlantic trading vessels, displaying a mean burthen of 114 and 137 tons respectively in 1722–1724 and 1787–1789,[45] whereas the typical eighteenth-century West Indiaman was almost 200 tons.[46]

Newfoundlandmen, moreover, were not specialist vessels. As the carriage of cod provided employment only in the late summer and autumn, sack ships were deployed in various branches of home and overseas trade at other times, including, no doubt, the eponymous wine trade. Similarly, fishing vessels were not fit for fishing alone; rather, they were of a build and a burthen that might be adapted inexpensively for redeployment in a range of alternative trades. A number of West Country fishing vessels, for instance, were fitted out as private men-of-war in the 1739–48 and 1776–83 wars,[47] while advertisements stressing the suitability of 100-ton ships like the *Hibernia* 'for the Newfoundland, Mediterranean or coasting trade',[48] or the handiness of the *Heart of Oak*, of 61 tons burthen, 'for the Banks, culm or coasting trades'[49] attest to the potential versatility of these craft.

Ownership of the shipping requirement reflected rather than explained Devon's – and the West Country's – preponderance in the trade and fishery of Newfoundland. At once prosaic, mobile, and easily liquidated, this capital stock did not afford the county's fishing interest an insuperable advantage in the prosecution of the business. Conversely, it presented no obstacle to entrepreneurs from other regions who might wish to break into the trade, particularly during its expansive phases. That this did not occur until the late eighteenth century raises three broad questions concerning the pronounced and prolonged 'Western' orientation of the trade. How did Westcountrymen, particularly Devonians, establish and maintain their virtual monopoly in the business? Why was the fount of this enterprise fixed so rigidly for so long in the West Country? What significance did the industry hold for the economy of its source areas? Complex and inter-related, the answers to such questions lie in the advantages accumulated by Devon's fishing merchants and fishermen amidst the political and economic processes which governed the development of Newfoundland, as well as its distinctive fishery and trade.

Public Pressure and Private Enterprise

Devonshire adventurers were involved in the fishery at Newfoundland from its inception. Regularly undertaking transatlantic ventures from the 1560s,[50] the county's fishing merchants and fishermen acquired an expertise which enabled them to retain their stake in the fishery as it expanded rapidly in the late sixteenth and early seventeenth centuries. This was a 'free' trade unrestricted by historic institutional structures, and therefore the emergent fishing interest was able to fashion a legal and political framework which furthered its primarily economic aims. Strengthened and given a self-conscious identity by the marked regional focus of the developing business, the so-called 'Western Adventurers' formed an interest group which proved particularly potent at critical times in the seventeenth century. By virtue of its public pressure, the West Country's fishing lobby protected an exclusive environment in which its private enterprise could proceed without the interference of any independent authority.

The Western Adventurers represented the interests of capital in the Newfoundland trade, employing the organs of local urban administration – which they dominated – to voice their disquiet to central government whenever occasion arose. At such junctures petitions and memorials issued forth from the mayors, corporations, and merchants of the fishing ports, stressing the general utility of the fishery in providing employment for the poor, wealth for the nation, and trained seafarers for the Navy. The adversities which prompted these pleas were many and varied; however, two crucial facets of the business – control over the shore of Newfoundland, and the regulation of the labour force – were the predominant concerns of the mercantile pressure group. Thus, if the island's harbours and creeks should fall under the private ownership of residents, access to the sites vital to the cod-drying process would be denied, while the refusal of fishermen to return to England would drain the essential labour resource, creating, perhaps, a rival, island-based fishery. Either way, the Western Adventurers reasoned, the free migratory structure of their business would be impaired and their enterprise ruined. When such threats materialised, notably in the early seventeenth century as sundry attempts were made to settle the island, and again in the 1660s and 1670s when the bye-boat fishery emerged, the state was urged to intervene to protect the free enterprise of the fishing merchants.[51] This seemingly contradictory proposition was resolved by the proviso that the fishery should be governed 'under the restrictions of such customs and laws as were agreed upon by the fishermen among themselves'.[52]

In acquiescing to such demands, successive governments, convinced by the contention that the migratory fishery was the 'greatest nursery of seamen of this nation',[53] confirmed the customary rights that the 'Western Adventurers' claimed to hold over Newfoundland and its trade. Edicts like the 'Western Charters' of 1634, 1661, and 1676 vested authority over the island's harbours and creeks in the first fishing ship's captain – the 'fishing admiral' – to arrive in each locality at the start of the season, while inhabitants were prohibited from settling within six miles of the shore, and residents or fishermen who injured the person or property of others on the island were to be deported and tried by the mayors of West Country ports.[54] Vague though it may have been, this self-regulating legal apparatus afforded the Western Adventurers the freedom they ultimately sought – freedom from the authority of an independent entity, be it in the guise of a colonial governor on the island or a trading company in London. Moreover, such a mechanism of control bolstered the migratory pattern of the fishery by effectively obliging fishermen to depart the island at the season's end, and by affirming the *de facto* property rights that migratory interests were increasingly exercising over purportedly free stretches of Newfoundland's shore. Here, with regularity of operation, stages, flakes, and boats were constructed and left over winter by transients intending to return in the next year, a logical practice which not only shaped future channels of migration but also placed the migratory property-holders in a pivotal position with regard to the development of the sedentary fishery.[55]

Once erected, this favourable framework effectively permitted the fishing merchants of Devon and Dorset to prosecute the fishery and trade of Newfoundland unhindered by the incursions of government and rival trading interests, their island-based property protected from the encroachments of settlers and fishermen alike. Such monopolistic tendencies intensified during the course of the seventeenth century as the West Country fishing interest, previously hostile to settlement of the island, actively sponsored permanent occupation of Newfoundland. From the 1630s, planters, most of whom were temporary migrants from the West Country, were furnished with servants and supplies by the migratory merchants,[56] though it was not until the 1660s and 1670s, with the introduction of the bye-boat fishery, that servicing island-based producers emerged as a clear trend. This innovation divided the fishing interest, as the more conservative merchants protested vehemently that the 'pernicious' practice was responsible for the demise of the trade, denouncing the evasion of the 1676 Charter by rival fishing ship owners

> who chose rather to quit part of their annual fishery by lessening the complements of their men and boats than to lose the advantage they made by carrying of passengers, and by disposing of their trifling adventures to the inhabitants.[57]

During the eighteenth century, particularly from the 1750s, the Western Adventurers continued to cultivate settlement in Newfoundland, exploiting their pivotal position in the fishery by leasing out fishing rooms – once 'the ancient possession of the Crown of Great Britain' but now the 'private property of merchants'[58] – to resident boatkeepers whom they provided with fishing tackle and servants. Paying for these services by mortgaging their fish before it was caught, the sedentary producers became embroiled in a cycle of debt, depending entirely on the migratory merchants for credit, supplies, and transportation facilities.[59] It was by virtue of this process that the West Country's fishing merchants maintained their hold over the Newfoundland trade even as their direct role in the fishery was being supplanted. Such a transition was accomplished by Devon and Dorset men whose predecessors had established a political and economic framework in which the fishery and island of Newfoundland could develop only in their interest. As much was astutely and somewhat cynically acknowledged by John Reeves in 1793:

> there had always been a set of men who have invariably set themselves against every attempt to introduce order and justice into that island; that these men have looked upon Newfoundland as their own property, to be enjoyed exclusively of the rest of His Majesty's subjects; and that every thing they have urged at different times has been to serve these private interests of their own . . . for attaining this end they have resorted to popular topics such as 'No residents' – 'A free fishery carried on from Great Britain' – but in their practice it has been found that they were the first encouragers of residency and population in carrying over the bye-boatkeepers, who settled there and became constant residents . . . It appears too, that the freedom they have mostly sought and exercised was that of being free of all rule and order themselves in the enjoyment of an exclusive monopoly, and at liberty to exercise a dominion over the boatkeepers and poor inhabitants, whom they kept in perpetual thraldom.[60]

Fishermen, Splitters, and Youngsters

In 1765, Governor Palliser was still arguing that

> the first and most important national object for the fishery . . . is the nursing and maintaining a number of seamen for speedy manning our fleets in time of danger.[61]

Such a belief, assiduously propagated by the Western Adventurers in the seventeenth century, framed government policy towards the Newfoundland trade until the late eighteenth century, underpinning reactionary legislative attempts to revive the ship fishery and reverse the flow of settlers to the island.[62] Though it is improbable that this argument was ever practically vindicated,[63] it had a sound if simplistic theoretical basis, for the labour force employed in the cod-fishing industry possessed precisely the qualities sought by generations of naval strategists. Thus it was large, with at least 10,000 men engaged during peak seasons; it attracted and trained large numbers of landmen; it was readily available, in that most of the men returned to England at predictable times each year after relatively short absences overseas; and it was skilled in the art of transoceanic seafaring. Such attributes also had a bearing on the distinctive West Country orientation of the Newfoundland trade, for in the particular skills and rare flexibility of the region's labour supply lay the reason why the business remained so firmly anchored in the localities where it originated.

The fishery was a labour-intensive activity. Cod – shore fish weighed an average of 10–12lb – were taken by rod and line, and then headed, split, gutted, salted, and left to dry on the island's shores before being loaded into sack ships and carried to Europe.[64] Skill was of the essence throughout the process. Small fish, especially capelin, had to be secured and prepared for use as bait before the fishermen could proceed to locations where they judged the cod might be plentiful; shore-workers were required to clean the fish thoroughly and expeditiously, applying the optimum amount of salt so that the cod neither burned nor reddened in the delicate drying process; and the shiphandling and navigational expertise of seafarers – who might also engage in fishing – was important, for the best fishing rooms in Newfoundland, and high market prices, rewarded swift transatlantic passages. Such skills were peculiar to the island's fishery and could only be truly acquired through the experience of a number of years in the business.[65] That Devonians regularly participated in these long-distance fishing voyages therefore gave rise to the formation of a nucleus of skilled labour in the vicinity of the ports engaged in the Newfoundland trade.

This concentration of local expertise can be discerned in various facets of the business. In the early seventeenth century, for instance, Devonians' knowledge of Newfoundland's waters was drawn upon by captains of Dutch carriers instructed to call at Plymouth to pick up a 'pilot for Terra Nova' or 'a man who will act as supercargo for the freighter and who will buy fish' on the island.[66] Similarly, London sack ships operated out of Devon ports, recruiting local seafarers conversant with the navigational and seasonal requirements of the trade.[67] An acquired expertise was also apparent in the work of the county's fishermen. Thus, in 1765, Griffiths Williams watched as boats operated by Irish and Devon crews fished the same Newfoundland waters, noting that the Devon vessel was completely loaded in seven hours, while its rival was lacking a full load even after a full day's work.[68] Ashore, these catches were often cured by transient workers from Devon, whose specialist role in the production process was reflected in designations like 'header', 'splitter', or 'salter' entered in the muster rolls of the ships which carried them to the site of their employment.[69]

If the Newfoundland trade required, and generated, a skilled workforce, the demand for this labour was both seasonal and liable to vary from year to year. Thus, the crews of Newfoundlandmen were normally recruited in March or April and discharged in the autumn,[70] while the migratory workforce was subject to pronounced short-term fluctuations, declining, for example, from 6,460 men in 1771 to 4,089 in 1773, and still further to 2,883 in 1778.[71] Some flexibility was therefore required of the labour supply, which implied that secondary employments were available if the workforce was to sustain itself during the annual off-seasons and periodic depressions which were an integral feature of the business. In this respect it is clear that the agricultural and maritime sectors of Devon's economy could absorb or release labour according to the dictates of the Newfoundland trade. During the annual cycle, servants might spend the summer in Newfoundland 'in the situation of day labourers, in which many have been employed at home in the winter season';[72] similarly, bye-boatkeepers displayed a 'propensity to . . . maintain their families in England, and to integrate the overseas fishery with homeland farming, trade work or other maritime pursuits'.[73] In 1774 it was said that Devon and Dorset supplied

> lads from the plough, men from the threshing floor and persons of all sizes, trades and ages and from the manufactories [who] flock annually, in the Spring, to Newfoundland [in] the hope of returning with six or ten pounds [from] the land of fish.[74]

Periodic fluctuations were partly accommodated by the ebb and flow of 'youngsters', the recruits and volunteers who supplemented the skilled element of the workforce during expansive phases in the Newfoundland trade. Generally, these 'green' men belonged to inland areas, whereas the regular fishermen and shore-workers hailed from the fishing ports and their environs. This pattern was still evident in the last quarter of the eighteenth century, despite the influx of large numbers of Irish migrants conveyed to Newfoundland in West Country vessels, and the increasing rigidity of Devon's agricultural labour market.[75] Thus the majority of skilled fishermen and seafarers enlisting in Dartmouth's Newfoundlandmen – notwithstanding John Tucker, a fisherman of Hatherleigh, and John Hooper, a 'header' of North Tawton – dwelt in the port itself, in Torbay parishes, or in the Newton Abbot district, while 'green' men resided in parishes such as Ashburton, Chudleigh, Hennock, South Bovey, and even Okehampton.[76] When contraction occurred such men returned to their homes or else remained in Newfoundland. Seafarers, however, generally turned to other maritime employments, with regular captains of Dartmouth's fishing ships such as Thomas Goldsmith, Philip Leigh, and Peter Tessier commanding private men-of-war in the 1776–83 conflict,[77] and Teignmouth seamen working in the coastal trade, while in 1804 the port's fishermen were said to be 'engaged in husbandry about the country near Teignmouth'.[78]

Such elasticity in the labour supply, together with the local concentration of skilled workers, evolved from the time the Newfoundland trade centred on the West Country. In turn, the source of the workforce increasingly became the focus of the trade. With the fishermen, splitters, and youngsters having a stake in the economy and society of Devon, the migratory pattern of the fishery tended to perpetuate itself. Only in the late eighteenth century, as the basis of the fishery shifted to Newfoundland – where, significantly, winter employments were developing – did Devon and the West Country cease to be the main fount of the Newfoundland trade.

'The Stay of the West-Countries'?

Implicitly, the longevity of the West Country's commitment to the Newfoundland trade, and the passion which it occasionally aroused, suggests that the business was of considerable significance to the local economy. In Devon it was important in various respects. During the long migratory era of the trade most of the county's havens despatched vessels to Newfoundland, though it was in the ports of Barnstaple, Bideford, Dartmouth, Exeter, and Plymouth that the business was chiefly conducted. Here, fishing ventures might account for a high proportion of shipping activity. In September 1620, for instance, 50 of the 70 ships which arrived at Plymouth had sailed from Newfoundland,[79] and no less than 84 per cent of the 389 musters submitted by captains of vessels entering Dartmouth between 1770 and 1774 pertained to Newfoundlandmen, the proportion rising slightly in the period 1788–1792.[80] Similarly, with 41 entrances and 24 clearances, Newfoundland was clearly the principal origin and destination of foreign-going craft using Exeter in 1790, though most worked out of the sub-port of Teignmouth.[81]

The operation of such vessels formed the basis of the wealth and power of some of the county's leading merchants. In north Devon the Bucks and the Darracotts were heavily engaged in the Newfoundland trade, while the Folletts, Haymans, and Jacksons of Topsham, and perhaps most notably, the dynastic firms of the Holdsworths, Hunts, Newmans, and Roopes of Dartmouth all derived substantial profits from the fishery.[82] In the process, these once humble Western Adventurers evolved by the mid-eighteenth century into 'gentlemen of the highest reputation and credit' in whom might be found 'great candour and respect'.[83] Meanwhile, thousands of Devonians worked in the transatlantic fishery, with the skilled fishermen, seamen, youngsters, and pauper apprentices[84] generally returning with shares or wages to spend in the markets and alehouses of their native county. The Newfoundland trade further contributed to the local economy in that it consumed the produce of various ancillary industries. Apart from ships, fishing tackle, and fitting-out equipment supplied by the county's port industries, the migratory nature of the fishery brought business to producers as diverse as the clothiers of Tavistock, the boot- and shoemakers of Ashburton and Buckfastleigh, and the market gardeners of Paignton, whose early-season cabbages were grown specifically for export to Newfoundland.[85]

While it was probably of wider importance to the county than most branches of overseas commerce, the place of the Newfoundland trade in Devon's economy should not be overestimated. As the fishery was essentially seasonal, its impact on port activity and the labour market was concentrated into the early spring and late autumn months. Long depressions beset the trade, most notably in the second half of the seventeenth century, inducing marginally-involved havens like Sidmouth, Exmouth, Kenton, and Dawlish to drop out of the business.[86] Increasingly during the eighteenth century the trade focused on Dartmouth and Teignmouth, restricting its 'knock-on' effects to an area to the seaward of a line joining Exeter, Ashburton, and Salcombe. Moreover, the main protagonists of the trade generally held other interests. North Devon's Western Adventurers developed trading links with mainland America and Ireland, merchant families such as the Folletts moved into the professions,[87] and investors such as William Newman became 'concerned with foreign and other houses abroad'.[88]

Though possessed of strong social and cultural ties with their homeland, the fishing merchants were economically committed to Devon only so long as a reservoir of skilled labour was fixed in the county. When the late eighteenth century witnessed the growing ascendancy of the sedentary fishery, mercantile capital either migrated permanently to Newfoundland, or else to London, Liverpool, or cod-marketing areas such as Portugal.[89] Similarly, the very transient character of the work naturally presented fishermen with the prospect of emigration to Newfoundland and thence, perhaps, to the American mainland. Those engaged in the ancillary trades in Devon were less mobile, though few were totally dependent on the Newfoundland trade, as the market for their goods extended to other branches of coastal and overseas commerce and, in many cases, into the domestic population. Thus, the Newfoundland trade was hardly the 'stay of the West-Countries';[90] yet for over two centuries it formed an important and integral feature of Devon's economy and society.

22: Devonians and the Newfoundland Trade

1 HA Innis, *The Cod Fisheries. The History of an International Economy* (Toronto, 1954), 1–10.

2 K Matthews, 'A History of the West of England–Newfoundland Fishery' (unpublished DPhil. thesis, University of Oxford, 1968) 34–40.

3 Matthews, 'West of England–Newfoundland Fishery', 46–59; DB Quinn, 'Privateering: The North American Dimension (to 1625)' in M Mollat, ed., *Course et Piraterie* (Paris, 1975), I, 360–86.

4 Matthews, 'West of England–Newfoundland Fishery', 68–9; and above chapter 17.

5 WG Handcock, *Soe Longe as there Comes Noe Women. Origins of English Settlement*

in Newfoundland (St John's, Newfoundland, 1989).

6 Matthews, 'West of England–Newfoundland Fishery', 3.

7 Handcock, *Soe Longe*, 24.

8 'Representation of the Lords Commissioners for Trade and Plantations to His Majesty, relating to the Newfoundland Trade and Fishery', 19 December 1718, printed in S Lambert, ed., *House of Commons Sessional Papers of the Eighteenth Century* (Wilmington, Delaware, 1975), vol. 90, 2 (hereafter 'Representation'); G Cell, *English Enterprise in Newfoundland, 1577–1660* (Toronto, 1969) 22, 100.

9 An estimate offered to the House of Commons by William Nyell, Member for Clifton Dartmouth, on 25 April 1621: LF Stock, ed., *Proceedings and Debates of the British Parliaments respecting North America* (Washington, 1924), I, 36; Cell, *English Enterprise*, 75.

10 'Representation', 2; see Cell, *English Enterprise*, 15–8, 150–3.

11 DJ Starkey, 'The West Country–Newfoundland Fishery and the Manning of the Royal Navy' in R Higham, ed., *Security and Defence in South-West England before 1800* (Exeter, 1987) 93–101.

12 Matthews, 'West of England–Newfoundland Fishery', 66; Cell, *English Enterprise*, 106–07.

13 Matthews, 'West of England–Newfoundland Fishery', 11, 19; 'Representation', 4, 11.

14 Matthews, 'West of England–Newfoundland Fishery', 162–70; Handcock, *Soe Longe*, 25–7.

15 Matthews, 'West of England–Newfoundland Fishery', 265–8; 'Representation', 17.

16 Matthews, 'West of England–Newfoundland Fishery', 306–12; Handcock, *Soe Longe*, 182.

17 Cell, *English Enterprise*, examines Newfoundland's proprietary colonies.

18 Handcock, *Soe Longe*, 27–30.

19 S Ryan, 'Newfoundland Consolidated Census Returns, 1698–1833. Abstract of CO 194 Statistics' (unpublished typescript, Memorial University of Newfoundland, 1969).

20 MA Chang, 'Newfoundland in Transition. The Newfoundland Trade and Robert Newman and Company, 1780–1805' (unpublished MA thesis, Memorial University of Newfoundland, 1974) 12.

21 Matthews, 'West of England–Newfoundland Fishery', 552–88; Chang, 'Newfoundland in Transition', 15–27.

22 Ryan, 'Newfoundland Census Returns'.

23 'Representation', 1.

24 Handcock, *Soe Longe*, 53.

25 Handcock, *Soe Longe*, 54.

26 JJ Beckerlegge, 'Plymouth Muniments and Newfoundland' *Transactions of the Plymouth Institution*, 18 (1936–7), 3.

27 Cell, *English Enterprise*, 101, and WJ Harte, 'Some Evidence of Trade between Exeter and Newfoundland up to 1600' *DAT*, LXIV (1932), 475–84.

28 Matthews, 'West of England–Newfoundland Fishery', 60.

29 *Calendar of State Papers Domestic, 1635–1636*, 30.

30 PRO, CO 1/32.

31 PRO, CO 1/34.

32 PRO, CO 1/35, 38, 41, 47, 55; see Handcock, *Soe Longe*, 55–60.

33 Matthews, 'West of England–Newfoundland Fishery', 74–89; Cell, *English Enterprise*, 97–100; and above pp. 131–3.

34 Handcock, *Soe Longe*, 59–60.

35 Matthews, 'West of England–Newfoundland Fishery', 266, 388–90.

36 Handcock, *Soe Longe*, 74, 219–42.

37 Third Report of the Committee Appointed to Enquire into the State of the Trade to Newfoundland, 1793, printed in Lambert, *Sessional Papers*, 90, 426.

38 Maritime History Archive, Memorial University of Newfoundland, Newman Papers, unsigned letter, 27 December 1790. I am grateful to Heather Wareham and her staff for bringing this information to my attention.

39 PRO, BT 6/87, cited in Chang, 'Newfoundland in Transition', 42.

40 PRO, CO 194/36, Elford to Sydney, 14 July 1785, cited in Chang, 'Newfoundland in Transition', 35.

41 Cell, *English Enterprise*, 3–4.

42 'Representation', 4.

43 PRO, HCA 26/62. Letter of Marque Declarations.

44 Evidence of Peter Ougier, First Report, 1793 Enquiry, printed in Lambert, *Sessional Papers*, 90, 145.

45 Ryan, 'Newfoundland Census Returns'; Second Report, 1793 Enquiry, Appendix 6(H), printed in Lambert, *Sessional Papers*, 90, 237.

46 R Davis, *The Rise of the English Shipping Industry in the Seventeenth and Eighteenth Centuries* (1962) 298.

47 See below, chapter 32.

48 *Sherborne and Yeovil Mercury*, 25 Jan. 1779.

49 *Sherborne and Yeovil Mercury*, 23 March 1789.

50 See above, p. 142.

51 See Matthews, 'West of England–Newfoundland Fishery', 133, 168–72.

52 'Representation', 1.

53 'Petition of the Gentry, Merchants . . . of Exeter, Totnes . . .'. PRO, CO 1/32.

54 The 1634 and 1676 'Western Charters' are printed in DW Prowse, *A History of Newfoundland* (New York, 1895) 154–5, 191–2.

55 Handcock, *Soe Longe*, 232–5.

56 Matthews, 'West of England–Newfoundland Fishery', 120.

57 'Representation', 5.

58 'Representation of the Lords Commissioners for Trade and Plantations to His Majesty, Relating to the Newfoundland Trade and Fishery', 29 April 1765, printed in Lambert, *Sessional Papers*, 90, 30.

59 Chang, 'Newfoundland in Transition', 1–34.

60 Evidence of John Reeves, Third Report, 1793 Enquiry, printed in Lambert, *Sessional Papers*, 90, 369.

61 Governor Palliser's Remarks on the 1765 'Representation', printed in Lambert, *Sessional Papers*, 90, 35.

62 For instance, see 'Palliser's Act', 15 George III, c.31.

63 See below, chapter 30.

64 See FNL Poynter, ed., *The Journal of James Yonge, 1647–1721* (1963) for a contemporary description of the fishery.

65 Handcock, *Soe Longe*, 253–4.

66 Charter Parties relating to the *Lily* and the *Unicorn*, drawn up in Amsterdam on 6 and 30 April 1624 respectively; transcripts are held in the Maritime History Archive, Memorial University of Newfoundland. I am grateful to Peter Pope for bringing this information to my notice.

67 Chang, 'Newfoundland in Transition', 48.

68 Cited in Matthews, 'West of England–Newfoundland Fishery', 426.

69 PRO, BT 98/3–8. Dartmouth Muster Rolls, 1770–1802.

70 PRO, BT 98/3. Dartmouth Muster Rolls, 1771.

71 Chang, 'Newfoundland in Transition', 11.

72 Evidence of Peter Ougier, First Report, 1793 Enquiry, printed in Lambert, *Sessional Papers*, 90, 145.

73 Handcock, *Soe Longe*, 26.

74 JM Murray, ed., *The Newfoundland Journal of Aaron Thomas, 1794* (1968) 173, cited in Handcock, *Soe Longe*, 256.

75 See Handcock, *Soe Longe*, 30–1, 88–90, 169.

76 PRO, BT 98/3–8. Dartmouth Muster Rolls, 1770–1802.

77 See below, chapter 32.

78 Handcock, *Soe Longe*, 163.

79 Cell, *English Enterprise*, 5.

80 PRO, BT 98/3–8, Dartmouth Muster Rolls, 1770–1802.

81 PRO, CUS 17/12.

82 Matthews, 'West of England–Newfoundland Fishery', 14–8.

83 Governor Palliser's evidence, Third Report, 1793 Enquiry, printed in Lambert, *Sessional Papers*, 264.

84 Handcock, *Soe Longe*, 61–3.

85 Matthews, 'West of England–Newfoundland Fishery', 10–11.

86 Handcock, *Soe Longe*, 55–7.

87 Matthews, 'West of England–Newfoundland Fishery', 15.

88 Evidence of Richard Routh, Third Report, 1793 Enquiry, printed in Lambert, *Sessional Papers*, 271.

89 Chang, 'Newfoundland in Transition', 60–6.

90 Sir Walter Raleigh's Address to the House of Commons, 23 March 1593, Stock, *Proceedings and Debates*, I, 7.

23 *Excavations at Ferryland*

PETER POPE

RECENT EXCAVATIONS AT FERRYLAND, Newfoundland, by the Memorial University of Newfoundland Archaeology Unit under the direction of Dr James Tuck have uncovered distinctive pottery and clay tobacco pipes which underline both the strength and the flexibility of Devon's commercial connexions with Newfoundland in the seventeenth century. Ferryland was colonized in 1621 by Sir George Calvert, later Lord Baltimore, and enjoyed a revival as a node in Sir David Kirke's London-based commercial network after he secured a new patent for the exploitation of Newfoundland in 1637. The ceramics from seventeenth-century Ferryland are generally what one would expect in a maritime community commercially dominated by West of England ports. Most are widely-marketed north Devon, Spanish Merida and tin-glazed earthenwares.[1] Less predictably, Totnes-type coarse earthenware pots were recovered in contexts of *c*1640–60. These are the first examples of this ware identified in North America (Fig 23.1) and, given its restricted distribution in Britain, are a strong indication of the presence of ships and fisherfolk from the communities along the Dart.[2] Statistical analysis of clay pipe bowl styles and marks confirms the south Devon connexion but suggests a post-Restoration shift in the Devon region to which Ferryland looked as a commercial metropole. Forms likely to have been supplied from south Devon ports predominate in assemblages dating before 1660, while the relative representation of forms more likely to have been supplied from the north Devon ports roughly doubles after 1660.

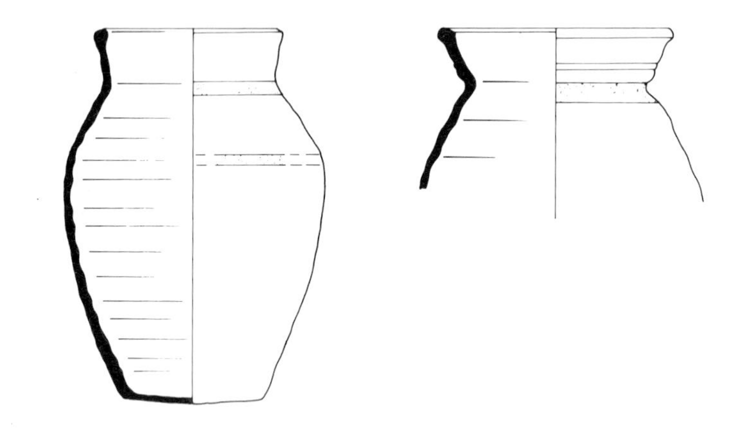

23.1 Totnes-type coarse earthenware pots from a forge/cookroom of *c*1640–60, Ferryland, Newfoundland (CgAf-2, Locus B). The left-hand pot is about 8 inches high. *(Peter Pope)*

In the seventeenth and eighteenth centuries particular West Country ports exploited specific areas on the rugged eastern coast of Newfoundland's Avalon peninsula. Thanks to the detailed fisheries censuses of the period 1675–84, we know the home ports of British ships fishing and trading in the various Newfoundland harbours at that time.[3] Ships from Bideford and Barnstaple dominated Ferryland and other southern Avalon harbours, while the ships of south Devon ports such as Dartmouth concentrated their efforts around centrally-located St John's.[4] The archaeological evidence suggests that Dartmouth withdrew, in the Restoration period, from an earlier active participation in the southern Avalon fishery, while north Devon fishermen and planters pushed northwards from their original fishery to the south of Ferryland. The socio-economic currents underlying the shifting geographical patterns of West Country activity at Newfoundland remain obscure. The archaeological evidence from Ferryland underlines the intensely local nature of early modern transatlantic connexions and the enduring vernacular character of the West Country fishery at Newfoundland, despite its continuing economic evolution, often under the pressure of metropolitan merchant capitalists such as the Kirkes.

23: Excavations at Ferryland

1 PE Pope, 'Ceramics from Seventeenth Century Ferryland, Newfoundland' (CgAf-2, Locus B), MA thesis, Memorial University of Newfoundland, Canadian Theses on Microfiche, 1986.

2 JP Allan and PE Pope, 'A New Class of South-west Pottery in North America', *Post-Medieval Archaeology*, 24 (1990), 51–60.

3 KM Matthews, 'A History of the West of England–Newfoundland Fishery', unpublished DPhil. diss., University of Oxford, 1968, 181–6; RC Harris and GJ Matthews (eds), *Historical Atlas of Canada*, I, *From the Beginning to 1800* (Toronto, 1987), pl. 23.

4 W Gordon Handcock, *Soe longe as there comes noe women: Origins of English Settlement in Newfoundland* (St. John's, 1989), 58, 64–68.

24 *Devon and the Navy in the Civil and Dutch Wars, 1642–88*

J D Davies

Devon's importance to the navy depended heavily on the nature and direction of England's foreign policy. When the nation was in conflict with France or Spain, as in the sixteenth, early seventeenth, and eighteenth centuries, the county and its chief naval harbour at Plymouth assumed a role of considerable strategic significance. However, the half-century between 1642 and 1688 saw both a massive internal upheaval in the form of a civil war and a major shift in foreign policy. The old rivalries gave way temporarily to conflict with the United Provinces of the Netherlands, a conflict stimulated largely by competition for trade: 'the trade of the world is too little for us two, therefore one must down', one English merchant of the 1660s remarked.[1] An inevitable consequence of this change of 'natural enemies', and of the three hard-fought wars which resulted from it, was that the chief theatre of naval conflict shifted to the North Sea, a shift which had natural and considerable consequences for Devon. For one of the few times in its more recent history, the county found itself temporarily relegated to the sidelines of naval strategy.

Devon at War, 1642–88

The Civil War

'Truly, my lords, if this town be lost all the West will be in danger to follow it.' The words of the Earl of Warwick, Lord High Admiral of England, written from Plymouth in August 1644,[2] neatly summarise several of the considerations underlying the course of the civil war in Devon. When that conflict began, in 1642, the major port towns, influenced by talk of Catholic plots and invasions and by a belief that the royal government in the 1620s and 1630s had failed to protect trade, declared for Parliament, so that much of the military strategy in the area came to centre on attempts by both sides to relieve or capture the ports.[3] However, as in the country as a whole, parliament's strategy was aided considerably by the adherence of virtually the entire navy to its cause, a choice of sides explained once again by maladministration in the 1630s (in this case, the failure to pay or victual the crews of the king's ships).[4] The use of the navy in Devon demonstrates its immense value to parliament in coastal areas. The fleet could be used to supply isolated and besieged strongholds: Plymouth was besieged almost continuously from December 1642 to January 1646, and one of the most important factors in its successful resistance was undoubtedly parliament's command of the sea. The regular arrival of supply ships was vital in maintaining the morale of the town, and during particularly dangerous royalist attacks parties of seamen could be rushed ashore to reinforce the defences, while their ships served as floating batteries.[5]

Conversely, the fleet (based at Portsmouth, and resupplied largely by sea) could impose a more effective blockade on ports which fell into royalist hands, a fate which befell all the other Devon ports in 1643. In July 1644, for example, Warwick had vessels on station off Dartmouth, Salcombe, and Topsham.[6] For the royalists, the southwestern ports were a vital link in their supply routes from the continent, particularly those which brought in arms and ammunition, though much of the traffic into and out of ports was simply a continuation of Devon's usual trade with Europe. Parliament was concerned about these contacts, and by the possibility that Devon might be an entry point for pro-royalist invading armies from Ireland or abroad,[7] and as the war progressed parliament's warships increasingly disrupted the shipping entering and leaving the ports. In July 1644 the *Dreadnought* and *Mary Rose* took two French vessels bound for Dartmouth, and in the following May the *Providence* took a royalist nine-gunner trying to slip out of the Dart.[8] The warships stationed in the southwest were also ideally placed to intercept vessels sailing to and from royalist Ireland. On 14 September 1645 alone, seven prizes carrying ammunition, pilchards, and salt for Ireland were brought into Plymouth, one of several successful hauls for parliament's warships that year.[9] Finally, as the king's cause collapsed, the navy tried to prevent the headlong flight of the royalists to the continent via the southwestern ports. Vice-Admiral Batten's blockade of Falmouth in July 1644 failed to prevent the escape of Queen Henrietta Maria to France, but in the following year a total of five vessels was deployed off Dartmouth and Topsham, 'for here is much preparation of divers people to run away'.[10] The fleet could also be used to support the operations of parliament's army. In 1644 Warwick's ships moved west to support the Earl of Essex's advance through Devon and Cornwall, with vessels carrying provisions to the troops. Indeed, one factor which contributed to Essex's humiliating surrender at Lostwithiel in August was the need for Warwick's supply ships to return to Plymouth because of contrary winds.[11] More successful was the co-ordinated attack on Dartmouth in January 1646, when 11 parliamentary ships prevented any royalist craft from escaping while General Fairfax's army (assisted by a shore party of 200 seamen) attacked the town.[12]

It would be misleading to suggest that the story of parliament's command of the seas off Devon was one of unqualified success. The fact that the Devon ports had to surrender to the king in 1643 amply proved the point that a fleet can only be in one place at one time. Warwick was then off the east coast, and the temporary commander-in-chief in the west, Captain Moulton, wrote with resignation in May that 'a fleet in this country would do much good, if there were no greater occasion elsewhere'.[13] Warwick arrived in July and immediately tried to relieve Exeter, but despite his superior forces he met the same fate as Moulton in the previous month: vessels crossing Topsham bar were trapped by the wind and tide, and unable to manoeuvre to escape the crossfire from royalist shore batteries. Moulton lost two ships in June, Warwick another three in his attempt.[14] Throughout the naval war, and despite the increasing number of interceptions by his blockading vessels, Warwick complained regularly that he had too few ships to deploy in the southwest.[15] In these circumstances the royalists were able to build up almost a miniature maritime state in the region. Privateers were fitted out for the king at Dartmouth and Barnstaple, financed by loans from and victualled by local merchants, armed with anything which could be spared from redundant merchant ships and shore batteries, and crewed by any mariners available locally, including captured parliamentarian seamen. A proper Admiralty jurisdiction was set up to deal with prize cases, and attempts were made to collect customs and other duties. Indeed, one motive which underlay Essex's advance into the region in 1644 was the desire to eradicate this hornets' nest of royalist naval activity.[16] Once the civil war in England ended in 1646 (in Devon, Exeter and Barnstaple fell in April), parliament rapidly made use of the former thorn in its side as a base for its operations against the continuing royalist threat from Ireland. Munitions and supplies were shipped from Barnstaple to Munster, while Plymouth became the main victualling base for parliament's Irish squadron.[17] In this way, as in so many others, the history of the civil wars in Devon demonstrated the truth of the royalist minister Edward Hyde's maxim that the 'loss of the whole navy was of unspeakable ill consequence to the king's affairs'.[18]

The Anglo-Dutch Wars

The commercial rivalry between England and the Netherlands culminated in the Anglo-Dutch wars of 1652–4, 1664–7, and 1672–4. Devon was on the periphery of these conflicts, at least in terms of its proximity to the main fleet actions of the war, although (as this chapter will demonstrate) individual ships and squadrons were based at Plymouth in each of the wars and the county continued to provide significant numbers of officers and men for the service. Moreover, the Dutch were loath to give up their most direct and important sea route, the English Channel, and sometimes attempted to run the gauntlet. This strategy caused the main naval engagement fought off Devon during the Dutch wars, on 16 August 1652. The great Dutch admiral Michael de Ruyter, at sea with 30 ships to guard a Dutch convoy through the Channel, engaged 42 English vessels under Sir George Ayscue. Despite the disparity in numbers, de Ruyter got the better of an indecisive battle, forcing Ayscue to run for Plymouth.[19] De Ruyter reappeared off Devon in 1667, when the main English battlefleet had been laid up at Chatham because of the government's desperate financial straits. Small flying squadrons were based at strategic ports to defend the coasts and harass Dutch shipping, that at Plymouth being commanded by Admiral Sir Thomas Allin and the Devonian Sir John Kempthorne. After leading the famous assault on Chatham, de Ruyter sailed west and appeared off Plymouth on 15 July, off Dartmouth three days later, and off Torquay, where he made a half-hearted assault, on the nineteenth. Fortunately, Allin had been able to strengthen the shore defences (though his ships had to stay in port for fear of the superior Dutch numbers), and the Dutch were unable to do much damage. By the time de Ruyter returned to Plymouth Sound, on 29 July, peace had been agreed, and Plymouth enthusiastically revictualled and paid its compliments to the Dutch admiral and fleet which had so recently threatened it.

The next visit of the Dutch navy to Devon was to be greeted with even more enthusiasm.[20] One of Prince William's chief objectives in November 1688 was to draw England into his 'grand alliance' against Louis XIV's France, and his accession to the throne as William III enabled him to carry this out. One consequence of the resulting shift in naval operations from the North Sea to the Atlantic and the Channel was the need for a new dockyard in the South West – a fitting outcome of William's fortunate Devon landfall.[21] Plymouth could already boast a record of continuous and invaluable service to the navy throughout the seventeenth century: its elevation to dockyard status was really the expansion of a well-established operation, not a wholly new beginning.

Plymouth as a Naval Base

The 'Western Squadron'

Although Plymouth was never an operational base on the same scale as the Thames and Medway dockyards and Portsmouth, it had a vital role to play throughout this period as the navy's chief port in the west. Its particular importance was as a base for the defence of trade entering or leaving the Channel, or to guard more local cross-Channel trade, and it quickly became established as an essential element in the increasingly-elaborate convoy systems which developed from the 1640s onwards in response to the constant depredations of pirates, foreign privateers, and enemy warships. The nature of the response was usually an attempt to combine the two strategies of 'cruisers' and 'convoys', and either stategy could be adopted as appropriate by a flexible 'western squadron' based at Plymouth. This force was already a regular part of the naval establishment by 1650, when Captain (later Sir) William Penn was appointed 'commander-in-chief in the western squadron' of six ships, with orders to guard the Channel from Beachy Head to Lands End.[22] In later years the squadron's operational area extended west into the Soundings, and many of its vessels were often detached to convoy cross-Channel shipping. In April 1660 six ships were on convoy duty, taking west country ships (including several carrying tin) from Plymouth to the Downs, and convoying other vessels to Wales, Ireland, Morlaix, and La Rochelle, as well as from La Rochelle to Plymouth; two ships were cruising, one in the mouth of the Channel, and one *en route* to Kinsale.[23] The vessels serving in the squadron at this time were typical of those which formed its establishment, at least until the time of the second Dutch war: two fourth-rates of 40–48 guns, three fifths of 24–28 guns, and three sixths of 12–16 guns. Despite the general Restoration trend of forsaking the two bottom rates, the squadron continued to consist largely of fifth-rates (like the *Mermaid, Pearl*, and *Hunter*, which comprised its strength over the winter of 1673–4), or prizes like the *Sorlings*, vessels which could release larger, English-built (and therefore more widely favoured) vessels for service in the main fleet or elsewhere.[24] The squadron was also used to guard outgoing or incoming fleets of merchantmen, such as those to and from Virginia, Barbados, and Newfoundland, and it would be reinforced to escort a particularly important fleet, perhaps even with a third-rate like the 60-gun *Plymouth* of 1653.[25] Particular care was taken of Devon shipping, and local merchants' solicitations for convoys were often successful, although on one occasion the Admiralty complained that Plymouth merchants were

> pretending their ships to be ready to sail and lying for want of convoy, and occasioning thereby great hurrying and charge to the king, when it has been found that they were not ready.[26]

However, the squadron was never entirely capable of fulfilling all of its commitments. The cruising and convoy roles might not be compatible if there were many hostile ships on the western coasts, and many ships requiring convoy. In 1673, for instance, the Admiralty was caught between the two stools of trying to reinforce convoys while simultaneously ordering ships to cruise independently to deal with the many small Dutch privateers or 'capers' in the area.[27] In the long peace after 1674 retrenchment of naval expenditure meant that there were few ships in service, the western squadron *per se* fell into abeyance, and vessels nominally allocated to cruise in the Soundings often found themselves diverted further afield to convoy shipping, perhaps to destinations as distant as the Canaries, Spain, and Portugal.[28] It proved difficult to prevent attacks from the ships of Ostend, Flushing, France, and even Algiers. In the summer of 1677, for example, Algerine warships were plying between Ushant and Lands End, 'in the very chops of the Channel' in Samuel Pepys's words, and (among other ships) captured the *Truelove* of York, bound from Plymouth to Bilbao, off Ushant. The four English warships available were supposed to pursue both these elusive corsairs and the interminable swarm of Ostend privateers which was terrorising the Channel at the same time.[29]

Plymouth continued to play its part as a base for the patrolling warships, and as a first or last landfall for vessels returning to or leaving England. Warships convoying merchantmen on the deep sea routes, to the Mediterranean or the Americas for example, invariably called at Plymouth on the outward voyage to take on last-minute supplies and instructions, to collect west country shipping bound in their direction, or to await stragglers, and also called at Plymouth on the return journey before sailing on to the Downs or the Thames.[30] Similar use of Plymouth was made by ships bound for distant stations, particularly the Mediterranean. Substantial fleets were maintained there intermittently in the 1650s, and almost continuously from 1662, when England acquired Tangier, until 1682–4, when the long war with Algiers ended and Tangier was evacuated. Plymouth was a valuable link in the chain of communication to these fleets and to Tangier, and (particularly in the 1660s) it served as the main victualling base and port of embarkation for the isolated North African outpost of Charles II's England.

The Infrastructure of Naval Support

The facilities for servicing the navy at Plymouth during this period were rudimentary. No dock of any sort existed, and warships requiring major repairs or refitting always had to sail to Portsmouth or further afield. A careening hulk, the Spanish prize *Elias*, was stationed at Plymouth from 1657 until she was condemned in 1684,[31] but no more elaborate facilities were provided until the building of the dockyard in the 1690s. Other support facilities were equally makeshift. In about 1656 several victualling storehouses were built on the Lambhay, but these were demolished in 1660 because they prejudiced the defences of Plymouth fort. Thereafter, storehouses on the Lambhay were rented from local merchants.[32] Naval facilities were therefore centred in Plymouth itself and its immediate environs: the hulk was moored in the Cattewater, and warships using the port traditionally used the same anchorage, rather than the more exposed Hamoaze.[33]

Plymouth was one of several outports at which the Commonwealth and Restoration governments established naval agents, though the intermittent nature of the appointments at other ports (Deal, Dover, Hull, Yarmouth, and Kinsale) suggests that Plymouth occupied a special, more permanent, place in naval strategy. From 1652–88 the post at Plymouth was in the hands of only three men, whose background and individual careers are described elsewhere in this volume: Henry Hatsell (1652–61), John Lanyon (1661–74), and his uncle Philip Lanyon (1674–88).[34] The powers delegated to these agents varied considerably. In particular, Hatsell exercised a degree of control over the operations of Plymouth-based ships which neither of his successors ever possessed. Hatsell was able to give sailing instructions to units of the western squadron and other vessels, and he regularly ordered warships to convoy merchantmen to and from Devon ports, or ordered them to particular stations.[35] The Lanyons had little, if any, say in the giving of operational orders: by the 1670s the Admiralty was taking all important decisions itself, and providing commanders of convoys with exhaustively complete instructions which largely eliminated the need for a 'land admiral' at Plymouth.[36]

Warships using Plymouth required materials such as masts, anchors, and canvas to enable them to make 'running repairs'. Most of the supplies had to be acquired locally, and both the limited nature of the hinterland and the alternative demands of merchant shipping ensured that shortages often occurred. In 1656 Hatsell found it almost impossible to get gun carriages, 'there being but one carriage maker in this town, and he very much employed by the merchants in this season of the year'. In the following year he had to obtain deals and elm boards from Portsmouth, cordage and hemp from his own contacts in Brittany, and on one occasion he obtained tar from a Norwegian captain who had traded to Devon for many years.[37] In 1665 John Lanyon encountered shortages of masts, sails, canvas, and cables, and overcame a gunpowder shortage only by borrowing some from local landowner Sir John Skelton.[38] Victuals were handled separately by the local agents of the victualling office in London, which allocated set amounts to each port for each year. In 1674 Plymouth was to receive victuals for 1,500 men, making it the fourth victualling centre after London (22,700), Portsmouth (4,000) and Dover (3,000).[39] The captain of a warship coming into Plymouth would therefore have to deal with both the naval agent, to get his ship refitted, and the victualling agent, to get provisions for his men.

Unfortunately, naval supply at Plymouth usually operated with very little money, and often with no money at all. The letters of Hatsell and the Lanyons over thirty years repeat the same story almost *ad nauseam*. The governments of the 1650s had been largely bankrupted by an ambitious foreign policy, those after the Restoration by parliamentary ignorance of finance, royal extravagance, and an ambitious but unsuccessful foreign policy. The navy as a whole suffered: crews, dockyard labourers, and contractors went unpaid, with Plymouth's distance from London telling against it, simply because disgruntled Devonians were unable to pester officials in the same direct ways that Thames merchants or Chatham-based mariners could. Hatsell complained regularly to the administration that his bills were not being cleared, and that he had to use his own credit to buy stores. He hinted at the different treatment of Plymouth, arguing that laying out his own money was

> the case of very few that serve you . . . for although you are straightened for money, yet I humbly conceive there is no reason why such a burden should lie more on me than on any other. . . .[40]

Even so, the situation became progressively worse under a series of short-lived and bankrupt governments in 1658–60. Plymouth's naval debt grew to over £4,000 by the spring of 1660, and the tradesmen of the town complained bitterly that they were not being paid.[41] Even the victualling agent refused to supply any more until his bills were paid, and he was later arrested by his creditors.[42]

The year 1660 brought both a restoration of the monarchy and a brief restoration of government finances, but the second and third Dutch wars soon placed John Lanyon in the same predicament. He claimed to be £2,600 out of pocket by February 1666, a sum which had more than doubled by November, when he warned the Navy Board's Samuel Pepys that 'my credit do suffer very much, and the complaint of the tradesmen and carpenters is heavy upon me'. Pepys did what he could, but money was always diverted to other, seemingly more immediate, priorities.[43] The naval administration's failure to pay its debts finally had its inevitable consquence in 1673–4, when the local tradesmen refused outright to provide any more supplies for the navy until their previous bills were paid, and the frigate *Swan* could not be refitted because the tradesmen were unwilling 'to trust his Majesty further'.[44] Peace brought a respite, though even then Plymouth was easy to neglect: the town's tradesmen continued throughout the 1670s and 1680s to grumble about the navy's failure to pay its debts, eventually suing Philip Lanyon for £166 due on ships refitted two years before.[45]

Despite the apparent neglect of Plymouth, and the comparatively limited use made of it between 1642 and 1688, several suggestions were put forward for a major expansion there. John Lanyon presented to the administration an account of the defects of Plymouth, and suggested remedies for them: he attributed the silting of the Cattewater to the spoil from tin workings and quarries washed down into the harbour, and proposed better dredging and an exemption of sand barges' crews from the press. He also proposed a dry dock on the Cattewater to support an enlarged, permanent western squadron.[46] In 1677 Sir John Narbrough proposed using Plymouth as a supply and refitting base for vessels of his Mediterranean fleet stationed to the west of Gibraltar, believing that it would be superior to the fleet's existing victualling base, Leghorn.[47] However, nothing came of these schemes. Although King Charles II seems to have been impressed with Plymouth on his two visits there in 1671 and 1677,[48] the Admiralty was less enthusiastic. Narbrough's proposal was rejected in favour of Lisbon, and another suggestion that a resident commissioner of the navy should be established at Plymouth was rejected on the grounds that 'whatever it be in war, no such officer is needful in peace'.[49]

Devon's Naval Manpower

The Officers

The navy's adherence to Parliament in 1642 led to a purge of aristocratic, royalist officers from the fleet, and created opportunities for men from humbler backgrounds. The Interregnum navy drew its captains from three main sources; merchant ship masters, naval warrant officers, and army officers,[50] and Devon provides fine examples of each type of career. The merchant captain John Stoakes of Plymouth first entered the navy in 1649 as captain of the *Hector*, rising to a series of increasingly important commands, including that of rear-admiral in the Mediterranean in 1655 and 1657–9. He held several major commands under Charles II before dying at the start of the second Dutch war.[51] The career of Nicholas Heaton of Plymouth was one of the most extraordinary of any seventeenth-century naval officer. Originally just a trumpeter's mate, he rose to command two frigates between 1653 and 1660, but was excluded from the navy after the Restoration because of his unwillingness to conform to the Anglican faith. Even so, his local reputation remained considerable, and as late as 1673 merchants were prepared to recommend him as the best man to take a large convoy westward.[52] From the army came the most famous Devonian naval officer of the age, George Monck, general-at-sea in the first Dutch war, architect of the restoration of King Charles II, and joint general-at-sea again, as Duke of Albemarle, in 1666. Monck's career as a whole and his service as a naval commander are thoroughly documented, and need no detailed recapitulation here.[53] However, it is worth noting that Monck's regard for his Devon ties was enduring: even when aboard his flagship on the eve of battle in 1666, he endeavoured to administer the lord lieutenancy of the county himself, by post, until the government persuaded him to appoint a deputy.[54]

After the Restoration the nature of the officer corps changed once again. Many of the officers of the interregnum period remained, to be joined by new men who had also risen from the merchant service or from warrant posts. These 'tarpaulins' now found themselves competing for naval posts with 'gentlemen' officers, young men from unimpeachable royalist backgrounds whom Charles II and his brother James, Duke of York, Lord High Admiral from 1660 to 1673, encouraged to join the service. Once again, Devon contributes examples of each of these kinds of naval officer. Into the navy from the merchant service came John Kempthorne, the son of a Devon attorney, who gained his first experience on a Topsham ship before commanding large merchantmen in the Mediterranean trades. His reputation rests largely on two famous single ship actions, his vigorous defence against a Spanish privateer in 1657 (which ensured him a prestigious command as soon as he entered the navy in 1664), and his fight in the *Mary Rose* against an Algerine squadron in 1669, for which he was knighted. Kempthorne became a vice-admiral and resident commissioner of the navy at Portsmouth, where he died in 1679, but he continued to hold land at Bigbury until his death.[55] Sir John Berry was the second son of a vicar of Knowestone whose early death left the family destitute, forcing Berry and his brother into the merchant service. By 1663 he was a boatswain in the navy, rising to command a ketch in the West Indies in 1665. He then served almost continuously as a captain until 1689, was knighted for bravery at the battle of Solebay in 1672, and became a vice-admiral and commissioner of the navy. He seems to have maintained few direct links with Devon, settling instead in London and Kent; nevertheless, he bequeathed five pounds in his will to the poor of his home parish.[56] Less spectacular careers included that of Stephen Ackerman, a merchant captain in the 1660s who commanded a vessel of the western squadron in 1665–7, became a grocer at Plymouth after the war, and returned to the navy in 1678, holding a series of commands in later years and hurriedly preparing the hired ship *True Dealing* at Plymouth in 1685 to defend the Devon coast against the Duke of Monmouth's rebels.[57]

Devon also provided its share of 'gentlemen captains'. Hugh Seymour, the third son of Sir Edward Seymour, third baronet of Berry Pomeroy, entered the navy in 1661 as a volunteer, rose to command in 1664, and was killed in the Saint James's Day Fight in July 1666. Monck praised him highly as 'a discreet young man and dilligent'.[58] Seymour's cousin, Francis Courtenay of Powderham Castle, commanded continuously from 1660 to 1673, when he died in command of the *Dunkirk* at the battle of the Texel.[59] Bearing in mind the appalling reputation which the 'gentlemen captains' of the Restoration have gained, it seems clear that both Seymour and Courtenay were competent and popular captains; but to redress the balance, Seymour's nephew William was reported to have been made a lieutenant in the 1680s only to gratify his father, the Speaker of the House of Commons, and was said to be 'a very idle gaming fellow'.[60] Other Devonian naval officers benefited less from direct paternal influence than from a network of local connections, and friendships with potential patrons who could advance their careers. During his time as naval agent Hatsell recommended several local officers for advancement, notably Captain Robert Plumleigh of an old Dartmouth merchant family. In later years Richard Tapson of Stonehouse and his eponymous son, a naval lieutenant, were advanced by Sir Richard Edgcumbe, who also promoted Ackerman's career. Tapson also enjoyed the patronage of the Governor of Plymouth, Colonel Piper, while Ackerman was being recommended in the 1680s by Lords Bath and Arundel, Sir John Covington, and 'all the gentry in the west'.[61] In an age when patronage was the single most important criterion for advancement in the service, such recommendations were worth a great deal.

The Seamen

Local ties also played an important part in the recruitment of seamen, with Devon captains, well known among local seamen and with strong ties in the maritime communities, usually being able to attract large numbers of volunteers. At different times Kempthorne, Tapson, and the Plymouth 'tarpaulin' Jeremy Roach were able to claim that they could man their ships almost entirely with Devon volunteers, brought in by the traditional methods of word of mouth and beating the drum at seamen's inns.[62] When Ackerman's *True Dealing* was suddenly paid off in 1685 at the end of Monmouth's rebellion, Samuel Pepys, as Secretary of the Admiralty, commiserated with him that this would make him 'suffer in your credit with the seamen of your country'.[63] In 1678 both Kempthorne and his admiral, Sir Thomas Allin, sent boats to Plymouth to raise men. Kempthorne had already made it clear in letters to his friends that he would take only volunteers, and they flocked to serve under him, 'Sir John being this country's man'. The officers of Allin's boat attracted hardly any volunteers, and quickly had to resort to pressing.[64] However, 'tarpaulins' were not alone in being able to attract volunteers: Francis Courtenay's name was sufficient to persuade many, particularly from the hinterland of Powderham Castle, to make their way to his ship.[65]

It is difficult to demonstrate in statistical terms the importance of Devon's contribution to the manning of the navy during this period. No detailed musters showing the origins of ships' crews were kept, and records of origin in ships' paybooks are few and far between. The little evidence which does exist helps to confirm the point that Devon captains had a higher proportion of Devon men in their ships than others. When Stephen Ackerman fitted the *Barnardiston* for sea in 1678, about half of his crew seems to have been drawn from Devon, the overwhelming majority being from his native Plymouth. Similarly, the numbers of Devon men on Kempthorne's *Saint Andrew* were also very high.[66] The proportion was much smaller on vessels with no obvious Devon connection. Of 299 seamen whose place of origin can be identified aboard the fleet flagship *Royal Sovereign* in 1673, 11 came from Barnstaple, three from Plymouth, one from Bideford, and two from Exeter, suggesting, perhaps a particularly successful press in north Devon. The great majority of the ship's company was drawn from London and its environs.[67] The few other ship's books which give similar information confirm this trend: in the ships of the main fleet in the North Sea, recruitment from the Thames and the east coast formed the backbone of most crews. Even so, Devon was clearly regarded as a nursery for naval seamen. When orders were sent out to the vice-admirals of maritime communities to raise fixed quotas of seamen for the fleet, Devon always received by far the largest demand for any single county (though London was never included in these quotas). In 1678, for example, Devon was called on to provide 1,300 men: the next most important sources of manpower, Bristol and Norfolk, had to provide 950 apiece.[68] It is clear that a significant number of these men must have been channelled into ships operating from Plymouth, but, even so, Devon's contribution to the manning of the navy between 1642 and 1688 remained impressive.

Unfortunately, even in Devon the wartime fleets could never make up their manpower requirements exclusively from volunteers, and various methods of compulsion were necessary. Certain of these, notably an embargo on outward-bound shipping and pressing from inward-bound merchantmen, were significant in the Thames, Downs, and Solent, but had less impact on Devon. In 1653, for example, it was thought to be too risky to impose an embargo on the outward-bound Newfoundland fishing fleet, even though many seamen had gone aboard it to avoid the press and to earn higher wages than those on offer in the navy.[69] Forced recruitment of seamen in Devon was therefore centred ashore, and undertaken by several different authorities: directly by naval captains; by specially appointed pressmasters; or by the agents of local government, the vice-admiral of the county, the justices of the peace, and mayors. In addition, Devon seamen serving on merchant ships or fishing vessels were often pressed at sea, in coastal waters, or in other ports.[70] For those attempting to press on land, the task was a game of cat-and-mouse involving large numbers of particularly elusive mice. Pressmasters encountered a conspiracy of silence from the parish constables, who were supposed to assist them but instead gave notice to local seamen to make their getaways, from ship owners who wanted to keep their best men, and even (particularly in the first Dutch war) from JPs, and the mayors of Plymouth and Barnstaple. The north Devon port was particularly notorious among pressmasters in the 1650s, with all 'the chiefs in power and authority' colluding with seamen and merchants to resist the press. Seamen's mobs carried clubs and staves to intimidate the pressmasters, and the Mayor of Barnstaple ingenuously claimed that pressing the seamen there was a bad idea as it would lead to 'affrighting [of] the country'.[71] In any case, the constant nature of the wartime press could lead to a rapid exhaustion of the manpower pool. Two pressmasters working in Devon in 1653 found that they were unable to get more than 200 men from the south of the county, there being 'in any seaport town not one man . . . [the] towns are already drained by several preceding presses', and they therefore intended to try their luck around Bideford and Appledore.[72] Attempts to streamline the system had little success. In the third Dutch war an effort was made to get JPs, employing parish constables, to draw up accurate lists of the seamen in each parish, but the repetition of the instructions in the Devon sessions books suggests that, as in the rest of the country, the proposed system was simply unmanageable and impractical.[73]

The haphazard nature of the press had several consequences. Officers entrusted with pressing were often so desperate to make up their quotas that they pressed complete landlubbers, old men, or boys. In 1667 Samuel Giles, woolcomber of Exeter, suddenly found himself removed from his workplace and installed aboard the frigate *Bristol*; a decade earlier, Hatsell had found several of the men pressed from Bideford and Barnstaple so 'unserviceable' that he had no alternative but to discharge them.[74] However, these problems were endemic in every maritime county: Devon's geography created more particular difficulties. Once pressed, men were given conduct money and ordered to proceed to their ships, or ports from which they could join them. Men from the north Devon ports, ordered to appear at Plymouth, vanished in transit across the county,[75] and even those who did appear in the right place at the right time still had to be got to the fleet. In the Dutch wars, Plymouth's distance from the main fleet posed an awkward problem of logistics, and Hatsell warned in the first Dutch war that if men were given conduct money to go overland to Portsmouth, they would simply disappear *en route*.[76] The administration usually resorted to the expedient of shipping seamen from Plymouth to the fleet, but this was a slow and unreliable system which led admirals to consider Devon an unreliable source of seamen. The obvious alternative, and one which was followed in all the Dutch wars, was to divert many Devon seamen into ships operating from Plymouth,[77] though the majority still seem to have served in the main fleet in the North Sea.

Where did these Devonian seamen come from? The petitions for relief to the quarter sessions from wounded sailors or their widows provide a useful 'random sample', although almost all of the surviving petitions originate from the south of the county.[78] As one would expect, the great majority were drawn from the main port towns, especially Plymouth and Dartmouth. South coast men predominated, their numbers swelled by men from the immediate hinterland. More surprisingly, naval seamen were also recorded as originating in Buckland-in-the-Moor and Moretonhampstead. Their careers reflect the variety of ways in which seamen could join the navy, and the hardships of service there. When Thomas Heathman of Ashburton and Nicholas Kitching of Bovey Tracey wished to volunteer in the third Dutch war, they made their way to Captain Thomas Newman, deputy Vice-Admiral of Devon, at Dartmouth, and secured berths with Kempthorne and Berry respectively. Only Kitching returned from the war, and he was wounded in the back and right knee and unable to work to maintain his family.[79] Christopher Powell, cordwainer of St Marychurch, 'yet having an inclination for the seas', had been on several merchant voyages and thereby made himself liable for the press, which duly caught up with him in the second Dutch war. Though wounded, he had recovered sufficiently by 1673 to be pressed again by Mr Showers of Topsham, and was sent aboard the *Anne*, where he was even more badly wounded, 'his senses taken from him . . . by his fall backwards into the hole of the ship'.[80] Powell was more fortunate than John Spry of Buckland-in-the-Moor, pressed aboard the *Royal Katherine* in 1673 and wounded several times, culminating in both his legs being shattered, so that he was forced to spend all his pay in getting home. However, even Spry might have regarded himself as more fortunate than John Haycraft of Sidmouth, killed by a shot through the bowels while serving under Francis Courtenay, or William Cork of Brixham, another of Courtenay's crewmen, who survived three engagements only to die of a fever which raged through the ship.[81]

Impressment, mutilation, or death did not only affect the victims themselves. An extensive press placed a severe strain on coastal communities, with wives and children thrown back on charity from their parishes, which were often unable to cope with the demands for relief. The county quarter sessions controlled a system of bounty payments to war casualties and their families which supplemented the pensions paid out of the Chatham Chest to all those maimed in the navy. The men themselves obtained yearly pensions and their widows yearly gratuities, but the sheer numbers killed or wounded in the Dutch wars placed a heavy burden on the county.[82] Nevertheless, the system does seem to have provided some relief to the needy. In 1667 a seaman's widow, Julian (sic) Tilt of Lympstone, petitioned for relief, being

> in a most deplorable condition, much in debt and with one poor child, utterly unable to make any satisfaction to creditors, and not as yet receiving any of her husband's pay due for his service.

The court ordered £3 to be paid, after which she should 'trouble this court no more', and should rely on the parish officers for relief.[83] The petitions for relief provide many examples of the impact of war on individual Devon families. The death of John Drew of Paignton left his widow with nine small children to bring up. Alice Yard of Dartmouth had three sons killed in the third Dutch war, and was left destitute as a result, they 'being able seamen, and single, unmarried persons . . . the staff of her age'. John Davy of Kenton's right arm became withered and useless as a result of wounds received in the battle of the Texel (1673): his parents were poor and unable to help him, his brother was a prisoner in Algiers, so he had no means of support.[84] For wives and widows seeking relief directly from the navy, Devon's geographical location again created difficulties. Payment of wages could only be secured at the Navy Office in London, and a journey there was an immense undertaking for poor people. In May 1674 the widows of six Devon men killed on the *Nightingale* petitioned the Navy Board for relief, having been absent from their families for two months,

> and all that time attended here at daily charge waiting payment, [so] that they have spent all they can make shift for, and are now ready to pawn the clothes off their backs, while they fear their children are ready to starve in the streets.[85]

The navy's tardy payment of its debts could have a serious effect on a coastal community, even if many seamen returned from the navy alive and unharmed. Unpaid seamen or widows meant unpaid tradesmen, landladies, and other creditors, and the whole community suffered.[86] Devon may have been a long way from the fighting of the Dutch wars, but it was still very much a county at war.

Though geography dictated that, in several respects, Devon would remain relatively on the periphery of naval affairs during the conflicts with the Dutch, its importance to the navy, particularly as a source of skilled seamen, remained considerable. Moreover, although Plymouth may not have seen the development of substantial support facilities during this period, its value (or potential value) as a westward base was certainly recognised, and its use as a base for the western squadron and for the organisation of convoys foreshadowed important aspects of its use in later centuries. Another pointer to things to come was the occasional use of Torbay, especially in the 1640s and 1650s, both as a fleet anchorage and as a gathering point for convoys.[87] These functions, together with the strategically important civil war naval campaigns in the South West, prove emphatically that Devon did not become, to paraphrase Michael Oppenheim, just another county in naval affairs between the great Elizabethan wars and the second hundred years' war with France.[88]

24: Devon and the Navy in the Civil and Dutch Wars, 1642–1688

1 R Latham and W Matthews, eds, *The Diary of Samuel Pepys* (1970–83), V, 35.
2 JR Powell and EK Timings, eds, *Documents Relating to the Civil War, 1642–8* (NRS, 1963), 169.
3 A Fletcher, *The Outbreak of the English Civil War* (1981), 201, 214–15, 233–4.
4 See above, chapter 13.
5 BL. Add. MS 35,297, *passim*.; Powell & Timings, *Civil War*, 5, 52, 55, 172–3,

188; EA Andriette, *Devon and Exeter in the Civil War* (Newton Abbot, 1971), 129, 130, 134.

6 See e.g., G Penn, *Memorials of the Professional Life and Times of Sir William Penn, Knt.* (1833), i, 70; BL. Add. MS 35,297, fos 49–52, 66; Powell & Timings, *Civil War*, 161–2, 164–6, 208.

7 Historical Manuscripts Commission (hereafter HMC), *Portland MSS.*, I, 194; *Calendar of State Papers, Domestic Series, 1645–7*, 9; Andriette, *Devon and Exeter*, 101.

8 BL. Add. MS. 35,297, fo. 66; Powell & Timings, *Civil War*, 162, 164.

9 Bl. Add. MS 35,297, fos. 62v, 82.

10 Powell & Timings, *Civil War*, 117, 161–2, 164, 208.

11 BL. Add. MS. 35,297, fos. 40v, 41v, 43, 44–5; Powell & Timings, *Civil War*, 103, 105, 117–18, 170–1.

12 Powell & Timings, *Civil War*, 229–30; HMC, *Portland MSS.*, I, 339–40.

13 Powell & Timings, *Civil War*, 52–4, 77.

14 Powell & Timings, *Civil War*, 53–4, 76–7, 82–4.

15 Penn, *Memorials*, i, 69–71, 107.

16 HMC, *Duke of Somerset, Etc.*, 67–8, 72–3, 82–3; DRO, Seymour Papers, 1392M/L1644/22; E Warburton, *Memoirs of Prince Rupert and the Cavaliers* (1833), ii, 338–9; Powell & Timings, *Civil War*, 117.

17 *Calendar of State Papers Relating to Ireland, 1633–47*, 520, 529; Penn, *Memorials*, i, 307; JR Powell, ed., *The Letters of Robert Blake* (NRS, 1937), 51.

18 E Hyde, ed. WD Macray, *The History of the Rebellion and Civil Wars in England Begun in the Year 1641* (1888), II, bk v, 382.

19 SR Gardiner and CT Atkinson, eds, *Letters and Papers Relating to the First Dutch War, 1652–4* (NRS, 1899–1930), II, 105–08, 116–17, 120–2, 142–4, 300–1.

20 BL Egerton MS 928, fos. 48–57; RC Anderson, ed., *The Journals of Sir Thomas Allin, 1660–78* (NRS, 1940), II, xxxv–xxxvi; Oppenheim, 71. For William's landing in 1688 see below, pp. 180–81.

21 See below, pp. 183–4.

22 HMC, *Portland, MSS.*, II, 68; Penn, *Memorials*, i, 303.

23 *Cal.S.P.Dom., 1659–60*, 550.

24 F Fox, *Great Ships: the Battlefleet of King Charles II* (1980), 183; JR Tanner, ed., *Catalogue of the Naval Manuscripts in the Pepysian Library at Magdalene College, Cambridge* (NRS, 1903–22), II, 175, 239; Fox, *Great Ships*, 180.

25 *Cal.S.P.Dom., 1658–9*, 549; Tanner, *Catalogue*, II, 10, 52, 68, 74.

26 Tanner, *Catalogue*, II, 164, 167, 175, 239.

27 Tanner, *Catalogue*, II, 14, 26, 70, 123, 128.

28 S Hornstein, *The Restoration Navy and English Foreign Trade 1674–88* (1991).

29 Magdalene College, Cambridge, Pepys MS 2853, 46–7, 127, 135, 141 & *passim*.

30 E Chappell, ed., *The Tangier Papers of Samuel Pepys* (NRS, 1935), 185; Hornstein, *Restoration Navy*, 54–9.

31 *Cal.S.P.Dom., 1657–8*, 415; PRO, ADM 106/371, fos. 602, 606.

32 HMC, *Lindsey Supplement*, 5; *Cal.S.P.Dom., 1661–2*, 482–3; PRO, ADM.106/381, fos. 1, 3. Oppenheim's erroneous suggestion (*Maritime History*, 70) that yards and buildings at Plymouth were authorised in 1662, but never built, resulted from a Navy Board order of 1692 being entered in the wrong place in the eighteenth-century entry book he used: BL. Add. MS. 9314, fos. 3v, 85–6.

33 PRO, ADM 106/300, fo. 105; RC Anderson, ed., *Journals and Narratives of the Third Dutch War* (NRS, 1946), 238–9; NAM Rodger, ed., *The Naval Miscellany*, v (NRS, 1985), 75.

34 See below, p. 179.

35 See e.g., *Cal.S.P.Dom., 1657–8*, 57, 155, 407, 415, 437, 441, 478; *Cal.S.P.Dom., 1658–9*, 549; *Cal.S.P.Dom., 1659–60*, 455, 550.

36 Tanner, *Catalogue*, II, 5, 8, 16, 22, 128, 182, 239, 265; Hornstein, *Restoration Navy*, 53–64.

37 BL. Add. MS. 38,848, fo. 45; Gardiner & Atkinson, *First Dutch War*, III, 133, 354–5, IV, 40; *Cal.S.P.Dom., 1657–8*, 415, 423.

38 *Cal.S.P.Dom., 1664–5*, 394, 403, 412, 417, 429–30, 436, 545; *Cal.S.P.Dom., 1665–6*, 48, 89.

39 Tanner, *Catalogue*, IV, 190.

40 PRO, SP 18/174/121, 18/175/152; *Cal.S.P.Dom., 1657–8*, 445, 465, 466, 488, 501, 530; Gardiner & Atkinson, *First Dutch War*, VI, 178.

41 *Cal.S.P.Dom., 1658–9*, 486, 487, 490, 507; *Cal.S.P.Dom., 1659–60*, 338–9, 383–5, 503, 528; *Cal.S.P.Dom., 1660–1*, 66, 260; BL. Add. MS. 9302, fo. 119v.

42 HMC *Portland MSS*, I, 695.

43 Bodleian Library, Oxford, Rawlinson MS A.174, fos. 413–14; *Cal.S.P.Dom., 1665–6*, 250; and see Rawlinson MS. A.174, fos. 411, 421; Pepys *Diary*, viii, 58, 144.

44 PRO, ADM 106/300, fos. 112, 116, 118, 120, 122; Tanner, *Catalogue*, II, 226, 227, 252.

45 PRO, ADM 106/336, fos. 393, 396, 407, 409, 413, 414, 419; ADM 106/361, fos. 451, 458, 462; ADM 106/371, fo. 573.

46 Bodleian, Rawlinson MS. A.174, fos. 352–3.

47 Tanner, *Catalogue*, IV, 502, 548.

48 JJ Beckerlegge, 'Charles II's Visits to Plymouth', *DAT*, 100 (1968), 219–25.

49 Tanner, *Catalogue*, IV, 22, 548, 553. A resident commissioner was a member of the Navy Board, permanently based in one of the royal dockyards; such an appointment at Plymouth would have implied a major enhancement of the port's status.

50 JD Davies, *Gentlemen and Tarpaulins: The Officers and Men of the Restoration Navy* (Oxford, 1991), 27.

51 RC Anderson, *List of English Naval Captains, 1642–60* (1964), 22; PRO, PROB 11/316, fo. 384; *Cal.S.P.Dom., 1664–5*, 201.

52 Gardiner & Atkinson, *First Dutch War*, I, 23; Anderson, *List*, 13; B Capp, *Cromwell's Navy* (Oxford, 1989), 387; PRO, ADM 3/275/13.

53 See JR Powell and EK Timings, eds, *The Rupert and Monck Letterbook, 1666* (NRS, 1969), 3–10. 185–95; M Ashley, *General Monck* (1977).

54 Powell & Timings, *Rupert and Monck*, 223.

55 GA Kempthorne, 'Sir John Kempthorne and his Sons', *MM*, 12 (1926), 289–317; PRO, PROB 11/361, fo. 152.

56 *Dictionary of National Biography*, 'Berry'; SS Webb, *The Governors-General: The English Army and the Definition of the Empire, 1569–1681* (University of North Carolina, 1979), 350–1; PRO, PROB 11/398, fos. 291–5.

57 Tanner, *Catalogue*, I, 316; PRO, ADM 7/630, fo. 31v; *Cal.S.P.Dom., 1668–9*, 357; Magdalene College, Pepys MS. 2858, 119–20, 191–2.

58 Tanner, *Catalogue*, I, 404; PRO, ADM 2/1745, fo. 44v; H St Maur, *Annals of the Seymours* (1902), 291; NMM, LBK/47, unfol., Albemarle's list of officers.

59 Tanner, *Catalogue*, I, 339; E. Cleaveland, *A Genealogical History of the Noble and Illustrious Family of Courtenay* (Exeter, 1735), 302.

60 Chappell, *Tangier Papers*, 173.

61 *Cal.S.P.Dom., 1653–4*, 521, 535; Magdalene College, Pepys MS. 2853, 341; Pepys MS. 2855, 23; Pepys MS. 2857, 214, 223; Tanner, *Catalogue*, II, 53, 293; Davies, *Gentlemen and Tarpaulins*, 25.

62 Magdalene College, Pepys MS. 2854, 78; BS Ingram, ed., *Three Sea Journals of Stuart Times* (1936), 112, 117, 131–2.

63 Magdalene College, Pepys MS. 2858, 191.

64 PRO, ADM 106/336, fos. 396, 399.

65 PRO, ADM 30/24/5. fos. 88–95; DRO, QS 128/3/9, 128/18/1, 128/38/1, 128/42/3, 128/50, 128/79/3.

66 PRO, ADM 33/105, 33/115.

67 PRO, ADM 33/107.

68 PRO, ADM 1/5138/916; and see BL. Add. MS 9316, fo. 22.

69 *Cal.S.P.Dom., 1653–4*, 203, 514; Gardiner and Atkinson, *First Dutch War*, V, 36; Oppenheim, *Maritime History of Devon*, 69.

70 See e.g. PRO, ADM.106/282, fos. 427–8; DRO, QS.128/97/3; D Starkey, 'The West Country-Newfoundland Fishery and the Manning of the Royal Navy', in R Higham ed., *Security and Defence in South-West England Before 1800*, (Exeter, 1987).

71 *Cal.S.P.Dom., 1653–4*, 220–1, 281–2, 338, 400; Gardiner and Atkinson, *First Dutch War*, III, 416, IV, 103, 217, V, 35–9, 333–4.

72 PRO, SP 18/35/112.

73 DRO, DQS 1/11, Apr. & July 1672, Jan. 1673, sessions minutes.

74 DRO, QS 128/55/1; BL. Add. MS 38,848, fo. 45; and see Tanner, *Catalogue*, II, 14. See also above, p. 103.

75 BL. Add. MS 38,848, fo. 45.

76 *Cal.S.P.Dom., 1653–4*, 281, 321.

77 *Cal.S.P.Dom., 1653–4*, 223, 281, 290, 526; Gardiner & Atkinson, *First Dutch War*, IV, 103; Powell & Timings, *Rupert and Monck*, 117–18; Tanner, *Catalogue*, II, 6, 8, 9, 14.

78 This paragraph is based on the seamen's petitions in DRO, QS 128.

79 DRO, QS 128/3/2. 128/12/1. See also above, chapter 14.

80 DRO, QS 128/105/1.

81 DRO, QS 128/18/1, 128/25, 128/113/2.

82 DRO, DQS 1/10, Apr. 1666, July 1666 (entry marked 'Sidmouth'), Oct. 1666 (entry marked 'Exmouth'), Apr. 1667, July 1672, Oct. 1674 sessions minutes; DRO, QS 128/110; SK Roberts, *Recovery and Restoration in an English County: Devon Local Administration 1646–70* (Exeter, 1985), 122–4.

83 DRO, QS 128/77/1; DRO, DQS 1/10, Apr. 1667 sessions minutes.

84 DRO, QS 128/97/1–2, 128/42/5, 128/69/5.

85 PRO, ADM 106/3544/1, 'mariners' folder.

86 See e.g., *Cal.S.P.Dom., 1657–8*, 193.

87 *Cal.S.P.Dom., 1645–7*, 585; Penn, *Memorials*, I, 440–6.

88 Oppenheim, 37.

25 The Naval Agents at Plymouth, 1652–88

J D DAVIES

DURING THE FINAL PHASE OF PLYMOUTH'S association with the navy before the building of the dockyard, naval affairs there were in the hands of agents drawn from the local community. Though their purely naval activities are detailed elsewhere in this *History*,[1] their careers were multi-faceted and provide some interesting insights into the relationship between Devon and the navy, and into some of the connections of the Plymouth mercantile community, during the Stuart period.

In 1652 Captain Henry Hatsell was appointed naval agent at Plymouth in an attempt to improve the quality of provisioning and refitting there during the first Dutch war. Though the origins of his military title are obscure, he had taken part in Parliament's campaigns against the Scillies and Jersey in 1648–51, and had served both as a pressmaster at Minehead and as a militia commissioner for Devon before taking up his naval post.[2] Like so many other officials of the republican regime, Hatsell possessed a deep and radical religious belief, criticising the 'base and profane' nature of the state's Devon seamen, and praying, even as the restoration of the monarchy loomed, that Parliament would turn to the Gospel for guidance.[3] Hatsell was, briefly, a great man in Devon: in addition to the naval agency, he served as vice-admiral of the county, as a JP, and as an MP in Cromwell's parliaments. His salary as naval agent, £270 per annum, was greater than those of the secretary to the Admiralty and several commissioners of the navy. He acquired the sequestered royalist estate of Saltram and, despite his frequent complaints about the lack of payment for naval affairs at Plymouth, he evidently became a wealthy man, trading on his own account with the continent. Surprisingly, in the light of his strong connection with the republic, he survived as naval agent until September 1661, well over a year after the Restoration and his dismissal from his local government posts. He retired to Saltram, and died there in 1667.[4]

His successors, the Plymouth merchant John Lanyon and Lanyon's uncle Philip, lacked Hatsell's influence, but both had other interests in addition to the naval agency. Philip Lanyon had served as deputy treasurer and commissioner for prizes at Plymouth during the second Dutch war (1664–7) and, in addition to succeeding his nephew as naval agent in 1674, he served during the 1670s as chief overseer for the construction of the Royal Citadel.[5] The younger Lanyon's interests and connections had gone well beyond Plymouth, and his financial enterprises had been on a grander scale. He was one of the original victualling contractors for Tangier, which had been acquired by England in 1662, and this role brought him into contact with Samuel Pepys, then a member of the Tangier committee. Lanyon's first appearance in the *Diary* occurs when Pepys sends orders to Plymouth for him to take up 150 tons of shipping there to transport bread from the Devon port to the African colony. Thereafter, Lanyon's regular trips to London in connection with Tangier business soon made him a friend of Pepys, possibly because they saw each other as kindred spirits. Both were determined to do as well as possible for themselves out of the contract, but Lanyon lacked Pepys's acumen and extraordinary knack of covering his tracks. By 1668 Lanyon's proceedings in the contract were under investigation, and Pepys sadly judged his erstwhile friend 'a very knave . . . [and] a fool also'.[6] Nevertheless, Lanyon cannot have lost out too heavily on his Tangier enterprise, or on his naval agency, despite his unceasing protests about the lack of money reaching Plymouth in the 1660s. Though he could grumble in 1666:

> I can truly say that since I undertook this affair, I could not procure the value of ten groats on the king's account, without my own engagement,

he clearly died a very rich man, bestowing largesse on the poor of several Devon and Cornwall parishes (including Egg Buckland and Stonehouse), giving £300 for new almshouses in Charles parish, Plymouth, £1,200 to his dead wife's relations, and £1,000 to each of his sisters.[7]

Despite differences in social status and interests, the careers of the naval agents possess certain common features. In particular, they illustrate the very blurred dividing lines between state and private enterprise which existed during this period and the opportunities which existed for enriching oneself through official service even when the state was straitened for money. They made contributions of various kinds to the development of Plymouth. Under these men, the agency proved to be a successful form of naval administration, appropriate for Plymouth's contribution to the service in the years before the establishment of the dockyard.

25: The Naval Agents at Plymouth, 1652–88.

1 See above, chapter 24.

2 *Calendar of State Papers, Domestic Series, 1649–50*, 35, 57, 394; *Cal.S.P.Dom., 1651*, 13; *Cal.S.P.Dom., 1651–2*, 53, 59.

3 *Cal.S.P.Dom., 1653–4*, 15; PRO SP18/220, fo. 63; SP18/224, fo. 88.

4 S Roberts, *Recovery and Restoration in an English County: Devon Local Administration, 1646–70* (Exeter, 1985), 50, 54, 148, 154; British Library, Additional MS. 9302, fo. 184; PRO, Prob 11/324, fo. 52.

5 B.L. Add. MS. 5752, fo. 180; *Calendar of Treasury Books, 1676–9*, ii, 1278. See above, p. 123.

6 R Latham and W Matthews, eds., *The Diary of Samuel Pepys* (1970–83), iv, 21, 156; v, 196, 202, 205, 210, 214, 223, 226; ix, 262, 379.

7 PRO, SP 29/154, fo. 95; PRO, Prob 11/344, fos. 208–9.

26 *Prince William's Landing in Torbay*

J L Anderson

On the morning of 5 November 1688 a fleet of Dutch ships was seen off Dartmouth, coasting eastward on a westerly wind.[1] About 50 warships were escorting well over 200 transport vessels that carried about 15,000 troops with their equipment, horses, guns, and supplies. In attendance were scores of small fishing-boats, flat-bottomed 'Schievelingers' that were to act as landing-craft (Fig. 26.1). The ships stood toward Torbay, but that had not been planned: the choice of their destination had been a matter of contingency. Environmental constraints, particularly the winds, had largely dictated the point where the descent was to be made.[2]

The Commander-in-Chief of the expeditionary force was Prince William of Orange (Fig. 26.2). Invited to England by dissidents, he had sailed from the Netherlands on the 1 November with the professed purpose of preserving 'the Protestant Religion and the Liberty of England' from the increasingly autocratic governance of King James II. The ships had put to sea on an easterly wind, and William's naval high command had resolved before sailing that, if the wind were in that quarter, the convoy was to move to the southwest of England, a specified objective being the roadstead of Exmouth.[3]

That harbour had much to commend it. It was undefended, capacious, and deep enough to accommodate the Dutch transports, yet too shallow to allow English warships to follow. The low banks of the estuary could expedite the landing of troops, and adjacent areas were suitable for their marshalling. Nearby was Exeter, one of the largest provincial cities in England and easily accessible from Exmouth by road or by water up the Exe estuary and then by the recently-improved canal to the city. However, a heavy sea makes Exmouth unapproachable, and on 4 November the pilot with the expedition advised that 'the see is to greett' for the ships to enter the Exe. Of necessity, William decided to land most of his forces in the harbour of Dartmouth and the rest on the less-sheltered shore of Torbay. Two castles commanded the approaches to the Dart, and to secure these William ordered the despatch of two frigates and three transports, each of the latter carrying perhaps 200 infantry.[4]

The morning of 5 November revealed that at least part of the convoy, including the Prince's frigate *den Briel*, had run beyond the marks for Dartmouth. With the strong east wind, the unwelcome prospect was that the voyage would have to continue to Plymouth – politically uncertain, strategically more remote and logistically more difficult. Suddenly the wind calmed and then veered to the west. The leading ships put about and stood northeast, bypassing Dartmouth which, with the wind westerly, is difficult of access to vessels under sail. Later that day the transports came to anchor

26.1 Prince William Landing, 5 November 1688, from the cartouche of Greenvile Collins's chart of the South Coast of Devon in *Great Britain's Coasting Pilot* (1693). *(National Maritime Museum)*

off Brixham in Torbay.

Accompanied by his Guards, and said in one account to have been preceded by Count Solms and a small party of grenadiers, the Prince landed that afternoon.[5] The sense of immediacy that surrounded the expedition's landing is conveyed in the terse report sent the same day by the Collector of Customs at Brixham:

> About three hundred sail of Dutch came just now into Torbay, several of them landing soldiers there, and the Prince himself going on shore. The rest of the soldiers and horse will, if they can, be landed this night, there being about 5 or 600 ashore already and are still landing.[6]

The first regiments ordered ashore were those of the Anglo-Dutch Brigade, a formation of long standing composed of about 3,000 English and Scots soldiers in Dutch service. Their precedence was for the purpose of propaganda, which counted for much in William's plans: it was important that the descent be perceived as an act of liberation, not of foreign conquest. Nevertheless, and despite the encouragement of apparently welcoming crowds on the hillsides, the 'combined operation' was carried out with a professional thoroughness. While most of the warships cruised protectively well to seaward, some lay just offshore, covering the landing with their guns. The patrolling was active. The *Dove*, homeward bound from Lisbon, was stopped on the 6 November five leagues off the Start, and her master detained and questioned. The naval sloop *Fanfan*, which had been sent westward to press men, was taken by the Dutch.[7]

Professional care also characterised the military when ashore. Respectful of the quality of King James's cavalry, the troops encamped in fields enclosed by hedges and stone walls, and stood to arms during the night so as not to be vulnerable to a surprise attack by enemy horse.

In order to meet the threat of the King's cavalry in a more general sense, William had shipped some 4,000 horses with the expedition. The carriage of these by sea proved difficult and costly, and their disembarkation presented further problems. On the first day of the landing some of the transports were run ashore and the horses unloaded when the tide fell. The following morning, according to Burnet, a place was found near Brixham 'where the ships could be brought very near the land, against a good shore, and the horses would not be put to swim above twenty yards'.[8] The process of disembarkation was completed on the following day. Meanwhile, about 100 ships carrying artillery and heavy baggage were ordered to Exmouth. After some delays caused by adverse winds they entered the estuary and discharged their cargoes at Topsham, as had been originally intended.

26.2 Prince William on a horse, with his fleet unloading horses in Torbay in the background, by Jan Wyk. *(National Maritime Museum)*

The passage of the Dutch convoy across the southern North Sea and down Channel was uncontested, and the landing was unopposed, as was the Prince's triumphal progress to Exeter.

26: Prince William's Landing in Torbay

1 Letter from Collector of Customs at Dartmouth, 5 November, *Manuscripts of the Earl of Dartmouth*, Historical Manuscripts Commission, XI Appendix, Part V (1887), 185.
2 JL Anderson 'Prince William's Descent on Devon, 1688, the Environmental Constraints', Stephen Fisher (ed.), *Lisbon as a Port Town, the British Seaman and other Maritime Themes* (Exeter, 1988); Edward B Powley, *The English Navy in the Revolution of 1688* (Cambridge, 1923).
3 Memorandum of a meeting aboard the flagship *Leyden*, 11 November (1 November in the English calendar), N Japikse (ed.), *Correspondentie van Willem III en van Hans Willem Bentinck*, Pt I, ('s Gravenhage, 1928), 623–4.
4 *Correspondentie* II (iii), p. 53; I (ii) p. 625. See also Greenvile Collins, *Great Britain's Coasting Pilot* (1753), 3; and for more detail on Dartmouth, Torbay and Exmouth, *The Channel Pilot, Pt I: South West and South Coasts of England* (1886), 123–31.
5 *Journaal van Constantijn Huygens den Zoon van 21 October 1688 tot 2 September 1689*, Werken van het Historisch Genootschaap Gevestigd te Utrecht, 23 (1876), 14. See also John Whittle, *An Exact Diary of the Late Expedition of His Illustrious Highness the Prince of Orange, etc.* (1689) and Gilbert Burnet, *Bishop Burnet's History of His Own Time*, Vol. I: *From the Restoration of King Charles II to the Settlement of King William and Queen Mary at the Revolution, etc.* (1724).
6 HMC *Dartmouth* MSS, XI, 185.
7 HMC *Dartmouth* MSS, XI 213, 222; XV, 58.
8 Burnet, *History*, 789.

27 *Devon and the Naval Strategy of the French Wars 1689–1815*

Michael Duffy

The landing of William of Orange at Torbay was followed by the flight of James II to France, and initiated a series of seven Anglo-French wars occupying 67 of the 127 years from 1689 to 1815. These were wars for which the Royal Navy was caught initially off-balance and unprepared. The prospect had been the nightmare of James II's former admiral, the Earl of Dartmouth, who foresaw the French navy controlling the western approaches and throttling British trade from France's main Atlantic coast bases while he had no such western dockyards and was powerless to take the main British battlefleet thither.[1]

The Western Parameters of the New Naval Warfare

The Dutch Wars had left all the main British bases capable of docking first- and second-rate ships of the line, the bulwarks of the battlefleet concentrated on the Thames. The sole dockyard to the westward, Portsmouth, had only a double-dock capable of receiving smaller first-rate battleships, so that, in the words of Edmund Dummer, architect of Plymouth dockyard, at the start of these Anglo-French wars it seemed:

> a mighty boldness to advance with the Grand Fleet further westward of the Isle of Wight than the *Soveraigne* had been knowne to have been, since the time of her built.[2]

The disadvantages of this eastward focus of dockyards was quickly experienced when the French used their western bases to land troops in Ireland and on 1 May 1689 fought off an attack by a smaller British cruising squadron at Bantry Bay. The British warships had to go back to Portsmouth to repair their damages and it was nearly two months before they regained their station.[3]

Steps were soon taken to expand and upgrade Portsmouth dockyard, but more was needed, for in the new warfare the major scene of naval operations soon proved to be not the Channel, directly between the warring countries, but at the Channel's mouth and in the western approaches. Initially this was because of French support for the Irish rebellion, and disaffected Ireland remained a weak point in British defences that needed guarding. Moreover, Lord Dartmouth's fears were confirmed when the French found it easiest to attack Britain's rapidly expanding trade with the Mediterranean, the Americas, Africa and India at the point in the western approaches where it dispersed from British shores or converged to enter British ports, a point close to their main bases and away from the main concentrations of British naval power.[4]

Above all, the theatre of battlefleet operations was determined by the two controlling factors of the age of the sailing warship: winds and bases. Since the prevailing winds were strong westerlies, neither navy liked operating its battlefleet in the bottleneck of the Channel. After surviving a violent gale there in 1692 Admiral Russell declared:

> no fleet of ships, being so many in number, nor of this bigness, ought to be ventured at sea but where they may have room enough to drive any way for eight and forty hours, or where they may let go an anchor and ride. In the Channel six hours with a shift of wind, makes either side a lee shore . . .[5]

The danger became still greater during the eighteenth century as warships increased in size, and particularly vulnerable were the unwieldy three-decked first- and second-rates, whose immense superstructures acted as sails driving them to leeward. In 1745, when ordered to concentrate his big ships up-Channel against invasion from Dunkirk, Admiral Vernon protested that there was not drift enough for them in such narrow seas and that it was far better to keep a strong squadron at sea to the westward, where they would have Plymouth and Portsmouth and Irish harbours for shelter and sea room enough to drive in safety during storms.[6]

If it was the instinct of the British navy to get its big ships out of the Channel and to the westward, it was more so that of the French, whose Channel bases, Le Havre and Dunkirk, were incapable of taking first-rates.[7] As far as possible, therefore, the French battlefleet operated to the westward, and the significant exceptions when it came into the Channel served only to confirm their general prejudice. Tourville's victory over the Anglo-Dutch fleet at Beachy Head in 1690 was wasted in delays while he repaired his battle damages at the inadequate facilities at Le Havre, and he then took the easy option of raiding Devon, where Torbay provided shelter against the westerlies. An armed force of 30,000 men assembled to oppose him, but Tourville exploited the mobility of his galley squadron and ships' boats to launch a dawn raid further up the coast at Teignmouth on 26 July, burning the houses and eight merchant ships. Three days later he reconnoitred Dartmouth but drew off in the face of vigorous fire from the batteries at the harbour mouth. His instructions urged him to attack the bigger prize of Plymouth, where Admiral Killigrew had taken refuge with 11 of the line and 130 merchant ships of the homeward Mediterranean convoy. However, winds from west-south-west, which delayed him, and a sick list rising above 4,000, reinforced his feeling that Plymouth would be too strong, and Tourville retired to Brest in the second week of August.[8]

If the 1690 campaign drew the French westward even when they won command of the Channel, that of 1692 showed the difficulty of escape if they lost it. Tourville was to bring an invasion force from Normandy to land in Torbay, but mistaken orders led him against an Anglo-Dutch fleet twice his strength off Barfleur on 19–20 May. Most of his smaller warships escaped through the dangerous Alderney passage to St Malo, but the big three-deckers had no refuge near at hand. Some got back to Brest by going up-Channel and north about Scotland, but ten first- and second-rates and five others were trapped and destroyed in the open bays of Cherbourg and La Hogue.[9] It was not until 1744 that a French fleet came up-Channel again as far as Dungeness in support of an attempted surprise invasion from Dunkirk, only to be scattered by a storm which drove them to seek refuge back in Brest – providentially escaping a repetition of the 1692 disaster at the hands of a waiting superior British fleet alerted of their coming by the Dartmouth customs cutter which saw them off the Start.[10]

French anxieties about taking their fleet into the Channel were perhaps best revealed in their attempted invasion of 1779. Thirty-one-thousand troops from St Malo and Le Havre, protected by a combined Franco-Spanish fleet of 66 battleships under the Comte d'Orvilliers, were to attack Portsmouth and the Isle of Wight. At the height of war in America Britain could assemble only 38 of the line to oppose him, so the initiative lay with D'Orvilliers. On 16 August he appeared off Plymouth, where near-panic reigned for a while. Unaware that he had not yet picked up his troops, Yard Commissioner Ourry even considered setting fire to the dockyard to keep it out of French hands. Only 4,800 regulars and militia were available for its defence, whereas the garrison commander, General Lindsay, thought 9,000–10,000 necessary. A British third-rate was taken at the entrance to the Sound and there was a minor exodus inland of tradesmen and their families. The garrison stood firm, however, and there was a rallying together as volunteers came forward, arms were distributed, and 630 Cornish miners arrived to improve the fortifications.[11] On 19 August an easterly wind drove d'Orvilliers back from off the Sound where, even on the day of his arrival, he had expressed doubts about his mission. He pointed out to his Minister of Marine the lack of Channel facilities if his ships were damaged in battle, and he stressed the vulnerability of his fleet to the winds:

> The British, whose harbours are all to leeward in westerly or south-westerly winds, can, without any risk send out their squadrons and their fleets; it is not the same for the combined forces of France and Spain. If this great assemblage of battleships is struck by a westerly gale, their only resource is to pass through the Channel and go eastward; but if the gale is from the south, south-south-west or even from the south-west, the greater number would not be able to round the most southerly point of the coast of England, from which fact it will be understood that the navy of the two Powers is very much exposed in these waters during the autumn and winter.

D'Orvilliers was offered the alternative of landing in Cornwall and perhaps attacking Plymouth from there, but he thought Falmouth an inadequate base-port and, with sickness increasing, the stormy season approaching, and the British fleet avoiding his efforts to pin it down, he called off the enterprise.[12]

The French preference was consequently to keep within safe range to westward and windward of their first-rate bases at Brest and Rochefort on the Atlantic coast, leaving the Channel for the most part uncontested. While the British navy used the opportunity to bombard the French Channel ports intermittently, it soon realized that to achieve decisive results it would have to follow the French. It had to do so to protect British commerce and also to attack French commerce, which in wartime tended to operate from the Atlantic coast ports of Bordeaux, Nantes, and Lorient, close to the fleet bases. It had to do so if it was to catch the French fleet and bring it to battle, and particularly if it was to make the most of its advantage in that the bulk of the French battlefleet was divided between Brest and Toulon in the Mediterranean. The Brest fleet was most dangerous when reinforced either from Toulon (as in 1690) or by the Spanish fleet (as in 1779), so that it was desirable to have a British fleet between Brest and its reinforcements to prevent their junction.

The Quest for a Western Dockyard

A pattern soon emerged, therefore, in which the focus of Anglo-French naval activity in home waters was at the mouth of the Channel, between the Scillies and Ushant, in the Soundings, and ranging out with diminishing intensity to Cape Finisterre at the north-western tip of Spain and to Cape Clear at the south-western tip of Ireland. The timing of the British response to this new pattern can be charted by William III's orders in December 1689 that Portsmouth dockyard should be made capable of receiving first-rates, and at the turn of 1690–91 that a first-rate docking facility be established also at Plymouth.[13]

The Bantry Bay battle in 1689 had quickly shown that Portsmouth was too far up-Channel to be the dock of first resort for emergency warship repair in the new situation, and within a month the search began for a new docking site further west. Plymouth was already the customary naval supply depot in the West, and in June a hulk was ordered thither to assist in hull cleaning (so essential to maintain a warship's speed) and refitting of spars. In May the Admiralty asked its Plymouth agent, John Addis, if a dock might be built there, and on 15 June instructed the Navy Board to send a member thither to survey a suitable site and estimate the cost. By the time Sir John Berry went down to the South West the search had widened, and he was to consider also Dartmouth and Bideford (the latter presumably with current Irish operations in mind). By August all harbours from Dartmouth to Falmouth were ordered to be surveyed. Berry reported in favour of a Plymouth site at Turnchapel in the Cattewater, but he could find no local builder and it was

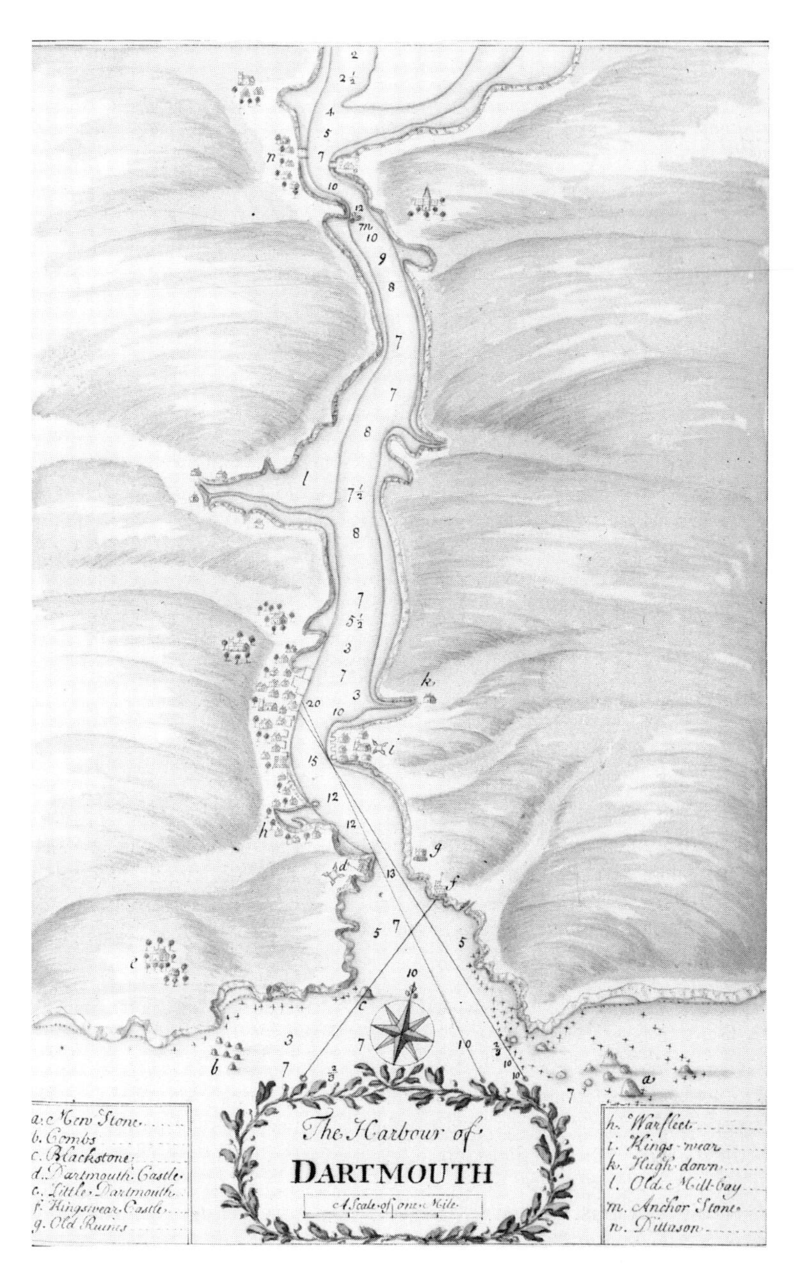

27.1 Dartmouth Harbour 1698, from a survey of places on the South Coast useful to the Navy, carried out by Edmund Dummer, Surveyor, and Captain Thomas Wiltshaw, Commissioners of the Navy, with Captain James Conoway and Captain William Cruft, Masters of Trinity House, BL K. Mar. III.67. A report of 1690 rejected the port of Dartmouth on account of the hazards of entering, noting that improvements for the Navy had been made in the Hamoaze at Plymouth (Helen Wallis). *(British Library)*

perhaps for this reason that when Edmund Dummer, Assistant Surveyor of the Navy, was sent to investigate in September he took the Portsmouth stonemason Robert Waters. Dummer was ordered to proceed to Dartmouth and Plymouth, 'taking notice of all the parts adjacent thereunto to represent what was found most suitable to the design of building a single dry dock'. At this stage the dock was to be capable of taking up to third-rate cruising ships.[14]

Dummer was initially favourably impressed by Dartmouth's commodious harbour (Fig 27.1) but a subsequent review rejected that port 'by reason of the conceived hazards of entering the same under the high lands and rocky shores'.[15] Dummer opted for Plymouth, though dispute then occurred between the choice of a Cattewater site, favoured by Dummer and the Navy Board, or the Hamoaze, favoured by the Admiralty. The Cattewater was where the existing naval facilities were situated, but it was a cramped site and, in a populated area, more expensive to develop. The proposed

Hamoaze site at Point Froward was rural, with room for expansion (see below, p. 192, Fig 28.1), estimates were cheaper, and its three-mile distance from Plymouth would impede the peculation of naval stores which Dummer thought rife at the Cattewater.[16] The problem of the Hamoaze, as Dummer explained, was that:

> the passage to that river is very crooked, the current false by many eddies, the tides on springs rapid, the soundings foul, the shores dreadful, and the coming in and going out too much commanded by the western winds.[17]

In January 1690 the Navy Board persuaded the Admiralty to accept the Cattewater, but nothing was done during the campaigning season and by November everyone agreed on the Hamoaze, contracts being signed with Waters on 30 December to build a stone dock there for £8,909.[18] It may be that a more substantial base on the site most capable of expansion was now being envisaged,[19] but it is not unlikely that the final determinant was Tourville's raid on the Devon coast that summer. While Admiral Killegrew's convoy took refuge in the Cattewater, Killegrew took his warships up the Hamoaze as the safest and most defensible anchorage, placing batteries on St Nicholas Island and either side of the Cremyll passage to protect them. Writing in defence of the Hamoaze site in 1694, Dummer explained:

> natural impediments have in this place their proper virtues. And this supereminent treasure of the Nation, the Navy and its Stores, must never be easy to come at . . .[20]

By 1694 plans for the new naval base had been greatly expanded. The dock was ordered to be upgraded to receive first-rates. In March 1691 the Admiralty requested a Navy Board investigation of the land requisite to establish not just a dry dock at Point Froward, but also 'a yard and other conveniences about it'. Sixteen months later it asked for estimates for the buildings of a fully-equipped dockyard, and on 29 July 1692 their construction was ordered to begin. In just over three years Plymouth was thrust right into the front line of the new naval warfare, transformed from a minor servicing depot for cruisers into the most advanced British naval dockyard, capable of major overhaul, repair and laying-up of the biggest warships of the main battlefleet.[21]

The expanding role for Plymouth coincided with the investigation and rejection of the other southwestern ports as supplementary supply depots or places of refuge for the navy. In the Bristol Channel nothing more was heard of Bideford as a base after 1689, and, though Bristol was suggested as a store depot in 1691 and 1693 and Milford Haven as a base in 1693, the recapture and development of Kinsale as a small cleaning and supply depot for ships up to fourth rate on the Irish coast in 1691 removed the need of a base closer to Irish waters. For a time Falmouth seemed a possible rival to Plymouth, but a Navy Board survey with the help of Trinity House in 1693 condemned it: while its harbour was large and safe, its entrance was undefended and difficult in north-westerlies. It lacked a road outside the harbour where ships could ride easily; the site was too cramped for more than a few cleaning slips; there were no local markets to obtain the right provisions and stores; and land communications were bad.[22] Such prejudices remained until the end of the eighteenth century: D'Orvilliers in 1779 was advised against resorting to Falmouth by a renegade British naval captain.[23]

Investigations were completed in 1698 with 'A Survey of the Ports on the South West Coast of England from Dover to the Lands End' by Dummer and Captain Thomas Wiltshaw of the Navy Board and Captains Conaway and Cruft of Trinity House.[24] This was dismissive of all alternatives to Plymouth. In Devon and Cornwall, Exmouth was 'encumbered with many inconveniences', its entrance almost filled with rocks and shoals more than a mile long, dividing the water into various and broken channels and difficult passages. Dartmouth was rejected as before. Fowey had the same disadvantages as Dartmouth with a harbour half its size, although it might shelter small warships embayed between Rame Head and the Dodman. Falmouth was 'clogged with many inconvenient shoals and sudden soundings', and Helford was too small. Only Dartmouth was considered to possess 'some particulars improvable for the services of the Navy', but in general all alternatives were thought more hazardous than those already in use. There was nothing to contradict Dummer's assertion in a survey of existing naval bases in the same year that Plymouth:

> is the most eminent harbour to the westward of Portsmouth and is adjoined by two rivers (little inferior to some of the best in England) namely Hamoaze and Cattewater, both of which afford good mooring and security fit to receive any fleet of the largest ships whatever.[25]

The Need for a Safe Western Fleet Anchorage

Despite this glowing recommendation, there were flaws to Plymouth as a naval base almost to the end of the French wars. The problem of achieving the right combination of winds and tides to enter or leave the Hamoaze was a perpetual cause of delays and mishaps. In 1800 Earl St Vincent claimed knowledge of ships waiting three months for a favourable wind to get out. Dummer expected improvement as pilots became more experienced, laid buoys and erected beacons, but Plymouth pilots became renowned for their caution. In 1747 the Admiralty ordered warping buoys laid to expedite movements, but in January 1782 Admiral Rodney, eager to get his flagship out of dock for the West Indies, still complained bitterly at the pilots' delays, while in the first eight months of 1805 alone five warships grounded while attempting passage.[26]

A still greater problem was the lack of a breakwater to the Sound, which was open to southerly gales and to rough water in any storms. It was the untrustworthiness of the Sound that led the Navy to site its new dockyard up the Hamoaze or Cattewater. Only in the summer months did Plymouth possess a reliable sheltered road close to the dockyard where a fleet could fit out, repair, or resupply in safety (Fig. 27.2). In January 1794 Admiral Graves, trying to get ships ready to join Lord Howe's fleet, complained of the difficulty in caulking in the Sound in bad winter weather so that it could only be done in the Hamoaze with all the delays of passage involved. 'In this respect', he concluded, 'Spithead has greatly the advantage of Plymouth Sound.'[27]

In summer the Sound was more benign, and one of Plymouth's greatest achievements in the French Wars was its rapid repair in the Sound of Admiral Keppel's fleet after the battle of Ushant on 27 July 1778. Keppel brought 23 of his battleships, extensively damaged in their masts and rigging, limping in on the 31st. When the Maker Heights watchtower signalled a fleet in sight at 7 a.m., Yard Commissioner Ourry (below, p. 209, Fig. 30.1) went out in his yacht and arranged with Keppel what had to be done. Since the fleet's longboats had been disabled, all of the dockyard launches, manned by the riggers, were brought out to get the wounded to hospital, while the master shipwright and all his mastmakers went round the fleet surveying what needed replacing and what might be fished and saved. Keppel would not allow his ships into the Hamoaze, closer to the yard, for fear of not being able to get them to sea as a fleet again. Consequently those more lightly damaged stayed out in Cawsand Bay, where they knotted

27.2 Men of War at Plymouth, 1766. Oil painting by Dominic Serres. *(National Maritime Museum)*

rigging, patched sails, and took in new yards and topmasts. Those requiring major mast replacement went into the Sound, where the 90-gun second-rate *Blenheim*, which had been preparing for sea, was hastily converted into a sheer hulk for taking out and replacing masts. Three were brought into sheltered water, two between St Nicholas Island and the mainland and the other into Barn Pool, under the lee of Mount Edgcumbe, to be keeled over to repair shot-holes below the waterline. Only one leaking fireship and the most severely damaged battleship, the *Egmont*, were taken into dry dock.

The only hitches in a marvellously smooth operation occurred in revictualling, when the fresh meat contractor threw up his contract and paid the £500 penalty at the prospect of having to supply so large a fleet so unexpectedly, and the master brewer declared his inability, at such an unseasonable time for brewing, to supply more than 30 tons of beer per ship. Within a fortnight, however, the fresh meat crisis was solved and Keppel was being supplied in plenty, though beer remained insufficient throughout.

By 15 August 15 ships were ready to sail, and Keppel finally left again on the 23rd with all his fleet except the *Egmont*, which was expected to follow shortly and of which he wrote:

> A ship crippled in battle, in her masts and yards, much wounded by shot in her bottom, not to be got at but by taking everything out, is carried into the harbour, her masts all taken out, the ship docked – her shot defects repaired, part of a new false keel put in – turned out of dock – completed with new masts and rigging, and returned into the Sound within twenty days, and now within two or three days of going to sea upon service – I own, appears to me, an exertion astonishing.

Repair and resupply had taken just over three weeks, a vast improvement on the aftermath of Bantry Bay in 1689 and abundant vindication of the decision to build a dockyard at Plymouth. Keppel was full of praise for 'the very extraordinary work that has been expedited by the Officers and People in the Dockyard.'

Nevertheless, both Keppel and Ourry admitted that a prolonged spell of fine weather had contributed much to the speedy refit, and the former declared that he could not have used the Sound (or Cawsand Bay) for so large a fleet after August as 'it has too much apparent danger to venture it'.[28] The safe period to use the Sound was indeed a relatively short one. Storms in early May 1780 reduced *Bienfaisant* (80 guns) and *Ramillies* (74) to virtual wrecks; storms in early September 1746 so battered Admiral Lestock's Lorient expedition that many cables were parted and anchors lost on foul ground in the Sound, while damaged storeships and transports ran for safety into the Cattewater and were difficult to extract again.[29] It was not impossible to bring the fleet into the Sound outside the summer months, and another Plymouth triumph was the total resupply of Hawke's fleet in six days when he brought it in in October 1759 (see below, p. 187). Hawke, however, decided not to risk it again,

> as I cannot be induced to think there is sufficient room for so large a squadron or water for the three-deck'd ships in Plymouth Sound at this time of the year.[30]

Stormy weather thus brought danger in the Sound, and from the first losses of the *Henrietta* (60 guns) and *Centurian* (48) on Christmas Day 1689 casualties mounted along with increased naval usage. It was an uncertain refuge from storms at sea, a lesson learnt in September 1691 when Russell, making for Torbay, was forced into the Sound by a southerly gale, losing the second-rate *Coronation* (90 guns) with all but 24 hands off Rame Head and *Harwich* (70) at the entrance to the Hamoaze, with two more third-rates driven aground but subsequently refloated.[31]

As an alternative the Navy made increasing use of Cawsand Bay just outside the Sound, sheltered against winds from south-west through north to south-east by east, with good holding ground of fine sand and mud for anchorage. Its disadvantages were its distance from the dockyard, which impeded supply, and its relatively small size. In 1794 the Port Admiral cleared it of frigates to accommodate as many battleships as possible. A survey of 1798 claimed that with careful mooring it could take nine first-rates and eight frigates, and St Vincent was warned in 1800 that only eight or nine of the line might anchor in safety at any one time. The admiral was concerned, as Keppel had been in 1778, about safety in the winter months, complaining in 1806 that:

> Cawsand Bay is a very unfit place for large ships to resort to, dangerous in the extreme, and such a swell that five days out of seven nothing can lay alongside of them – several have been put to the hazard of knocking their bottoms out.[32]

While Cawsand Bay was used by individual warships or small squadrons seeking resupply or minor repair from the dockyard, there was an essential need for a sheltered fleet anchorage to enable it to keep station to westward in the face of westerly gales. Hawke explained in 1759 that whereas

> single ships may struggle with a hard gale of wind, . . . a squadron cannot. It must always from wearing lose ground in working against a strong westerly wind in the Channel, where it cannot make very long stretches, but more especially if it should blow so as to put it past carrying sail.

He added: 'if for the future this should happen I shall put into Torbay'.[33]

A number of alternatives to Torbay were considered as refuges when the fleet was driven from its usual cruising station westward of the Isle of Ushant, outside the main French base at Brest. When the Scillies were finally charted in the 1790s, St Mary's Road, just over a hundred miles from Ushant, was surveyed by Sir Edward Pellew, but it was too westerly, destitute of servicing facilities, and considered usable only in summer. Memories of the wreck of Sir Cloudesley Shovell's *Association* scared admirals away. Mevagissey Bay, a hundred miles from Ushant, was the closest mainland roadstead but was thought capable of holding only 14 of the line and rejected by Sir Roger Curtis in 1797 because of doubts as to its safety. With Cawsand Bay too small and Plymouth Sound unsafe, all the advantages lay in using Torbay. It was already the traditional shelter against westerlies in the age of sail. Four miles wide and, except for the foul ground of the Ridge halfway up the bay, a good holding anchorage on a mud and sand bottom capable of taking a fleet of any size, it had the additional advantage of enabling ships running back from Ushant 135 miles away to sail several more points away from the wind than more westerly alternatives.[34]

Torbay thus became the essential complement to Plymouth for naval operations to the westward in the French wars: a ready refuge for admirals careful of their fleets; a vital last safety line for admirals determined to hang in close to Brest as long as possible; 'a place' wrote the Secretary to the Admiralty, Josiah Burchett,

> very convenient for the refreshment of the fleet, tho' it does not altogether please some people on shore, who (without reason) think it a loadstone, which does too much attract.[35]

As early as 1689 the King and his ministers were complaining at the fleet retiring to Torbay instead of keeping station off Brest.[36] For their part, admirals not infrequently complained at government attempts to refit their fleets at Torbay to keep them at sea, rather than allowing them back to Spithead where they might refit more quickly but where they would be more remote from the operational zone and where ministers feared they would try to remain.[37] In August 1781 it was also used as a defensive position for the main battlefleet when Admiral Darby brought it in during stormy weather with the news that a combined Franco-Spanish fleet of 56 (in fact 49) of the line was in the offing. Darby anchored his 22 battleships in a double-lined crescent with three-deckers on the outside and two-deckers within, guarding the gaps between them. The battle of Torbay, however, never took place because again the French (and Spanish) were unwilling to risk a fleet action up-Channel, particularly since they would be at a disadvantage in trying to manoeuvre against a fleet at anchor.[38]

Torbay, like Plymouth, also had its weaknesses. Ideal as a protection from westerlies, it was wide open to winds from the east. If sheltering ships did not get out when the wind began to move in that direction, they were in danger of being embayed and driven ashore. In 1781 Darby was more afraid of an east wind than of attack by the enemy.[39] In February 1745 Admiral Medley, escorting a large convoy, nearly came to grief in exactly those circumstances. In the chaotic rush to escape, an East Indiaman fouled and sank the *Cape Coast* bound for Africa, while the *Expedition* for Lisbon and the *Tyger* transport for Newfoundland drove ashore at Berry Head, the latter with 170 soldiers, six sailors and six women drowned. Medley's battered ships limped on to Plymouth, where two warships required docking and three more needed repair at the Island and in the Sound.[40] Fifty years later a far greater catastrophe loomed when Earl Howe took the main battlefleet, 27 of the line, into Torbay at a time when the French fleet of 30 of the line was at sea and the entire outward bound trade at a standstill sheltering in Plymouth. On 13 February 1795 he was caught by a sudden easterly gale and faced losing the war for Britain in an afternoon. Howe is reported to have paced the deck of his flagship all day, wringing his hands and exclaiming: 'Oh, my king! Oh, my country! Every ship of this fleet will be lost.' As his ships strained on their anchors, nine of them parted their cables but were brought to before going ashore. The experience shattered Howe's nerve and he never took the fleet out again.[41]

In fact, considering the enormous usage of Torbay in these wars, with convoys of up to 400 ships anchored there on occasion, serious damage was remarkably small – much smaller than in Plymouth Sound. The worst was in the winter of 1804–5, when the *Venerable* (74 guns) was wrecked at Paignton. Her crew was rescued by *Impetueux* (84), which within days nearly joined her as she was driven deep into the bay. Ashore, fires were kindled and directions written in large black letters on the white houses as to where to run her ashore to save lives. Fortunately the weather moderated enough to enable *Impetueux* to warp out to the safety of an anchor left by another battleship, but within a month another storm drove the frigate *Blonde* (32) ashore on Goodrington Sands. Whereas the local population had behaved badly in looting the wreckage of the *Venerable*, on this occasion they redeemed themselves when Brixham fishermen dragged two smuggling boats four miles overland to bring off *Blonde*'s crew.[42]

The Western Squadron in the Evolution of a New Naval Strategy

With the building of Plymouth Dock and the availability of Torbay as a fleet anchorage, it remained for the Navy to develop a strategy that could best exploit their capabilities. For some time they were regarded as advanced bases while Portsmouth became the home base of the main battlefleet and the point of concentration for convoys and major expeditions departing British shores. The 1690s building programme developed Portsmouth as the principal British dockyard and naval arsenal. It was much closer than Plymouth to London, the centre of naval administration, and to the great concentration of dockyards and victualling and armament factories on the Thames. It had the advantages of the large Spithead anchorage; safe in all winds, close to the dockyard to facilitate refitting, and a further large anchorage off St Helens on the eastern coast of the Isle of Wight to facilitate the concentration of large numbers of ships. Consequently the practice was for ships to be fitted out at the start of each campaign at Plymouth or the Thames dockyards to join those prepared at Portsmouth. If the main battlefleet sailed *en masse* to the westward it would use Plymouth dockyard as its facility for individual or small groups of ships in need of minor repair or supply, and Torbay as its place of refuge from westerly storms or as a place of call, usually after cruises of up to six weeks (the longest generally thought practical if crews were to remain healthy), to rest and refresh the crews and resupply the ships from victuallers sent round from Plymouth or Portsmouth.[43]

For operations against the French fleet, the grand fleet was usually at sea from May to September, after which in the early wars it was thought too stormy to risk the first- and second-rates. However, for purposes of all-year-round trade protection the pattern of the Dutch Wars was revived and expanded: the maintaining of a western squadron based on Plymouth, with Kinsale on the Irish coast as its additional lesser supply base. Sir George Byng's instructions of 1 December 1704 are not untypical of the tasks of this force. He was allotted four ships from Spithead, two from Plymouth, and three already cruising 30–50 leagues west of Scilly. With this squadron of third-rate or smaller cruising ships he was to cruise the Soundings, clear them of enemy warships or privateers and protect homeward bound trade. The outward bound Turkey Company convoy was to be escorted 100–150 leagues from Lands End. One or two ships at a time should be sent to Plymouth to clean, victual and return, and the squadron would continue on this service as long as provisions lasted, sending in every 20 days to Plymouth to report and receive orders. If forced back by lack of provisions or bad weather he should revictual at Plymouth for three months' service and proceed to sea until ordered to the contrary.[44]

Over time the western squadron was increased in strength, with a major turning point in the latter part of the 1744–48 war with France which was confirmed in the ensuing 1756–63 war. Byng had nine ships in 1701; in 1745 Admiral Martin had 12. In addition to Byng's tasks, Martin was given a more aggressive role to 'annoy the enemy's ships and commerce', and this led him 30–60 leagues southwest of Ushant on to the French trading routes. Nevertheless his was still a cruising squadron of third-rates or less, lacking the strength to take on the French fleet, for which he would need to be reinforced by first- and second-rates brought up from Portsmouth.[45] However, two substantial considerations shortly led the Admiralty to abandon its policy of keeping back its strongest units at Spithead, 210 miles from Ushant, rather than having them based on Plymouth, only 120 miles distant. The first was the very serious threat of a French and Jacobite invasion between 1744 and 1759: serious not simply because of the size of the potential invasion force, but also because no one knew how much internal Jacobite support it might receive. This led to a reconsideration of the best way to handle the invasion menace and to Admiral Vernon's famous statement in September 1745, that Martin's western squadron should be reinforced by five 90-gun second-rates because

> a western squadron formed as strong as we can make it by the junction of these five great ships to those Admiral Martin has to the westward and what others can be spared and got speedily to the Soundings, might face their united force, cover both Great Britain and Ireland and be in a condition to pursue them wherever they went, and be at hand to secure the safe return of our homeward bound trade from the East and West Indies . . .[46]

The second determining factor was the switch of the main thrust of the British war effort away from Europe, where it had been in the Wars of William III and Marlborough, and into an overseas contest for imperial supremacy. In this new policy the Navy could play a decisive strategic role by throttling France's ability to menace Britain's colonies or to protect its own. This was strikingly revealed in 1745 and early 1746, when a number of damaging French expeditions got away to the colonies, which Martin's small force was unable to prevent. The key, as Admiral Anson subsequently urged, lay in the western approaches:

> Our colonies are so numerous and so extensive that to keep a naval force at each equal to the united force of France would be impracticable with double our navy . . . The best defence, therefore, for our colonies as well as our coasts, is to have such a squadron always to the westward as may in all probability either keep the French in port, or give them battle with advantage if they come out.[47]

The build-up of the western squadron began when Anson took command in July 1746, and in August he had 29 ships of which 17 were of the line, including his 90-gun flagship *Prince George*, as well as six 50s, four frigates and two sloops, enabling him to patrol aggressively against any opposition in the Bay of Biscay.[48] By 1759 Hawke's western squadron, looking to stop French invasion, comprised 25 of the line including one first- and two second-rates.[49] By 1805 Admiral Cornwallis's 'Atlantic Fleet' numbered 44 of the line, including 13 first- and second-rates: 20 blockading Brest, seven Rochefort, seven Ferrol, and three as far south-west as the coast of Portugal.[50]

The escalating size of the western squadron, until it became effectively the main battlefleet, had major consequences for Plymouth, Torbay, and indeed for Devon as a whole. In April 1748 its commander, Admiral Warren, reported his intention not to send any of his ships to yards eastward of Plymouth that summer except for third-rates needing cleaning. The burden of sustaining the force was placed squarely on Plymouth dockyard, and its size and importance increased rapidly. Between 1739 and 1748 its workforce doubled, overtaking that of Woolwich. In the subsequent Seven Years War (1756–63) it overtook Deptford and Chatham. By 1762 a purpose-built,

1,200-berth naval hospital was completed, only outmatched by the 1,800-berth Haslar hospital at Portsmouth, and the 1760s and 70s saw an expansion programme which doubled the yard's size.[51] Table 27.1 contrasts Plymouth's position towards the end of the Spanish Succession and American wars. Only intermittently in the wars after 1778 did it overtake Portsmouth, but it was fast approaching parity, and some indication of its relative capacity to equip the Navy towards the end of the French wars can be seen in the distribution of moorings for laying up ships about 1807 (Table 27.2).

Table 27.1
Size of dockyard workforce

1711		1782	
Portsmouth	2,001	Plymouth	2,438
Chatham	1,287	Portsmouth	2,385
Deptford	1,083	Chatham	1,673
Woolwich	926	Deptford	1,295
Plymouth	717	Woolwich	1,179
Sheerness	234	Sheerness	511

Sources: Merriman, *Queen Anne's Navy*, 373; Knight, 'Royal Dockyards', App. IV, 397–8.

Table 27.2
Moorings for laying up ships c.1807

	battleships	frigates & sloops	total
Portsmouth	48	36	84
Plymouth	59	20	79
Chatham	22	29	51
Deptford		37	37
Sheerness	11	19	30
Woolwich		30	30
	140	171	311

Source: Morriss, *Royal Dockyards during the Revolutionary and Napoleonic Wars*, 37.

The growth of the dockyard and its impact on the local economy and society are described in later chapters. Its needs penetrated as far down as the local workhouses, where the unemployed poor picked oakum for caulking warships.[52] Moreover, from the mid-eighteenth century naval demands on the local economy increased, not simply because of the massively larger western squadron, but also because of the developing needs of the Navy to keep its ships at sea.

Devon's Role in the Blockade of Brest

The strengthening of the western squadron widened the strategic options of its commanders. They now had the capacity to blockade the French fleet in the Bay of Biscay and could do so by loose or close blockade.[53] Loose blockade saw the main fleet out in the summer months in a series of broad sweeps in the Bay of Biscay, retiring periodically to Torbay while frigates watched the main French fleet based at Brest and warned of its sailing. This mode had the advantage of imposing less wear on ships and crews, which were kept in the shelter of Torbay or Spithead in the winter months. Moreover, by giving the enemy chance to put to sea it gave greater opportunity to bring them to decisive fleet action.[54] The movements of Earl Howe, an exponent of loose blockade, in 1793–4 were as follows:[55]

1793	14 July	sailed St Helens
	10–23 August 4 Sept – 8 Oct 11–15 Dec	in Torbay
	17 Dec	returned Spithead
1794	2 May	sailed St Helens
	15 June	returned Spithead (via Plymouth)
	3 Sept	sailed Spithead
	21 Sept – 21 Oct 31 Oct – 11 Nov	in Torbay
	29 Nov	returned to St Helens

Long rests in Torbay gave ample time for re-provisioning from Portsmouth and the Thames as well as from Plymouth (and caused Howe to be nicknamed 'Lord Torbay'). The disadvantage of a loose blockade was that, should the French be allowed to get out, they might also get clean away to do whatever damage they could.

Close blockade was first developed by Lord Hawke in 1759 and revived by Earl St Vincent in 1800 to last through the crisis years of the Napoleonic Wars. It involved stationing the fleet close in to Brest to prevent the enemy leaving port at all. This kept the British navy in control, deprived enemy squadrons of necessary sea-training, and exploited Brest's weakness – its poor communications which made it dependent on supply by sea. Close blockade, by shutting off that traffic, deprived the French of the means to put to sea. In a two-week period in 1800 the inshore squadron sent back to Plymouth as prizes six *chasse-marées* laden with salt-fish, cord, wood and other stores (20 October), two brigs with wheat (26 October), a brig with resin and pitch and a sloop with flour (4 November).[56] The disadvantage of close blockade was the strain on ships and crews, which might so damage the fleet as to lose it control of the seas, and losses were frequent when operating so close to the French coast.

To be effective, close blockade had to be continuous. From the time he left Torbay on 20 May 1759 until the time he caught and destroyed the Brest fleet at Quiberon Bay on 20 November (Fig. 27.3), Hawke was only briefly off station three times during storms: in Torbay 6–11 June, Plymouth Sound 13–18 October and Torbay again 10–14 November. St Vincent in 1800 was off Ushant continuously from leaving Torbay on 27 May to returning thither on 25 September, and though forced into Torbay more frequently thereafter, his ships nevertheless were back on station again the moment the winds allowed.

The maintenance of the fleet at sea over such long periods created enormous problems of supply. The 24,000 Anglo-Dutch seamen in Torbay in 1693 were more than the entire population of any Devon town – indeed, only three towns in England and Wales were bigger. The 23,000 seamen in St Vincent's western squadron in 1800 were exceeded in Devon only by those in the Plymouth conurbation, and there were still only 16 English towns with a population greater than 20,000. To supply the needs of such fleets could enrich farmers and contractors, but it could also cause enormous hardship for the local population, particularly in times of bad harvests. The continuing presence of 25,000 mouths on the coast for the first two months of 1795 drained Devon of food, so that by 14 March a quarter of wheat cost five shillings above the national average and by 11–18 April eight shillings more, provoking a wave of food riots in south Devon and up the Tamar Valley.[57] Moreover, supplying the fleet was not simply a matter of providing for its immediate wants. Hawke was ordered to ensure that his ships had never less than two months provisions on board; by 1800 the requirement was for five months, since the western squadron was the strategic reserve for the entire world and had to have the capacity of following any French force wherever it went.[58]

Through the victualling yard, naval bakehouse, and brewhouse at Plymouth, as well as through private baking contracts for biscuit, Devon helped supply these store-provisions. But equally so did the other yards from their hinterlands. Devon agriculture, however, became of more crucial importance from the mid-eighteenth century onwards as the Navy began regularly supplementing dry-stores with fresh provisions to keep its crews healthy and at sea. The onset of disease was frequently the main determinant of the length of a cruise in the early French wars. In 1689 the summer cruise of the Anglo-Dutch fleet in the Soundings terminated abruptly with its arrival in Torbay at the end of August to unload over 2,000 sick, 500 already having been buried at sea.[59] Scurvy was the usual cause, though two successive cruises by Hawke in 1755–6 each lasted barely two months owing to typhus. By mid-century the need for a healthy diet to ward off sickness was becoming appreciated, and once fresh beef and fresh vegetables became regarded as useful anti-scorbutics naval demand for them was enormous.[60] Nearest was freshest, and some indication of the local demand can be seen from the cost of fresh beef delivered to victualling depots as recorded in the Victualling Board's ledgers for 1804 (Table 27.3).

Table 27.3
Fresh beef received, by value

London	£38,129
Plymouth	£27,286
Portsmouth	£13,748
Chatham	£9,582
Dover	£8,583
Torbay	£4,931

Source: PRO ADM 112/190.

Over 4,880 oxen passed into the naval pens at Plymouth in 1804 and found their way to the blockading fleet. In the three months October–December 1800 St Vincent was sent 377 tons of fresh beef; in the three months May–July 1805 4½ tons of cabbages, 12½ tons of potatoes, nearly one ton of turnips and 3½ tons of onions passed from Plymouth to the fleet off Ushant.[61] The results were impressive. After more than six months at sea, Hawke had fewer than 20 sick out of 14,000 at Quiberon Bay in November 1759. After being 121 days continuously off Brest, St Vincent landed only 16 sick at Torbay in September 1800.[62] As far as possible supply was by a shuttle-service of victuallers between Plymouth and Ushant and, additionally, warships sent back in rotation to clean or repair returned stocked with live animals and vegetables for the fleet.[63] The latter, however, could never bring enough, and the shuttle was liable to break down in bad weather, particularly in winter, when trans-shipment was difficult and frequently small ships could not make the voyage at all.[64]

Great significance was therefore attached to the occasions when the fleet was forced back to Torbay as providing the best opportunity for resupply. In a close blockade this had to be done in a hurry. Admiral Cornwallis, in entrusting command temporarily to Sir Charles Cotton in July 1804, ordered him

> to bear up for Torbay – should the wind be to the westward – to collect the squadron, and take the opportunity, during the continuance of wind, to supply the ships in water, and such other wants as are to be obtained at that anchorage, taking care to be to sea the moment the wind should come round to the northward or eastward . . .

While the wind was westerly the French could not get out from Brest, whose exit faced westward. Hence the need to be back quickly to forestall their escape when the wind shifted.[65]

In these circumstances the fleet's arrival in Torbay (Fig. 27.3) resembled a pit-stop in a motor race, but was even more hectic. Contractors were on short notice. In 1759 Richard Cross, the Exeter butcher, was contracted to supply 'good fat well-fed ox beef' at 48 hours notice, and on 6 June Sir Edward Hawke came into Torbay demanding 46,926 lb of it (nearly 70 oxen), while a horseman was sent galloping to Plymouth for victuallers to be sent round at once.[66] In 1803 the contract to supply cabbages, greens, onions, leeks, turnips and carrots for HM's ships at Plymouth and the Channel Fleet at sea, held by John Helson, 'gardener', of Thornhill near Plymouth and John Boon, 'gardener' of Plymouth, stipulated supply within twelve hours of demand.[67] By then the operation had become more sophisticated. As the fleet was seen making landfall on the Devon coast heading for Torbay, so the message was relayed along the coast – after 1795 by signal stations between Torbay and Plymouth. Victuallers kept ready in Dartmouth and at the foot of Millbrook Lake across the Tamar at Plymouth, with one month's provisions for 15,000 men, put out for Torbay. Lighters were also taken up to carry round beer (another reputed antiscorbutic), while at Brixham other vessels were kept ready to assist in loading fresh beef and water.[68] As the battleships came to anchor they sent their boats ashore to refill their casks with fresh water at Brixham, where a reservoir was built during the American War and pipes laid to the quay. Their bore was enlarged in 1801 to speed up watering.[69] Live oxen would already have been driven overland from the depot at Ivybridge, and these were slaughtered on the beach by contractors. Sometimes extra slaughterers were sent post-haste from Plymouth Victualling Yard to speed up provisioning.[70]

The scene would be chaotic, particularly since the sailors were rapidly surrounded by a crowd of petty traders seeking to sell them spirits and much else besides: the arrival of a large floating town in Torbay was a magnet to peddlars of all sorts. In 1800 St Vincent tried to keep these off by establishing a marine guard so that:

27.3 The Western Squadron entering Torbay. Engraved by T Medland from a drawing by W Anderson, printed in *Naval Chronicle* XIII (1805), plate Clxxviii.

> an entire stop was put to the scenes of drunkeness, obscenity, blasphemy, and consequent casualties (by the men fighting with each other and falling over precipices) which, to the disgrace of His Majesty's Navy, obtained heretofore in watering the fleet at Brixham . . .

but two months later there was rioting again.[71]

As soon as the wind changed the fleet was off, irrespective of whether it had completed its resupply. St Vincent's successor, Cornwallis, was nicknamed 'Billy Blue' for keeping the Blue Peter flying all the while to hold his ships in readiness to sail. St Vincent expected his ships to be under sail and well out of the bay within an hour and a half of the unmooring signal being hoisted. Captains and junior admirals ashore could be left behind in the haste, and bum-boat women, butchers, and shoemakers on board selling their wares were liable to be carried away.[72]

The Napoleonic Wars made Torbay a depot in its own right, with a naval hospital at Paignton from 1800, storehouses, slaughterhouses and the reservoir, and protective fortifications on Berry Head (above, p. 125, Fig. 15.4). However, the blockade of Brest proved so successful in stifling activity at that port that Napoleon turned to developing new first-rate bases up-Channel at Cherbourg and Antwerp and moved the focus of naval activity on the Atlantic coast deeper into the Bay of Biscay to Lorient, Rochefort and the north coast of Spain.[73] As the British blockade of the latter increased, so new bases were sought further west. In Ireland a new store base was developed at Hawlbowline Island in 1811.[74] In England Sheerness to the east was upgraded, and in the west attention again turned to Falmouth, used as a base for frigate squadrons in the 1790s. Moorings for 15 of the line were laid there in 1805, when it began to be used to refit and resupply battleships.[75] Its possibilities were limited, however, and after taking the western squadron thither St Vincent reported in March 1806, backing the recommendation of the engineers Rennie and Whidbey to make a breakwater for Plymouth Sound:

> I see no other chance of resisting the insatiable ambition of the ruler of France but making Plymouth Sound a secure mole at any expense, for the difficulty of getting out of Falmouth Harbour is so great in winter time, that it cannot be depended on.

Work began on the breakwater in 1812. By August 1815 1,100 yards were above sea level and it was already showing an effect in sheltering the Sound in storms.[76]

Devon and the Spoils of War

The final major consequence of Devon's central strategic role in operations in the western approaches was that it became the major emporium for prizes taken in home waters and a major landing place for prisoners brought in from all points westward. The western approaches were the main hunting ground for British warships and privateers in home waters, and they sent their captures into the nearest secure port – either Falmouth or, more often, Plymouth.[77] If confirmed as legitimate prizes, the captures were then sold for the benefit of their captors. How extensive this traffic could be can be seen from Table 27.4.

Britain's sudden declaration of war in 1803 caught France and its allies off guard, and captures again poured in. The Cattewater in June 1803 was described as 'quite a wood of French prizes and detained Batavians' – 105 in all, reckoned with their cargoes as worth £1½ millions. Prize sales were major events: in January 1799 'a great number of respectable merchants from London, Bristol and Exeter attended, and the different vessels and stores sold remarkably well . . .', and in the following December Plymouth was 'full of merchants from London, Liverpool, Chester, Bristol etc.' for a sale which disposed of upwards of £100,000 of property.[78]

With the prizes came prisoners, and a substantial business developed around them, too. Trained, experienced seamen were valuable strategic commodities. Captors had the choice between offering to exchange prisoners in order to get their own skilled seamen back, or of retaining them in order to hinder their enemy from manning his warships. Because the Royal Navy usually expected to acquire a superiority in the war at sea, it would not usually exchange all for all but only man for man, so that it frequently acquired a surplus of enemy seamen. In the Seven Years War 64,373 French prisoners passed through the hands of the superintending Sick and Hurt Board. Of these, 8,499 died, and, after exchanges, more than 26,000 still remained in British hands in 1762. Since contemporary estimates gave the number of trained native seamen at the call of the French navy as 56–60,000, a recent study has concluded that: 'This heretofore little-known factor may have played a crucial role in preventing the [French] navy from manning its ships with trained men'.[79] It contributed much to the poor French naval performance from 1758 onwards. In the Napoleonic Wars, when soldiers, too, were captured in the Peninsular campaigns, 122,440 French prisoners were brought to Britain between 1803 and 1814, of whom a French report stated in 1814 that 12,845 had died and 70,041 still awaited return.[80]

Many of these prisoners came to Devon, the degree of the county's involvement being indicated in Table 27.5. Mill Prison at Plymouth was the first in Britain purpose-built for prisoners of war. Constructed in the Seven Years War, it was redeveloped as Millbay Prison in 1799. Most prisoners, however, were quartered in old warships, and there were eleven such prison hulks at Plymouth in 1811. The maintenance of these captives became a substantial local business, though it could be abused: in 1798 the Plymouth contractor was imprisoned for six months and fined £300 for failing to provide them with good provisions of full weight.[81]

Table 27.4
Prizes, detained and recaptured ships sent into Plymouth 1793–1801

To Michaelmas	1793	1794	1795	1796	1797	1798	1799	1800	1801	1793–1801
Totals	30	22	87	70	95	176	115	157	196	948

By Country	French	Spanish	Dutch	English	American	Danish	Swedish	Prussian, etc.
Totals	340	42	65	156	109	116	46	74

Source: *Naval Chronicle* VII (1802), 175–6.

Table 27.5
Locations of French prisoners, 19 January 1799

Portsmouth	10,576
Plymouth	8,398
Norman Cross (nr Peterborough)	4,127
Stapleton (nr Bristol)	4,121
Liverpool	4,000
Chatham	1,298
Edinburgh	736
	30,265
Officers on parole	
Tiverton	114
Litchfield	66
Bishop's Waltham	60
Peebles	60
	300

Source: *Naval Chronicle*, I (1799), 254.

Sick prisoners were unwelcome, and when in 1756 some were callously despatched in carts and without subsistence money to Tavistock, its inhabitants fearing infection refused to receive them, as did Launceston and Okehampton. Government money to maintain healthy prisoners on parole, however, was a valuable supplement to the income of the Devon towns, whose woollen industry was often hit by being shut off from its biggest market in northern Europe by the wars. In 1757 Tavistock, Torrington, Exeter, Crediton, Ashburton, Bideford, and Okehampton all acted as parole towns.[82] In the 1790s this income was a lifeline to Tiverton, reckoned as being worth £150 a month by its town clerk when 176 prisoners from the captured frigate *Virginie* arrived, and there was a bonus when this Breton crew put out the great fire that threatened to engulf the town in November 1797.[83]

In the great economic crisis of 1811–12 Tiverton, Ashburton, Okehampton and Crediton all housed French prisoners, though by the latter year they were fast being concentrated in the new Dartmoor prison at Princetown, begun in 1806 and opened in 1809 at a cost of £135,000. By December 1812 it housed 9,500 prisoners and a 1,200 garrison.[84] Such a large concentration threatened to exhaust local food supplies, though it brought profit to Tavistock tradesmen, and also to the enterprising businessman of Plymouth Dock who supplied straw for the prisoners to earn a small income plaiting, thus initiating what became a thriving Plymouth industry, the making of straw hats for sale to the Channel Islands, the West Indies and Spain.[85]

The most famous prisoner to reach Devon in these wars was, perhaps fittingly, the last. Following his defeat at Waterloo the Emperor Napoleon fled to Rochefort, but being unable to escape the British naval blockade he surrendered to Captain Maitland of the *Bellerophon* and was brought to Torbay on 24 July 1815 and then on 2 August to Plymouth, finally returning to Torbay to depart for St Helena on the *Northumberland*. It was an appropriate climax to Devon's part in the French Wars. Having for so long threatened invasion, the closest Napoleon ever came to Britain was to the two main operational bases of the fleet that had kept these islands secure against his threats and contributed so much to the final British victory.

27: Devon and the Naval Strategy of the French Wars 1689–1815

1 E Chappell, ed., *The Tangier Papers of Samuel Pepys* (Naval Records Society, 1935), 161.
2 The first-rate *Royal Sovereign*, originally built as the *Sovereign of the Seas* in 1637: BL, Lansdowne MS 847, f.17v.
3 EB Powley, *The Naval Side of King William's War* (1972), 134–43, 173–4.
4 e.g. see JH Owen, *War at Sea under Queen Anne 1702–1708* (Cambridge, 1938), 101ff.
5 *HMC, Finch MSS*, IV, 270–1.
6 BM Ranft, ed., *The Vernon Papers* (NRS, 1958), 451–2.
7 G Symcox, *The Crisis of French Sea Power 1688–1697* (The Hague, 1974), 43–55.
8 Symcox, *Crisis of French Sea Power*, 92–101; C de la Roncière, *Histoire de la marine Française* (Paris, 1937), VI, 79–80; *HMC*, 12th Report, Appendix Pt VII, *MSS of SH Le Fleming*, 275, 282, 326 (misdated); *HMC Finch MSS*, II, 382. The best account of the Teignmouth raid is that intercepted from a French participant in *HMC Finch MSS*, III, 443.
9 Symcox, *Crisis of French Sea Power*, 50, 116–24; EH Jenkins, *A History of the French Navy* (1973), 80–87.
10 H Richmond, *The Navy in the War of 1739–48* (3 vols., Cambridge, 1920), II, 62–84, 93.
11 GR Barnes and JH Owen, eds, *The Private Papers of John, Earl of Sandwich*, II, (NRS, 1933), 64–5, 67, 68–71, 74; A Temple Patterson, *The Other Armada* (Manchester, 1960), 143–4, 181–93; *Exeter Flying Post*, 27 August 1779.
12 G Lacour-Gayet, *La marine militaire de la France sous le règne de Louis XVI* (Paris, 1905), 273–4.
13 J Ehrman, *The Navy in the War of William III 1689–1697* (Cambridge, 1953), 418, 428.
14 Oppenheim, 74–5 (Oppenheim perhaps too readily ascribed the investigation of Bideford to corrupt jobbery); Ehrman, *Navy in the War of William III*, 416; AE Stephens 'Plymouth Dock: A Survey of the Development of the Royal Dockyard during the Sailing Ship Era' (unpublished PhD thesis, University of London, 1940), 39; BL, Lansdowne MS 847, f.4.
15 Stephens, 'Plymouth Dock', 40; BL, Sloane MS 3233, f.33v.
16 J Coad, 'Historic Architecture of HM Naval Base Devonport 1689–1850', *MM*, 69 (1983), 342; Stephens, 'Plymouth Dock', 37–8, 41–2.
17 BL, Lansdowne MS 847, f.39. This review was made in 1694 and repeated in 1698 (in BL, Kings MS 43, f.146) except that 'the shores dreadful' became 'the rocks dangerous'.
18 Oppenheim, 75; Coad, 'Historic Architecture of HM Naval Base Devonport', 342; Ehrman, *Navy in the War of William III*, 417.
19 Coad, 'Historic Architecture of HM Naval Base Devonport', 342; in February 1690 three storehouses were added to the plan.
20 *HMC Finch MSS*, II, 384–8; BL, Lansdowne MS 847, f.39v.
21 NMM, ADM/4/1773, 5 March 1691 (I am grateful to Jonathan Coad for this reference); Coad, 'Historic Architecture of HM Naval Base Devonport', 342–4.
22 Ehrman, *Navy in the War of William III*, 415–6.
23 Lacour-Gayet, *La marine militaire de la France*, 274.
24 BL, Sloane MS 3233.
25 BL, Kings MS 43, f.145v.
26 BL, Kings MS 43, f.146; BL, Add. MS 31, 173, St Vincent to Nepean, 29 Oct. 1800; GB Mundy, *The Life and Correspondence of the Late Admiral Lord Rodney* (1830), II, 179–80; R Morriss, *The Royal Dockyards during the Revolutionary and Napoleonic Wars* (Leicester, 1983), 40.
27 PRO, ADM 1/100, Graves to P Stephens, 5 January 1794.
28 Keppel's reports from 31 July to 23 Aug. are in PRO, ADM 1/94 pt.3, and Ourry's in ADM 174/116. See also *Sandwich Papers*, II, 128–9, 142, 148–52, 155–6.
29 RJB Knight, 'The Royal Dockyards in England at the Time of the American War of Independence' (unpublished PhD thesis, University of London, 1972), 316; PRO, ADM 1/88, Lestock to Corbett, 9 September 1746.
30 PRO, ADM 1/802, Hanway to Clevland, 14 October; ADM 1/92, Hawke to Admiralty, 5 November 1759.
31 Powley, *Naval Side of William's War*, 303–4; Ehrman, *Navy in the War of William III*, 380; *HMC Finch MSS*, III, 251–2, 255, 259.
32 *Naval Chronicle*, I (1799), 343; DM Steer, 'The Blockade of Brest by the Royal Navy 1793–1805' (unpublished MA thesis, University of Liverpool, 1971), 191; JR Schaber, 'Admiral Sir William Cornwallis and the Blockade of Brest 1801–1806' (unpublished BLitt thesis, University of Oxford, 1977), 56 n.1; BL, Add. MS 31, 173, St Vincent to Admiralty, 28 March 1806.
33 PRO, ADM 1/92, Hawke to Admiralty, 5 Nov. 1759.
34 Steer, 'The Blockade of Brest', 200–201; GJ Marcus, *Quiberon Bay* (1960), 35.
35 J Burchett, *A Complete History of the Most Remarkable Transactions at Sea . . . to the conclusion of the Last War with France* (1720), 417.
36 AN Ryan, 'William III and the Brest Fleet in the Nine Years War', in R Hatton and JS Bromley, eds, *William III and Louis XIV* (Liverpool, 1968), 51–2. For Admiral Russell's justification of Torbay see *HMC Finch MSS*, II, 240.
37 PRO, ADM 1/92, Hawke to Admiralty, 23, 24 Aug. 1762; Sir JK Laughton, ed., *Letters and Papers of Charles, Lord Barham, 1758–1813*, I, (NRS, 1907), 327–8 reporting Admiral Geary.
38 WM James, *The British Navy in Adversity* (1926), 306–7; *Sandwich Papers*, IV (NRS, 1938), 60; PRO ADM 1/95, Darby to Admiralty, 25, 29 Aug., 2, 5, 9 Sept. 1781; Lacour-Gayet, *La marine militaire de la France*, 375.
39 *Sandwich Papers*, IV, 60.
40 *Naval Chronicle*, I (1799), 330 n.1; PRO, ADM 174/289 1–3 March 1745.
41 GJ Marcus, *A Naval History of England* (1971), II, 39; Oppenheim, 90; C Lloyd, ed., *The Health of Seamen* (NRS, 1965), 237–8.
42 *Naval Chronicle* (1804), XII, 472–4, 497–8, (1805), XIII, 64, 77. The building of a breakwater was urged as early as 1696; A Robinson, *Reasons for Making a Harbour or Mould in Tor-Bay* (2nd edn, 1700), but nothing was done even after the failure of an experiment to overwinter two second-rates there in 1799–1800: see Sir J Ross, *Memoirs and Correspondence of Admiral Lord de Saumarez* (1838), I, 295–6.
43 *HMC Finch MSS*, II, 244; III, 195, 219–20; IV, 471; *Sandwich Papers*, II, 84, 107; III, 45.
44 B Tunstall, ed., *The Byng Papers*, I (NRS, 1930), 55–7. For a description of the activities of the western squadron, see Owen, *War at Sea under Queen Anne*, 27, 69, 101–22, 193, 199, 207–37.
45 Richmond, *Navy in the War of 1739–48*, II, 147–50; PRO, ADM 2/1331, Admiralty to Martin, 17 Aug. 1745, Admiralty to Hamilton, 3 Aug., to Vernon, 7 Aug. 1745.
46 Richmond, *Navy in the War of 1739–48*, II, 69.
47 Quoted in R Middleton, 'British Naval Strategy 1755–62: The Western Squadron', *MM* 75 (1989), 350.

48 Richmond, *Navy in the War of 1739–48*, III, 21, 38.
49 RF Mackay, *Admiral Hawke* (Oxford, 1965), 200–03. The squadron was subsequently strengthened by two more second-rates.
50 P Bloomfield, ed., *Kent and the Napoleonic Wars* (Gloucester, 1987), 100–13; JR Schaber, 'Cornwallis and the Blockade of Brest', 124, shows 62 ships and vessels and 28,000 men in his force in July 1805. For a fuller account see M Duffy, 'The Establishment of the Western Squadron as the Linchpin of British Naval Strategy', in M Duffy, ed., *Parameters of British Naval Power 1650–1850* (Exeter, 1992), 60–81.
51 D Baugh, *British Naval Administration in the Age of Walpole* (Princeton, 1965), 264, 273–5. See also below, pp. 195–200.
52 Knight, 'Naval Dockyards', 115.
53 The best discussions of the systems of blockade are by AN Ryan, 'The Royal Navy and the Blockade of Brest, 1689–1805: theory and practice', in M Acerra, J Merino and J Meyer, eds, *Les marines de guerre européennes XVII–XVIIIe siècles* (Paris, 1985), 175–93, and by his pupil, DM Steer, 'Blockade of Brest'.
54 So Hood urged Cornwallis in 1801, see JR Schaber, 'Cornwallis and the Blockade of Brest', 45 n.1.
55 Steer, 'Blockade of Brest', 56–8 and Appendix 2.
56 *Naval Chronicle*, IV (1800), 342, 433–4. See also Hawke's instructions in 1759, Mackay, *Hawke*, 202.
57 PJ Corfield, *The Impact of English Towns 1700–1800* (Oxford, 1982), 8; C Emsley, *British Society and the French Wars 1793–1815* (1979), 41–2; J Stevenson, *Popular Disturbances in England 1700–1870* (1979), 97–8. For similar problems in 1801, see R Wells, 'The Revolt of the South-West, 1800–1801: A study in English popular protest', *Social History*, 6 (1977), 713–44.
58 PRO, ADM 2/1331 Admiralty to Hawke, 18 May 1759; BL, Add. MS 31,179 St Vincent's Order Book, (frigates were to be victualled for four months). In early 1801 Calder took part of the squadron to the West Indies when Ganteaume escaped from Brest; in 1809 Duckworth reached Madeira, en route to the Caribbean, before he learnt that the Brest fleet had escaped only as far as the Aix Roads.
59 *HMC Finch MSS*, II, 240.
60 S Gradish, *The Manning of the British Navy during the Seven Years' War* (1980), 133, 135, 140–71; NAM Rodger, *The Wooden World* (1986), 82–105; NAM Rodger, 'The victualling of the British Navy in the Seven Years' War', *Bulletin du Centre d'Histoire des Espaces Atlantiques*, 2 (Bordeaux, 1985), 37–53.
61 ADM 112/190; Steer, 'Blockade of Brest', 274, 289.
62 Lloyd, ed., *Health of Seamen*, 121; C Lloyd and JLS Coulter, *Medicine and the Navy 1200–1900* (4 vols. Edinburgh, 1957–63), III, 159.
63 Gradish, *The Manning of the British Navy*, 165–6; Steer, 'Blockade of Brest', 289; *Naval Chronicle*, X (1803), 257, 435, 511; XII (1804), 161, 331–2.
64 Gradish, *Manning of the British Navy*, 167; PRO, ADM 106/272 Victualling Board to Navy Board, 14 Dec. 1759; ADM 1/802 Hanway to Admiralty, 28 Dec. 1759; ADM 1/92 Hawke to Admiralty, 10 Sept. 1759, 31 Oct. 1760.
65 J Leyland, ed., *The Blockade of Brest*, I (NRS, 1898), 369; PRO, ADM 1/92 Hawke to Admiralty, 14 Oct. 1759.
66 Mackay, *Hawke*, 208; Rodger, 'Victualling of the British Navy', 44.
67 PRO, ADM 112/87, 15 Nov. 1803. See also below, chapter 29.
68 *Naval Chronicle*, IV (1800), 434; XI (1804), 81; Steer, 'Blockade of Brest', 273–4, 280–1.
69 Steer, 'Blockade of Brest', 275 ff.
70 *Naval Chronicle*, XI (1804), 78–9; XII (1804), 499.
71 BL Add. MS 31,172 St Vincent to Admiralty, 28 Sept., 7 Nov. 1800; Add. MS 34,940; General Order, 21 Aug. 1800.
72 HW Richmond, ed., *The Private Papers of George, second Earl Spencer*, III (NRS, 1924), 377–8; BL, Add. MS 34,940, General Orders 28 Oct. 1800; Add. MS 31,172 St Vincent to Admiralty, 20 Aug. 1800; Add. MS 31,173, St Vincent to Nepean, 25 Aug. 1800; *The Times*, 5 Jan. 1804, report from Brixham of 1 Jan.
73 R Glover, 'The French Fleet, 1807–1814: Britain's problem and Madison's opportunity', *Journal of Modern History*, 39 (1967), 233–52.
74 Morriss, *Royal Dockyards*, 4.
75 *Naval Chronicle*, XIII (1805), 328.
76 BL, Add. MS 31,173 St Vincent to Admiralty, 28 March 1806; Morriss, *Royal Dockyards*, 57; Oppenheim, 90–1; J Naish, 'Joseph Whidbey and the Building of Plymouth Breakwater', *MM* 78 (1992), 37–56.
77 See also below, chapter 32.
78 *Naval Chronicle*, I (1799), 166; II (1799), 640; X (1803), 82.
79 J Pritchard, *Louis XV's Navy 1748–1762* (Kingston, 1987), 73, 81–2.
80 F Abell, *Prisoners of War in Britain 1756 to 1815* (Oxford, 1914), 40ff; O Anderson, 'The establishment of British supremacy at sea and the exchange of naval prisoners of war, 1689–1783', *English Historical Review*, 75 (1960), 77–89.
81 Abell, *Prisoners of War*, 15, 220, 228; Oppenheim, 118.
82 Abell, *Prisoners of War*, 289; NMM, VAU/9/17, 23 Jan. 1756.
83 Lt Col Harding, *The History of Tiverton* (Tiverton, 1845), I, 158; J Bourne, ed., *Georgian Tiverton: The Political Memoranda of Beavis Wood 1768–98* (Devon and Cornwall Record Society, New Series, 29, 1986), 152, 157, 160 n.10; A Reed, 'French prisoners of war on parole in Tiverton 1797–1812', *The Devon Historian*, 36 (1988), 10–14.
84 PRO, ADM 98/205; B Thompson, *The Story of Dartmoor Prison* (1907), 10–12; Abell, *Prisoners of War*, 52, 235–60.
85 Besides contractors, the local population could sell wares to the prisoners at a weekly market: Thompson, *Story of Dartmoor Prison*, 66–70; CBM Sillick, 'The City-Port of Plymouth: An essay in geographical interpretation' (unpublished PhD thesis, University of London, 1938), 55, 66.

28 The Development and Organisation of Plymouth Dockyard, 1689–1815

JONATHAN COAD

The Design and Building of the New Dockyard, 1690–1700

THE NEW DOCKYARD ON THE HAMOAZE was remarkable in being the only Royal Naval home yard built on an empty site to a single overall plan during the entire period of emergent British naval ascendancy between the early sixteenth and early nineteenth centuries (Fig. 28.1). As such, its creators took the opportunity to incorporate in its construction all the latest ideas in dockyard technology and planning.[1]

The focus of every major naval dockyard was its dry dock, where major inspections and repairs below the waterline on warships could be carried out most efficiently. From the very beginning the architect of Plymouth dock, the Assistant Surveyor of the Navy, Edmund Dummer, provided alternative estimates for building, either in the traditional manner in wood, or in stone according to the new techniques developed by the French in constructing their dock at Rochefort in the 1670s–80s.[2] While there is no evidence that Dummer had actually seen the Rochefort dock, there are enough similarities with the design adopted at Plymouth to indicate that British naval architects knew all about it.[3] On 30 December 1690 a contract was made with the Portsmouth mason, Robert Waters, to build a stone dock sufficient to accommodate up to a third-rate ship of the line (66–80 guns). As built, like that at Rochefort, it incorporated stepped sides shaped to the lines of a ship's hull, which reduced the amount of water to be drained, economized on shoring necessary to prop up the ship, and improved working access to the hull. It also incorporated a double gate, instead of the three-leaved single-gate system hitherto used in Britain, which had the double advantage of being quicker to open or shut and of requiring only 4–6 men to operate, instead of 50–70 as formerly.[4]

Dummer did, however, make his own distinctive contribution to dock design at Plymouth. This came about as the result of objections raised by the Naval Agent (later first Resident Commissioner) at Plymouth, Captain Henry Greenhill. To lessen construction costs Dummer chose a small inlet in the rocky foreshore behind Point Froward. Here he was doubly fortunate to have good bedrock to support the dry dock (the absence of which was a failing at Rochefort) and a sufficient range of tides (up to 17ft on an ordinary spring tide) to allow gravity drainage – an important bonus when chain pumps were the only available mechanical alternative. Greenhill, however, asserted that the site was exposed to a three-mile fetch of water which on a high tide in westerly winds would render the dock gates insecure against the force of the waves. Instead, he suggested a site further up-river in a quarry opposite Saltash, where there was only a mile fetch of water and where there were lodgings for workmen and a market adjacent in Saltash. Defending his choice, Dummer retorted that Sheerness dock was equally exposed, that the contractor was confident he could secure the gates, and that Stoke and Stonehouse were near enough for lodgings and Plymouth for a market. He thought Greenhill's alternative too cramped for expansion, more expensive to excavate, and too close to substantial habitation and to a major highway to be secure against embezzlement.[5]

Second thoughts thereafter, however, led Dummer to take the dock gates problem more seriously and to propose the creation of an enclosed wet dock or basin in front of the dry dock. Besides protecting the gates of the inner dock, this offered a number of further advantages. It would speed up the dry-docking process by enabling an initial hull inspection or minor repairs or cleaning at low tide, if the outer gates were open, while, as a wet dock with the outer gates shut to retain water at low tide, passage could be made into or out of the dry dock on all occasions. Equally, in a wet dock a ship could be careened or repaired above the waterline in the basin more efficiently than from a hulk in the river, the passage of men and material was easier than if the ships were out in an open harbour, and a ship might be simultaneously stored while repairing – all with ease, because a ship stayed at a constant level in relation to the quays, and damage to hulls from constant grounding

28.1 The Hamoaze and Plymouth Sound in the late seventeenth century, from a watercolour by W de Buse. This shows Stonehouse Creek and the open country to the west not long before the building of the Dockyard. To the left is Mount Edgcumbe House with its shore battery. *(City of Plymouth Museums and Art Gallery)*

at low tides was prevented. Dummer claimed that work done in five weeks in an open harbour might be done in five days in a wet basin.[6] This new design of a wet dock or basin in front of a dry dock evolved to meet the specific needs of the Hamoaze, but it appeared so advantageous that it was also applied to the new dry dock building at the same time at Portsmouth. When the new scheme was put to the King, probably in January–March 1691, William III, who knew something of the harbour through visiting Plymouth en route to Ireland in 1689, added an extra requirement that the new dry dock be enlarged to be able to take a first-rate ship of the line (96–100 guns).[7]

Dummer's other significant achievement at Plymouth, made in consultation with Greenhill and the yard officers, was to site the many different workshops, offices and storehouses required for the building, repair and maintenance of ships of war in such a way as to enable movement within the yard, and the servicing of ships in dock or at the wharves, with the minimum of chaos and obstruction. This was a matter in which Dummer had developed a distinct expertise. In 1682 he had been sent by the Admiralty as Midshipman Extraordinary on the *Woolwich* to Tangier and the Mediterranean, to write accounts and draw views of ports. Having sketched the Italian coastline, he left the *Woolwich* at Genoa in spring 1683 and went by land for two months to draw Marseilles and Toulon, then regarded as the best-planned naval arsenal in Europe.[8] At Plymouth Dummer proudly proclaimed that he had produced 'not only the most regular, but also the most convenient of all the other yards in England (if not those of any other country beside) by being so disposed that each officer may despatch his business without incommoding any other person whatsoever in his duty'.[9]

In practice the dock was planned first and the yard subsequently designed about it. A full dockyard had not at first been intended, but probably the expansion of the dock plan led the Admiralty to enquire seriously in March 1691 about the land required for 'a yard and other conveniences about it'. Detailed on-site planning, however, does not appear to have been begun until Dummer's visit on 3 March 1692 when he, Greenhill and the principal officers considered 'the figure of the yard, needful habitations and other houses . . .'. Planning then advanced far enough so that, when the Admiralty asked for estimates on 11 July, the Navy Board was able to supply a detailed list eight days later, allowing the Admiralty to order construction work to begin on 29 July 1692.[10]

The overall plan can be studied in the accompanying sketch map (Fig. 28.2) and the plate (Fig. 28.3) produced in 1698. The dockyard might be considered as a square surrounding the dry dock and wet basin which intruded from the centre of its western side. The docks had a building or graving slip to each side, and the river frontage was lined with wharving to capitalize on the advantage of the Hamoaze in having deep water to the shoreline at high tide. The yard buildings form the other three sides of the square, with those handling the heaviest materials closest to the wharves for ease of conveyance. On the north side was placed the great smithy with its seven fires, deliberately isolated from the rest to reduce fire risk – the greatest danger in an undertaking where so many expensive and highly-flammable materials were stored.

The eastern side of the yard was dominated by the 400ft-long terrace of residences for the 13 principal officers, with small office wings at each end, at the edge of a cliff 90ft above the docks. It was, perhaps, the earliest terrace in England to be designed to have an architectural

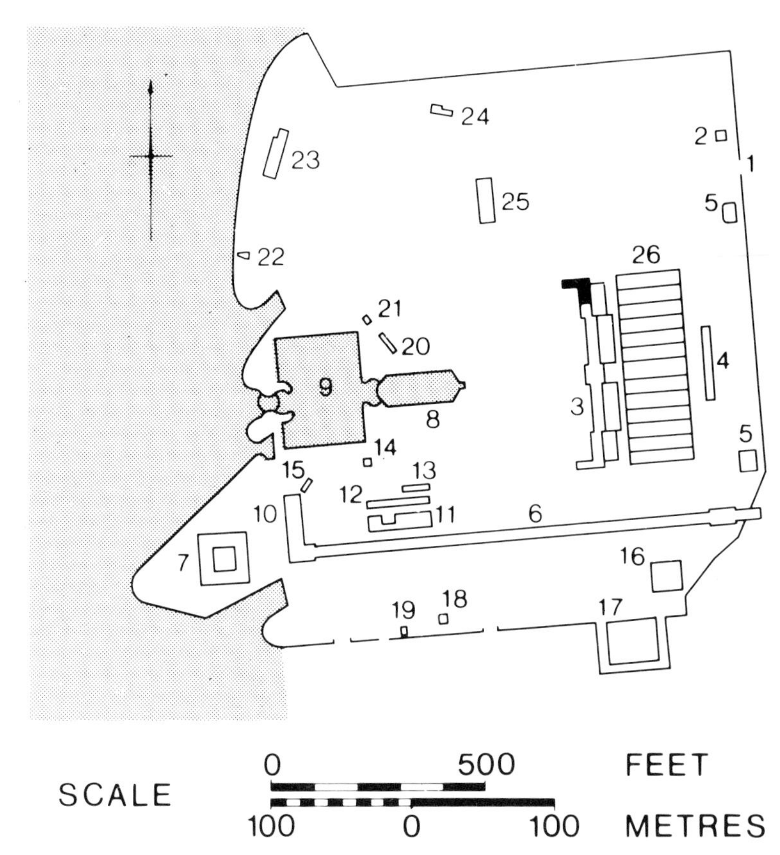

PLYMOUTH DOCKYARD c1700 Key: (Buildings in solid black still survive)

1 Main Gate	8 Dry Dock	15 Oar-Makers' Shop	21 Little Pitch House
2 Guard House	9 Wet Dock	16 Boat Houses	22 Double Wheel Crane
3 Officers' Terrace	10 Hemp House	17 Mast Houses	23 Great Smiths' Shop
4 Officers' Stables	11 Tarred Yarn House	18 Two Saw Pits	24 Painters' Shop etc
5 Ponds	12 Rigging House	19 Double Wheel Crane	25 Plank Storehouse
6 Ropery	13 Tap House	20 Foreman of the Yard's Cabin	26 Officers' Gardens
7 Great Storehouse	14 Great Pitch House		

28.2 Sketch Plan by the author of the Dockyard *c*1700. Reproduced by courtesy of the *Mariner's Mirror*.

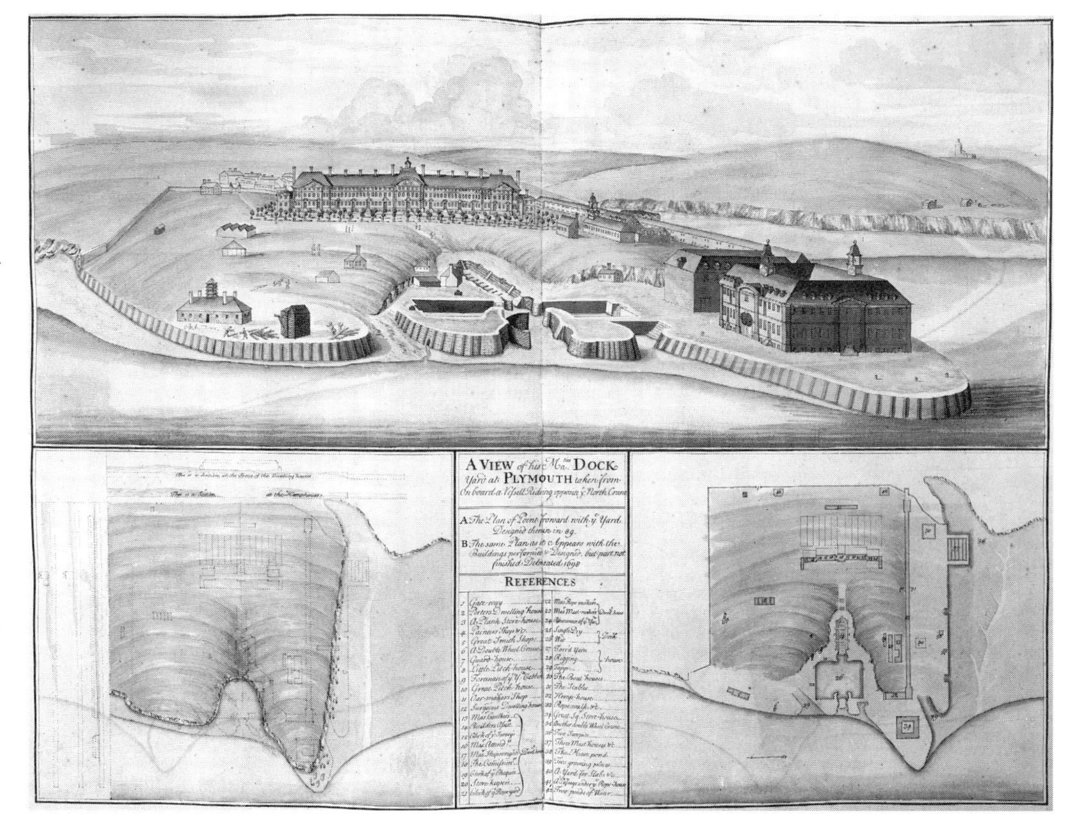

28.3 A watercolour of HM Dockyard Plymouth, 1698, for Edmund Dummer, artist unknown. To identify the buildings see Fig. 28.2. *(BL, King's Top., 43, fos 129v–30)*

unity, with a palace front. Its classically-pedimented facade marks it out as the prestige symbol for the dockyard. Its affinities with Robert Hooke's Bethlehem Hospital at Moorfields, London (1674–6), have led to suggestions that Hooke was the dockyard architect, but naval records make no mention of him. The records all indicate that the Navy Board relied on its Surveyor (from 1692), Edmund Dummer, for the layout and design of the individual buildings. He clearly consulted Greenhill and the yard officers, who had day-to-day supervision of construction, and in the case of the terrace in particular they had a major influence in securing a third storey to the building against Dummer's opinion.[11] Nevertheless, Dummer was proud of his achievement in managing to assemble all the principal officers 'in one entire pile of building' in the most eminent place where they could observe the yard's business and more readily communicate and confer with each other.[12]

The south side of the square plan contained most of the yard's major storehouses and workshops, carefully sited according to needs and functions. Jutting out from the south-west corner, where Point Froward was extended with wharving created out of rubble excavated from the dock and from levelling for buildings, stood Dummer's 'great square magazine' – the principal storehouse, perhaps modelled on the very similar *Zeemagazijn* built for the Amsterdam Admiralty in 1656. Sixty feet square and two storeys high, with two large cellars below and a loft above, it could reputedly hold the gear for 40 ships of the line. Standing out on the Point, it was well placed to receive and dispatch stores without interrupting other business, and was approachable on any state of the tide.[13] Most of the south side was taken up by workshops providing the means of motive power for the ships. Warships had to combine striking-power with mobility, and hence to move hulls heavily laden with cannon at speed they had to carry more sail-area than merchantmen. This put immense strain on the most vulnerable parts of a ship's equipment – the masts, yards, rigging, and sails – the workshops for and stores of which occupied the major part of any capital naval dockyard. The longest building in any yard (and hence the biggest potential obstruction to cross-yard traffic) was the ropewalk, where hemp was spun into yarn and twisted into strands, ropes and cables. At Plymouth it was 1,056ft long and sited to one side of the yard to avoid obstruction, though it also had an underpass halfway along its length. Rope manufacture also involved impregnating the yarn with tar for protection from rot, and buildings for this were attached to the ropewalk, as was another for turning rope into rigging. A large store for hemp, the essential raw material for rope and canvas, was sited at the western end of the ropewalk, with a sail-loft above and sufficient space beyond for sails to be dried outside without being spoilt through too close proximity to dust and tar from the workshops. Lastly, facing southward out of the square, with their separate wharf and double-wheeled crane, were the mast houses and associated mast pond where the masts could lie in the mud of the foreshore to retain their resin.[14]

Not all went as smoothly as Dummer's self-flattering descriptions indicate. The Admiralty determined on the site before investigating its ownership, and only then discovered that it belonged to a minor whose trustees could not sell and who for some time were reluctant to see permanent buildings on the site. Not until 1694 was agreement reached on a lease at £100 a year, and not until 1857 did the Admiralty obtain the freehold. Problems still occurred in that the initial site was too restricted for the ropewalk, the desired 40 feet extension of which remained unbuilt in 1697 until the existing lessee of its intended site could be brought to reasonable terms.[15]

Moreover, it was only when the decisions were made to extend the docks and then build a yard that the difficulties of the site became apparent. The initial third-rate dock, 170ft long, 46ft wide and 24ft deep at the gates, would have been built into the foreshore at an estimated cost of less than £9,000. The first-rate dock as built was 230ft long, 50ft wide and 22ft deep at the gate, but the wet basin, 256ft x 200ft, was built on the original site and the dry dock had to be hewn out of the cliff behind it, the whole estimated at almost two-and-a-half times the original cost.[16] An advantage of these excavations was that enough slate-stone was removed to line the wharves and provide some of the ground for the great storehouse. To the cost of the ropewalk had to be added the cost of levelling the site and £600 spent on

Table 28.1
The Construction of Plymouth Dockyard, 1691–1700

	Construction dates	Estimated costs
Dry Dock	1691–94	£9,750 9s 11¾d
Wet Dock/Basin	1691–95, 97–1700	£12,137 4s 9d
Drains & Sluices		£681 4s 7d
Slate Walling		£4,074 17 5½d
Two House Cranes	1693	£296
Officers' terrace	1693–96	£5,443 17s 11½d
Common Shore 800ft long behind the same		£485 4s 5½d
Great Storehouse	1694–96/7	£4,520
Ropewalk	1695–99	£4,080
Hemphouse	1695	£1,507
Tar cellar		£600
Yarn house		£406 18s 0d
Mast house	c.1695	£1,183 4s 0d
Offices for Clerks		£600
Porter's Lodge	1697	£128
Saw pits		£32
Smithery	1697–	
Officers' stables	1697–	
Gateway	1697–	
Boat houses	1699–	
Chapel	1700	

Sources: Stephens, 'Plymouth Dock', 34–97; BL Lansdowne MS 847, fol 62. The latter is Dummer's December 1694 report on progress which includes his estimates for the project. Items above with no estimated costs do not appear in this report. If an item of £1,873 4s 8d for 'Pumping and keeping docks free of rain' is included from the 1694 report, Dummer's December 1694 estimate for the creation of the dockyard in its earliest form comes to the suspiciously rounded figure of £50,000.

building tar cellars underneath.[17] In July 1692 the Navy Board estimated the expense of the buildings for the new yard at £23,406, but the costs continued to rise (Table 28.1). By December 1694 Dummer put the total cost, including docks, at £50,000. However, with fresh difficulties encountered and new buildings ordered, a fresh valuation in 1698 reached £67,095 6s and the final cost is unknown.[18] The yard officers declared with some justice in April 1695 that 'there never was so difficult and so heavy a piece of work done in England'. The need for major and expensive levelling operations was to be a problem with every expansion of naval facilities at Plymouth Dock, and was not to be paralleled until construction of Bermuda Dockyard over a century later.[19]

With their own costs rising, and the Admiralty notoriously slow in paying its bills, the contractors inevitably suffered. By 1696 Waters was running into difficulties. In 1698 and 1699 his work was reported as almost at a standstill, and by 1700 the Admiralty was completing some of his contracts at its own expense.[20] Whether through attempts at cost-cutting or plain bad workmanship, some of the contractors' work was soon found to be unsatisfactory. Brick-making on the site was of poor quality, so that in 1697 a considerable part of the ropewalk wall and the top 3ft of the yard boundary wall had to be pulled down and rebuilt.[21] The wall of the wet dock developed bulges, and after an attempt to shut its outer gates failed in 1697 they had to be rehung and were not successfully closed until 1700.[22] Dummer himself was suspended from duty in December 1698 on a charge of accepting bribes from local contractors.[23]

Finally, the yard suffered from a number of sins of omission. Some of these show Dummer's planning to be less perfect than he claimed. In 1696 the yard officers submitted a request for more buildings: a shed for repairing boats; a bricklayer's workshop; a painters' shop; a storehouse for treenails and wedges; a pitch house; and a tar house for the sailmaker.[24] Further, expansion to the status of a full dockyard created serious problems of workers' accommodation. The Admiralty balked at the costs of making provision itself, and not until 1700 were the first houses built outside the north corner of the yard, the beginnings of what was to become the town of

Plymouth Dock.[25] Lastly, the other principal government departments associated with the Navy were slow to adapt their operations to the emergence of a new major dockyard. Large-scale consolidated yards, adjacent to the dockyard, were not finally determined upon by the Ordnance until 1719 or by the Victualling Board until 1823 (see below).

The Second Phase of Development

The twenty-six years of peace following the Treaty of Utrecht in 1713 were not propitious times for naval expansion schemes. Nevertheless, successive governments used the navy to aid commerce by patrolling the main trade routes in the Atlantic and Mediterranean.[26] Plymouth, as the most westerly home base, was best placed for the essential shore support, a factor which undoubtedly influenced the decision to embark on a developing repair and expansion programme for the yard starting five years into the peace. In 1718–19 the original dock was repaired, and between 1719 and 1723 a new dock was built at the head of the graving slip to the north of the old dock. At the same time a new storehouse and plank-shed were added. In 1727 the yard's area was expanded from 35 to 54 acres by renting more land to the south of the yard from Sir William Morice. This new land was developed as a timber ground and mast pond with new large mast and boat houses. Access was via a long camber off from which ran a mud-dock for unloading and two new building/graving slips.[27]

The War of the Austrian Succession (1739–48), and especially the Seven Years War (1756–63), threw enormous burdens on the Navy which it sought to shoulder by increasing the size of the fleet. In turn this strained shore facilities, particularly at the south-coast yards. Moreover, in 1746, in a move which did more than anything else up to this date to firmly establish the importance of this Devon base, Admirals Anson and Warren secured agreement that in future Plymouth, and not Portsmouth, should be the refitting dockyard for the Western Squadron.

Increased pressure on facilities in the 1740s led to further additions to the Yard (Fig. 28.4). A £4,858 enlargement was carried out to the South Jetty. The north dock was rebuilt (1740–43) and, following the end of the Austrian Succession War, as a quick means of enlarging capacity, the graving slip at the stern of the north dock was converted into a dock too. Open in 1752, the whole constituted an elongated double dock, the Head Dock 200 x 52 x 26ft deep, the Stern Dock 190 x 52 x 25ft deep. The smithy proved unable to keep pace with the increase in iron fittings on warships, and in particular was handicapped by having only one large forge for anchor work. This led in 1748 to an order to extend the smith's shop with four forges. Similarly, the ropeyard had been unable to supply sufficient cordage, so a new shed for warping yarn was ordered, as well as an oven for heating bolt ropes for tarring: until then they had been heated outside the Yard in the Bakehouse, and were cool and stiff before going into the tar kettle.[28] In 1749 the Plymouth Dockyard officers sought to excuse the poor state of the dockyard buildings, saying: '. . . the continual hurry they had been in at that port during the fitting and refitting of ships prevented them carrying out the necessary repairs of the yard'. Worse, increase in warship sizes was making obsolete the dry docks, where: ' . . . it was becoming difficult to dock a ship of the third rate or upwards in any other than the outer dock'. This led to the building of a new dock to the north of the double dock, 239ft 4in x 86ft 7in wide x 26ft 10in deep, begun in 1758 and known as 'Union Dock' after the 90-gun ship which first used it in March 1763.[29]

The Great Replanning and Expansion of 1761

In November 1761 the Navy Board wrote a long report to the Admiralty in which it set out the problems of Plymouth Dockyard and proposed solutions. After referring to

> . . . its great utility for the equipment and refitting of the Royal Navy in time of war, as well as for the convenience of the harbour for laying up a number of the largest of his Majesty's ships in time of peace . . .

the Board lamented the condition, inadequacy, and siting of the various buildings,

> . . . the greatest part of them are improperly placed, some of the principal ones still remaining upon the surface of the original rock, others standing upon the part that has been levelled more than thirty feet below them . . . the whole is very crowded and very inconvenient.[30]

As the Navy Board noted, the growth of the new town of Plymouth Dock had hemmed in the dockyard to the north and east, while the harbour prevented a westward expansion. This left only the south for the ten acres proposed for expansion which could be partly reclaimed along the foreshore. Such a development would leave the existing ropery inconveniently straddling the middle of the enlarged dockyard, so a replacement was proposed, lying along the new eastern boundary.[31]

Aware of the huge cost, the Navy Board noted that:

> . . . we thought it much the most advisable to lay down one general plan to answer every purpose, to be prosecuted as opportunity shall offer, constant experience showing us the advantage that would have attended designs of the same kind had they been laid down for the rest of His Majesty's yards.[32]

The cost of this expansion scheme was enormous – £379,170 1s 2d – particularly when added to the £352,240 4s 3d estimated for a similar exercise at Portsmouth. In contrast, just over half a century before, the Navy Board had estimated £23,406 for the creation of the original Plymouth Dockyard.[33] On Thursday 11 November 1761 the Admiralty Board met to consider the Navy Board's proposal. Those present were Lord Anson, Dr Hay, Admiral Forbes, Lord Villiers and Mr Pelham. The details of the discussion are not recorded, but the meeting ended with the Admiralty endorsing the proposals and ordering the start of the work.[34] It is perhaps doubtful whether any other group of men at that time could have commissioned projects of such magnitude and been reasonably certain that future funds, over and above normal naval requirements, would be available to prosecute the work. But by the middle of the eighteenth century the Royal Navy had become ' . . . by a large margin the largest industrial organization in the western world'.[35] Great Britain's growing industrial base and increasingly sophisticated methods of government funding meant that the Georgian Navy escaped the financial crises that were such a feature of its Stuart and Tudor predecessors and of its French rival.

Both the Admiralty and Navy Board deserve due recognition for these far-sighted plans and decisions. The works inaugurated in the 1760s at the Devon and Hampshire dockyards were only to be rivalled in scale a century later as the Royal Navy changed from sail to steam and from timber to metal. With minor variations, the 1761 master plan for Plymouth Dockyard was finally to be completed around 1817, but the great bulk of the work had been finished by 1795.[36] By the time of the French Revolutionary War, both Plymouth and Portsmouth were probably the best equipped dockyards in Europe.

The scheme approved in 1761 increased the number of dry docks to five as well as including four building slips on the new ground. Of the new dry docks the northernmost merits special mention. Variously described as the 'New Union', or 'North New Dock', or 'Great Parlby Dock' (after its builder), it was 250ft long, 85ft 3in wide, and had 27ft 6in clearance over the sill of the gates. The *Naval Chronicle* hailed it as 'the largest dock in the Universe'. Originally designed in the 1780s to accommodate the largest British first-rates, the 100-gun *Queen Charlotte* and *Royal George*, it was lengthened by ten feet and deepened one foot during construction – according to Dockyard tradition so as to be able to take the mammoth French 120-gun, 2,747-ton *Commerce de Marseilles*, then building at Toulon and which 'coincidently' was the first ship to enter the dock following its capture in 1793.[37] To back up these new shipbuilding and repair facilities there was to be substantial provision of plank and boat houses, a large mast pond, a new smithy and a vast new ropemaking complex. Dummer's great storehouse was no longer adequate either for dockyard requirements or for holding reserves of equipment for the fleet. In its place, and occupying the western part of the original rope yard, the Navy Board planned a double quadrangle of eight large storehouses; in the event, only seven were built.

Following normal custom, the overall plan for Plymouth Dockyard was carefully worked out in London by the Navy Board's two Surveyors,

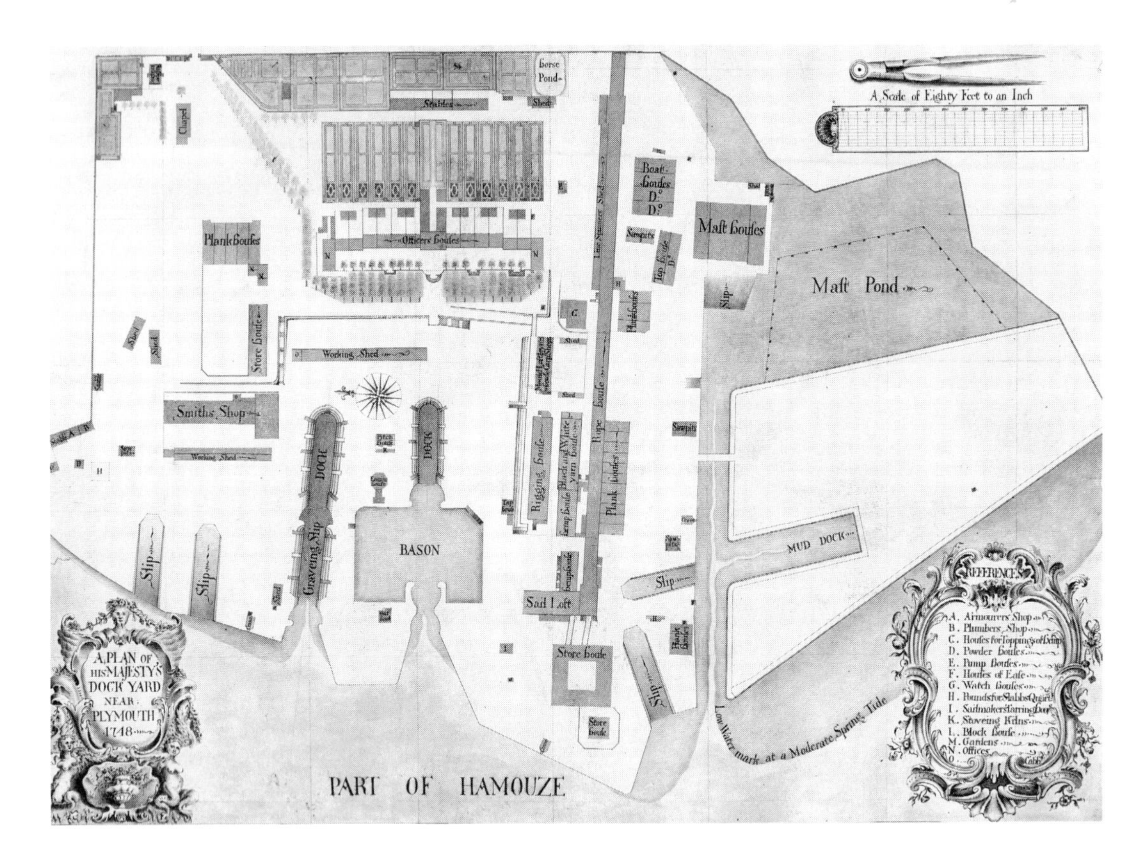

28.4 Plymouth Dockyard in 1748, a plan showing the results of the first period of expansion. *(National Maritime Museum)*

Table 28.2

Reconstruction and Expansion of Plymouth Dockyard, 1758–1817. The Principal Buildings and Engineering Works.

Ref to fig. 28.4		Construction Dates	Estimated Costs	Sources (see below)
54d	New Dock	1758–63		a
55e & d	Slips	1762–64		a
43a & b	East & West Store houses	1763–67		a
42	Fitted Rigging & Sail loft	1788–?	£7,355	a,b
14	*White Yarn House*	1766–73	£500 15s	a,b
15	*Tarring & Wheel House*	1766–73	£407 7s	a,b
16,17	*Black Yarn Houses*	1766–73	£1,841 7s 8d	a,b
18	Spinning House	1766–73	£12,158 12s 4d	a,b
19	Laying House	1766–83	£17,024 6s 4d	a,b
25	Mast Houses & Slips	1768–70	£6,111 9s 6d	a,b
?46	Clerk's Office & Store	1769–74		a
55c	South Slip	1770–73	£15,744	a,b
11	*Master Ropemaker's House*	1772–73		
53	*Wharf Walls in South Channel*	1771–77	£44,353	a,b
54b&c	Alterations to Double Dock	1772–73		a
21,23, 57,62	Mast & Boat Pond, locks & Plank House over, Boathouse & Mould Loft	1773–82		a,b,d
?43e	North West Store-house	1774–76		a
55a	*South Slip by Boundary*	1774–75		a
31	*Smith's Shop*, coal yard	1776–78		a
10	Advance Guard House	1777–78		a
29	Counter Guard House	?1778		e
20	Top & Capstan House	–1780		a
22,28-part	Boat Builders' Cabin & Pitch House	1780–81		a
54e	New Dock	1783 'in hand'		a,b
6	*Pay Office*	1784–85		a
36	Joiners' Shop	–1791		f
38	Offices	c.1796		g
32	Bricklayer's Yard	–1792		c
30	*Armourers' & Plumbers' Shop*	–1792	£500	c
41	Rigging House	1788–92		h
43c	East Cross Store-house	1790–92	£6,266	i
5	Reservoir	1805–10		j
58	Boat Basin	1802–?09		k
9	Painters' Shop	1810–13	£2,558	c
43a	East Cross Intermediate Store-house	?1810–17		l
44	Offices	?post 1808		m
13	*Ropery Offices*	1814–15	£1,695	c
4	Chapel	1814–17		n
43e	West Cross Store-house	1815	£25,628	c
55b	Slip	1816–17		c

Sources: a: ADM/BP/6b 14 June 1786; b: NMM ADM/Y/PD/3; c: Annual Estimates in *Parliamentary Papers*; d: ADM/174/18–19; e: ADM/B/195, 21 October 1777; f: ADM/L40/158 shows it completed by 1701; g: ADM/140/230; h: NMM 66/086, 18 March 1788; i: ADM/141/270, ADM/Y/PD3; j: ADM/B/216, 21 September 1804; k: ADM/B/224, 1 December 1806; 1: NMM ADM/7/PD3; m: ADM/B/230.
Buildings in italics still survive.

William Bately and Thomas Slade. These plans were then sent to the Plymouth Dockyard officers for them to design the individual buildings and engineering works. Thus, in November 1761, the yard officers were instructed that two of the new building slips were

> . . . to be immediately taken in hand . . . As it may be for the Advantage of His Majesty's service to carry on the work of the said slips by contract, you are to send up a plan, profile and section thereof . . . for our consideration.[38]

For major buildings, the Surveyors were much more specific, their instructions revealing their due concern for convenience, economy and aesthetics:

> . . . you will observe, figure 3 marks the south front of a square of four buildings intended for the principal magazines for stores, which, as a guard against fire are not to join at the angles; whose fronts are to be uniform, to be three storey in height, with arched cellars under them, built with stone and rubble work, plain, strong and convenient, of which you are to send us a design, with plans etc. of the floors . . . their fronts must conform to each other.[39]

Construction work was almost exclusively the responsibility of civilian contractors, most notably Templar and Parlby, sometimes working as a unified firm, at other times apparently operating independently.[40] Occasionally, when their normal maintenance duties permitted, dockyard craftsmen would undertake certain small specific works.[41] Most of the limestone for construction came from the levelling of part of the site, its use helping to defray the expense of the project.[42] Similarly, the Navy Board appears to have followed normal practice in supplying contractors with all timber required, its position as the country's largest purchaser of timber making this a more economical arrangement.[43]

By the 1790s the new smithery was proving inadequate, and in 1797 it was extended. Following the success of Bentham's work at Portsmouth, money for an adjacent foundry was allocated in 1811.[44] Across the Hamoaze the Navy Board authorized construction in the 1780s of a ballast pound. This survives on the foreshore at Torpoint, a memorial to the great quantities of shingle ballast needed by ships discharging cargo at the dockyard opposite.[45]

The scale of the dockyard expansion is best seen in Pocock's great painting of the dockyard as it appeared c.1800 (Fig. 31.4, below). Fig. 28.5 shows the dockyard immediately after the Napoleonic wars, while Table 28.2 gives the key dates for the construction of the principal buildings and engineering works. Sadly, very few of these survived the air raids of 1941 and 1942, but in its heyday Plymouth rivalled Portsmouth as the greatest of the Georgian dockyards.

Inevitably there were critics of the work at this Devon yard. As early as 1774 the Earl of Sandwich, visiting the base with his fellow Admiralty Board members, felt that 'the greatest scheme of improvements . . . is founded upon too extensive a plan . . .'. Money spent on the ropery, he felt, would have been better spent at Chatham '. . . instead of employing it [here] in useless magnificence'.[46] Nearly twenty years later the Inspector General of Naval Works, Brigadier General Sir Samuel Bentham, recorded rather similar opinions, although he noted: 'I have heard of its [Plymouth Dockyard] being considered by persons whose opinions cannot but be respectable, that this is the most perfect dockyard in the kingdom'.[47] Defence expenditure then, no less than now, was always a subject for lively public debate. However, what can be said with some certainty is that Great Britain would have been very much less well equipped to fight the great naval wars with France at the end of the eighteenth century had it not been for the farsighted actions of the Navy Board and Admiralty in the 1760s. Throughout the French wars Plymouth's naval facilities were kept fully utilized; the dockyard itself proved adequate to the task and it was the other naval establishments associated with it which were shown to be in need of modernization.

The Growth of the Ancillary Facilities of the Naval Base

Although the dockyard was always the focus of naval activity, other facilities, the responsibility of separate boards, were needed to equip the ships and to care for the sick and wounded sailors. Early on, the Board of Ordnance established its own yard to provide munitions for both the Navy and the land defences of Plymouth and, later, for Plymouth Dock. It was joined by the Victualling Board, responsible for provisioning the fleet, and later in the eighteenth century by the Sick and Hurt Board, responsible for the naval hospital at Stonehouse.

Victualling

Ships of the Royal Navy had used Plymouth as a victualling base long before the establishment of a dockyard here (see above, chapters 12, 13, 24 and 25). Supplies were obtained from victualling agents almost certainly operating from premises in the commercial port, but such arrangements were unequal to the naval build-up following establishment of the dockyard. In 1702 the Victualling Board established an Agent, John Stucley, at Plymouth, with power to make local purchases. He operated from an office and victualling yard at Lambhay, between the Citadel and Sutton Pool. It was a cramped site, and boats could load only above half-tide. In 1705 detailed plans were drawn up for a slaughterhouse, pickling and packing houses, a bakehouse and a cooperage at Empacombe on the Cornish side of the Hamoaze. This produced an outcry at Plymouth Quarter Sessions, which urged that most of the oxen came from the Devon side, and Plymouth paid £100 14s 3d to Mr Justice Opie 'for travelling about and money spent at the Assizes of Devon, Somerset, Dorset and Bristol and in London to continue the Victualling Office on its present site'. The Empacombe site was a large one, dry, with ample water frontage for development and close to the Dockyard, but whether because of Plymouth's political pressure, or the extra expense of bringing cattle across the Tamar, or the added delay in receiving orders by post from London, the plan was dropped in 1707, and again in 1722 when a similar scheme was mooted to establish a complete office there.[48]

Victualling Board operations consequently continued to be improvised until 1733, when it was decided that the brewhouse it rented in Plymouth was too small and ordered construction of a brewhouse of its own at Southdown, across the Hamoaze near the entrance to Millbrook Creek. The renewal of war in 1739 highlighted all the shortcomings at Plymouth, whose

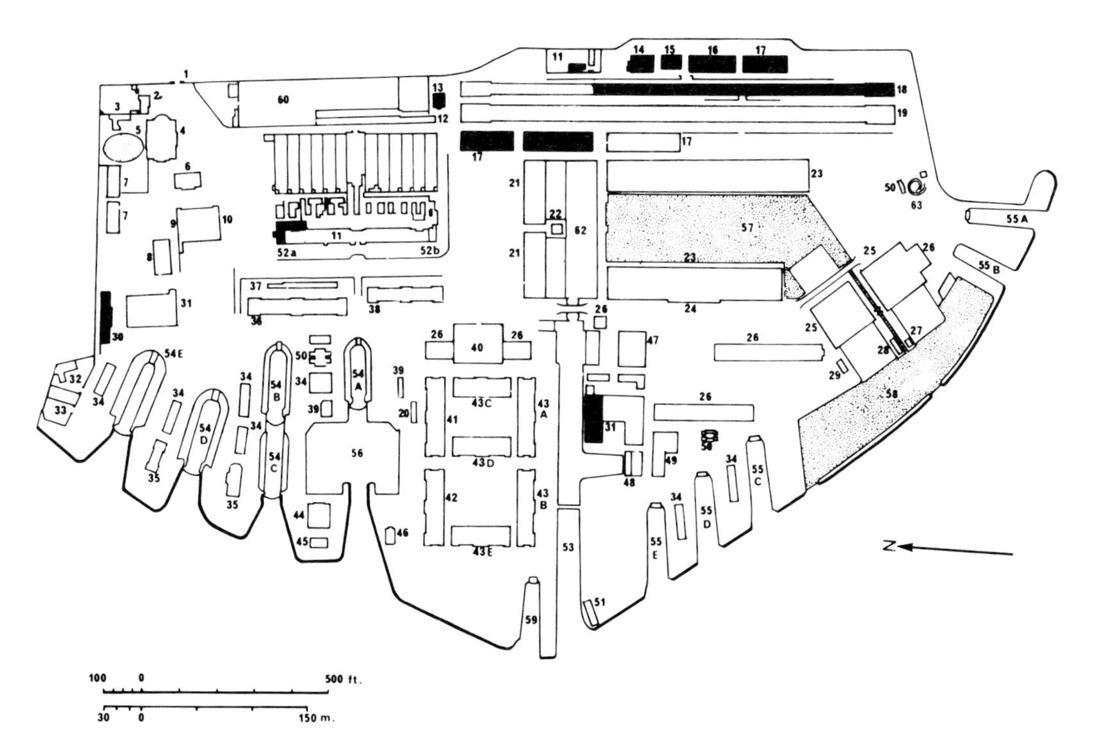

PLYMOUTH DOCKYARD c1820
Key: (Buildings in solid black still survive)

1 Main Gate
2 Master Warden's House
3 Stables
4 Chapel
5 Reservoir
6 Pay Office
7 Team Stables
8 Painters' Shed
9 Painters' Shop etc
10 Guard House
11 Officers' Terrace
12 Officers' Stables
13 Master Ropemaker's Offices
14 White Yarn House
15 Tarring House
16 Black Yarn House
17 Hemp House
18 Spinning House
19 Laying House
20 Topping House
21 Boat House
22 Office
23 Plank Store with Mast Locks underneath
24 Plank Store with Mould Loft over
25 Mast House
26 Sawpits
27 Cabin
28 Hemp House and Pitch House
29 Guard House
30 Plumbers' Shop
31 Smiths' Shop
32 Bricklayers' Yard
33 House Carpenters' Shop
34 Shipwrights' Sheds
35 Dock Pumps
36 Joiners' Shop
37 Sheds
38 Offices
39 Cabin
40 Timber Yard
41 Rigging House
42 Sail Loft
43A–E Quadrangle Storehouses
44 Offices
45 Cabins
46 Cabins
47 Carpenters' Shop
48 Stores
49 Stores
50 Steaming Kiln
51 Offices
52 Offices (1692)
53 Camber Channel
54A–E Dry Docks
55A–E Building Slips
56 Wet Dock
57 Inner Mast Pond
58 Outer Mast Pond
59 Graving Slip
60 Commissioner's Garden
61 Gazebo
62 Boat Pond

28.5 Plymouth Dockyard *c*1820, a sketch plan by the author, reproduced by courtesy of the *Mariner's Mirror*.

production quickly proved too small, where access to the Lambhay depot was too limited, and where the distance from the Dockyard and the difficulty of ships' boats working in the Sound in bad weather caused further delays. In 1743 the Admiralty instructed the Victualling Board to assess the facilities, but the attempt to find a 'commodious place at or near the Hamoaze' was forestalled by the dramatic upsurge of demand to victual the rapidly expanding western squadron. The Board had to build rapidly on its existing sites to meet immediate needs, and this outlay discouraged further search for a new consolidated site. In 1749, when the Admiralty Board visited Plymouth on a tour of inspection, they noted with satisfaction:

> the Victualling office at Lambhay where a cooperage, several new storehouses and two bakehouses had been erected . . . Then proceeded to view the brewhouses and other victualling storehouses erected at South Downe in Hamoaze. Found two complete brewhouses, a cooperage and several storehouses which were very conveniently situated for the purpose and in exceedingly good order. Observed also a watering place well adapted to the service of the Fleet.[49]

The provision of a brewery and bakehouse meant that Plymouth ranked alongside Weevil Yard at Gosport and the main victualling premises at Deptford as a manufacturing centre as distinct from a storage depot. Not all the premises at the Devon base were owned by the Victualling Board: during and after the Napoleonic wars, for example, the flour mills were leased from Plymouth corporation.[50]

Arrangements which had been considered good in 1749 had come to be less than adequate by 1815. The Victualling Board had not matched the Navy Board's expansion and modernization programme at Plymouth during the latter part of the eighteenth century, while during the Napoleonic wars demands on it had probably increased proportionately to a greater extent than on the dockyard. As well as supplying warships based at Plymouth, the victualling esablishment here was probably the main supply base for victualling depots at Gibraltar and Ascension Island. After the end of the war, the Victualling Board resolved to create a wholly new and unified Victualling Yard. In 1823 a site was selected on Stonehouse peninsula for constructon of what was to become the Royal William Victualling Yard.[51] Nothing survives of the earlier premises.

Ordnance: the Development of the Morice Yard

Apart from providing weapons for the Citadel, the Board of Ordnance had little connection with Plymouth before the creation of the dockyard in the 1690s. For the Board, a priority was a yard near to the dockyard with its own berths for loading and unloading the heavy guns and their carriages from the warships. At first a small gunwharf and a storehouse were established below

28.6 Morice Yard, Plymouth Dockyard, one of the original Storehouses, used for gun carriages, gunners' equipment and in times of emergency for gunpowder. *(English Heritage)*

Mount Wise, but by 1717 this was becoming inadequate. Attempts to expand here were thwarted by a combination of the landowner's opposition and by a desire on the part of the Navy Board to establish larger facilities adjacent to the northern boundary of the dockyard.[52]

In 1719 a site here was leased from the local landowner, Sir Nicholas Morice, from whom the yard takes its name, and construction work began in earnest in 1720. As with the dockyard, the rocky nature of the site meant extensive levelling. On the foreshore a wharf and two semi-circular quays were formed. Beside the latter, at right angles to the wharf frontage, were built two storehouses (Fig. 28.6). On the wharf edge were placed two treadwheel cranes, and a little behind them was built a small powder magazine. Open space beyond was used for storing gun barrels, while nearby was a limekiln and a forge for the armourer. On top of the promontory, overlooking the centre of the yard with views across the Hamoaze to what was then a part of Devon, was built a terrace (Fig. 28.7) for the five senior yard officers. Building activity reached a peak in 1722 and then declined rapidly; the yard was partly operational by 1724.[53]

The principal function of the ordnance yard was the storage and maintenance of weapons for both the navy and the Plymouth garrison. The two storehouses took the gun carriages and the gunners' equipment – the rammers, mops, sponges, buckets and tackle – together with the small arms, musket shot and grape. Gun barrels were stored outside in rows, while cannon balls tended to be kept in the open in pyramidal heaps. For safety reasons the gunpowder was kept separately in its own magazine. The small staff of armourers and carpenters were to maintain the equipment; manufacturing as such was not undertaken here. A warship heading for the dockyard or to be put in ordinary would offload munitions at Morice Yard for safekeeping and would similarly call at the yard to re-equip before commissioning.

The location and layout of the yard, and the design of the original buildings – which mostly survive – was the responsibility of Colonel Christian Lilly, senior officer for the Plymouth district, assisted by Mr Schutze, his draughtsman. All the designs were approved by the Chief Engineer in London, Colonel Armstrong. The Vanbrugian qualities of the terrace and storehouses might suggest that Sir John Vanbrugh, Comptroller of the King's Works, was responsible. However, the records make no mention of his involvement, although it is reasonable to suggest that he may have been consulted by Colonel Armstrong.

In the autumn of 1720 William Cowley, a London stonemason, was awarded the contract for the bulk of the construction work. He was to be joined by Abraham Curtis, possibly also from London, who undertook all carpentry and joinery. The works were under the supervision of Andrew Jelfe, Clerk of the Survey at Plymouth, who seems to have taken his orders direct from the Board of Ordnance in London.

The unusually complete building accounts enable us to trace the early progress of the yard with some precision.[54] One of the most interesting entries is a payment to Abraham Curtis in November 1724 of £6 17s 9d for laying '551 feet running of fir quarter 3½ by 2½ inches planed and spiked to the floors for truck ways'.[55] Wagon ways had been in use for centuries in the quarrying and coal trades, but this is one of the earliest references to truck ways within buildings to help in stores' handling. Was Lilly a pioneer, or was he copying a system used in other Board of Ordnance establishments?[56]

Although the storehouses at the new yard were adequate, the small powder magazine soon proved to be far too small. By the 1730s ships' powder was being stored in Plymouth Citadel, involving dangerous manhandling through the narrow streets of the old town. After the outbreak of war in 1739, extra powder had to be kept in the storehouses themselves, adding to the risks of explosion. The local Board of Ordnance engineer, Horneck, pleaded successfully with his Board for a new and larger magazine sited away from the centre of the yard. This was brought into use in the mid-1740s and remains much as completed (Fig. 28.8). It follows the standard design of such structures, with double-skin walls and a barrel vault, and is notable for the somewhat quirky brick pilasters and a pediment on its main elevation. Within this is a cartouche with the arms of the Duke of Montagu, Master General of the Ordnance from 1739 to 1749.[57]

In 1771, conscious of the rapidly expanding dockyard at Plymouth, the

28.7 Morice Yard, Plymouth Dockyard, the Officers' Terrace, completed in 1724. *(English Heritage)*

Board of Ordnance wrote to their engineer, Lieutenant Colonel Patoun, asking him how much land might 'be necessary to be purchased for enlarging the gunwharf and storehouses in proportion to the augmentation made to the dockyards'.[58] As a result, work began in 1775 on a new powder depot further up the Tamar at Keyham. This was well sited to receive production from the Royal Powder Mills at St Budeaux, while its distance from the main ordnance yard was an added safety factor. This separation of the gunpowder magazines from the other ordnance buildings can be paralleled by developments at this time at Portsmouth.[59]

Within Morice Yard itself, a number of small buildings were added in the 1770s. These provided extra space for the smiths and a furbisher, responsible for the maintenance of side arms. Adjacent to the furbisher's shop a large carriage store was constructed. During the Revolutionary and Napoleonic wars a considerable number of temporary buildings were erected, including an artillery hospital complete with nurses' quarters. Ordnance activity here probably reached a peak in 1813 when, along with a depot at Falmouth, Morice Yard was designated the main supply depot for Wellington's victorious army in Spain.[60] Fortuitously, Morice Yard largely escaped damage in the 1941 and 1942 air raids which so devastated Devonport, and it remains today the best preserved and most complete of all the Georgian ordnance depots.

The Naval Hospital

As Plymouth grew in importance as a fleet base, provision had to be made for the sick and wounded. At first, following normal practice, the Navy relied on the contract system and other makeshift arrangements. In 1702 the

28.8 Morice Yard, Plymouth Dockyard, the Powder Magazine, built *c*1744. *(English Heritage)*

28.9 The Royal Naval Hospital, Stonehouse, a fairly recent (*c*1939) aerial view. Note Stonehouse Creek at bottom left, now a school sports field. *(Medical Officer in Charge)*

Admiralty ordered an enquiry into the whole subject, and although this reported strongly in favour of building hospitals exclusively for the Navy, its recommendations were ignored for many years. Purpose-built naval hospitals were first constructed at Minorca and Gibraltar.

The outbreak of war in 1739 was instrumental in forcing officials in England to follow suit: between August 1739 and September 1740, 15,868 sick and wounded were landed, mostly at Portsmouth and Plymouth, and existing arrangements were unable to cope. In 1741 the Admiralty proposed three naval hospitals at Queenborough in Kent, Portsmouth, and Plymouth.[61] After a further four-year delay, work began on Haslar Hospital at Gosport. Only after this was completed were funds found for a hospital at Plymouth.

Land for the naval hospital was purchased at Stonehouse in 1758, the site abutting the creek so that sick and wounded could be ferried by boat direct from warships to the hospital. The architect was Alexander Rovehead. Although little known in this country, his work was admired in Paris and he deserves due recognition, for medically his design for Stonehouse was considerably in advance of that of Haslar. The Hampshire hospital consisted of a great central building with four wing pavilions. At Stonehouse the hospital wards, ultimately holding 1,500 patients, were grouped in ten separate three-storey blocks arranged formally around a rectangular courtyard. This latter arrangement greatly facilitated the ventilation which late-eighteenth-century medical experts thought to be the key to better hospital hygiene. The blocks were linked at ground level by a colonnaded passage. At Haslar the wards extended the full widths of the ranges and had to do double duty as corridors. At Stonehouse, the two wards on each floor were divided by a spine wall, and access was by way of a staircase at one end of each building. As a consequence of all this it was far easier to isolate patients here and limit the spread of infectious diseases to which eighteenth-century hospitals were so frequently vulnerable.

Forming an axis with the main entrance was the administrative building and chapel, distinguished by a clock tower and bell cupola set above a pediment. The first patients started using the hospital in 1760, and it was largely completed by 1761. In the 1780s it was visited by the French physician M Tenon, who had been commissioned by Louis XVI to study the major hospitals of Europe with a view to reforming those of Paris. He declared Stonehouse to be 'this beautiful hospital, the most perfect that I know for its intended purpose'.[62]

In 1763 a large pedimented terrace was built outside the main entrance for the senior medical staff. Extra accommodation was added here in 1804, when Edward Holl designed two further houses flanking these and forming a small square; one of these houses provided accommodation for the hospital governor.[63]

Although Stonehouse Hospital suffered some war damage, it remains substantially intact (Fig. 28.9). The creek, however, is now filled in, and patients arrive by road or helicopter rather than by boat.

The first century and a quarter of Plymouth Dock's existence had been remarkable. In 1690 Plymouth was little more than a victualling station and convenient port of call for cruising squadrons. Less than a century later its dockyard facilities, victualling and ordnance establishments, and its new naval hospital, had grown to rival those of Portsmouth. It owed its growth almost entirely to changed strategic patterns and the navy's need for a base close to the Western Approaches and the Atlantic. The long series of wars with France, which ended in 1815, served to consolidate its position as one of the two most important naval bases in Britain.

28: Development and Organisation of Plymouth Dockyard, 1689–1815

1 J Ehrman, *The Navy in the War of William III, 1689–1697* (Cambridge, 1953), 419. In the completion of the first two sections I am grateful for information supplied by Dr Michael Duffy and the late Mr J Marsh.
2 AE Stephens, 'Plymouth Dock: A Survey of the Development of the Royal Dockyard during the Sailing Ship Era' (unpublished PhD thesis, University of London, 1940), 41.
3 J Merino, 'Graving Docks in France and Spain before 1800', *MM*, 71 (1985), 36–9.
4 Merino, 'Graving Docks', 36–9; BL, Lansdowne MSS, 847, 'An Account of the Generall Progress and Advancement of His Majesties New Dock and Yard at Plymouth . . . December 1694'; Ehrman, *Navy in the War of William III*, 417, 422–3.
5 For Greenhill's report of 23 Nov. 1690, and Dummer's reply of 8 Dec. 1690, see Stephens, 'Plymouth Dock', 46–52.
6 BL, Lansdowne MSS, 847; Ehrman, *Navy in the War of William III*, 422. The first wet dock was probably built at Blackwall in 1660; see G Jackson, *The History and Archaeology of Ports* (Kingswood, 1983), 44.
7 BL, Lansdowne MSS, 847, f.5; KV Burns, *The Devonport Dockyard Story* (Liskeard, 1984), 7–8.
8 BL, King's MSS, 40, 'A Voyage into the Mediterranean Seas'.
9 BL, King's MSS, 43, f.145v, 'Survey and Description of the Principal Harbours . . .'.
10 NMM, ADM 4/1775, 5 March 1691; ADM A/1785, 11, 29 July 1692; Stephens, 'Plymouth Dock', 67n.
11 HM Colvin, *A Biographical Dictionary of English Architects* (1954), 297; NMM, ADM A/1785, 11 July 1692; LAD/7, 9 May 1694; Unsorted MSS, 1695–1832, 8 Feb. 1695; JG Coad, 'Historic Architecture of HM Naval Base, Devonport', *MM*, 69 (1983), 348–51. Mr HG Slade has drawn my attention to its similarities with the facade of the *Hotel des Invalides*, Paris, begun in 1690.
12 BL, Lansdowne MSS, 847, f.20v.
13 BL, Lansdowne MSS, 847, f.23v; Ehrman, *Navy in the War of William III*, 423.
14 Ehrman, *Navy in the War of William III*, 425; Burns, *Devonport Dockyard Story*, 11–12. The rope-making process can be followed through the illustrations in the *Encyclopedie* (1752); see CC Gillespie, ed., *A Diderot Pictorial Encyclopedia of Trades and Industry* (New York, 1959), II, plates 475–8. See also JG Coad, 'Chatham Ropeyard', in *Post-Medieval Archaeology*, III (1969), 143–65.
15 Stephens, 'Plymouth Dock', 52–4, 86–7; NMM, ADM 174/1, 22 June 1698.
16 BL, Lansdowne MSS, 847, ff.5v–6v, 17v–18v; NMM, ADM A/1765, 25 Jan. 1690.
17 BL, Lansdowne MSS, 847.
18 BL, Lansdowne MSS, 847, f.34v; King's MSS, 43; NMM, ADM A/1788, 29 July 1692.
19 Stephens, 'Plymouth Dock', 74; JG Coad, *The Royal Dockyards, 1690–1850: Architecture and Engineering Works of the Sailing Navy* (Aldershot, 1990), chapter 19.
20 Stephens, 'Plymouth Dock', 68, 80–1, 87–8, 90, 94.
21 Stephens, 'Plymouth Dock', 71, 80, 83.
22 Stephens, 'Plymouth Dock', 84, 90–3.
23 B Pool, *Navy Board Contracts, 1660–1832* (1966), 49.
24 Stephens, 'Plymouth Dock', 78.
25 Burns, *Devonport Dockyard Story*, 13–4. Building speculation began about 1696 according to Stephens, 'Plymouth Dock', 81, 84–6.
26 DA Baugh, ed., *Navy Administration, 1715–1769* (NRS, 1977), xiii.
27 PRO, ADM 174/7, 19 Sept. 1718, 14, 27 Aug. 1719, 25 May 1721; ADM 174/8, 7 July 1721, 29 Jan. 1722; ADM 174/103, 5 Oct. 1722, 12 July 1723; Burns, *Devonport Dockyard Story*, 16.
28 DA Baugh, *British Naval Administration in the Age of Walpole* (Princeton, 1965), 275; PRO, ADM 7/658; ADM 114/41; ADM 174/14, 22 Jan. 1748; ADM 174/288, 3, 15, 19 Sept. 1741; ADM 174/289 (note inside cover); ADM 174/290, 29 Sept. 1752; Burns, *Devonport Dockyard Story*, 16–7.
29 PRO, ADM 7/658.
30 NMM, ADM B/176, 2 Nov. 1761.
31 NMM, ADM B/176, 2 Nov. 1761.
32 NMM, ADM B/176, 2 Nov. 1761.
33 BL, Lansdowne MSS, 847.
34 PRO, ADM 3/69, 11 Nov. 1761.
35 NAM Rodger, *The Wooden World: An Anatomy of the Georgian Navy* (1986), 29.
36 Coad, 'Historic Architecture, Devonport', 360–1.
37 *Naval Chronicle*, IX (1803), 73; Burns, *Devonport Dockyard Story*, 21.
38 PRO, ADM 174/16, 30 Nov. 1761.
39 PRO, ADM 174/16, 30 Nov. 1761. Early designs can be seen in PRO, ADM 140/269.
40 See Coad, *Royal Dockyards*, chapter 2.
41 In 1792, for example, dockyard workers were ordered to complete the northeast middle storehouse: PRO, ADM 174/23, 8 May 1792.
42 NMM, ADM B/167, 2 Nov. 1761.
43 In 1762 the dockyard officers supplied Templar with all materials for making the new jetty head – stone as well as timber in this instance: PRO, ADM 174/113, 27 April 1762.
44 NMM, ADM B/228, 28 Oct. 1807; PRO, ADM 1/3527, 2 July 1808; PRO, ADM 140/241–2.
45 NMM, ADM BP/3, 30 Nov. 1782. Papers relating to this are in the Antony Estate archives, Cornwall CRO, Truro. I am indebted to Dr J Frears for showing me the results of her research.
46 PRO, ADM 7661, 25 June 1774.
47 PRO, ADM 1/3225, 28 May 1793. Complaints about the quality of the work resulted in Smeaton being requested to investigate and compile a report. For this, see NMM, ADM BP/6b, 30 Jan. 1787.
48 PRO, ADM 110/2, 4 Jan., 20 April 1704; WDRO, Receiver's Book, 1706/7; NMM, Unsorted MSS, 21 April 1707; Baugh, *British Naval Adminstration*, 439. I am grateful to Mr J Marsh for the first two of these references.
49 PRO, ADM 7/653, 10 Aug. 1749; Baugh, *British Naval Administration*, 437–9.
50 PRO, ADM 111/266, 10 Oct. 1831.
51 PRO, ADM 111/258, 20 Sept. 1823.
52 PRO, WO 48/30, 7 May 1717; WO 47/30, 15 Oct. 1717; WO 47/32, 7 April 1719.
53 PRO, WO 49/229 and WO 40/230 contain the building accounts.
54 For a more detailed account, see Coad, 'Historic Architecture, Devonport', 367–75.
55 PRO, WO 49/230, 20 Nov. 1724.
56 See MJT Lewis, *Early Wooden Railways* (1970).
57 PRO, ADM 1/4008, 3 May 1743.
58 PRO, WO 47/78, 13–14 Dec. 1771.
59 JG Coad, 'Historic Architecture of HM Naval Base, Portsmouth', *MM*, 67 (1981), 55–8.
60 Coad, *Royal Dockyards*; PRO, WO 6/174, 21 Aug., 30 Sept, 1813.
61 NMM, ADM E/8b, 4 April 1741.
62 Coad, 'Historic Architecture, Devonport', 377–81; J Tenon, *Memoires sur les hopitaux de Paris* (Paris, 1788), liii–liv.
63 NMM, ADM B/172, 16 Sept. 1763; PRO, ADM 140/320, 323, 325.

29 *The Local Community and the Operation of Plymouth Dockyard, 1689–1763*

A J MARSH

WHEN THE BUILDING OF A DRY-DOCK at Portsmouth was mooted in 1656, the inhabitants of that town were willing to contribute £500 to the cost. No gesture remotely like this came from the people of Plymouth when a new dockyard with a dry-dock was proposed in 1689. Despite (or perhaps because of) former naval presence, suspicion and even obstruction was the initial response. The established fishing and shipping interests feared impressment; competition for labour, stores, and moorings; and French attacks. Such feelings were exacerbated by the arrival in mid-1689 of the bluff 'Tarpaulin', Captain Richard Cotton, as Master Attendant with a hulk laden with cordage, spare anchors, and other stores for the refitting and cleaning of cruisers. He at once cleared the Cattewater from the buoy off Mount Batten to Turnchapel 'by hard shearing and cutting of cables'. Cotton lived on the hulk, but the Mayor gained his revenge by billeting troops on his family living in the town.[1]

29.1 George St Lo, a portrait engraved by J Nutting. *(National Maritime Museum)*

The Navy Board tried to limit the damage by replacing Cotton and by appointing as Naval Agent (subsequently Resident Commissioner) Henry Greenhill, who did much to win over Plymouth Corporation. Even his efforts, however, were impeded by the Navy's rather arbitrary practices. As already indicated in a previous chapter, the dry-dock and basin at Point Froward were built before the Admiralty had established title to the land; the Navy Board paid not in cash but by tickets which, particularly in the early 1690s, might still not be cashed six quarters in arrears. Even substantial and experienced contractors could be brought low, in turn bringing down their subcontractors. In 1698 Robert Waters, builder of the dry-dock, was 'in danger of arrest every day, and some of his creditors are already arrested for £15 or £20 when he owed them £100 which is very hard'. Equally hard pressed were the Yard workmen, mostly strangers brought in from other yards and unable to secure credit from local tradesmen and landlords.[2]

Nevertheless, work on the dockyard advanced slowly and inexorably and local relations improved. Early in 1695 preparations were begun to transfer men and materials from the Cattewater base to the Hamoaze. On 31 March the Navy Board ordered the first warship, a fifth-rate, to be built at the new dockyard, which effectively opened for business with the dry-docking of the 48-gun *Weymouth* on 4 June. In midsummer the new commissioner, Captain George St Lo (Fig. 29.1), moved residence from Plymouth to the dock. By February 1696 he was looking to the complete removal thither of the storekeeper and all his stores. Building delays still hindered the transfer and slowed the build-up of dockyard activity, but August 1696 saw the launching of the first warship, the 32-gun *Looe*, and December 1697 saw spinning begin in the still incomplete ropewalk.[3]

As the dockyard came into full operation, employment and contract-supply opportunities increased and local attitudes mellowed. When Greenhill returned as Commissioner in 1705, he and Admiral Sir George Byng were admitted Freemen of the Borough, a practice which became normal, while parliamentary representation for Plymouth soon fell under Admiralty influence. Some jealousy and hostility still remained, particularly between Plymouth and the new town of Plymouth Dock emerging outside the dock gates, but there was general recognition of the contribution the dockyard now made to the local economy; so much so by 1707 as to make the Plymouth authorities fight strongly and successfully against the attempt of the Victualling Board to remove its operations from Plymouth to Empacombe on the Cornish side of the Tamar (see above, p. 197).

The Yard in Action

The ships using Plymouth as a base needed to be cleaned, fitted, stored, and provisioned. Each of these operations exercised different sections of the dockyard labour force, and most of them drew on the local economy.

Cleaning

Cleaning involved 'breaming', or burning off the weed and barnacles from the hull with furze or brushwood. There was abundant dwarf trailing furze in West Devon and Cornwall – Tavistock was the recognised market for furze seed – and the Timber Purveyor did not need to go far beyond Saltash or Bere Ferrers on the Tavy to buy furzes.[4] After breaming, the hull was 'payed' (smeared) with 'whitestuff', a mixture of rosin oil and brimstone, or with the cheaper 'blackstuff', pitch and tar, and 'boot-topped' along the waterline with tallow and brimstone. Rosin, pitch, and tar from Stockholm or the Plantations and brimstone from Italy were imported by great London merchants, bought 'cheapest and best' by the Navy Board on the London market, stored at Deptford Yard and distributed to the outports by storeship. Train oil, used for paint, came from the whale fisheries. Tallow was mainly supplied by Newcastle merchants who bought at the great cattle markets, notably in Ireland. Every seafaring community needed these stores; Plymouth itself had merchants who dealt in them, and in emergencies the Dockyard bought from them. Robert Willcocks supplied Plantation rosin; William Davis supplied train oil, and when he could not deliver the Commissioner was authorized to buy from Jacob Coppins at Davis's expense.[5] Tallow caused headaches for the Navy Board. Plymouth consumed far more in paying a ship than did other yards, and the price asked by local dealers might be 70 shillings a ton when the Board could buy in London at 50. In 1705 Nathaniel White offered tallow at Plymouth at 34s, but was found to be an agent of an Irish merchant, Cray, who was offering it in London at 27s.[6] Cleaning was the work of caulkers. It was best done in a dry-dock, but the lesser rates could be 'hauled down', i.e. canted over by tackles between the lower masts and capstans or holdfasts on a muddy shore. Larger rates might be heaved down alongside a hulk while moored afloat.[7] A ship ordered to the West Indies needed 'sheathing' against shipworm. Its hull was coated with a layer of tarred horsehair secured by thin deal plank. The Timber Purveyor bought hair in the larger market towns – Launceston, Liskeard, Plympton, and Tavistock. When a ship returned from the West Indies the Yard would beat down its bulkheads, wash with vinegar, smoke between decks, and tar inside and out against contagious distempers.[8]

Fitting

Fitting involved countless small works by carpenters, painters, glaziers, riggers, and other craftsmen. A ship ordered to carry a Governor to Barbados would need extra cabin space, a Commodore would expect 'a vermilion frieze inside and out' on his pinnace, an admiral would expect the 'greening' of his pinnace and his great cabin, and might try to get winding staircases at the ship's sides between his cabin and the quarterdeck. Standing Orders to the Yards record the issue and reissue of sumptuary regulations prohibiting accommodation ladders or stipulating that the hulls of flagships, if refreshed, must be in 'plain contract colours, black and yellow'.[9] Alterations and additions should only have been done on a warrant from the Navy Board, but ships' officers constantly tried and often succeeded in getting unauthorized improvements made. Sails and rigging, masts and spars were the items most frequently demanded by captains. Sails might be sent from Deptford or ordered from private contractors, but were mostly made in the Yard. Stephen Newell, appointed Master Sailmaker in 1693, served until his death, aged 73, in 1740.[10] The best canvas came from Noyals and Vitry in Brittany, and Holland 'duck' came from northern Europe. In 1696 a price preference of two pence a yard was given to English canvas, which came mainly from East Anglia or Bridport. Most canvas was purchased by the Navy Board and distributed from Deptford Yard, but Plymouth had always had close links with Brittany, and Philip Pentyre was a prominent local supplier of canvas.[11] Hemp was by far the heaviest charge on Navy funds. A typical contract with one of the great merchants dealing with Riga and Konigsberg, agreed by the Navy Board in May after the Yards had submitted their estimated needs, would be to supply a quantity of hemp – 800 tons to Portsmouth, 500 to Chatham, 300 to Plymouth – to be delivered to the Thames by Christmas or to the outports by Lady Day, at £32 a ton to the Thames, £33 to Portsmouth, and £34 to Plymouth.[12] The contractors demanded escort from the Baltic to the port of delivery and thence back to the Thames. The hemp was made into cordage in the Yard. The ropehouse (Fig. 28.2, above, p. 193) planned by Dummer was of two storeys, but capable of supporting a third, and of housing ten wheels. In 1748 there were ten wheels working, two of which were put out of use when peace was declared. Thomas Yeo of Plymouth supplied rope, presumably from his own ropeyard, before he was made Master Ropemaker in 1700. On Yeo's death in 1704, Commissioner William Wright recommended Yeo's son-in-law, Mr Reed, for his post.[13] Masts and spars from the Baltic or from New England were provided by London merchants on terms similar to those for hemp.

Alterations to the dimensions of ships were classed as major repairs and postponed until peacetime in most cases, but, if the need was pressing, the captain influential, or the dockyard enjoying a respite, they might be sanctioned in wartime. The design of many rates of ships were faulty and requests for alterations were all too frequent. 'Girdling' was adding plank along the waterline to stiffen a ship; 'doubling' was adding plank to the entire hull. In 1698 Captain Clark of the *Shrewsbury* asked for a mainmast three feet longer, 'as she would do nothing under a pair of courses with reefs taken out'. It was peacetime, and the Navy Board approved the work after asking the opinion of Thomas Podd, Master Shipwright of Plymouth. However, when in 1703 the Plymouth Commissioner, Richard Edwards, informed them that he had 'enlarged the topmasts and yards and added a strake or two under the lower wales to assist her sailing' they wanted to know:

> why her masts and yards were enlarged, resulting in the doubling of her, loss of time, and additional charge, but a prejudice to the wear of the ship . . . It is a sad consideration to find the masts, yards and sails of ships increased to make them tender and then to propose girdling or doubling to cure the same.

When Edwards tried to lecture the Board, as a seaman dealing directly with seamen, they delivered a withering rebuke. Samuel Hood of the frigate *Vestal* asked for longer masts and yards, and six inches added to the false keel. This seems a very similar alteration, yet a later Board granted it, perhaps because of their opinion of the captain, perhaps because of the importance of the service intended for the ship – Rodney flew his flag on her at the bombardment of Le Havre in July 1759. A less common complaint was that of Captain Fletcher in 1709 that the *Rose* was:

> so deep in the waist that when it blows a fresh gale and she carries any sail she fills her deck so full of water that her men are swimming.

The Master Shipwright was asked to recommend a remedy.[14]

Storing

Beating down Channel in the face of the prevailing westerlies might take weeks, and for that reason the Admiralty preferred to use Plymouth for squadrons operating in the Soundings, the Atlantic, and the Mediterranean. An infinite variety of stores was required, often suddenly and urgently, to maintain these ships. At least once a quarter, and often much more frequently, Plymouth's requirements were met by the dispatch of a storeship from Deptford laden with wainscot board, spruce deals, ash oars, red kersey for waist-cloths, copper kettles, 'bells, watch; bells, cabin . . .' etc.[15] These storeships might themselves be delayed for weeks waiting for a wind or working their way to windward by 'tiding' down. Other stores came direct from holders of standing contracts. Ambrose Crowley of Sunderland sent ironwork of all kinds: nails, hacksaws, hinges, locks, pitch-pots.[16] Coals for the smithy came from Pontop in Durham, or Tanfield Moor, or from South Wales.[17] Ships making ocean passages carried fishing tackle supplied by Samuel Austin of Tower Street, London, and azimuth compasses and spare cards supplied by Mr England. After 1756 Mr Dunsterville's 'new and popular compass cards' were adopted in all yards. Plymouth Dockyard held a lodestone for touching compass needles.[18]

Local men won a small share of the standing contracts and were often invited to tender in times of shortage, when they could name their own price. The Navy Board did not forget those who dealt fairly at such times, and some Plymouth families held contracts for several generations. Robert Moorshead of New Street became Blockmaker for the Yard in 1699, and on his death in 1713 his son was invited to continue.[19] The contract for painter's work was held by Thomas Coward until his death in 1698. The Board ordered that he should not be supplanted until his widow, Katherine, had expended his stock of colours. In due course she was awarded a new contract, and a John Coward still held the contract in 1743.[20] William Davis held a standing contract for ironwork. In 1703 the Commissioner complained that Davis could not supply nails to time and that those he did supply were not stamped with the Queen's mark, and he suggested that nails be bought from Crowley. Davis exerted himself to comply with his contract and was allowed to continue.[21] He also supplied colours, altering 227 ensigns 'since the Union of the Two Kingdoms according to the pattern sent for that purpose'. Plumbers' work, glaziers' work, oars, treenails, and candles were provided by local men. Cash for paying seamen and workmen in the Yard was usually brought, months in arrears, by ship from Portsmouth. In an emergency it was raised locally. In 1703 pay for the soldiers in Newfoundland was sent from London to the Downs, but it arrived after the ship ordered to carry it had sailed. When she arrived at Plymouth, she took instead £696 provided by the local Collector of Excise, who had to ask repeatedly for reimbursement.[22]

Victualling

Victualling the ships resorting to Plymouth offered the naval administration its greatest challenge: the health, morale, discipline and efficiency of the fleet depended on it. Every September the Navy Board made a 'Declaration of Victuals', an estimate of the number of men in sea pay for the coming year, and its subordinate Victualling Board could then purchase and preserve the sea victuals, which had to be dried or pickled, soon after the harvest and the Martinmas killing.[23] The Victualling Board preferred to place large orders with those offering the lowest tenders at widely advertised negotiations in London. Cereals for biscuit and oatmeal came mostly from East Anglia, though Mr Bowditch of Exeter was invited to tender for bread, pease, and oatmeal in 1702.[24] Cheese came from Suffolk before 1758 and from Cheshire and Gloucestershire thereafter. The contractors for cheese and butter had to undertake to supply whatever was demanded at a fixed price for a whole year, to put it into casks and replace any that deterioriated within six months. Only very substantial merchants could undertake this, and most Devon men were in a small way of business. They were also remote from London, and those who tendered by letter could rarely prevail against those who attended in person. The Board recognized that Devon dealers were at a disadvantage, and in 1702 it took positive steps to avail itself of the abundant farm produce of the western counties by appointing an agent at Plymouth, John Stucley, with powers of local purchase.[25] Salt beef was prepared at Plymouth. John Hooper of Barnstaple sent beef when the price there was acceptable. White salt for pickling was supplied on standing contract by the Newcastle dealer, Cotesworth. In 1702 he failed to deliver 1,000 barrels, and the Agent was told to buy locally at Cotesworth's expense. He bought French salt at £10 6s a barrel from Mr Darracott of Plymouth. Plymouth had an established trade in 'Bay salt' from Biscayan ports, and was in this case able to meet a large and urgent demand at the height of the killing season. A similar crisis occurred in 1734 when a London contractor, John Nicholson, failed to deliver white salt from Lymington in the Solent. In that year Philip Pentyre of Plymouth was supplying Bay salt. Salt meat packed at Plymouth had a good name: in 1758 an enquiry into Boscawen's complaint about meat supplied to the western squadron found that meat in cases packed in the outports was better than that packed at Deptford.[26]

Ships in commission spent half their time in harbour or at anchorages such as Torbay. To conserve their sea victuals and to promote the health of the seamen, ships within reach of a victualling yard were ordered 'petty warrant' victuals – bread instead of biscuit, fresh meat, and green vegetables. Local merchants were well placed to supply fresh produce. Though negotiations were started in London they were likely to be completed locally. For instance, in 1734 the Victualling Board gave notice in the *Courant* and the *Gazette* that it would on 25 September treat for oxen and hogs for London, Portsmouth, Plymouth, and Dover. Three dealers attended in person, one of them representing Hugh Littleton of St Germans and Mr Gatherall of Liskeard. Seven others tendered by letter, four of them from Plymouth. Once a price had been established in London, the Agent in Plymouth was authorized to treat locally, and on 11 November he agreed with local dealers for deliveries twice weekly of oxen and hogs on the hoof to Stonehouse or the Dock. Thomas Harris of Barnstaple supplied the hogs. In the next year tenders were received from Plymouth, Rame, Totnes, and Wembury. In 1738 the Board accepted the 30 oxen a week offered by the lowest bidder in London and instructed their Plymouth Agent, Nathaniel Cooper, to make them up to 200 a week at the same price with local dealers and to make an offer for 70 of these to Mr Elliott of St Germans. In 1739, at the start of the War of Jenkins Ear, the requirement rose to between 500 and 800 a week, and the tenders in London were too high. The Plymouth Agent was ordered to treat locally and accept the best price he could get.[27]

In wartime the Board had to pay the price demanded. In peacetime, particularly if it suspected a local price-ring, it would not submit. In treating for malt in October 1734 it ordered its Agent to let the Plymouth dealers know 'that we bought here at 16s 6d a quarter and that if they enter into a combination to distress the Service we shall send that specie from hence'. When the tenders came in a fortnight later from Plymouth, Insworke and St Germans, they were at least three shillings above the London price, and the Agent was told 'to let them know that we can't think of dealing in those parts at such high prices', and that they were sending 200 quarters of malt in biscuit bags in the *William and Mary* hoy. A month later the Board, having sent malt, pease, and biscuit by ship, ordered the Agent to give notice in Plymouth, Exeter, Topsham, Looe, Falmouth, and other places that he would treat for biscuit, oatmeal and meal. By now the local dealers had been humbled, and tenders were accepted from Thomas Collier of Topsham and Jacob Austin of Plymouth for malt, from Paddon and Skinner of Tavistock for oatmeal, and from Joseph Veale of Exeter for biscuit. Six years later, still wary of price-rings in malt, the Board ordered its Agent to publish his tender date locally and at Newport on the Isle of Wight, Southampton, and to inform a Mr Judd of Fareham. In the event Richard Pett of Plymouth won the contract.[28]

Beer was an important component of sea victuals, issued at the rate of a gallon a day per man. It was bulky, short-lived, and best brewed locally. Local brewers charged too much, and the Board brewed at a rented brewery at Insworke and after 1736 at a new brewery at Southdown. Even in peacetime the Board's brewery could not meet the demand, and private brewers were invited to tender. In 1734 the Board rejected the tender of Stephen Edwards of Plymouth as 'too high' and that of 'the Plymouth Brewers' as 'extravagantly high'. Next year the copper at Insworke burst and the Board instructed its Agent to buy at the best price he could get.[29] Plymouth beer had a bad name in the Navy. In 1725 the purser of the *Dunkirk* complained that the beer from the Board's brewery at Millbrook (Insworke) was very sour, 'and our people get the gripes which puts them under a necessity to drink water which is very comfortless at this time of year'. Complaints reached their height in 1759, when Hawke kept his long vigil off Brest and persuaded the Board to discontinue beer supplied from Plymouth and to send it instead from Portsmouth.[30]

The Agent in Plymouth struggled to meet the sudden heavy demands of squadrons ordered overseas from a small yard; in a remote and small-scale local economy; and where supplies from Deptford were unreliable because of hiccups in the convoy system. In December 1704 the *Portland* came into Plymouth having lost both the ships carrying butter and cheese which she had been ordered to convoy from Dover. One came in later; the other overshot to Falmouth and was taken in the course of her return. These ships had been delayed for a month in Dover, and because of the delay Sir Stafford Fairborne's squadron had to sail with oil instead of cheese.[31]

Even so, there were impressive achievements in victualling, above all in 1759, the year of Hawke's blockade and victory (see above, p. 187). But as early as 1705, when Byng was cruising off Brest with 10,065 men, while some victuals were sent from Portsmouth, two members of the Victualling Board came to Plymouth and hired ships there and organized fortnightly supplies of beer and water, sheep and greens.[32]

The Naval Base in Peacetime

Peace brought adjustments, but not much diminution of activity. The ships which came in to be paid off or reduced to lowest complement had to be surveyed, the weakest sold, the soundest refitted first, and, for all hulls worth retaining, complete sets of stores, rigging, and furniture had to be set apart. Two ships were manned with two-thirds complement as guardships, ready to be sent to sea at short notice. The remainder were placed 'in ordinary', manned by skeleton crews which maintained an anchor watch day

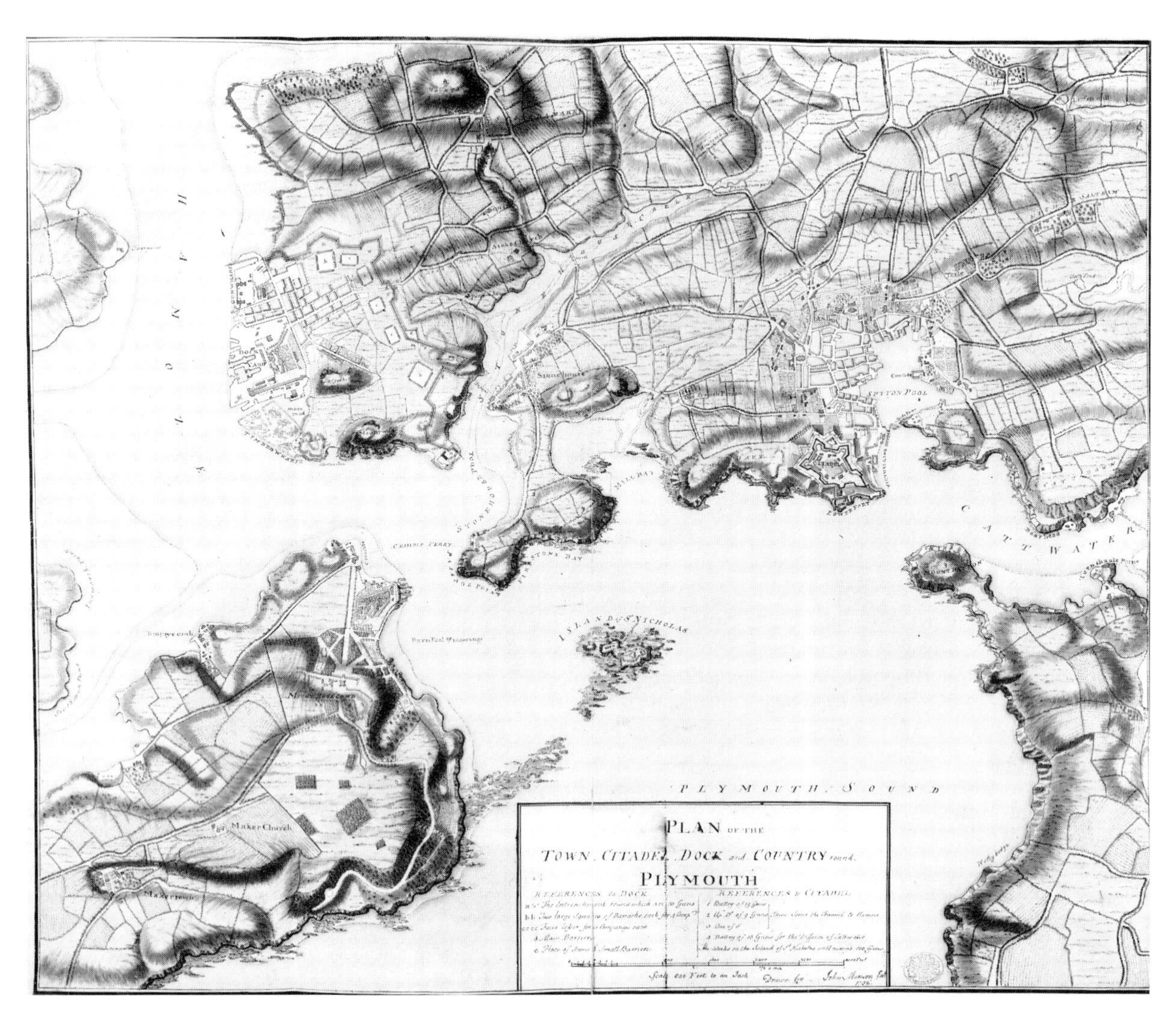

29.2 Plymouth, 1756: Plan of the Town, Citadel, Dock and Country around, drawn by John Manson, Engineer. Note the draughtsman's characteristic style for the depiction of hills (Helen Wallis). *BL, King's Top., XI, 77.*

and night, wet the sides and decks in dry weather, and opened the gunports for ventilation. Canvas awnings and light coloured paint were used to reduce the effect of sun on the decks. To improve ventilation, the bulkheads of bread and powder rooms were cleared from the holds, and the strakes of the inner ceiling were removed from the orlop and gun decks. Eight guardboats were also employed, two at a time to patrol the harbour at night to prevent pilfering and to check that the sentries of the Ordinary were in a watchful posture.[33] After the peace of Ryswick (1697) two third-rates and eight fourth-rates were laid up in the Hamoaze, all the large rates going to Portsmouth or the Thames. The emphasis of Navy Board orders was now on retrenchment. In 1697 the Clerk of the Cheque was reminded that his accounts were four quarters in arrears, standing contracts were terminated and renegotiated on better terms, and interest allowed to creditors was reduced from six to five per cent. Heads of departments were asked to estimate the number of workmen they needed to retain, and in due course the Surveyor of the Navy defined the peacetime establishment.[34] Subsequently officers were urged to retain the more active and skilful workmen and to dismiss those who kept brandy shops or 'only come to their duty when they cannot be better employed'.[35] In the ropeyard some of the redundant spinners were kept on if they accepted the lower grade of 'hatchellors' (hemp combers). 'Extra', or overtime, rates were terminated except for dockings.[36] At the same time efforts were made to pay the workmen their arrears.

Because it had always been a base for cruising ships of the lower rates, Plymouth (Fig. 29.2) was less affected by the transition from war to peace than the eastern yards. The ships checking smuggling, including the 'owling' of wool in the Irish Sea, were based on Plymouth, as were most of those operating against the Sallee rovers, protecting the Newfoundland fishery, escorting the trade to the Canaries, Lisbon, or the Straits of Gibraltar, or serving the garrisons in New York, Barbados, and the Leeward Islands. The men who were retained were on the whole fully employed. The sailmakers were set to building up the stocks of spare sails depleted in war. The shipwrights could undertake major repairs which had been postponed in the rush of wartime refits, or could concentrate on new construction.

Shipbuilding and major repair

It was customary for a Commissioner at the end of a war to propose to the Navy Board that a new ship be laid down. In that way he could retain the best of his workforce and keep them employed.[37] But even in wartime there were slack periods for shipwrights, especially in the summer months when most ships were at sea, and new ships were built by the Plymouth yard from the outset at the rate of one a year. The first, apart from two small Advice Boats, was the fourth-rate *Anglesea*, ordered in 1693 and launched at Mr Flint's yard. She was followed by a long line of fifth-rates, the first of which were the *Lyme* in 1695 and the *Looe* in 1696, built in the Dockyard by the Master Shipwright, Elias Waffe. The rebuilding of a third-rate, the *Rupert*, ordered in October 1698, taxed the skills and resources of the new Dockyard. Large oak timbers were sent from the eastern yards, and the local Purveyor, Thomas Netherton, scoured Devon for suitable timber: 'to Cornwood [10 miles] to view timber for the *Rupert*', 'to Lord Fortescue [Castle Hill, north Devon: Fig. 29.3] for a particular piece of timber . . . for a sternpiece for the *Rupert*'.[38] Waffe's successor, Thomas Podd, was in charge of her rebuilding at Plymouth, and there were doubts about his competence. His fifth-rate, the *Pembroke*, launched in April 1710, required shortened masts and light girdling when she was fitted for the Mediterranean in November, and he was asked to explain 'why, when newly built, she is so tender'.[39] The most influential of Plymouth Master Shipwrights was Benjamin Slade, who in 1747 was ordered to build a 24-gun ship to the lines of a captured French privateer, the *Tiger*. He reported to Anson: 'our present 24-gun ships are too full aft, and the *Tiger* as much the contrary'. He was at the start of a movement to learn from the French, and his correspondence with Anson enabled him to recommend his kinsman, Thomas Slade, who rose to be Surveyor of the Navy, 1755–71.[40]

The presence of a naval base did not stimulate many local merchant builders to build warships; rather it inhibited them, perhaps because the Navy Board did not want shipwrights lured away from the Yard. John Bingham of Plymouth rebuilt a fireship in 1709, and Digory Veale built a victualling hoy in 1736, but when in 1740 the latter contracted to build a 24-gun ship, he found the task beyond him and was glad to turn her over unfinished and receive £1,533 for his work. John Snook built two sloops at Saltash in 1757.[41] On the other hand, Plymouth Dockyard played an important part in supporting warship building in remoter western ports as far as Liverpool, sending supervisors, masts, spars, rigging, and anchors, and bearing on its books the boatswains and carpenters appointed to the ships before launching.[42]

29.3 Castle Hill, Filleigh, the seat of the Fortescues, by GB Campion, engraved by J Henshall and published in 1830. *(Devon and Exeter Institution)*

Timber supply

Shipbuilding and major repairs consumed great quantities of oak and some elm. Local supplies were limited, for though oak and ash were predominant trees in Devon and Cornwall, high winds on the uplands stunted the trees, and only in sheltered valleys were useful trees raised. The Navy Board dealt with timber merchants and actively sought timber through purveyors attached to the dockyards and by seeking contact with public spirited or embarrassed landowners. In times of heavy demand, Plymouth was encouraged to seek timber in areas remote from the eastern dockyards.

During the wars against Louis XIV some oak was sent by local landowners: Mr Harris of Hayne in Stowford, Squire Cloberry of Stoke Climsland, and Squire Speckett of Saltash. Mr Bearcroft, agent at Tavistock of the Duchess of Bedford, sent timber in good times and bad, but Mr Elliott of Port Elliott was too exorbitant, and Major Glynn of Glynn near Bodmin persisted in sending his timber to Chatham.[43] Local supplies were not adequate, and the Plymouth purveyors, notably Thomas Netherton, looked to the Severn and Dee and beyond. They bought from Shropshire and Hereford (loading at Chepstow or Hung Road on the Avon), from Lanthornan Park, Newport, from Sir Roger Mostyn in Flint, from Lord Cholmondely at Neston on the Wirral – even from the Earl of Thanet at Appleby in Cumberland. In this last transaction, in 1703, the cost of felling, peeling and sawing 69 trees was £43 3s 1d. Carrying the timber by cart twenty-five miles to Rockliffe on the Eden cost £118 17s, and thence by two river vessels to Whitehaven £28 4s 6d. There it was loaded on to the *Hamoaze* Transport provided by the Navy Board.[44]

The delays and high cost of sea transport under convoy led the Navy Board to discourage purchases in Wales after 1712, and to direct to Plymouth timber from merchants who habitually supplied Portsmouth: Christopher Coles of Pulborough, John Dibble of Abinger, and George Moore of Arundel.[45] The only slightly reduced demands of peacetime were met largely by local merchants and landowners such as Mr Hayman of Exeter, Mr Tozer of South Sydenham, and merchants of Teignmouth and Topsham.[46] Elm was even harder to find than oak and was brought from Helston, Bridgewater, Lyme, and Weymouth.[47] The demand for timber intensified again in the War of Jenkins Ear. Some oak was still to be had in Devon and Cornwall, but much more was directed from Portsmouth and Chatham by the Navy Board, and many small quantities came from parts of the southern counties remote from navigable water – Ampsfield in Hampshire, Singleton in Sussex, Longleat in Wiltshire, and Melbury Sampford in Dorset.[48] One consignment is very well documented, that from Braydon Wood at Ilford Bridge near Ilminster, offered to Plymouth Yard by the agents of Sir Charles Wyndham, Susanna Strangways Horner, and the Earl of Ilchester. Felling cost perhaps only £22 10s, but land carriage over twenty miles to Lyme via Tatwoth, near Chard, cost £240. The vendors could not find private vessels to hire, and had to hire three from the Navy Board for £429. They found that transporting the king's timber in the king's ships did not exempt them from customs duty at Plymouth or from anchorage dues to the Collector of Saltash, and that an offer of venison to the Master Builder at Plymouth, which was refused, did not prevent some of their timber being rejected as defective through rotten knots, shakes, and general tenderness. This timber had been surveyed by Paul Baker the Purveyor in wartime, but was not delivered until July 1749, a year after the end of the war.[49]

The southeastern counties were almost stripped of oak trees in the Seven Years War, and Plymouth was once more dependent on Wales. Timber was brought from Ledbury and the Forest of Dean, loading at Gatcombe near Gloucester, from Neath, and from the woods and parks adjacent to Swansea. Again there were delays in moving it by sea. One vessel was held up at Milford Haven waiting for convoy for three months. Once the Navy Board was reconciled to the expense, these areas could yield quantities of timber, and after the wars Plymouth was judged to be 'better supplied with timber than any of the other Yards'.[50] Only rarely can the landowner's motive for selling be established, but in the case of Thomas Carew it is clear that the expense of building Crowcombe Court on the slopes of the Quantocks between 1723 and 1739 forced him in 1755 to sell all oak trees of above fifty feet in girth in his 12 woods at Stoodleigh in Devon to Jonathan Rashleigh of Hammersmith. Rashleigh, whose home was at Menabilly in Cornwall, had long supplied timber to Plymouth, and in July 1757 he signed a contract with the Commissioner there to deliver timber from Stoodleigh which had been surveyed by Matthew Page.[51]

The Workforce

The dockyard workforce rose, not steadily but in surges to meet 'emergent occasions', from 54 in 1691 to 323 in 1697, 499 in 1702, 741 in 1710, 1,130 in 1749, 1,696 in late 1757, and 1,837 in 1759. In 1710 there were 270 shipwrights, 29 caulkers, 48 riggers, 12 sawyers, 165 labourers and 71 workers in the ropeyard (Cf Table 31.2, below). At first the craftsmen were mainly recruited from the Thames or from Portsmouth. When two caulkers deserted in 1704 they were sought in Rotherhithe and Ratcliffe. Many left their homes reluctantly and expected 'encouragements' to stay. In 1693 John Ward and his 'servant' (apprentice) were brought from London to serve as caulkers, but left at once when their demand for ten shillings a week subsistence was refused. When the workload increased dramatically in 1747 shipwrights were recruited both in western ports – Fowey, Falmouth, St Ives, Bideford, Ilfracombe, Bristol – and further afield in Liverpool and Hull.[52] Once established, a shipwright could look forward to a secure job for life and the opportunity to install his sons as apprentices. Therefore, as time passed, more dockyard workmen regarded themselves as Plymouth men. But promotion often involved transfer to and from other yards: the appointment of an Assistant Master Shipwright of Plymouth to be assistant to the Surveyor of the Navy triggered transfers for the Master Mastmaker of Chatham and a Quarterman of Deptford.[53] Some shipwrights were much-travelled men. Adam Sale, shipwright at Plymouth, asked in 1748 to be allowed a servant, pleading twenty-three years' service, twelve of them at sea as ship's carpenter and many in Deptford Yard, and impairment of vision and mobility after exposure to winter cold in the mountains above Leghorn when acting as Purveyor and Overseer of Timber for Admiral Rowley in 1746.[54]

Shipwrights were paid 2½d an hour in 1748 for a ten-hour day, with the chance of working extra 'tides' of one-and-a-half hours or 'nights' of five hours at 5d an hour. They were regularly mustered by the Clerk of the Cheque and were grouped in gangs under quartermen by 'shoaling', a system similar to the picking of sides for a playground game. This ensured a fair distribution of able men, young apprentices, and old men 'almost past their labour'. The rates of pay were lower than those obtaining in merchants' yards, and extra men pressed in wartime were usually impatient to be paid off. Some supplemented their earnings by running brandy shops, by taking gifts for doing unauthorized work for commanders of ships, or even by doing work outside the Yard.[55]

Unrest was provoked mainly by delay of pay or the withdrawal of extra allowances. Both of these grievances caused the troubles of February 1693. In July 1691 Greenhill had reminded the Navy Board that pay was in arrears and the men harassed by 'the continual importuning of their creditors'. A month later, having promised them pay for the previous November and December, he paid them with imprest money intended for contractors supplying the Yard. In February 1693 pay was fourteen months in arrears. Greenhill hoped that the promise of one quarter's pay would satisfy them, but the carpenters came to him in a mutinous mood. He arrested the ringleader and his son, and discharged them. This removed their 'protection', and both were at once pressed on board the *Portsmouth*. Thereupon the remainder refused to work and Greenhill asked the Navy Board for instructions, commenting: 'they are ungovernable. I can attribute their unruliness to nothing so much as the ill custom of large allowances for extra work.' The men evidently petitioned the Navy Board, complaining that they were often stranded after working in ships at moorings. Greenhill replied that this was because men of the *James Galley* had cut adrift the hulk's boat sent to carry them ashore. The Navy Board stood firm, and early next month Greenhill was sending to Bideford, Topsham, and Dartmouth for shipwrights and carpenters.[56] Delays of pay were again severe in 1698, and were particularly harmful in Plymouth, where so many of the men were strangers in a town whose merchants were not used to granting credit. St Lo warned the Navy Board: 'the workmen will be forced to knock off; their credit having for some time been on the wrack, and victuals not to be gotten without ready money'.[57]

There were occasional complaints of shoddy work: of caulking 'slightly performed, only paid over with pitch, and no oakum drove into the seams'; of the Master Shipwright 'doing his work like a blockhead'. The Admiralty Visitation of 1749 was critical of the Plymouth workforce: the Master Carpenter was old and gouty, the Boatswain on crutches, many workmen 'very insufficient persons', some had been taken in when almost past their labour, and most of the recently-entered servants were under size and three of them were 'borne on the books' after their masters had 'run'. In contrast, the workmen at Portsmouth were 'the best body of men in any of the Yards, their servants remarkably stout lads'. It must be said for Plymouth that this Visitation followed a period of very hasty expansion under a Commissioner (Vanbrugh) who was himself sick.[58]

Some craftsmen, notably sailmakers, were not kept constantly at work but were hired or dismissed as occasion required. As work outside the Yard was scarce at Plymouth, these men had to be given higher rates than in the eastern yards. The spinners and hatchellors who worked in the ropeyard were paid piece-work rates – in busy times they could perform two-and-a-half days' stints in a day. In quiet times they hoped to supplement their pay by undertaking private work, and as this was not to be had in Plymouth they asked to be paid for one-and-a-half days and threatened to leave if it was not granted. Because they were paid by the piece they were angered by the entering on the books of boys who would slow down output and might endanger life as they were 'careless and addicted to play, knowing no danger so fear none'. In 1745 the entering of four apprentices to four spinners led to tumultuous picketing of the gates by 65 other spinners, who threatened to beat any who tried to enter. On the fourth day soldiers appeared at the gate to protect the blacklegs. Only 40 spinners held out, and they sent word that they would return the next day and asked clemency. But that night a labourer from Chatham brought word that the spinners there were out, and next morning 56 spinners absented themselves. The Commissioner then heard their grievances and negotiated a compromise.[59]

The theft of stores, particularly of cordage and tallow which found a ready market in the town, was frequent and mainly by boat. Offenders who were unskilful enough to be caught were mulcted of their pay, and persistent offenders might be dismissed. Attempts to prosecute in the civil courts were discontinued, as the county magistrates did not favour keeping offenders in gaol until the assizes, and juries found pretexts to acquit even confessed pilferers.[60]

The opportunities for illicit gain were greater for the dockyard officers: the Master Shipwright might receive substandard timber from contractors or allow unauthorized work in ships or in officers' houses; the Master Carpenter might make furniture for himself or his superiors. The Clerk of the Cheque, whose signature was required for all payments, had innumerable perquisites: the first to hold the office, John Addis, grew rich enough to own 42 houses, 13 of them beer shops. The most famous was John Clevland, who rose as clerk at the Navy Board to his father, Captain William Clevland. As Clerk of the Cheque at Plymouth (1730–43) he was able to buy a mansion near Bideford and to become MP for Saltash. He was promoted Clerk of the Acts at the Navy Board, and under Anson's patronage became Secretary to the Board of Admiralty.[61]

Plymouth's Years of Strain and Triumph

The mid-century wars were the real testing time of Plymouth's capacity to function as a major naval base. 1746 and 1747 were perhaps the crisis years. The increase of both the western squadron and of the many other tasks thrown upon it (such as the supply of Admiral Lestock's Lorient expedition) resulted in the yard running out of cables in September 1746, when storm damage put Lestock in urgent need for two of his third-rates. A month later the arrival of Anson with the western squadron, two of whose ships had sprung their foremasts, showed up a severe shortage of masts. With only one single-tree mast of 32in thickness in store and no others above 29in, the Master Shipwright proposed to work his mastmakers and boatbuilders two 'tides' every day until a sufficient number of composite masts could be made up.[62] In the following year Anson complained that Commissioner Vanbrugh was dilatory in cleaning his frigates and urged the Admiralty to 'keep an extraordinary magazine of all kinds of stores at that post during the war, and principally cordage, masts and sails', but again at the end of the year a parcel of Bridport canvas was so urgently needed that it could not await convoy and had to be sent expensively by land. The timber shortage became chronic as demand far outpaced existing supply contracts, and a shortage of timber hoys and lighters hindered attempts to speed up new delivery. At the same time escalating labour needs resulted in desperate appeals to Admiralty overseers of shipbuilding in merchant yards as far away as Liverpool and Hull to procure shipwrights and caulkers for Plymouth, where the shipwrights were working extra tides by candlelight.[63]

The lessons learnt and new facilities provided in 1747–8 prepared the Plymouth base for its testing in 1759, when Hawke's protracted blockade of Brest and Rochefort with a large fleet was the supreme test of the skill and determination of the seamen and of the ability of the Plymouth base to sustain them. Its successful outcome justified the strategy of the western squadron and gave further impetus to the development of Plymouth Dockyard.

Admiral Hawke, 1759

The early months of 1759 imposed no undue strain on the Dockyard. Work continued on the building of a new 70-gun ship, and one dock was committed for four months to a major repair of the *Hampton Court*. Plymouth had fitted 11 of the 25 ships with which Hawke sailed on 17 May.

As they started their vigil off Ushant, Commissioner Rogers was granted fourteen days leave to attend to his private affairs. Yet there were signs that the situation was grave: there were reports of French preparations to invade; the dockyard workers were exercising with small arms two afternoons a week; armed cutters, privateers, and transports were being hired; tenders were bringing in men pressed at Cork, Greenock, Liverpool, Gloucester, Bristol, and Penzance; and men were taken from frigates to complete the manning of ships of the line.[64]

But when the Commander-in-Chief at Plymouth, Vice-Admiral Harrison, died suddenly on 13 March, no successor was appointed to support or quicken the Commissioner, except Captain Edgcumbe for the time that his ship was in for repair. Not until 15 August was a Commander-in-Chief appointed, and then he was not an admiral, but Captain Thomas Hanway, with the status of Commodore. He was to forward the King's service, hasten the dispatch of ships and quicken their commanders, and to have particular concern for the appropriate manning of ships. His appointment was prompted by Hawke's letter of 23 July, in which he attributed the frustration of his plan to get two ships cleaned in dry dock every spring tide to 'the want of a Commanding Officer at Plymouth to see all orders executed with the dispatch and punctuality necessary'. Hawke, who was quick to suspect lethargy and 'neglect' in dockyard officers, was reassured by the appointment of Hanway, who had served under him at sea and who got four of Hawke's ships back to sea before the end of August in spite of bad weather.[65] When Hawke was driven into the Sound for shelter in mid-October, Hanway showed a proper sense of urgency:

> That no time be lost in equipping the fleet, I have directed the crews of the *Burford* and *Winchester* to put the stores for the several ships into the dock vessels to be carried into the Sound as far as demanded; and have applied to the contractor for furnishing ballast to send all his barges to assist in carrying beer and water when the weather will admit of it. I have proposed to Sir Edward Hawke to send the ships long-boats with anchors and hawsers to endeavour to warp the victuallers out of the Catwater, and have ordered the Masters Attendant to send two launches to assist in that service. The cutters are employed in removing thirty-two sick men from the *Foudroyant*, which are all I have had any account of, and which shall be replaced.

Arriving unexpectedly on 13 October, and despite continuing bad weather, Hawke's fleet was completely reprovisioned for three months service with all except its full quantity of beer, which the brewhouse could not produce quickly enough, so that on the evening of the 18th the Admiral was able to get out of the Sound on a light wind with the help of his ships' boats.[66] The seamanship of Hawke's crews was so skilful that storm damage was kept to a level which did not exhaust Plymouth's stores or workmen, and ships which came home with Keppel from Goree or with Boscawen from Lagos were repaired and replenished and sent to reinforce Hawke.

Hanway's main preoccupation in October 1759 was clearly that of getting provisions out to the ships. Hawke had predicted that victualling would be the greatest strain which a long blockade would impose on the base. He put the refreshment of his men above the cleaning of his ships, and rather than exhaust the men clearing their ships for docking, he ordered them:

> to heel and boot-hose-top only, remaining at rest for ten days in port, and at their departure bringing such a quantity of fresh meat as would keep sweet at this season, two or three live bullocks and twenty live sheep.

His letters to the Admiralty in July had complained repeatedly about shortages of butter and cheese, the excessively bad beer brewed at Plymouth, and the 'great delays and neglect' his captains complained of in getting empty casks ashore and full ones aboard. John Ommanney, the Victualling Agent, replied pleading the interruption by winds and the sheer volume of work: loading 22 victuallers for the fleet, supplying the ships in harbour, and unloading victuallers sent from Deptford.[67] The Admiralty acted quickly to assist and support the hard-pressed Ommanney. On 6 August they ordered one of the Victualling Commissioners, Robert Pett, to Plymouth with powers to dispatch victuals without waiting for orders. Within a week he proposed that the *Catwater* be kept constantly going to the fleet with roots, greens, and apples without convoy. On 14 August the *Juno* convoyed nine victuallers to the fleet, one with dry goods, three with beer, two with 248 sheep, two with 40 live oxen, and one with cabbages, onions, turnips, and carrots. Fresh vegetables were sent in the hope of preventing scurvy, though the authorities put their trust in fresh meat. Hawke had asked for it on 23 July, as soon as the first signs of scurvy occurred among men fed on salt meat, but already the Admiralty had given orders for it. Later in the year, beef and pork were shipped from Cork to augment local supplies.[68] Beer was thought as essential as beef to the health of seamen, and Pett investigated Hawke's complaints in September. Along with Commodore Hanway, Commissioner Rogers, and several captains, he surveyed 495 butts at Southdown, of which they found 437 fit for sea stores, 26 fit for present use by ships in harbour, and only 28, mostly of the June brewing, unfit for use.[69]

The activities of Hanway, representing the Admiralty, and of Pett from the Victualling Board were a significant contribution to the organization of Hawke's crucial blockade. It is possible that the Navy Board also had a direct representative to quicken and support the Resident Commissioner, in that at least twice in the year (in January and April) Digby Dent, a Commissioner of the Navy, was in Plymouth, on the first occasion paying the ships.[70] All the major naval departments thus had representatives at Plymouth capable of taking immediate decisions without reference back to London.

As the blockade was prolonged through autumn into winter, getting provisions from Plymouth to the ships became the main obstacle, but Pett's experience as Inspector of the Business of the Hoytaker fitted him for this challenge. In the event it was victuallers which first sighted Conflans when he sallied from Brest towards Quiberon and was destroyed by Hawke's fleet on 20 November.[71] After the battle Hawke blockaded the estuaries to which the French survivors had fled, but it was as well that his main work was done because it became increasingly more difficult to supply him in the Bay of Biscay over the winter. Some provisions and beer were got out, but on 7 February Sir John Bentley, commanding after Hawke returned home, reported that scurvy was weakening his squadron and asked for beef, mutton, and onions.[72] That scurvy forced the fleet back to port only after nine months at sea, more than ten weeks after the decisive battle and at the end of the winter, stands as one of the great eighteenth-century achievements of the naval authorities and their servants in Plymouth in victualling the fleet. Lind attributed the victory of Quiberon to 'the most perfect and unparalleled state of health' enjoyed by the English seamen, 14,000 of them, many of whom had been at sea above six months.[73]. By the end of the Seven Years War Plymouth had been proven as the best operational base and was about to be extended and improved to become the largest of Britain's dockyards.

29: The Local Community and the Operation of Plymouth Dockyard, 1689–1763

Sadly John Marsh died while finalising these footnotes, so some may not be as full as he would have wished. The text was completed for publication by Dr Michael Duffy.

1 PRO ADM 106/388, Cotton's reports, 9 August, 25 October 1689.

2 ADM 106/520, 11 February, 13 September 1698; NMM VAU/H/1/1699.

3 AE Stephens, 'Plymouth Dock: A Survey of the Development of the Royal Dockyard during the Sailing Ship Era' (Unpublished PhD thesis, University of London, 1940) 73–5, 78, 82, 85–6.

4 ADM 174/281, Netherton's reports 9, 10 September 1695; W Marshall, *Rural Economy of the West of England* (1796), I, 37, II, 9.

5 ADM 174/4, 21 December 1711.

6 ADM 106/982, Vanbrugh, 4 January 1742; ADM 106/3578 Wright, 24 June 1705.
7 ADM 106/3578, Wright, 11, 22 June 1703.
8 ADM 174/281, Netherton, 17 October–26 November 1696; ADM 174/1, 27 October 1697.
9 ADM 174/2, 28 April 1709; NMM VAU/T/1, 17 September 1757, 30 March 1758.
10 ADM 106/432, Greenhill, 17 March 1693; NMM VAU/Q/1, 24 January 1740.
11 ADM 174/1, 5 March 1697.
12 ADM 174/1, 29 May 1697.
13 ADM 174/14, 4 July 1748; ADM 106/3578, Wright, 21 July 1707.
14 ADM 174/1, 3 August 1698; ADM 174/4, 30 May 1712; ADM 174/15, 9 August 1758; ADM 174/2, 7 October 1709.
15 ADM 174/1, 16 April 1697, 26 July 1698.
16 E Hughes, *North Country Life in the 18th Century* (1952) I, 18, 63–5.
17 ADM 174/15, 6 December 1758; ADM 106/903, Plymouth Officers, 26 May 1738; ADM 174/14, 20 March 1749.
18 ADM 1742/2, 22 July 1709; ADM 174/2, 30 June 1714; NMM VAU/F/13, 28 May 1756; ADM 106/982, Vanbrugh, 31 May 1743.
19 ADM 174/1, 20 May 1699; ADM 174/4, 16 October 1713.
20 ADM 174/1, 1 January 1699; ADM 106/982, Vanbrugh, 10 April 1743.
21 ADM 106/3578, Wright, 27 July, 7 September 1703.
22 ADM 106/3578, Wright, 27 July 1703.
23 D Baugh, *British Naval Administration in the Age of Walpole* (Princeton, 1965), 386–90; ADM 110/4, 8 December 1703; ADM 111/25, 25 July 1734.
24 ADM 111/1, 2 December 1702.
25 ADM 110/4, 1 April 1702; ADM 111/1, 26 November 1702.
26 ADM 111/1 9, 11 December 1702; ADM 111/25 24 February, 17 October 1735; ADM 110/19 p.131.
27 ADM 111/25 (Plymouth and Dover), 6 October 1735; ADM 111/26, 4 October 1738, 12 September 1739.
28 ADM 111/25, 13, 27 November 1734; ADM 111/26, 2, 16 October 1734, 6 June 1740.
29 ADM 110/2, 20 April, 5 December 1734; ADM 111/25, 8 November 1734, 5 February 1735.
30 NMM VAU/D/2, 10 November 1725; ADM 110/19, 3 September 1759.
31 ADM 110/2, 2, 5 December 1704.
32 ADM 110/2, 11 July 1705
33 ADM 174/1, 13 January, 22, 29 February 1698, 5 May 1699, 15 January 1700; ADM 106/520, St Lo 18 January, 22 April 1698; NMM VAU/D/1, 24 June 1698; ADM 174/14, 1 December 1747.
34 ADM 174/1, 4 August, 24 September, 1 October, 30 December 1697.
35 ADM 174/14, 30 September 1748.
36 ADM 174/4, 4 July 1713.
37 ADM 1/3595, 4 October 1703.
38 ADM 174/1, 19 August 1698; ADM 174/281, 1698–1699; ADM 1/3578, 29 October, 12 November 1703; ADM 1/3595, 4 October 1703.
39 ADM 174/3, 15 November 1710.
40 Staffordshire CRO, D 615/P(S)/1/1/22. I am grateful for information supplied by E Keough, Invincible Conservation (1744–1758) Limited.
41 ADM 174/2, 5 October 1709; NMM VAU/V/1, 10 November 1736; B Pool, 'Warship-Building by Contract', *MM*49 (1963), 107; ADM 106/2190, 1758.
42 ADM 106/1052, Vanbrugh, 8 December 1747; ADM 174/15, January, 3 June, 26 July 1757, 26 June 1758.
43 ADM 174/4, 9 January, 3 November 1713; ADM 174/281 (Speckett of Saltash).
44 Stephens, 'Plymouth Dock', Appendix C; ADM 174/1, 5 April 1700; ADM 174/2, 25 March 1709; Blake Tyson, 'Oak for the Navy', *Cumberland and Westmorland Ant. & Arch. Soc.* LXXXXVII (1988), 117–26; ADM 106/3578, Wright, 23 November 1703.
45 ADM 174/4, 2 May 1712; ADM 174/3, 26 April 1710, 21 September 1711.
46 ADM 174/4, 2 May 1712, 8 September 1713.
47 ADM 174/4, 12 May 1712.
48 ADM 174/4, 4 July 1748, 4 January, 20 March 1749.
49 Dorset CRO, D 124, Box 179; ADM 174/4, 27 March 1749.
50 ADM 174/15, 20 July, 26 August, 1 November 1758; British Library, Kings Ms 44.
51 Somerset CRO, DD/TB 10/10; ADM 174/14, 14 April 1748; ADM 174/15, 1 July 1757.
52 ADM 106/3578, 1 September 1704; ADM 106/432, 26 March 1693; ADM 106/1052, 27 December 1747; ADM 174/14, 14 December 1747.
53 ADM 3/61, 25 April 1749.
54 ADM 174/14, 17 January 1748.
55 ADM 174/14, 6 July, 30 September 1748.
56 ADM 106/432, 14 February 1693.
57 ADM 106/520, 8 February, 22 March 1698; NMM VAU/H/1, 1699.
58 ADM 3/61.
59 ADM 106/405, 25 September 1691; ADM 106/520, 26 April 1698; Baugh, *British Naval Administration*, 287–8; NMM VAU/D/3, 14–18 May 1745.
60 ADM 171/4, 4 January 1712; ADM 106/432, 27 March 1693; NMM VAU/H/1, 1699.
61 Oppenheim, 84; Baugh, *British Naval Administration*, 82–3; R Sedgwick, *The House of Commons 1715–1754* (London, 1970) I, 559–60; L Namier and J Brooke, *The House of Commons 1754–1790* (London, 1964) II, 220–1.
62 ADM 1/88, Lestock, 9 September 1746; DA Baugh (ed.), *Naval Administration, 1715–1750*, Navy Record Society (1977), 259–60.
63 ADM 1/87, Anson, 2 May 1747; ADM 174/14, 22 January, 7, 14 November, 8, 19 December 1747; Baugh, *British Naval Administration*, 283.
64 ADM 3/67, 16, 17, 18, 30 May, 1, 11 June 1759.
65 ADM 1/807, Hullock, 13 March 1759; RF Mackay, *Admiral Hawke* (Oxford, 1965), 212; ADM 3/67, 15 August, 10 September 1759; ADM 1/82, Hawke, 23 July 1759; ADM 1/802, Hanway, 31 August 1759.
66 ADM 1/802, Hanway, 14 October 1759; ADM 1/92, Hawke, 13, 14, 17, 21 October 1759.
67 Mackay, *Hawke*, 216–8.
68 ADM 3/67, 6 August, 24 December 1759; ADM 110/19, 13 August 1759; ADM 1/82, Hawke, 14 August 1759; S Gradish, *The Manning of the British Navy during the Seven Years War* (London, 1980), 163–4.
69 Gradish, *Manning*, 154–8; ADM 110/19, 3 September 1759.
70 ADM 174/15, 19 January 1759; D Erskine (ed.), *Augustus Hervey's Journal* (London, 1953), 300.
71 ADM 110/19, 3 September, 15 October, 14 November 1759; ADM 1/802, Hanway, 9 November 1759; Mackay, *Hawke*, 239.
72 ADM 106/272, 14 December 1759; ADM 1/802, Hanway, 28 December 1759; ADM 110/19, 26 December 1759; ADM 3/67, 7 February 1760.
73 Gradish, *Manning*, 167–8.

30 *Devon Men and the Navy, 1689–1815*

N A M Rodger

The great difficulty in assessing the county's contribution to the Navy during the eighteenth century is that we know so little about the relations of the Service with the country as a whole or any other county in particular, that it is difficult to know whether Devon was typical or exceptional. It may be hazarded that the Navy's chief non-economic impact on the county as a whole was as a service, an employment which Devon men followed for shorter or longer periods and in greater or lesser numbers. Something can be said about naval recruitment in Devon, but the available evidence comes almost entirely from the period from the 1770s onward, and without comparable figures from the late-seventeenth and early-eighteenth centuries it is difficult to know how much things had changed or were changing.

One thing which immediately strikes the observer is the surprisingly small number of prominent officers from Devon in the eighteenth-century Navy. The county which had given the Tudor Navy so many of its leading figures, and which still contained several considerable seaports, provided very few senior officers until the latter years of the eighteenth century. Only one of the great Devon seamen of the sixteenth century left a collateral descendant to carry his name into the eighteenth: Francis Drake, a younger son of the Drakes of Nutwell, who reached flag-rank and a knighthood during the American War.[1] Among his contemporaries were Captain Paul Henry Ourry (Fig. 30.1), one of three naval sons of a Huguenot immigrant, who married the heiress of George Treby of Plympton Erle, inherited his seat in Parliament and became Commissioner of the dockyard (1775–83),[2] and Admiral Lord Edgcumbe, who may just count as a Devon man since his seat of Mount Edgcumbe lay in the Devon half of the parish of Maker.[3] Sir Charles Pole, who reached flag rank during the Great Wars with France, was born in Stoke Damerel and came of a Devon family.[4]

Much more numerous were the naval incomers to the county, of whom one of the earliest seems to have been Captain Joseph Taylor, a Dorset man who bought a modest estate in the Teign valley about 1720.[5] Captain Philemon Pownoll, of a Cheshire family, who made a fortune by capturing the Spanish register ship *Hermione* in 1762 (Fig. 30.2) and invested it in an estate at Ashprington,[6] Captain Warwick Calmady, a member of a Cornish family, part of which had long been settled in Devon, acquired Mothecombe in the parish of Holbeton about 1750,[7] and at about that time Rear-Admiral John Pritchard retired to a house at Stoke Damerel near Plymouth.[8] Several members of the Graves family, of whom no fewer than seven reached active or retired flag rank, settled in Devon. Thomas, subsequently Admiral Lord Graves, himself born in Cornwall, married the heiress of Cadhay and died there in 1802.[9] His first cousin, Admiral Samuel Graves, purchased the Cockenhayes estate in Buckerell, near Honiton, and rebuilt there a house called Hembury Fort, while his nephew Vice-Admiral Sir Thomas Graves (son of a clergyman from County Londonderry) settled at Woodbine Hall, Combe Raleigh.[10] In the late eighteenth century a number of other officers bought or inherited Devon estates, including Rear-Admiral Sir Thomas Troubridge, Admiral Sir John Laforey in St Budeaux near Plymouth, and Vice-Admiral Richard Incledon Bury at Swimbridge in north Devon.[11] Of all these, only Drake and Pole seem to have been unimpeachably Devon men, and taken together they do not suggest that the native gentry of Devon had any strong tradition of sending their sons to sea.

Only in the closing years of the eighteenth century, and particularly during the Great War against France, did the senior officers of the Navy begin to take a strong interest in Devon as a place to settle. This interest seems to have been concentrated around Plymouth and in the district around

30.1 Paul Henry Ourry (1719–83) as First Lieutenant, by Reynolds, now at Saltram House. *(National Trust)*

30.2 Captain Philemon Pownoll, from an engraving by John Spilsbury after a portrait by an unknown artist. *(Maurice Ash)*

30.3 Cadewell House, Cockington, Torbay, built by Captain, later Rear-Admiral, Sir Thomas Louis, who maintained there a considerable establishment, including peacocks. On his death aboard the *Canopus*, off Alexandria, in 1807, he was succeeded by his son, Admiral Sir John Louis, who resided there until his death in 1863. *(Devonshire Association)*

Torbay with which so many of them had become familiar during the years when the Channel Fleet used it as a base and Lord Vincent kept his headquarters at Torre Abbey. It is in this period, and apparently in this latter area alone of all Devon outside Plymouth, that the Navy began to make an impact on county society, and officers began to figure prominently at dinners and dances.[12] The watering-place of Torquay was largely founded in these years by naval wives anxious to lodge as near their husbands as possible,[13] and a number of senior officers bought estates nearby, including Lord Exmouth at Canonteign in the parish of Christow, Sir Thomas Louis (of French ancestry but born in Exeter) at Cadewell in Cockington (Fig. 30.3), and Sir John Duckworth at Wear in Topsham (Fig. 30.4).[14] Even with this infusion, however, the Navy remained sparsely represented among the landed families of the county, and in 1822 only five out of a list of 200 gentlemen's seats in Devon could be identified as belonging to sea officers.[15]

This evidence, however, effectively refers only to landowners, most of whom would have been elder sons, while sea officers were overwhelmingly drawn from landless younger sons.[16] Those who made their fortunes at sea

30.4 Admiral Sir John Duckworth (1748–1817), of Wear, Topsham. A memorial bust by Chantrey in St Margaret's Church, Topsham. *(J Youings, courtesy of the Vicar and Churchwardens)*

would certainly become landed gentlemen, but the large majority did not. This may account for the rather different figures produced by Michael Lewis from an analysis of those officers who in the 1840s gave O'Byrne information about their places of origin.[17] Of about 1,500 officers, 123 (8 per cent) came from Devon, which was the greatest number from any county in Britain, and the second greatest (after Hampshire) in proportion to the population of the county.[18] These statistics need to be approached with caution: Lewis's sample was certainly not typical of the commissioned officers of the Great War against France because O'Byrne listed only those who were still alive on 1 January 1845 – and were therefore among the youngest – and because the sample who mentioned their homes seems to have been biased towards those who came of landed families.[19]

Fortunately Lewis's figures can be compared with others from documentary sources, and these broadly confirm them. Between 1789 and 1791 334 officers whose baptismal certificates survive passed their lieutenant's examination. Of these, 28 (8 per cent) came from Devon (Table 30.1). It was the leading county after Middlesex, most of whose births came from the four or five parishes of the West End and doubtless represent families up for the season as much as permanent residents. The same factor somewhat inflates the figure for Somerset (including Bath), and perhaps those of Dublin and Midlothian (including Edinburgh). Another sample of 676 young gentlemen qualifying in navigation at the Royal Naval College in 1816–17, and therefore born in the closing years of the eighteenth century, gives similar results. London has replaced Middlesex, evidently because of a looser definition embracing the Middlesex suburbs, and Hampshire has overtaken Devon, but the proportion of Devon men, 63 or 9 per cent, remains much the same as before (Table 30.2.)

Lewis's conclusion is therefore confirmed, which naturally raises the question of why a county so prominent as a recruiting ground for junior officers should have yielded so few native admirals. Perhaps if we had figures for earlier periods they would show that Devon had only recently risen to this prominence, so that the young Devon officers had not yet had time to reach flag rank. Perhaps the indifference of the established county families meant that the Devon officers came from less influential backgrounds – though outside influence on naval promotions was severely limited in its effects.[20] It is notable that in both samples half of the Devon officers had

Table 30.1
Places of Birth of Lieutenants Passing 1789–91

Middlesex	39			
Devon	28	(8%), of which 14 born in Plymouth, Stoke Damerel or Stonehouse.		
Hampshire	23	of which 11 born in Portsmouth, Portsea or Gosport.		
Kent	20	of which 5 born in Rochester, Gillingham, Queenborough, Woolwich or Deptford.		
Somerset	13		Surrey	8
Dublin	13		Yorkshire	8
Cornwall	11		Norfolk	6
Dorset	9		co. Cork	6
Midlothian	9		Suffolk	5
Essex	8		West Lothian	5
London	8		Glamorgan	5

England	229 (69%)
Ireland	41 (12%)
Scotland	40 (12%)
Wales	12
Americas	10
Elsewhere	2
Total	334

Sources: Baptismal certificates attached to Lieutenants' Passing Certificates in PRO, ADM 107/12–14

Table 30.2
Places of Birth of Lieutenants Passing 1816–17

London	78	
Hampshire	64	of which 37 born in Portsmouth, Portsea or Gosport.
Devon	63	(9%) of which 31 born in Plymouth or Stoke Damerel.
Kent	48	of which 20 born in Chatham, Rochester, Woolwich, Gillingham or Deptford.

Surrey	20	Berkshire	8
Dublin	19	Staffordshire	8
Cornwall	18	Yorkshire	8
Midlothian	17	co. Limerick	8
Somerset	15	Cheshire	7
Norfolk	14	Isle of Wight	7
India	14	Durham	6
Suffolk	13	Lancashire	6
Essex	12	co. Wexford	6
Sussex	11	Canada	6
Dorset	10	Warwickshire	5
Middlesex	10	Aberdeenshire	5
Northumberland	10	Angus	5
Wiltshire	9	Jamaica	5
co. Cork	9		

England	500 (74%)
Ireland	72 (11%)
Scotland	58 (9%)
Wales	8
Channel Is., IoM	7
Americas	14
Elsewhere	17
Total	676

Source: Records of candidates for lieutenant passing in navigation at the Royal Naval College Portsmouth, in PRO, ADM 6/119.

been born in the immediate vicinity of the dockyard at Plymouth, and most of the remainder in the south-west corner of the county. By comparison, Hampshire also shows one half born near the dockyard but the other half broadly scattered across the county, while Kent, with no fewer than four dockyards, shows only a moderate concentration near Chatham in the second sample (which might be as much military as naval) (Table 30.2). The implication seems to be that Devon as a whole was much less influenced by the Navy than its contribution of officers might suggest, but that Plymouth and its neighbourhood were connected strongly to the Navy, and weakly to the rest of the county.

Likewise in politics, which often carried ambitious persons into parts of the country with which they had no natural links, Devon had weak naval connections. Its Parliamentary seats tended to be occupied by local men, and offered less opportunities to the sea officer than, say, Cornwall.[21] Even Plymouth, commonly reckoned an Admiralty borough, by no means always returned a sea officer, and from 1754 to 1788 was represented by Lord Barrington, the Secretary at War.[22] From 1784 to 1790 Captain John MacBride sat for the city, and from 1790 to 1796 Admiral Gardner, one of the Lords of the Admiralty, but in 1797 Charles Pole was unable to get elected in spite of being both an admiral and a local man. He finally succeeded in 1806, backed by strong administration pressure and ferocious threats from Lord St Vincent, but lost his seat again in 1818 when government support was withdrawn.[23] At Dartmouth in 1757 'the Corporation have desired a seaman, so I proposed Captain Howe'.[24] Rodney represented Okehampton for two years,[25] and Pocock sat for the other Plymouth seat 1760–1768.[26] John Clevland, Secretary of the Admiralty 1751–1763, with a large influence at Barnstaple where his father had established the family, himself sat for Saltash or Sandwich, and put his elder son in for Barnstaple.[27] Sir Edward Pellew was elected for Barnstaple in 1802, partly as the candidate of the anti-Clevland faction, but it cost him £2,000 and he did not repeat the experiment. Lord Cochrane took the notoriously venal seat of Honiton in 1806, but dishonoured his agent's bills and was soon replaced by his fellow-officer, Sir Charles Hamilton.[28] Most Devon seats, however, remained firmly in the hands of the county families, and naval men, like nabobs and other rich outsiders, had to buy their way into corrupt boroughs or force their way in as clients of government. There seems to have been virtually no established naval influence in county politics, even in the seaports, except for the Admiralty influence in Plymouth.

In the recruitment of naval ratings it seems that Devon was as prominent as any county with numerous seaports and seamen was bound to be. We still lack any detailed account of the mechanisms by which the Navy in the eighteenth century recruited its men, but work on the middle years of the century suggests that in peacetime it was manned almost entirely by regular seamen and seafarers, particularly from the deep-sea trades, and Devon ports undoubtedly contributed their share.[29] The actual means of attracting men to ships seem at that time to have been largely personal, with people joining ships where they had friends or connections, and above all joining captains and officers to whom they had become attached by previous service.[30] It was customary to open a 'rendezvous' (a recruiting depot) in London, from which parties of men would from time to time come down to join their new ship, but muster books generally suggest that most men came in in ones or twos over time, and that there were few geographical links between them and their ship. In wartime, impressment was used to obtain the essential minimum proportion of seamen from the merchant service at a time when there was an acute scarcity of experienced men. To a limited extent this was done ashore, chiefly in the seaport suburbs where seamen dwelt, but the principle effort was at sea, stopping homeward-bound British merchantmen within soundings and taking men out of them.[31] At the same time the Navy recruited numbers of landmen, and officers who came of landed families, as so many of them did, seem often to have gathered landmen from their home districts if not from their ancestral estates.[32] Here a lack of Devon captains drawn from the local gentry, and perhaps the presence of sufficient work on Devon farms and in its industries, would have led naturally to an absence of the large bodies of landmen which can be found following magnates from remoter or poorer counties. In Cornwall, for example, a number of senior officers including Lord Mount Edgcumbe, whose political and territorial connections were as much in Cornwall as in Devon, and Boscawen, with his strong sense of Cornish identity, built up extensive followings largely composed of their fellow countrymen.[33] Boscawen's death in 1761 was described as 'an event which greatly affects this county, there being a vast number of Cornishmen whose bread, and hopes of preferment depended entirely on him'.[34] Nothing similar to this happened in Devon at the same period.

Evidence for the geographical pattern of naval recruitment is scarce before the mid-eighteenth century, but some light is shed by a series of Orders in Council in 1693, 1694 and 1696, instructing the Vice-Admirals of the maritime counties to impress men for the Navy. In these orders Devon was allotted by far the largest individual quota: 1,300 men (Table 30.3). This is clear evidence that Devon men were believed to use the sea more than those of other counties, but unfortunately it is not clear on what the belief was based, nor how accurate it was. It is not even certain that the Vice-Admirals succeeded in levying the number of men for which they had been assessed. The order in which the counties appear in Table 30.3, therefore, cannot be taken at face value as an estimate of the ratios of their seafaring populations, if only because the kingdom's largest and most populous port, London, is conspicuously omitted.

Devon recruitment can be studied with rather more confidence from the muster books of ships commissioning at Plymouth during the American War, the first period at which information about ratings' place of birth was recorded. A total of 12 ships which commissioned there between the years 1770 and 1778, and whose musters are complete enough to be usable for this purpose, record the place of birth of 2,923 ratings, of whom 693 – rather less than a quarter – were born in Devon. They came from 128 parishes which

Table 30.3
Impressment from the Maritime Counties, 1693–96

Devon	1,300
Northumberland & Durham	800
Bristol	500
Hampshire & Isle of Wight	500
Dorset	500
Suffolk	500
Norfolk	500
Yorkshire	500
South Wales	300
Sussex	300
Essex	300
Cinque Ports	300
Lancashire & Cheshire	300
South Cornwall	250
Gloucestershire	200
North Wales	200
Cumberland & Westmorland	200
Somerset	200
Kent	200
Lincolnshire	150
North Cornwall	100
Total	8,100

Sources: PRO, T 1/47 fo. 72; T 11/13 pp.30, 95, & 237 (printed in *Calendar of Treasury Books* X, pp. 45–6, 488–9, 1290–1).

can be identified, of which 56 yielded one man each, and only 26 yielded five men or more (Table 30.4). These centres of recruitment were nearly all seaports or in their vicinity, and most were on the south coast and around Plymouth. In Table 30.5 the Devon recruits' places of birth are sorted into four geographical groups: those on the south coast west of the Start, the south coast east of the Start, the north coast, and inland parts (more than five miles from navigable water). Thirty-nine per cent came from the southwest coast, and a further 30 per cent from the southeast coast. More than half the recruits were rated petty officers or able seamen, and were therefore already experienced men when they joined their ships, and all but 5 per cent were volunteers. These proportions show a slightly higher proportion of newcomers to the sea than in the run of English counties.

Two of the 12 ships were commanded by Devon captains: Pownoll of the *Apollo*, and James Hawker, son of a Plymouth merchant family, of the *Mermaid*.[35] Another captain, Samuel Barrington of the *Prince of Wales*, was Lord Barrington's brother and consequently had Westcountry connections. Nevertheless, the evidence of territorial recruitment in Devon, unlike in Cornwall, is weak. Indeed, few of these ships appear to have made any particular attempt to recruit Devon men beyond the immediate area of Plymouth. Most of them sent up recruiting parties to London, as was the custom, but only two captains sent parties into Devon, in both cases no farther than the South Hams. Pownoll had a rendezvous at Totnes (near his home), and Captain MacBride of the *Bienfaisant* (himself an Ulsterman) had a party in and around Dartmouth.[36] This was the obvious area to try, for in the 1770s Dartmouth and its outports still had more seamen than any other port in Devon.[37]

This pattern of recruitment, with almost all men volunteers, ought to be a fair reflection of Devon's 'natural' naval connections. The impression given is of a county surprisingly unaffected by the presence of the Navy at Plymouth and Torbay. A numerous population of seamen contributed substantially to naval manpower, but recruitment ashore was concentrated in Plymouth and its immediate surroundings. It seems to have been the sea and not the land which linked Devon men to the Navy. Those who went to sea encountered the Service, and many served in it, but those who stayed ashore were affected by it only if they lived in or near Plymouth. How typical Devon was in this is difficult to say without the full analysis of the Navy's recruitment and manning, which we still lack. From Table 30.6 it will be seen that Devon was by far the most significant contributor to manning these

Table 30.4
Devon Parishes Yielding Five or More Men, 1770–79

Plymouth	133	(Total for Devon: 693)
Stoke Damerel	56	
Exeter (all parishes)	39	
Barnstaple	22	
Buckfastleigh	21	
Dartmouth	21	
Modbury	16	
Staverton	15	
Bideford	13	
Tavistock	13	
Totnes	13	
Ashburton	12	
Stoke Gabriel	12	
Highweek	10	
Plympton St Mary	10	
Topsham	10	
Dartington	9	
Stonehouse	9	
Paignton	8	
Tiverton	8	
Berry Pomeroy	7	
Crediton	7	
Brixham	5	
Churston Ferrers	5	
Cornwood	5	

Sources: the following musters in the PRO:

ADM 36/7587	*Defence* 74	March 1770 (Commissioned)
ADM 36/7382	*Gibraltar* 20	June 1770
ADM 36/7562	*Argo* 28	February 1775
ADM 36/7932	*Solebay* 28	August 1775
ADM 36/7761	*Mermaid* 28	April 1776
ADM 36/7899	*Prince of Wales* 74	November 1776
ADM 36/8695	*Queen* 90	November 1776
ADM 36/8299	*Bienfaisant* 64	November 1776
ADM 36/8022	*Apollo* 32	January 1777
ADM 36/7860	*Blenheim* guardship	March 1777
ADM 36/8072	*Yarmouth* 64	April 1777
ADM 34/651	*Rattlesnake* 12	April 1779

Table 30.5
Devon Recruitment by Region and Skill 1770–79

Region	PO, Ab & Idlers Vol.	PO, Ab & Idlers Pressed	Ordy., LM & Svts. Vols.	Ordy., LM & Svts. Pressed	Totals
SW Coast	156	2	109	4	271 = 39%
SE Coast	124	6	65	15	210 = 30%
Inland	49	0	61	1	111 = 16%
N Coast	31	2	21	0	54 = 8%
unidentified	14	1	29	3	47 = 7%
Totals	374 = 54%	11 = 2%	285 = 41%	23 = 3%	693
England	59%	3%	35%	3%	

Sources: as for Table 30.4

Devon ships, providing more than twice as many men as Cornwall and more than three times as many experienced men. The other counties, and countries, which contributed to manning these ships were mostly those with large seaports and seafaring populations, and it is an open question whether Devon weighed any more heavily in the manning statistics of the Navy as a whole than the size of its seafaring population would indicate. It certainly contributed heavily to those ships commissioning at Plymouth. Since only two of them made any attempt to recruit in the county (even a few miles away from Plymouth), since almost all these men were volunteers (and few were turned over from other ships), a great many of these men must have

Table 30.6
Recruitment Compared by Counties and Countries, 1770–79

County	PO, Ab & Idlers Vol.	Pressed	Ordy., LM & Svts. Vols.	Pressed	Totals
Devon	374	11	285	23	693 (24%)
Cornwall	129	3	191	4	327
co. Dublin	43	6	124	2	175
London	77	1	45	8	131
co. Cork	56	6	46	4	112
Northumberland	56	5	5	0	66
co. Waterford	31	2	24	6	63
Lancashire	41	5	8	3	57
Middlesex	40	1	9	5	55
Gloucestershire	29	5	16	2	52
Yorkshire	31	6	5	0	42
Kent	31	2	8	0	41
Somerset	21	0	15	3	39
Cumberland	28	7	3	0	38
Argyll	26	1	3	0	30
Dorset	23	1	5	0	29
Lanarkshire	21	4	3	1	29
Hampshire	24	0	4	0	28
Norfolk	23	0	4	0	27
Suffolk	20	2	4	0	26
New England	16	1	9	0	26
Surrey	19	0	5	0	24
Essex	21	0	2	0	23
co. Kilkenny	7	0	15	1	23
Angus	21	0	1	0	22
Durham	19	0	1	0	20
Pembrokeshire	11	1	7	1	20
co. Down	12	1	7	0	20
co. Tipperary	4	0	16	0	20
Aberdeenshire	20	0	0	0	20
England	1,080	58	641	50	1,829 (63%)
Ireland	226	21	315	15	577 (20%)
Scotland	225	13	21	1	260 (9%)
Americas	50	5	22	0	77 (3%)
Wales	48	3	18	4	73 (2%)
Foreign	49	5	19	0	73 (2%)
Other*	27	0	7	0	34 (1%)
Totals	1,705 (58%)	105 (4%)	1,043 (36%)	70 (2%)	2,923

* Channel Isles, Isle of Man, born at sea.

Sources: as for Table 30.4

made their own way to Plymouth to join their ships, presumably drawn by some previous knowledge or connection. Nevertheless, the figures in these tables, fragmentary and incomplete though they are, suggest that the Navy's influence on Devon as a whole was not necessarily much greater than it would have been over any maritime county not possessed of a dockyard or other close links with the Navy. It was only the specific area of southern and western Devon, especially Plymouth itself and the South Hams, and to a lesser extent the towns on and near the south coast, which had any special relationship with the Navy.

It is interesting to compare the pattern of recruitment during the American War with the 1795 and 1796 Quota Acts, the first attempt to introduce anything like a national conscription for the Navy. There were in fact three Quota Acts in 1795, which levied respectively the counties of England and Wales, the seaports of Britain, and the counties, burghs, and towns of Scotland (including seaports).[38] The assessment on the ports was apparently based on the tonnage registered in each,[39] but it is not clear how the county assessments were calculated. They look roughly proportional to population, but as the first national census was not held until 1801, in this respect the administration can only have been guessing. In 1796 two Quota Acts were passed, for England and Wales and for Scotland, and that for England was based on a new principle. The counties were levied as a whole for either the Navy or the Army, Devon being among the naval counties.[40] The assessments of the leading counties are set out in Table 30.7, which shows that the three Quota Acts produced widely different levies on the individual counties. Devon was fifth in the 1795 county assessment, fifth again in the total levied on its ports, and fourth according to the 1796 formula, which was consistent enough, but London was sixteenth as a county in 1795, first by an enormous margin as a port, and in 1796 was levied for the Army. The 847 to be found from the ports of Devon was made up thus: Dartmouth 394, Exeter 186, Plymouth 96, Barnstaple 74, Bideford 48, and Ilfracombe 49.[41] Dartmouth indeed ranked tenth among all the ports of England. Probably the port assessments of 1795 are the only ones which can be assumed to have borne some relation to the actual seafaring populations of those places, and the two county assessments are evidence of the difficulty an eighteenth-century government had in acquiring usable statistics, rather than a useful measure of the real value of the respective counties as recruiting grounds. Certainly their relationship with each other, and with the 1690s assessments, seems eccentric.

Thirty years after the American War, about the time of Trafalgar, another analysis of ships commissioning at Plymouth suggests how much had changed (Tables 30.8–10). By this time naval recruitment was handled almost entirely centrally by the Impress Service, and there seems to have been very little recruitment by individual ships – none at all by large ships. Almost all newly-raised men came from the receiving ship *Salvador del Mundo*, and more than half of all the men in the sample were turned over directly from other ships. This makes it impossible to produce figures for the proportions of pressed men, but it was clearly much higher than during the American War, and there is ample other evidence of deterioration in the manning situation. The ratio of skilled to unskilled men had almost reversed (Tables 30.6 and 10). The proportion of Englishmen had fallen from 63 per

Table 30.7
Quota Act Naval Assessments

County	1795 County	1795 Ports	1796 County
Yorkshire	1,081	1,629	612 (+ 789 army)
Lancashire	589	1,891	763
Middlesex	451	–	(army)
Kent	450	606	570
Devon	393	847	509
Somerset	351	44	455
Lincolnshire	342	60	323 (+ 121 army)
Surrey	323	–	(army)
Suffolk	263	116	341
Norfolk	260	794	337
Cheshire	246	25	(army)
Staffordshire	245	–	(army)
Essex	244	322	316
Hampshire	236	267	306
Gloucestershire	201	694	261
London	198	5,704	(army)
Cornwall	194	224	252
Derbyshire	194	–	(army)
Warwickshire	193	–	(army)
Cumberland	184	710	238
Leicestershire	183	–	(army)
Northumberland	176	1,283	228
Salop	176	–	(army)
co. Durham	173	742	224
Sussex	172	224	223
Nottinghamshire	161	–	(army)
Wiltshire	160	–	(army)

Source: Statutes 35 Geo. III, c.5 & c.9; 37 Geo. III, c.4.

cent to 47 per cent, and of Devon men from 24 per cent to 7 per cent. This must be partly a reflection of the general decline in the numbers of skilled men (predominantly English), and the increase in the unskilled (mainly Irish), and it probably also reflects a central rather than a local recruitment system, eliminating whatever Devonian influence on Plymouth ships there had been in the 1770s. Even so, the fall in Devon's naval recruitment seems precipitate, and may also reflect the decline during the same period of Devon's ports and seaborne trade. There is nothing in the figures for 1805 to suggest that naval influence was any more widespread in Devon than it had been thirty years before (Tables 30.5 and 30.9).

The reasons for this must have been bound up with economics and communications. Devon's industries remained prosperous until well into the eighteenth century,[42] and when they did decline the naval wage was falling so far behind inflation that even the poor were not tempted away to sea. From 1653 to 1797 an able seaman in the Navy earned 22s 6d a lunar month, net of fixed deductions. As a result of the 1797 mutinies this was raised to 28s a month net, and in 1806 raised again to 32s net.[43] Ordinary seamen and landmen earned less. By comparison, wages in the Exeter woollen trade were 6s to 10s a week in the 1780s, though the work was not always continuous, and of course the worker was not found in food and lodging.[44] This was before the rapid price inflation of the war years.[45] Merchant seamen's wages varied a great deal between different ports and trades, but in the first half of the century they seem to have averaged about 29s a month in peacetime, and 42s in wartime.[46] At London in 1768 the seamen successfully struck for 40s a month.[47] In 1792, just before the War with France, a seaman in the Baltic trade might earn 30s a month, but during the war this rose to as much as five guineas.[48] By 1815 merchant seamen's wages in various trades ranged from 35s to 60s, though in real as opposed to cash terms the advantage over men-of-warsmen was less.[49]

As for communications, Devon roads were notoriously bad, and into the nineteenth century there were parishes with little or no wheeled transport.[50] This was no doubt one thing which deterred sea officers from settling there until the spread of the turnpikes in the latter years of the eighteenth century, and the bad roads were a very practical obstacle to the spread of naval

Table 30.8
Devon Parishes Yielding Five or More Men, 1804–5

Plymouth	63	
Exeter	28	
Stoke Damerel	24	
Barnstaple	12	
Ashburton	9	
Tavistock	9	
Totnes	8	
Kingsbridge	6	
Tiverton	6	
Brixham	5	
Stonehouse	5	Total for Devon: 272

Sources: the following musters in the PRO:

ADM 36/16457–8	*Hibernia* 110	November 1804 (Commissioned)
ADM 36/17134	*Martin* 18	February 1805
ADM 36/17008	*Avon* 18	March 1805
ADM 36/17220	*Wolverine* 18	March 1805
ADM 36/17189	*Surinam* 18	March 1805
ADM 37/192	*Thunderer* 74	April 1805
ADM 36/17403	*Caesar* 80	May 1805
ADM 36/17216	*Weazle* 18	May 1805
ADM 36/17030	*Brisk* 18	May 1805
ADM 36/17408	*Audacious* 74	June 1805
ADM 36/15867	*Captain* 74	June 1805
ADM 36/16431	*London* 90	August 1805
ADM 36/17353	*Pompée* 80	October 1805

Table 30.9
Devon Recruitment by Region and Skill 1804–5

Region	PO, Ab & Idlers	Ordy., LM & Svts.	Totals
SW Coast	49	63	112 (41%)
SE Coast	32	33	65 (24%)
Inland	11	30	41 (15%)
N Coast	11	16	27 (10%)
unidentified	7	20	27 (10%)
Totals	110 (40%) (cf England 42%)	162 (60%) (cf England 58%)	272

Sources: as for Table 30.8

Table 30.10
Recruitment Compared by Counties and Countries, 1804–5

County	PO, Ab & Idlers	Ordy., LM & Svts.	Totals
London	123	162	285
co. Dublin	45	232	277
Devon	110	162	272 (7%)
co. Cork	43	178	221
Lancashire	54	124	178
Gloucestershire	36	97	138
Kent	42	67	109
Yorkshire	48	38	86
Somerset	20	58	78
Hampshire	39	35	74
co. Waterford	20	53	73
co. Antrim	16	53	69
Northumberland	48	19	67
Norfolk	45	20	65
Germany*	28	35	63
co. Wexford	11	49	60
Midlothian	35	19	54
co. Down	12	41	53
Cumberland	34	15	49
Dorset	19	30	49
Surrey	15	33	48
co. Limerick	6	41	47
Middlesex	13	31	44
Renfrewshire	23	20	43
co. Durham	38	4	42
Portugal (+ islands)	9	33	42
co. Londonderry	7	34	41
New York	17	22	39
Sweden	20	19	39
Essex	20	18	38
Lanarkshire	15	23	38
co. Kilkenny	2	33	35
co. Tipperary	3	32	35
co. Wicklow	3	32	35
Cheshire	7	27	34
Glamorgan	8	24	32
Isle of Man	6	24	30
co. Donegal	0	29	29
co. Kildare	2	26	28
Pembrokeshire	8	19	27
Pennsylvania	12	15	27
Denmark	14	13	27
Argyll	9	17	26
Lincolnshire	12	13	25
Wiltshire	7	18	25
Angus	14	11	25
co. Carlow	4	21	25
Suffolk	11	13	24
Jersey	3	19	22
co. Meath	0	20	20
England	880	1,219	2,099 (47%)
Ireland	217	1,076	1,293 (29%)
Scotland	202	163	365 (8%)
Wales	57	92	149 (3%)
Channel Is. & IoM	15	46	61 (1%)
Americas	94	134	228 (5%)
Foreign	106	173	279 (6%)
Totals	1,571 (35%)	2,903 (65%)	4,474

* including Danzig, Reval and other Baltic towns

Sources: as for Table 30.8

influence outside Plymouth. It was the focal point of sea communications from all the western parts of Britain and Ireland – in Tables 30.6 and 30.10 the prominence of the western counties over the eastern is marked – but in practice remote from much of the county in which it lay. As late as the 1750s the Devon roads were considered to present a worse threat than enemy action, and all supplies for Plymouth, even gold, went by sea. In 1757 the *Tartar* attacked, and fortunately took, a French privateer off the Isle of Wight while herself carrying £40,000 to Plymouth to pay the last quarter's wages to the Yard.[51] The spread of turnpikes began to improve the situation in the second half of the century, and by the American War Plymouth was linked by turnpike to Exeter and London.[52] For long afterwards, however, the county remained self-sufficient in spirit, independent of the Navy as of all central government and unbeholden to it. Even Plymouth long had poor relations, and poor communications, with the naval town around the dock,[53] and during the Seven Years War the magistrates of the city did not hesitate to arrest sea officers who appeared in Plymouth in search of deserters.[54] There is no doubt that the naval influence on Devon was growing throughout the eighteenth century, both absolutely and relatively as other industries and ports declined. By the mid-century 'Greater' Plymouth was probably more populous than Exeter, and in the 1801 census the city of Plymouth with the parishes of Stonehouse and Stoke Damerel (including Dock) had a combined population of 43,000, compared with Exeter's 17,000.[55] This must have been very largely the consequence of the naval presence and naval investment. What is less clear is whether Devon felt itself, even in 1815, to be a particularly 'naval' county. The Navy was certainly prominent locally, around Plymouth and to a lesser extent in Torbay, but the county as a whole gives an impression of rural independence from national institutions of all sorts and, in inland parts, from the sea. Whether this was unlike the other 'dockyard counties' of Hampshire and Kent cannot yet be answered, but it looks as though, at least as late as 1815, Plymouth and the Navy faced outwards towards the sea and other seaports more than they looked inwards into Devon.

30: Devon Men and the Navy, 1689–1815

1 D & S Lysons, *Magna Britannia* VI: *Devonshire* (1822), cxxi.
2 Lewis Namier and John Brooke, *The History of Parliament: The House of Commons 1754–90* (1964), III, 240.
3 Lysons, *Magna Britannia*, VI, 326.
4 RG Thorne, *The History of Parliament: The House of Commons 1790–1820* (1986), IV, 841; BH Williams, *Ancient Westcountry Families and their Armorial Bearings* (Penzance, 1916), I, 54.
5 JS Bromley, 'The Profits of Naval Command: Captain Joseph Taylor and his Prizes', in J Schneider, ed., *Wirtschaftskräfte und Wirtschaftswege II: Wirtschafskräfte in der Europäischen Expansion, Festschrift für Hermann Kellenbenz* (Stuttgart, 1978), 529–44 (reprinted in JS Bromley, *Corsairs and Navies 1660–1760* (1987), 449–62).
6 JS Corbett, *England in the Seven Years War: A Study in Combined Strategy* (1907), II, 321; Robert Beatson, *Naval and Military Memoirs of Great Britain from 1727 to 1783* (1804), III, 419; Lysons, *Magna Britannia*, VI, 15.
7 Richard Polwhele, *The History of Devonshire* (1797–1806), III, 456. (I owe this reference to the kindness of Mr Stephen Pugsley and Dr Michael Duffy.) Polwhele states that Calmady bought Mothecombe, but Williams, *Ancient Westcountry Families* I, 48, that he, or at least his family, inherited it from the Pollexfens.
8 List of seats appended to Benjamin Donn, *A Map of the County of Devon* (1765) (*ex inf.* Mr Stephen Pugsley and Dr Michael Duffy).
9 Lysons, *Magna Britannia*, VI, 378.
10 Lysons, *Magna Britannia*, VI, 77, 138, 386.
11 Lysons, Magna Britannia, VI, cxxx, cxxxi, cxxxvii, 467.
12 See, e.g., DH Cozens, 'The Kitson Diaries', *DCNQ* XXXIII (1974–77), 78, 122, 159.
13 WG Hoskins, *Devon* (1954), 118.
14 Lysons, *Magna Britannia*, VI, xc, cxix, Thorne, *House of Commons 1790–1820*, IV, 756; and GD Woollcombe, 'Sir Thomas Louis', *DAT* 64, 249–56.
15 Lysons, *Magna Britannia*, VI, ccxxvi–ccxxix.
16 NAM Rodger, *The Wooden World: An Anatomy of the Georgian Navy* (1986), 258–9.
17 Michael Lewis, *A Social History of the Navy, 1793–1815* (1960); William O'Byrne, *A Naval Biographical Dictionary* (1849).
18 Lewis, *Social History*, 62.
19 Lewis, *Social History*, 27, 60–1. Lewis also took some information from John Marshall's *Royal Naval Biography* (1825), which included officers not below Commander's rank alive on 1st January 1823.
20 Rodger, *Wooden World*, 333–5.
21 In 1761 the MPs of Cornwall included three sea officers and four naval officials: LB Namier, *The Structure of Politics at the Accession of George III* (2nd ed., 1957), 355.
22 Namier & Brooke, *House of Commons 1754–90*, II, 55.
23 Thorne, *House of Commons 1790–1820*, II, 118–121; IV, 844.
24 Namier & Brooke, *House of Commons 1754–90*, I, 252.
25 Namier, *Structure of Politics*, 127–8. David Spinney, *Rodney* (1969), 164, 173.
26 Namier & Brooke, *House of Commons 1754–90*, III, 305.
27 Namier, *Structure of Politics*, 128, 210 n.5, Romney Sedgwick, *The History of Parliament: The House of Commons 1715–54* (1970), I, 559.
28 Thorne, *House of Commons 1790–1820*, II, 102–3, 111–12; III, 462.
29 Rodger, *Wooden World*, 153, 155.
30 Rodger, *Wooden World*, 119–24.
31 Rodger, *Wooden World*, 164–82.
32 Rodger, *Wooden World*, 155–7.
33 For Edgcumbe's followers see Namier, *Structure of Politics*, 34–6, 318–19. For Boscawen's see Rodger, *Wooden World*, 132, 156, 280–1, 286–7, 330, 336.
34 Namier & Brooke, *House of Commons 1754–90*, II, 103.
35 Crispin Gill, 'Some Diaries and Memoirs of Plymouth in the French Revolutionary and Napoleonic Wars', *DAT*, CXV (1983), 7.
36 PRO, Musters of *Apollo* and *Bienfaisant*, ADM 36/8022 and 8299.
37 WG Hoskins, *Industry, Trade and People in Exeter, 1688–1800* (Manchester, 1935), 170. See also chapter 14, above.
38 35 Geo. III c.5, c.19 and c.29. (I am indebted to Mr AN Ryan for his advice on the Quota Acts.)
39 JS Bromley, ed., *The Manning of the Royal Navy, Selected Public Pamphlets 1693–1873* (NRS 1974), 151, n.2, 154 n.
40 The 1796 acts are 37 Geo.III c.4 and c.5.
41 Not 41 as quoted by Oppenheim, 116.
42 Hoskins, *Devon*, 129–30, 208.
43 Conrad Gill, *The Naval Mutinies of 1797* (Manchester, 1913) 35; GE Manwaring & Bonamy Dobrée, *The Floating Republic* (1935), 257.
44 Rodger, *Wooden World*, 125, 137; Hoskins, *Exeter*, 130–131.
45 AJ Taylor, *The Standard of Living in Britain in the Industrial Revolution* (1975); MW Flinn, 'Trends in Real Wages, 1750–1850', *EcHR*, 2nd Ser. XXVII (1974), 395–413; GN von Tunzelmann, 'Trends in Real Wages, 1750–1850, Revisited', *EcHR* 2nd Ser. XXXII (1979), 33–49.
46 Marcus Rediker, *Between the Devil and the Deep Blue Sea: Merchant Seamen, Pirates and the Anglo-American Maritime World 1700–1750* (Cambridge & New York, 1987), 304–5.
47 PRO, ADM 7/299 No.40.
48 Simon Ville, 'Wages, prices and profitability in the shipping industry during the Napoleonic wars: a case study, *Journal of Transport History* 3rd Ser.II (1981), No.1, 48–51.
49 Jon Press, 'Wages in the Merchant Navy, 1815–54', *J. Transport Hist.*, 3rd Ser.II (1981), No.2, 48.
50 Hoskins, *Devon*, 151–2.
51 WH Long, *Naval Yarns* (1899), 50.
52 Hoskins, *Devon*, 151.
53 Hoskins, *Devon*, 151.
54 PRO, ADM 1/801, H Harrison to Admiralty, 3 August 1757.
55 Hoskins, *Devon*, 174.

31 *Industrial Relations at Plymouth Dockyard, 1770–1820*

ROGER MORRISS

IN ALL THREE WARS WITHIN this period, Plymouth briefly outgrew its easterly neighbour, Portsmouth, eventually doubling both the size of the total workforce and the number of its shipwrights (Fig. 31.1). Of all the problems of these years, that of managing this growing body of men was one of the most formidable, for the workforce was organised, articulate and always ready to protect its interests. Moreover, the period was one of innovation, in which new ideas for the organisation of labour were extended throughout the six major dockyards in England. In opposing the principal innovation, piecework for shipwrights, Plymouth took a lead. Not until after the turn of the century were all the problems involved in this innovation removed, and not until the Napoleonic War was the potential of the workforce in Plymouth Dockyard fully realised.

The difficulties between the Board of Admiralty and Navy Board in London and the workforce at Plymouth arose from the pursuit of ambitions on both sides. For its part the Admiralty recognised the need to meet wars of an ever-larger scale with more productive forms of employment than the traditional payment by the day. The skilled artificers on the other hand wished to preserve their relative independence during working hours to practise their craft, at the same time striving to achieve a standard of living commensurate to the apparent value of their skills.[1] These ambitions were not mutually exclusive. Yet a reconciliation of interests was handicapped by an unwillingness on the part of the Board of Admiralty to enter into prolonged negotiations – the reverse of its customary paternalism – or to apply to Parliament to obtain higher rates of pay. In consequence the system of employment at Plymouth was subject to prolonged periods of inefficient operation: first a period of suspicion on the part of the workforce, followed by one of unconscious maladministration on the part of the Navy Board.

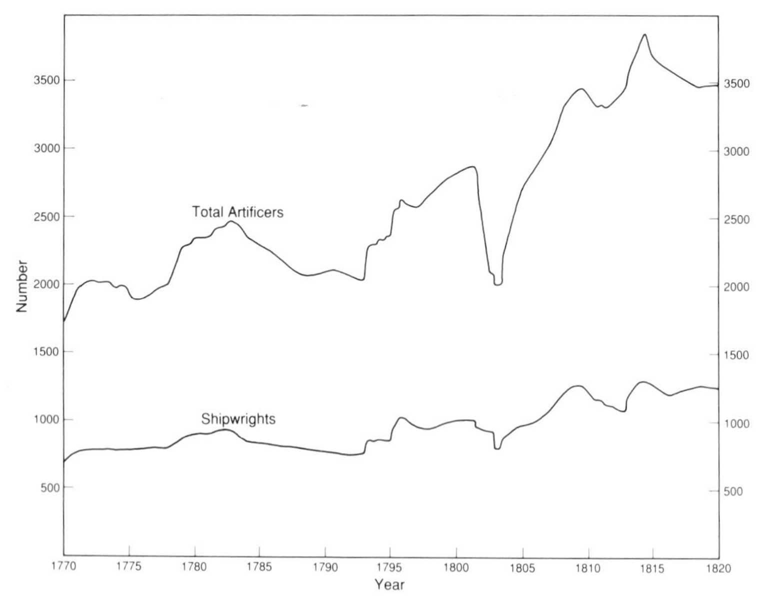

31.1 The number of shipwrights and the total number of Artificers in Plymouth Dockyard, 1770–1820.

Riots related to the problem of payment occurred in 1801, while greater efficiency was only achieved through inquiries, reports and liberalising administrative changes in the first half-decade of the new century.

Such problems also affected work and relations in the other five major dockyards in England, but geographical factors seem to have exacerbated difficulties at Plymouth, and to have made the workforce there, even in major disputes involving other yards, the most determined in their cause. First, being the most distant from the competition of the profit-making merchant building yards along the Thames, attitudes within the Plymouth workforce appear to have been more reactionary. Secondly, south Devon was a food-exporting region, not easily relieved from other areas during periods of food scarcity, while the supply of the fleet from Plymouth aggravated local shortages. The families of dockyard artificers consequently suffered severely during scarcities. Thirdly, the physical extent of the port often obliged artificers to work on ships under the authority of naval officers at considerable distances from the yard, for periods probably longer than common elsewhere. Vulnerability to naval discipline perhaps bred a more aggressive, defensive attitude. Certainly occasional incidents even in day-to-day relations with the navy indicated the necessity for the workforce to be constantly ready to defend itself.

The Workforce and the Navy

Some sea officers clearly held artificers in contempt. Trifling brushes with their authority were exaggerated into offences punishable by treatment humiliating and degrading to their victims. Such incidents inflamed the yard men and were inclined to grow unless prompt defusing action was taken. For example, on board the *Diomede* on 10 April 1782 a sea officer blocking the way past a carpenter's bench refused to move for Edward Higgins, a shipwright, to get through. On observing that there was no other way past, Higgins was beaten 'very much' and later that day took his case to an attorney. Next day an apprentice working on board the same ship accidentally stepped on the foot of a 'young gentleman' who immediately complained to the commanding officer. The apprentice was taken to the gangway and threatened with flogging, at which the shipwrights on board promptly left their work and took the boy on shore. Commissioner Ourry and Admiral Milbank, the port admiral, quickly stepped in to conciliate, the latter making a signal for all lieutenants in port and issuing a general memorandum concerning the treatment of yard artificers. Ourry had the memorandum read to the yard men at the Call Office, and then, 'fearing it might not be heard by all', read to each of the gangs in turn down at the yard, at which the men were satisfied.[2]

At the end of the century, when the Government was restricting civil liberties, the liability of the artificers to mistreatment appears to have increased. They were subjected to an Admiralty order which placed them, whilst on board ships, officially under the command of sea officers. In 1800 the Plymouth workmen, conceiving themselves 'placed if not under Martial Law yet not far therefrom removed', petitioned the Board of Admiralty to be again placed under 'their respective artificer officers and them only', improper behaviour to be reported by them to the yard commissioner or principal officers. In support of their petition they cited an incident on the brig *Sylph*, when a gang of caulkers was prevented from working the evening

31.2 Plymouth Dockyard 'in the county of Cornwall' (*sic*), by J Clevely, engraved by Carington and published 1772. (*National Maritime Museum*)

task after the Lieutenant ordered them off the quarterdeck, threatening to flog one of their number. Their Quarterman 'told him he had better not flog the man, and that he had a right to go to any part of the ship where his duty called him', at which the Lieutenant armed his Marines and confined the gang to the foredeck, where it was 'exposed to the inclemency of the weather' throughout a January night from 7 p.m. until 11 a.m. The Quarterman was kept prisoner until the yard boat arrived to take the gang ashore. The Board of Admiralty in fact complied with the petition, for which it received an expression of thanks from 'all the mechanics and workmen of Plymouth Dock yard'.[3]

The Problem of Payment

Working in a hostile environment, the artificers were clearly conscious that their security depended on their own efforts. Impressment was the main threat, from which they were theoretically protected, and unwarranted discharge another. Thus in 1793 the Plymouth ropemakers struck work even following the release from imprisonment of one of their number. He had insulted the captain responsible for pressing him, for which he was discharged by the yard commissioner. His 300 fellow ropemakers secured his reinstatement by remaining on strike for three days.[4] But this organisation for self-protection was also employed to achieve improvements in other terms of employment. The skilled men were particularly aware that their main defence was the demand for their skill, and they accordingly preserved it from dilution. Newly-entered men, unable to prove completion of a formal apprenticeship, were ritually 'horsed' from the yard: seized, placed astride poles carried on artificers' shoulders, paraded round the yard and out of the gate, there to be forcefully and humiliatingly deposited with their tools.

As the key trade and largest single group in the dockyard, the shipwrights took the lead in many of the issues between workforce and authority in Plymouth yard. After 1770 the main issue that specially concerned them was the proposed introduction of piecework. This overlay the issue which engaged all the trades, the antiquity of their basic rates of pay and the failure of government to raise them. Most of these rates had been established in the 1690s and not since been altered. As basic rates for the working day, they determined total earnings, pay for overtime being proportions of the daily rate. About a third was obtained for one and a half hours' overtime known as a Tide, and a complete day's pay was obtained for five extra hours known as a Night. During the mid-century wars, 1739–48 and 1756–63, the basic rates had not been a prime cause of dispute. Furthermore, not fully conscious of their growing bargaining power, artificers at Plymouth had remained relatively placid, on the periphery of combinations.[5] However, when they were deprived of their overtime by the peace in 1763, with food prices rising throughout southern England, petitions for higher basic rates of pay were organised in 1765, 1769 and 1772, a movement in which the Plymouth shipwrights began to take a lead. Although food prices in 1769 were more reasonable around Plymouth than about other Royal yards – as a contemporary, William Shrubsole, pointedly observed – the shipwrights there were so distressed 'that even they' initiated the proceedings of that year with 'circular letters' exhorting the other yards 'to unite in order to petition their Royal Master . . . for an increase of pay'.[6]

Unfortunately, from a political point of view, payment in the dockyards was a complicated package of earnings, allowances and perquisites, and, as the eighteenth century wore on, public attention focused on the allowances and perquisites rather than on the basic rates of pay. Apart from their daily wage and recompense for overtime, some dockyard artificers received the pay of their apprentices and all received a small lodging allowance, permitted from 'time out of mind'. But because of the intricacy of calculations, and the necessity for paybooks to be checked in London, payments were made quarterly and always late, especially at Plymouth, to where money was shipped from Portsmouth. Thus, for example, the wages for the western yard for Christmas quarter 1774 were not paid until May 1775.[7] To survive, artificers resorted to moneylenders, who made them advances on evidence of earnings – a certificate bought with a fee from a clerk to the Clerk of the Cheque. The cost of these advances materially reduced the value of artificers' total earnings; in 1770 William Shrubsole put the loss at 40s a year, or more than three weeks' pay for a shipwright; by 1805 credit cost 10 to 15 per cent and there were other 'vexatious conditions' as well.[8] It was inevitable that many artificers ran into debt, placing great store in consequence on their daily 'payment in kind', their perquisite of wood 'chips'. Attempts in 1756 and 1757 to regulate the amount of what was often a waste of good material caused riots at the eastern yards, and a proposal in 1783 to abolish the perquisite simply petered out.

However, if the Board of Admiralty was unwilling to obtain alterations in basic rates while allowances and perquisites existed, it had to permit concessions concerning other aspects of their employment during wartime when hostilities gave the artificers leverage. In 1781, at the height of the American War of Independence, the Comptroller of the Navy Board, Sir Charles Middleton, complained to Lord Sandwich that at that time they dared 'not contest a single point of duty with either shipwrights, caulkers or ropemakers'. Similarly, during the Revolutionary and Napoleonic wars, in the months spanning the Peace of Amiens bargaining power passed noticeably from the artificers to the Navy Board and back to the men when war resumed.[9]

The Question of Piecework

At Plymouth the shipwrights demonstrated their power in their resistance to piecework in 1775. By that time some yard trades – sawyers, ropemakers, and labourers – had long been paid by the piece, while between 1772 and 1774 'scavelmen', joiners, bricklayers, and house carpenters also started work by incentive schemes. A scheme for shipwrights had been 'agitated for many years', and in 1775 Lord Sandwich, First Lord of the Admiralty, felt himself right to persevere through every difficulty to establish it. A trial in all six yards thus occurred during the second quarter of that year, when 95 task gangs were formed representing 62 per cent of all shipwrights.[10] At Plymouth 26 gangs were formed comprising 390 shipwrights, 104 apprentices, and 27 quartermen. The same scheme was applied in each yard, standard prices per task being paid according to the total tonnage of the ships under construction. Later the Navy Board was to compare average wages at each yard. Portsmouth shipwrights made the least, at 3 shillings and sixpence a day, Chatham workers the highest at 4 shillings and threepence. Plymouth shipwrights did slightly better than those at Deptford and Sheerness and worse than those at Woolwich, making three shillings and tenpence farthing a day.[11] However, discontent at the scheme came to a head in mid-June 1775, during the visitation of the yards by Lord Sandwich and members of the Navy Board.

Opposition stemmed from a range of factors. Shipwrights claimed that the prices allowed for tasks were insufficient; that they laboured incessantly in weather 'uncommonly favourable', yet lost on the low-priced jobs what they gained on the high. The size and time allowed for each task was also too limited; each task ought to have been two or three times the size of those set, 'great inconvenience' arising from the 'shortness of the time'. Timber slabs were not cut to size by sawyers before they were needed; and when shaped there was no allowance for the discovery of defects in the timber. With such inconveniences, they could no longer apply their skills in the old way; yet 'bred in His Majesties yard' they could not 'slight their work'. Though paid only for the tasks they performed, in weather that prevented them from working they were not paid by the day or permitted to go out of the yard. Moreover, when accidents prevented individuals from working, they were not given a note entitling them to sick pay; 'one unfortunate moment may reduce whole families to the greatest distress'. Above all, they seemed to be trapped. Their work was of such an incessant, so laborious a nature, that they required more assistance; yet what they earned in the longer days would not afford them the means to procure it. 'What then must be our situation in the midst of an inclement winter?'[12]

At Portsmouth on 13 June the response of the Navy Board was but mildly reassuring. Nonetheless, after almost all the men in 21 task gangs failed to report for work, in consultation with Sandwich the Board conceded that the shipwrights need not work 'task' during the winter months. Most then returned to work, but a hard core stayed out, sending a request to Plymouth to support their demand that taskwork be abolished altogether.[13] At Plymouth, news of events came on 20 June in a private letter to a shipwright, Pascho Asford.

Commissioner Ourry had the Board's concession read out and persuaded the shipwrights to continue working until the Navy Board arrived. But on 23 June, on the Board's arrival at Plymouth, 390 shipwrights absented themselves from the yard. Ourry promptly directed the yard officers to inform them that they might return to Day work with one Tide extra. Yet still the shipwrights refused to go to their work 'till all their grievances were redressed'. The Board for its part refused to say anything further until work was resumed, declaring on the 25 June that the names of those men wishing to return to work would have to be submitted for consideration to the full board in London.[14] Over the next few days the shipwrights' mood grew angry, and in a memorandum they broadened their complaints – the 'grievances of an useful and distressed community' – to the fundamental causes of discontent.

> We pray a final dissolution of Task work and desire to be reinstated in the former mode of work, which has existed ever since the Institution of a yard in this place; this only exception, to implore your honours for two shillings and sixpence per Day, in consequence of the exceeding dearness of provisions and all the necessaries of life, being unable to support our Families on the present wages; likewise to revoke an order which signified the discharge of any man that should be out of the yard one month, sick or on Doctor's note; also the cutting off the odd pence at the end of every quarter from our wages (if less than sixpence).[15] The payment of the yard to be within six weeks after the expiration of the Quarter, for should it exceed one day of six months our distresses are aggravated by paying three pence in the Pound more Interest.

The Navy Board was neither sympathetic nor encouraging. In its view, the men knew it was not in the power of the Admiralty or Navy Board to grant higher basic rates of pay, and they totally misunderstood the order for discharge after one month's sick leave, which, after examination, was to deter malingerers. The memorandum in fact gave the Board reason to relinquish responsibility for resolving the dispute. Sandwich himself noted: 'as they now had avowed the real cause of their mutiny, namely the want of an increase of wages, it was very evident to us all that nothing could be done by us, as that is a matter of so much importance that it requires the interposition and direction of superior powers'.[16]

This neglect of complaints in the western yards was to broaden and prolong the whole strike. Previous to 27 June Portsmouth yard had returned almost to normal, but that morning two Plymouth shipwrights arrived to meet the Portsmouth yard committee and next morning all the Task gangs, the majority of the other shipwrights, and 16 caulkers, 'upwards of 500' men, stayed out of the yard. Furthermore, the two Plymouth shipwrights with two or three from Portsmouth went 'Express to the Eastern yards'. From Deptford and Woolwich, on 30 June they went to Chatham and Sheerness, with marked success. On 5 July a petition from the last three yards echoed that initially presented at Portsmouth, but requested in addition the reinstatement of their brethren at the two western yards. On 6 July 20 Task gangs absented themselves from Chatham yard; on 7 July all the Task gangs and two full Day gangs at Woolwich. Only Deptford was not affected. Sheerness was quiet but, according to Sandwich, only because the shipwrights did not want to lose free housing in hulks on the foreshore. By 14 July, with strikes holding firm at all four belligerent yards, orders were given for the official discharge of all absentee shipwrights.[17]

At Plymouth this order precipitated violence. Outside the yard the shipwrights had advertised for subscriptions to a strike fund, the Commissioner issuing a counter-statement 'to certify' the Navy Board's view of their claims. Within the yard, boat- and mast-house men who had been put to work at the dockside received threatening letters, were insulted by apprentices, had treenails thrown at them, and their tools thrown in the dock. Newly-entered men were insulted and pelted with treenails by the apprentices of absentees. On 18 July boys calling from the portholes of the *Rippon* (where they could not be identified) threatened the new men with horsing, which was carried out that evening. Two men were seized, placed on poles and carried to a field 'they call the Field of Liberty'. The commissioner pursued them there, where he entered upon a constant noise of 'Liberty'. Looking about, he saw the two new men clambering over the hedge amid a shower of missiles. Some came in his direction and he was later to reflect how fortunate he was to have received no damage; he was even more glad to have escaped the horror of being tarred and feathered, which he was informed some of the men had been inclined to inflict.[18]

Thereafter the violence subsided into a peaceful and confident defiance. Now discharged, the shipwrights arranged to collect tool chests and requested the appointment of a day to receive outstanding wages. Initially they still considered their position strong: for, they threatened, were their demands not granted, necessity would urge them to seek their 'Bread from new masters tho' it may be in foreign climes'. Yet as time passed doubts gradually undermined their confidence. On 25 July Commissioner Ourry had a long talk with four Task gangs who agreed to get the others to petition for re-entry; and on 1 August he received four representatives of all absentees alone in his parlour. 'They in a submissive manner delivered the petition which I received and read' and reproved them, observing to them that it was 'rather inflaming matters than submissive'. So they were to remain until mid-August.[19]

However, unbeknown at Plymouth, on 22 July the Admiralty had ordered the Navy Board to review its trial of taskwork, along with the shipwrights' complaints and propositions. Four days later the Navy Board had made numerous recommendations favourable to the workforce: that task prices be increased by between 4 and 12.5 per cent; that day pay and two tides be allowed whenever defects in materials were discovered; and that the shipwrights receive assistance on articles of heavy work requiring great strength. These were authorised by the Admiralty and sent to the yards on 4 August, revised instructions following on 16 August. These also provided for the examination of timber for defects, the timely supply of iron work, and the option for gangs in rotation to take a turn out of working by task.[20] At Plymouth the orders threw the shipwrights into confusion. Though Ourry was promised a submissive petition for the London boards, he received a defiant one. A drift back to work had started at Portsmouth on 11 August, and the Plymouth men anxiously awaited the post from there, calling the Portsmouth men 'd--nd villains'.[21]

On 16 August 40 to 50 Plymouth shipwrights sailed to the east in a hired vessel, those remaining simply admitting that the time was elapsed since they ought to have received answers from the eastern yards. They attempted a final appeal, yet from this time applications for re-entry increased from a trickle to a flood. Advertisements for new entrants also brought young men, some from 40 miles distance. By 22 August, though still 98 shipwrights short of the yard establishment, Ourry had 692 shipwrights on the yard books, including 291 classed as task workers. By 27 August those numbers had increased to 731 and 330, only 38 short of the establishment. He was also informed that the shipwrights had returned to work 'with great spirit', their main concern now being the re-entry of 18 men over 40 years of age who had been refused a new start. Other casualties included six shipwrights blacklisted as leaders and forbidden entry to any Royal yard, and another 21 refused re-entry for a month for abusing the privilege of having an apprentice at the time they struck.[22]

Nonetheless, the Plymouth shipwrights were still able to resist piecework. They claimed the option, given early in the dispute, of working by the day rather than by task, and they were to maintain this preference for another 13 years. An attempt to persuade the shipwrights to adopt task work in October 1779 met with 'a sullen, determined resolution against it'. Piecework for repairs, termed 'jobwork', was introduced elsewhere in 1780, but that, too, was resisted at Plymouth. Apprentices were given to the few who volunteered for piecework, but they were assaulted and were given passages to the eastern yards. 'I must do the men justice to say that they go on with the work of coppering ships with great spirit', Ourry reported in April 1780, 'but as to working by the piece or task there is no getting the better of the prejudice they have taken against it'.[23]

Yet the shipwrights of Plymouth yard were swimming against the tide. After 132 petitioned to adopt it, Woolwich shipwrights accepted taskwork from September 1775. At Chatham by 1781 the number of task gangs was gradually increased to six. At each of the yards caulkers were permitted piece rates for new work in 1775, and for all work by the end of the war. At Portsmouth, shipwright resistance finally collapsed after an order of January 1783 effectively withdrew overtime for those not working by job or task. At Plymouth three months earlier over 100 shipwrights requested to work by job, yet the opposition of others still prevented its adoption.[24] After peace resumed in 1783, possibly sustained by earnings from extensive repairs to the fleet, opposition to piecework assumed the character of a cause. In 1786 physical intimidation of volunteers was accompanied by 'the hoisting of yellow flags' and the hanging of 'effigies on board the ships in Dock'. Violence erupted again in 1788, four shipwrights being beaten for performing what 'was of the nature of task or job work'. Eleven shipwrights and apprentices were responsible, of whom nine were discharged. Blame was also attached to the second Foreman of the Yard, who had canvassed gangs for interest in piecework and had entered into a 'sort of treaty with several'. But his initiative proved instructive to the Navy Board of the strength of effective resistance at Plymouth, for it preceded the formal introduction of piecework for shipwrights there later that year. By 1803 in all 17 out of 21 trades at Plymouth worked by the piece.[25]

Table 31.1
Average Wages Paid per Day in Plymouth Dockyard 1758–1803

(Average for 313 working days; includes wages of Apprentices; excludes Lodging and Chip money)

	1758	1780	1790	1797	1803
	s d	s d	s d	s d	s d
Shipwrights	3 0	3 8	3 2¼	5 2	6 6
Caulkers	3 1½	3 3½	3 7¼	5 1½	6 3
Joiners	2 10¾	3 9	3 1¾	5 1¼	5 7¾
House Carpenters	2 7½	3 7½	2 7¾	4 5¾	3 8
Masons	2 4¾	3 9	3 6½	5 3½	5 0
Bricklayers	2 2¼	3 2	2 8	4 4½	3 4
Smiths	2 7	2 8	2 3½	4 7	4 3
Scavelmen	2 0¾	2 2¾	2 3¾	3 11¾	3 0
Labourers	1 6½	1 7¼	1 10	2 6¼	2 7
Sailmakers	2 10¾	3 3½	2 11½	3 10½	4 9½
Riggers	2 5½	2 6¾	2 4½	3 0½	3 6
Ropemakers	3 6¼	3 7¼	2 8½	3 9¼	–
Sawyers	3 5¾	2 9¾	2 8¾	4 2½	4 8

Source: *6th Report of the Commissioners* . . . see footnote 25.
The years were selected by the Commissioners, who divided the annual wages bill by the number of men employed and by 313 days. Their intention was 'to show clearly the increase which has taken place of late years'. They acknowledged: 'it may be conceived, as the workmen are frequently employed on Sundays and the average we have formed being for the 313 working days, that it exceeds the wages actually paid to them'. But they claimed this 'certainly is not the case, and we consider it to be a low average, inasmuch as we believe the time lost by the workmen, by being absent from the yard from sickness and other causes, to be fully equal to their employment on Sundays, and such average is further reduced by the number of persons entered and discharged in the course of the year, who have not received pay for the whole time'.

By that time the shipwrights had benefited significantly from piecework, especially from job or repair work, used on an extensive scale from 1793. Ten years later it was discovered that the quartermen had indulged in creative accounting to ensure that shipwrights made earnings close to the ceiling set by the Navy Board – usually a rate of two days' pay for one actual working day – on top of which they still made overtime. As they received the earnings of their own apprentices working alongside men in the gangs, the yard officers' vested interest ensured that those gangs made the maximum earnings possible. Partly in consequence, while the workforce at Plymouth increased by 29 per cent between 1780 and 1801, the yard's annual wages bill enlarged in the same period by 105 per cent. Consequently, although probably more labour was exacted through piecework, financially the artificers in Plymouth dockyard were certainly better off employed that way than they were on Day rates, and better paid, too, than workers in nearby merchant shipyards.[26]

The Riots of 1801

Nonetheless, in spite of earnings from piecework, during the 1790s some in the dockyard community still occasionally suffered distress. Fluctuating food prices, on top of long-term inflation, brought periods of severe deprivation. The region around Plymouth was particularly affected by food scarcities, partly owing to large quantities of foodstuffs being sold into the naval victualling yard. After the poor harvest in 1794, a gentleman living nearby explained high food prices by

> the long continuance of the outward bound Fleets on the coasts near Plymouth, from which market and that of the Dock Twenty-thousand inhabitants more than usual were fed for several months; a number nearly equal to all the stationary inhabitants of both those places. During their continuance here, after the vicinity had been much drained of oxen, sheep, corn and potatoes, supplies were drawn from the several counties of Somerset, Dorset, Gloucester and Worcester.

Food rioters in Plymouth that summer were joined by recruits to the 67th Foot stationed there. From the yard artificers, the shipwrights petitioned for more apprentices, a request the Admiralty thought fit to grant, sending for a list of those with large families and sons of proper age.[27] Other means of supplementing earned income were employed too. Embezzlement appears to have increased, while some artificers set up their 'wives and families in little business such as small shops and public houses in order to make' themselves 'in some degree a little more comfortable'. Following bad harvests in 1798, 1799 and 1800, food prices rose so high that bags of potatoes costing at most two shillings in 1793 were sold in 1801 for twelve or thirteen shillings. With prices so high for so long, most artificers turned their thoughts once more to a petition for an increase in their basic rates of pay. An 'honest man', who had worked many years in Plymouth yard and disagreed with the petition, informed the Board of Admiralty on 18 January 1801:

> That in the Dock-yard here there is a formidable *conspiracy* on foot among the workmen of every description to extort from *Government* an advancement of wages: their professed object is to petition: but their real and ultimate one is to threaten. To facilitate this Design, Delegates are appointed to travel and excite the same spirit in the Workmen of other Dockyards belonging to His Majesty. Certain I am their complaints are totally groundless.[28]

As occurred thirty years earlier, the men at the other five yards concurred in the petition: in September 1800 when food scarcity affected the whole of southern England, price fixing and food rioting had occurred at Portsmouth, Chatham, Sheerness and Woolwich. Deciding this time to go to the top, early in February 1801 a request was presented to William Pitt for permission to send a petition into the House of Commons, and to the Board of Admiralty for sanction and support 'when Parliament request your Lordships' opinions in our behalf'. To both, the artificers' delegates enclosed copies of their intended petition to the House of Commons. It claimed that, even with extra wages from piecework and overtime, with high prices and increased rates of interest their earnings were no longer adequate to their needs. However, Pitt resigned on 5 February, simply referring the matter to the Admiralty. But there Lord Spencer made way for St Vincent, who did not take his place at the Board until 20 February, and a decision on the request was not referred to the Navy Board until 1 April. Until then the delegates returned regularly, first to Downing Street, then to the Admiralty. Such was the concern at the combination that later their movements were followed by a 'trail' assigned from the Home Office. In the event, the eventual response – that the artificers would be allowed 'a bounty in proportion to the number of their families' until food prices declined – came too late. At Plymouth on 31 March a riot occurred which was to be followed by one at Sheerness and another at Plymouth on 15 April.[29]

At Plymouth on 30 March price fixing and the seizure of foodstuffs had culminated in the restoration of order by the militia. On 31 March the riot act was read and mounted soldiers dispersed the crowd. By 4.30pm order seemed to be restored, but, as Jonathan Elford reported to his brother, his fellows, hearing that a Dockyard man had been taken as a rioter, struck work.

> Upon this the Magistrates, supported by a troop of the Queen's Bays, the Piquets of the Wilts and East Devon, and the Artillery with four field pieces loaded with Grape and Canister, took part at the upper end of Fore Street near the Main Guard house where the prisoners were. The Dock yard men came out of the yard in a body whooping and hazzaing and came to the spot where the Magistrates were, upon which the Dock Volunteers Cavalry & Infantry formed in their rear . . . But instead of acting with energy the Magistrates, to their eternal disgrace, ordered the prisoners to be released. The rioters then demanded the release of all the other prisoners which was also conceded to them. They then took the Man on their shoulders and carried him thro the town hazzaing and making shouts.

Over the next few days the dockyard workforce exercised a noticeable ascendancy over the official figures of authority at Plymouth. Anonymous warnings of 'diabolical things' were received by the magistrates, including on 3 April information of the intention of the yard men to seize the guns at the Gun Wharf and any other arms and ammunition they could find if they were opposed by the military. The contents of the Gun Wharf and Guard Room were promptly evacuated to the Garrison. On 4 April the East Devonshire militia arrived, and on 7 April the Buckland Volunteers, while by 9 April the Magistrates had sworn-in 300 Special Constables.[30]

In London the riot seemed to confirm opinion about the Plymouth artificers: St Vincent observed on 6 April to Lieutenant-General Simcoe, commanding the troops in the Southwest, that he knew 'from long experience that the majority of artificers in Plymouth is governed by the very worst spirit and intention'. St Vincent was inclined to caution. 'You must be aware', he warned

> that we rely on the exertions of Plymouth yard for the repair of the ships composing the Channel Fleet, and although there appears no combination with the other Dock-yards, there have been sensations in them which would blaze forth if any strong measure was taken at Plymouth.[31]

But blaze forth these sensations did. At Sheerness on 13 April the Commissioner was physically forced to promise the release of an impressed yard man, and three days later a second rescue occurred at Plymouth. While the magistrates were examining a local waterman taken up during disturbances at the market,

> a mob consisting of several thousands [sic] forced and broke through the front gates of the Court by means of large pieces of wood which they made use of as battering rams, and suddenly filled the courtelage in the front of the Committee Room, broke the front Door and window of the Inner Building and rescued the prisoner.

Next day the smiths gathered about two-thirds of the artificers on a green near the yard Chapel for a further rescue attempt. While a crowd of local inhabitants gathered outside the yard gates to join the men, the magistrates and armed forces formed near the Main Guard House. About mid afternoon, however, after speeches for and against a sally, and a fruitless deputation to the magistrates for the release of some female rioters, the yard men gradually dispersed.[32]

To the Navy Board these events seemed to have been 'instigated by the insinuations of evil disposing and designing men'. Certainly there was reason to fear a link-up with the fleet. On 16 April, according to Jonathan Elford,

> their first step was to endeavour to incite the crews of the two only ships in commission in the harbour, the *Cambridge* and *Urania*, to join them, which they manifested by assembly on an elevated piece of ground at the southern extremity of the yard.

However, later investigations were to uncover no deep designs, and observers close to events preferred to attribute them to the high price of food. Of the riots at Plymouth, Lord Fortescue, Lord Lieutenant for Devon, observed on 7 April: 'The people were certainly not in their hearts disloyal . . . The dearth was the cause . . . the poor are certainly in a very miserable state.'[33]

Free from the authority of the civil power within the yard, the activities of the men correlated closely with disturbances in the region; as the Plymouth magistrates observed to the Duke of Portland, the Home Secretary, on 23 April: 'in fact the yard men act as a Barometer upon the place . . . and many miles around . . .'. Fortescue agreed, writing from Plymouth two days later: 'The state of this place is so much dependent upon the Dock yard (whose vortex extends several miles round) that it is only by degrees approaching to that quiet settlement which obtains elsewhere'. Fortescue put the influence of the yard down to the variety of trades composing the Dock community. Tradesmen in local towns identified with their counterparts around the dockyard. 'I am persuaded that these towns would be as quiet as the rest of the Country if the Dock yard community would let them.' According to information received by the Plymouth magistrates, the dockyard men seemed to have influence in South Cornwall as well as in Devon. The men who regulated prices in the market at Fowey allegedly declared: 'they were but a few men but had only to hold up their hand and the whole Dock yard would join them'. The correspondence of the leaders of rioters at Modbury also suggested communication and co-ordination among price fixers, especially as one assured a flour dealer 'that he might carry flour to Plymouth and need not smuggle it; he would assure him a free passage'.[34]

At the end of April, when the yard seemed again restored to relative quiet, a Navy Board committee was dispatched first to Plymouth to discharge all who had been involved in organising the petitions for increased rates of pay and in the riots. In all, 103 men were discharged from Plymouth yard at midday on 5 May. The committee then visited the other yards in turn, and 39 men went from Portsmouth, 79 from Chatham, 39 from Sheerness, 49 from Deptford, and 35 from Woolwich: 340 men in all. From the end of April artificers' letters between the yards were intercepted. Although there was now little hope of achieving the object of their petitions, on 28 April John Spry, a Plymouth delegate, wrote to all his fellow delegates of the hope that their union would 'remain to the end of the chapter', and that their labours might not be entirely lost: 'as our friendship has begun in endeavouring to ameliorate the distresses of our Brother workmen in common with ourselves, and not from any sordid or improper Source'. But with the news of the Plymouth discharges the Sheerness men could only hope 'that our suffering friends will bear themselves with that decent and manly spirit which becomes them.' They 'had no violent measures to recommend,' but hoped 'our Plymouth friends will still correspond with us, which innocent and lawful privilege we would persevere in maintaining . . . we cannot conceive that any criminality can justly attach to you'.[35]

Administrative Changes after 1801

The food scarcity and riots at the turn of the century were to enter the folk memory of inhabitants at Plymouth.[36] The Napoleonic War was to bring nothing comparable to past hardships. The harvest of 1801 was better than in preceding years and food prices fell. In May 1801 chips were abolished, along with other unofficial emoluments received by dockyard officials. In compensation most artificers received between 3d and 6d a day according to

31.3 Plymouth Dockyard: the covered Slip, constructed 1774–5, the roof in about 1815. This is the only eighteenth-century slip remaining in a royal dockyard. *(English Heritage)*

Table 31.2
Artificers Employed in the Royal Dockyard at Plymouth, 1773–1814

	14 Dec. 1773	14 Mar. 1782	14 Sept. 1790	14 Dec. 1800	26 Mar. 1814
Blockmakers	4	4	3	4	6
Braziers	1	3	1	1	–
Bricklayers	27	32	24	29	57
〃 Labourers	10	10	10	10	22
Caulkers	79	102	86	106	116
Coopers	–	–	1	1	2
House Carpenters	71	81	66	92	245
Joiners	57	63	54	75	107
Labourers	260	300	280	400	606
Locksmiths	3	3	3	3	4
Masons	7	9	8	10	29
Messengers	–	–	–	–	12
Oakum Boys	30	30	30	30	45
Oarmakers	1	1	1	1	1
Painters	–	–	–	–	29
Pitch Heaters	3	2	2	2	2
Plumbers	2	1	1	3	5
Quarter Boys	12	12	12	12	–
Riggers	54	79	86	128	141
〃 Labourers	50	100	86	132	–
Sailmakers	37	52	44	67	68
Sawyers	86	88	102	140	208
Scavelmen	70	60	60	95	170
Shipwrights	790	937	758	1,011	1,316
Smiths	85	110	87	189	234
Teams	16	23	17	24	31
Tinmen	–	–	–	–	1
Treenail Mooters	1	1	1	1	–
Warders	–	–	–	–	26
Wheelwrights	3	4	4	4	3
Rope Yard					
Boys	9	16	15	30	42
Foremen	2	3	3	4	5
Hatchellors	23	40	43	34	–
Hemp Dressers	–	–	–	–	14
Labourers	16	37	23	13	82
Layers	–	–	–	–	4
Line and Twine Spinners	–	–	–	–	16
Spinners	132	218	194	215	189
Wheelboys	–	–	–	–	18
Winders Up	11	17	14	14	–
Yarn Knotters	–	–	–	–	13
Total	1,952	2,438	2,119	2,880	3,869
Sources:	NMM, ADM B/188, 11 Jan. 1774	NMM, ADM BP/3, 27 April 1782	NMM, ADM BP/10, 8 Oct. 1790	NMM, ADM BP/21A, 14 Mar. 1801	NMM, ADM BP/34A, 2 April 1814

their trade, the ropemakers appealing in 1804 against exclusion from this provision. This payment in lieu, being made quarterly with earnings, did not reduce artificers' dependence on moneylenders. However, in 1805 'subsistence money' was introduced – the weekly payment of three-quarters of artificers' usual earnings. Reducing dependence on credit, it was received with 'universal satisfaction'. At this time earnings themselves were also increased. The ceiling had been removed from earnings by job in 1803, and in 1805 prices for work performed by task were raised by 20 to 25 per cent. The basic rate of Day pay remained unchanged, but the Commissioners for Revising and Digesting the Civil Affairs of the Navy, appointed in 1805, recommended new rates double the old – in effect the 'two for one' earned by many pieceworkers since 1793. With overtime calculated by the hour rather than by the old 'nights' and 'tides', the new rates were eventually introduced

31.4 Plymouth Dockyard *c*1800, by Nicholas Pocock. Note Dummer's Terrace of the 1690s, left of centre. *(National Maritime Museum)*

in 1812, along with numerous other detailed changes in yard management. These permitted the payment of all earnings weekly, which was introduced only a month after it was recommended in June 1813.[37]

With payment less of a concern, early in the Napoleonic War agitation among artificers focused more on hours of work. The riggers and smiths had not been permitted payment by the piece; they now found that to achieve earnings comparable with those of pieceworkers their hours had to be extremely long, up to 17 hours a day. During the brief peace, the stint for which the sailmakers made a single day's pay had been increased; to make the same earnings their hours were lengthened in proportion. Under the pressure of mobilising many sea-worn vessels, the shipwrights simply found the hours demanded of them – from 5.30 a.m. till 9 p.m. – beyond their strength. The Navy Board was obliged to adjust times of bell-ringing and allowances for breaks.[38]

Improvements in payment, and attention to hours (at least for the shipwrights) had their benefits for the navy. Although in all over 800 men left or were discharged between 1801 and 1803, thereafter vacancies in the war establishment were steadily filled. Indeed, though having an establishment of 900, from 1805 Plymouth actually employed over 1,000 shipwrights, with numbers continuing to grow. The navy required to replace many ships of the line over 74 guns, and in January 1806 the Admiralty was able to order that a set number of shipwrights be devoted to new construction. By 1809 the number at Plymouth exceeded those at Portsmouth by almost 100 and further entries had to be restricted.[39]

Such numbers working by the piece made a marked increase in building speed. Consequently, between 1804 and 1815 new ships were launched more frequently than had ever before been possible in wartime. One hundred, 98- and 74-gun ships, begun shortly before the American War of Independence, had respectively taken twelve, thirteen, and eight and a half years to complete. Even during the Revolutionary war 110- and 80-gun ships had taken twelve and seven years each. Yet after 1805 the *Caledonia* and the *St Vincent*, both of 120 guns, were built within three and a half and five years; while the *Union* (98) took less than six years. Perhaps most striking was the contrast between the times taken to build the 50-gun ships *Medusa* and *Jupiter*: the former, begun in 1776, took nine years four months; the latter, in 1811, took only twenty-six months. Large frigates, not previously attempted in wartime at Plymouth, were now produced in pairs in rapid time: the *Circe* and *Pallas* of 32 guns in 1804 in five months; the *Nisus* and *Menelaus* of 38 guns between 1808 and 1810, each in seventeen months.[40]

Improvements in payment also benefited the artificers, permitting great numbers to provide against hard times by subscribing to friendly societies. In 1817, when the Plymouth Dockyard Provident Institution, a savings bank, was founded, it received 3,724 deposits in 22 months. Some of these were made by the existing Friendly Societies, these being the accumulated weekly, monthly or quarterly deposits (some as little as one penny a week) of almost every man in the yard. At the same time a pension fund for widows, orphans and pensioners attracted a thousand subscribers.[41]

For the workforce of Plymouth dockyard these deposits represented a significant gain from the administration changes after 1801. The men gained too from the refusal of the Navy Board in 1815 to reduce the yard establishment as quickly as in 1802. Although criticised for failing to comply with contemporary *laissez-faire* economics, the Board preferred to ensure that the fleet was laid up in good condition. The artificers of Plymouth yard were thus preserved from the immediate postwar unemployment and distress so prevalent elsewhere. However, in the long term such security was counterbalanced by a relative change in status for the shipwright. With the supersession of Day work by piecework, skilled men no longer had the control over the deployment of their work effort that they once had. Partly in consequence, but mainly due to the growth of a more scientific attitude to ship design, they could no longer claim with credibility to embody the art or mystery of shipbuilding. Nonetheless, in material terms the workforce at Plymouth dockyard was certainly better off in 1820 than at any time in the preceding half-century. Furthermore, the settlement of the range of problems surrounding the adoption of piecework assured a productivity in shipbuilding and a stability in labour relations that had not been possible in the thirty years before 1800.

31: Industrial Relations at Plymouth Dockyard, 1770–1820

1 EJ Hobsbawm, 'Custom, Wages and Workload in Nineteenth-century Industry', in *Labouring Men* (1968), 344–370, and J Rule, *The Labouring Classes in Early Industrial England, 1750–1850* (Harlow, 1986), 120–6; W Shrubsole, *A Plea in Favour of the Shipwrights belonging to the Royal Dock yards* (Rochester, 1770), 15. I am grateful to Dr RJB Knight for providing me with much information and for commenting on drafts of this paper.
2 PRO, ADM 174/117, 19 April 1782.
3 PRO, ADM 1/5126, ff. 112, 115: Address of thanks, 22 March 1800. Civil officials as well as artificers occasionally suffered abuse from naval officers: RJB Knight, ed., *Portsmouth Dockyard Papers 1774–1783: The American War* (Portsmouth Record Series, 1987), 100–1.
4 C Emsley, *British Society and the French Wars 1793–1815* (1979), 32.
5 DA Baugh, *British Naval Administration in the Age of Walpole* (Princeton, 1965), 327; BM Ranft, 'Labour Relations in the Royal Dockyards in 1739', *MM* (1961), 281–91; R Middleton, 'The Adminstration of Newcastle and Pitt: the Departments of State and the conduct of the war 1754–1760, with particular reference to the campaigns in North America' (Unpublished PhD thesis, University of Exeter, 1968), 139–141. See also Chapter 29 above.
6 JM Haas, 'Methods of wage payment in the royal dockyards 1775–1865', *Maritime History* V (1977), 99–115; Shrubsole, *A Plea in Favour*, 3.
7 HE Richardson, 'Wages of Shipwrights in HM Dockyards, 1496–1788', *MM* (1947), 265–74; RJB Knight, 'The Royal Dockyards in England at the time of the American War of Independence' (Unpub. PhD thesis, University of London, 1972), 163–4.
8 Shrubsole, *A Plea in Favour*, 19; RA Morriss, *The Royal Dockyards during the Revolutionary and Napoleonic Wars* (Leicester, 1983), 102.
9 RJB Knight, 'The Royal Dockyards', 200–1; RA Morriss, 'Labour Relations in the Royal Dockyards, 1801–1805', *MM* 62 (1976), 337–46.
10 RJB Knight, 'The Royal Dockyards', 156; PRO, ADM 7/662, f. 74; JM Haas, 'The Introduction of Task Work into Royal Dockyards, 1775', *Journal of British Studies* (1969), 44–68.
11 NMM, ADM B/190, 26 July 1775.
12 NMM, ADM B/190, 14 June 1775.
13 NMM, ADM B/190, 15, 17 June 1775; PRO, ADM 174/115, 20 June 1775. For Lord Sandwich's account of events at Portsmouth see Knight, *Portsmouth Dockyard Papers*, 136–8.
14 PRO, ADM 174/115, 20 June 1775; NMM, ADM B/190, 30 June 1775.
15 The odd pence were kept by the clerks of the Treasurer of the Navy as their perquisite from the payment.
16 Petition of 31 June and Navy Board response of 1 July 1775: PRO, ADM 7/662, ff. 36–9, 43.
17 NMM, ADM B/190, 30 June, 5, 6, 7, 15 July 1775; PRO, ADM 7/662; Knight, *Portsmouth Dockyard Papers*, 48.
18 NMM, ADM B/190, 17 July 1775; PRO, ADM 174/115, 2, 3, 18, 28 July 1775.
19 NMM, ADM B/190, 22 July, 1 Aug. 1775.
20 NMM, ADM B/190, 26 July, 16 Aug. 1775. The taskwork prices authorised by the Board of Admiralty were in fact slightly higher than those recommended by the Navy Board. For the Navy Board order, see Knight, *Portsmouth Dockyard Papers*, 50.
21 According to Sandwich, the drift back to work at Portsmouth followed that at Woolwich, caused by 'a Bill of Indictment found at the Assizes of Maidstone by the Grand Jury of the County of Kent against twelve of the people of Woolwich for a conspiracy with an intent to procure an increase of wages'. PRO, ADM 7/662.
22 PRO, ADM 174/115, 17, 22, 27 Aug. 1775; NMM, ADM B/190, 1, 8 Sept. 1775.
23 PRO, ADM 174/115, 29 Aug. 1775; ADM 174/117, 25, 30 Oct., 3, 7 Nov. 1779, 7, 21 April, 5 May 1780.
24 NMM, ADM B/190, 5 Sept. 1775; RJB Knight, 'The Royal Dockyards', 162; PRO, ADM 174/117, 18 Oct. 1782.
25 PRO, ADM 174/120, 25, 31 May 1788; Register of Dismissals, Plymouth Yard, PRO, ADM 106/3006; NMM, ADM BP/8, 27 May 1788; 6th *Report of the Commissioners appointed to inquire into Irregularities, Frauds and Abuses practiced in the Naval Departments and in the business of the Prize Agency*, BPP, Commons Reports, 1803–4 (83), III, 16–121.
26 BPP, 1803–4 (83), III, 127; Appendix 2, p. 179; Appendix 104, pp. 372–385.
27 W Symons to Duke of Portland, 21 July 1795, PRO, HO 42/35, quoted in Emsley, *British Society and the French Wars*, 42; NMM, ADM BP/15A, 2 April 1795.
28 *The Times*, 23 Jan. 1801; PRO, ADM 1/5126, 3 Nov. 1798, 18 Jan. 1801.
29 *The Times*, 4, 10, 22 Sept. 1800; PRO, ADM 1/5126, ff. 230, 245, 248, 252, 253; HO 28/27, report of trail, n.d.; ADM 106/2664, 1 April 1801; R Wells, 'The Revolt of the South-west, 1800–01: a study in English popular protest', *Social History* 2 (1977), 713–44.
30 PRO, HO 42/61, ff. 39, 408, 498; ADM 106/1916, 11 April 1801.
31 D Bonner Smith, ed., *Letters of Lord St Vincent 1801–4* (Navy Records Society, 2 vols., 1921, 1926) II, 168.
32 PRO, HO 42/61, ff. 593, 614.
33 PRO, ADM 106/3244, 11 May 1801; HO 42/61, ff. 466, 614.
34 PRO, HO, 42/61, ff. 614, 628, 690, 703, 719, 725.
35 PRO, ADM 106/3244, 26 April, 18 May 1801.
36 See 'The Bold Shipwrights of Dock, A Legend of old Devonport', a narrative poem in which a romance between a shipwright and a pilot's daughter is set against the events of April 1801: in a newspaper cutting, c1890–4, pasted in a volume, NMM, WQB/49.
37 RA Morriss, *Royal Dockyards*, 102, 104.
38 PRO, ADM 1/5126, ff. 85, 282; ADM 106/1917, 3 March 1804; ADM 106/2234, 28 April 1804.
39 NMM, ADM BP/29B, 8 Dec. 1809.
40 KV Burns, *Plymouth's Ships of War: A History of naval vessels built in Plymouth between 1694 and 1860* (NMM monograph, No 4, 1972), 15–19.
41 Scottish Record Office, Melville MSS, GD/51/2/987, 991.

32 *Privateering Enterprise in Devon, 1689–1815*

DAVID J STARKEY

ON 11 JULY 1689 JOSEPH REED, commander and sole owner of the *Diligence of Limerick*, appeared before the Judge of the High Court of Admiralty in London and offered a sworn statement as to the tonnage, crew size, armaments, ownership, and other characteristics of his vessel.[1] This 'particular true and exact account'[2] was part of the process by which a letter of marque, or privateer commission, was issued to Captain Reed, empowering him to equip and set forth his ship to attack and appropriate French seaborne property. It was the first of over 23,000 such declarations made in the Court during the 'long' eighteenth century, each identifying the officers and owners of a vessel licensed to commit acts of reprisal upon ships and goods of a specified nationality. The introduction of this procedural requirement, in support of the bail which had always underpinned grants of reprisal, was but one sign of the sharper definition and more efficient regulatory mechanism which distinguished eighteenth-century privateering from its ancient and varied antecedents.[3] Moreover, the survival of all the declarations offered between the accession of William III and the battle of Waterloo (the last British letter of marque was issued in February 1815[4]), together with a vast array of related evidence in the archive of the Prize division of the High Court of Admiralty,[5] facilitates a comprehensive analysis of privateering activity undertaken from the British Isles during 1689–1815.

The privateering experience of this era was characterised by more than the wealth of its documentary record. As reprisals were generally, though not necessarily, permissible in wartime against the vessels and cargoes of enemy subjects, Britain's recurrent and prolonged conflicts with France gave eighteenth-century privateering a focus which set it apart from the anti-Spanish and anti-Dutch orientation of commerce-raiding in the late Tudor and Stuart ages. Thus, French seaborne traffic was the principal object of predatory operations in seven of the eight conflicts in which letters of marque were granted between 1689 and 1815, the sole exception being the 1718–1720 war against Spain. The period was afforded a further coherence by the unequivocal status that privateering assumed within the code of international maritime law. By the 1690s the activity had been regularised by a series of bilateral agreements reached between the principal maritime powers, while the operations of the stateless sea-robber, or pirate, with whom the privateersman was, and is, so readily associated, were increasingly marginalised. Such a clarification was inextricably linked to the concurrent emergence of state navies, a development which, in turn, radically altered the face of sea warfare. With maritime conflicts now determined largely by fleets of purpose-built men-of-war, privateers were no longer a vital weapon in the state's naval arsenal. In contrast to many of its antecedents, therefore, eighteenth-century privateering was neither a form of dubiously authorised piracy nor a decisive factor in the prosecution of the war at sea. Rather, it represented a legitimate business opportunity for ship owners and seafarers willing to risk their capital and labour in a quest for prize and profit; a quest which might coincidentally serve the nation's war effort.

In this eighteenth-century guise, clear patterns were evident in the conduct of British privateering enterprise.[6] Typically, it assumed two broad forms; private men-of-war were set forth specifically to apprehend prizes, while 'letters of marque', or armed merchantmen, were commissioned to add a predatory option to the primary trading purpose of their voyages. In terms of activity levels, the privateering business fluctuated widely during the course of each war as investors, particularly those engaged in private men-of-war, responded to the various determinants which enhanced or depressed prize-taking prospects in relation to alternative commercial opportunities. Spatially, this enterprise was generally distributed in line with the structure of the shipping industry. Accordingly, London ship owners invariably accounted for a major portion of the licensed fleet, while the interest of Bristolians was marked until the 1750s, declining thereafter as merchants in other western ports, especially Liverpool, expanded their shipping concerns. However, as privateering operations were feasible in the most diminutive of seaworthy craft, there was considerable scope for investors in the lesser outports, where capital accumulations were generally modest, to engage in commerce-raiding activity. Indeed, commissioned vessels were fitted out in over 100 British ports and havens during the eight wars of the 1689–1815 period, with speculators from Alderney to Aberdeen, from Leith to Londonderry, and from Helford to Harwich seeking to profit at the expense of foreign ship owners and consignees.

Venturers based in Devon invested in this business of reprisal in each of the wars of the long eighteenth century. Though constituting a relatively small proportion of the activity sanctioned by the High Court of Admiralty, the county's commerce-raiding enterprise encompassed many facets of the privateering phenomenon. Moreover, their comparative proximity to popular cruising stations meant that Devon's ports were regularly used by commissioned craft from other regions seeking to recruit labour, land prizes, or repair damage. The county's experience of privateering therefore offers numerous insights into the nature of this unorthodox business opportunity and its place in the economies of provincial maritime districts. Three aspects of this experience are examined in the present chapter. First, the scale of Devon's privateering business is viewed contextually; attention is then focused on particular local ventures to illustrate the contrasting aims, organisational structures, and operational methods of different forms of licensed activity; and, thirdly, Devon's experience is considered in an assessment of the significance of privateering enterprise in the eighteenth century.

Context

The number of vessels licensed to operate as privateers during the 1689–1815 period can be estimated with some precision from the letter of marque declarations.[7] Though many of these statements were offered in respect of ships previously commissioned, the identification and elimination of such duplicate declarations reveals that almost 11,000 different craft sailed with letters of marque during the long eighteenth century. As Table 32.1 indicates, 423 of these vessels were set forth by Devon venturers. This represented less than 4 per cent of the overall total, though the proportion varied between conflicts, ranging from 1 per cent in the 1718–1720 war – embodied in the *Neptune* of Topsham – to 5.5 per cent in the American Revolutionary War. In the long-term context, therefore, Devon's 'input' into the eighteenth-century privateering business was generally greater than it had been in the Dutch Wars of the third quarter of the seventeenth century, when the county's ship owners and seafarers exhibited little interest in the private war at sea. However, in relation to the Elizabethan and early Stuart era, Devon's contributions to the post-1689 privateering business were less significant, for the county had dominated provincial commerce-raiding in 1589 and in the 1625–1630 war, with Devon venturers owning

Table 32.1
Devon's Commissioned Vessels, 1689–1815

War	Devon total	National total	Percentage Devon-owned
1689–1697	15	406	3.7
1702–1712	45	1,343	3.4
1718–1720	1	98	1
1739–1748	54	1,191	4.5
1756–1762	35	1,679	2.1
1777–1783	148	2,676	5.5
1793–1801	31	1,795	1.7
1803–1815	94	1,810	5.2
	423	10,998	3.8

Source: PRO, HCA 25/12–209; HCA 26/1–104.

approximately 11 and 26 per cent of the English vessels licensed in each respective period.[8]

If Devonians never again participated to such a degree in commissioned activity, their eighteenth-century investments were far from negligible. Viewed from a regional perspective, for instance, it is clear that Devon was the West Country's pre-eminent commerce-raiding county, accounting for 80 per cent of the region's input in the Spanish Succession War, and at least 45 per cent of the South West's commissioned fleet in the other major wars of the 1689–1815 period. These Devon vessels, as Table 32.2 shows, belonged to 12 ports and havens, with 52 licensed craft owned by venturers in four North Devon bases, and 371 set forth by residents of maritime communities in the south of the county. The interest of each port tended to vary between wars, with Bideford emerging as Devon's leading privateering port during the wars against Louis XIV; Exeter and, more especially, Dartmouth predominant in the mid-century conflicts; and Plymouth assuming a local ascendancy in the Napoleonic era. Relative to other provincial bases, these ports were important centres of privateering activity. For example, although 51 ports engaged in the business of reprisal during the 1702–1712 conflict, Bideford's fleet of 13 licensed vessels was exceeded only by the contributions of London (671 vessels), Bristol (157), Guernsey (147), Jersey (64), Liverpool (31), and Dublin (15). Similarly, in the Napoleonic War, Plymouth, with 77, eclipsed Bristol and 68 other ports, ranking fifth behind London (599), Liverpool (401), Guernsey (152), and Greenock (78) in the number of licensed craft fitted out.

Such a basic measure, of course, neglects the quality of the units

Table 32.2
Devon's Commissioned Vessels by Port, 1689–1815

Port	War								
	1689	1702	1718	1739	1756	1777	1793	1803	Total
Appledore	–	–	–	–	1	–	–	–	1
Barnstaple	1	5	–	1	1	–	–	2	10
Bideford	7	13	–	8	2	1	–	–	31
Brixham	–	–	–	–	–	4	–	–	4
Dartmouth	2	9	–	16	3	68	15	10	123
Exeter	4	5	–	10	20	20	3	2	64
Exmouth	–	–	–	2	–	1	–	–	3
Ilfracombe	–	–	–	–	–	5	2	3	10
Plymouth	1	9	–	9	4	42	10	77	152
Teignmouth	–	–	–	–	3	4	–	–	7
Topsham	–	4	1	8	1	2	1	–	17
Totnes	–	–	–	–	–	1	–	–	1
	15	45	1	54	35	148	31	94	423

Source: PRO, HCA 25/12–209; HCA 26/1–104.

comprising the eighteenth-century commissioned fleet. In fact, many different types of vessel carried privateer licences, with diminutive cutters, ketches, and luggers authorised in just the same manner as ocean-going, fully-rigged ships. The letter of marque declarations indicate a vast range in the strength and size of commissioned craft. Manning levels, for example, varied between the nine-strong company of the *Defiance* and the complement of 400 seafarers required by the owners of the *Lord Clive*.[9] A vessel's weaponry might consist of a handful of small arms and cutlasses, yet ships like the *Prince Regent* were provided with 32 18lb carriage guns as well as '12 musketoons, 80 muskets with bayonets, 30 pistols, 60 cutlasses, 25 pole-axes, and 50 boarding pikes'.[10] As manning and armaments depended to some degree on a vessel's burthen, a similarly extensive distribution characterised the tonnages declared, with various licensed craft of less than 10 tons appearing as little more than row-boats in comparison with ships such as the 1,549-ton *Ganges*.[11]

Within this broad spectrum, clear regional traits were apparent in the scale of activity. The average tonnage of London's licensed fleet, for instance, was higher than the national mean in each conflict. Likewise, vessels belonging to the ports of eastern England were invariably of above average tonnage, while the converse was true of the craft set forth from Kent and Sussex bases, and, more particularly, from the Channel Islands. In Devon the pattern was slightly less clear. Typically, the county's commissioned vessels varied considerably in build, strength, and tonnage, with the 14-ton *Hunter* of Plymouth at one extreme and the Dartmouth vessel *Fame*, of 654 tons burthen, at the other.[12] Yet with regard to the average tonnage of the county's privateering input, Devon's commissioned vessels were more substantial than the national mean – 208 as against 186 tons – in the 1689–1697 war, and smaller than the overall norm in each subsequent conflict. Indeed, in the American Revolutionary War the average tonnage of the county's licensed fleet was barely half of the overall mean of 205 tons, while the disparity was even more pronounced in the 1793–1801 and 1803–1815 wars, when local averages of 139 and 149 tons compared with national figures of over 300 tons. For most of the long eighteenth century, therefore, Devon's contribution to the British privateering business was less marked in terms of tonnage commissioned – or capital invested – than is indicated by the unrefined spatial analysis of the number of vessels licensed.

Differences in average tonnage reflected the composition of the commissioned fleet belonging to the various ports and regions engaged in privateering activity. Prominent amongst London's licensed vessels, for instance, were East Indiamen, invariably the largest units of the British mercantile marine. The declared tonnage of these specialist 'letters of marque' increased from approximately 350 tons in the early eighteenth century to just under 500 tons in the 1740s and 1750s, and to over 1,100 tons in the Revolutionary and Napoleonic era.[13] The mean tonnage level of the capital's commissioned fleet was further enhanced by substantial 'letters of marque' employed in the Mediterranean and northern European trades, and by the outset of numerous large-scale private men-of-war, notably in the 1739–1748 and 1756–1762 conflicts. Such 'deep-water' private ships-of-war – vessels exceeding 250 tons burthen with crews of at least 100 men[14] – formed an important element of Bristol's privateering enterprise in the mid-eighteenth century, while Liverpool ship owners concentrated their investments in 'letters of marque' deployed in the slave and West Indian trades, and merchants in east-coast bases such as Scarborough, Whitby, and Yarmouth specialised in armed merchantmen of 250 to 500 tons burthen carrying timber from the Baltic. However, average tonnage levels were invariably much lower in the Channel Islands and southeast England. Here, locational advantages during Anglo-French wars, together with limitations in the supply of local shipping, determined that privateering enterprise was almost entirely embodied in small-scale 'Channel' privateers set forth to prey on enemy trade in the Channel Narrows, in the approaches to French ports, or in the Bay of Biscay.[15]

In Devon some variety was apparent in the functional complexion of the licensed fleet. 'Letters of marque' set forth from the county's ports for a number of destinations during the 1689–1815 period. In the 1690s the *Lambe*, at 130 tons and 30 men, was one of six Bideford ships declared to be undertaking voyages to Newfoundland, the Streights, and then back to

England.[16] Another Bideford vessel, the *Expedition Frigott* of 170 tons and 50 men, carried a letter of marque as she sailed for Madeira, and from thence to the West Indies, in 1709.[17] Seventy years later the 303-ton *Heptarchy* of Dartmouth was licensed during her whaling venture, returning from Greenland with four large and one small 'fish', despite having most of her crew pressed by the *Fairy* sloop-of-war.[18] More numerous, however, were the private men-of-war despatched by Devon venturers to seek out and apprehend the enemy's seaborne property. Such craft ranged from the 600-ton *Boscawen* of Dartmouth, with 26 carriage guns and 300 men,[19] one of the largest and most powerful commerce-raiders commissioned in the High Court of Admiralty, to vessels like the *Black Joke* of Topsham, the *Providence* of Brixham, and the *Prosperous* of Ilfracombe – burthen 20 tons or thereabouts, armed with four small carriage guns at most, and worked by crews of 16 to 24 men.[20] In line with various broad influences, the scale of the typical predatory unit changed over time. Thus, in the 1740s and 1750s, substantial 'deep-water' private ships-of-war dominated Devon's privateering enterprise, while comparatively diminutive 'Channel' craft came to the fore in the American Revolutionary War and remained prominent in the 1793–1815 wars.

The composition of the licensed fleet was clearly pertinent to the prize return of the privateering business. A local preponderance of private men-of-war, for example, generally resulted in a relatively high local 'catch', while areas specialising in the operation of 'letters of marque' were much less productive of prizes. Accordingly, in terms of the number of properties subject to common condemnation,[21] the Channel Islands emerged as the leading privateering bases in the eighteenth century (though only during Anglo-French conflicts), with centres of licensed trading such as the ports of eastern England generally returning few prizes. Devon venturers, as Table 32.3 indicates, accounted for 3.6 per cent of the privateering prizes condemned in the High Court of Admiralty during the 1702–1809 period, a share which accorded almost exactly with the proportion of licensed vessels owned in the county during the 1689–1815 era as a whole. Considerably less significant than the 20–25 per cent of the total catch, by value, attributed to Devonians in the 1625–1630 war,[22] this return nevertheless suggests that a rough balance was reached between local contributions to national privateering input and output. However, there was some variation from war to war. Thus, in the 1702–1712 conflict, three prizes were condemned to 45 Devon-owned commissioned vessels, a 1:15 prize-per-privateer ratio which compared with an overall figure of 1:1.5. Later in the century the reverse was true as the return of Devonians relative to their privateering input – one prize for every two licensed vessels in the 1740s, 1:3 in the 1756–1762 conflict, and 1:2 in the American Revolutionary War – exceeded that of the licensed fleet as a whole.

The distribution of Devon prizes by port, as shown in Table 32.4, indicates that the county's south-coast bases, notably Dartmouth and Plymouth, were the most productive prize-taking centres. Relative to other provincial bases, individual Devon ports compared favourably in terms of prize condemnations, though only in particular wars. Thus, in the 1739–48 conflict, Dartmouth's 15 licensed vessels accounted for 17 prizes, a return bettered only by the Channel Islands (124 condemnations), London (107), Bristol (82), and Dover (34). In the Seven Years' War Bideford's total of eight prizes – all save one taken by the 200-ton, 130-man, *Tygress*[23] – ranked ahead of much larger ports such as Dublin, Glasgow, and Scarborough; while the 39 prizes sentenced to Dartmouth predators in the American Revolutionary War rendered the port the second most important prize-taking centre after Penzance in an expansive West-Country commerce-raiding business. The output of Devon's privateering enterprise, like the county's input, was therefore somewhat marginal in relation to the major focal points of eighteenth-century predatory activity, London, Bristol, and the Channel Islands, yet significant in a regional and provincial context. Moreover, in the detail underlying such quantitative comparison there is much in Devon's privateering experience to illuminate the nature and conduct of eighteenth-century commerce-raiding enterprise.

Table 32.3
Prizes Condemned to Devon's Commissioned Vessels, 1702–1809

War	Devon total	National total	Percentage Devon-owned
1702–1712	3 (2)	956	0.3
1718–1720	0	7	–
1739–1748	27 (5)	408	6.6
1756–1762	11 (7)	382	2.9
1777–1783	76 (6)	1,312	5.8
1793–1801	6	303	2
1803–1809	2 (1)	93	2.2
	125 (21)	3,461	3.6

Figures in brackets denote prizes taken in consort with non-Devon captors.

Source: PRO, HCA 25/14–209; HCA 26/4–104; HCA 34/23–65.

Table 32.4
Prizes Condemned to Devon's Commissioned Vessels by Port, 1702–1809

Port	War							
	1702	1718	1739	1756	1777	1793	1803	Total
Bideford	–	–	4	8	–	–	–	12
Dartmouth	–	–	17	–	39	1	1	58
Exeter	2	–	3	–	8	–	–	13
Ilfracombe	–	–	–	–	1	–	–	1
Plymouth	1	–	1	–	26	5	1	34
Teignmouth	–	–	–	1	2	–	–	3
Topsham	–	–	2	2	–	–	–	4
	3	0	27	11	76	6	2	125

Figures include prizes taken in consort with non-Devon captors.

Source: PRO, HCA 25/14–209; HCA 26/4–104; HCA 34/23–65.

Ventures

Privateer commissions permitted venturers engaged in many different forms of shipping activity to commit acts of reprisal upon foreign-owned trade in the eighteenth century. While it is conventional to distinguish the primarily commercial armed merchantman from the overtly predatory private man-of-war, further refinement of the licensed fleet is necessary if the true character and significance of British privateering enterprise is to be discerned. This can be achieved by examining Devon's privateering experience, for most forms of commissioned enterprise were apparent in the county's privateering stock, or else operated out of its ports, while local venturers generally conformed to trends current in the activity at large.

The term 'letter of marque' may be applied to the various types of licensed vessel engaged in activity other than the apprehension of prize. Such ventures were invariably organised on a wage labour basis, with seafarers remunerated by regular payments and afforded a share in any prize taken as a form of bonus to stimulate their predatory opportunism or to stiffen their defensive resolve against the violence of an assailant. Some of these craft operated on behalf of the state. In 1747, for instance, the *Falmouth*, of 320 tons and 120 men, was deployed as 'an advice boat in Government service . . . in her voyage from Plymouth with the trade to Portsmouth', during which she captured two French *corsaires*. The *Falmouth*'s articles stipulated that two-thirds of the proceeds of these prizes belonged to the ship's owners, while the remaining third was to be divided amongst the crew according to a predetermined schedule of shares.[24] Revenue cutters were likewise commissioned, with seven of Devon's 31 licensed vessels sailing on the orders of the Customs Commissioners in the 1793–1801 conflict. Ranging from 45 to 130 tons, such craft were worked by complements of between 11 and 33 men, companies which included the famous – William Pitt, Charles Fox, Henry Dundas, Edward Brandon Sheridan, Edmund Burke, and Samuel Whitbread allegedly served aboard the *Eagle* of Plymouth – and the bizarre – Joshua Jellyman, Zephaniah Tartlett, John Paste, William Gooseberry, Thomas Bakewell, and Edward Eatwell were nominated as officers of the *Shark* of Barnstaple – according to Customs House declarants seeking to relieve the tedium of applying for scores of letters of marque at a single Admiralty Court hearing.[25]

However, the majority of 'letters of marque' were engaged in trade, though the significance of cargo carriage to the purpose of the venture might vary from the incidental to the fundamental. Some of these vessels were despatched on 'cruising voyages' to the Caribbean, the Newfoundland Banks, or the Mediterranean. Here, prizes were sought, though if circumstances dictated, the relatively large, wage-earning crew might be redeployed in loading a cargo for the passage home. Powerful craft such as the *Eagle Gally* of Bideford – burthen 350 tons, with 30 guns and a declared complement of 100 men – exhibited the hallmarks of the 'cruise and voyage' venture in her 1697 sortie to 'Newfoundland, and the Streights'.[26] Similarly, the *Admiral Edwards*, owned by Newman & Roope of Dartmouth, was of a build and a strength – 300 tons, 22 carriage guns, and 90 men – which suggested that predation was intended to form an important part of her 1779 voyage to Newfoundland.[27] Perhaps the most unusual example of this genre, however, was the venture undertaken by the 300-ton, 100-man *Benson Gally* in 1744. Cruising on the Newfoundland Banks, this Bideford predator was clearly engaged in a combined operation with the fishing fleet belonging to her owner, Thomas Benson, as four of her prizes were first landed on the island before being navigated back to Bideford by prize crews drawn from Benson's fishing ships.[28]

While the delivery of cargoes was a secondary function of such 'cruise and voyage' ventures, other 'letters of marque' were set forth principally to carry goods to a set destination. Though these armed trading vessels had long since formed an important part of the commissioned fleet, it was not until the American Revolutionary War that they were commonly described as 'letters of marque' by ship owners keen to relate that their vessels possessed the defensive qualities of a licensed ship, while assuring potential customers that such commissioned status would not lead to a reckless pursuit of prizes. Freighters and passengers in Exeter, for instance, were invited to ship their goods or themselves to Lisbon in the *Princess Royal*, 'a LETTER of MARQUE, burthen 200 tons, with ten guns . . . she is going on a pleasant voyage, and will be a long time out of England'.[29] Occasionally, chance encounters with an enemy vessel during these commercial voyages might add greatly to the profits and wages of those engaged in the venture. Such good fortune befell the owners and men of the *Swift* of Plymouth, a deep-waisted, single-decked sloop employed to carry coals and rice to Malaga in 1777.[30] As Figure 32.1 suggests, her return voyage was interrupted by the capture of the American schooner *Leopard*, both captor and prize, together with their respective cargoes, being sold by the candle in Plymouth during April 1778.

Such 'letter of marque' captures were comparatively rare, the bulk of privateering prizes being condemned to private men-of-war. Set forth without cargoes to 'cruise' against enemy commerce, these ventures were organised on a risk- and profit-sharing basis. Accordingly, instead of wages, privateersmen were normally remunerated with a share in any prizes taken, a reward which not only instilled a prime productivity incentive into the activity, but also removed the constraints imposed on earnings by the payment of monthly wages. Service in a private man-of-war therefore offered an unusual opportunity for seafarers to share directly in the produce of their labour, but it also entailed a high element of risk as cruises did not always yield prizes and naturally involved the physical hazards of war. Moreover, seamen entered this 'no purchase, no pay' occupation at times when employment was readily available in the Navy or in the mercantile marine. In effect, therefore, privateersmen gambled the earnings they could have acquired elsewhere against the chance that their predatory endeavours might generate sufficient profit to render their share more valuable than the sum of the wages so forsaken. This gamble represented the seafarer's investment in the venture, a stake which substantially reduced the expenditures borne by the promoters of the enterprise, and added a co-operative veneer to relations between capital and labour in the commerce-raiding business.

Two principal types of private man-of-war operated in the eighteenth century. Organised along similar lines and intent on profiting from the seizure of the enemy's seaborne property, the 'deep-water' and 'Channel'

For Sale *by the* Candle,

AT the Fountain Tavern, on Smart's Quay, in Plymouth, on Thurſday the 9th Day of April, 1778, by Three o'Clock in the Afternoon preciſely,

The good Schooner LEOPARD,

(Lately taken from the Rebels by the Swift Letter of Marque, Edward Smith, Commander.)

Plantation built, ſquare ſtern'd, burthen about 90 Tons, a remarkable faſt Sailer, and well found, calculated for the Newfoundland or Fruit Trades, and may be ſent to Sea at a very trifling Eepence; now lying in Catwater, where ſhe is to be delivered.

For Viewing and Inventories Application may be made to

JOSEPH SQUIRE, Broker.

Plymouth, March 27, 1778.

For Sale *by the* Candle,

AT the Fountain Tavern, on Smart's Quay, in Plymouth, on Thurſday the 9th Day of April, 1778, immediately after the Sale of the Leopard,

The following GOODS,

20 Pipes - }
20 Hogſheads } Genuine old Vidonia Wines.
40 Quarter Caſks }

Being the entire Cargo now landing out of the Swift Letter of Marque, Edward Smith, Commander, from Teneriffe, for this Port. The Wines may be taſted any Time before the Sale, and Catalogues delivered, by applying to

JOSEPH SQUIRE, Broker.

Plymouth, March 27, 1778.

For Sale *by the* Candle,

AT the Fountain Tavern, on Smart's Quay, in Plymouth, on Thurſday the 30th of April, 1778, by Three o'Clock in the Afternoon preciſely,

The good Sloop SWIFT,

Bermudian built, burthen about 100 Tons, more or leſs, a prime Sailer, only Three Years old, pierced for 12 Guns, and is now mounted with Ten Four-pounders and Six Swivels, ſhifts without Ballaſt, and remarkable well found, every Thing belonging to her almoſt new, is juſt returned from a ſucceſsful Cruize, and may be ſent to Sea at no Expence in Materials. For viewing the ſaid Veſſel, and Inventories, Application may be made to

JOSEPH SQUIRE, Broker.

Plymouth, March 27, 1778.

N. B. Any Perſon inclinable to treat for her by private Contract, may apply as above.

For Sale *by the* Candle,

AT the Fountain Tavern, on Smart's Quay, in Plymouth, on Thurſday the 30th of April, 1778, immediately after the Sale of the Swift,

The following GOODS,

20,000 White Oak Pipe Staves
1,500 Ditto Hogſhead Staves
1,000 Pounds of remarkable fine clean Bees Wax.

Being the entire Cargo of the Schooner Leopard, Joſeph Comſtock, late Maſter, from Edington, in North Carolina, bound to Teneriffe, taken and ſent into this Port by the Swift Letter of Marque, Edward Smith, Commander.

For viewing the aforeſaid Goods, and Catalogues, Application may be made to

JOSEPH SQUIRE, Broker.

Plymouth, March 27, 1778.

32.1 Sale of the 'Letter of Marque' *Swift*, with her goods and her American prize, from the *Exeter Flying Post*, 3 April 1778. *(Devon Library Services, WCSL)*

forms of predator were different in degree rather than in kind. While the former was a private ship-of-war despatched to prey on the valuable transoceanic trade of the Bourbon powers, the archetypal 'Channel' privateer limited her attentions to the enemy's coastal and fishing vessels, and to neutral ships carrying contraband produce. Devon venturers engaged in both forms of activity, the character of their investments reflecting the wider influences which essentially conditioned privateering enterprise. Thus, in the 1740s, local merchants and seafarers were conspicuously involved in the upsurge of large-scale commerce-raiding activity fostered by the relative abundance of high-value units of enemy commerce. With poorly protected French 'Martinicomen' conveying cargoes of sugar, coffee, indigo, and specie across the Atlantic, and the Spaniards transporting the bullion of Mexico and Peru in register-ships 'running' for home,[31] Devon's merchant capitalists, like their rivals in Bristol and London, perceived the existence of 'good pickings for privateers of force'.[32]

Accordingly, substantial quantities of capital were invested in powerful private ships-of-war set forth to intercept Bourbon colonial trade in the Bay of Biscay, the Channel Soundings, or further west, off the Azores. Typical of the scale of operations were ventures like the *Exeter* of 320 tons, 26 carriage guns, and 230 men, and the 200-ton, 150-man *Godolphin*,[33] just two of the eight commissioned craft owned by George Coade, jr, John Tozer, & Co of Exeter. Dartmouth merchants were also active in this business. Thus the *Lyoness*, of 350 tons, 20 carriage guns, and 145 men, and the *Tygress*, a 300-ton private ship-of-war armed with 20 carriage guns and worked by 200 men, were despatched by a syndicate of local gentlemen and merchants headed by John Seale, Charles Hayne, and Richard and Robert Newman, in conjunction with Sir William Billers and William Poston, aldermen of the City of London.[34]

Meanwhile, a mercantile group led by Arthur Holdsworth and Nathaniel Terry of Dartmouth was responsible for the outset of six private men-of-war, including the *Mars*, of 260 tons and 150 men, the *Dartmouth Gally*, of 180 tons and 200 men, and the 600-ton *Boscawen*, a former French man-of-war worked by some 300 seafarers.[35] Prominent amongst this consortium were the London merchants Israel Jalabert and Parnell Nevill, whose privateering speculations extended to at least 20 ventures in the 1739–1748 war, including a strong interest in the *Royal Family* squadron. This fleet of four private ships-of-war, mustering 1,550 tons, 92 guns, and 850 men, represented the largest concentration of privateering capital and labour assembled in the eighteenth century.[36] With George Walker, erstwhile captain of the *Mars* and the *Boscawen*, assuming command of the *Royal Family* vessels – and attracting a following of 'Old Boscawens' to join the squadron as it fitted out in Bristol[37] – Dartmouth's commerce-raiding enterprise was inextricably linked with the most dynamic facet of the British privateering business in the mid-eighteenth century.

The 'deep-water' private ship-of-war was distinguished by the magnitude of her crew. Complements generally exceeded 100 men, with upwards of 250 shareholding seafarers shipped aboard the larger 'privateers of force'. Such crews were organised along naval lines to maximise the prize-taking ability of the vessel.[38] Thus a hierarchical command structure was invariably apparent, with four lieutenants, five midshipmen, and a captain of marines subservient to the commanders of large-scale predators such as the *Boscawen* of Dartmouth. Specialist crew members – the master, the gunner, the surgeon, the boatswain, and the carpenter – were responsible for the central aspects of the ship's work, while supplies and provisions were entrusted to quartermasters, armourers maintained the small arms, and trumpeters or drummers were recruited to accompany the 'music of the great guns'. Subordinate to the officers and specialists, and comprising the bulk of the complement, were the able and ordinary seamen, the landmen, and the boys who hauled sails, operated guns, and boarded prizes.

So as not to 'disturb and divide the harmony that ought to be amongst the Company for the success of the undertaking', these variously rated privateersmen were obliged to observe the articles drawn up to govern the venture. In general, these regulations prescribed a series of measures to punish cowardly or insubordinate behaviour, to reward vigilance and valour, and to compensate the injured and bereaved. The men of the *Tygress*, for instance, were to forfeit their share in the venture if they transgressed the articles, while £5 was to be awarded to the seafarer who first boarded a prize, and £15 was payable to those unfortunate enough to lose a limb. Such contracts, moreover, determined how the proceeds of the enterprise were to be administered and divided between the venturers. In most instances the net produce of the 'deep-water' cruise was evenly split, the privateer owners claiming one moiety, and the other belonging to the ship's company. A local variation seems to have applied in Dartmouth, however, for the articles of the *Tygress* specified that five-eighths of the net prize fund belonged to the vessel's owners, while the contract relating to the *Boscawen*'s 1744 cruise awarded two-thirds of the profits to her owners, the proportion being revised to five-eighths in a subsequent agreement.

In spite of these comparatively disadvantageous terms, the *Boscawen*'s men participated in numerous violent engagements which epitomised the aims and means of the 'deep-water' commerce-raiding campaign of the 1740s. In August 1744 the Dartmouth vessel encountered *Les Deux Amis* three leagues off Cape Pinas in northern Spain. The 350-ton West Indiaman resisted the *Boscawen* for over three hours in an action which left numerous casualties on both sides, including two or three Frenchmen who were 'blown up'. Unfortunately for the captors the prize was less valuable than had been anticipated, for *Les Deux Amis* was proceeding for Bayonne with ballast and 65 passengers on board, having previously discharged her cargo of sugar, coffee, and 60,000 pieces of eight at Corunna.[39] In the following year, however, the *Boscawen*, cruising in consort with the *Sheerness* of Bristol, perpetrated one of the most notable privateering attacks of the eighteenth century. Sailing to the northwest of Finisterre, the two private ships-of-war met with a fleet of eight French Martinicomen, fully laden and homeward bound. Despite forming a line of battle and offering spirited resistance, five of the enemy ships were captured, one was sunk, and no fewer than 113 Frenchmen were killed. As a consequence of this bloody and damaging action, 1,650 hogsheads of sugar and 100 tons of coffee, worth at least £40,000, passed into the hands of the captors.[40]

Engagements on this scale were beyond the scope of the 'Channel' privateer. This form of enterprise entailed the outset of relatively small craft to prey on enemy small fry and neutrals in the Channel Narrows or in the approaches to the ports of Brittany, Normandy, and the Bay of Biscay. The prospects facing such ventures tended to improve in the second half of the eighteenth century as the growing effectiveness of British naval and privateering activity encouraged Bourbon consignees to ship their goods in neutral vessels. Reliant on documentary defences rather than armaments, these targets were susceptible to the attentions of diminutive predators whose crews required a detailed knowledge of the laws of contraband and a keen eye for incriminating evidence more than prowess in physical combat. By the American Revolutionary War the day of the 'privateer of force' had all but passed, though substantial ventures such as the 400-ton, 150-man *King George* of Exeter were occasionally mounted (see Fig 32.2). As Devon's experience shows, privateering venturers now tended to invest their capital and their labour in relatively limited undertakings, adopting more flexible organisational structures to counter the risks inherent to their enterprise.

The changing character of commerce-raiding enterprise was amply demonstrated when reprisals against Dutch seaborne property were granted in December 1780.[41] With vast numbers of merchantmen – 'full 16,000 traders' were at sea according to one report[42] – suddenly exposed to seizure and common condemnaton, a veritable commerce-raiding mania infected every British maritime district. 'Never was the spirit of privateering at such a pitch' was the consensus of contemporary opinion, as venturers eagerly fitted out 'every vessel that can swim upon the water for 24 hours' for a cruise against that 'treacherous and self-interested nation'.[43] Nowhere was the enthusiasm for the Dutch War greater than in the West Country, for in the Soundings and western reaches of the Channel an abundance of erstwhile neutral Dutchmen, laden with Carribbean produce, were believed to be proceeding for home unaware that hostilities had commenced. Feverish activity was apparent in the ports and estuaries of South Devon as local venturers swiftly despatched over 60 'Channel' privateers, and private men-of-war from Lancaster, Liverpool, London, Newcastle, and elsewhere were refitted 'with all possible expedition' to secure these seemingly rich and easy pickings.

THE Lords of the Admiralty having been pleaſed to appoint the BEAVER SLOOP of WAR, Capt. Peyton, to be a conſtant Convoy between Exeter and London, in the Manner the Otter was during the laſt War, All VOLUNTEERS, willing to enter on Board her for this Service, will be entitled to the following Bounties;

Five Guineas—Able Seamen,
Three Guineas—Ordinary Seamen,
Two Guineas—Landmen or ſtout Lads,

To be paid by the Treaſurer, on the Captain's granting a Certificate that the Perſon entering is entitled to the Bounty.

Apply to the Beaver, now lying at Exmouth; Mr. John Williams, in Exeter; or Mr. John Oſborn, Deputy Key-maſter, Topſham.

For a CRUISE of SIX MONTHS,

NOW lying at Starcroſs, and will ſail in a few Days,

The PRIVATE SHIP of WAR

KING GEORGE,

A Compleat Frigate-built Ship, about 400 Tons Burthen, Copper-ſheath'd, Mounting 22 Six-pounders, all upon one Deck, with 2 Nine-pounders on the Fore-Caſtle and 6 Four-pounders on the Quarter Deck, beſides Swivels and ſmall Arms.

This Ship will be fitted out at a very great Expence, and have Accommodations for 150 Men, to be commanded by

Capt. BENJAMIN BUTTELL.

All Gentlemen Seamen and young Able-bodied Landmen, who are deſirous to make their Fortunes, may apply to the ſaid Captain Buttell, Mr. William Johns, or Mr. John Oſbourn, at Topſham, who will give them good Encouragement; and he particularly hopes for the Company of thoſe Gentlemen who were with him upon his laſt fortunate Cruiſe.

Able Seamen	£.7 7 0
Ordinary ditto	5 5 0
Able Landmen	4 4 0
Ordinary ditto	3 3 0

☞ Some OFFICERS wanting.

32.2 Recruiting advertisement for the *Beaver* sloop-of-war and the *King George* private ship-of-war, from the *Exeter Flying Post*, 11 June 1779. *(Devon Library Services, WCSL)*

The scale and urgency of this predatory response was typified by the experience of Captain Peter Tessier of Dartmouth. His craft, the *Spitfire*, a single-masted lugger of 50 tons, equipped with one carriage gun and six swivels, and worked by 15 men,[44] departed the Dart as soon as possible after the declaration of war. Alas, due to 'the multiplicity of business in the Admiralty Office', the grant of Tessier's commission was delayed. He therefore remained unlicensed on the morning of 31 December 1781 as the *Spitfire* stood in sight of *De Twee Gesusters* as she was seized by the *Providence*, a 25-ton, 16-man privateer of Dartmouth, just three leagues off Start Point. Having taken some prisoners off the Dutchman and placed some of his men aboard while the *Providence* returned to Dartmouth, Tessier claimed a share in the prize, a 300-ton vessel conveying coffee, sugar, cocoa, and tobacco from Curacao to Zuricksee. Some hours later however, the *Stag* private man-of-war of Jersey appeared at the scene, and her captain, after threatening to sink the *Spitfire*, imposed his own men on the stricken Dutchman and laid claim to the prize. In the protracted legal battle which ensued, the Prize Appeals Court dismissed the interest of the non-commissioned *Spitfire* as well as that of the *Stag*, condemning *De Twee Gesusters* as prize to the *Providence*, though half of the proceeds were declared droits and perquisites of the Admiralty.[45]

This was one of many such cases decided on appeal, a clear sign of the intensity of the small-scale, short-range privateering assault. Indeed, it was in the courts that privateering venturers fought their sternest battles in the Anglo-Dutch War. Countering the claims of alleged joint-captors was often more difficult and costly than taking the prize itself, with litigants such as Peter Ougier, managing owner of the *Snap Dragon* of Dartmouth, marshalling evidence from Falmouth, Plymouth, and Shrewsbury and then spending many weeks in London to prepare his defence against the *Bird*.[46] As cases might turn on the evidence of the prize vessel's crew, efforts were sometimes made to influence witnesses' recollections of events. William Newman, owner of the *Spitfire*, allegedly suggested to the captain of *De Twee Gesusters* that the 'more we have of this prize, the more generous we shall be to you',[47] while an attempt to bribe the mate of *Die Lieffde* by the agents of the *Bird* only incensed the witness and left him 'violently attached' to the cause of the *Snap Dragon*.[48] Subsequently, the Prize Appeals Court decided in favour of the Dartmouth venturers engaged in this 40-ton coaster, which was one of the many small privateers offered for sale in the spring and early summer of 1781 as the privateering mania abated (see Fig. 32.3).[49]

If somewhat less heroic than the 'deep-water' operations of the 1740s, the bout of 'Channel' privateering aggression unleashed in the winter of 1780–1781 represented the apogee of Devon's eighteenth-century privateering business. Though the county was never again to witness such intense predatory activity, a strong interest in 'Channel' commerce-raiding was apparent in Plymouth in the Napoleonic War. As the account books of the 107-ton, 31-man *Snap Dragon* indicate, the main target of this enterprise was neutral shipping as it proceeded down Channel. No fewer than 13 vessels were detained during the predator's 1807 cruise, yet only the *Dispatch*, a recapture, generated prize money, the remainder being restored or liberated. In a subsequent cruise another 13 neutral vessels were arrested and restored, four on the payment of captors' expenses, while six were sentenced as droits and perquisites of the Admiralty and a single vessel, the *Jongfer Charlotte*, was condemned as prize.[50] Modest earnings accrued from this predation, though in common with other Plymouth ventures of the time, the lion's share of the profits belonged to the vessel's owners, as most crew members took the option of transferring their shares to the owners in return for a guaranteed monthly wage.[51] Such a system, which had prevailed in the Channel Islands throughout the eighteenth century, obviated much of the financial risk facing privateersmen and served to assimilate commerce-raiding enterprise with the rest of the shipping industry.

Significance

Eighteenth-century privateering capitalists were always keen to stress the wider utility of their enterprise. In his proposals for the establishment of the 'Exeter and Devonshire Naval Association', for instance, 'Civis' suggested that the outset of private ships-of-war would prove beneficial to the public in distressing 'our natural enemies' and affording protective services 'equal to those of frigates, which we at present stand in need of' (see Fig. 32.4). Devon's privateering experience indicates that there was a modicum of truth in these propagandist contentions. Thus, the multiple captures achieved in the 1740s and 1750s by large-scale private ships-of-war such as the

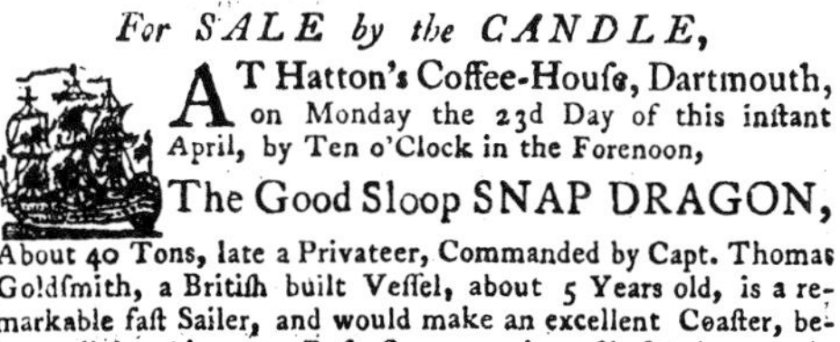

For SALE by the CANDLE,

AT Hatton's Coffee-Houſe, Dartmouth, on Monday the 23d Day of this inſtant April, by Ten o'Clock in the Forenoon,

The Good Sloop SNAP DRAGON,

About 40 Tons, late a Privateer, Commanded by Capt. Thomas Goldſmith, a Britiſh built Veſſel, about 5 Years old, is a remarkable faſt Sailer, and would make an excellent Coaſter, being well found in every Reſpect, or may be eaſily fitted out again for a Privateer.

Immediately after the Sale of the Veſſel will be ſold in Four Lots, all her WARLIKE STORES and other MATERIALS, that did belong to her as a Cruiſer.

For Particulars apply to Mr. PETER OUGIER, of whom Inventories may be had.

Dartmouth, April 10, 1781.

32.3 Sale of the *Snap Dragon* of Dartmouth, from the *Exeter Flying Post* 10 April 1781. *(Devon Library Services, WCSL)*

For the EXETER FLYING-POST.

PROPOSALS for the Conſideration of the CITIZENS of EXETER.

Communicated to the PRINTER,

S I R,

A WAR with our natural Enemies, will naturally have this good Effect,—that it will conſolidate our lat jarring Intereſts at Home, and make us unanimous in *true Patriotiſm*, the *Love and Defence of our Country*, and the Execution of our beſt Endeavours againſt our perfidious hereditary Enemies, the French and Spaniards;—In Order to which, I beg Leave to ſubmit the following Hints to the Conſideration of this Antient, Loyal, and Opulent City, in Hopes of their obtaining Improvement and Perfection under more capable Hands, and the Patronage of the Public.

TO DISTRESS OUR ENEMIES, and in ſo doing ENRICH OURSELVES, is the Subſtance of my Propoſition, which in other Words, is,

For the Citizens of Exeter, and Inhabitants of the County of Devon, to Subſcribe at Pleaſure, for the Purpoſe of fitting out a number of Privateers, proportionable to the Sums ſubſcribed, to cruize againſt the Enemies of Great-Britain, (than which 'tis preſumed there cannot be a Stronger Proof of our Loyalty or Patriotiſm) every 25l. to be deem'd a Share in the General Fund, the Money to be lodged in the Hands of Perſons of known Subſtance and Property, and to be under the Direction of *other* Perſons properly qualified to conduct the Undertaking! The Captures and Prizes to be divided among the Ships Crew, and Subſcribers, in proportion to their Subſcriptions.

In order to render this Plan as broad bottom'd, and univerſal as poſſible, thoſe whoſe Circumſtances will not admit of their Subſcribing a whole Share, may join with their Friends and Acquaintance, and raiſe a Share between them, which whole ſhare ſhould be ſubſcribed in the Name of one of them. Thus too thoſe who have never been in Sight of Salt Water, nor had the leaſt Hand in Commercial or Naval Tranſactions, nay even the LADIES, and Female Delicacy itſelf, may lend effectual Aſſiſtance to drub the French, and diſtreſs our natural Enemies; which Laudable Aſſociation may be entitled, the EXETER AND DEVONSHIRE NAVAL ASSOCIATION, and if thought neceſſary might be incorporated by Act of Parliament for the Security of the Subſcribers.

Was a Plan of this Kind to take Place, Imagination can ſcarce conceive how large Sums might be ſubcribed, (for Individuals are rich and Loyal, however poor the Nation may be) and what Advantages might accrue to Individuals from Captures at the Beginning of the War, before the Enemies Trade is demoliſhed, (a Temptation ſufficient to induce even Miſers to ſubſcribe largely) and to the Public from a Number of Privateers cruiſing in the Channel, Bay, Mediterranean, &c. where their Services would be equal to thoſe of Frigates, which we at preſent Stand in need of.

The time to Profit by privateering, and to diſtreſs the Enemy moſt effectually, is certainly at the Beginning of a War. May a Plan of this Kind then be ſpeedily adopted, heartily encouraged by all Ranks of People, and honeſtly, patriotically, and ſucceſsfully proſecuted, to the great Emolument of the Subſcribers, the real Honour of our City and County, the permanent good of our Nation, and the utmoſt Humiliation of our perfidious Enemies, is the ſincere and ardent Wiſh of

Your humble Servant,

CIVIS.

32.4 Proposals for the 'Exeter and Devonshire Naval Association', from the *Exeter Flying Post*, 3 April 1778. *(Devon Library Services, WCSL)*

Dartmouth Gally, the *Boscawen*, and the *Tygress* of Bideford self-evidently inflicted some damage on the enemy's commerce. Similarly, the despatch of scores of diminutive commerce raiders from Devon's ports in the winter of 1780–1781 contributed to the severe depletion of Dutch trade, while the perennial visitation and search of neutral vessels passing through the Channel helped check the flow of contraband goods to France and Spain. Commissioned enterprise might also serve the war effort in a defensive sense. For instance, 'letters of marque', such as Devon's licensed Newfoundlandmen, possessed a degree of defensive self-sufficiency which could only lessen the Navy's protective burden. Moreover, the capture of *corsaires* like *L'Aigle*, of 22 guns and 175 men, a prize to the *Tygress* of Dartmouth,[52] reduced the hazards confronting British trade, while the interception of diplomatic communications, such as the congressional dispatches taken out of the American privateer *Compte d'Estaing* by the men of the *King George* of Exeter, might prove to be of some strategic value.[53]

If such actions demonstrated the military efficacy of commerce-raiding enterprise, they were largely incidental to the outcome of the wider naval struggle. By the eighteenth century, in contrast to earlier epochs, privateering was a marginal factor in the conduct of the war at sea, the peripherality of the activity becoming more obvious as state navies expanded with each successive war. Indeed, there is evidence to suggest that the operations of private men-of-war retarded rather than promoted the prosecution of maritime conflict. Valuable naval time and effort, for example, might be expended in the policing of privateersmen such as James Vercoe, captain of the *Fox* of Plymouth, who was arrested at sea by Lord Hervey of the *Daphne* man-of-war for allegedly pillaging a Dutch merchantman.[54] Of more significance, perhaps, was the impact of privateering on the seafaring labour market. Requiring large numbers of men, private ships-of-war invariably accentuated the seemingly insoluble 'manning problems' faced by the Navy in wartime. Thus, 'seamen flocked from all quarters to enter on board' the *Boscawen* at Dartmouth in 1744,[55] a time when labour shortages were evident in the King's ships. Likewise, the outfit of the *King George* private ship-of-war in 1779 clearly added to naval recruitment difficulties in the Exe estuary. Attempting to raise a complement for the *Beaver*, a sloop-of-war intended 'to be a constant convoy between Exeter and London', the Lords of the Admiralty offered a bounty of five guineas to able seamen on recruitment, two guineas less than the sum currently promised by the *King George*'s owners (see Fig. 32.2). Such was the paucity of volunteers for the naval sloop that Exeter's Chamber of Commerce felt obliged to supplement the government's bounty by three guineas, thereby rendering it more lucrative for able men to enlist in the *Beaver* than in the private ship-of-war.[56]

Privateering was therefore of dubious utility as a tool of war. Its true significance, however, lay in the economic sphere. As a necessarily impermanent branch of the shipping industry, the business of reprisal represented an option which might be taken up by ship owners and seafarers during the brief periods when predatory prospects were bright. At these junctures commerce raiding could assume an important role in various aspects of the maritime economy. It provided an investment opportunity, attracting the funds of the small investor in addition to the capital of merchants and ship owners at the heart of the local business community (see Fig. 32.4). As a labour-intensive activity, privateering added to the pressure on the supply of seafarers, helping to drive up wage rates. Moreover, the outfit of private ships-of-war stimulated activity in the ancillary maritime industries. With commerce raiders like the *Dragon* and the *Mars* 'just built for that purpose' in Teignmouth,[57] vessels such as the *Favourite* of Exeter having extra armaments fitted together with 'exceeding fine covering for fighting the guns',[58] and damaged craft like the *Lord Hawke* seeking repairs in Dartmouth,[59] privateering entailed a considerable amount of work for shipbuilders. Similarly, the demands of privateering promoters for sails, cordage, warlike stores, victuals, and provisions generated business for a range of local suppliers and traders.

Such activity was especially important to the economies of ports depressed by the onset of war. In Dartmouth, for instance, privateering enterprise fulfilled a counter-cyclical role in the 1739–48 and 1777–83 conflicts, expanding as market closures, impressment, and losses to the enemy brought recession to the Newfoundland trade. Accordingly, it was the Holdsworths, the Newmans, the Sparkes, Leigh & Pinson, Peter Ougier, Arthur French, and other leading cod-fishing merchants who set forth the majority of Dartmouth's private men-of-war in these conflicts. Likewise, many of the commanders of these licensed vessels – men such as Thomas Goldsmith, Andrew Pidgely, Henry Studdy, and Peter Tessier – were engaged as captains of Newfoundlandmen in peacetime, a duality which must have applied to a large proportion of their crews.[60] Although predatory success could never be guaranteed, the outset of privateers meant employment for capital and labour which otherwise may have lain idle, and also triggered the 'knock-on' effects felt by those engaged in servicing and supplying the shipping industry.

The returns generated by the privateering business were also of some import to the local economy. In 1747, for instance, the owner of Sutton Pool in Plymouth remarked that his port investment was the 'best bargain I ever made', the Pool being in a 'thriving condition' as a result of the dues paid on the landing of prize goods.[61] Later in the century, notably in the wake of the 1780–1781 privateering mania, brokers and auctioneers in Dartmouth and Plymouth were busily engaged in marketing the goods and vessels condemned to local privateering venturers.[62] Such sales might benefit consumers – if not domestic importers and retailers – as influxes of prize produce not only served to depress prices but also added to the range of goods available. The first coffee imported into Topsham, for example, comprised the cargo of a Martinicoman taken by the *Hawke* in 1756.[63]

More directly, returns accrued to the venturers engaged in privateering enterprise. Of course, these might be decidedly negative; thus, enemy seizures of vessels like the *Tygress* of Dartmouth,[64] the loss of craft such as the *Bellona* of Exeter – 'overset in a violent gust of wind' off Dawlish Warren, with the demise of 25 men[65] – and mutinous debacles like the cruise of the *Snap Dragon* of Plymouth, clearly constituted a wastage of resources.[66] Other ventures yielded the windfall profits which privateering enterprise promised. Thus, the *Dartmouth Gally* 'did take from His Majesty's enemies several rich and valuable prizes' in 1744,[67] while in 1781 the *Lady Howe*, a 250-ton, 85-man Dartmouth privateer, generated a net prize fund of over £26,000 from the capture of *De Negotie en Zeevaert*.[68] Perhaps the most profitable of all of Devon's commerce-raiding ventures, however, was the *Snap Dragon* of Dartmouth, fitted out for a mere £157 10s in the opening stages of the Dutch War.[69] The net proceeds accruing from her capture of *Die Lieffde* amounted to £21,088 3s 5d.[70] If rare, such extravagant rates of return explain why privateering enterprise remained a regular facet of Britain's wartime economy during the long eighteenth century.

32: Privateering Enterprise in Devon, 1689–1815

1 PRO, HCA 26/1.
2 PRO, HCA 26/60. Article 6, 'Instructions to Privateers', 27 March 1777.
3 See above, chapter 10; also, see FR Stark, *The Abolition of Privateering and the Declaration of Paris* (New York, 1897); and DJ Starkey, *British Privateering Enterprise in the Eighteenth Century* (Exeter, 1990), 19–34.
4 PRO, HCA 25/207.
5 See JC Appleby and DJ Starkey, 'The Records of the High Court of Admiralty as a Source for Maritime Historians' in DJ Starkey, ed., *Sources for a New Maritime History of Devon* (Exeter, 1986), 70–85.
6 See Starkey, *British Privateering Enterprise*, 35–58, 249–56.
7 Unless otherwise stated, the figures cited in this section are derived from Starkey, *British Privateering Enterprise*.
8 See above, chapter 10.
9 PRO, HCA 26/69, 28: Declarations 28 April 1781, 15 April 1762.
10 PRO, 25/178: Declaration 20 Jan. 1812.
11 PRO, HCA 26/75, 101: Declarations 13 Dec. 1799, 7 March 1805.
12 PRO, HCA 26/23, 91: Declarations 15 May 1745, 13 Dec. 1804.
13 See R Davis, *The Rise of the English Shipping Industry in the Seventeenth and Eighteenth Centuries* (1962), 264.
14 See Starkey, *British Privateering Enterprise*, 40–6.
15 See WR Meyer, 'Mascall's Privateers', *Archaeologia Cantiana*, XCV (1979), 312–21; JS Bromley, 'The Channel Island Privateers in the War of the Spanish Succession' *Société Guernesiaise Report and Transactions*, (1949), 444–78; P Raban, 'War and Trade in the Mid-Eighteenth Century', *Société Guernesiaise Report and Transactions*, (1986), 131–63; chapters by Bromley, Jamieson, and Meyer in AG Jamieson, ed., *A People of the Sea. The Maritime History of the Channel Islands* (1986), 109–94.
16 PRO, HCA 25/13: Declaration 2 April 1697.
17 PRO, HCA 26/13: Declaration 5 Jan. 1709.
18 PRO, HCA 26/45: Declaration 3 Sept. 1779; *Exeter Flying Post*, 13 Aug. 1779.
19 PRO, HCA 26/22: Declaration 11 July 1744.
20 PRO, HCA 26/25, 17, 55: Declarations 2 July 1747, 6 May 1780, 1 Jan. 1781.
21 See R Pares, *Colonial Blockade and Neutral Rights, 1739–1763* (Philadelphia, 1975), 77–147; Starkey, *British Privateering Enterprise*, 293–4.
22 See above, p. 93.
23 PRO, HCA 26/6: Declaration 24 Sep. 1756.
24 PRO, ADM 43/11(2).
25 PRO, HCA 26/81, 88: Declarations 26 Feb. 1793, 22 June 1803.
26 PRO, HCA 25/13: Declaration 12 April 1697.
27 PRO, HCA 26/66: Declaration 3 Nov. 1779.
28 PRO, HCA 26/32: Declaration 19 May 1744; HCA 32/102, 113, 127, 143.
29 *Exeter Flying Post*, 20 March 1778.
30 PRO, HCA 25/57: Declaration 25 July 1777.
31 See R Pares, *War and Trade in the West Indies, 1739–1763* (Oxford, 1936), 109–14.
32 PRO, C 103/130. Richard Taunton to Thomas Hall, 8 Nov. 1746.
33 PRO, HCA 25/33, 31: Declarations 9 Feb. 1745, 9 July 1744.
34 PRO, HCA 25/34, 26/4: Declarations 23 Nov. 1745, 20 June 1744.
35 PRO, HCA 26/22, 4, 22: Declarations 17 Nov., 2 April, 11 July 1744. See DJ Starkey and P Raban, 'London Capitalists, Channel Island Seafarers and Devon's Private Ships-of-War 1739–48', *DCNQ*, *XXXVI* (1991), 351–4.
36 Starkey, *British Privateering Enterprise*, 131–2.
37 See HS Vaughan, ed., *The Voyages and Cruises of Commodore Walker* (1928).
38 This discussion is based on the Articles of Agreement collected in PRO, ADM 43, particularly those relating to the *Boscawen* and *Tygress* of Dartmouth in ADM 43/3, 5.
39 PRO, HCA 32/105(1).
40 PRO, HCA 32/94(1), 97(2), 98(3), 106, 157(1). See Vaughan, *Voyages and Cruises*, xxviii, 48–54; and JW Damer Powell, *Bristol Privateers and Ships of War* (Bristol, 1930), 163–4.
41 See DJ Starkey, 'British Privateering against the Dutch in the American Revolutionary War, 1780–1783' in S Fisher, ed., *Studies in British Privateering, Trading Enterprise and Seamen's Welfare, 1775–1900* (Exeter, 1987), 1–17.
42 *Morning Chronicle and London Advertiser*, 25 Dec. 1780.
43 *Glasgow Mercury*, 21 Dec. 1780.
44 PRO, HCA 26/55: Declaration 1 Jan. 1781.
45 PRO, HCA 45/12: Case of *De Twee Gesusters*.
46 DRO, Seale Papers: Correspondence of Peter Ougier with John Seale, 1781.
47 PRO, HCA 45/12.
48 DRO, Seale Papers: Peter Ougier to John Seale, 16 Aug. 1781.
49 See the *Sherborne and Yeovil Mercury*, April–May 1781.
50 PRO, C 103/180, C 124/bundle: Pearse v. Green.
51 PRO, HCA 25/210: Articles of Agreement, *Alert* (1807), *Betsey* (1807), *Caesar* (1807), *Satellite* (1807), *Snap Dragon* (1807), *Unity* (1806).
52 PRO, ADM 43/5(1).
53 *Exeter Flying Post*, 13 Aug. 1779.
54 PRO, HCA 45/12: Case of *Jonge Juffrow Anna*.
55 Vaughan, *Voyages and Cruises*, 40.
56 *Exeter Flying Post*, 6 Aug. 1779; see DJ Starkey, 'War and the Market for Seafarers in Britain 1736–1792' in LR Fischer and HW Nordvik, eds, *Shipping and Trade 1750–1950: Essays in International Maritime Economic History* (Pontefract, 1990), 25–42.
57 *Exeter Flying Post*, 5 March 1779, 18 Feb. 1780.
58 *Exeter Flying Post*, 28 Aug. 1778.
59 C Elliott, 'Some Transactions of a Dartmouth Privateer during the French Wars at the end of the Eighteenth Century' in Fisher, *Studies in British Privateering*, 19–40.
60 PRO, BT 98/3–5.
61 PRO, C 108/355: Thomas Veale to Joseph Burt, 22 Dec. 1747.
62 See the *Exeter Flying Post* and the *Sherborne and Yeovil Mercury*, April–Sep. 1781.
63 PRO, CUST 64/4: Collector, Exeter, to Board of Customs, 23 Oct. 1756. I am indebted to Stephen Fisher for this reference.
64 PL Ford, 'Some Briefs in Appeal Causes', *Proceedings of the Massachusetts Historical Society*, V (1889–90), 99–100.
65 *Exeter Flying Post*, 10 Sep. 1779.
66 PRO, C 103/180, C 124/bundle: Pearse v. Green.
67 DRO, 1032 F/Z 7: Deposition of Arthur Holdsworth, 28 Aug. 1750.
68 PRO, HCA 42/140.
69 DRO, Seale Papers: Draft of Agreement between Peter Ougier and John Seale, 1781.
70 PRO, HCA 42/135.

33 *Devon's Maritime Trade and Shipping, 1680–1780*

Stephen Fisher

When viewed overall, the century after 1680 was a period of striking expansion and innovation in England's commercial and shipping activity. These changes may be briefly summarised as a pronounced increase in the volume of transactions, a consolidation of the earlier widening of the areas of trade, distinct changes in the composition of commerce, particularly with the rise of colonial and Asian goods, and a marked growth of the English mercantile marine. For some this has been seen as a period of 'Commercial Revolution', preceding and contributing to the classic English Industrial Revolution.[1] For Devon, too, the century after 1680 saw a notable overall growth of maritime commerce and shipping. Indeed, the first forty or fifty years of this period to about 1720 or 1730 may be regarded as the heyday of Devon's commercial activity, when the county's trade and shipping were at their most notable on the national commercial stage. Devon certainly made some contribution to the contemporary 'Commercial Revolution'. After about 1730, though, despite the continuing expansion of its commercial and shipping business, Devon's national importance declined quite markedly as other ports and regions of the country underwent more rapid growth.

Devon's noteworthiness as a quite significant trading and shipping county in the years 1680 to about 1730 sprang from a number of factors. It has been well said that 'ports are a mirror of the economy', their commerce relating to the fortunes of their hinterlands and their regional economies, with shipowning fostered by good trading opportunities. In the period from 1680 to the 1720s Devon's economy was amongst the most thriving and advanced in the nation. Serges and other medium-priced woollen cloths were produced competitively in various parts of the county, particularly in and around Exeter, Tiverton, and Cullompton, while there were copper and other mining interests in the west of the county, particularly in the Tamar valley. Agriculture was reasonably progressive and flourishing, in east Devon especially. These industrial and farming activities generated significant trades, both inwards and outwards, coastal as well as foreign, at the various ports of the county, and especially on the southern coast, in greatest proximity to these economic activities. The county's westward location on the English Channel, a great artery of English and European commerce, also encouraged trading and shipping activities. Devon's commerce was helped, too, by the existence of a number of populous and increasingly prosperous towns, most particularly Exeter, with resident gentry and a burgeoning middle class, a centre of rising wealth and conspicuous consumption. Three other factors lay behind Devon's not unimportant role in English commercial expansion to 1720 or so. First, there was the establishment of the naval dockyard at Plymouth in 1690 and its subsequent rapid growth in the wars with France and Spain to 1714, along with the use of Torbay as a fleet anchorage: the needs of the navy generated considerable and growing commerce and shipping. Devon's commercial activity was also promoted by the existence of rich fishing grounds off both of the county's coasts, particularly for pilchards and herrings, with good markets at home and abroad. Finally, the historic traditions of maritime skill and enterprise to be found among the local seafarers, merchants, and ship owners should not be forgotten.

From about 1730, however, Devon's role in national maritime affairs began to decline quite fast, even though its own commerce and shipping continued to grow overall. This relative although not absolute decline is largely explained by the broad stagnation of the county's cloth manufacturing industry, which came about for various reasons, principally higher wage costs compared with competing areas elsewhere in England and a tendency to institutional conservatism. The economic hinterland of Devon's ports, although becoming more populous and prosperous, was limited in comparison with the expansive hinterlands of other provincial ports, notably Bristol and Liverpool, Hull and Newcastle. This tendency towards the marginalisation of the Devon economy, in national terms, towards 1780, meant that Devon's commercial and shipping enterprise, although still expansive after 1730, lacked the vigour and note of earlier decades. The one particular growth point was indeed the continuing rise of Plymouth as a naval port, and its expanding needs for supplies of all kinds. Without the presence of the dockyard, or of the frequent wars and intense naval activity of the mid- and later century, Devon's maritime story in these decades would have been a decidedly lesser one.[2]

Devon's commerce and shipping in the period 1680–1780 already has a useful modern literature, although it is very much centred on Exeter.[3] It provides for the years 1680–1780 a detailed discussion of the movements and mercantile enterprise in Exeter's trade and shipping, and the significant, especially industrial and social, factors underlying them. There are brief references in these works to the trades and shipping of the other Devon ports, and sometimes comparative figures are given, but no satisfactory overview exists of Devon's trade and shipping as a whole in these years. The best available studies of the other Devon ports, moreover, do not go into commercial matters at all deeply.[4]

This chapter will provide a comparative overview of the principal Devon ports of the period; their trades, foreign and coastal; and their ship owning interests, relying on two main sets of sources. First, some use will be made of the evidence of contemporaries who visited the ports during the period, to provide some general views. Secondly, use will be made for trade and shipping of the abundant central Customs records of the period which are available from the beginning of the eighteenth century. These national statistics were based on the returns of Customs officials in the different customs ports, and provide both a quantitative and descriptive view of the commerce of the individual Devon ports. Had space permitted, use might have been made of surviving business records and contemporary newspapers, which are informative on individual merchants and ship owners.[5] This chapter, then, provides an overview of the trades and shipping interests of the different Devon ports, in their heyday from 1680 to about 1730 and thereafter in their slower but continuing expansion to 1780.

Some Contemporary Impressions

The principal port of Devon in the period's earlier decades was Exeter, which, in Customs terms, meant not only Exeter itself but also Topsham, its sister port on the Exe estuary. As had been the case for many centuries, Exeter Customs port also included a number of lesser havens such as Lympstone and Exmouth on the river Exe (Fig. 33.1), as well as Sidmouth to the east and Teignmouth to the west. These places, though, carried on relatively little trade and were mostly local fishing places where some boat and shipbuilding was also practised, with Teignmouth, however, notable in the Newfoundland fishery and trade.[6]

There are a number of contemporary impressions of Exeter to draw on.

To set the scene use will be made of Count Magalotti's account of 1669. It is outside the period, it is true, but forms a useful base for later comparison. He noted Exeter's dependence on the commerce in

> bays and different sorts of light cloth [which] is sold to all parts, being sent to the West Indies, Spain, France, and Italy; but the greater part goes into the Levant. The very best cloth is also made, both for home consumption and for exportation; but the trade in this is not considerable, in comparison with the other.[7]

This is not at all a bad description of Exeter's trade, given that it focuses on the principal export product, but the work of modern scholars has made clear that Holland and the German states were important markets too, that the emphasis put on the Levant trade is exaggerated, and that there was also a large coastal and overland trade to London in cloth, as well as a very varied general foreign and coastal trade. Celia Fiennes, the redoubtable traveller, offers a description of Exeter some thirty years later, in 1698. She thought it 'a town very well built . . . spacious noble streets, and a vast trade is carried on [in] serges'. She gave a graphic description of the city's Custom House (Fig. 33.2), remarking that it had an

> open space below with rows of pillars [where] they lay in goods just as they are unladen out of the ships in case of wet. Just by are several little rooms for land waiters, &c., then you ascend up a handsome pair of stairs into a large room full of desks and little partitions for the writers and accountants – it was full of books and papers. By it are two other rooms which are used in the same way when there is a great deal of business.[8]

Some twenty years later, Thomas Cox, the author of *Magna Britannia*, was struck by the city's 'stateliness [and] the richness of its citizens'. He noted that it was a 'resort of strangers' and that 'all kinds of merchandise is so plentiful in it, that nothing necessary is wanting'.[9]

Daniel Defoe also visited Exeter about this time, or a little earlier. The city in his view, in an oft-quoted observation, was 'full of gentry, and good company, and yet full of trade and manufactures also'. On Exeter's trade he was quite specific:

> this city drives a very great correspondence with Holland, as also directly to Portugal, Spain and Italy; shipping off vast quantities of the woollen-manufactures, especially to Holland, the Dutch giving very large commissions for the buying of serges, perpetuanas and such goods.[10]

He does not mention, however, the Mediterranean trades, the Atlantic trades, notably to the West Indies and North America, or the extensive coastal trades.

Malachy Postlethwayt is of particular interest for understanding Exeter as a port, and indeed all the other port towns of Devon as well. He emphasised the financial independence and autonomy of Exeter and the county's merchant class, in general trade and particularly in two branches, the pilchard and herring fisheries, and the Newfoundland fishing:

> I speak now . . . for the whole coast, that in all the towns that lie thereon, beginning at Southampton and reaching the Land's End, and even after that into the Severn Sea, and so to both sides of that sea . . . there are abundance of considerable merchants, who trade independent of London, having two particular branches, which they manage with great success, exclusive of their ordinary correspondence; namely, the pilchard and herring fisheries, and the Newfoundland fishing. They deal very largely also in other things, as in the serges

33.1 The Exe Estuary from Exmouth, an oil painting by CW Bampfylde, 1771. *(Exeter University)*

33.2 Exeter Quay and Custom House. An undated coloured print, probably after 1800. Note the open arcading of the Custom House and the covered Fish Market. *(Devon and Exeter Institution)*

33.3 Exeter Cathedral Yard, by A Glennie, engraved by W Deeble, early nineteenth century. The building on the left, which still stands, was the Exeter Bank, which opened in 1769. *(Devon and Exeter Institution)*

> and manufactures of Exeter, and of other parts of Devonshire, and especially in copper and block-tin, plentifully found in the mines of Cornwall and some in Devonshire, and hardly anywhere else in England.

Exeter, in Postlethwayt's judgement, was one of the principal cities of the kingdom, 'for its building, wealth, extent and number of inhabitants'.[11]

These contemporary views of mercantile Exeter may be closed with the forthright, rather eulogistic but informed opinion of Andrew Brice, a native of the city and a printer and newspaper editor, published in 1759. He had some interesting things to say about the merchants and tradesmen of the city and the county, who he presciently observed to be a rising class. He thought Devon's 'tip-top merchant adventurers &c. . . . may now be justly esteemed a good species of gentry'. On the 'better-sort' of Exeter, he wrote:

> as to table [they] live moderately well in ordinary, and entertain friends and strangers in proper seasons handsomely and very daintily on occasion, without being wastefully profuse . . . Their dress is very proper to a rich trading city, genteel and comely, not gaudily foppish. Their diversions, mostly, are polite enough, yet free from affectation of most fashionable, and taken but in due season.

Brice also provides a charming little cameo of the city's merchant exchange, in the Cathedral Close (Fig. 33.3):

> The void place before the cathedral has been laid out in three divisions, and these environed with rails and posts, between which are left streets, or paved highways . . . Here as on a sort of Change, almost daily, do gentlemen, merchants, and chief traders, walking take meridian air, and talk of business or of news, perhaps or laugh at merry tale, till infallible St Peter, with one warning stroke, sends them with whetted appetites to dinner.[12]

For Plymouth, Count Magalotti's observations of 1669, well before the dockyard's establishment, again provide a good starting point. Regarding the town's trade and shipping, he picked out especially the inter-country carrying business of the locally-owned vessels:

> The life of the city is navigation. The inhabitants export lead and fish in greater quantities than any other article, and with these they go to the Canaries, and to the Western Islands [Azores]. To Barbados in the new world, and in every part of Europe, they act as carriers, conveying merchandise from place to place, at an immense profit to themselves.

He shrewdly noted a striking demographic aspect of Plymouth (generally true of all contemporary port towns) that 'only women and boys are to be seen; the greater part of the men living at sea'.[13] Celia Fiennes was in Plymouth in 1698, some eight years after the naval dockyard's inauguration. She thought Plymouth eminently maritime, 'mostly inhabited with seamen and those which have affairs on the sea'. Naturally enough, she remarked on the activity of the newly-built dockyard (Fig. 33.4), and the need it had for supplies of all kinds:

> The Dock yards are about two miles from the town . . . it is one of the best in England. A great many good ships built there . . . a great deal of buildings on the Dock [including] house for their cordage and making ropes, and all sorts of things required in building or refitting ships.[14]

Rather later, in 1720, after the War of the Spanish Succession, Thomas Cox observed how the naval dockyard had 'much enriched' Plymouth and made it a busy place for shipping, it having been 'in the late wars a rendezvous for all outward-bound convoys, and convenient for the homeward-bound ships to put in, and provide themselves pilots up the Channel'. On Plymouth's foreign trade he was specific, drawing attention to the export of pilchards:

33.4 Plymouth Sound, 1697, with the new Dock and Ships. *BL, King's Top., 43, fos 127–8.*

> The merchants here drive a considerable trade to Virginia, the sugar-islands, and the Streights [the Mediterranean]. Their pilchards, which they take in great numbers on their coasts . . . they send into Spain and Italy, where they are a beneficial commodity.[15]

For Daniel Defoe, also about 1720, Plymouth was 'indeed a town of consideration, and of great importance to the public'. He considered it was much aided by its being 'a general port for the receiving all the fleets of merchants' ships from the southward, as from Spain, Italy, the West Indies, &c. who generally make it the first port to put in at for refreshment or safety, from either weather or enemies'. The trade of its 'several considerable merchants and abundance of wealthy shopkeepers'[16] depended upon the 'so many occasions' on which 'seafaring people' put into Plymouth.

The other principal south Devon port was Dartmouth. Thomas Cox offers us a good description about 1720:

> Dartmouth, a sea-port, borough, corporation and market-town. It has a commodious haven . . . The shipping of this port, and trade of the town, was the most considerable in the county (except that of Exeter) till Plymouth became of late so prosperous and flourishing; but now 'tis much lessened. However, some foreign commerce is still maintained . . .[17]

About the same time Defoe thought Dartmouth 'a town of note', and had a good opinion of the town's merchants and trade, especially its commerce in Newfoundland cod:

> Here are some very flourishing merchants, who trade very prosperously, and to the most considerable trading ports of Spain, Portugal, Italy, and the plantations; but especially they are great traders to Newfoundland, and from thence to Spain and Italy, with fish; and they drive a good trade also in their own fishery of pilchards.[18]

In 1750 Richard Pococke, too, thought Dartmouth (Fig. 33.5) had 'a pretty good trade to Newfoundland, Spain and Portugal'.[19]

As to the north Devon ports, there are fewer contemporary accounts to draw on, these places figuring less on travellers' itineraries. The two most useful observers are Thomas Cox and Daniel Defoe, both writing about 1720. Cox noticed at Barnstaple that: 'most of the trade' had now moved to Bideford, 'tho' there still remain some merchants . . . that maintain a tolerable traffic'. Bideford's trade, in Cox's view, was 'thriving', and the town was 'now one of the best trading towns in England, sending every year great fleets to Newfoundland and the West Indies, and particularly to Virginia'.[20] Daniel Defoe thought, too, that 'of late years . . . Bideford has flourished and . . . Barnstaple rather declined', and that they now matched each other in commerce. Both places had 'a large share in the trade to Ireland, and in the herring fishery, and in a trade to the British colonies in America'. He thought that if Bideford 'cures more fish, Barnstaple imports more wine and other merchandises', while both were established ports for landing Irish wool. Barnstaple he thought 'a large, spacious, well-built town' (Fig. 33.6a, b) and Bideford similarly 'pleasant, clean, well-built', with 'a very noble quay'. Defoe also noted the latter's coasting trade with Liverpool, 'several ships [being] employed to go [there] and up the river Mersey to Warrington, to fetch the rock salt'. This was then used in both Bideford and Barnstaple to 'cure their herrings', the demand for which 'in foreign markets [had] considerably increased'.[21]

Ilfracombe, the remaining Devon Customs port (Fig. 33.7), was remotest of all and hence the least visited. About 1720 Cox thought it 'a pretty safe harbour for ships, by reason of a pile built there'.[22] Defoe, too, thought well of Ilfracombe's 'very good harbour and road for ships', and 'good trade'. He noted, further, that Barnstaple merchants did much of their business at Ilfracombe, for 'ships from Ireland often put in, when, in bad weather, they cannot, without the extremest hazard, run into the mouth of the Taw'.[23]

Devon's Foreign Trade by Inward Shipping Tonnages

Given the fragmentary nature of many of the surviving Customs sources, including the detailed port books, it is not possible to piece together overall movements over the whole period for either the volumes or the values of transactions for the Devon ports. Instead, use will be made of the Devon returns from surviving central Customs records of the tonnages of shipping, British and foreign, employed in trading to foreign parts and entering the English ports, including repeated voyages, from 1709 to 1779. These tonnage figures give an approximation of the relative importance of commercial activity at the principal Devon ports. Until 1772 the figures are for individual years on a once-every-seven-year basis; after 1772 the figures

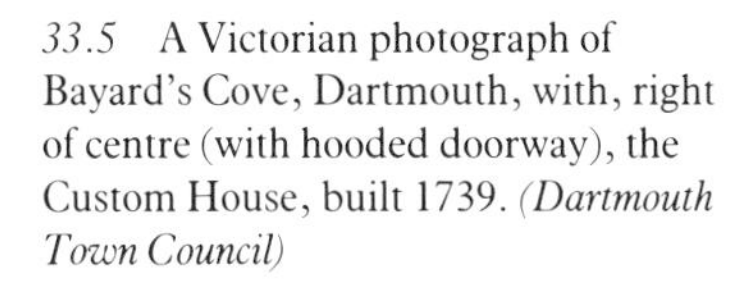

33.5 A Victorian photograph of Bayard's Cove, Dartmouth, with, right of centre (with hooded doorway), the Custom House, built 1739. *(Dartmouth Town Council)*

33.6a Barnstaple Quay, known locally as the 'Strand', as depicted by GB Campion, engraved by L Henshall, and published in 1830. Ships were still very much part of the local scene. *(Devon and Exeter Institution)*

33.6b Barnstaple, Queen Anne's Walk, at the north end of the Quay, a merchant exchange built *c*1708. In the colonnade is the ancient 'Tome' stone on which merchants struck their bargains, and which formerly stood in front of the Quay Hall to the right of the scene in Fig. 33.6a. *(J Youings)*

are annual. It should be borne in mind that the statistics relate to the Customs ports, and not to the individual ports as such. Thus Exeter includes Topsham, the only other notable trading place in the Exeter Customs port, with the other Devon Customs ports referring overwhelmingly to the traffic of the port of that name.

Over the period 1709–1780 the three leading Devon ports in tonnage movements inwards in foreign trade were Exeter, Plymouth and Dartmouth. Table 33.1 presents the inward trading tonnages from foreign parts for these ports in certain peacetime years over the period, and the average for 1772–4. The tonnage figures for Bristol are presented, too, for purposes of comparison.

As will be seen, until 1751 Exeter remained the leading Devon port in the peacetime tonnages entering of shipping employed in foreign trade, losing its position to Plymouth in 1772 (in fact Plymouth also led in 1765). Exeter's total tonnage entering remains fairly constant over these years as a whole, whereas Plymouth's showed much growth in 1772–4 (this growth became apparent from 1758). It is very likely that Plymouth's rise reflected the growing importance of imports of naval stores – timber, iron and other commodities – for the great dockyard. It is noteworthy also that Dartmouth's foreign trading tonnage inwards grew notably from 1751 onwards. In these peace years the tonnages entering these three ports was very largely British-owned, except for Plymouth from 1751, when foreign-owned shipping assumed substantial proportions. In 1772–4 Plymouth's foreign trading entries of shipping made up some 40 per cent of all the tonnage entering these three south Devon ports. Viewed individually, these three ports were much behind Bristol in the trading tonnages in question, but if their entries are combined they accounted for 48 and 49 per cent of Bristol's such entries in 1716 and 1772 respectively, and 33 and 39 per cent in 1730 and 1751 respectively. In 1772–4 the foreign trading tonnage entering these three ports averaged 48 per cent on average of Bristol's similar tonnage.

For Barnstaple and Bideford most of the figures of trading tonnage entering from foreign parts between 1709 and 1779 are clearly unreliable – they are repetitive for both ports until 1765. But in 1765 Barnstaple's trading shipping entries from abroad came to 1,878 tons, and in 1772 to 2,426 tons, compared with Bideford's 569 and 626 tons respectively. While Ilfracombe's figures are usable for all the indicated years, the highest trading tonnage from foreign parts reported as entering this port was but 930 tons, British and foreign vessels combined, in 1751. For 1772–4 the figures for the north Devon Custom ports are presented in Table 33.2.

In the frequent wars of the eighteenth century, though, considerable changes could occur. The war years are here represented by 1709, 1744,

Table 33.1
Peacetime Tonnages of Trading Shipping Entering the Ports Indicated from Foreign Parts, Select Years, 1716–74, including Repeated Voyages

	Exeter		Plymouth		Dartmouth		Bristol	
	British	British & foreign	British	British & foreign	British	British & foreign	British	British & foreign
1716	6,166	6,259	2,271	3,085	2,034	2,094	23,819	24,008
1730	5,493	5,493	1,715	2,058	1,908	2,148	28,879	29,034
1751	6,108	6,348	917	2,117	3,438	3,438	27,167	30,433
1772	4,875	5,705	5,241	8,784	4,368	4,448	34,074	38,707
1772–4 (average)	5,448	6,845	4,873	8,130	5,131	5,570	36,834	42,958

Source: BL, Add. MSS, 11,256, 11,255.

33.7 Ilfracombe, north Devon: the Town and Harbour by T Allom, engraved by J Lowry and published 1830. *(Devon and Exeter Institution)*

Table 33.2
Peacetime Tonnages of Trading Shipping Entering the Ports Indicated from Foreign Parts, 1772–4, including Repeated Voyages

	Barnstaple		Bideford		Ilfracombe	
	British	British & foreign	British	British & foreign	British	British & foreign
1772–4 (average)	2,037	2,087	635	635	313	400

Source: BL, Add. MSS, 11,256, 11,255.

1758, 1779 and 1777–80, as shown in Table 33.3. In these years it is clear that Plymouth generally assumed the lead in Devon's foreign trading activity as measured by the tonnages, British and foreign, of vessels entered from foreign parts. Plymouth's entries held up well in 1709 and 1744, and grew impressively in 1758, 1779, and 1777–80, with much use of foreign-owned shipping. Such statistics chiefly reflect the growing role of the supply needs of the naval dockyard in Plymouth's foreign trade over the period, which more than compensated for the adverse effects war is generally thought to have had on English foreign trade, with its higher freight costs and insurance, hazards from privateers and warships, and the bunching of trade into distinct periods through the use of convoys. In fact, Dartmouth's trading tonnages entering from foreign parts were rather erratic in the first three war years recorded, while Exeter's generally grew, although both did better in 1777–80, when, in Exeter's case especially, there was a great resort to foreign-owned vessels. If individual comparison for these three leading Devon ports in these tonnage figures is made with Bristol, each of them came much behind Bristol. If the three south Devon ports' trading tonnages entering from abroad are combined, however, they amounted to 33, 35 and 37 per cent of Bristol's similar tonnage in 1709, 1744 and 1758, reaching as much as 69 per cent in 1779. In 1777–80 the combined trading tonnage entries of the three south Devon ports constituted 61 per cent on average of Bristol's entries.

Table 33.3
Wartime Tonnages of Trading Shipping Entering the Ports Indicated from Foreign Parts, Select Years, 1709–80, including Repeated Voyages

	Exeter		Plymouth		Dartmouth		Bristol	
	British	British & foreign	British	British & foreign	British	British & foreign	British	British & foreign
1709	1,980	2,428	578	3,518	545	545	17,146	19,817
1744	2,395	2,895	2,131	2,226	1,575	1,745	17,678	19,476
1758	2,534	4,322	1,624	5,889	905	905	21,686	30,348
1779	1,871	5,148	5,813	12,242	3,804	4,890	21,948	32,313
1777–80 (average)	2,183	4,596	6,814	12,612	3,097	4,076	25,235	35,163

Source: BL, Add. MSS, 11,256, 11,255.

For Barnstaple and Bideford in the war years of 1758 and 1779, foreign trading activity as measured by vessel tonnages entering from abroad fell away very considerably, in fact to a nil level in Bideford's case in 1779. Taking the four years 1777–80, however, Barnstaple's British and foreign tonnage together averaged 978 tons, and Bideford's 108 tons only, there being no entries at all at Bideford in 1780 as in 1779. Curiously, Ilfracombe's foreign trading activity changed little in all these indicated war years, but the total tonnages recorded were very low throughout.

Devon's Trade and Shipping Movements, 1759–63

Consideration will now be given to the trades, foreign and coastal, and the shipping movements of the Devon ports in a five-year period of the Seven Years War, that is 1759–63. In 1764 each Customs port in the land had been asked by the Customs authorities in London to survey their trade, and the summary views as later prepared in Customs headquarters have survived.[24] The survey actually covers rather more than five years, that is for the 'five years to Christmas 1763 and down to the time of the survey', some time in 1764, although the actual end-point is not given. This can be viewed, however, as a five-year period, and in fact the port shipping figures are clearly stated as referring to vessels 'trading to and from this port or creeks for five years', that is 1759–63. The survey gives no indication of either the values or volumes of the commodities which comprised the commerce of the respective ports: in the main the goods traded are simply listed. Nevertheless, it provides an idea of the great range and the types of goods that were traded at the Devon ports, as well as other useful information.

Altogether for Exeter Customs port between 1759–63 over 70 commodities were listed as foreign trade imports, and nearly 40 commodities as shipped abroad. In Exeter's coastal trade over 45 commodities were imported, and over 20 exported. The goods brought in from abroad can be divided into groups. Among the foodstuffs, for instance, were wine, oil and olives, lemons and oranges, raisins, currants, nuts, sugar, ginger, rum, beef, butter, pork, codfish, and aqua fortis. Many kinds of timber were imported, such as pipe staves, deals, spars, masts, pine boards, clapboards, wainscot boards and mahogany planks. Other raw materials entering Exeter were cork, indigo, gum, tallow, salt, iron, pitch, turpentine, madder, train oil, whalebone and whalefins, cow or ox hides, furs, bear and seal skins, and lampblack. It is noteworthy that relatively few manufactured goods were imported into Exeter from abroad: among them were linen, matting, soap, Flanders tiles and stoneware.

The goods shipped abroad from Exeter in 1759–63 included, as would be expected, among the manufactured goods, woollens, as well as other textiles such as haberdashery ware and weaving apparel. Other manufactures exported abroad were very varied, including tanned hides and leather, cordage, fishing nets and lines, ironmongery wares, wrought pewter, tinware, earthenware, glass bottles, bricks and gunpowder. Some of the goods so exported were no doubt of local manufacture, but as in previous centuries others had been brought into Exeter from elsewhere, either from other parts of Britain or abroad. This practice of exporting abroad previous imports can be seen, too, in the list of foodstuffs exported, such as wine, oil, molasses, and rice. Other foodstuffs shipped abroad, which no doubt included local products, were wheat, flour, bread, barley, oatmeal, pease, cheese, porter, cider, codfish, and salt. The raw materials exported included tobacco, lime, coal, and unwrought tin.

A number of the commodities figuring in Exeter's foreign trade in 1759–63 can be seen again in the lists of goods reported as either being imported or exported in Exeter's coastal trade. Coastal trade inwards, for example, included, among foodstuffs, wheat, barley, wine, groceries, raisins, nuts, strong beer, codfish, and salt. The raw materials imported coastwise included wool, yarn, oil, tobacco, snuff, iron, lead, tin, coal, dyestuffs such as madder and redwood, as well as hemp, oak plank, and staves. The manufactures imported coastwise included linen, haberdashery wares, ironmongers' wares, earthenware, bricks, and glass bottles. Coastal shipments outwards included, among foodstuffs, wine, groceries, oats, barley, malt, cider, beans, butter, and salt; the raw materials included wool, oil, tobacco, pipe clay, clay, and old cast iron; and among the manufactures there were woollens, linen, haberdashery wares, ironmongery and snuff.

It is evident from these commodities composing Exeter's foreign and coastal transactions in 1759–63 that the city's maritime commerce was both varied and complex, and that the two sets of trades, foreign and coastal, were interdependent. Goods imported into Exeter, either from abroad or coastwise, could either supply the city's or its hinterland's needs, or provide cargoes for re-export in either the foreign or coastal trades. Such imported goods then re-exported would accompany the exports of the city's and its hinterland's own products or manufactures, either abroad or along the coasts to British destinations. In short, Exeter was acting as an entrepôt dealing in a great variety of goods, even if certain commodities such as woollens, wines, sugar, tobacco, timber, and coal stand out in terms of either value or volume.[25] Exeter's merchants may have contained specialists amongst them, but as a body they were carrying on a very varied and complex set of transactions.

The customs returns for Exeter for 1759–63 also provide useful data on the shipping movements of the port, and on the extent of local smuggling.[26] It needs to be remembered that, in addition to the legal trades that figure in the eighteenth-century Customs returns, there was what may well have been significant illicit business that went unrecorded.

On the shipping employed in Exeter's foreign and coastal trade between 1759 and 1763, Table 33.4 is informative. As will be seen, an average of 80 vessels, British and foreign, were reported as trading to and from Exeter in foreign trade each year, averaging 73.4 tons per vessel. There were roughly three British to every foreign vessel, but the latter were distinctly larger at an average 84.2 tons, compared with 69.5 tons for British vessels. On average, not quite as many vessels traded to and from Exeter coastwise as in her foreign commerce each year, some 63 in all, and they were distinctly smaller, averaging 47.4 tons.

As to contraband trade within the Exeter Customs port, the local Customs authorities evidently thought it had 'rather increased' in these war years, the goods in which it was 'reputed' to occur being 'tea, coffee, brandy, rum, geneva and tobacco'. It was thought such illicit trade was principally carried on from Guernsey, Jersey and Alderney. Nine vessels were suspected of being so employed, as well as 'a great number of open boats which trade to and from Guernsey, [and] serve to take goods out of larger vessels on the coast'.

Table 33.4
Shipping Trading to and from Exeter Customs Port, 1759–63

	In foreign trade
British-owned shipping	
Total number	297
Average number p.a.	59.4
Total tonnage	20,649
Average tonnage p.a.	4,130
Average tonnage per vessel	69.5
Foreign-owned shipping	
Total number	105
Average number p.a.	21
Total tonnage	8,838
Average tonnage p.a.	1,768
Average tonnage per vessel	84.2
Total number of vessels	402
Average number p.a.	80.4
Total tonnage of vessels	29,487
Average tonnage p.a.	5,897
Average tonnage per vessel	73.4
	In coastal trade
Total number of vessels	313
Average number p.a.	62.6
Total tonnage of vessels	14,834
Average tonnage p.a.	2,967
Average tonnage of vessels	47.4

Source: BL, Add. MS 9293.

The Customs report on Plymouth's foreign trade in 1759–63 was in some ways more usefully broken down. In particular it drew attention to the 'considerable quantities of prize goods of all kinds [and] naval stores of all sorts from Petersburgh and other parts of the East Country' which had been brought into the port, attributing this to the war then in progress. It then picked out certain foreign import trades, from Portugal and Spain in 'wines and fruit and likewise salt'; from Hamburg in 'linens and other articles'; and from Rotterdam in 'terras, bricks and stone ware'. Exports abroad from Plymouth were thought 'inconsiderable', chiefly English manufactures and products such as broad cloth, hose, stationery ware, pilchards, cider, coal, lime and salt, as well as wine and linens. They were despatched to Leghorn, Madeira, Newfoundland, the West Indies, South Carolina, Portugal, Spain, Ireland and Guernsey. Attention was also drawn to the trade from Plymouth 'to Africa' in 'prohibited East India goods and various sorts of British manufactures [received] coastwise and by land carriage from London'. Special mention was made of the prize goods and naval stores which were re-exported 'in large quantities'. Plymouth's coastal commerce inwards consisted of 'woollens, linens, haberdashery wares, apothecary's ware, British spirits, grocery and other necessaries of life from London and other ports'. Outwards it consisted of 'long ells, oats, cider, coals and hillary stones or slates'. Clearly Plymouth, too, had complex entrepot functions.

Data was also provided on Plymouth's shipping movements in her foreign and coastal trade between 1759 and 1763, as shown in Table 33.5. As will be seen, 103 British and foreign vessels were reported as trading to and from Plymouth on average each year in these war years, averaging almost 116 tons per vessel. There were nearly twice as many British as foreign vessels, but the latter, as at Exeter, were significantly larger. Plymouth's total tonnage engaged in foreign trade in 1759–63 was just over double the corresponding Exeter figure. In Plymouth's coastal trade there were less than half the vessels employed in her foreign trade, and at an average of 59 tons they were significantly smaller.

The smuggling reputedly carried on from Plymouth, or rather, as was

Table 33.5
Shipping Trading to and from Plymouth Customs Port, 1759–63

	In foreign trade
British-owned shipping	
Total number	330
Average number p.a.	66
Total tonnage	34,557
Average tonnage p.a.	6,911
Average tonnage per vessel	104.7
Foreign-owned shipping	
Total number	185
Average number p.a.	37
Total tonnage	25,098
Average tonnage p.a.	5,020
Average tonnage per vessel	135.7
Total number of vessels	515
Average number p.a.	103
Total tonnage of vessels	59,655
Average tonnage p.a.	11,931
Average tonnage per vessel	115.8
	In coastal trade
Total number of vessels	222
Average number p.a.	44.4
Total tonnage of vessels	13,125
Average tonnage p.a.	2,625
Average tonnage of vessels	59.1

Source: BL, Add. MS 9293.

pointed out, at Cawsand and Kingsand, was 'principally with Guernsey', and employed eight 'sailing boats of about 8 tons each' as well as several rowing boats from six to ten tons. The articles involved were 'tea, brandy, rum, geneva' and, interestingly, 'china'. The customs authorities, though, considered that Plymouth's contraband trade 'does not increase here as it does in general all thro' Cornwall'.

Dartmouth's maritime commerce, both in and out, foreign and coastal, like the commerce of Exeter and Plymouth, was also composed of a great miscellany of commodities, reflecting again no doubt a significant entrepot function, as well as transactions with other entrepots along the English coast. Among the port's foreign imports, apart from those which might be expected, were unusual items such as fish tongues and feathers, while prominent among the port's exports abroad were hats and millinery, boots and shoes, British sail cloth, anchor stocks, fishing craft, gunpowder and 'other ammunition', as well as East India goods, French prize cotton, and prize brandy. Dartmouth's coastal imports were as similarly varied as Exeter's and Plymouth's, but included (shades of the 'agricultural revolution') cloverseed, as well as anchors and gunpowder. As might be expected, given the important local Newfoundland interest, the port's shipments to other British ports included 'dry codfish', but among the less conventional items were handspikes and sailors' clothes.

For Dartmouth's shipping movements, in 1759–63, as with Exeter and Plymouth, the customs report stipulated both British and foreign-owned vessels, but combined the shipping in the foreign and coastal trades, as is shown in Table 33.6. Some 76 vessels, British and foreign, were involved in the foreign and coastal trades of Dartmouth on average in these years, averaging 56.6 tons per vessel. The total tonnage employed in Dartmouth's foreign and coastal trades in 1759–63 – 21,666 tons – was less than half of Exeter's trading tonnage in these years, and very considerably behind Plymouth's total trading tonnage in this period of 72,780 tons. As to the smuggling carried on in the Dartmouth customs jurisdiction, it was thought 'there are several cutters and other small vessels employed . . . which trade has rather increased than decreased, notwithstanding the utmost diligence and alertness of the officers'.

Information was also given in this survey on whether the Devon Customs

Table 33.6
Shipping Trading to and from Dartmouth Customs Port, 1759–63, Foreign and Coastal Combined

British-owned shipping	
Total number	351
Average number p.a.	70.2
Total tonnage	20,166
Average tonnage p.a.	4,033
Average tonnage per vessel	57.5
Foreign-owned shipping	
Total number	32
Average number p.a.	6.4
Total tonnage	1,500
Average tonnage p.a.	300
Average tonnage per vessel	46.9
Total number of vessels	383
Average number p.a.	76.6
Total tonnage	21,666
Average tonnage p.a.	4,333
Average tonnage per vessel	56.6

Source: BL, Add. MS 9293.

ports were paying their way. At both Exeter and Plymouth the customs receipts exceeded the cost of the customs service, but this was not so at Dartmouth. In the view of the London Inspector-General of the Customs, this came about 'not owing to any misconduct or inattention in the . . . officers of the port', but rather to the want of imports.

As to the commerce and shipping movements of the north Devon ports in 1759–63, no information was given for Barnstaple on her coastal trade, but there was a reasonably good listing of goods in foreign trade. Barnstaple's foreign imports consisted mostly of foodstuffs and a range of raw materials. The only manufacture imported was 'plain linen'; while horses figured among the lists. Concerning Barnstaple's shipments abroad, manufactures stand out, no doubt including local products as well as others imported coastwise or from abroad. They included stuffs, serges, druggets, kerseys, English and German linen, and among the less conventional items were cotton shirts, leather jackets, rugs, blanketing, tin kettles, fishing lines, hooks, nets, twine thread, and 'compasses for boats'. Raw materials and foodstuffs were also shipped abroad.

The data on Barnstaple's shipping movements in these five years relates to the combined foreign and coastal trades. Only one foreign vessel was included, of 46 tons, the rest being British ships, that is 345 vessels of 10,687 tons, and averaging 31 tons. As to contraband, it was stated that the principal commodities were 'rum, brandy, tea, tobacco and soap', but such business was thought to be 'rather decreased'. The customs receipts were thought to be 'so inconsiderable as hardly to defray the expenses', the port's trade being 'so much declined from what it was', and the number of officers 'much too great for the business now carried on'.

On the other hand, Bideford's foreign trade seems to have been far more thriving and varied in this war period. Foodstuffs and raw materials predominated among imports from abroad, the latter including 'bladders', while among the manufactured goods were pig iron, cast and wrought iron, and lead musket balls. A great variety of exports were listed, especially manufactures, some locally produced but others clearly imported from elsewhere in the country. They included many woollen textile products, among them broad cloth, bays single and double, stuffs, and kerseys, as well as a variety of cotton goods, including 'Manchester cottons', 'Welsh cottons', 'stamp'd cottons', 'Manchester linens', and 'Manchester checqued linens'. The manufactures further included women's cloaks, negligees, silk handkerchiefs, swanskin cotton caps, leather gloves, greatcoats, bed ticks, sheeting, blanketing, Birmingham wares, and a great variety of metal wares including pots, nails, hatchets and hoes, locks, frying pans, fowling pieces, compasses, and looking glasses. Foodstuffs and raw materials, British and foreign in origin, were also shipped abroad, including 'tobacco of the British plantations'. Certain of these exports also figure among the goods imported coastwise into Bideford. Potatoes also feature in Bideford's coastal imports, the only time they occur in all these Devon Custom port returns.

Concerning Bideford's shipping movements, between 1759 and 1763 there were altogether 64 British ships in foreign trade movements, totalling 3,944 tons, an average of 61.6 tons per vessel, but some 512 'coasters' totalling 11,740 tons and distinctly smaller at an average of nearly 23 tons per vessel. The commodities 'principally smuggled' were tea and brandy, both it was thought in 'greater quantities than there have been heretofore', but no vessels of the port were 'reputed smugglers'. The customs receipts exceeded the management expenses.

As to Ilfracombe in 1759–63, the port's inward foreign trade was regarded as 'very trifling', but consisted of some diverse goods: 'French prize coffee, Irish linen, oranges and lemons, French prize muscovado sugar, and other articles'. The shipping 'trading to and from this port and the creeks', i.e. in the foreign and coastal trades combined, numbered 216 vessels, totalling 8,301 tons, at an average 38.4 tons per vessel. In Ilfracombe's case, alone among the Devon ports in this Customs survey, there is mention of the number of vessels from the above total, which 'belong to the port and creek', namely 54 vessels totalling 3,280 tons and averaging 60.7 tons per vessel. The document also states that for Ilfracombe the proportion of foreign to British vessels 'is as 1 to 3 – and the tonnage nearly the same'. The local Customs officers reported the contraband trades to have decreased, the principal commodities being 'rum, soap and candles from Ireland', but 'no vessels reputed smugglers . . . use this port'. The customs receipts fell 'considerably short of the charges of management', owing to 'the very little business in the way of customs' at Ilfracombe.

Ship Ownership by Customs Port

In the century after 1680 Devon was very much a ship owning as well as a trading county. Customs statistics on ship owning are available from the beginning of the eighteenth century and, as will be seen, to the 1770s there was some limited overall growth in the total tonnage of Devon's vessels registered in the foreign trades, while a more substantial expansion occurred in the vessels registered in the coastal trades. Devon's shipping was employed either in its home ports' commerce, whether foreign or coastal, or in the trades of other ports, in Devon or elsewhere in Britain, or abroad. It is clear from a variety of anecdotal and individual evidence that Devon vessels were engaged in the carrying trades of British and foreign ports, but how important such business was to Devon ship owners cannot easily be determined from such records. However, comparison of Tables 33.1 and 33.2 above, of the tonnages of shipping employed in Devon's peacetime foreign trades over the eighteenth century to the early 1770s, with Table 33.8 below, of Devon's peacetime ship ownership over the same period, indicates a very rough relationship or coincidence, with no great excess of ship owning tonnage. But the deficiencies of the north Devon trading tonnage figures before 1765 and the absence of data on shipping tonnage employed in coastal trade rule out any close comparison. Nevertheless, for what it is worth, this suggests that, before 1780, the scale of Devon's ship owning was broadly related to the maritime commercial activity of the county, and that, while Devon's shipping was engaged to some extent in a carrying business for other ports, British and foreign, such 'tramping' ship owning had not yet become as significant as it was to become in the nineteenth century.

Table 33.7 presents, for various peacetime years between 1716 and 1774, the total tonnage of vessels belonging to the south Devon Customs ports, in foreign and coastal trade. As will be seen, in the foreign-going trades Exeter clearly led as a shipowning port to the mid-century, but its ownership failed to expand much over the whole period. However, Plymouth's foreign-going fleet, from a level of roughly half Exeter's fleet in the early century, then showed an actual decline thereafter. Dartmouth was clearly the rising Devon shipowning port in foreign trade ownership, its fleet growing more than five-fold between 1716 and 1772–4. In all three ports, the tonnage of vessels owned in the coastal trade was distinctly subordinate to the foreign-going tonnage, but all witnessed some appreciable expansion over the period.

Shipping ownership in the north Devon ports in certain peacetime years is shown in Table 33.8. From quite substantial levels in the century's first half, both Barnstaple's and Bideford's foreign-going ownership then fell away. Barnstaple had a substantial tonnage in the coastal trade to the mid-century, but by the early 1770s this, too, was declining. The Ilfracombe figures are particularly interesting for the quite significant growth of coastal-trade ownership over the period, which much exceeds the tonnage in foreign trade.

Table 33.7
Peacetime Tonnages of Vessels, in Foreign and Coastal Trade, Belonging to the South Devon Ports, and Bristol, Select Years, 1716–74, Counting each Vessel but Once a Year

	Exeter		Plymouth		Dartmouth		Bristol		
	Foreign trade	Coastal trade	Foreign trade	Coastal trade	Foreign trade	Coastal trade	Foreign trade	Coastal trade	Foreign & Coastal trade
1716	4,578	1,550	2,228	550	1,034	831	20,575	568	21,143
1730	5,970	1,620	2,144	430	1,464	405	23,120	785	23,905
1751	5,183	1,174	1,441	330	2,518	683	18,300	720	19,020
1772	5,395	2,823	1,527	950	6,625	1,645	35,090	2,180	37,270
1772–4 (average)	5,063	2,648	1,540	930	5,580	1,509	35,582	1,867	37,449

Source: BL, Add. MS 11,255.

Table 33.8
Peacetime Tonnages of Vessels, in Foreign and Coastal Trade, Belonging to the North Devon Ports, and all Devon Ports as a Percentage of Bristol's Shipping, Select Years, 1716–74, Counting each Vessel but Once a Year

	Barnstaple		Bideford		Ilfracombe		Total Devon tonnage			All Devon ports as a percentage of Bristol	
	Foreign trade	Coastal trade	Foreign trade	Coastal trade	Foreign trade	Coastal trade	Foreign trade	Coastal trade	Foreign & Coastal trade	Foreign trade	Foreign & coastal trade
1716	2,005	2,000	2,910	450	280	442	13,035	5,823	18,858	63.4	89.2
1730	2,625	2,106	1,715	645	270	448	14,188	5,654	19,842	61.4	83.0
1751	2,038	2,340	1,759	461	150	648	13,089	5,636	18,725	71.5	98.4
1772	2,162	1,431	754	588	440	1,440	16,903	8,877	25,780	48.2	69.2
1772–4 (average)	1,681	1,692	571	758	350	1,150	14,785	8,687	23,472	41.6	62.7

Source: BL, Add. MS 11,255.

Tables 33.7 and 33.8 permit some interesting comparison with the tonnages owned at Bristol in these years. If the peacetime foreign-going tonnage belonging to the Devon ports is combined in each year it compares favourably with Bristol's similar tonnages, from between 61.4 per cent in 1730 to 71.5 per cent in 1751. It then fell back to 41.6 per cent in 1772–4, by which time Bristol's foreign-going ownership had undergone striking growth. Bristol's shipping in the coastal trades, though, was small compared with Devon's coastal vessel ownership. Comparison of the combined foreign and coastal vessel ownership for all the Devon ports with Bristol's total ship ownership indicates, as Tables 33.7 and 33.8 show, that Devon's ship owning compared very well with Bristol's to the mid-century, the Devon fleet in 1751 being roughly equal to the Bristol fleet, at least in total tonnage. In 1772–4, though, with the significant growth of Bristol's ship owning, Devon's ownership by tonnage fell back to 62.7 per cent of Bristol's fleet.

In sum, as is shown in Table 33.8, Devon's total peacetime ship ownership, coastal and foreign-going, did expand somewhat between 1716 and 1730, when Devon's commercial activity was still notably expansive, but then, in 1751, it fell back to its earlier level. The expansion in total tonnage that then occurred to 1772–4 was almost entirely in coastal vessels, which corresponds well with the more limited development of Devon's foreign commerce.

The maritime trading and shipowning activity of the Devon ports in the period 1680–1780 as a whole had a notable part in the Devon economy in these years, particularly in the most thriving years to about 1730. The county's ports, merchants, ship owners, and mariners helped sustain the manufacturing, mining, agricultural, and naval interests of the county. Devon's maritime traffic, too, gave significant employment to mariners, to those loading and unloading vessels, to customs officers, shipbuilders, and ship repairers. Service activities, such as banking and insurance, were also stimulated, middle-class occupations were boosted, and the rising consumer appetites of the age were whetted by the imports, legal and illicit, of sugar, tobacco, tea, and other goods. These wider economic and social effects of Devon's maritime commerce in this period have been particularly considered for Exeter by those historians of the city's commerce previously referred to. But work remains to be done on such issues for the other Devon ports, and also on a number of questions which arise from the discussion above. Was there, for instance, a migration of mercantile capital towards the expansive Plymouth from other Devon ports from the mid-century? And, how extensive was the carrying or the 'tramping' business of Devon vessels in British and foreign commerce in these years? Such questions await future investigation.

33: Devon's Maritime Trade and Shipping, 1680–1780

1 On these commercial and shipping developments see, in particular, the work of Ralph Davis, particularly 'English Foreign Trade, 1660–1700', *EcHR*, 2nd Series, VII (1954), 'English Foreign Trade, 1700–1774'. *EcHR*, 2nd Series, XV (1962), and *The Rise of the English Shipping Industry* (1962).
2 Stephen Fisher and Michael Havinden, 'The Long-Term Evolution of the Economy of South West England: from Autonomy to Dependence', in MA Havinden *et al*, eds, *Centre and Periphery. Brittany and Cornwall and Devon Compared* (Exeter, 1991), and the authorities cited therein.
3 WG Hoskins, *Industry, Trade and People in Exeter, 1688–1800* (Manchester, 1935); WB Stephens, *Seventeenth-Century Exeter: A Study of Industrial and Commercial Development, 1625–1688* (Exeter, 1958); EAG Clark, *The Ports of the Exe Estuary, 1660–1860: A Study in Historical Geography* (Exeter, 1960) and R Newton, *Eighteenth Century Exeter* (Exeter, 1984).
4 See, for example, Crispin Gill, *A New History of Plymouth* (Newton Abbot, 1966) and Ray Freeman, *A History of Dartmouth* (Newton Abbot, 1983). An exception is HJ Trump, *West Country Harbour* (Teignmouth, 1976). There is a brief but informative sketch of the coastal trade of the Devon ports for part of this period in TS Willan, *The English Coasting Trade, 1600–1750* (Manchester, 1938).
5 There is a considerable discussion of Exeter merchants, for instance, in the works cited above by WB Stephens, WG Hoskins and EAG Clark. See also below, pp. 242–3 and volume II of this work.
6 See below, p. 167 and also Trump, *West-Country Harbour*, passim.
7 L Magalotti, 'The travels of Cosmo III, Grand Duke of Tuscany, through England', in R Pearse Chope, ed., *Early Tours in Devon and Cornwall* (Newton Abbot, 1967), 107.
8 Celia Fiennes, *The Journeys of Celia Fiennes*, C Morris, ed., (1947), 245, 248. See above, p. 131.
9 Thomas Cox, *Magna Britannia* (1720), 477.
10 Daniel Defoe, *A Tour through England and Wales* (1928 ed.), I, 222.
11 Malachy Postlethwayt, *The Universal Dictionary of Trade and Commerce* (2nd edn. 1757), I, 639, 638.
12 Andrew Brice, *The Grand Gazeteer or Topographic Dictionary* (Exeter, 1759), 440, 550, 544.
13 Magalotti, 'Travels of Cosmo III', 102.
14 Fiennes, *Journeys*, 252, 253. See also above, chapter 28.
15 Cox, *Magna Britannia*, 468.
16 Defoe, *Tour through England*, I, 227, 231.
17 Cox, *Magna Britannia*, 472.
18 Defoe, *Tour through England*, I, 225, 227.
19 Richard Pococke, 'Travels through England', in Pearse Chope, ed., *Early Tours*, 186.
20 Cox, *Magna Britannia*, 491, 489.
21 Defoe, *Tour through England*, I, 260, 262, 261–2.
22 Cox, *Magna Britannia*, 493.
23 Defoe, *Tour through England*, I, 263.
24 BL, Add. MS 9293.
25 See above, note 3.
26 See below, chapter 35.

34 *Three Exeter Pioneers in the Italian Trade*

E A G Clark

In March 1771 the *Lively* began to load serges at Topsham Quay for Genoa and Leghorn.[1] Fragmentary business records have survived for three of the merchants listed as despatching cloth: Samuel Milford, Abraham Kennaway, and Matthew Lee, all of Exeter. Milford's Journal, 1760–74 (Figs 34.1, 2), is a massive folio volume containing 464 pages, closely written in the same hand and format throughout. It meticulously records all of his cash transactions, including the purchase of 'white' cloth, payments to weavers, and to fullers, dyers, and other cloth finishers, and the shipment, insurance, and sale of cloth to merchants on the continent.

Honeycombed with cross-references to other ledgers and bill books, his Journal enabled Milford to keep his finger on the pulse of his enterprises. Inscribed 'in the name of God, Amen', it is a monument to his commercial acumen, scrupulous honesty, stamina, and attention to detail. It records his decisions to return amounts overpaid, to make allowance for unfavourable shifts in the rate of exchange, and to give abatements when cloth was not up to standard. There are shrewd assessments of other merchants. When Salvator Pacifico of Ancona asked for long credit, Milford refused, minuting: 'he is not worthy to be trusted with one shilling'.[2] The son of a Thorverton serge maker, and married to the daugher of an Exeter fuller, Milford started trading in a small way, but his annual profits increased from £164 in 1760 to £1,006 in 1770, and were around £2,000 in the prosperous early 1770s. He was throughout a pillar of the Unitarian Church in Exeter.[3]

Matthew Lee's Ledger, 1748–1775, is a much slighter record of cash transactions, neatly arranged in two columns, laconically balancing payments for a funeral and 'my son's board', with gains such as 'profits on whale oil sent to Oporto'.[4] More informative on the structure of the woollen trade are the fragmentary Kennaway accounts (1746–1794), which enumerate continental debtors by name under countries.[5]

Milford, Lee, and Kennaway (Fig. 34.3) can be regarded as typical of the more prosperous Devon woollen cloth merchants. They spread their risks and also ensured a monthly turnover by loading a few bales on most vessels clearing for their markets. In 1771, for example, Kennaway despatched 286 bales of cloth from Topsham on 31 ships, for Genoa, Leghorn, Naples, Messina, Ostend, Amsterdam, Rotterdam, Hamburg, and Cadiz, Milford 125 bales on 24 ships, and Lee 135 bales on 13 ships.[6] All three took part in the long-established Dutch and German trades via Topsham, but all were also pioneers in the Italian trade which developed after 1750. In the first half of the eighteenth century the Italian market was supplied from London, the cloth being shipped coastwise. Direct shipments from the Exe rose from 1,000 pieces in 1743 to 72,575 pieces in 1750 and 109,410 pieces in 1754, when the market ranked second to that with Germany.[7] Large, partially-laden, well-armed vessels from London, 'with liberty to touch at Exeter', anchored in the Exe estuary to complete their cargoes, which were sometimes sent down to Starcross by lighter from Exeter and Topsham Quays.[8] By the early 1770s there were nine vessels sailing annually from Topsham to Italian ports. Some of these, for example the *Danzig Packet* for Ancona, were London vessels, loading part cargoes, but others, such as the *Lion*, in which Kennaway had shares, were Exeter ships engaged in the lucrative new trade.[9] An earlier reliance on commission agents in Amsterdam had been superseded by direct links with markets. In 1764 Milford sold cloth to merchants in ten Italian towns. Kennaway's debtors in 1794 included 129 merchants in Italy and Germany and 63 in Spain. Italian merchants accounted for 73.5 per cent of Kennaway's debts in 1787, Spanish for 18.2 per cent, and 'home debts' for a mere 8.3 per cent.[10] The small cloth shipment to London was probably for overseas markets, for example to catch an early ship to Hamburg.[11] Milford and Lee both had their bills of

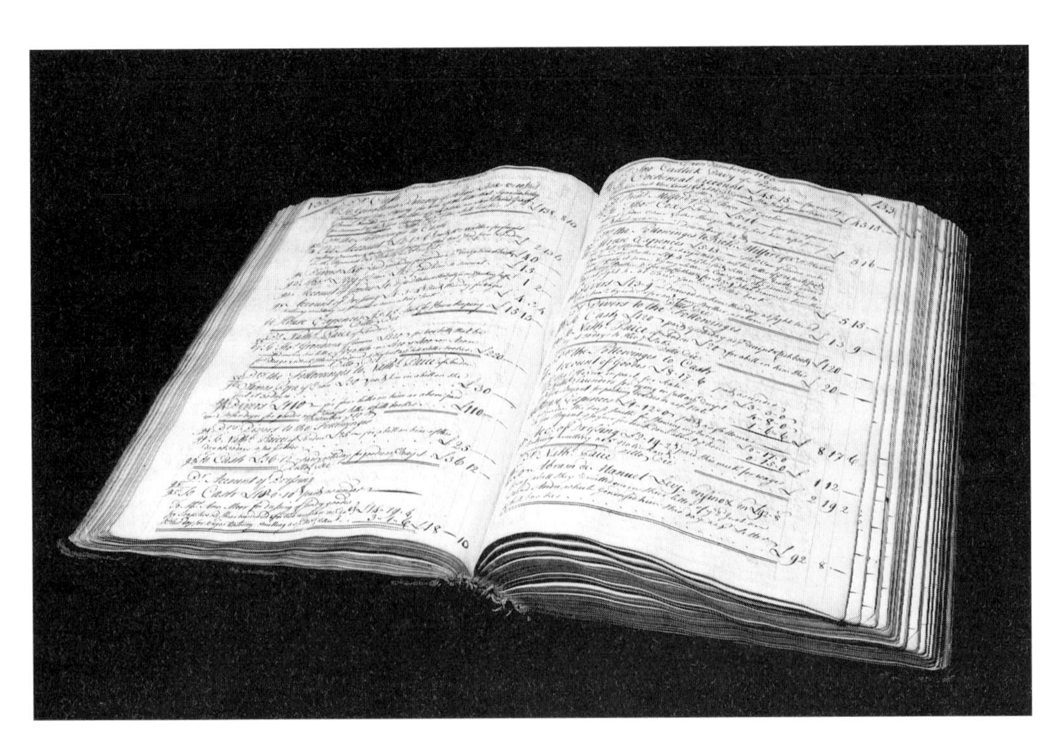

34.1 The journal of Samuel Milford of Exeter, 1760–74. *DRO, 71/8.*

34.2 Samuel Milford's merchant mark, from the fly-leaf of his Journal, Fig. 34.1.

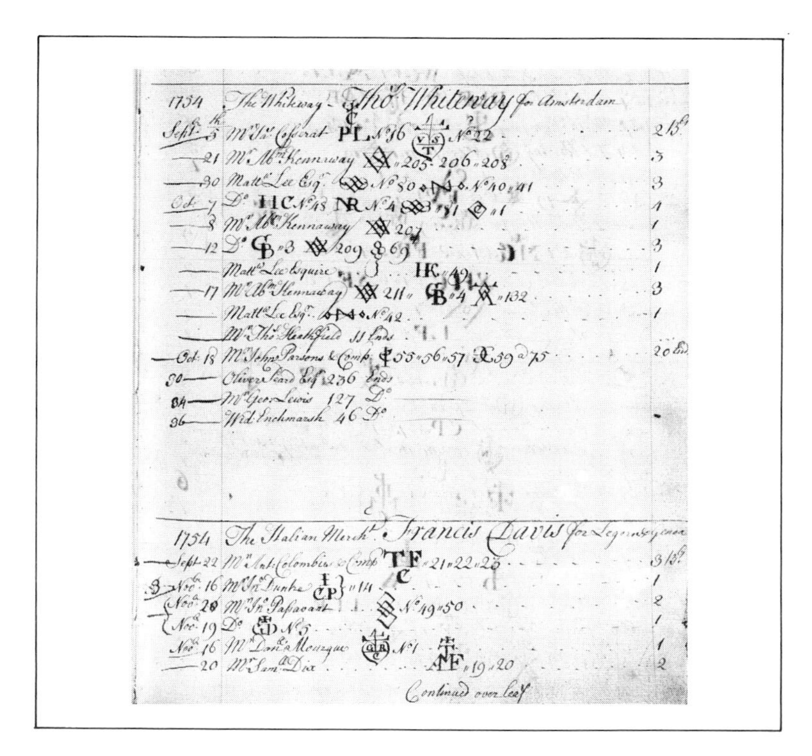

34.3 Merchant marks of Exeter merchants recorded in the 'Old Bale Book', 1752–63, DRO, 02/33, fo. 48. Note that Kennaway and Lee were lading goods in 1754 for Amsterdam, and that the *Italian Merchant* was bound for Leghorn.

exchange handled by London merchants, who also arranged marine insurance.

The cloth trade was the fulcrum for all three merchants, but Milford also exported hides, and Kennaway and Lee wheat and oats. All imported oil, packing canvas, and other raw materials for the cloth industry. William Kennaway, an older brother of Abraham, who was described as a wool stapler, was one of the small and wealthy group importing wool from Dover and Rye.[12] The Kennaways had part shares in several vessels, including the *Exeter*, *Phoenix*, *Devonshire*, *Hope*, *Lion* and *Freeport*.[13] Lee and Kennaway also invested in the voyages made by the Greenland Fishery vessel *Exeter*.[14] All three merchants engaged in cloth finishing and had industrial premises a stone's throw from Exeter Quay. William Kennaway's house, warehouses and offices were outside Southgate.[15] Milford had press shops, burling, packing, and finishing rooms, and hired racks in the Friars.[16] Cloth was purchased 'white' from weavers as far afield as Okehampton and South Molton and then sent out for fulling, stretching on racks, dyeing, and pressing.[17]

The years of peace between 1763 and 1778 saw the development of the South European trades as the principal markets for the Devonshire woollen industry.[18] The three merchants continued to ship cloth to Italian and Spanish ports, and in smaller quantities to Amsterdam, Rotterdam and Hamburg.[19] The War of American Independence led to the closing of Spanish and Dutch ports to British shipping, while the Italian trade was vulnerable to attacks by privateers. Ostend became the neutral entrepôt for cloth.[20] Milford may have seen the dangers of an exclusive reliance on distant overseas markets in wartime. His premises were offered for sale in 1784 and he applied his commercial talents to developing the City Bank which he founded in 1785.[21] Meanwhile, Lee's capital gains had reached £20,000. He went into partnership with Baring in the Plymouth Bank, invested in London property, and purchased an estate at Ebford, overlooking the Exe estuary.[22] The Kennaways' trade gains increased from £1,582 in 1751 to nearly £30,000 in 1785. They became partners in the Western Bank, but in 1791 they shipped more cloth from Topsham than any other merchant (1,074 bales), nearly a tenth of the annual export.[23]

Britain was at war almost throughout 1793–1814. The ties between Devon and its overseas markets were dissolved, and cloth manufacturers found a new, though reduced, market with the East India Company. The Kennaways suffered crippling losses when the Italian and Spanish markets closed – their Italian debts alone were £52,393 in 1793. They continued to ship cloth coastwise to London on a reduced scale, but the importation of wine from Spain now became their chief commercial interest.[24] Samuel Milford died in 1800, leaving about £70,000. The family papers indicate the transformation in social standing and lifestyles which took place with the new generation, but still coupled with a concern for wise investment and sound mercantile training. One son became a leading Exeter merchant and JP, and another a Devon banker. After schooling at Eton, two grandsons were placed with carefully selected firms on the continent 'to study the rudiments of mercantile affairs'. A third grandson, John, completed a Grand Tour, and published *Peninsula Sketches* (1816) and an account of travels in the Pyrenees and Italy.[25] Doubtless he visited some of the cities where, two generations before, a considerable part of the foundations of the family fortune had been laid by Samuel Milford, who, on the evidence of his Journal, rarely, if ever, left his native Devon.

34: Three Exeter Pioneers in the Italian Trade

1 DRO, Wharfinger's Journal, Topsham, 1770–1775.
2 DRO, 71/8 Journal of Samuel Milford, 1760–1774, 143.
3 Joyce Youings, *Tuckers Hall Exeter* (Exeter 1968), 178; DRO, Milford Journal; R Newton, *Eighteenth Century Exeter* (Exeter 1984), 74–5.
4 DRO, Ledger of Matthew Lee, 1748–1775.
5 DRO, 58/7, Kennaway Papers. Abraham Kennaway was exporting cloth to Amsterdam, Cadiz, and Oporto as early as 1750 (PRO, E 190/1003/13). William Kennaway Jr was importing wool in 1743 (DRO, Papers relating to Crediton Canal Shares, loose page from Wool Book, 1743–46), but not exporting cloth from the Exe in 1750–51 or 1770–75 (PRO, E 190/1003/13); DRO, Book 177, Book of Entries and Waste Book, 1750–51; DRO, Wharfinger's Journal, Topsham, 1770–75). By 1791 W Kennaway was a major exporter of cloth (DRO, Wharfinger's Ledger, Topsham, 1790–95).
6 DRO, Wharfinger's Journal, 1770–75.
7 EAG Clark, *Ports of the Exe Estuary, 1660–1860* (Exeter, 1960), 113–115.
8 Customs House, Exeter, Letter Book 6, 4 May 1771; *Exeter Flying Post*, 5 April 1776; 20 December 1776; 18 May 1781; 9 November 1781.
9 DRO, Wharfinger's Journal, 1770–75.
10 DRO, Milford Journal; DRO, Kennaway Papers, Box 9, Account Book.
11 DRO, Milford Journal, 158.
12 DRO, Papers relating to the Crediton Canal Shares, loose page from a Wool Book, 1743–1746.
13 DRO, Kennaway Papers, Box 9, Account Book.
14 DRO, Ledger of Matthew Lee, 21.
15 SD Chapman, *The Devon Cloth Industry in the Eighteenth Century*, Devon and Cornwall Record Society, NS 23 (1978), 53.
16 *Exeter Flying Post*, 25 December 1784.
17 DRO, Milford Journal; Bodleian Library, Oxford, Milles Devonshire MSS, Parochial Returns, I, 123, 148; II, 33, 43, 61, 63, 143.
18 Clark, *Ports of the Exe*, 115–117.
19 DRO, Wharfinger's Journal, Topsham, 1770–1775; DRO, Milford Journal.
20 Clark, *Ports of the Exe*, 117.
21 *Exeter Flying Post*, 25 December 1784; WG Hoskins, *Industry Trade and People in Exeter, 1688–1800* (Exeter, 1935), 49.
22 DRO, Ledger of Matthew Lee.
23 DRO, Kennaway Papers; Chapman, *Devon Cloth Industry*, xviii; DRO, Wharfinger's Ledger, 1790–1795.
24 Clark, *Ports of the Exe*, 118–123; DRO. Wharfinger's Journals, 1790.
25 Milford Papers (in private possession), letters.

35 *Devon and Smuggling, 1680–1850*

ALAN G JAMIESON

IN 1836 JOHN RATTENBURY, Devon's most famous smuggler, reflected upon his life. He had made his first smuggling voyage in 1794 at the age of sixteen. More than forty years later he described smuggling as:

> a career which, however it may be calculated to gratify a hardy and enterprising spirit, and to call forth all the latent energies of the soul, is fraught with difficulty and danger.[1]

Yet Rattenbury had no regrets at having participated in the trade, for in his time it was a major maritime activity, a defiance of the law which enjoyed widespread popular support and could bring lucrative rewards.

Smuggling was in decline by the time Rattenbury wrote his memoirs in the late 1830s, and smugglers were becoming semi-romantic figures of popular folklore. This transformation has continued in the present century, and some scholars consider smuggling to have been no more than a minor historical phenomenon. However, when Rattenbury first entered the trade, in the 1790s, smuggling was one of the most important problems facing the British government. The customs commissioners called it 'the National Evil,' and to Methodist leader John Wesley it was 'the accursed thing'.[2] In almost every maritime county of Britain smuggling was rampant, posing a grave threat to national revenue, legal trade, and public order. The problem had its origins in the late-seventeenth century, and for more than one hundred years smuggling was the principal form of popular defiance of government economic policies.

During the eighteenth century the smuggling trade was large, and made official import figures for commodities such as tea, tobacco, and spirits distinctly unreliable. Government estimates were usually based on the assumption that for every cargo of contraband that was seized, perhaps eight or ten others got through safely. In 1783, when the total government income was only £12.7 million (67 per cent of which came from customs and excise duties), it was estimated that smuggling was depriving the government of at least £2 million in revenue per annum, a colossal sum.[3] Modern scholars have attempted a more detailed quantitative analysis of the smuggling trade, but it is doubtful whether their figures are much more reliable.[4] No greater precision can be expected in weighing the importance of smuggling in different parts of Britain. Although Devon and Cornwall have a great popular reputation as smuggling areas, almost throughout 'the smugglers' century' they were overshadowed by the maritime counties of southeast England; Essex, Kent, Sussex, and Hampshire being closest to the smuggling supply bases on the Continent and to London, the principal market in the country for smuggled goods.[5]

Devon and Cornwall were, however, leading members of the second rank of smuggling areas. They were not too far from supply bases in the Channel Islands and northwest France, and they provided both local markets and routes to more distant consumers of smuggled goods. In Devon the local market consisted of farmers, miners, quarrymen, fishermen, seamen, and townspeople, both in small market towns and in larger centres such as Plymouth and Exeter. In the wider context north Devon was often used as a distribution point for contraband intended for markets further up the Bristol Channel, and at least some of the goods smuggled into south Devon eventually found their way to London.

Smuggling was hardly a new phenomenon in the later-seventeenth century, but its nature changed considerably at that time. Previously smuggling in England had been of exports, chiefly wool and woollen goods, and this illicit trade had mainly been carried on at major ports whose customs officials were easily bribed by merchants. The square-rigged vessels of the time were usually unsuited to isolated bays away from the legal quays. The root cause of the change in the nature of smuggling was the decision of the British government, influenced by mercantilist doctrines, to take greater control of the nation's trade. The Navigation Acts provided the legal framework for this control and a more effective customs service was required to enforce them. The customs ceased to be farmed in 1671, and the new customs commissioners sought to establish reliable officers in every port. Customs control became even more important after the start of the French wars in 1689. The government sought to pay for the wars by greatly increasing customs duties on imported goods such as brandy, tea, and tobacco. Although some smuggling of exports continued, the new wave of smuggling principally involved the illegal importation of high-duty goods for which there was a great and growing demand throughout the eighteenth century. If such smuggling had been restricted to the major ports it might have been stifled by the slowly-increasing efficiency of the customs service. However, the spread of the fore-and-aft rig during the second half of the seventeenth century produced a class of vessel ideal for widespread smuggling. Sloops, luggers, and cutters were fast, highly manoeuvrable, and could land contraband cargoes in any sheltered bay. The customs now faced the almost impossible task of watching not only the main ports but also hundreds of miles of coastline.

These smuggling craft could only carry small cargoes of contraband, so a supply base was required where bulk cargoes, such as tobacco, could be broken down into smaller lots. Continental ports in France or Holland were obvious choices, but they were often difficult to visit in wartime. The ideal supply bases were the Isle of Man and the Channel Islands, because although they were British possessions, they were outside the British customs system. The Channel Islands, especially Guernsey and Alderney, were the principal supply bases for Devon smugglers.

Countermeasures

The new wave of smuggling did not have a great impact before 1700, but from 1680 the British government was working hard to improve the customs service and stamp out port frauds. In 1683 William Culliford toured the ports of southwest England, purging them of all customs officers suspected of collusion with smugglers. Leading officials were removed at Barnstaple, Exeter, and also Plymouth, where 'Mr Hamlyn the collector is a person that hath apparently abetted and countenanced that knott of men which have been in so long a combination and contract to defraud the king'.[6] He was dismissed, despite pleas from the local merchants that he should remain in his post.

A customs cruiser had been based at Plymouth as early as 1685, but it was not until the late 1690s that a chain of such vessels was established along the coasts of England and Wales. In 1698 one was based at Dartmouth and another at Ilfracombe. New legislation was needed to increase the effectiveness of these vessels, and it was not until 1718 that it was made illegal for vessels of 50 tons or less to 'hover' within two leagues (about 6 miles) of the coast, and the importation of brandy in vessels under 15 tons was forbidden.[7]

What impact these measures had on the Devon smugglers is hard to tell. The principal sources of information concerning their activities are the letters written by the local customs collectors to the Board of Customs in London. Unfortunately the letterbooks for most Devon ports have not survived for the period before 1750, and there are none at all for the port of Bideford. The Plymouth books begin only in 1799, Ilfracombe's in 1778, and Dartmouth's in 1775. The Exeter books date from 1743, and the earliest records are those for the port of Barnstaple, which begin around 1720.

The north Devon coast was never as notorious for smuggling as the south, but the Barnstaple books are not without interest. In 1718 it was reported that several French ships were hovering offshore intent on transferring contraband to vessels carrying limestone from Wales to north Devon. In the following year a customs officer was established at Croyde, and later moved to Braunton to watch the nearby lime kilns to which cargoes of limestone and coal were brought in summer.[8] In 1726 a cargo of tea was smuggled ashore at a lime kiln at Powderham near Exeter, and throughout the rest of the century the coasting vessels supplying lime kilns in both north and south Devon were often used for smuggling.[9]

By the late 1720s smuggling had increased greatly throughout Britain, so much so that in 1733 a parliamentary committee was set up to examine the problem. It concluded that smuggling was rampant in every maritime county of the kingdom, and noted that since Christmas 1723 some 250 customs officers had been injured and six killed in the course of their duties. Between 1723 and 1733 over 250,000lb of tea and over 650,000 gallons of brandy had been seized, but it was estimated that ten times as much had escaped detection. In the same period more than 2,000 smugglers had been prosecuted by the customs and 230 smuggling vessels had been seized, but smuggling continued to increase.[10]

In evidence to the committee the commander of the customs cruiser at Dartmouth, Captain Ashe, reported that there were several dozen small smuggling craft in Devon and Cornwall which regularly went over to Guernsey to collect cargoes of tea, tobacco, wine, spirits, and other goods. Large numbers of armed men, with horses, met the vessels on their return. The few customs officers could only stand and watch as the contraband was landed and carried away to hiding places further inland.[11] The committee's figures of seizures in Devon are incomplete, but most of those noted took place in Exeter, and at places on or near the Exe estuary. North Devon receives a few mentions, but there is no reference at all to the Plymouth area. The total figures for goods seized in Devon given in the principal list are 13,789lb of tea, 4,869 gallons of brandy, 8,088lb of tobacco, and 996 gallons of wine. However, another list of wine seizures covers all Devon ports and gives a total of 9,864 gallons of wine seized in the county during this period. The main smuggling incident in north Devon noted in the returns concerned the island of Lundy. In 1727 William Cuthbert landed large quantities of brandy and wine there for later distribution along the shores of the Bristol Channel.[12]

The parliamentary report of 1733 eventually resulted in the smuggling act of 1736, which offered indemnity to all smugglers who would inform on their former comrades and introduced the death penalty for all attacks on customs officers. The act was ineffective, and in 1745 parliament set up another committee. Britain was then at war, and some smugglers were accused of being unpatriotic. It was said that when Admiral Martin's fleet sailed from Plymouth, a smuggler crossed over to France to warn the enemy. However, smugglers, who were recognised as being 'extraordinary good sailors', could expiate such sins by serving in the Royal Navy, and many were sent into the fleet after being captured. One witness claimed 'that great quantities [of tea] are brought by lime vessels, which come to Devonshire', and he believed 'not a ship went from Devonshire to Holland or France, but what run[s] prohibited and French goods'.[13]

The committee's report was followed by the 1746 smuggling act, which was draconian in its provisions. Almost every smuggling offence became a capital crime, but the act did little to reduce smuggling and by its very severity drove the smugglers to use more violence. In 1759, during the Seven Years War, it was reported from Devon that large armed gangs were openly running contraband goods ashore, particularly in Torbay. The goods came from Guernsey, and previously such landings had been most common around Lyme Bay. The government was asked to send 'an impress smack' to Torbay as the smugglers would make excellent seamen for the navy.[14]

In 1764 the Exeter collector of customs confirmed that the smugglers of Dorset, Devon, and Cornwall obtained most of their contraband from Guernsey and Alderney, and another report noted that many of the boats most active in smuggling from Guernsey belonged to the village of Cawsand, which was in Cornwall but within the port of Plymouth. Warren Lisle, commander of a customs cruiser, noted that the smugglers around Lyme Bay received most of their contraband from Alderney, and that Beer in Devon (Fig. 35.1) was one of the principal smuggling villages on Lyme Bay. Another correspondent, Richard Kent, said smugglers usually carried contraband away from Guernsey in cutters and open lug-sail boats, most of the latter coming from either Cawsand or Beer.[15]

In 1767 the government attempted to bring the Channel Islands within the British customs system, but because of opposition from the inhabitants the attempt was abandoned after a few years. Smuggling continued unabated, and with the return of war after 1775 it increased. Another smuggling act was passed in 1779, but it could not be enforced. Indeed, because of the circumstances of the American War of Independence, when Britain was at war with France, Spain, and Holland, smuggling reached an unprecedented level. No troops or naval vessels could be spared to support the customs. By the time the war ended in 1783 the smugglers posed a threat to public order which was greater than ever before. The smugglers were carrying on their trade openly and using not just small vessels, but also large armed ships which could defy most customs cruisers with impunity.

The south coast of Devon was plagued by three of these formidable vessels in 1783. They were based in Guernsey but had been built in England and were run by Devon smugglers, notably William Brown and a man named Willard. The largest vessel was the lugger *Ranger*, which had been built in Cawsand and carried 22 guns. The others were two cutters, the *Dogger Bank* and the *Swift*. The latter had been built in Bridport, carried 16 guns, and was usually commanded by Brown. The *Swift* was involved in one of the more outrageous smuggling incidents of the time, a defiance of authority which no government could ignore. On 13 May 1783 the customs cutter *Spider*, based at Dartmouth and commanded by John Swaffin, was at anchor in Brixham road, Torbay. At first light a large cutter and a sloop were seen to have anchored near Paignton (Roundham) Head. Swaffin entered his cutter's boat and was rowed towards the two vessels. He recognised the cutter as the heavily-armed *Swift*, so he decided to board the sloop, which belonged to Thomas Parkinson of Brixham, a noted smuggler. A boat carrying three men was then seen to leave the cutter, and Swaffin decided to intercept it. When he got near, however, 12 armed smugglers hidden in the bottom of the boat suddenly sprang up and seized Swaffin and his men. The captives were taken aboard the *Swift* and her commander, William Brown, said he had escorted the sloop from Guernsey to Torbay. The *Swift*'s own cargo was 1,500 six-gallon casks of spirits and four tons of tea, and Brown began landing this on Paignton Sands. The *Spider* and another customs cruiser, the *Alarm*, based at Exeter, witnessed all this, but at first refused to challenge the *Swift*. Instead they took refuge under the guns of the battery on Berry Head. Later, however, they dispatched their boats to disrupt the landing operations. The *Swift* fired a broadside at these craft as they approached and forced them to withdraw, but the intervention unsettled Brown and he decided to leave Torbay. He took his vessel northeastwards and landed the remainder of his cargo at Holcombe near Teignmouth. Meanwhile, Parkinson's sloop was seized by the customs officer at Paignton. In the early hours of the following day Swaffin was released by Brown and cast adrift in his own boat.[16]

Incidents such as this, and the generally high level of smuggling, made it imperative that the government take action. However, its first reaction was to set up yet another parliamentary committee of inquiry, to which the port collectors replied in October 1783 that smuggling had increased greatly in the last three years. Richard Valentine, the customs officer at Salcombe, in the port of Dartmouth, reported that in his area:

> the practice of smuggling has been carried on by people who live in little villages along the coast who are in general poor and assist in unloading the smuggling vessels and bringing the same to shore where

35.1 Beer Harbour, from George Rowe, *Scraps Illustrating . . . Devonshire* (Sidmouth, 1829). *(Devon Library Services, WCSL)*

> the horses are in readiness to carry off the same. The species of ship employed on this coast are chiefly fishing craft belonging to Torbay who chiefly land their cargoes at or near the Start or Prawle.

At one time, Valentine reported, he had been able to make seizures, but now he was confronted by such large gangs of smugglers that he could not act without the assistance of troops. The large smuggling vessels *Dogger Bank*, *Swift*, and *Ranger* dominated the coast and worked with impunity.[17]

The customs officer at Brixham, also in the port of Dartmouth, believed smuggling had received a particular boost in the summer of 1783 because of several landings made in Torbay by the *Swift*. More recently the *Ranger* had put ashore a large quantity of tea and spirits, and all landings were covered by large gangs.

> The big smuggling vessels were chiefly employed in the larger branches of this pernicious traffic, but the usual and most frequent practice of smuggling on this coast is in the fishing boats of which there are a great number belonging to Torbay and we believe most of them more or less carry on the smuggling trade. They are from 18 to 25 tons each mostly built here or at Teignmouth.

Their method was to remain outside the hovering limits until the revenue cutter had left the area, then come in to land their cargoes, usually at night. If there was any danger of being surprised by the revenue cutters or their boats, the smugglers would lash casks of spirits into rafts and sink them by attaching stones. The rafts would be dragged up at a later date.[18]

At Exeter the collector confirmed that large armed smuggling vessels had become a menace, but he said little about the particular situation within his own port. Most of his comments referred to smuggling in the ports of Dartmouth and Plymouth, in particular to the village of Cawsand. He claimed that most of the contraband landed there was carried into Devon, even supplying Exeter. The collector wanted troops stationed at Cawsand 'that enormous seat of smuggling', as 'it would greatly annoy and distress the immense contraband trade carried on there'. The Exeter collector also wanted more troops to back up his own officers, and asked that an additional officer should be established at Dawlish, which 'is become a place of considerable resort for smugglers, remarkable for the running of goods'.[19]

Reports from the north coast of Devon were very different to those from the south coast. The Barnstaple collector denied that there had been an increase in smuggling in his area, and believed that no local vessels were engaged in that illicit trade.

> We believe all the smuggled goods brought here come by land carriage from the coasts of Cornwall as this port lays too far up the Bristol Channel for smuggling vessels to venture without great danger.[20]

However, the complacent attitude of the Barnstaple collector was not shared by his colleague at Ilfracombe, who wrote that large quantities of tea and brandy had been brought from France and lodged on the island of Lundy. The contraband was then collected by pilot boats from Ilfracombe and landed on the coasts of Devon, Cornwall, Somerset, and Wales.[21]

After digesting the reports the customs commissioners estimated that smuggling on the south and east coasts of England had increased three fold during the past three years (1780–83), and that the increase had been most pronounced in southwest England. Their lowest estimates of goods smuggled nationally during that period were 13 million gallons of spirits, 21 million pounds of tea, and 300,000lb of coffee. They saw the most worrying development as the increasing use of large armed vessels by the smugglers, believing that there were about 100 of these, more than half of them being active between the Isle of Wight and Lands End. Smaller smuggling craft were almost too numerous to be counted, but there were believed to be at least 200 of them. Of the ten places specifically noted as building and fitting out large armed smuggling vessels, two, Beer and Cawsand, were within the limits of the Devon ports. It was recognised that customs officers could not intervene without military assistance, but even then 'much blood has been spilt and many lives lost in this most dangerous of all warfare'.[22]

Accompanying the report was a list of 215 smuggling vessels said to be active on the south and east coasts of England. Although not totally reliable, this list does give some idea of the relative importance of smuggling in different areas at this time. More especially, it shows smuggling in southwest England to have been very considerable. Some 114 vessels belonged to southeast England (Essex, Kent, Sussex), but no fewer than 76 came from southwest England: Dorset 25, Devon 28, and Cornwall 23. Of the Devon vessels 15 came from the Plymouth area, five from around Torbay, and eight from the Beer area. The Barnstaple collector believed that any smuggling in north Devon was carried out entirely by Cornish vessels, and that the landings were made at places like Hartland and Clovelly in the port of Bideford.

The first report of the parliamentary committee on smuggling appeared very speedily in December 1783. The 'mixed system of war and trade' introduced by the owners of the large armed smuggling vessels was noted as a particularly dangerous threat to public order, but smuggling of all types seemed to have increased greatly since 1779. It was now a highly organised trade whose practitioners 'pursue all the regular plans of book-keeping'. The committee described the system:

> Riders are sent, from time to time, to receive orders within the circle of their respective rides; which orders have already been collected in parts more distant from the coast. Notice is then circulated of the day and hour when the vessel may be expected to appear offshore with cargo. A place of landing is fixed upon; signals are settled; scouts are appointed; the degree of force that may be needed is arranged; and, lastly, the terms of freighting adjusted and also of insurance in case the person who gives the order will not take the articles at his own risk. The imported goods, if distributed upon the coast, are, in most instances, sold at about half the price of goods that have paid legal duty. If the goods are brought to London, under insurance, which is a common practice, they are delivered either to retail traders, or to private housekeepers, at about two thirds the price of legal goods.

Smuggling then was now worse than ever and was carried on with a violence that 'not only threatens the destruction of the revenue, but is highly injurious to regular commerce and fair trade, very pernicious to the manners and morals of the people, and an interruption of all good government'. It was time that parliament took decisive action.[23]

In its final report, in 1784, the committee recommended various measures to defeat smuggling, including the reduction or abolition of the duties which had called it into being, an extension of the hovering limits to four leagues (about 12 miles), and the licensing of the fore-and-aft-rig vessels so beloved by smugglers. In addition it decreed that large numbers of troops and naval vessels should be directed to assist the customs officers and cruisers.[24] The Younger Pitt moved quickly to carry out many of these suggestions. By the end of 1784 some duties had been reduced, most notably that on tea; a new smuggling act introducing licensing of certain vessels had been passed; and the army and navy had been ordered to give every assistance to the customs. Over the next few years there was some reducton in smuggling, with the large armed smuggling vessels being removed from the scene at an early date. But with the outbreak of war with France in 1793 the final reckoning with the smugglers was postponed for another twenty years.

Devon 1784–1792

The new resolute government policy against smugglers came none too soon for the beleaguered customs officers of Devon. In December 1784 Captain Swaffin of the customs cutter *Spider* suffered another humiliation at the hands of the smugglers. Near Torbay he intercepted a boat which was recovering a sunken cargo of spirits, but when he took her to the shore he was confronted by a mob of more than 100 confederates. Swaffin and his handful of men were attacked by the mob and were forced to flee. All of them suffered injuries, but at least they had escaped with their lives.[25] In the following year the customs officer at Bantham, west of Salcombe, was not so lucky. He rode out to look for smugglers at Hope Cove, and was found later lying at the foot of the cliffs. With his dying breath he said that the smugglers had thrown him over the edge, but his attackers were never found. A similar fatality had occurred near Beer in 1755.[26]

The new smuggling act of 1784 seems, however, to have put heart into the customs men. Early in January 1785 the collector at Exeter toured the shores of his port, accompanied by a detachment of the 70th Regiment, hunting for cutters and luggers which were illegal under the new act. Unfortunately the smugglers had already taken their vessels to sea, probably to Guernsey, and the collector was able to seize only four vessels. His lack of success led him to conclude: 'we think the great business of destroying smuggling must be effected by the revenue and other cutters upon the water.'[27] In the same month the Exeter collector had to reply to a worried enquiry from the Customs Board about whether wool was being smuggled out of Devon. In the previous year a Devon vessel, thought to be the *Chance* of Salcombe, had been wrecked in Normandy. She had been carrying a cargo of wool and was thought to be bound for a French port. Contraband goods smuggled into England were usually paid for in cash, although bills of exchange were often acceptable in the Channel Islands, but there was also a return trade of wool being exported illegally, chiefly from counties in southeast England. The Exeter collector thought it unlikely that Devon smugglers were now paying for goods with return cargoes of wool, since the county was usually short of wool and stocks had to be brought in from other parts of England.[28]

Captain Swaffin of the *Spider* finally seemed to be having some good luck in July 1787 when he seized the luggers *Hawke* and *Nancy* of Beer in Start Bay. Both were carrying spirits and tobacco, and Swaffin claimed they were taken well within the hovering limits. The vessels were escorted to Dartmouth and prosecutions were begun, but in 1788 the court ruled that the craft had been taken outside the limits and should be returned to their owners. Finding he was personally liable to compensate the owners, Swaffin wished to dispute the judgement but could not find any witnesses from among his crew. Since the seizure the *Spider* had left the customs service and her crew had been dispersed. Some seamen had gone on long overseas voyages in merchant ships 'and [of] those that remain many [are] employed by the smugglers and [have been] bought over by them'. Lacking witnesses, all Swaffin could do was ask the customs to help him pay the compensation.[29]

While some customs men suffered at the hands of the courts, others continued to face violence on the beaches. In September 1788 customs officers trying to stop a landing at Hope Cove were savagely beaten by the smugglers. They were, however, able to identify their attackers, who fled to Teignmouth, searching for a vessel to take them out of the country. Troops were sent after them and they were captured.[30] In March 1789 the customs officer at Babbacombe attempted to stop smugglers landing casks on the beach, only to be attacked by them. Those responsible were eventually brought to court, but the jury promptly acquitted them. The Dartmouth collector raged:

> We think it almost impossible to convict an offender by a Devonshire jury who are composed of farmers and generally the greatest part of them either smugglers or always ready to assist them in removing and secreting their goods.[31]

As well as facing popular support for the smugglers, the customs service was hindered by fears that its own men might be in league with them. John Prout, the customs officer at Paignton, was accused several times of engaging in illegal activities. However, the Dartmouth collector always came to his defence and, in April 1790, stressed how important Prout's post was: 'Paignton is situated in the centre of Torbay and [is] where a great number of clandestine traders reside and there is more smuggling in that neighbourhood than in any other part in this port'. In the last five years Prout had seized 3,467 gallons of brandy, 233 gallons of rum, 1,331 gallons of geneva gin, and 346lb of tobacco.[32]

The Royal Navy assisted the customs officers, but relations were not always good between the two services. In July 1790 the customs boat at Salcombe chased the Cawsand shallop *True Blue* which had just arrived off the coast from Guernsey, but was unable to catch the vessel. Seeing a sloop of war, the *Fly*, nearby, the customs boat alerted her and the navy took up the chase. The *Fly* soon captured the smuggler, but, when the customs boat came near, the warship threatened to open fire if she attempted to interfere. The *Fly* took the *True Blue* to Portsmouth, and the navy resisted the claim of the Salcombe customs officers that they should have a share of the prize money.[33] On other occasions the navy and the customs were able to co-operate. In June 1791 the naval cutter *Nimble* seized the Brixham cutter *Persevering Peggy*. She was not carrying contraband, but had sinking stones aboard as if she had just been engaged in putting down rafts of kegs. Also, although the vessel was cutter-rigged, with a running bowsprit, she did not have the licence required by law. The Dartmouth collector backed up the navy's claim that the *Persevering Peggy* was a smuggling craft and not a fishing boat as her owners claimed. At Brixham nearly 100 sail of fishing boats were employed in the fishery for the London, Bath, and other markets, and the captured cutter had never been one of them.[34] The sinking of contraband cargoes, to be recovered later, had become increasingly common, and in October 1791 it was noted that Bigbury Bay was a spot much favoured by the Cawsand smugglers for such activities since it was the most unguarded part of the port of Dartmouth. On that part of the coast there was only one customs officer stationed between Salcombe and the limits of the port of Plymouth 12 miles away.[35]

Informers were vital to the successful prosecution of the war against the smugglers. Some reported where landings were to take place, while others provided details of the smuggling vessels and their cargoes when they were about to leave supply bases such as Guernsey. In January 1792 the Exeter collector warned his men that five smuggling vessels, said to be loaded and ready to sail from Guernsey, might soon appear in their area. He passed on the informer's description of the vessels: the cutter *Pearl* of Plymouth, 'with narrow yellow sides and topmast; she has row scuttles'; the cutter *Fanny* of Brixham, 'black with yellow mouldings and red counter'; the cutter *Hope* of Plymouth, 'yellow sides with red mouldings'; and the sloops *Betsey* and *Good Intent*, 'black, belonging to Dartmouth.'[36]

The French Wars

Whatever progress had been made in suppressing smuggling in Devon and elsewhere since 1784 was largely lost after the start of the long French wars in 1793. Duties rose once again to pay for the war, so the demand for smuggled goods increased at a time when the preventive forces were much weakened. The troops and naval vessels were directed to other duties, and the customs cutters were less effective. Some of them were 'borrowed' by the navy, while others could not get crews because seamen had been taken by the naval press gangs. Smuggling was never again to attain the heights it reached in 1783, but it was to remain a serious problem throughout the French Revolutionary and Napoleonic wars.

In 1799 there were two customs cutters stationed at Plymouth, the *Busy* and the *Ranger*, but the latter spent much of the year away from the port serving with the navy in the Helder expedition and the former was laid up for repairs for a long period. In addition to these vessels there were nine customs rowboats stationed at various points on the winding creeks, rivers, and bays of the port of Plymouth. There was one rowboat each on the rivers Yealm and Erme, at Plymouth, Plymouth Dock (Devonport), Weston Mill, Saltash, and St Germans, while the infamous smuggling village of Cawsand merited two boats.[37] When the six-oared customs boat from Cawsand approached the smuggling vessel *Lottery* of Polperro in late December 1798, she was fired on and one of her crew, Humphrey Glynn, was killed. This incident greatly infuriated the customs authorities and, when the *Lottery* was captured by a revenue cruiser in May 1799 and taken to Plymouth, her crew were closely questioned. One seaman turned informer and identified Thomas Potter of Polperro as the killer. A cavalry detachment from Plymouth seized Potter in a midnight raid on Polperro, and he was later sentenced to death for the murder of Glynn. The collector at Plymouth believed that the successful conclusion of the Glynn affair had been of 'much consequence to the revenue, to the established government, and for the good order of society'.[38] The *Lottery* herself served as customs cruiser at Plymouth in 1799 during the absence of the *Busy* and the *Ranger*.

The short peace of 1802/3 did not allow time for any intensified action against smuggling, and it continued to thrive when the new war broke out. In 1804 the Plymouth collector reported much smuggling in his port, and it was particularly bad in two areas. The first was the district embraced by Bigbury Bay, the river Yealm, and Cawsand. In the river Yealm and Cawsand Bay rafts of spirit kegs were sunk regularly, to be 'crept' up later with metal grapnels. Indeed, it was said that 17,000 small casks of spirits were smuggled into Cawsand and the Yealm each year. The second area notorious for smuggling was around Polperro and Mevagissey in Cornwall. Most of the contraband landed there was said to go to consumers in Plymouth.[39]

It is a measure of the high level of smuggling at this time that even the north coast of Devon, not usually a major smuggling area, witnessed increased activity after 1800. In 1804 the Barnstaple collector actually admitted that there had been an increase in smuggling and reported that spirits and tea were brought to the area from Guernsey by cutters and luggers. In summer, landings usually took place on the north coast of Cornwall and the contraband was then sent further up the coast by land or by coasting vessel. In winter, landings occurred at places such as Hartland, Clovelly, Lee, Combe Martin, and Lynmouth in north Devon and Porlock in Somerset. Farmers took the contraband inland to be hidden until it could be sent further up the Bristol Channel by land or in coasting vessels. The island of Lundy was also still used as a depot for contraband goods.[40]

Smuggling was struck a major blow when, by acts in 1805 and 1807, the British government extended the British customs system to the Channel Islands. The Devon smugglers were to find alternative supply bases in France, with Roscoff replacing Guernsey and Cherbourg replacing Alderney, but French ports were difficult to use in wartime. The naval blockade of France was one obstacle to Devon smugglers, while on the south coast of their own country the navy was also causing problems. A chain of naval signal stations was set up, and the regular use of Torbay as a fleet anchorage hindered its use by smugglers. In 1810 came further problems with the setting up of the preventive water guard by the customs. During the later years of the Napoleonic War smuggling became increasingly difficult, and it would only revive with the coming of peace in 1815.

Jack Rattenbury of Beer

It is usual to see smuggling largely from the side of the customs officers because of the nature of the surviving sources, but the autobiography of the Devon smuggler John Rattenbury gives a view from the other side, including his experiences during the French Revolutionary and Napoleonic wars.[41] 'Jack' Rattenbury (Fig. 35.2) was born in Beer in 1778 and went to sea at the age of nine to become a fisherman. When war broke out in 1793 he joined a privateer, but she was captured off the Azores and taken to Bordeaux. Jack escaped and by 1794 had found his way back to Beer. It was then he made his first smuggling voyage to the Channel Islands, but on his return he joined the crew of a coasting vessel. That ship was captured by a French privateer, but Jack got away to the English coast, only to be seized by the press gang when he got ashore. The navy did not hold him long. After his desertion Jack returned to Beer and spent the next few years fishing, smuggling, coasting, and victualling passing ships.

In 1800 he signed on at Topsham for a voyage to the Newfoundland fishery. The vessel was to take fish to Oporto, but on the way she was captured by a Spanish privateer and taken to Vigo. There Jack escaped, made his way to Portugal, and returned in 1801 to Beer, where he got married. Despite his new state, Jack then joined a Weymouth privateer which cruised off the Azores but took no prizes.

Between 1801 and 1805 Jack remained in Beer and occupied his time fishing, piloting, smuggling, and victualling ships. On one occasion he was seized by the press gang, but his wife helped him escape. In 1805 he once again joined a privateer and went for a long cruise off Madeira, the Canaries, and the Azores, but no prizes were taken. On his return to Beer he resolved never to go privateering again, as it seemed to involve great effort for no reward. He preferred smuggling as a paying occupation. However, soon after his return he was seized by a naval tender while on a smuggling voyage and was lucky to escape, an accomplishment he seems to have perfected.

In 1806 Jack made a smuggling voyage to Alderney and on his return sank most of his cargo. His boat was then captured by a naval cutter whose commander said he would free him if he revealed where the kegs had been sunk. Jack told him, but the officer went back on his word and took the smuggler to stand trial in Dartmouth. Found guilty of smuggling, Jack was given the choice of paying a £100 fine, being sent into the navy, or going to prison. He chose the last, but found the gaol so vile that he volunteered for the navy. As the naval tender left Dartmouth harbour he escaped over the side.

Back in Beer, Jack purchased a share in a galley, a large open rowing boat

35.2 John Rattenbury of Beer, drawn by W Bevan, from *Memoirs of a Smuggler* (Sidmouth, 1837). *(Devon and Exeter Institution)*

of a type more commonly used by smugglers in the Straits of Dover, and she made a number of successful voyages to Alderney before being lost at sea. He soon obtained a new smuggling vessel, but while returning from Alderney was captured and taken to Falmouth. Sentenced to imprisonment, he was to be taken to Bodmin gaol, but escaped when his guards got drunk, and made his way back to Beer.

After a number of further smuggling voyages Jack was again taken by the navy and sent to a frigate, only to desert from her in Ireland and return to Devon. He was then introduced to four French officers who had escaped from prison in Tiverton, and he agreed to take them back to France, a not uncommon activity for smugglers in wartime. They were hidden in Beer while Jack prepared for the voyage. Then the officers were discovered and Jack was arrested. Rather implausibly he explained that he thought the French-speaking gentlemen came from Jersey, and he was about to return them to that island. Surprisingly he was released, and returned to smuggling.

In 1809 he began running a public house, but trade was bad and by 1812 he was in debt. In hopes of getting extra money he returned yet again to smuggling, only to be captured by the navy and taken to Brixham. His wife went there and helped him escape. In 1813 debts forced him to give up the public house and, since smuggling was now much reduced, he endeavoured to support his wife and four children by piloting and fishing. When the war came to an end smuggling revived and he returned to his old trade, voyaging to Cherbourg now that Alderney was closed to smugglers. However, the preventive forces remained vigilant on the Devon coast and most of his cargoes had to be sunk for collection later. One cargo sunk in January 1815 could not be collected for three weeks, and Jack found that the cold had made the spirits thicken and they were practically unsaleable.

The Coming of Peace

Although he was an ardent smuggler, Jack Rattenbury does not seem to have made much money from that difficult and dangerous trade. The big rewards went largely to the men of capital who funded the smuggling trade, and after 1815 they began to withdraw from that business. As a consequence the nature of smuggling began to change, declining from a vast illicit trade to an increasingly small-scale criminal activity. This change was slow but steady, and by the 1840s smuggling was only a minor problem. The withdrawal of the monied supporters of smuggling was a reaction to changes in government economic policies and in social attitudes, and to the increasing effectiveness of the preventive forces.

After 1815 more men and ships were on duty to suppress smuggling than ever before, although rivalries between government departments rather undermined their effectiveness by preventing co-ordinated action. With the foundation of the Coast Guard in 1822 a major step forward was taken, and that body became the principal agency fighting the smugglers, with the customs men forced to take second place. However, it took time for the Coast Guard to have an impact, and the 1820s witnessed a revival of smuggling, although it never reached the level of earlier periods. This revival did not affect the north coast of Devon, where smuggling was of only minor importance after 1815, but there was a considerable activity on the south coast of the county.

In July 1823 the customs collector at Dartmouth reported that vessels from his port had been to Cherbourg to collect spirits and the cargoes had been sunk near Start Point.[42] In December 1824 William Fletcher, the Coast Guard commander at Kingsbridge, noted that a number of landings had taken place in south Devon, but he believed the quantities of contraband involved had been small. One cargo had been run into Torbay; another at Bantham; a third had been sunk near Salcombe and later brought ashore; and a fourth cargo had been landed at Hallsands in Start Bay. A French cutter had been seen off Hope Cove, and it was thought she had sunk a cargo in Bigbury Bay, but nothing was found after Coast Guard boats had spent three days 'creeping for it'. Several local vessels were well known as smuggling craft, but increasingly the smugglers at Bantham, Hallsands, and Salcombe were hiring French vessels to bring over their contraband. Despite all this activity it was not thought that the quantities of contraband involved were very great: 'I do not think that any cargo run on this coast exceeds from 80 to 120 or 130 tubs [of spirits]'.[43]

One cause of the recent rise in the amount of smuggling was thought by Fletcher to be 'the improvement of agriculture which has brought a greater demand into the market'. However, smuggling had become a rather hand-to-mouth affair and spirits were sold at low prices 'with the view to get immediate payment and a small profit, as there is [now] no large capitalist, and no person who has much property at stake' in the smuggling trade. The Coast Guard had done much to discourage smuggling, but 'the disposition still remains', and it would revive if preventive measures slackened. The commander believed Hallsands was a favourite haunt of smugglers and wanted a Coast Guard boat stationed there.

Contraband goods continued to be landed, but changes in government economic policy were assisting the swing against smuggling. As the Dartmouth collector observed in April 1825:

> We hope the reduction of the duties on British spirits and on rum will occasion those articles to be had on such easy terms as to lead to the exclusion of foreign brandy and geneva [gin] and we are humbly of opinion that this measure will tend more to suppress smuggling than any preventive measures which might be adopted.[44]

The abolition of the excise duties on beer and cider in 1830 did much to foster the consumption of home-produced alcoholic beverages in place of the foreign liquor which had for so long been smuggled into the country. Other duties were also being reduced, a process which reached its peak in the 1840s.

Relations between the customs officers and the Coast Guard were not always good, but they co-operated sufficiently to make life increasingly difficult for the smugglers. Even in 1831 the Dartmouth collector was reporting that there was little smuggling activity in his port.[45] The remaining smugglers had become very secretive for fear of informers, and many were no longer ready to risk their own vessels in the trade, preferring to hire French vessels to bring over the contraband.

Jack Rattenbury was a witness to the steady decline of smuggling after 1815.[46] Between 1815 and 1819 he made a number of successful smuggling voyages between Cherbourg and Beer and collected enough money to pay off the debts he had incurred while running the public house. In 1819 he was captured while on a smuggling voyage and taken to Dartmouth. Once again he escaped and spent the following year in a less dangerous occupation, running a gentleman's yacht, only to return to smuggling soon after. In 1825 he was captured off Dawlish by a Coast Guard boat, convicted of smuggling, and sent to Exeter gaol. He was not released until 1827. After this period in gaol Jack Rattenbury's fortunes began to decline. By 1829, aged 51, he was in such dire straits that he willingly joined the navy as a seaman, only to be discharged in 1830 because of illness. For a time he worked in the coasting trade, but he eventually returned yet again to smuggling. Within a short time he was captured, convicted, and sent to Dorchester gaol, from where he was not released until 1833. He returned once more to the smuggling trade, but found it increasingly dangerous because of informers and the ever-present preventive forces. In 1836, having narrowly escaped arrest himself, Jack gave evidence for the defence at his son's trial before Exeter Assizes for assaulting a customs officer on the beach at Budleigh Salterton. William was convicted and sentenced to seven years transportation to Australia, but a pardon was later obtained. No doubt realising that smuggling was now too dangerous a trade, Jack Rattenbury decided to restrict his activities in future to fishing, piloting, and coasting. He also wrote, apparently with journalistic assistance, an account of his life, being one of the few smugglers to do so.

In the mid-1840s the preventive services reached their peak in numbers and efficiency. In May 1844 the Coast Guard forces in Devon were quite formidable. North Devon was covered by the Barnstaple district, running from Porlock in Somerset to Bude in Cornwall, and it could muster 12 officers and men but no revenue cutter. The four districts in south Devon had much stronger forces. Plymouth district had 75 officers and men and two revenue cutters, the *Harpy* and the *Arrow*; Salcombe district had 61 officers and men but no cutters; Dartmouth district had 69 officers and men and the cutter *Defence*; and Exmouth district had 74 officers and men and the cutter *Nimble*.[47] In addition to the Coast Guard there were customs officers, excise officers, detachments of troops, and naval vessels. By 1849 it was found possible to reduce the cutter fleet by one third.

The decline of smuggling continued into the next decade, and in its first annual report, in 1857, the Board of Customs confidently reported:

> With the reduction of duties, and the removal of all needless and vexatious restrictions, smuggling has greatly diminished, and the public sentiment with regard to it has undergone a very considerable change. The smuggler is no longer an object of general sympathy or a hero of romance; and people are beginning to awake to the perception of the fact that his offence is less a fraud on the revenue than a robbery of the fair trader.[48]

The great age of smuggling in British history was produced by popular resistance to an economic system decreed by the state, but which the state did not have sufficient force to impose effectively. By the time the state did muster sufficient force, after 1815, the old economic system based on mercantilism was breaking down and a new one based on free trade was taking its place. Thus the economic causes of widespread smuggling were disappearing at the very moment the government was at last mustering sufficient force to defeat the smugglers. Jack Rattenbury and his fellows in Devon became relics of the past, but their activities had been an important chapter in Devon's maritime history.

35: Devon and Smuggling, 1680–1850

1 J Rattenbury, *Memoirs of a Smuggler* (Sidmouth and London, 1837), 105.
2 G Smith, *King's Cutters: The Revenue Service and the War against Smuggling* (1983), 71, 79.
3 P Mathias, *The First Industrial Nation: An Economic History of Britain, 1700–1914* (2nd edition, 1983), 39; First report of the committee appointed to enquire into the illicit practices used in defrauding the revenue, 24 Dec. 1783, *House of Commons Papers*, vol.38.
4 For example GD Ramsay, 'The Smugglers' Trade: A Neglected Aspect of English Commercial Development', *Transactions of the Royal Historical Society* (1951), and WA Cole, 'Trends in Eighteenth Century Smuggling', *EcHR* X (1958).
5 For smuggling in southeast England see, for example, E Carson, *Smugglers and Revenue Officers in the Portsmouth Area in the Eighteenth Century* (Portsmouth, 1974), KM Clark, *Smuggling in Rye and District* (Rye, 1977), and H Benham, *Smugglers' Century: Essex 1730–1830* (Essex Record Office, 1986).
6 Report of William Culliford, 1683, PRO T64/139 and 140; N Williams, *Contraband Cargoes: Seven Centuries of Smuggling* (1959), 83–6.
7 Smith, *King's Cutters*, 16, 21, 32.
8 G Farr, 'Smuggling Survey of North Devon' (unpublished MS., 1970), 2.
9 Returns of seizures 1723–33, PRO T64/143.
10 Report of the committee to enquire into the frauds and abuses in the customs to the prejudice of trade and diminution of the revenue, 7 June 1733, *House of Commons Papers*, vol.12.
11 For the Channel Islands and the smuggling trade see AG Jamieson (ed), *A People of the Sea: The Maritime History of the Channel Islands* (1986), Chapter 8.
12 Returns of seizures 1723–33, PRO T64/143.
13 Report of the committee on smuggling, 24 March 1745, *House of Commons Papers*, vol.25.
14 E Keble Chatterton, *King's Cutters and Smugglers 1700–1855* (1912), 79.
15 BL Add. Ms. 38463.
16 John Swaffin to board of customs, 20 May 1783, PRO CUST 65/2.
17 PRO CUST 65/2.
18 PRO CUST 65/2.
19 PRO CUST 64/9.
20 PRO CUST 69/67.
21 PRO CUST 69/169.
22 Customs report on smuggling, 26 Nov. 1783, PRO T48/82.
23 First report of the committee appointed to enquire into the illicit practices used in defrauding the revenue, 24 Dec. 1783, *House of Commons Papers*, vol.38.
24 Third report of the committee appointed to enquire into the illicit practices used in defrauding the revenue, 23 March 1784, *House of Commons Papers*, vol.38.
25 Dartmouth collector to board of customs, 24 Dec. 1784, PRO CUST 65/2.
26 Petition of the widow of Richard Cullin, Sept. 1785, PRO CUST 65/2; JRW Coxhead, *Smuggling Days in Devon* (Exmouth, 1956), 22–3.
27 PRO CUST 64/9.
28 Exeter collector to board of customs, 29 Jan. 1785, PRO CUST 64/9.
29 John Swaffin to Dartmouth collector, 11 Sept. 1787, and lawyers to board of customs, 13 March 1788, PRO CUST 65/3; petition of John Swaffin, 10 Nov. 1789, PRO CUST 65/4.
30 PRO CUST 65/3.
31 Letters of 7 & 30 April 1789, PRO CUST 65/4.
32 PRO CUST 65/4.
33 Richard Valentine to Dartmouth collector, 6 Sept. 1790, PRO CUST 65/4.
34 List of smuggling vessels seized by HM ships 1783–93, PRO ADM 7/353; PRO CUST 65/4.
35 PRO CUST 65/4.
36 PRO CUST 64/156.
37 Report on customs establishment at Plymouth, Sept. 1799, PRO CUST 66/1.
38 PRO CUST 66/1.
39 Chatterton, *King's Cutters and Smugglers*, 142–4.
40 G Farr, 'Smuggling Survey of North Devon', 8.
41 J Rattenbury, *Memoirs of a Smuggler*, *passim*.
42 PRO CUST 65/23.
43 PRO CUST 65/25.
44 PRO CUST 65/25.
45 PRO CUST 65/29. For smuggling incidents in Devon in the 1830s see HN Shore, *Smuggling Days and Smuggling Ways* (1892, reprinted 1929), 102, 107, 111.
46 J Rattenbury, *Memoirs of a Smuggler*, *passim*.
47 Returns of coast guard districts May 1844, in report of the select committee on the tobacco trade, *BPP* 1844, vol.XII.
48 First annual report of the board of customs, 20 Feb. 1857, Customs Library, King's Beam House, London.

36 Devon Ports and the Rhythms of the Sea

E A G CLARK

THE FIRST RHYTHM WAS THE twice daily rise and fall of the tide. Until docks were constructed, all Devon ports were 'tide havens'. Quays were constructed near the low-water line, and at low tide most were 'dry', as at Barnstaple, Bideford, Clovelly, Stonehouse Pool, Sutton Pool, Dartmouth, Brixham, and Torquay.[1] At the river port of Topsham there was two feet at low water, but a byelaw insisted 'ships shall not at any time ground before the Keyhead, but come and go with every tide'.[2] At all of the ports vessels lay on the mud or moved to deep water anchorages between tides. Port activities depended on the daily tidal rise of some 9 to 15 feet on the south coast and 15 to 25 feet on the north, which brought Devon ports within the draught limits of most sailing ships. Fortnightly, the surging amplitude of spring tides carried vessels of 150 tons or more to the quays of Ilfracombe, Bideford, Barnstaple, Fremington (from 1855), Plymouth, Salcombe, Dartmouth, and Topsham, and smaller vessels to Kingsbridge, Totnes, Brixham, Torquay, Teignmouth, Exeter, and (from 1809) Axmouth. Furthermore, on many of the branching arms of the estuaries were rural quays, often associated with lime kilns, where stone and culm were discharged at high springs and agricultural produce was laden. There were at least 11 rural wharves and/or lime kiln sites on the Exe and Dart, six on the Tavy, four on Kingsbridge estuary, three on the Torridge, and two each on the Teign, the Avon and the Erme.[3] The volume of this largely unrecorded trade at rural quays is indicated by the claim by Robert Davy in 1827 that he brought 1,000 lighter loads annually to his wharves and kilns at Countess Wear on the Exe.[4]

Most of the ports were river ports. With the exception of the Tamar and Dart, the estuaries had less than six feet of water on the bar at low tide. Sailing vessels waited in customary anchorages outside the bar. Pilot boats patrolled to guide vessels over the bar between half and full tide. In 1850 there were five off the Exe, 'with their flags flying at the mast head by day, and a light at night'.[5] Once across the bar, vessels often rode at deep water anchorages such as off Appledore, or along the three-mile stretch of the Dart below Greenway, or in Exmouth Bight, or Shaldon pool, to wait for a tide, to tranship, or pick up a river pilot. As the level of the water rose, imperceptibly at first and then as a swiftly moving flood, age-old practices were followed, according to local circumstances. On Barnstaple Bar it was dangerous to cross before quarter flood.[6] On the Teign, the clay barges left their moorings off Shaldon within two hours of flood, and sailed up light to the quays on the Stover and Hackney Canals, to return laden on the ebb.[7] On the Exe and Dart vessels needed the full six hours of tidal rise to navigate the shoal-filled upper estuaries to Topsham and Totnes.[8]

The contrast between spring and neap tides imposed a second rhythm on navigation. Springs tended to be periods of increased activity. In 1825 74 per cent of the 109 London 'constant' (regular) traders which visited Topsham entered or cleared in weeks with spring tides.[9] At Teignmouth large vessels were advised to attempt a passage 'two days before and after spring tides'.[10] Quays with shallow approaches, such as Axmouth, Lympstone, and Totnes were known to be accessible to small coasters at spring tides only.[11] For short hauls it was advantageous to employ vessels of shallow draught, which could enter the larger ports on any tide. The constant traders plying between Plymouth, Dartmouth, and Exeter were of 34 to 80 tons,[12] and drew about eight feet. Neaps were periods of curtailed operations. Large vessels were delayed for several days.[13]

The third rhythm was seasonal, the fitful change from the long, relatively calm days of summer to the dangers of winter storms, mists, and long dark nights. At ports with detailed records, December, January, and February were consistently the slackest months. Winter was perceived as hazardous. A Brixham merchant wrote to the owner of Budleigh Salterton lime kilns in December 1813: 'it is impossible for any vessel to come to your place with culm at this season of the year, indeed, it is considered very hazardous even in summer'.[14] The coal trade was seasonal. There were 42 shipments of coal at Plymouth in the winter half of 1769–70, and 136 shipments in the summer half. At Teignmouth shipments averaged seven per month in October–March, and 18 per month from April to September.[16] Exeter–London constant traders accomplished the voyage in a week in summer, and in three weeks in winter.[17]

The leisurely rhythms of tides and seasons brought regularities to the pattern of shipping movements but cut across the need for the expeditious receipt and despatch of goods. Constant traders were introduced between major Devon ports and London and Bristol in the eighteenth century. In 1791 there were 11 sailing from London to Exeter, nine to Plymouth and six to Dartmouth.[18] By 1825 the 17 to the Exe were each making some three to five visits a year, with an average turnabout in the estuary of 21 days.[19] In 1830 Chamberlain's Wharf vessels advertized their intention of 'clearing every week from Topsham, whether laden or not'.[20] At the peak before railway competition there were regular sailings from London to Axmouth, Exeter, Dartmouth, Plymouth, Bideford, and Barnstaple, and twice-weekly services from Bristol to Barnstaple and Ilfracombe.[21] The advent of steamers aided the quest for reliable despatch. A regular service between Plymouth, Falmouth, and Portsmouth began in 1825, and between London and Topsham in 1831.[22] Nevertheless, neap tides continud to be a problem in the latter case, and the steam ship company experimented with vessels of 12, 11 and then ten feet draught, before settling on the *Zephyr*, which drew 8 feet.[23] Such dialogues between the seafarer and the rhythms of the sea, exchanges which began with the earliest landfall on the Devon coasts, are the chapters in a story which never ends.

36: Devon Ports and the Rhythms of the Sea

1 Except where otherwise stated, the account of the physical setting of the ports in this section is based on the following: Admiralty, *The Channel Pilot* (1859); G Collins, *Great Britain's Coasting Pilot* (1693 and 1764); T Moore, *History of Devonshire* (1829–1836). Maps: Survey of the Coast of Devonshire from Exmouth Bar to Stoke Point, 1779; G Collins, Plymouth, 1693 (includes inset map of the Kingsbridge estuary); Plymouth Sound, Hamoaze and Cattewater, surveyed in

1770; Brixham Harbour, 1836 (facsimile in PA Kennedy, *Oakum* (Exeter, 1970), 27; W Board, Chart of Exmouth Harbour and the Navigable part of the River Exe (1830).
2 DRO, T.78, Copy of Decree concerning Topsham Quay, 1623.
3 Ordnance Survey, 6 inches to the Mile, 1st edition, 1890, Sheets 127 SE and NW; 117 NE; 128 SW; 131 SE and NW; 132 SW; 136 NE; *Donn's Map of the County of Devon* (1765); P Russell, *Dartmouth* (1950), 127.
4 EAG Clark, *Ports of the Exe Estuary, 1660–1860* (Exeter, 1960), 82.
5 DRO, Pilotage Letter Book, 1861–1895, 4 June 1872.
6 *English Channel Pilot* (1859), 88.
7 Interview with Mr Thomas, Superintendent, Exeter Canal.
8 DRO, Mayor v. Earl of Devon and Exe Bight Oyster Fishery, affidavits of pilots.
9 Computed from DRO, Wharfinger's Journal, Topsham, 1825.
10 T Brice, *History and Description of the City of Exeter* (Exeter, 1802), 130.
11 DRO, Letter Book 29, 246 (1822); Bodleian Library, Oxford, Vol.1, Parochial Returns, 116; Clark, *Ports of the Exe Estuary*, 60, 66.
12 *Exeter Itinerary and General Directory* (Exeter, 1828),
13 Clark, *Ports of the Exe Estuary*, 16–18, 38–39.
14 DRO, Rolle Papers, Letter from CT Bartlett to J Kay, 7 December 1813.
15 WDRO, Account of Coals brought into port of Plymouth, 1769–1770.
16 DRO, 1508 M 1/3 Metage Book, Kenton Manor, 1782–1801.
17 House of Lords MSS, Minutes of Evidence, Bristol and Exeter Railway Bill, 1836, 16 Mar. 1836, 48, 59.
18 *Universal British Directory of Trade, Commerce and Manufactures* (1791–98), III, 621–632.
19 DRO, Wharfinger's Journal, Topsham, 1825.
20 Printed note loose in DRO, Wharfinger's Journal, Topsham, 1834–5.
21 *Robson's London Directory* (1830); *Robson's London Directory* (1840).
22 *Woolmer's Exeter and Plymouth Gazette*, 2 April 1825; Clark, *Ports of the Exe Estuary*, 177–8.
23 DRO, Transcript of Shorthand Notes taken by Thomas Latimer at the Guildhall, Exeter, 4 May 1833, 25.

36.1 The Rhythm of the Sea: Down End, Saunton, North Devon, *c*1950 *(H F Youings)*

Index